3 Miles to an Inch

The History
of
NEWBERRY COUNTY
South Carolina

Volume Two: 1860–1990

Pen and ink drawing of the Opera House,
by William Frank Lominack, Jr.

The History
of
NEWBERRY COUNTY
South Carolina

Volume Two: 1860–1990

by Thomas H. Pope

UNIVERSITY OF SOUTH CAROLINA PRESS

Grateful acknowledgment is made to Newberry Federal Savings Bank for making a generous grant to the University of South Carolina Press to ensure publication of this volume.

F
277
N5
P66
v. 2

Copyright © 1992 University of South Carolina

Published in Columbia, South Carolina, by the University of South Carolina Press

Manufactured in the United States of America

Library of Congress Cataloging-in-Publication Data

(Revised for vol. 2)

Pope, Thomas H., 1913–
    The history of Newberry County, South Carolina.

    Includes bibliographical references and index.
    Contents: v. 1. 1749–1860 — v. 2. 1860–1990
    1. Newberry County (S.C.)—History. I. Title
F277.N5P66   975.7'39   72-13449
ISBN 0-87249-248-6 (v. 1)
ISBN 0-87249-777-1 (hard v. 2 : alk. paper)

To

Mary Waties

with a heartful of love

Contents

Illustrations

Following page 332

Maps

Preface

Newberry is still primarily an agricultural county. It has exchanged its reliance upon cotton as a cash crop for dependence upon poultry and eggs, milk and beef cattle, and timber and pulpwood. As a result, its economy is healthier.

Since World War II the county has lost two textile plants, Newberry Mill and Mollohon, and gained a number of non-textile establishments. This, too, has made Newberry's economy more diversified and stable but has not substantially affected the rural nature of the county.

The population has changed somewhat since 1860. Then the racial division was roughly two-thirds black and one-third white. Today the population is approximately one-third black and two-thirds white. While the composition is very different, the population of the county has not increased much over that of 1900.

The story of almost two-and-a-half centuries since the first European settlers arrived in the Dutch Fork and on the Enoree and Bush rivers is one of overcoming the adversity of war and economic depression, of coping with Reconstruction, of improving the lifestyle of the people, and of looking to the future with hope. Writing this story has been a labor of love.

Acknowledgments

For a score of years I have sought to learn and to record the history of Newberry County. Many people have assisted in various ways for which I am grateful, but a few deserve special thanks.

The distinguished historian, Dr. George C. Rogers, Jr., has read and reread my manuscript and has made many helpful suggestions. His unflagging courtesy and his unflagging interest are deeply appreciated.

Dr. Daniel W. Hollis, another historian of distinction, and Augustus T. Graydon, Esquire, of the Columbia Bar, very kindly read the chapter on Blease and offered helpful suggestions.

Charles E. Lee, former director of the South Carolina Department of Archives and History, read the manuscript for the University of South Carolina Press and made numerous suggestions I appreciated and which greatly improved the form and substance of the text. He and his co-workers at the archives, William L. McDowell, Jr. and Wylma Wates, were of great assistance in my research.

My lifelong friend, Clarence McKittrick Smith, Jr., who was trained in historiography at Harvard and Duke, also read my manuscript and gave me valuable advice about its revision.

Dr. Allen Stokes of the South Caroliniana Library provided his usual help to amateur historians; I am grateful for his assistance.

I am greatly indebted to Dr. John Hammond Moore for his criticism of my manuscript and for his assistance in the rewriting of it.

At the Newberry-Saluda Regional Library, Caroline Tucker Neel Taylor and Eliza McCrackin Parr were extremely cooperative and helpful. They secured books that I needed, and I am indebted to them.

Much of my research into this period of Newberry's history necessarily was in the newspaper files of the past century and a half. Fortunately, the *Newberry Observer* has stored on microfilm all of its issues, and that newspaper has been extremely generous in permitting me to use such materials.

It was necessary to delve into the probate records of the county, and no one could have been more accommodating than the late Probate Judge Frank H. Ward, his successor, Probate Judge Margaret Schumpert, and her deputy, Freida Koon.

Clerk of Court Jackie Bowers, her predecessors, Mildred R. Harmon and Ellouise S. Setzler, and their staffs aided me in my search for deeds and other recorded instruments, particularly those pertaining to the churches.

Genell Ruff and the late Reverend J. C. Copeland assisted with the identification, size of the congregations, and the names of the present pastors of the African Methodist Episcopal churches and the Enoree Baptist Association, respectively.

The chapter on agriculture could not have been written without the help of the late Dennis Crawford of Clemson University, Henry Eason, and Philip Epps. Mr. Crawford had the only library of agricultural statistics that I could find in South Carolina, and he generously brought it to me for my education.

Mary Davis Dominick, executive director of the Newberry County Development Board-Chamber of Commerce, was most cooperative and furnished employment figures and other data involving industry.

Colleen Fowler, the clerk of Whitmire, helped with the names of Whitmire's mayors, while D. H. Hamm, Jr., assisted in the identification of Prosperity leaders of long ago. Martha Roller was of great assistance in obtaining information about the physicians of the county.

The late Thomas Worth Abrams, who was a walking genealogical encyclopedia of the Whitmire area, was extremely helpful about Whitmire's past.

William Frank Lominack, Jr., graciously sketched the Opera House for the frontispiece and dust cover. I appreciate his help and that of Gary T. Pope in taking the photographs used in the book.

My gratitude is expressed to the Newberry Federal Savings Bank for generously making a grant to assist the University of South Carolina Press in publishing this volume.

The late Gerald C. O'Quinn and his successor as county veterans service officer, Al Morrison, gave invaluable assistance in locating and identifying the veterans of the county.

I am grateful to Keitt Purcell, Edward O. Cannon, J. Thomas Johnson, and William C. Carter for their interest, encouragement, and help.

Dr. David Fischer compiled the exhaustive index for this volume, and I thank him for his assistance.

Last, but by no means least, I am grateful to Kimberly G. Derrick, Susan C. Fellers, and Cassie D. Dominick for typing and retyping the manuscript.

To all of these, and to a great many whom I have not named, I extend my sincere thanks for helping me. Any errors made have been mine; they are inevitable but regrettable.

The History
of
NEWBERRY COUNTY
South Carolina

Volume Two: 1860–1990

1

Newberry Goes to War

As 1860 drew to a close, South Carolina declared its independence for a second time. Public opinion was molded and expressed in mass meetings over the state. In Newberry District the largest such meeting in its history was held at the courthouse on November 19, 1860. Every hamlet and every settlement was represented.

After hearing speeches from Milledge L. Bonham of Edgefield and W. D. Simpson of Laurens, as well as from local speakers, the group adopted a resolution calling for immediate secession. It then selected Newberry's four delegates to the convention called to meet in Columbia the following month. They were Simeon Fair, Robert Moorman, John P. Kinard, and Joseph H. Caldwell. These nominees forthwith signed a resolution for the secession of South Carolina from the Union.[1]

At an election held on December 6, 1860, these nominees of the mass meeting were duly elected. Newberry's delegates were substantial, highly respected citizens. Fair was a leading lawyer of the district and the others were prominent planters.

Colonel Fair, a volunteer officer during the Seminole War of 1836, succeeded James J. Caldwell as solicitor of the Middle Circuit and had been effective in securing Newberry College for the town of Newberry. Former Senator Robert Moorman was a native of Union District but had long been prominent in Newberry politics. Major John Peter Kinard was a former sheriff and one of the largest slaveholders of the district; in 1860 he owned 105 slaves. Joseph H. Caldwell was a member of one of the leading families in the district; this was his first political venture.

The Secession Convention met in the First Baptist Church of

1

Columbia on December 17, 1860, but, because of the outbreak of smallpox in the capital, adjourned to meet in Charleston. Before making this
move, however, the convention unanimously adopted a resolution offered by Chancellor John A. Inglis that South Carolina secede and that
a committee of seven be appointed to draft an ordinance to that effect.[2]

When the convention reconvened in Charleston, the committee
promptly submitted a draft repealing the Act of May 23, 1788, by which
South Carolina had ratified the Constitution; the "union now subsisting
between South Carolina and the other States, under the name of the
'United States of America' " was dissolved.[3]

News of its unanimous adoption by the convention was telegraphed
to the South Carolina members of Congress. They promptly resigned.[4]
The ordinance of Secession was signed that night, December 20, at Institute Hall. Dr. John Bachman, so intimately connected with Newberry
by having been the first president of the Board of Trustees of Newberry
College, prayed for divine blessing upon the new declaration of independence.[5] South Carolina rejoiced.

While South Carolina expected a Southern Confederacy to be established, the state was a sovereign nation until this could be done. As such
it had to provide for the powers formerly exercised by the national government. Provision had to be made for the state's defense, for commerce
with its former confederates in the union and the nations of Europe, for
a postal system, for foreign relations, for citizenship, for a monetary system, for naturalization, and for various other sovereign responsibilities.[6]

Just before the convening of the Secession Convention, the General
Assembly elected as governor Francis W. Pickens of Edgefield. Pickens
had served as minister to Russia and as a member of Congress. Despite
his classical scholarship and ability as an orator he would prove unable
to inspire the confidence required at this critical time.[7]

The convention charged him with the conduct of foreign affairs but
reserved the right of independent action. Pickens was authorized to
make diplomatic appointments and treaties subject to confirmation by
the convention, if in session, and by the Senate, if the convention were
in recess. Instead of transferring authority to the General Assembly, the
convention reserved to itself powers over commerce, war, citizenship,
treason, and confederation with other states. It authorized the General
Assembly to provide for the exercise of the judicial power by such courts
as it might designate.[8]

The convention provided for an executive council consisting of the
lieutenant governor and four persons appointed by the governor with

the advice and consent of the convention. The council was responsible to the governor.

The cabinet of Governor Pickens consisted of A. G. Magrath, Secretary of State; D. F. Jamison (the president of the convention), Secretary of War; C. G. Memminger, Secretary of the Treasury; Lieutenant Governor W. W. Harllee, Postmaster General; and A. C. Garlington of Newberry, Secretary of Interior.[9]

Albert Creswell Garlington, member of a distinguished Laurens District family, was born in Georgia and was first honor graduate of the University of Georgia in 1843. He read law under C. P. Sullivan of Laurens; married Sallie Moon, daughter of Dr. Peter Moon of Newberry; and removed to Newberry where he quickly became a leading member of the Bar. Elected first as representative and then as senator from Newberry District, he was a leading political figure at the outbreak of the war. After the abolition of the first executive council, Garlington served both as a major in the Holcombe Legion and as the adjutant and inspector general of South Carolina. He was considered to be one of the greatest orators in the state.

The executive council was named by Governor Pickens in December 1860, but its first meeting was held on January 3, 1861.[10] Thereafter it met almost daily until the Confederate States Constitution was ratified.

Until the Confederacy was formed, South Carolina conducted its foreign affairs as an independent nation; although Pickens wanted to send an envoy to Europe, this idea was not put into effect and diplomatic overtures were made by mail. But communications with other Southern states were not left to written documents; instead commissioners were dispatched to them.[11] These commissioners suggested that a Southern Convention be held in Montgomery, Alabama, on February 4, 1861, and South Carolina's Secession Convention selected delegates to attend such a meeting.[12]

The Secession Convention, by resolutions, and the General Assembly, by act, provided for the creation of volunteer forces to be called into state service for six months within the state's boundaries. Governor Pickens appointed Milledge L. Bonham of Edgefield as major general commanding volunteer forces, consisting of four brigades. A. C. Garlington of Newberry was appointed brigadier general commanding one of these brigades.[13]

Ten regiments of infantry were to be organized, and no difficulty was expected in raising them in the early days of January 1861. Indeed the only difficulty experienced was that too many volunteer units were formed and ten regiments became eleven. The regiments of both Colonel Maxcy Gregg and Colonel Johnson Hagood bore the name of 1st South Carolina Volunteers (SCV). The other commanders were Colonel J. B. Kershaw, 2nd Regiment; Colonel James H. Williams of Newberry, 3rd Regiment; Colonel J. B. E. Sloan, 4th Regiment; Colonel Micah Jenkins, 5th Regiment; Colonel James H. Rion, 6th Regiment; Colonel T. G. Bacon, 7th Regiment; Colonel E. B. C. Cash, 8th Regiment; Colonel J. D. Blanding, 9th Regiment; and Colonel A. M. Manigault, 10th Regiment.[14]

In addition, there were regular troops—a regiment of infantry commanded by Colonel Richard H. Anderson, and a battalion of artillery commanded by Lieutenant Colonel R. S. Ripley.[15] Later, of course, other units of infantry, cavalry, and artillery were created. And at least two commands of mixed arms, infantry and cavalry, were formed; these were the Hampton Legion and the Holcombe Legion.

Before the Montgomery Convention could be held, Newberry organized its first company of volunteers, the "Rhett Guards" named for the redoubtable Robert Barnwell Rhett, Father of Secession. When the lists were opened on January 5, 1861, the first volunteer was Basil M. Blease; the company commander was Captain Whitfield Walker, the firebrand who had tried unsuccessfully to raise a company to go to Kansas just four years before. This group became Company B, Gregg's 1st South Carolina Volunteer Regiment, and was enlisted originally for six months.[16]

Great excitement attended the organization of this and other companies raised in the district in January 1861. Colonel James H. Williams of Newberry was in Arkansas looking after his extensive planting interests there when Governor Pickens named him to command the 3rd SCV Regiment.[17] Before he could reach South Carolina, twelve companies were raised for his regiment, five of them in Newberry District.

The *Rising Sun* reported that Captain S. N. Davidson had organized a company in the Jalapa section, that Captain R. Clayton Maffatt had raised a unit in the Frog Level (later Prosperity) area, that Captain Drury Nunamaker had organized a company in the Dutch Fork, that Captain James Drayton Nance had formed the Quitman Volunteers in the town, and that Captain J. C. S. Brown had organized the Snow Hill Company in the Broad River section.[18]

Many young men felt that if they did not get to Charleston with the first troops, Fort Sumter would be captured and the war ended before they saw service. Others agreed with B. F. Perry, future governor who had opposed secession, that, as South Carolina was determined to go to hell, he would go along with her.[19] A few, very few, agreed with old Chief Justice John Belton O'Neall that the South would find "neither strength in her arm nor mercy in her woe."[20]

The ladies of the town would have nothing to do with O'Neall's caution. Instead, they had C. H. Kingsmore, the talented local artist, design a silk flag for Company B which was presented to the unit as it entrained for Charleston on January 12.[21] When the Rhett Guards arrived there, they were stationed on Morris Island. Although the company arrived too late to witness the repulse of the *Star of the West* when that ship sought to reinforce Fort Sumter on January 9, it took part in the opening battle of the war when Fort Sumter was bombarded on April 12.[22] The first shot was fired at 4:30 a.m. that day from Fort Johnson on James Island by the battery of Captain George S. James.[23]

Meanwhile, on March 11, 1861, the delegates in Montgomery adopted a constitution for the Confederate States of America. The South Carolina Convention, which had adjourned on January 5, reassembled on March 26 and ratified the Constitution on April 3 by a vote of 138 to 21.[24] Thus ended South Carolina's existence as a republic, and the attack on Fort Sumter was launched by Confederate troops under the command of General P. G. T. Beauregard, not by South Carolina's Volunteer Force.

Soon after the fall of Fort Sumter on April 14, President Jefferson Davis called for 8,000 men from South Carolina to enter the Provisional Army of the Confederacy. Gregg's 1st SCV and Kershaw's 2nd SCV Regiments left for Virginia on April 22 and 25 respectively. Hagood's 1st SCV Regiment failed to volunteer and was temporarily discharged. All of the other volunteer state troops entered the Confederate authority for twelve months.[25]

On July 1, 1861, President Davis called for 3,000 troops from South Carolina to enlist for the duration of the war. Two regiments were organized under his call—Colonel James L. Orr's Regiment of Rifles and Colonel Maxcy Gregg's 1st South Carolina. When the enlistment of Gregg's troops expired, they were still in Virginia; they returned home and reorganized under the new enlistment. Company B was reactivated at Newberry on July 27, 1861, and returned to Virginia. It missed the First Battle of Manassas while at home for reactivation.[26]

Other regiments organized that summer for the duration of the war included the 13th South Carolina. By the end of 1861 there were ten South Carolina regiments in Virginia. That state had become the chief battleground of the Confederacy after it seceded and the capital was moved from Montgomery, Alabama, to Richmond, Virginia.[27]

The South Carolina Convention was reassembled at Columbia by its President, D. F. Jamison, on December 26, 1861, largely because of widespread lack of confidence in Governor Pickens. In November, the coast of the state was blockaded, Port Royal and Beaufort were in enemy hands, Charleston was considered in peril, and the white people in the Low Country feared a slave uprising. The convention reacted by creating an Executive Council of five persons—the governor, the lieutenant governor, and three individuals chosen by the convention. This body was in reality a Council of Safety of which Governor Pickens was only a member; it was given extraordinary powers. Former Senator James Chesnut, Jr., Attorney General Isaac W. Hayne, and former Governor William H. Gist were the three elected members of the council.[28]

Chesnut became chief of the Department of the Military (and virtually commander-in-chief), Lieutenant Governor W. W. Harllee and Gist heads of the Department of Treasury and Finance, and Hayne, chief of the Department of Justice and Police. Later Gist was made head of the Department of Construction and Manufacture.[29]

The council adopted conscription of men between eighteen and forty-five,[30] and many volunteered to escape the odium of the draft. By the end of April 1862, South Carolina had 21,914 men in Confederate service for the duration. By the end of August there were 42,973 South Carolinians in Confederate service.[31]

On April 16, 1862, the Confederate Congress enacted its first conscription law. The Executive Council cheerfully supported it and offered the state rolls to Confederate conscription officers. The state exemptions differed slightly from those under Confederate law; the two most troublesome differences related to overseers and students at the state military academy. The Executive Council was unwilling to consent to the drafting of overseers because they were deemed necessary for the protection of women and children, and fortunately the Confederate Congress passed a more liberal exemption law in October 1862.[32]

In May 1863, however, the liberal exemption accorded overseers was amended drastically. Since it was not enforced during the crop season, conflict between the state and the Confederacy did not arise until late in 1863. M. L. Bonham, who had become governor in December of 1862, and the Confederate conscription officials very sensibly avoided a confrontation until a new law was enacted by South Carolina in December 1863; this act declared the state's exemption laws applicable only to the military forces of South Carolina and not to troops raised under the laws of the Confederate states.[33]

Governor Bonham cooperated fully with the Confederate government; during 1863 and 1864 he did not certify for exemption any minor officials. At the end of 1864, however, the situation changed. At Bonham's suggestion the legislature provided that all persons designated by the governor would be exempt from Confederate service; this position was taken because South Carolina was threatened by enemy forces and was not being given the reinforcements needed for defense.[34]

As early as February 6, 1862, the Executive Council began to consider the vexatious question of impressment. At first the members authorized the compulsory use of slave labor only in the area threatened with invasion,[35] but this view soon gave way to a more realistic one authorizing impressment over the state at large.

On July 11, 1862, a divided council, by a vote of three to two, asked the chief of the Department of the Military to devise a plan for raising a corps of black laborers to be placed under Confederate control. His report was modified and approved on July 28; this plan provided for different classes, the use of each class for a four week period, and the impressment of only one hand where the owner had but two slaves. A circular was to be broadcast and clerks of court and sheriffs were directed to make returns of the road hands in their districts with their owners' names and addresses.[36]

Although the idea of impressment was unpopular, there was grudging compliance so long as the council remained in existence. When it was abolished, however, the supply of labor practically ended. In December 1864 the legislature finally enacted a law with teeth in it; by then Sherman was in Savannah and the war was lost.

The council also made an energetic and intelligent effort to obtain war supplies despite the blockade. It attempted to prohibit the export of cotton except under bond that the proceeds of sale would be invested in war materials and brought back through the blockade. The Confederate government opposed this measure and caused it to fail. At home powder and lead were produced by various means, and foundries and workshops were established.[37]

The historian Charles E. Cauthen concluded that the council "exercised its power with not only considerable energy and wisdom but with restraint as well."[38] Unfortunately, however, it became so unpopular that it and its creator, the convention itself, were abolished on December 18, 1862, by the General Assembly.[39] At the same time the legislature elected a new governor, M. L. Bonham of Edgefield, and a new lieutenant governor, Plowden C. J. Weston of Georgetown.[40]

During his two-year term, Bonham supported the Confederate government and did his best to place the state's military resources at the disposal of the Confederacy. He personally did not like the Davis administration, but officially he did not let his feelings keep him from doing his duty. He was commissioned a brigadier general at the end of his term.[41]

One of Bonham's immediate problems was the large number of deserters lurking in the foothills and mountains in the northwestern part of South Carolina. Gangs of bushwhackers and horse thieves operated around Walhalla and Pendleton. Large numbers of deserters banded together in Greenville, Spartanburg, and Pickens districts.[42]

Newberry, however, was loyal. A deserter named Metts was reportedly hanged at Frog Level,[43] and Kershaw's Brigade announced its loyalty to President Davis from its bivouac in Virginia.[44]

In 1864, A. C. Garlington of Newberry was one of the leading candidates for governor, along with Samuel McGowan, John S. Preston, and A. G. Magrath. On the first ballot, Magrath received fifty-five votes, Garlington forty-nine, Preston thirty-four, and McGowan two. On the second ballot, Garlington's vote rose to fifty-three, but on the sixth ballot, Magrath was elected.[45] This was the closest that a Newberry man would come to the office of governor during the nineteenth century, except for James H. Hammond before the war.

Throughout the war years the county's real property continued to be assessed for ordinary tax purposes at $164,880, the valuation established by the classification of rural lands in the Act of 1815 and followed since that year.[46] Ordinary taxes were derived from levies on lands, slaves, Free Negroes, sales, the income of professional men, monies lent, corporate capital, dogs, billiard tables, and playing cards. By far the largest yield was from the tax on slaves.[47]

Another tax was levied to repay bonds issued in 1861 and 1862 to finance the state's unusual military expenditures in the opening days of the war. No bonds were issued after 1862 for such purposes since few troops remained in state service and the Confederate government was reimbursing South Carolina for military expenses incurred in the common cause.[48] This tax to repay the bonds was levied on the property assessments made for ordinary tax purposes; it amounted to $46,000 in Newberry District in 1863.[49]

A special war tax was levied by the Confederate government beginning in 1861. The tax was based upon the actual value of real property

and slaves, and each state was initially given the choice of paying its pro-
rata part of the tax or of letting the central government collect it. South
Carolina chose to pay its share and to collect the tax from its taxpayers;[50]
the assessment was different from the assessment used for ordinary
taxes. For example, Newberry's real property was assessed at $3,877,856
and its 14,450 slaves at $7,021,065. Other taxable items included mer-
chandise, bank stock, other corporate stock, money at interest, cash on
hand, horses, gold watches, gold and silver plate, pianos, and carriages.[51]

Newberry's total valuation for the war tax was $13,998,581, and it paid
$69,992.90 in 1862 and $30,000 in 1863.[52] Thereafter the tax was levied
directly by the Confederacy. All taxes were increased in 1864, taxes for
ordinary purposes being doubled or tripled.[53]

But reduction of cotton acreage had a much greater impact in Newberry than mere taxes. The district's economy was based entirely upon
that crop. After voluntary efforts to reduce cotton acreage failed to produce the desired result, the General Assembly enacted legislation to
compel such reduction. First it decreed that only one and a half acres of
short staple (and three acres of long staple) cotton could be planted for
each farm "hand" between the ages of fifteen and fifty-five. The acreage
was subsequently reduced to one acre of short staple cotton to each
"hand" between fifteen and fifty-five, and then raised to one acre per
"hand" between the ages of twelve and sixty-five.[54]

Since no battles were fought in the district, and it had no minerals or
factories of consequence, the extent of Newberry's participation in the
bloody struggle can best be judged by the number of soldiers and the
number of casualties from the district. In 1860 Newberry District had a
white population of 7,000 men, women, and children. Over 1,500 white
males from the district followed the Stars and Bars and more than 500
paid the supreme sacrifice in battle. Many others returned to their
homes broken in body, maimed and diseased—soon to die themselves
from the ghastly effects of the long struggle, lack of nourishment, and
exposure.

Many, many more men born in Newberry District volunteered from
the western states to which they had emigrated prior to the war.[55] They
too served with distinction. Also showing great courage were the
women of Newberry who remained at home, managing their farms and
their slaves and stoically suffering for four long years. Each month the
casualty list grew; each week the wounded and crippled came through
the district on the Greenville and Columbia Railroad.

In 1861 the legislature established a Soldier's Board of Relief in each district. The first board set up for Newberry District consisted of Dr. Peter Moon as chairman, and Robert Stewart, Burr J. Ramage, Robert Moorman, George Gallman, George Wise, Daniel Goggans, Andrew Longshore, George S. Cannon, and Joseph Caldwell.[56] The board sought to help the families of destitute or needy soldiers. The objective was not only humanitarian, in that it sought to alleviate the needs of the families, but also utilitarian, in that it would reduce the anxiety of soldiers on active duty for the welfare of their families. It was a necessary part of the war effort. For example, the amount expended in Newberry District in the period May 1–August 1, 1863, came to $2,759. This took care of 474 applicants for relief, the maximum award being $6 per quarter.[57]

The women of Newberry established a house of rest for the wounded and the weary. Since the courts conducted practically no business during the war,[58] they converted the courthouse into a hospital for the sick. They furnished clothing and other supplies for the men in the army. Among the leaders of this group were Mrs. F. B. Higgins, who lost a son at Second Manassas; Mrs. P. B. Ruff; Mrs. Lambert J. Jones; and Mrs. J. J. Brantley.[59] The Newberry College building was used as a Confederate hospital, the surgeon in charge at the close of the war being Dr. Benjamin F. Kilgore.[60]

The community established a larger cemetery to take care of the casualties of the war. The legislature chartered the Rosemonte [sic] Cemetery Association on February 6, 1863, and named Dr. Peter Moon, F. B. Higgins, R. Stewart, A. C. Garlington, and Simeon Fair as the first board of Directors. Colonel Fair then conveyed 8.2 acres between the Calmes graveyard and lands of Newberry College to the association. Thereafter the old village cemetery was little used and was ultimately abandoned.[61]

All of the resources of the district were devoted to the welfare of the Confederacy. Slowly, the district was exhausted both in manpower and in resources. The end was inevitable after Gettysburg and Vicksburg in 1863. From that time on it was only a question of how long the South could stave off defeat. But this was not apparent from the gallantry of Newberry's soldiers in the field.

Newberry men fought in every Southern army; they were present at all major engagements. Certain units, however, were more closely identified with the district because they were raised in it. Gregg's 1st South Carolina, William's 3rd South Carolina, Hunt's 13th South Carolina, Keitt's 20th South Carolina, Lipscomb's 2nd Cavalry Regiment, the Hampton Legion, and the Holcombe Legion included Newberry companies. They fought from Fort Sumter to Appomattox, at Cold Harbor and Chancellorsville, Antietam and Fredericksburg, Knoxville and Chickamauga, Gettysburg, Atlanta, and Bentonville in North Carolina.

Two Newberry men wrote brigade histories: Captain D. Augustus Dickert, *The History of Kershaw's Brigade*, and Lieutenant J. F. J. Caldwell, *The History of a Brigade of South Carolinians known first as Gregg's and subsequently as McGowan's Brigade*. Both are classics and both tell the story of brave men who were unawed by the presence of death, of men who refused to yield to the overpowering material might of the enemy until ordered by their commanders to lay down their arms.

Caldwell, writing of Appomattox, made the point that "when three-fourths of Lee's army had disappeared from the ranks, when Grant's thousands swarmed around them on every side, they, poor remnants, marched forward to battle with steady tread and flying banners, until recalled to be surrendered."[62] This remnant included Newberry's first unit, Company B, Gregg's 1st South Carolina Volunteers, and the 13th South Carolina Regiment.

When Dickert paid tribute to Kershaw's Brigade, Newberry units in the 3rd and 20th South Carolina Regiments were given recognition: "This heritage of valor left to posterity as a memorial of Southern manhood to the Southern cause will be cherished by your descendants for all time, and when new generations come on and read the histories of the great Civil war, and recall to their minds the fortitude, the chivalry, and the glories of the troops engaged, Kershaw's Brigade will have a bright page in the book of their remembrance."[63]

Gregg's 1st South Carolina Volunteers volunteered to go to Virginia in April 1861, even though the regiment had originally been organized for service within the state. The regiment then volunteered for the duration of the war[64] and was reactivated as a unit of the Confederacy on July 27, 1861. The regiment was sent back to Virginia and became a part of Gregg's Brigade in late May 1862. This brigade, consisting of the 12th, 13th, and 14th South Carolina Volunteers, was organized on the South Carolina coast. It was ordered to Virginia in April 1862. There it became a brigade of five regiments with the addition of the 1st Regiment and Orr's Regiment of Rifles.[65]

The 13th South Carolina Volunteer Regiment was originally commanded by Colonel O. E. Edwards and later by Colonel B. T. Brockman. In 1864 Colonel Isaac Foster Hunt of Newberry succeeded to the command and led the regiment until the surrender. Lieutenant Colonel William Lester served as Hunt's executive officer.

Colonel Hunt was born in Newberry District on November 16, 1833, the son of Jacob Hamilton and Hannah Herbert Hunt. Educated at The Citadel, he was elected captain of the Newberry Rifles, Company D, 13th South Carolina Regiment. Promoted to major in 1862, to lieutenant-colonel in 1863, and to colonel in 1863, he saw hard fighting, was severely wounded several times, and was regarded as a fine officer. He entered business in Charleston after the war and then moved to Greenville in 1878. He was married to Harriet Austin and died on April 13, 1908.

Colonel Lester was born in Newberry District on October 9, 1819, the son of Allen and Martha Dennis Lester. He organized the DeKalb Guards, Company G, 13th South Carolina Regiment, in the Frog Level section of the district. Successively promoted to major and lieutenant-colonel, he was highly regarded as a steady, dependable officer. The Prosperity Chapter of the United Daughters of the Confederacy was named in his honor. He married Sarah Hunter and, after her death, Hannah Young. He died on March 1, 1886.

Gregg's Brigade was part of A. P. Hill's famous Light Division. In the campaign of 1862 the brigade saw action at Cold Harbor, Frazier's Farm, Malvern Hill, Second Manassas, Ox Hill, Harper's Ferry, Sharpsburg (or Antietam), Shepherdstown, and Fredericksburg. The next year it fought at Chancellorsville, Gettysburg, Hagerstown, and Falling Waters. In 1864, it was in the battles of the Wilderness, Spottsylvania Court House, Jericho Ford, Riddle's Shop, the Weldon Railroad, Deep Bottom, Fussel's Mills, Reams Station, and Jones's Farm. Finally it surrendered at Appomattox.

The Newberry units in Gregg's Brigade suffered heavy casualties. Company B of the 1st South Carolina, the Rhett Guards, had fifty-five men who were killed in battle or who died from disease.[66] It took pride in the flag of the 1st South Carolina being the first Confederate banner raised in Gettysburg;[67] it felt dishonored by its two deserters, W. C. Counts and William Hyler.[68]

Newberry's losses in the 13th South Carolina–Company D, the Newberry Rifles; Company G, the DeKalb Guards; and Company H, were, respectively, forty-nine, forty-seven and ten from battle and disease. Company H had only eighteen men from Newberry District.[69]

Caldwell tells of the attempt on the part of the Confederate government prior to the battle of Gettysburg to introduce a system of conferring medals as rewards and incentives of gallantry. One was offered to each company, to be given to the soldier whom the majority of his company should select as the most distinguished for gallantry in the battle of Chancellorsville. It excited no competition or enthusiasm, he writes, either because of an indifference to reputation or to a "high, stern patriotism which felt the cause far above baubles of metal."[70]

Newberry furnished five companies to Williams's 3rd South Carolina when it was organized. Captain J. C. S. Brown's Snow Hill Company and Captain Mat. Jones's Company from Laurens were absorbed by the other ten companies on organization of the regiment. Twelve companies volunteered and reported to duty, while Confederate regulations only permitted a regiment to have ten companies of 100 men each.[71]

The four Newberry companies in this regiment were B, the Williams Guards; C, the Pickens Guards; E, the Quitman Rifles; and H, the Dutch Company. They had losses in battle and from disease of forty-eight, thirty-seven, fifty-four, and forty-five, respectively.[72]

The spirit of the regiment was exemplified by Julius Zobel of Company E. He was a native of Germany, not yet twenty-one and not yet naturalized when he volunteered. He lost his leg at Knoxville and after being captured was sent to prison in the North. There he was visited by the German Consul who offered him his liberty if he would take the oath of allegiance to the North. Zobel refused to betray the country he had sworn to defend or to desert his comrades. Instead, he said, "Let me die a thousand deaths in this hell hole first!"[73]

It was also personified by Louis Spillers of Company D, who was fatally wounded in the battle of Chickamauga. When the litter-bearers found him late at night, he was leaning against a tree, calmly smoking his clay pipe. When asked why he did not call for assistance, he replied that he thought his turn to be cared for would come so he "just concluded to quietly wait and try to smoke away some of my misery." He died before morning.[74]

Dickert characterized Adjutant Y. J. Pope of the 3rd South Carolina as the "most beloved" of all the officers in that regiment. He was wounded seven times, including the loss of an eye at Cedar Creek. Another who displayed courage and fidelity was Simpson Piester, body servant of Lieutenant James Spencer Piester of Company C. When his master was killed at Fredericksburg, the faithful servant unhesitatingly went to his body and tenderly bore it to the rear so that it might be sent home.[75]

Colonel James H. Williams, another highly regarded officer, was born in Newberry District on October 4, 1813. He served in the Seminole War of 1836; as captain of Company L, the Palmetto Regiment, in the Mexican War; and as a major-general of militia before the Civil War. He led the 3rd South Carolina Regiment through the term of its first enlistment; at the reorganization of the regiment, Captain J. D. Nance was elected colonel. Colonel Williams returned to South Carolina where he commanded the 4th and 9th Regiments of State Troops until the end of the war. Dickert calls him a "born soldier, considerate of and kind to his men" and "cool and fearless to a fault." He was a most useful leader in peace and war.

Colonel James Drayton Nance commanded the 3rd Regiment in the battles around Richmond in 1862, at Second Manassas, Maryland Heights, Sharpsburg, Fredericksburg, Gettysburg, Chickamauga, Knoxville, and the Wilderness, where he was killed on May 6, 1864. A member of the Newberry Bar prior to the war, he was the idol of his regiment and had been recommended for promotion to brigadier general at the time of his death. The chapter of the United Confederate Veterans at Newberry bore his name.

Colonel William Drayton Rutherford, kinsman and former law partner of Nance, succeeded to the command of the regiment. He led it with distinction and great gallantry until his death at the battle of Strasburg, Virginia, on October 13, 1864. A chapter of the United Daughters of the Confederacy at Newberry is named in his honor.

The 3rd South Carolina took pride in being part of the First Brigade (Kershaw's), of the First Division (McLaw's), of the First Corps (Longstreet's) of the Army of Northern Virginia. As such, it saw action at First Manassas, Seven Pines, the Seven Days, Second Manassas, Harper's Ferry, Sharpsburg, Fredericksburg, Chancellorsville, and Gettysburg.

In late 1863 the Corps was sent to aid the Army of the Tennessee and as a part of that army, the 3rd South Carolina fought at Chickamauga and took part in the siege of Knoxville.[76] Returning to the Army of Northern Virginia, the 3rd South Carolina took part in the battles of the Wilderness, Spottsylvania Court House, Cold Harbor, Petersburg, and the Shenandoah Valley Campaign including the battles of Deep Bottom, Berryville, Strasburg, and Cedar Creek.

In 1865 Kershaw's Brigade returned to South Carolina in order to protect the state from Sherman. It was disposed on the Salkehatchie River, then pulled back to Cheraw and sent into North Carolina to join General Joseph E. Johnston. The 3rd South Carolina fought at Bentonville and surrendered to Sherman at Durham on May 2, 1865.[77]

Kershaw's Brigade was composed of the 2nd, 3rd, 7th, 8th, 15th, and 20th South Carolina Volunteers and the 3rd Battalion commanded by Colonel George S. James. James was born in Laurens County and his battery is credited with having fired the first shot of the Civil War. He was killed at South Mountain.[78]

The 20th Regiment was organized in 1862, along with the Holcombe Legion and other regiments. Lawrence M. Keitt, fiery former congressman from South Carolina, was its commanding officer.[79] John P. Kinard of Newberry was quartermaster of the regiment. He organized Company F in Newberry District and was succeeded by Captain John M. Kinard, who was killed at Strasburg on October 13, 1864.[80] William M. Kinard was thereupon promoted to captain and served in that capacity for the rest of the war. Of 132 men in service, twelve were killed in action and twelve died of disease.[81]

The 20th South Carolina was first stationed on the coast of South Carolina and there took part in the siege of Morris Island. Sent to Virginia in May 1864, it was assigned to Kershaw's Brigade.[82] Colonel Keitt commanded the brigade at Cold Harbor, was killed leading the attack, and thus was a casualty in his first battle in Virginia. His unit remained with Kershaw's Brigade and took part in all of its subsequent fighting.

The Holcombe Legion was a mixed unit of infantry and cavalry, constituted by South Carolina on November 21, 1861, and mustered into Confederate service on May 1, 1862. Colonel P. F. Stevens was the original commander, and Lieutenant-Colonel W. Pinckney Shingler was the executive officer. In July 1862, the infantry and cavalry were separated, with the cavalry going to Virginia immediately under Shingler's command. The cavalry became the 7th S.C. Cavalry Regiment under Colonel Shingler; when he resigned on May 30, 1864, Colonel Alexander C. Haskell became commander of the regiment.[83]

The 7th Cavalry was part of Gary's Brigade[84] and saw hard fighting in Virginia. Company C of the Holcombe Legion, known as the Newberry Rangers, was redesignated as Company E, 7th South Carolina Cavalry. Of a total of 107 men, thirty-four were from Newberry.[85]

Two other companies of the Holcombe Legion which were from Newberry were G and H. Company G became part of the Holcombe Legion Infantry and lost twenty-three men from wounds and disease. Company H was organized by Captain James M. Maffatt, who died of disease at Lockhart, Mississippi, in 1864 after being elected sheriff of Newberry District. This company had twenty-four casualties from battle and disease; eighteen men were captured and imprisoned until the end of the war.[86]

Company G. 2nd South Carolina Cavalry Regiment, was organized by Captain Thomas J. Lipscomb. He was promoted to colonel of the regiment, and Captain J. Wistar Gary commanded the company for the remainder of the war. Of twenty-nine men from Newberry, ten were captured; one of these, M. P. Cline, died in prison.[87] The 2nd South Carolina Cavalry was part of Butler's Command.

Colonel Thomas J. Lipscomb was born on March 27, 1833. He received a liberal arts education at the South Carolina College and the University of Virginia. He then attended Jefferson Medical College in Philadelphia and was graduated from the Medical College of South Carolina in 1854. Although he took post-graduate courses in that field in New York and Paris, he never practiced medicine. At the outbreak of the war, he was a planter in Newberry District. From captain of Company G, 2nd Cavalry Regiment South Carolina Volunteers, he was promoted to colonel of that regiment in 1863 after Butler lost his leg at Brandy Station. He served as such until the surrender.[88]

Colonel Lipscomb was married to Harriett Harrington in December, 1861. They had one son, Thomas J. Lipscomb, Jr. Colonel Lipscomb served as mayor of Columbia, and as superintendent of the Penitentiary. He died on November 4, 1908, at his home in Columbia.

Captain Ellison S. Keitt organized and commanded Company M, Mounted Rifles, 20th South Carolina Regiment. This unit saw service on the South Carolina coast and suffered no casualties. Another unit which saw service on the coast was Company G, 2nd Regiment of State Troops. Captain George H. Chapman commanded this company, which included seventy-seven men from Newberry, during its six months of active duty. This unit sustained losses from an epidemic of meningitis that struck the camp near Pocotaligo.[89]

And so these Newberrians whose courage was the hallmark of their devoted service to their state were at last released from war. They made their way homeward to an uncertain future. Theirs was to be a long, exhausting struggle.

2

Defeat and Despair

Looking forward to the inevitable defeat of the Confederacy, the U.S. Congress established the Freedmen's Bureau in March 1865. It was to function for one year after the war was over and was designed to promote the welfare of the freedmen by distributing rations to the needy, arranging transportation for the displaced, approving labor contracts, inspecting plantations, and looking after black schools.[1]

The first head of the bureau in South Carolina was General Rufus Saxton, a West Pointer who was "truly anti-slavery." Martin Abbott, in his incisive study, concluded, "Failing to recognize that racial adjustment between black and white in post-war South Carolina was a complex matter of many dimensions, he developed an approach that, while commendable in its commitment and sincerity, was deplorably naive. His idealism, thus misdirected, proved to be as much a source of weakness as of strength."[2]

Operating out of the Beaufort area, which had been in Union hands since early in the war, Saxton was ready to enlarge his activities to the rest of the state when the Confederacy collapsed.

Meanwhile General Sherman put the torch to the city of Columbia in February 1865 and continued his march across South Carolina. Although he regarded his Carolina campaign as his greatest achievement, it embittered generations of South Carolinians. Many still look upon him as a modern Attila the Hun, or as a monster who destroyed, looted, burned, and waged war upon a helpless civilian population. Whether his campaign is regarded as a military masterpiece or an act of unexampled brutality, most can agree that he laid waste to a great state.

Not knowing which way Sherman would go from Columbia, preparations were made to defend Newberry. Captain F. N. Walker, the Confederate enrolling officer, managed to rally one hundred men to protect the court house town. Pickets were posted and scouts sent out. Fortunately for Newberrians, the Union army moved toward Winnsboro rather than to Newberry.[3] But the vicinity of Pomaria was visited by one wing of Sherman's army with the usual results.[4]

Henry Summer, Esquire, had moved from Newberry to his farm near Pomaria. It lay in the path of Judson Kilpatrick, the notorious cavalryman, whose men burned the home, with its valuable library and the outbuildings, and left the family without food or shelter. Indeed a noose was placed around Summer's neck and he was threatened with hanging unless he gave the invaders gold he did not have. The family was finally able to walk four miles to William Summer's house, but the exposure and mistreatment undoubtedly shortened Summer's life; he died four years later. This was only one example of the treatment received by those who happened to live along Sherman's line of march.[5]

Two former Newberrians, however, seemed to enjoy the campaign. Mrs. Amelia Burton Boozer Feaster, and her ravishingly beautiful daughter, Marie Boozer, the future Countess de Pourtales, left Columbia with Kilpatrick. The people of Winnsboro were incensed when the two ladies rode through that town in a carriage commandeered from the Elmore family.[6] The people of Newberry enjoyed one report which filtered back from the vicinity of Fayetteville. Hampton's cavalry, it was said, rode into a sleeping camp, and General Kilpatrick made a hasty escape from the warm bed of a lovely lady. In Newberry she was generally thought to have been Marie Boozer.[7]

But there was little to amuse Newberrians in 1865. General Lee surrendered the Army of Northern Virginia to Grant at Appomattox on April 9, and General Johnson surrendered the Army of Tennessee and all troops in the Department of North and South Carolina to Sherman at Durham on April 26. To white Newberrians the world had ended. Worse was yet to come; it soon would be apparent that the heel of the conqueror was more debilitating than the sword of the victor.

During the weeks between the sack of Columbia and formal surrender, there was little activity, governmental, political, or economic, in the state.[8] Governor Magrath fled from Columbia and was a fugitive until arrested and incarcerated in Fort Pulaski.[9] He spent several days at Major L. J. Jones's home in Newberry in early March.[10] The General Assembly tried to meet in Greenville but, when only thirty members appeared, it lacked a quorum and so could do nothing, reported the *Charleston Courier* of May 10, 1865.

John Porter Hollis, an authority on the early period of Reconstruction in South Carolina concluded:

> The imprisonment of the governor, the existence of martial law, and the consequent disruption of the State government, left South Carolina in a sad condition. Her people were for the time deeply humiliated. They had already known what it meant to be the object of special vengeance, and forebodings of the future appeared to be equally gloomy. It was feared that South Carolina, jeered at as the "nest wherein was hatched the snake of secession," would lose her status as a State entirely and become part of the national public domain. Vast tracts of her territory along the coast and the sea islands had even then been confiscated and rumors of entire confiscation were everywhere prevalent.[11]

Soldiers returned home from Virginia and North Carolina to find desolation. A state with a white population of 146,000 males of all ages in 1860 had lost 40,000 men by death or disease. South Carolina lost 23 percent of its arms-bearing population compared to an average loss of 10 percent of all Confederate armies and 5 percent of all Union armies.[12] In addition South Carolina's property had lost seven-eighths of its total pre-war value.[13]

In 1860 Newberry District's real estate was valued at $4,766,300 and its personal property, consisting principally of slaves, at $14,000,000.[14] These valuations were made by the owners and the assistant marshal in charge of taking the census of 1860.

Ten years later the district's real estate was valued at $2,575,621 and the personal property at $1,727,958.[15] Thus in a decade the taxable wealth of Newberry District declined from $17.75 million to $4.3 million. The depreciation took place during the first five years of the decade as the result of the war, emancipation, and poor crops.[16]

The results of wartime were still much in evidence. The barren farm conditions were all too evident in the decaying plantations, overgrown fields, sagging buildings, rotting fences, and scrawny livestock. Swarms of freedmen were in motion; the entire labor system was in a chaotic condition.[17]

Francis B. Simkins and Robert H. Woody, in their study of the state during Reconstruction, describe with vivid clarity the five principal reasons, besides the effect of fighting itself, for the plight of South Carolina. "First, there was the influence of the blockade; second, the necessities of war had prompted the neglect of processes of production essential to the normal functioning of the community; third, there was a great sacrifice of man power; fourth, most of the surplus wealth was expended in the cause of the Confederacy and the defeat blasted hopes of its future redemption; fifth, the social discipline of the community was disrupted by the destruction of slavery."[18]

South Carolina's transportation system had been destroyed in large measure during the war. At the surrender, the Laurens Railroad was inoperable; its rails were ripped up and twisted, its crossties destroyed, and its rolling stock worn out. The Laurens and Newberry Hack, called a handsome coach by the *Newberry Herald* of February 28, 1866, provided the only public transportation between these two courthouse towns. The hack made three round trips a week. The other line through the district, the Greenville and Columbia Railroad, was in poor condition but could function after a fashion.

Following the assassination of President Lincoln in April 1865, his successor, Andrew Johnson, early manifested his intention to carry out Lincoln's program to restore the Union and not to treat the South as conquered territory. On May 29, 1965, Johnson issued an Amnesty Proclamation that indicated his conception of different degrees of guilt among those whose conduct was to be forgiven. All citizens were urged to take the "test" oath and all who would do so were granted full pardon except those in the exempted classes. These individuals had to petition the President individually for a pardon.[19]

Among those from Newberry District to petition the President for amnesty were: the bookdealer W. J. Duffie; Elijah P. Lake, the former Ordinary of the district during the early years of the war; G. F. Wells, Andrew Lee Lark, Baruch Duncan, John S. Renwick, George B. Tucker, Henry Whitmire, John Hopkins Williams, and Washington Floyd, farmers; lawyer Lambert J. Jones; and Colonel James H. Williams. Lake was excluded as an officeholder while the others from Newberry were excluded because they owned property valued at more than $20,000. Only Williams and Duffie had been soldiers, the former as an officer and the latter as a private. Jones had served for three months as regimental commissary in the state reserves.[20]

At the local level three crucial problems had to be solved: the political, the social, and the economic. As a conquered territory, South Carolina had no functioning government. With the freeing of slaves, an enormous adjustment was required on the part of the former masters and former slaves. Economically the district had to solve the problem of survival. Attention first turned to the political problem; until South Carolina had a semblance of stability the other two problems could not be addressed.

The *Tri-Weekly Herald* of June 21, 1865, carried a call for a public meeting at Masonic Hall for the first Monday in July to consider the political condition of South Carolina. The person calling the meeting, T. P. Slider, would within a few years become a "scalawag" and hold office as county treasurer. "Scalawag" was defined by Simkins and Woody a generation ago as a native white who was "impelled to forego feelings of race prejudice and local attachment in order to win office or plunder through the Negro vote." As defined by Eric Foner, the leading modern authority on Reconstruction, a "scalawag" was a native Southerner who cast his lot politically with the freedmen. Foner points out that the terms "carpetbagger" and "scalawag" have become so unavoidable a part of the lexicon of Reconstruction that he has continued to employ them, without intending to accept their pejorative implications.

Newberry District's Republican Party included "carpetbaggers," or those who had come from the North with all of their belongings in a carpetbag, the best example being John J. Carrington; sincere Unionists such as B. Odell Duncan; and "scalawags."

Meanwhile Silas Johnstone, Esquire, the Intendant, appointed a Committee of Eleven to make arrangements for the public meeting to be held instead at Hurd's Hall on July 3.[21]

The proposed meeting was held on that date, Colonel James H. Williams being elected chairman, and Henry Summer, secretary. Williams appointed a Committee of Fifteen, and resolutions were adopted recognizing the end of the war and the desirability of early restoration of South Carolina to the Union. Colonel Williams was elected a deputy to serve the new president, Andrew Johnson, with former Congressman Armistead Burt of Abbeville, who had been elected at a public meeting in Abbeville a few days before. The group recommended that James L. Orr, former speaker of the U.S. House of Representatives, also be sent to Washington. W. W. Boyce of Fairfield District was endorsed for governor, and the group also named a Committee on Correspondence and a Committee to Raise Funds for the Washington conference.[22]

Before the Newberry citizens met, President Johnson had appointed, on June 30, the Honorable Benjamin F. Perry of Grenville as provisional governor of South Carolina. Perry was directed to enroll eligible South Carolina voters at once and order an election for a constitutional convention that would restore the state to the Union. The President's choice was an able, high-minded Unionist who had retained the respect of all factions and his appointment was an indication of Johnson's good intentions.[23]

Two weeks after the appointment of Governor Perry, the 4th Separate Brigade, United States Army, was assigned to the Western District of South Carolina with headquarters at Newberry. Brevet Brigadier General Charles H. Van Wyck was the commander. Newberry, Laurens, Abbeville, and Edgefield constituted the 2nd Sub District, and the 56th New York Regiment was assigned to it. Its commander, Lieutenant Colonel Rockwell Tyler, established his headquarters in the Newberry College building. Company L was stationed in Newberry.[24]

The election for delegates from Newberry District to the Constitutional Convention resulted in the naming of E. P. Lake, Henry Summer, and Robert Stewart. James H Williams and Ellison S. Keitt were defeated.[25] No blacks voted, and few whites participated.

Before the convention could meet, Newberry was shocked by an act of barbarity and thrilled by another of extraordinary courage. On the evening of September 8, 1865, a young ex-Confederate soldier from Texas, Calvin Crozier, was returning home from Virginia; he was in a box-car at the Newberry Depot with some women under his care.[26] During the night soldiers of the 33rd United States Colored Troops (organized originally in the Sea Islands around Beaufort as the 1st South Carolina Regiment of Volunteers by Thomas W. Higginson)[27] intruded into the car and insulted the women. Crozier remonstrated, they refused to leave the car, and Crozier wounded one slightly with a knife. The regiment was bivouacked in Halcyon Grove (near the railroad tracks south of Boundary Street), and the soldiers soon assembled at the depot where they seized Jacob S. Bowers by mistake. As they were about to lynch an innocent man, Crozier declared that he was the one who had wounded the soldier.[28]

The infuriated mob seized Calvin Crozier, carried him back to the bivouac area, shot him and buried him in a shallow grave. The white officers of the regiment not only refused to intervene, but the commander, Colonel Charles Trowbridge, took full responsibility for what occurred.[29]

To the credit of the citizens of Newberry, Calvin Crozier has not been forgotten. A chapter of the United Daughters of the Confederacy honored itself by assuming his name. A shaft marks the spot where he was murdered, and his remains are now in Rosemont Cemetery with a suitable marker.

The recent murder of a Confederate veteran by Union soldiers and misconduct by others had much to do with the actions taken by the Constitutional Convention when it met in Columbia on September 13. As if to accentuate the low state to which South Carolina had descended, Colonel Tyler constituted a Provost Court at Newberry just as the convention met; it consisted of Captain James J. Cox, Burr J. Ramage, and Silas Johnstone and had all the power normally exercised by the civil authorities.[30] Although the two civilians were outstanding citizens and greatly respected, the appointments brought home to Newberrians the full effect of living under martial law.

The delegates meeting in Columbia adopted an ordinance declaring all acts that were in force on December 19, 1860, of full force until altered or repealed by lawful authority; all acts passed since December 19 were to continue in force until modified or repealed except that those acts recognizing slavery had ended. The ordinance prohibited the General Assembly from ever passing any act imposing civil disabilities, forfeiture of property, or punishment of any kind on any citizen or resident for his conduct in reference to secession or the war. It also provided that all persons holding office on April 26, 1865, should hold and exercise the same for the residue of their respective terms provided that they took, before December 1, the oath prescribed in President Johnson's Amnesty Proclamation of May 29, 1865.[31]

On the same day (September 27) the convention adopted a constitution. It provided, for the first time, for direct election of the governor and lieutenant governor for four-year terms; for suffrage for all white men twenty-one years of age or more (except paupers and noncommissioned officers or privates in the United States services, and those disqualified by law for criminal convictions); for a House of Representatives of 124 members, one-half to be apportioned by population and one-half by taxes paid in each district, possessing the qualifications of white electors with residence in the state for three years; and for a Senate composed of one member from each district except Charleston, which was given two senators, the qualifications being the attaining of the age of thirty and residence within the state for five years.[32]

The convention also informed the next legislature that presidential electors should in future be elected by direct popular vote. Thus the convention abolished property qualifications for holding office and effectively reapportioned the Senate. As a result power passed to the upcountry. The constitution was not submitted to the people,[33] but elections were called in October for governor, lieutenant governor, and members of the General Assembly.

In Newberry District, Colonel James H. Williams, unsuccessful in his race for delegate to the convention, defeated Robert Moorman for the Senate by the close vote of 401 to 369. Six candidates ran for the House, and Christian H. Suber, Ellison S. Keitt, and A. C. Garlington were elected.[34] Wade Hampton carried Newberry District for governor by 360 votes to 355 for James L. Orr.[35] Hampton had asked the voters not to vote for him but came within 800 votes of winning.[36] W. D. Porter of Charleston was elected lieutenant governor.[37]

Meanwhile the 56th New York Regiment was replaced by the 25th Ohio Regiment, Lieutenant A. Madison commanding the local garrison.[38] In December, Madison was succeeded by Lieutenant Will H. Fonts.[39]

Four militia companies were organized in the District in 1865. Captains D. A. Dickert, Thomas W. Gary, J. K. G. Nance, and John McCarley were the respective commanders. At the beginning of the year the governor appointed M. W. Gary of Edgefield as major general of the 1st Division, James H. Williams of Newberry as major general of the 5th Division, R. P. Todd of Laurens as brigadier general of the 10th Brigade, Thomas W. Gary of Newberry as colonel of the 38th Regiment, and W. W. Lester of Newberry as colonel of the 39th Regiment.[40]

The General Assembly, meeting in November, established a penitentiary in Columbia, this being the first time South Carolina took steps to operate a state penal institution.[41] This was good legislation; but, unfortunately for the state, the legislature then enacted an elaborate Black Code rigidly regulating the conduct of the freedmen. For the first time, a Negro was defined as a person having one-eighth or more Negro blood; previously, determination of race was a question of fact for a jury. Miscegination was prohibited, and a special district court was given exclusive jurisdiction of all matters in which one or both parties were Negro and of all criminal causes in which the accused was a Negro.[42] The court also was directed to try cases of bastardy and vagrancy. Appeal was authorized from the district court to the circuit judge. The Black Code was a grievous error and was perceived by the North as an attempt to continue slavery under a different name.

Another matter that hurt the cause of the South was the misconduct of some white people. Solicitor Simeon Fair wrote Governor Orr on December 30, 1865, that a wanton, unprovoked murder had been perpetrated in the town of Newberry three days before. A band of ten or twelve mounted men had ridden up to the door of the jail, demanded the key of the guard, and had then shot him when he said that he did not have it. The men wheeled and escaped, but one of their horses was killed. The solicitor went on to report that the band had then killed a Negro about five miles from town. Two or three of the leaders called "scouts," lived in the neighborhood of the Saluda River on the Edgefield side; the others apparently were thoughtless youths with no better employment. Fair had called out the police companies of mounted men and put them under the authority of the officer commanding the Federal garrison.[43]

At about the same time Thomas W. Holloway was writing the governor about the threat of a black uprising in the Pomaria section.[44] Amid such fears, the garrison at Newberry was doubled.[45]

As should have been anticipated, General Daniel Sickles, the state's military commander, declared the Black Code void on January 1, 1866, and forbade any laws discriminating in any way between the races. He also stated that he would enforce fair labor contracts.[46]

Congress refused to seat Benjamin F. Perry and John L. Manning when they were elected United States senators in 1865 by the General Assembly. It then passed the Civil Rights Act over President Johnson's veto. General Sickles continued to overrule the state's civil authority by military fiat, even though the President declared the rebellion ended on April 2, 1866.

While the state was suffering from these actions, the people of Newberry not only shared those vicissitudes but experienced others peculiar to themselves. On June 18, 1866, the town's most destructive fire until that time started from an incendiary origin in the old Thespian Hall and rapidly spread. The *Newberry Herald* reported: "One-half of the business portion of our handsome little town is now a mass of ruins, and many of those who once dwelt securely and were recuperating their wasted energies, are now driven forth in an almost helpless condition."[47]

The largest loser in the flames was General H. H. Kinard, whose hall and hotel were valued at $20,000, and the total loss was in excess of $130,000. After the fire, a so-called "police company" of forty volunteers was organized: Captain Y. J. Pope, First Lieutenant T. M. Paysinger, and Orderly Sergeant Thomas S. Moorman, were its officers.[48] This was actually Newberry's first volunteer fire company.

By June 1867, the burned section was almost entirely reclaimed by the erection of substantial buildings. Nevertheless, the *Newberry Herald* of June 5, 1867, complained of the dull times, saying there was no business, and the very streets were deserted except by the merchants and their clerks, who stood upon the curb stones from early morning until evening.

The General Assembly in the 1866 session rewrote the District Court Act to abolish the distinction of color as a basis for court jurisdiction and vested exclusive jurisdiction in that court for all cases of larceny, misdemeanor, vagrancy, bastardy, and matters of contract between employer and employee or master and apprentice, where the amount exceeded $20. The court was given concurrent jurisdiction in cases not exceeding $100. It was made a court of record.[49]

Legislators also passed an act appointing a commissioner of immigration and encouraging European immigration. For the benefit of disabled veterans, they appropriated $20,000 for the purchase of artificial legs, and railroad companies were required to transport the wearers of the limbs free of charge.[50] But the most far-reaching legislative action was the refusal of the General Assembly to ratify the Fourteenth Amendment. Similar action by all former Confederate states except Tennessee brought about Radical Reconstruction and ended any opportunity of government by native white South Carolinians for the next decade.[51]

Failure to ratify the Fourteenth Amendment brought swift action from Congress. In March 1867 it declared that "no legal government or adequate protection for life or property existed in the unreconstructed States." They were divided into five military districts, North and South Carolina constituting the Second Military District under Major General Daniel H. Sickles, a former New York politician who had been in command at Charleston since the end of the war.[52]

Fearful that the people of the South might prefer remaining under martial law to meeting standards set by the Radical Congress for readmission to the Union, Congress directed military commanders to register all electors, white and black, except those whites unable to take the "test" oath, to hold elections for delegates to constitutional conventions, and to submit the new constitutions to the electors for ratification.[53] With these developments, the white leaders in Newberry, as in other districts, realized that they had come face to face with the new problems.

Blacks, anxious to assert themselves politically, gradually resolved to act independently of their former masters. In this evolution from subservience to political independence, they were encouraged and led by the most able members of their own race, by "carpetbaggers" who had first come into South Carolina with the Army and the Freedmen's Bureau, and by "scalawags." The last group was composed of South

Carolinians who for whatever reasons, chose to cooperate with those fashioning a new sociopolitical order.

The Union League of America followed the Union Army into South Carolina and it became a significant force when Congress enfranchised the Negroes. The league held secret meetings, and its ritual, teachings, and emotional appeal made the Negroes an important force in the Radical Republican Party.[54] In Newberry the league was an important factor in preventing the white leaders of the district from securing black cooperation, but for a short time it appeared that the whites might succeed.

B. Odell Duncan, a native Unionist who held office as United States Consul in Germany during the war, published an open letter in the *Newberry Herald* in March 1867, frankly advocating the establishment of full and complete equality of whites and blacks. He called upon Major L. J. Jones to take the lead in having Governor Orr call a constitutional convention to effect such a change.[55] Of course Major Jones did nothing of the kind since he and the other leading white citizens of Newberry, much like Wade Hampton, still thought they could control the Negroes by kindness and fair treatment.

The blacks, however, had other ideas. Simeon Young, Edward Young, Joseph Boston, Harvey Davis, and William Waring, local black leaders, announced that a picnic would be held at Blandusium Springs near Newberry on July 4. The various freedmen's associations, the Kindly Union Society, the Fellowship Association, and the Newberry Temperance Society combined to give the picnic. Invitations were extended to a number of the white citizens, and many attended.

The *Newberry Herald* reported the event and gave it full coverage. The streets of the town were filled at an early hour by freedmen who poured into Newberry from the plantations within a thirty mile radius. The societies formed a procession and marched to the picnic grounds followed by a large crowd. Two thousand blacks were present; all vied in showing their esteem for their white friends. The orators representing the societies were Simeon Young, Joseph Boston, Robert Toliver, and Howard Brown. The paper reported that the addresses were well delivered and well received, with not a word of a political or intemperate character heard. Everyone was greatly pleased.

Then General A. C. Garlington, Newberry's most gifted orator, counseled the freedmen not to engage in party strife and not to offer for office. He told them their civil rights were guaranteed, as was their freedom, and that whites had no disposition to deprive them of their rights.

He then said:

> I would especially put you on your guard against those who may come
> amongst you to stir up strife, or to advocate a policy which will lead to that
> end. Beware of wolves in sheep's clothing. We have had enough of strife;
> the country wants peace, and all our people rest. We want industry to
> revive, and plenty and prosperity to come back to us again. We should
> work together to this end, and avoid everything that may tend to prevent
> its accomplishment. By this course alone can you promote your own in-
> terests and prosperity, and the good of your race. We will deal fairly and
> honestly with you in all our relations, and we expect you to do the same
> with us.

The newspaper reported that the tables were then spread for dinner;
afterward other speeches were made and all was harmonious.

The reporter editorialized in closing: "The colored citizens of Newberry compare favorably in point of intelligence and good breeding, and
in their reciprocity of feeling and attachment to their white friends, with
their brethren in other districts."

The same euphoria was apparent in the newspaper's account of a
public meeting held at the Court House two weeks later. B. F. Randolph of Orangeburg, whose assassination in 1869 would trigger a legislative investigation, made the principal address stressing education,
labor, honesty, and voting. His remarks were regarded as mild and
generally well put.

The denouement followed quickly. Later in July the Union Republican Convention, held first in Charleston, reconvened in Columbia.
Newberry was represented by B. Odell Duncan, James Henderson, Simeon Young, Matthew Gray, and Joseph Boston. Only Duncan was
white, and he withdrew from the convention when that body went on
record as favoring the division and sale of all unoccupied lands.

In August a large radical meeting was held in Newberry for William
J. Armstrong, a Northerner assaulted in a Columbia barroom by two
Columbia youths who then were jailed by General Sickles. Armstrong
was accompanied by Thomas J. Robertson, future Republican U.S. senator of Columbia. The *Newberry Herald* reflected the hardening feeling
by reporting that Armstrong and Robertson "left as they came, like
thieves in the night."[56]

In September, Robert Toliver, Charley Cannon, James Longshore,
Harvey Clark, and others gave public notice that application would be
made to the legislature for an act incorporating a Freedmen's School in

town.[57] In that same month, voter registration was completed, Newberry District registering 1,131 white males and 2,251 black males.[58]

On September 21, 1867, the white Conservatives of the State held a meeting in Columbia at which twenty-one of the thirty-one districts were represented. Colonel Simeon Fair of Newberry was elected one of the vice presidents of the convention, and General James Chesnut, Jr., former U.S. senator, was chosen as president.[59]

The delegates protested the Reconstruction Acts passed by Congress, declaring them illegal and designed "to sow the seeds of discord in our midst and place the best interests of society in the hands of an ignorant mob." They then called on all registered white voters to ignore the approaching referendum; this action was taken in the hope that a majority of qualified electors would not participate and thereby, under the terms of the Reconstruction Acts, prevent the holding of a constitutional convention.

The action of the Conservatives cost them any hope of controlling the Negroes. It also left the state without benefit of the wisdom and experience of many of its leaders in the upcoming constitutional convention. And it fed the propaganda mills of the radicals who would later charge that the traditional leadership of South Carolina, by refusing to participate in this election, contributed directly to the excesses of Reconstruction.[60]

Carrying out the congressional mandate, General Edward Canby, successor to General Sickles as military commander, ordered an election held in November to determine whether a constitutional convention should be held and choose delegates to it if the convention were approved. Not a single white person voted at the courthouse box. Only thirty white voters participated in the district, but the convention received 1,969 votes. Lee Nance and James Henderson, blacks, received 1,605 and 1,561 votes, respectively, as delegates. B. Odell Duncan, a native white, got 1,579 votes.[61] General Canby declared the delegates elected and furnished each of them with credentials to attend a convention to meet in Charleston on January 14, 1868.[62]

The whites of Newberry at last realized that they would not be able to control the blacks. The latter were determined to participate fully in the governing of South Carolina. Outnumbering white voters in Newberry District, it was inevitable that they would win some of the offices in that district.

3

The Convention of 1868

The end of the war found blacks restive and whites apprehensive. Confusion abounded. Many newly freed blacks understandably thought that freedom meant surcease from all work; it was an invitation to migrate, and to congregate in towns. Many believed the cruel rumors that each freedman would be given forty acres and a mule. They were to be bitterly disappointed because ownership of land was by all odds the single most desired objective of the former slaves. In agricultural Newberry, land was wealth, and the blacks hoped for their share.

Many freedmen of course owned little except the clothes on their backs. They rarely acquired much property before emancipation, and the proclamation simply dealt with their status. Their experience as field hands and their lack of education equipped most of them only for manual labor, if not on the farms of their former masters, then somewhere else. Obviously, a welfare program had to be devised to help them.

Assistance also was needed by many whites, for their destitution was acute. War had not only taken its toll of the lives and bodies of the white men of Newberry but had wrecked the economy. Economic survival, for the moment, was even more important than the question of political control. Representatives of the old ruling class, as well as the poor whites, were in need. Lieutenant General Richard Heron Anderson, of the Army of Northern Virginia, in which he commanded a corps, accepted work as a day laborer for the South Carolina Railroad.[1]

John E. Glenn, son of Dr. George W. Glenn of Newberry, and a twice-wounded prisoner of war, lost everything in the war and had to find work to feed his wife and children. His friend, Major L. J. Jones, wrote Governor Orr to enlist support in getting Glenn a job as conductor on the Greenville and Columbia Railroad. Jones stated that Glenn had experience in railroad matters, for during the war he "had the control and management of the Memphis & Little Rock Rail Road for about six months."[2] His was a more or less typical case.

Governor Orr was besieged with pleas for provisions for hungry white natives, but the state had no means of helping its citizens.[3] Some of the distress was alleviated as the Freedmen's Bureau distributed food to both whites and blacks. By November 1866, the bureau had issued almost 800,000 rations to freedmen and 170,000 to whites at a total cost of $150,000. In 1867 alone $300,000 was spent in South Carolina for relief. Martin Abbott, in his study of the bureau, characterized this relief program as a bright chapter in its history.[4]

During this critical period, some local freedmen emigrated to the West, to Florida, and to Liberia. The *Weekly Herald* reported in the spring of 1866 that about 100 Negroes had boarded the railroad cars for an unknown destination; it said the agent who gathered them together was from the West.[5]

The same paper reported that 150 freedmen from Newberry had sailed for Liberia on the *Golconda,* a ship owned by the American Colonization Society. The emigrants had left Newberry on November 11.[6] This venture was not a happy one. Burrell Raines, one of the emigrants, returned within a year and reported through the *Weekly Herald* of August 14, 1867, that some had died and still more were sick. Nearly all of the survivors were anxious to come back to Newberry because, he said, they could not stand either the climate or the water.

Toward the end of 1866 Ralph Ely, late Brevet Brigadier General and now civil agent for the Freedmen's Bureau, certified that he had selected and made entry of United States lands in the vicinity of New Smyrna, Volusia County, Florida, for "certain freedmen resident of Newbury (sic) County, South Carolina." He requested transportation and subsistence for them and their families. Ninety-five men, women, and children proceeded by the Greenville and Columbia Railroad from Newberry to Columbia; thence they went to Charleston by rail and then by steamer to New Smyrna.[7] This colony had troubles in its new home, but some of the emigrants from Newberry succeeded there.[8]

While the new freedmen were making efforts to move elsewhere, local citizens were encouraging immigration of white Europeans. A meeting was held at the courthouse on July 2, 1866, at which a District Immigration Society was organized. J. F. J. Caldwell asserted that the present system of African labor was ruinous to the country, and he wanted to attract immigrants from North Germany, Denmark, and Sweden as workers. Although Isaac Herbert questioned the ability to hold lands by introducing foreign laborers, most of those in attendance were in favor of such a plan.[9]

Under this scheme male Europeans who immigrated to South Carolina were to receive $150 per year. The employer was to advance cost of transportation to be repaid out of the first year's wages, and field hands were to receive weekly, two pounds of pork and bacon, three pounds of corned beef, one quart of molasses, one pound of rice, and ten pounds of corn-meal or flour. Each male laborer also was to get one-half acre for himself, one-half acre for his wife, and one-quarter acre for each child, with the privilege of keeping a cow, pig, and poultry. Laborers were to be provided comfortable living quarters and free fuel. Female house servants were to be paid $100 per year and furnished board. Passage from Europe to Charleston was thirty dollars in gold for an adult and fifteen dollars in gold for a child, such sums to be paid upon arrival in Charleston.

The first batch of German immigrants to South Carolina arrived in Charleston on November 28, 1867, on the barque *Gauss*. The trip took forty-nine days, and 152 immigrants were aboard. In May 1868, the Reverend T. S. Boinest became president of the local immigration society, and until his death in 1871, he devoted his considerable talents to this program. Twenty-two rosy-cheeked, intelligent looking Germans arrived in Newberry in May 1868. By the end of that year 127 immigrants reached Newberry. Twenty more came in February 1869, and fifteen in March.

The society, which established offices in Newberry, Charleston, and Columbia, employed F. W. Bruggemann as general agent. In December 1869, twenty-four Swedes arrived. By the end of 1869 more than 272 immigrants had reached Newberry, but the death of T. S. Boinest ended serious efforts to attract immigrants to Newberry and the local society soon disbanded.[10]

Meanwhile, political events captured the attention of Newberrians. On March 17, 1867, B. Odell Duncan of Newberry wrote Governor James L. Orr, requesting that he persuade the *Charleston News* "or some other respectable paper" to publish a letter which he enclosed.[11] In it Duncan pleads for immediate full and complete equality before the law for all, regardless of race or color, and prophesizes harsh treatment of the South if it fails to grant such equality. Orr, with his usual desire to cover his flanks, requested William H. Trescot, at that time editor of the *Daily News*, to publish the letter.[12]

Duncan, born in Newberry District of well-to-do parents, Baruch Duncan and his first wife, Piannah McCrackin Duncan, graduated from Furman University in 1858; he then pursued postgraduate studies at the Universities of Berlin and Bonn until the outbreak of war.[13] In 1862 he accepted appointment as consul for the United States government for the Grand Duchy of Baden and the Rhenish Palatinate of Bavaria. He remained in this position until 1866 when he was removed by President Johnson.[14] He then returned to Newberry and began taking part in the organization of the new government. Although he was a sincere Unionist by conviction, he was ambitious for office and resolved to obtain one equal to his talents.

When the Union Republican Party held its convention in Columbia on July 24, 1867, Duncan was the only white delegate from Newberry District; his colleagues were four blacks, James Henderson, Simeon Young, Matthew Gray, and Joseph Boston. Although firmly committed to equality of the races, Duncan was still a conservative who expected someday to inherit land. Therefore he rebelled when the convention adopted a resolution calling for the division and sale of unoccupied lands to the poorer classes. Duncan wrote a letter to the president of the Union Republican Party of South Carolina, R. H. Gleaves, asking that his name be stricken from the party roll. Gleaves honored his request, stating that he was glad the convention had such a platform that no Judas could remain.[15]

Although Duncan's letter of resignation was published in the *New-berry Herald* of July 31, 1867, he felt that his position required further explanation. He accordingly wrote a long letter to the editor stating his belief that "the only safety for the country is to form a party based on the principles of the Civil Rights and Reconstruction Bills." He chided men of moderate views for not participating in the organization of the Republican Party and urged that only those with "their eyes open to the spirit and necessities of the times, would be able to rescue us from the dangers now threatening."[16]

Newberry's delegates to the Constitutional Convention were B. Odell Duncan, Lee A. Nance, and James Henderson. They received a bad press. The *Newberry Herald* reprinted an article about them which had appeared in the *Charleston Mercury.*[17]

In it Duncan was described as tall, slim, with reddish hair and a red beard, and about thirty years of age. He was ridiculed severely for his Union activities during and since the war. Nance was described as the son of a Negro father and a mulatto mother, about thirty-eight years of

age, stoutly built, good looking, industrious, and with more than ordinary intelligence. Henderson, twenty-five years of age and a mulatto, was
said to be the most intelligent delegate from Newberry.

John Porter Hollis, in writing of the convention, states:

> An analysis of the elements of the convention will result in this general
> classification: (1) native whites without distinction or reputation; (2) ex-
> Federal officers; (3) adventurers in search of promotion or plunder; (4)
> negro lawyers and missionaries; (5) former slaves. Only twenty-three of
> the white delegates were *bona fide* citizens of the State. Among these were
> F. J. Moses, Jr., who as aide to Governor Pickens had helped to haul down
> the Union colors at Fort Sumter, and who afterwards became a very cor-
> rupt "scalawag" governor; Camp, a "moonshiner" from Spartanburg,
> who shortly before his election to the convention had been "broken up"
> for illicit whiskey distilling; T. J. Robertson, who had grown rich as a war
> speculator and who afterwards became United States Senator; C. C.
> Bowen, who had been accused of bribing a man to assassinate a Confeder-
> ate officer, and tried for murder; J. M. Rutland, who after the Brooks-
> Sumner episode in the United States Senate, made up a purse to buy a
> cane for Brooks, but afterwards became a strong unionist. Seven of the
> White delegates had been Confederate soldiers.[18]

Duncan, while not representing the views of the majority of whites in
Newberry District, could not properly be called a "scalawag." He at least
had rejected secession openly and had the courage to refuse to fight his
section's battles. He did not pander to the black vote by advocating
seizure of unoccupied lands. His chief fault was in believing that
he could induce those who detested his views to follow him into the
Republican Party.

Governor Orr delivered a statesmanlike address to the convention
when it convened. For once he spoke from his heart rather than with an
eye to his own future, when he stated: "The fact cannot be disguised,
however, that the white population has almost unanimously abstained
from exercising the privilege (of voting), and your Convention is, therefore, strictly speaking, the representative only of the colored population
of South Carolina. This being the case, it cannot be denied that the
intelligence, refinement and wealth of the State is not represented by
your body . . . "[19]

Orr urged the convention to write a constitution under which all
men, white and black, could live in peace and with dignity. He urged
that every man in the state be allowed to vote without any disability in
electing the next legislature, and that after January 1, 1870, no man be

permitted to vote unless he could read and write, that a liberal home-
stead law be enacted, that imprisonment for debt be abolished, that relief
be given debtors for debts contracted before the war, that all existing
debts founded upon the purchase of slaves be wiped out, that provision
be made to educate the colored people, and that the obligations of the
state be fully redeemed.

Albert Gallatin Mackey, one of America's foremost Freemasons and a
bona fide Unionist before and during the war, was elected president of
the convention. He appointed Duncan to the Committee on the Legislative Part of the Constitution, James Henderson to the Committee on the
Bill of Rights, and Lee Nance to the Committee on Petitions.

According to the *Proceedings of the Convention*, neither Henderson
nor Nance made a speech, offered an amendment, or made a motion.
While Duncan was not one of the leaders, he nevertheless took an active part in some important deliberations. He served on the committee
to prescribe a mode in which the constitution should be submitted for
ratification and to provide for the election of state officers.

Duncan opposed the provision that the General Assembly provide for
compulsory attendance of all school children between the ages of six and
sixteen. Later he made a prophetic speech against the article which proposed to require schools and colleges to be open and free to all young
people without regard to race, color, or previous condition.

In part he said:

If we begin by educating the masses, we end by overcoming our prejudices. But if we begin by attempting to overcome their prejudices by force,
and educating them afterwards, I am convinced that the whole plan will
result in a failure.

Now, what is likely to be the result of obtaining this section, and
thereby opening the schools to all? Simply that they would be attended
only by the colored children. If the attempt is made to enforce a mixture
this way, I have no idea that fifty white children in the State would
attend the public schools. The freedmen's schools are now, if I mistake
not, open to all; and yet I believe not one white pupil in the State
attends them. . . .

Again, in attempting to enforce mixed schools, you bring trouble,
quarreling, and wrangling into every neighborhood. . . .

Gentlemen, this is too serious a question, to the peace and welfare of the
country, for me not to speak out plainly the dangers before us. . . .

Let us simply strike out the section, and leave the whole matter to the
Legislature. . . .

The Special Committee recommended that an election be held on April 14, 15, and 16, 1868, at which time the constitution would be ratified or rejected. At the same time the electors would vote for governor, lieutenant governor, secretary of state, comptroller-general, treasurer, attorney general, superintendent of education, and adjutant and inspector general. Members of the General Assembly and of the U.S. House of Representatives would also be elected. The convention adopted this plan, which provided for elections of all county officers required by the constitution to be elected by the people; these county elections were to be held within thirty days after ratification of the constitution.

Among the last acts of the convention was the adoption of a resolution asking Congress to remove the political disabilities of the following men from Newberry; Jacob Kibler, Henry Summer, John P. Kinard, E. P. Lake, W. W. Houseal, H. H. Kinard, and S. P. Kinard.

The constitution, as adopted by the convention,[20] included a Declaration of Rights declaring the indissolubility of the Union, the equality of all men, the prohibition of slavery, and the paramount allegiance due the Constitution and government of the United States. The article on the legislative department changed the old judicial districts to counties, abolished dual office-holding (which had been permitted under former constitutions), and gave Newberry County a senator and three representatives.

The governor and the other state administrative officers were to be elected by the people. A supreme court of three members serving six-year terms was established, equity and law courts were combined, counties were to be organized into judicial circuits, a circuit judge for each circuit was to be elected by the General Assembly for a four-year term, a probate judge was to be elected by the people in each county for a four-year term, circuit judges were to be rotated among the various circuits, and justices of the peace were to be elected by the voters.

A board of county commissioners was to be elected in each county for a two-year term. The board was to have jurisdiction over roads, ferries and bridges, in all matters relating to taxes, and in all disbursements of public funds. Thus the power over county matters, so long jealously guarded by the General Assembly, was vested in a local board.

In education the constitution provided for a school commissioner in each county. The county commissioners, with the state superintendent of education, comprised the State Board of Education. A free public school system was established and school districts were set up. The

General Assembly was to levy an annual school tax and was required to prescribe compulsory school attendance for all those between six and sixteen.

The militia was to consist of all able-bodied males between eighteen and forty-five except for those exempt by law. Women were given separate property rights and their property was not to be liable for the debts of their husbands. Divorce was to be permitted.

With an eye to appeasing the land hunger of those recently given their freedom, the convention adopted an ordinance directing the legislature to establish a Board of Land Commissioners and to provide for the purchase of land and its sale to actual settlers. One condition of the sales was to be that one-half of the tract purchased would be placed under cultivation within three years.[21]

On the whole the constitution was a moderate one, modeled in large part on those of the Northern states. South Carolina was to live under it for almost thirty years and retain many of its features in the Constitution of 1895.

During the convention Duncan was looking ahead to public office. Spoken of as a possible choice for secretary of state in February, a month later he was regarded as a leading candidate for Congress from the Third Congressional District.[22] On March 12, 1868, however, his hopes were dashed when the congressional caucus selected a tailor, Simeon Corley, as the Republican candidate for Congress over Duncan. Several ballots were required before the nominee was chosen.[23] The blow was softened somewhat by Duncan's election as a delegate to the National Republican Convention to be held in Chicago.

Newberry was shocked in February when General Canby summarily appointed an intendant and four wardens for the town of Newberry. Canby's *excuse* was the expiration of the terms of office of James M. Baxter, intendant, and of wardens Thomas M. Paysinger, Edward H. Christian, Osborne Wells, and Robert H. Wright. Canby appointed Charles W. Montgomery as intendant, and as wardens, William C. Johnson, Frederick Werber, Summmerfield Montgomery, and George Boland.[24] These appointments were made on the eve of the constitutional convention. Even though the appointees were white, they did not meet with the general approval of the community.

The political lines were drawn tighter when Canby ordered the election for the ratification of the constitution and for state officers. The Democratic Club of Newberry was organized in March, with former Senator Robert Moorman as chairman and Dr. Sampson Pope as secretary. The club elected delegates and alternates to a state convention held on March 31.

On April 6 the Democratic Club met at the Court House and nominated Captain Ellison S. Keitt for the Senate and Dr. John King Gary, Wallace A. Cline, and Young John Pope for the House. A week later a mass meeting was held and General Garlington, Judge Y. J. Pope, Major L. J. Jones, and J. F. J. Caldwell made speeches urging support for the Democratic ticket. A few Radicals replied and were followed by Tom Keitt, body servant of Ellison S. Keitt, who made a stirring appeal for the Democrats.

Newberry voted overwhelmingly in favor of ratification. The Republicans cast 2,045 votes and the Democrats only 815 votes in Newberry County; 2,049 voted in favor of ratification, and 803 against.[25]

General Robert K. Scott, "carpetbagger" from Ohio, was elected governor. Lemuel Boozer of Lexington was elected lieutenant governor. The Newberry legislative delegation consisted of Charles W. Montgomery, scalawag, as senator; Joseph D. Boston, James Hutson, and James Henderson, blacks, as representatives.[26]

The General Assembly held a special session in July 1868. That month B. O. Duncan wrote to Governor Scott that he had heard that Mr. Parker was not able to give bond to qualify as state treasurer and that he "would be willing to accept the position at least temporarily"— provided he did not succeed to Frederick Sawyer's position as collector of customs. Duncan expressed the hope that all elements of the Republican Party would forget their differences and work harmoniously, and he urged the necessity for securing fair and impartial elections.

By November Duncan was alarmed at the turn of events. He again wrote Governor Scott, this time protesting that he did not want "to see my old neighbors and friends afflicted by incompetent men in office, and my party disgraced for appointing men whose honesty even was suspected, but of whose entire want of respectability or capacity there could not be the least doubt." He predicted that the Republican Party could not succeed unless it could draw respectable, intelligent, and patriotic elements of the white population into its ranks. His plea fell on deaf ears.

In June 1869, Duncan wrote Scott a final letter endorsing Dr. Peter Moon and John Spearman for appointment as magistrates. In it he decried the political claims of others who sought the positions.[27] Again he was unsuccessful.

In 1869, Duncan, unsuccessful in his quest for high office and disgusted with affairs at home, re-entered the consular service and went to Italy.[28] He took no further part in local politics until the campaign of 1876. It is a source of regret that an individual of his education and views did not remain at home during Reconstruction.

4

Scott's Administration

The story of the corruption and incompetence at the state level of government during Reconstruction has been told by numerous historians. Few have attempted to recount conditions at the local level during the Reconstruction period.

When John A. Chapman wrote Part Two of *The Annals of Newberry* in 1892, not enough time had elapsed since Reconstruction for him to record the story of that period in Newberry. He said, "My heart fails me, my hand trembles and holds the pen unsteadily when I undertake to write, however briefly, of those dark ten years, immediately succeeding the war, through which we were compelled to pass."[1] Perhaps the passage of a century will enable a fair appraisal to be made now.

In 1868 Robert Kingston Scott was elected governor of South Carolina. Scott came to office from the Freedmen's Bureau. Before that he had been a physician, Realtor, and merchant in Ohio, a miner and physician in California, a prospector in Mexico and South America, a colonel of a regiment of Ohio volunteers, and finally a brevet-major general of the Union army.[2] Had he possessed character and moral courage he could have made a real contribution to stability in South Carolina government. Although he was disposed to act fairly, unfortunately he could not control the unscrupulous men who surrounded him in Columbia. He reputedly had a weakness for whiskey.

The special session of the South Carolina General Assembly that convened on July 6, 1868, was the harbinger of evil days to follow. Franklin J. Moses, Jr., former secretary to Governor Pickens and a member of the House from Charleston County, was elected speaker of that body.[3]

Three days later Scott took the oath of office as governor and Lemuel Boozer of Lexington became lieutenant governor.[4]

On July 7, 1868, the Senate ratified the Fourteenth Amendment,[5] and the following day the House of Representatives did likewise.[6] The New-berry delegation, consisting of Senator Charles W. Montgomery and Representatives Joseph D. Boston, James P. Hutson, and James Hender-son, voted for ratification.

On July 24 General Canby announced that all authority conferred upon him by the Reconstruction Acts was remitted to the civil authori-ties.[7] South Carolina would suffer under corrupt rule for nine long years.

As Simkins and Woody, in their classic study of the period, point out:

> Thus was South Carolina restored to the Union, her freedmen given suffrage, and her former ruling oligarchy deprived of political power. As the result of religious, philanthropic, or partisan zeal, new men and new measures were to have their way for a few troublous years. Viewed from almost any angle, Reconstruction was a failure. . . . That South Carolina would consent to be ruled by alien whites and native blacks was unthink-able; and that the rule of such people would not coincide with the inter-ests of the native whites was equally certain. . . . Even in its palmiest days the Radical government felt secure only when protected by Federal troops. Had that government been more capable, more efficient, and more honest, no doubt a different story could be told.[8]

The failure of the Radical government, supported almost until the end by the strong arm of the Federal government and operating under a modern, and in most respects excellent, constitution, was due not so much to its organization as to its personnel. To native white Newberri-ans, a carpetbagger was a contemptible parasite, and for a scalawag the Conservative native had a perfect antipathy."[9]

Newberry's two senators during the Reconstruction period were both white, Montgomery being a "scalawag" and his successor, Henry C. Corwin, a "carpetbagger." Senator Montgomery, who served only one term, was placed on a number of important committees—the Judiciary (although he practiced law for only a short time before becoming a gro-cer), Military (although he had no service experience during the war), Claims, Incorporations, Rules, and a number of special committees.[10]

During the ensuing regular session of 1868, Montgomery was elected president *pro tempore* of the Senate when the president *pro tempore*, D. T. Corbin, became acting lieutenant governor upon Lemuel Boozer's election as judge of the Fifth Judicial Circuit.[11] His popularity with colleagues enabled Montgomery to be elected one of three commissioners to revise the statutes, at an annual salary of $3,500. The others elected were Corbin, who did all the work, and W. J. Whipper, representative from Beaufort.[12]

The three House members from Newberry in the Forty-Eighth General Assembly received few appointments. Boston was placed on the Committee on Penitentiary; Henderson was named to the Committee on the Ordinance to Establish a Land Commission;[13] while Hutson received no committee assignments. They took little part in the debates and were considered of little importance.

The Reconstruction legislature under Scott, like its successors of that era, was not distinguished for notable legislation or constructive achievements. It was noted, instead, for its corruption, extravagance, and mismanagement of public funds.[14] In all these undesirable characteristics it was a suitable trail-blazer for the legislatures that followed throughout the Radical regime.

Under the Constitution of 1868, home rule was provided for the first time in South Carolina. The new county Board of Commissioners, elected by the people, took over the functions formerly exercised by the Commissioners of Roads, Bridges and Ferries; the Commissioners of Public Buildings; the Commissioners of the Poor; and the Commissioners to Approve Securities of Public Officers. In addition the new board levied taxes for ordinary county purposes and made disbursements of public funds.[15] The experiment in home rule failed because of the personnel. Significantly, the counties have now a century later reestablished this system of local self-government and, for the most part, removed the legislature from local affairs.

In addition to the three-member board of commissioners, the voters elected a sheriff, a coroner, a clerk of court, a judge of probate, and a county school commissioner. The constitution also provided for the election of justices of the peace; in order to circumvent the election process, the General Assembly in 1868 passed legislation allowing the governor to appoint magistrates until the courts could be organized. This method of securing inferior judicial officers so pleased the Radicals that they established a system of trial justices appointed by the governor instead of providing for the elected justices of the peace as required by the constitution. Newberry County was initially entitled to seven trial justices.[16]

County government also included certain appointed officials—a county auditor, a county treasurer, and county assessors. The assessors and auditors were responsible for evaluating property for tax purposes, and the treasurer for collecting the taxes and taking care of county funds.

On June 2–3, 1868, local voters chose county officials. Thomas M. Paysinger was re-elected sheriff; Thomas M. Lake, son of the incumbent clerk of court, became clerk of court; John T. Peterson, the incumbent ordinary, was elected probate judge; H. H. Kinard continued as coroner; William Summer was elected school commissioner; and George Brown, T. M. Jenkins, and Samuel Dogan became county commissioners. General Canby, the military commander, approved the officers elected.[17]

Although those elected were nominated by the Republican Party in a notice appearing in the *Newberry Herald* of May 13, the ticket was obviously agreed upon in advance by the leaders of the two parties. Peterson so testified when asked if he were not the nominee of the Republicans.[18]

Meanwhile, Governor-elect Scott called upon his associates in the Freedmen's Bureau to furnish confidential reports regarding those elected to county office. The report on Newberry County read:[19]

Sheriff.

Thomas M. Paysinger. He is the present Sheriff; a man of fair standing in this community. There are a number of stories current of his having shot Union soldiers while a scout in this neighborhood. Also of his having shot a negro since the war closed, but no conclusive proof. He was nominated and elected by the Republican party and is now on a Committee to get the freedmen into the Democratic party. He cannot take the test oath.

Clerk of Court.

Thomas M. Lake. Of very good character and standing. He cannot take the test oath.

Judge of Probate.

John T. Peterson. Is the present Ordinary. A man of good standing and character. He was the Ordinary during the war under the Confederate government. He was elected this time under a promise to support the Union Republican party. He says he can take the test oath.

County Commissioners.

T. M. Jenkins. A man of no standing or character in the community. He can take the test oath. Samuel Dogan (colored). Character and standing fair. Very ignorant. He can take the test oath. George Brown. Of good character and standing. He can take the test oath.

School Commissioner.

William Summer. Of good character and standing. A good man for the position. Formerly Asst. Asses. Int. Rev. He can take the test oath.

Coroner.

W. (H.) H. Kinard. Present Incumbent. Of fair character and standing. He cannot take the test oath but has made application to the Constitutional Convention to have his disabilities removed.

Scott's information about the three commissioners was accurate and prophetic. Brown was elected chairman, and, at an early meeting of the commissioners, the county was divided into townships as required by an act passed during the special session of the General Assembly held in July.[20]

The eleven townships established by the board were Number One, Newberry; Number Two, Caldwell; Number Three, Maybinton; Number Four, Cromer; Number Five, Reeder; Number Six, Floyd; Number Seven, Moon; Number Eight, Mendenhall; Number Nine, Stoney Battery; Number Ten, Cannon; and Number Eleven, Heller.[21]

In accordance with the legislative act, the board ordered an election to be held in each township for a town clerk, three selectmen, one surveyor, and one constable. Obviously the township system had its origin in the New England system; just as obviously it would not be satisfactory in rural South Carolina, and it was soon abandoned. However, the townships remained a political subdivision for tax purposes and as a unit for inferior courts for many years. In the 1868 election, the Democrats won in Township Number One by a margin of 200 votes;[22] the returns from the other townships were not reported in the local paper.

Economic conditions in the county were bad in 1868. Even though the price of cotton was twenty-nine cents a pound,[23] the crop that year was small, being only one-half that of 1860.[24] To make matters worse, the crops for the two preceding years had been poor. Prices would decline. In only two years between 1868 and 1900 would cotton bring as much as twenty cents a pound—in 1869 and 1871.[25] During most of this period cotton brought less than ten cents a pound. Since the county was dependent upon cotton as its only cash crop, there was little money in circulation.

On March 27, 1869, the Land Commission was established as directed by the Constitutional Convention.[26] Five state officials constituted the Advisory Board—Governor Scott, Attorney General D. H. Chamberlain, Secretary of State Cardoza, Comptroller General Neagle, and State Treasurer Parker. They named Charles P. Leslie, former New Yorker, as land commissioner. Leslie was succeeded the next year by Robert C.

DeLarge, a black from Charleston.[27] While Leslie kept inadequate records, DeLarge kept none.

The Act envisaged purchase of plantations, division of such lands into small sections of twenty-five to one hundred acres, and the sale of these lots on the installment plan. The purchasers needed only to pay land taxes and interest for three years. Then certificates of purchase would be issued and the settlers would have eight years within which to pay for the land. The state would issue bonds to furnish funds for the original purchase of the plantations.

In Newberry County, the commission bought 1,874 acres in the Maybinton section from Sheriff T. M. Paysinger for $14,055 on May 31, 1870.[28] He had paid much less for the land a short time before. Three years later F. L. Cardoza, who as secretary of state had assumed Leslie's duties, reported as follows:[29]

> The Beard and Moorman Tract in Newberry, purchased from Mr. Paysinger, is situated on the line of the Greenville and Columbia Railroad, about fifteen miles from Newberry Court House. A part of this tract, located on the Enoree River, containing about 268 acres, is worthless— being hills of white sand. Back from the river, the land is washed by gullies, many of which are from ten to twenty feet deep. Towards the North, the most of this land is worn out field. A creek passes along the Eastern boundary, adjoining which the land is good. The two tracts have been divided into fifty lots, nineteen of which are sold.

The Radicals attempted to buy a large plantation of 1,700 acres, known as the Croft Lands, on Saluda and Bush rivers. Leslie purportedly contracted with its owners, Henry Ware & Son of New Orleans, to buy it for $10,000 in 1870. T. P. Slider, always apprehensive of the Democrats, wrote Governor Scott on February 18, 1870, that the Democrats were seeking to prevent the sale and stated: "This land must be purchased as a good many of the colored people have already settled upon it and are in a great stew. . . ."[30]

Curiously the settlement on the Croft Lands was known as the "Promised Land."[31] In her monograph, Carol K. R. Bleser tells of finding a settlement near Greenwood still bearing that name; the Newberry County settlement is relatively forgotten after almost a century.

Newberry's leading merchant, Robert Stewart, died in August 1869, being succeeded by Pettus W. and Reuben S. Chick. There were at this time eighty places of business in Newberry, but business was dull and the streets were deserted.[32]

At the term of court in May 1870, the grand jury presented the public officers of the county and particularly the commissioners and trial justices for malpractice.[33] In doing so, the grand jury stated that "while some of the actions of some of these officers may have been prompted by sinister and corrupt motives, the greater part has been the result of ignorance and incompetence."

The Grand Jury was more explicit in condemning "the practice of converting the vestibule of the Court House into a Restaurant as an intolerable nuisance which should be abated." Judge T. O. P. Vernon, the presiding judge, promptly issued an order forbidding any person to use the porches of the courthouse for vending or exhibiting for sale refreshments, confectionaries or any other article of trade; the sheriff was directed to enforce it.[34]

As soon as Governor Scott was elected he was bombarded with requests for appointment to county positions. Among the most persistent office-seekers was Thomas P. Slider. After endorsing Joseph M. Ward for appointment as county treasurer, Slider reversed field and sought the appointment for himself.[35]

The governor named Ward to the post; the local newspaper termed it a "most judicious appointment."[36] When the Newberry legislative delegation sought to have Slider appointed instead of Ward, Scott promptly sent Slider's name to the Senate, and he was confirmed by that body on January 22, 1869.[37] This was Slider's reward for becoming a "scalawag."

Summerfield Montgomery, brother of the state senator, was named county auditor. He died during his first term in office. Assessors appointed by the governor were John P. Kinard, John Coate, Edward R. Kingsmore, and Solomon P. Kinard.[38]

Even though the county was represented by Republicans, local Democrats were able to win in two elections in 1868. They carried the county by a majority of 1,026 votes in the presidential canvass. And in November the town of Newberry was returned to white Conservatives. Major James M. Baxter was elected intendant, and the new wardens were J. S. Hair, J. N. Martin, Mathias Barre, and J. B. Smith.[39]

With so much political excitement that year, things got out of hand. Feeling was so high by the time the special session of the legislature began that B. M. Blease, Newberry's first volunteer in the recent war, published a card in the local newspaper denying that he was a Republican and stating that the author of the rumor was a "poor, dirty, lying, thieving, cowardly traitor to his race, and to everything decent." Blease was elected constable of Township Number One on the Democratic ticket a few months later.[40]

In September the Newberry Democratic Central Club adopted a resolution "that this is a white man's government, was transmitted to us as such from our ancestors, and that it is our solemn duty to transmit it as a white man's government to those who are to come after us."[41]

In October Dan Ward was ambushed on Main Street between Calhoun and Walnut streets by a group of blacks; the ambuscade followed a confrontation between Samuel Dogan, mulatto county commissioner, and William Fitzgerald earlier that day on the town square. Ward was wounded but was able to identify Dogan as one of his assailants.

The morning after the attempted assassination of Ward, Fitzgerald and his friend Sam Murtiashaw, both of the Broad River section, rode to Lee Nance's shop on lower Main Street and shot Nance down *in cold blood.*[42] Nance had been a delegate to the Constitutional Convention and active in the affairs of the Union League.

The murder of Nance and the killing of a number of other politically active Radicals in the upcountry provoked a legislative investigation into the "disordered state of affairs in the Third Congressional District, and the causes of the intimidation, outrages and murders perpetrated preceding and at the late general election."[43] The investigating committee succeeded in more deeply driving a wedge between the races; it examined 106 witnesses in Newberry County alone, of whom 52 were white and 54 were black.[44]

Joe Crews, a former slave trader from Laurens, was a member of the investigating committee. Ironically he was himself killed from ambush a few years later.[45] The majority of the committee concluded "that it was the intention of many of the leading Democrats in Newberry County to dispense with leading Republicans at all hazards."[46]

Governor Scott wanted to build a political machine, and, as so many others have done in similar positions, he proposed to do it by creating a state police force, controlling the inferior courts, and revamping the militia. The police act authorized Scott to appoint a chief constable, a chief deputy constable in each county, and as many deputy constables as the governor directed.[47] Scott named John B. Hubbard as chief constable for South Carolina.

Before long, Newberrians were complaining that these constables were arresting Newberry County men on warrants issued in Columbia, taking them back to jail in Columbia, and holding them without bail.

And within the year, Hubbard would be requesting fifty constables for Newberry.[48]

The legislature ignored the constitutional requirement that justices of the peace be elected by the people; in the Special Session an act was passed authorizing the governor to appoint magistrates. Two years later the governor was authorized to appoint trial justices with the advice and consent of the Senate. The office of magistrate was abolished effective May 1, 1870. Newberry was entitled to seven trial justices. The act further provided that the governor could appoint a trial justice during the interim between legislative sessions and the appointee would act until the end of the next session of the Senate; if the Senate failed to confirm, then the appointment would terminate. The governor could revoke an appointment at his whim.[49]

The Militia Act authorized a complete reorganization of the militia into the National Guard, with all officers being appointed by the governor.[50] Newberry County was authorized four companies of the 10th Regiment, 3rd Brigade; Lexington County was authorized two companies and Orangeburg County four companies in the same regiment.[51]

Although the National Guard was open to both whites and blacks, when the blacks joined, the whites would not. Consequently, the officers and men of the new National Guard were black. Early commanders of Newberry's four companies, A, B, C and D, were Joseph D. Boston, James P. Hutson, Munson L. Long, and John Henderson. Boston was appointed lieutenant colonel and executive officer of the 10th Regiment in July 1873. The brigade commander was Brigadier General W. B. Nash, the division commander was Major General Prince R. Rivers, and the regimental commander was Colonel E. J. Cain.[52]

One other measure calculated to enable the governor to solidify his control of the state was the Joint Resolution of February 1869, which authorized him to employ an armed force to preserve the peace.[53] It was to remain in being until the National Guard could be organized.

To ensure that there would be no racial discrimination, the legislature passed an act to enforce the provisions of the Federal Civil Rights Bill. The burden of proof was placed upon the accused whenever a colored person claimed discrimination. Any corporation found guilty was to forfeit its charter; as a result there was little evidence of discrimination in railroad cars or public restaurants.[54]

Scott wrote Sheriff Paysinger about the acts of violence occurring in Newberry County, including specifically an alleged attack on the residence of G. G. Dewalt. Acting Solicitor J. F. J. Caldwell, in a letter dated

March 29, 1869, vigorously protested to the governor. He stated that, on the basis of the governor's allegations, he had asked the grand jury to investigate, and that Mr. Dewalt had testified; no particle of evidence had been adduced to substantiate the governor's charges. He stated:[55] "The conviction is, therefore, forced upon me, that only malicious persons have made these representations to you—persons whose sole delight consists in fomenting discord between the two races and the two Political parties in this State. The Courts have always been open here for all persons of whatever race or social position. We are a law-abiding people. We desire that every man shall be secure in life, liberty and property. We want peace, and we insist upon justice. Give us that!"

In November, 1869, trouble loomed once more. The *Newberry Herald* of November 24, 1869, reported that there had been a disgraceful disturbance and stated: "A band of lawless, stupid leaguers, after an adjourned meeting, in which they had had the assistance and counsel of sundry carpetbaggers, sallied out with a large drum, and many of them armed with pistols, shotguns, etc., paraded the streets until long after midnight, making night hideous with yells, shouts, firing of weapons, and offensive language. . . . We demand of Governor Scott an investigation of this occurrence. If a few of the constables were removed perhaps it would be better for the public peace."

In a series of letters printed in the local newspaper, "Junius" wrote pointedly of the situation and strove to undermine Republican support. One week he asked the blacks what confidence they could have in Speaker of the House F. J. Moses, Jr., and in Joe Crews, "who was once a cruel and unfeeling slave driver and dealer in slaves." The next week he called the people of Newberry and of South Carolina beasts of burden and said they would deserve their fate if they, for any great length of time, submitted to the "infernal rule that has been imposed upon them by the yankee-scum that has defiled the land since the conquest."

In his next letter, "Junius" complained of the outrageous riot in the streets on November 16, blamed it on the Union League, and then said he didn't fault the Negroes because "I know that by far the greater part of the lawless meanness they now exhibit is infused into them by men with white skins but with souls as black as hell."[56]

The brutal murder of Samuel H. Dunwoody, the night watchman at the depot of the Greenville and Columbia Railroad, by four blacks in December exacerbated the racial tension in the community. The burning of the ginhouse of Thomas W. Holloway near Pomaria was a grim reminder of the danger.[57]

In January 1870, the *Newberry Herald* called for a change in government and the following month for the defeat of the Republicans. On
March 9 it carried the minority report of the committee appointed to
investigate the Third Congressional District. This report was submitted
by Javan Bryant. Pointing out the natural dislike of the former master for
the political strength of his former slave, and the equally understandable
distrust of the freedman for one who formerly held him in bondage,
Bryant went on to say:

> But it affords me great pleasure to report that while the brutal instincts of
> a few lawless ruffians led them to imbrue their hands in the life blood of
> their fellow beings, the great masses, the respectable and intelligent citi-
> zens, kept their feelings circumscribed within due bounds, and exercised
> toward their opponents that Christian charity so characteristic of all well
> regulated communities.

> In conclusion, allow me to call the attention of your honorable body to
> the existence, in the Third Congressional District, of a thoroughly
> organized party called the "Union League," which party has an
> "offspring" known as the "Investigating Committee," the real object and
> intention of which is to accumulate capital for the coming campaign.

The whites were not blameless for the racial tension existing in the
spring of 1870. John T. Henderson, colored Magistrate of Maybinton,
wrote Scott on April 15 that:

> the colored men here are much trample (sic) and intruded upon, in vari-
> ous ways. I myself have been abused from the beginning of my commis-
> sion up to the present and have strove (sic) assiduously to consider their
> abuse such as not worth the attention of a good citizen; but they are
> becoming more and more onerous and actually destroying the peace of
> the community. Persons stiling (sic) themselves Democrats. My house was
> fired into last night at the late hour of twelve by some person or persons
> unknown. The house I live in is rented. I saw a gentleman with a letter (a
> few days since) from the owner stating that he would set fire to the house
> and burn it up rather than suffer a Radical magistrate to dwell therein.

He appealed to Scott for immediate protection and closed with the
statement "my idea is that Made Peace is much better than no peace at
all."[58]

Two days later John P. Kinard wrote Scott that he had built a school
house on his place for the colored children of the neighborhood, had
enrolled seventy scholars, and hired a good white teacher, and that it

was the first school of its kind in this part of the state. He reported that the school had been burned on the past Saturday night by "some malicious devil." He thought it was a white person and asked the governor to offer a reward and to send Chief Constable Hubbard to investigate.[59]

In his report of 1870, Chief Constable Hubbard recommended a force of fifty men for Newberry County. Joe Crews, in neighboring Laurens, preached the supremacy of the blacks and urged them to seize whatever they wanted, and that if any fuss was made, "matches were cheap."[60] The jury which tried the four Negroes for the murder of Dunwoody, two of whom had confessed, was unable to agree; after a nine-day trial which attracted great attention, a mistrial was declared. The *Newberry Herald* was extremely critical of the proceedings. Colonel T. J. Lipscomb lost his house and kitchen by incendiarism. Seventy federal soldiers were encamped at Halcyon Grove in the town; they were detailed to maintain order in the county.[61]

Governor Scott made active use of the Negro militia and his state police force. Scott reportedly said publicly in Washington that the white people of South Carolina were fit only to be ruled by Winchester rifles; he proceeded to arm his militia and police force.[62] D. D. Wallace concluded that the arming of the blacks prompted the whites to join the Ku Klux Klan.[63] In any event, the result was divisive.

Whites and blacks who wanted honest government met at the courthouse in June, adopted a resolution against corruption, and called it a necessity to hold a reform convention to fight the Radicals. Six white men and six black men were elected as delegates to the state convention. This group of Republicans and Democrats met in Columbia and nominated on the Union Reform Party ticket Judge R. B. Carpenter, formerly of Kentucky, as governor, and General M. C. Butler, cavalry hero from Edgefield, as lieutenant governor.[64]

The counties organized and prepared for a strenuous campaign, Y. J. Pope being the executive committeeman of the Union Reform Party from Newberry.[65] The Union League of Newberry nominated candidates for all elective offices in September, and a week later the Union Reform Party did likewise.[66] Both named some white and some black candidates.

B. O. Duncan wrote from Naples, Italy, to Lewis Duckett, a well-to-do black citizen, that he was in favor of reform and hoped that every honest man would vote for Carpenter. His letter was printed in the local newspaper. The Union Reform leaders asked all storekeepers to keep their stores closed on election day.

But with all the election officials representing the Radicals there was little hope for an honest election. Newberry had only 3,600 registered electors; Scott received 2,915 votes to Carpenter's 1,645.[67]

The only consolation for the native whites was the victory in the local municipal election. According to the *Newberry Herald* of November 2, 1870, the "White Ticket" defeated the "Black Ticket." T. M. Paysinger was reelected intendant, and J. N. Martin, D. M. Ward, D. B. Wheeler, and W. T. Tarrant were elected wardens. They defeated D. R. Phifer, candidate for intendant, and Summerfield Montgomery, Jack Thompson, James Henderson, and Dan Moates. In the town 205 whites and 146 blacks voted. Paysinger got 225 votes while Phifer only received 122 votes. All the state and county offices were captured by the Radicals. Conservatives expected the worst for the next two years; their fears were to be realized.

The state Senate was organized for the 1870–71 session with its new presiding officer, Lieutenant Governor Alonzo J. Ransier, native Charleston black; Senator Montgomery of Newberry was re-elected president *pro tempore*.[68]

The House of Representatives re-elected Moses as speaker. Joseph D. Boston was assigned to the Committee on Grievances and the Committee on Incorporations. John T. Henderson, newly elected black member, was placed on the Committee on Federal Relations and the Committee on Public Buildings. H. C. Corwin, an Ohio "carpetbagger" destined to become the leading Radical in Newberry County, was placed on the Committee on Military Affairs, the Committee on Railroads, and the Committee on Banks and Insurance Companies.[69]

The second Republican legislature became more open in its corruption now that there was no immediate danger of being called to account. U.S. Senator Robertson's re-election was accomplished by bribes aggregating $40,000. The clerks of the two legislative bodies, Josephus Woodruff of the Senate and A. O. Jones of the House, established the Republican Printing Company; it received the public printing contract in 1871 for $450,000. During Scott's first term the cost of public printing had only been $45,000 per year. The huge difference formed a reservoir for bribing legislators.[70]

The public debt skyrocketed under the manipulations of Scott, Attorney General Chamberlain, and State Treasurer Niles G. Parker, who collectively constituted the Financial Board. The board's agent, H. H. Kimpton, was Chamberlain's college friend. The Land Commission's activities were equally malodorous. The free barroom in the State

Capitol with its liquors and choice foods remained open nearly twenty hours a day.[71] Altogether the legislature was a reproach to civilized society.

Conditions at the county level were little better; the opportunities to steal were simply fewer. Adam M. Riser, Newberry postmaster appointed by the Republicans, was convicted in the United States Court for robbing the mail.[72] Judge Bryan sentenced him to serve ten years.[73] The county commissioners did their best to emulate their legislative masters.

The new board elected in 1870 consisted of three blacks—Simeon Young, chairman, David Hailstock, and Andrew Gregory.[74] They had only been in office a few months before being indicted for official misconduct along with Samuel Dogan from the old board.

The Grand Jury returned this presentment at the May 1871 Term:

> In the present Board of County Commissioners they find, after a careful investigation, a system of corruption, bribery and theft stupendous to behold—a system of wholesale robbery which was to them almost preposterous. In examining the books, papers, etc. of the Old Board of Commissioners they found indubitable evidence of perjury on the part of one Samuel Dogan and Thomas M. Jenkins, by probating and paying the same account twice. Dogan has sold the proceeds of the Poor House Farm and has never accounted for the monies arising from such sales and also sold a horse belonging to the same institution, and has likewise not accounted for the proceeds of such sale. And as to the Board they find that they indulge in all species of fraud and corruption . . . [75]

The Grand Jury also presented Coroner and Trial Justice Munson S. Long, about whom was said: "As an officer they unhesitatingly pronounce him utterly incompetent in every respect. He can neither read nor write sufficiently to be intelligible to any one except himself; and as a natural consequence his books are in no order, or in other words are not kept at all. They find that he has received fines but has neither turned them over to the County Treasurer, nor otherwise accounted for the same. They, therefore, unhesitatingly, for the peace, dignity and prosperity of the community, recommend his speedy removal."[76]

Young, Hailstock, Dogan, and Long were convicted of official misconduct.[77] Gregory was indicted but fled to escape trial. Young was pardoned by Scott in October at the request of the leading Radicals in the county[78] and returned to the board of commissioners in 1872.[79] Dogan was convicted of perjury at the September 1871 term[80] but was pardoned by Scott on March 18, 1872.[81] Despite what the Grand Jury said about his virtual illiteracy, Long was elected county commissioner of schools in 1872.[82]

The Grand Jury that returned these presentments and indicted these officeholders included D. R. Phifer, a white Radical, and Dred Rutherford, Edward Young, Henry Garmany, and Sampson Pratt, blacks.[83] Phifer made this statement to the local newspaper: "From the revelations made to me as a Grand Juror, of the fraud and corruption committed by parties claiming to be Republicans, and from the failure to consummate in practice what seemed plausible and possible in theory, I am constrained to publicly sever all political connections with the so-called Republican party of this County and State."

The Grenekers of the *Newberry Herald* applauded Phifer's announcement and expressed the hope that others would follow this example. However, Phifer soon accepted appointment to the Board of Commissioners and was then appointed postmaster of Newberry in January and county treasurer in April of that year.[84] Apparently his publicly expressed disenchantment with the Republican Party was not permanent.

After the conviction of Young and Hailstock their offices as commissioners were declared vacant and an election was held in August of 1871. Two highly respected Democrats, Colonel William Lester and J. N. Martin, were elected. However the State Board of Canvassers refused to meet to declare the results and the offices remained vacant until Governor Scott appointed a new board in November. The editors of the local newspaper termed the action infamous and counseled court action.[85]

In March 1871 a group of prominent conservatives met with Governor Scott to discuss worsening relations between the races in the upcountry of South Carolina. Colonel Simeon Fair of Newberry and the other leaders told Scott that the arming of the Negro militia was responsible.[86] The *Newberry Herald* of January 18, 1871, had deplored the war footing of the militia and hoped that there would not be a "bloody war of extermination."

In May the county seat was visited on a Saturday night by "a band of disguised men, in character of Ku Klux." They fired into Simeon Young's house and wounded members of his family. Sheriff Paysinger pursued them and captured one of the band who had been wounded.[87]

Meanwhile President Grant was looking ahead to his campaign for reelection. On October 12, 1871, he issued a proclamation that "a condition of lawlessness and terror existed" in nine upcountry counties, including Newberry, and he commanded the dispersal of those obstructing the execution of the law. Five days later he issued yet another proclamation and subsequently suspended the writ of habeas corpus in those nine counties.[88]

The Federal authorities began an intensive effort to round up alleged Klansmen. Several hundred were arrested; most never came to trial but were released on bail after being held in jail. Many Newberrians were arrested, and the local newspaper kept its readers posted about those in jail and those released on bail. The *Newberry Herald* thought that Grant's suspension of the writ of habeas corpus sounded "the death-knell to the present system of American civilization." Although the *Herald* expressed a desire for rest from politics in April,[89] it was soon attempting to promote reform again.

Colonel Ellison S. Keitt was one of the first to call for the election of old Horace Greeley and Governor B. Gratz Brown, nominated to oppose Grant and the Radical Republicans. Keitt compared Grant as a statesman to McDowell as a general at Bull Run and asked for "the purification of the country." By invitation, Keitt, one of the period's great orators, made many speeches in New York state; they were well received.

On the eve of the election, Colonel Keitt's final New York speech received front page coverage. He charged that Scott had pardoned 300 of 385 convicts in the state penitentiary, that 100 of 165 legislators were blacks, that a room in the State House was used as a faro bank, that the state debt had increased under the Radicals from $6,000,000 to $29,000,000 in four years, and that the judiciary was vile and corrupt.[90]

Meanwhile, on the local scene, in January 1872 Sheriff Thomas M. Paysinger was indicted for habitual neglect and official misconduct in office. The office of sheriff was declared vacant, and the acting coroner, William Summer, assumed the duties of the sheriff. In April Governor Scott appointed John J. Carrington as sheriff[91] and he continued in that office as long as the Radicals remained in control.

B. O. Duncan, consul at Naples by appointment of the Grant administration, was so disgusted with the worsening situation in South Carolina that he wrote a letter made public in the *Newberry Herald* of June 12, 1872. In it he stated categorically that he "would under no circumstances support any man or party that would aid directly or indirectly the detestable scoundrels, who at present control the Radical party in South Carolina."

The state Republican Party, at its convention in Columbia on August 21, 1872, nominated F. J. Moses, Jr., for governor. This was too much for a group of Republicans who called themselves "Bolters," so they named Reuben Tomlinson, a "carpetbagger" from Pennsylvania, as their nominee. The Radicals named R. H. Gleaves, black, for lieutenant governor, while the Bolters chose another black, J. N. Hayne, as their candidate for this office.

The *Newberry Herald*, writing of the Radical convention, said:[92] "Thus closed one of the most corrupt and disgraceful assemblages that ever sat in Convention in any age or clime—civilized or barbarian. It presented to the eyes and mind of every honest expectation—black or white—Northern or Southern—a state of things almost incredible and that has no parallel in infamy and in the history of any country. It foreshadows that 'coming events cast their shadows before them.' God forbid such scenes in our land, ever to be enacted over again."

The state Democratic Executive Committee declined to nominate candidates for state office. It condemned the corruption and robbery of the Republicans, and resolved to try to secure local and legislative reform. General M. C. Butler, its chairman, appointed a chairman in each county; Simeon Fair was chairman for Newberry.[93]

During the campaign for state office, S. W. Melton, candidate for attorney general on the Radical ticket, charged Senator Montgomery of Newberry with taking a prominent part in issuing fraudulent pay certificates. Montgomery published a card denouncing Melton as "a liar, poltroon, and a coward." Melton and Montgomery happened to meet in a Columbia restaurant in September, and a fight ensued. Montgomery's companion, George Tupper, shot Melton's friends Captain J. D. Caldwell and Major James M. Morgan. Caldwell died, and the coroner's jury held Tupper.[94]

The fighting was not limited to those seeking state office. There was fierce in-fighting among Newberry Radicals for local leadership. They held three different nominating conventions that were characterized by the *Newberry Herald* as disgraceful and unruly.

The two factions were led by Joseph D. Boston and James P. Hutson. Both groups supported the same nominees for the state Senate, probate judge, coroner, and two county commissioners, but offered different candidates for the other offices. The Boston group triumphed in the election,[95] and Hutson was eliminated as a real power in county politics.

D. T. Corbin, U.S. attorney and former president of the Senate, made a speech in Newberry in which he virtually agreed with Colonel Keitt. He advised the blacks to vote and to elect the best county officers they could get. The *Newberry Herald*, which had backed Greeley over Grant from the beginning, endorsed Tomlinson over Moses. U.S. Senator F. A. Sawyer of South Carolina spoke in Newberry also and charged that the Regular Republican Ticket (the Radical ticket) was headed by the worst white man (Moses) and tailed by the worst black man (Cain) in the state.

But despite everything, Franklin J. Moses, Jr., carried the county by a majority of 1,800 votes. Grant was re-elected.

Again the only consolation for conservative whites was that the town administration remained Democratic. J. P. Pool was elected intendant; Osborne Wells, Peter Rodelsperger, William T. Tarrant, and Robert H. Wright were elected wardens.[96]

"Pro Bono Publico" suggested seriously in the local newspaper that a state organization be formed to petition Congress to establish a military protectorate, with the feeling that anything would be better than Moses and his gang.[97]

5

The Administrations
of Moses and Chamberlain

If South Carolina had suffered under the two administrations of Scott, the state was ill prepared for the debauchery that was to follow under Moses. Son of respectable parents, Franklin J. Moses, Jr., had graduated from South Carolina College, married the daughter of a respected Sumter lawyer, and served as private secretary to Governor Francis W. Pickens. In the latter capacity he had torn the United States flag from its staff upon the fall of Fort Sumter; this seems to have been his chief claim to fame before joining the Radicals in 1867. His later career was infamous in all respects.

Morally bankrupt, Moses was a member of the Constitutional Convention of 1868, Speaker of the House of Representatives from 1868 to 1872 and adjutant and inspector general at the same time. He violated every public trust given him, and this confessed bribe-taker subsequently adopted a life of petty crime in the North after 1876, finally dying of asphyxiation in Winthrop, Massachusetts. The best gauge of respectable opinion toward him is found in the changing of their family name by certain of his Sumter kinsmen during his tenure as governor.[1]

The *Newberry Herald*, on July 8, 1874, quoted an article in the *Jewish Times* to prove that Moses was not a Jew although his father was. It then concluded that "it is to be regretted that the same crumb of comfort cannot be given to Christians."

Recognizing a kindred spirit, the notorious Foster Blodgett, recently settled in Newberry after a checkered career in Georgia,[2] sought to get Moses to remove D. R. Phifer from the county treasurer's office and to appoint his son, Edwin F. Blodgett.[3] In this scheme Blodgett had the aid of County Auditor James W. Hayward. Phifer was supported by Joseph D. Boston, Probate Judge J. C. Leahy, and Sheriff J. J. Carrington.[4]

The result of Blodgett's efforts was a mass meeting called by the county chairman of the Republican Party in March 1873. Boston addressed the convention and his resolution supporting Phifer was adopted. The resolution expressed the view that Moses "will not be controlled by the wishes of E. F. Blodgett, Esq., late of Georgia, and not yet a qualified citizen of this State."[5]

The *Newberry Herald* termed the convention regarding the county treasurer's office as "more worthy of an uncivilized land than of this Southern country in its day of freedom and equal rights." It went on to state "if this is the fruit of the appointing power, it were better taken away, and the ballot, bad as it is now, be the test, with all its attendant ugliness, briberies and frauds."[6] But, of course, the system was not changed. Nor did the bickering over Newberry's treasurer abate; it simply extended to the office of county auditor.

The 1872 election saw the elimination of James P. Hutson as leader of those opposed to Representative Joseph D. Boston. Thereafter Senator Corwin and Boston were the leaders of the two Radical factions. Corwin had the advantage of being in the Senate and thereby in position to pass upon the appointments of county officials made by Moses. Although it took him a year to do so, he finally managed the ouster of County Auditor Hayward and County Treasurer Phifer.

In January 1874 Hayward reluctantly yielded to pressure by the Corwin faction and submitted his resignation to Moses.[7] In doing so he stated, as have so many other political appointees, that he was eager to preserve "peace and *harmony* in the ranks of the Republican Party of my County, and prevent contentions." At the same time that he tendered his resignation, he wrote Moses a long letter begging him to keep him in office.[8] Moses accepted the resignation and promptly named Robert E. Williams, native black, to the position. Corwin had the Senate confirm the appointment at once,[9] and Williams served as county auditor throughout the remainder of the Reconstruction period.

Corwin's efforts to oust D. R. Phifer as treasurer took more time; he finally succeeded after the election of 1874. Moses appointed Edwin Blodgett upon the expiration of Phifer's term in that year, but then the new governor, D. H. Chamberlain, removed Blodgett and appointed Phifer once more.

Meanwhile, Moses was making it clear to the public generally, and the Radicals in particular, that he could remove trial justices at will. His use of the powers to remove and to appoint was designed to hold any dissidents in line. In September, Moses removed local trial justice G. P. Jacoby, reappointed him the following week, and then removed him once more, making way for the eager spoilsman T. P. Slider, whom he appointed to that post in November.[10]

W. H. Thomas was appointed trial justice in May 1874, and then removed after he spoke for the reform group of Republicans against the regular Radical nominees. As soon as the election was over, Moses reinstated him.[11]

The previous year, in December 1873, Governor Moses pardoned former Sheriff T. M. Paysinger, who had been convicted of official misconduct at the November term of General Sessions Court.[12] Paysinger had been sentenced by Judge Montgomery Moses to serve a four-month term and pay a fine of $300. In March 1874, Governor Moses commuted the sentence of Captain Tupper, a friend of Senator Montgomery, who had been convicted of manslaughter in Columbia in 1873.[13]

Meanwhile, public indignation against high taxes, corruption, and extravagance caused a second Taxpayers' Convention to be called to meet in Columbia. A public meeting at Newberry Courthouse on February 2, 1874, elected delegates to that gathering and heard Representative Joseph D. Boston pledge himself to use every effort in the legislature to reduce the enormous tax assessments in the county. Delegates elected were R. L. McCaughrin, E. S. Keitt, George Johnstone, J. K. G. Nance, and Dr. William M. Dorroh.[14]

The *Newberry Herald,* on February 11, gave an example of the high taxes—fifteen cents on the dollar of actual value—and pointed out that this amounted to confiscation. By June, the newspaper was urging that the recommendation of the Taxpayers' Convention regarding tax unions be implemented locally. These unions were to be open to all, regardless of race, and were to be organized in each township, then at the county level, and finally as a state union. They were to be financed by voluntary payment of a percentage of the taxpayer's general tax. The state union, designed to seek prosecution of all state officials accused of any violation of law, was to be empowered to retain counsel for that purpose.[15]

Moses himself was soon indicted for misconduct, along with the treasurer of Orangeburg County. He relied upon his exemption from arrest as governor and refused to appear for trial.[16] His refusal gave impetus to the formation of the tax unions to secure better and more honest government and the Newberry County Tax Union was organized on August 3, 1874.[17]

Simeon Young, chairman of the Newberry County Republican Party, called a convention to meet on August 31. That group sent Senator Corwin, Cassey David, and Henry Gilliam to the state Republican convention.[18] The state convention nominated D. H. Chamberlain for governor and R. H. Gleaves for lieutenant governor. The *Newberry Herald* expressed the general anti-Republican feeling when it commented that Republicanism "is in a sorry plight when it can find no better men than Moses or Chamberlain to represent it."[19]

Some Republicans felt the same way, and an "Independent Republican" meeting was called to oppose Chamberlain; Newberry's delegates were W. H. Thomas, Wade H. Coleman, and Edward Young.[20] This group nominated Judge John Green for governor and Major M. R. Delany for lieutenant governor.[21] The Union Republican Party made nominations for local offices, but the Independent Republicans did not.[22]

The local Tax Union then called a public meeting to nominate candidates to oppose the Union Republicans. At this county-wide meeting the Conservatives, as they called themselves in hope of attracting men of both races, organized and endorsed the nominees of the Independent Republican Party for governor and lieutenant governor. It was decided that only three local offices would be contested; George S. Mower was nominated for a seat in the House of Representatives, John K. G. Nance was nominated for probate judge, and L. B. Maffett was named as the party's candidate for the office of county commissioner.[23] The strategy called for the election of one of three legislators and one of three commissioners in the hope that this would confuse the Union Republicans. Vain hope!

The good feeling existing between the races, about which the *Newberry Herald* rejoiced in late August, disappeared almost overnight. John Robinson's "Great World Exposition" showed in Newberry on Tuesday, October 20. On the day of the circus Town Marshal Henry Bluford was killed while trying to arrest some drunken, disorderly characters who were trying to force persons from the sidewalk. A riot resulted, and further bloodshed was only prevented by the united action of the intendant, Y. J. Pope, Sheriff Carrington, Deputy Sheriff Sligh, and the entire police force. The *Newberry Herald* said that they deserved the thanks of the community, as did the officers of the local Federal garrison who helped restore peace. This episode obviously had some influence on the approaching election.[24]

The following day the intendant called a mass meeting, addressed by Y. J. Pope, W. H. Thomas, George Johnstone, Joseph D. Boston, and

Thomas S. Moorman. Resolutions were passed condemning unlawful conduct, calling for speedy punishment for those who slew Bluford, expressing disapproval of those who took the law into their own hands, and pledging to sustain county and town officials. The town council opened subscriptions for the benefit of Bluford's family.

In the campaign that followed, George Johnstone, E. S. Keitt, J. K. G. Nance, George S. Mower, and Sampson Pope did yeoman service in speaking at various places in the county. The *Newberry Herald* maintained that the fight was not between Democrats and Republicans but against oppression and wrong and for honest government. But the efforts of these men were not enough to stem the tide. In the race for governor, Chamberlain carried the county by a vote of 3,181 to 1,476 for Green.[25]

Of Chamberlain, the *Baltimore Gazette* said: "Of all the Southern Governors, Chamberlain of South Carolina, is most doubtful as to how he will behave. From his record he is a man who has not discountenanced frauds on the State. How far he participated in them is another matter. We would not be surprised, in view of the recent political revolution in the West, East and South, to see Mr. Chamberlain trim his sails to the breeze and repudiate the rogues and thieves that have fattened so long on the treasury of South Carolina." The *Newberry Herald*, after quoting this, simply stated: "It will be a surprise if he does not."[26]

The week before the statewide balloting, the town of Newberry re-elected Y. J. Pope as intendant and chose E. S. Coppock, G. W. Pearson, T. C. Pool and J. C. Wilson as wardens.[27] The Democrats managed to win every municipal election during the years when the Radicals controlled the county, thereby making life a little more bearable to the native whites.

Daniel H. Chamberlain was a much more complex character than his predecessors. Graduate of Yale, law student at Harvard, officer in the United States Army, he had the instincts of a gentleman and craved the company of polite society and the approval of the leading citizens of South Carolina. Unfortunately, he was inordinately ambitious and had a flaw in his character—he lacked moral courage, and he was never able to go as far as necessary to prevent corruption.

Chamberlain has had many apologists—both during his tenure of office and since.[28] His famous telegram to the New England Society of Charleston that "the civilization of the Puritan and the Cavalier, of the Roundhead and the Huguenot, is in peril," does not quite equate with his willingness to campaign on the same ticket with men like R. B. Elliott whom he had denounced as scoundrels. His opposition to W. J. Whipper and F. J. Moses, Jr., as prospective.judges does not quite offset Chamberlain's membership on the corrupt Financial Board when he was attorney general. On balance, Chamberlain was a great improvement over Scott and Moses, but it should never be forgotten that he participated in numerous disgraceful activities. He is remembered as the Radical from whose grasp Hampton delivered South Carolina. He is a tragic figure.[29]

When the legislature met in 1874, Joseph D. Boston was appointed to the Rules, Incorporations, and Ways and Means Committees. His colleagues, James A. Henderson and Sampson S. Bridges, were not so fortunate. Henderson was named to the Committee on Mines, Mining, and Manufacturers; Bridges was assigned to the Prison Reforms and Railroads Committees.[30] Senator Corwin was appointed to a number of Senate committees. He was chairman of the Committee on Incorporations, chairman of the Penitentiary Committee, and a member of the Committee on Privileges and Elections, the Committee on Railroads, and the Committee on Immigration.[31]

One of Chamberlain's first problems in Newberry County involved the county treasurer. D. R. Phifer's term had expired, and Moses had appointed Edwin F. Blodgett. Chamberlain removed Blodgett and appointed Phifer. Senator Corwin prevailed on the Senate to reject Phifer, and thereupon Chamberlain appointed Captain Jesse C. Smith, formerly of Ohio, who had served creditably as clerk of court for the past two years.[32] The *Newberry Herald* thought his appointment would give general satisfaction and congratulated Smith.

The editor of the *Herald* was also pleased with Chamberlain's message to the General Assembly the next month, and with the appointment of H. Claremont Moses as clerk of court to succeed the new county treasurer and former clerk; the appointment was made by Judge Montgomery Moses, father of the new clerk. And he liked the removal by Chamberlain of Simeon Young, J. B. Heller, G. P. Jacoby and John S. Henderson as trial justices, and the later appointment of James F. Kilgore as trial justice.[33]

Newberry Conservatives did not like the entire county delegation's voting for F. J. Moses, Jr., for judge of the Third Circuit. The prospect of the former robber governor desecrating the temple of justice was too much for honest men. The election of W. J. Whipper and Moses to the bench resulted in the reorganization of the Democratic Party within the state. When Chamberlain refused to sign commissions for Moses and Whipper, there was great rejoicing.

Representative Boston also figured in the news during 1875. He had entered the University of South Carolina Law School along with H. C. Corwin in 1873 while both were members of the House of Representatives. Boston was admitted to the Bar on July 20, 1875. At the March 1875 term of the Court of General Sessions, Boston's brother, Isaac, was convicted by an all-black jury of stealing cotton; this was the first jury composed entirely of blacks to convict one of their race and this decision drew newspaper comment. Representative Boston wrote Chamberlain on October 2, 1875, requesting a pardon for his brother Isaac. Chamberlain promptly issued it.[34]

The single most important newsworthy action of the 1876 session of the General Assembly was the impeachment of Judge Montgomery Moses, brother of Chief Justice Franklin J. Moses and uncle of the former governor. Senator Corwin was credited with instigating the removal; S. J. Couch of Chester introduced in the House on January 31, 1876, a resolution to appoint a committee of five to investigate all matters pertaining to the proper discharge of the official conduct of Judge Moses.[35] The committee recommended impeachment, and the House as Committee of the Whole considered the matter. Then the House by unanimous vote adopted the resolution of impeachment.

A Committee of Seven, including Speaker Elliott, prepared the articles of impeachment, which were also adopted unanimously.[36] The Senate sat as a Court of Impeachment from March 8 to March 21, 1876.[37]

One of the prosecution's witnesses, George Johnstone, notorious for his biting and sarcastic repartee, was asked about Judge Moses' promptitude and dispatch of business. He answered: "I cannot conceive that if he had wilfully [sic] desired to impede the progress of justice and delay the business of the Courts, he could have succeeded better than he did. What his intention was is to be inferred from his acts."

When asked the effect of the Judge's course upon the rights of suitors and the community, he stated: "It was equivalent to a complete abolition of the judicial branch of the government, except in this particular, that we had all the repressive machinery without the corresponding benefits. . . . "

And then when asked about his personal feelings toward Judge Moses, Johnstone said: "Well, sir, I have a great contempt for him as a judicial officer, but, personally, I have no ill will towards him; I think he is an incubus upon the community, and on that ground I dislike him."

Major J. F. J. Caldwell, another witness, agreed that the jurist was not prompt, held up his decisions, and that: "I am satisfied from my observation that the citizens of the County generally have learned great contempt for the Court, and none of them feel that they will receive justice, certainly not on the civil side of the Court, within a reasonable time after bringing suit. A great many persons are prevented from bringing suit on account of the enormous and inexplicable delay."

R. C. Watts, future chief justice, testified that Moses had had a very bad effect on suitors and citizens and agreed with the others that he was not at all regular in attending terms of court. Still others swore that the judge had, from time to time, borrowed funds in the hands of various public officials and issued orders extending the time for accounting for them.

When the House finished presenting its case, counsel for Judge Moses requested a reasonable adjournment to enable them to meet the charges against their client. The Senate refused to grant this request, and all counsel for the respondent withdrew from the case on Monday, March 20. They stated for the record their reasons for doing so. The next day the Senate proceeded to ballot.

By vote of thirty-one to one, Moses was found guilty of corruptly demanding money from litigants for decisions favorable to them in Laurens in October 1873 and at Newberry in 1874. By vote of thirty-two to none, he was found guilty of appropriating to his own use public monies entrusted to the care of public officers. By vote of twenty-seven to five, he was convicted of wilful neglect of the duties of his office, thereby causing great delays in the transaction of judicial business.

He was also convicted, by vote of thirty-two to none, of wilfully refusing to sign orders presented to him by consent, and by vote of thirty to one, of dishonestly passing orders for payment of some claims in full while other creditors were allowed only sixteen cents on the dollar. Judge Moses was acquitted of the other charges. Senator Corwin voted to convict on all articles except the charge that he willfully dismissed the Grand Jury to prevent the prosecution of public officers.

The judgment of the Court of Impeachment was that Montgomery Moses, having been found guilty of high crimes and misdemeanors, be removed from office as judge of the Seventh Circuit. The House, resolved into Committee of the Whole, proceeded to the Senate to hear the verdict.[38] On the next day, Governor Chamberlain appointed Lucius C. Northrop as judge of the Seventh Circuit. Senator Corwin had to defend in the public press his participation in the impeachment proceedings.[39]

John A. Leland, writing just a few years later, concluded that the Radicals "have thrown one tub to the whale," by impeaching and convicting a judge whose term was about to expire and whose successor had already been elected. He likened it to "Judge Butler's story of the bully, who, when kicked and cuffed about by men whom he had insulted, declared that he *could* whip somebody, and went home and *whipped his wife*."[40]

In his *Memoirs*, Chief Justice Watts recalled:[41]

> The only thing which I testified to, and all I knew about the charges against Judge Moses, was that the number of cases on the docket at Laurens, and the few cases that he had tried during his term of office, showed conclusively that he neglected the trial of cases. I never did believe that Judge Moses was in any manner corrupt or that he was corruptly guilty in the decision of any case, although a great number of people honestly believed that he was corrupt. He knew very little law—had been a partner of his brother, Chief Justice Moses, who was a most learned and able lawyer. Judge Montgomery Moses wrote a beautiful hand and was practically a clerk in his brother's office. He was a most genial man and was especially kind to young lawyers. It was a matter of most sincere regret on my part that he had to meet the odious insinuations that were preferred against him.

Chamberlain had other judicial trouble in 1876, although it involved only the trial justices in Newberry County. Citizens of Township #4 petitioned the governor concerning misconduct in office by Trial Justice James F. Kilgore. Kilgore explained, in a long letter to the chief executive, why he had dismissed a warrant against one Morris Renwick, charged with stealing a cow. In the absence of Senator Corwin, Probate Judge Leahy felt it necessary to write the Governor defending Kilgore, T. P. Slider, and W. H. Thomas.[42] The charges against Slider and Thomas were more serious; they were accused by reputable citizens, including James N. Lipscomb and W. R. Smith, of requiring payment of fees before issuing warrants.[43] Both denied the charges. Slider offered to resign, and a month later did so.[44]

The state Democratic Executive Committee named Y. J. Pope to organize Newberry County for the election of 1876. He promptly issued a protest about the elections of Whipper, Moses, and Wiggins as circuit judges and called a meeting to take action. A large crowd met at the courthouse on February 7, and it was resolved that "no political party which has so blackened its hands with such ignoble candidates for the exalted position of Judge, is any longer entitled to the confidence or the support of a free people." The convention agreed to organize the county thoroughly and called for a county convention to meet in March. A resolution was adopted applauding Chamberlain's efforts to secure honesty and intelligence and pledging to assist and sustain him, although Sampson Pope, M. A. Carlisle, and Colonel T. J. Lipscomb spoke against the resolution.[45]

The *Newberry Herald* carried stories of the county conventions of the two political parties and many letters concerning the political situation. While some wrote that it was foolish to think that South Carolina could be saved by a minority party, others insisted that an all-out effort should be made. One correspondent concluded that "this generation has to pass away before South Carolina can adapt herself to the new situation."[46]

Colonel Ellison S. Keitt, ever mindful of the national situation, was among the first in the state to advocate the nomination of Samuel J. Tilden and Thomas Hendricks for president and vice president. After the National Convention had done so and Sampson Pope had returned from the St. Louis Convention to report on its activities, the county convention ratified the nominations.[47]

While the local newspaper gleefully reported a rumored split between the carpetbaggers and the native blacks in the Radical ranks, it announced in the same issue that the county Democratic convention had elected delegates to a state convention to name the statewide slate of candidates. James N. Lipscomb, Thomas W. Holloway, W. D. Hardy, and R. L. McCaughrin were those elected.[48]

During the time that the county organizations were being effected, Chamberlain was called to task by Intendant Y. J. Pope for the shipment of rifles and ammunition to a colored man, H. Bailey, supposedly of Laurens. The shipment was seized by the town authorities at the Newberry depot, and the town council insisted that, if the arms be the property of the state, they should be removed to the state armory at Columbia. When Governor Chamberlain replied, Pope advised him firmly that the arms would be sent to him "provided proof is made that such arms etc. are the property of the State."[49] Since many feared these weapons might have played a role in the upcoming campaign, this incident did much to solidify public opinion in this section behind the Democrats.

The state Democratic Convention reconvened in Columbia on August 15 to decide whether to nominate candidates for state office or to support Chamberlain. The "straightouts" swept all before them, Newberry's delegates being in the majority.[50]

On August 17, Chamberlain and his entourage reached Newberry to hold a mass meeting. The party arrived by train and walked to a grove on the outskirts of town, followed by the Democrats, some on foot and several hundred on horseback. Once there, Y. J. Pope requested order and announced that speaking time would be divided between the two parties; Senator Corwin agreed. Governor Chamberlain, Congressman Hoge, and Superintendent of Education J. K. Jillson spoke for the Radicals; James N. Lipscomb, Colonel D. Wyatt Aiken, and Sampson Pope spoke for the Democrats.[51]

On August 22, the Democratic county convention named its candidates for local office. James N. Lipscomb was nominated for state senator; Y. J. Pope, Dr. William Dorroh, and E. S. Keitt for the House; Colonel William Lester, Rolly Wood, and L. P. W. Riser for county commissioners; D. B. Wheeler for sheriff; E. P. Chalmers for clerk of court; Sampson Pope for probate judge; H. S. Boozer for school commissioner, and J. B. Werts for coroner. The Newberry Herald called for united support of the nominees.[52]

On September 9, the Radicals held a county convention to elect delegates to the state, congressional, and judicial circuit conventions. Sampson S. Bridges presided, and the two factions engaged in a bitter battle. The carpetbag wing was led by Senator Corwin and Probate Judge Leahy, while the native faction was led by Representative Joseph D. Boston and School Commissioner H. B. Scott. Corwin won a complete victory, although Scott made a powerful speech excoriating the whites of the party for using the blacks for their personal advantage. Chamberlain was nominated for re-election at the state convention held on September 13.[53]

Democrats made every effort to organize for the coming election. Rifle clubs were formed in keeping with General Martin Gary's plan of campaign. In addition to providing for the organization and arming of rifle clubs, the plan called for registering every Democrat, securing commissioners of election, preventing fraudulent election returns, attending Radical meetings in numbers, ensuring that Radical leaders would be held accountable for terrorism or disorder, and dressing the members of the clubs in red shirts.[54]

T. J. Lipscomb headed the Newberry Rifles, J. S. Hair the Three Mile Club, T. J. Maffett the Belmont Mounted Rifles, W. W. Riser the Jalapa Mounted Club, and D. A. Dickert and E. J. Lake other rifle clubs. Twenty-one Democratic clubs were organized in the county. The merchants of Newberry pledged not to furnish provisions and other necessary farming supplies on credit to those who voted against their interests in the approaching election. Y. J. Pope asked that services be held in each church in the county on Thursday, October 26.[55]

Both parties held numerous mass meetings throughout the county. The largest of these was attended by General Hampton on September 13, the greatest turnout in the history of the county up to that time. That morning some 5,000 to 6,000 persons were at the speaking at Cline's Spring; Hampton expressed surprise at the large number of blacks present. That night the torchlight procession included 2,500 mounted men and 1,000 on foot. Colonel T. J. Lipscomb was chief marshal, and his assistants were Captain J. Wistar Gary, O. L. Schumpert, and W. D. Hardy.[56] Democrats took heart.

Democratic meetings also were held at Maybinton, Prosperity, Jalapa, Mt. Tabor Church, Wicker's Camp Ground, and Liberty Hall. Twelve hundred men, including 200 blacks, attended a barbecue at Saluda Old Town. General Gary, General Butler, J. N. Lipscomb, and Sampson Pope addressed the group, and the local newspaper carried a full account of the day's activities.[57]

Meanwhile the Radicals held another county convention. Again Corwin thrashed Boston and emerged as the Republican candidate for state senator.[58] All of the nominees were black except "carpetbaggers" Corwin, Carrington, and Leahy.

The Radical mass meeting on October 27 attracted only 500 people. The *Newberry Herald* termed it a failure. B. O. Duncan wrote from his safe seat in Italy that Chamberlain was entitled to re-election. And W. H. Thomas incensed native whites when he stated that "the Democratic Party is a devilish, infernal mob, to crush out rights and liberties," and that "the worst Republican is better than the best Democrat."[59]

An articulate, educated black, Major M. R. Delaney, spent the last week of the campaign in the county making speeches for Hampton. He was thanked by the *Newberry Herald* for his able and efficient work and for his efforts in the interest of reform and good government.[60]

But despite all the organizational work and all the campaigning, the Radicals carried the county by a margin of 500. The black majority was 1,500, so undoubtedly both whites and blacks voted for Hampton and his ticket. There was no crisis on election day. Forbearance was the watchword. The local Federal garrison was stationed at Prosperity, Longshore's, and Pomaria. When returns were counted, the Republicans carried the Court House, Gibson's, Glymphville, Jalapa, Maybinton, Whitmire's, and Williams' Store.

Newberrians faced the fact that the locally elected officials were worse than their predecessors. The *Newberry Herald*, in its November 29 issue, compared the new officers with those they succeeded. After acknowledging that H. Claremont Moses "had proved himself a faithful and competent officer" who had "managed the affairs of his office in a manner that does him credit," it went on to say that T. J. Clayton, school teacher at Mount Olive, was rumored not to have acted honestly in financial matters. The article continued:

> In the School Commissioner's office we have M. S. Long to take the place of Harry B. Scott, who is known by white and black to be an honest, upright man. . . . It is no reflection on the character of either of these men to say that neither one of them possesses the requisite learning and intelligence for that important office. . . . Boston was regarded as the best man on the last ticket. In the Legislature he was usually found on the right side of every question, and won the respect of members of both political parties. As a proof of this, a Democratic legislator, formerly Lt. Gov., writing to a gentleman here, spoke in the highest terms of Boston, as a man who always tried to do his duty in the Legislature. Henderson also stands well in the community. As for Tom Keitt, his chief characteristic is "gas"; he has a great deal more brass than brains. Thomas is the worst character of the whole lot; he is a bad man, has some inteliigence and education, but no principle. He distinguished himself during the last campaign as the apostle of hate, appealing to the basest passions of his race, to stir up bad blood toward the whites. The Democrats are not likely to forget him soon for calling them a "devilish, infamous mob." He has been for some time Trial Justice in Town. It is bad enough when such men administer the laws, but worse still when they make them. . . . No more incompetent set of officers has ever disgraced the county.

More important than the local situation was that of South Carolina. Hampton had defeated Chamberlain by unofficial returns but the machinery of government was still in Radical hands. And Federal troops supported the Radical government. Had the "straightouts" won? All of South Carolina looked to Columbia for the answer.

6

Redemption

Wade Hampton, third and greatest of that name, was a natural leader. Educated at South Carolina College and one of America's wealthiest men before secession with large interests in South Carolina, Mississippi, and Louisiana, he had recruited and outfitted a famous unit, the Hampton Legion, at the outbreak of the war. He demonstrated his leadership ability by valiant service in the Army of Northern Virginia and ultimately became Lee's chief of cavalry. In 1865 he was almost elected governor of South Carolina even after refusing to be a candidate. No man appealed more to native white Carolinians; none had a more moderate attitude toward the recently freed blacks.

Hampton was persuaded to accept the nomination in 1876 by those "Straightouts" determined to make an all-out fight to overthrow the Radicals. Proud men could no longer endure the situation under which they had writhed for almost a decade. The "Straightouts" were led by two other Confederate generals, Martin Witherspoon Gary and Matthew Calbraith Butler.

Gary's father was born on Bush River in Newberry District. He had many relatives and connections in Newberry County. After being expelled for his part in the famous "Biscuit Rebellion" at South Carolina College, Gary attended Harvard, graduating from that institution in 1854. After reading law under Chancellor James Parsons Carroll at Edgefield, he practiced there and was elected to the House of Representatives in 1860. Entering service as a captain in the Hampton Legion, he was promoted successively to general. One of the best-known officers from South Carolina and known as the "Bald Eagle of Edgefield," he conceived the Red Shirt Plan of campaign to redeem South Carolina. He was the Democratic candidate for the state Senate from Edgefield County.

Butler, too, had relatives and connections in Newberry County. His grandfather represented the district including Newberry in Congress and served as major general of militia in the early part of the century. In 1870 Butler was the Reform candidate for lieutenant governor. He also was the central figure in the Hamburg riot of July 1876.[1] Butler nominated Hampton in the state convention and later took a leading part in the campaign. Butler and Gary advocated a bold campaign of intimidation to influence black voters, while Hampton sought to appeal to them. Both methods were used in the campaign of 1876; there is no way of determining which produced more tangible results but certainly the seeds for future disagreement were sowed. Hampton and Gary would differ violently in the future, but for the moment all factions worked in harmony for a common goal, the redemption of South Carolina.

In the general election of 1876 the Democratic candidates for the Senate and House of Representatives received fewer votes than the Radical candidates in Newberry County. E. S. Keitt stated in his memoirs that they were counted out but that they protested the results. Chamberlain took military possession of the State House on the night before the legislature convened in December of 1876. The delegations from Laurens and Edgefield were excluded and neither party had a majority with certificates of the secretary of state.

The Democrats organized the House at Carolina Hall with General William H. Wallace as speaker. The Radicals did the same with E. W. M. Mackey as speaker; they remained in the State House. The Wallace group returned to the State House, and for several days the two bodies occupied the hall of the House and attempted to transact business simultaneously. Later the Wallace House went back to Carolina Hall.

Members of the Newberry Democratic House delegation agreed to withdraw their protest concerning the vote count if Sampson S. Bridges and Tom Keitt, black Republicans, would go over to the Wallace House.[2] Other legislators also tried to persuade Radical members to come over to the Wallace House since it was necessary for that body to have sixty-three certified members to be recognized as a legal body. Every effort was bent to that end, and finally Bridges was persuaded to change his affiliation.[3] He was the sixty-third member of the Wallace House and was sworn in on December 6. Ellison Keitt, Pope, and Dorroh then withdrew their claims to seats in accordance with this bargain.

Meanwhile, the Senate seat from Newberry was being contested by Senator Corwin and Captain James N. Lipscomb. The Senate appointed James F. Kilgore as special referee to take testimony and report the results. The hearings continued for months, and finally on October 12, 1877, Corwin resigned and Lipscomb was seated as senator from Newberry. Corwin returned to his native Ohio in June 1878.[4]

Chamberlain and Hampton were each inaugurated as governor, Judge Thomas J. Mackey administering the oath of office to General Hampton. The legislature adjourned, and the two rival governments used every means to win legal recognition. Federal troops sustained Chamberlain, but he was unable to collect taxes sufficient to support his regime. Meanwhile, Hampton asked the citizens to pay voluntarily 10 percent of the amount paid in taxes during the previous year to an agent appointed in each county. The money was to be used to take care of the inmates of the penal and charitable institutions.[5]

Governor Hampton appointed Uriah B. Whites of Prosperity as tax agent for Newberry County. The response was enthusiastic. On January 10 a mass meeting at the courthouse recognized Tilden and Hendricks, the Democratic nominees for president and vice president, as having been elected and Wade Hampton as lawful governor. Those attending pledged moral and financial support to Hampton. By January 15, Whites had collected $2,511.66; Newberry paid more to Hampton than any county except Charleston. Among those who contributed were former Representative Boston and Representative S. S. Bridges.[6]

Boston did more than pay. He wrote an open letter to Senator T. J. Robertson urging him to secure recognition of Hampton. It elicited an editorial in the *Newberry Herald* of February 21, 1877: "The course of J. D. Boston, a native South Carolinian, is in striking contrast with that of W. H. Thomas, a Pennsylvania mulatto; and the course of Senator Robertson, also a native of South Carolina, is in striking contrast with that of Senator Patterson, a Pennsylvania carpetbagger—all Republicans."

The race for town offices in January saw W. T. Tarrant defeat Silas Johnstone for intendant and W. A. Cline, J. N. Martin, Alan Johnstone, and A. M. Bowers elected as wardens.[7] This was the first of a series of elections in which Silas Johnstone, half-brother of George and Alan Johnstone, was involved during the period of readjustment.

Hampton asked his lieutenants in each county for a report on county officers. Young John Pope, county chairman for Newberry, submitted his report on December 23, 1876.[8] In it he pulled no punches.

Hampton subsequently removed R. E. Williams as county auditor and

Jesse C. Smith as county treasurer. He also appointed Joseph M. Ward as jury commissioner, and James Packer as trial justice in town.[9]

At Hampton's suggestion, a county convention was held on February 21 to recommend suitable persons for appointive office. Chairman Pope reported the action of the convention in a letter to Hampton on March 7.[10]

The Supreme Court of South Carolina finally recognized the Hampton government, and President Hayes recalled the Federal troops on April 10. The withdrawal of the troops doomed the Republican administration and the next day Chamberlain turned over the executive department to Hampton. South Carolina was delivered from evil, in the opinion of many, but much remained to be done to restore honest and responsible government.

Representative W. H. Thomas was expelled from the House of Representatives on May 1, 1877, on the grounds of gross contempt and his defiant attitude toward the lawful House.[11] He was immediately arrested for improper use of the funds he handled as trial justice. Posting bond, he left Newberry and was convicted in absentia at the February 1878 term of General Sessions Court.[12] The President then appointed him "Consul at St. Paul deLoando, a decayed settlement on the west coast of Africa," the Newberry Herald sardonically reported on July 3, 1878.

Representative Thomas Keitt was rather ingeniously removed from office in 1877. First he was convicted of bigamy at the September term of General Sessions Court.[13] In December the House expelled him because of his conviction.[14] Governor Hampton then pardoned Keitt.[15] While this restored his civil rights, it of course had no effect upon his expulsion from the House. The New York Times, after gleefully and erroneously reporting that Colonel E. S. Keitt, former master of the black representative, had been convicted of bigamy, was sued for libel by Colonel Keitt; he sought $50,000 in damages.[16]

Hampton was slow in making appointments to Newberry County offices. The Grand Jury at May 1877 term of General Sessions Court made its presentment reciting a list of grievances: the deplorable condition of the county jail and poor house; the need for a county physician; the necessity for an election for clerk of court, school commissioner Munson S. Long being disqualified because of conviction of official misconduct, and coroner James W. Eichleberger having failed to qualify according to law; and the fact that the county had no treasurer, no auditor, and only one trial justice. It urged that the governor take action.[17]

On May 23 the Newberry Herald reported that M. A. Carlisle, Esq., had been appointed trial justice at Newberry and J. B. Fellers at Prosperity. On May 30 the paper reported that John T. Bynum had been appointed trial justice in Township Three, John W. Riser in Township Four, James N. Lipscomb in Township Seven, and Thomas W. Holloway in Township Eleven. These, with James Packer, filled the county's quota of seven trial justices. John S. Hair was appointed jury commissioner, *vice* Joseph M. Ward. U. B. Whites was named county treasurer.

On July 4 the *Newberry Herald* commented again on the situation, stating that no county was in such political confusion as Newberry. It characterized the House members as the "ignorant and simple Bridges, shallow-pated, loud-mouthed Keitt, and the infamous Thomas," and concluded that "the county officers were little superior to them, with one or two exceptions." Although Thomas had been expelled from the House on May 2, no election had yet been ordered. There was no auditor and only one commissioner, Henry Kennedy, had qualified.

The following week, Hampton appointed Levi E. Folk as county auditor; he had been recommended by the county convention in February. On July 12 the County Democratic Convention nominated Y. J. Pope for the House vacancy, E. P. Chalmers for clerk of court, and L. Bates Maffett for county commissioner. Upon receiving the nomination, Pope resigned as county chairman, and J. F. J. Caldwell was elected to succeed him. As soon as the convention adjourned, some who disliked the nominees or the nominating process attempted to nominate L. B. Maffett for the House, Captain D. A. Dickert for clerk of court, and L. P. W. Riser for county commissioner.[18] Those nominated as "Independents" promptly declined the nominations, whereupon another independent ticket was advanced.

This second ticket included C. H. Suber for the House, T. M. Lake for clerk, and J. A. Crotwell for commissioner. County Chairman Caldwell deplored this effort to split the Democrats, and the *Newberry Herald* on August 1 blamed the Radicals. C. H. Suber in that issue of the newspaper published a letter regretting the unwarranted use of his name and stating that he would refuse to serve if elected. Nevertheless, the regular Democratic ticket carried the county by only a small margin. Chalmers took possession of the clerk's office by physical force when he received his commission on August 15.[19]

The next month the hapless ex-senator Charles W. Montgomery was indicted for fraud by the Richland County Grand Jury. The case against him was *nol prossed* in November, and he moved back to Charleston where he spent the rest of his life. Death removed Foster Blodgett, the notorious Georgia "scalawag," in November 1877.[20]

In December another county convention was held to select the Democratic nominee for the House vacancy caused by Tom Keitt's expulsion and the nominee for school commissioner. George Johnstone was selected over Dr. W. M. Dorroh; the Reverend J. C. Boyd was nominated for school commissioner over H. S. Boozer, J. Belton Werts, and John A. Chapman.[21]

In the January 2, 1878, issue of the *Newberry Herald*, Silas Johnstone, half-brother of the regular Democratic House nominee, accepted the "Independent" nomination for the House. He challenged the legality of the county convention's action and stated that he had voted for Hampton in 1876. Dorroh, defeated by George Johnstone, promptly called on the voters to support the convention's nominees. A close election ensued, but George Johnstone defeated Silas Johnstone by eighty-seven votes. Silas carried the town of Newberry, while George overwhelmed him at Prosperity.

Meanwhile, shortly before the general campaign of 1878, the regular Democrats won another town election. J. P. Pool was re-elected intendant with L. M. Speers, Peter Rodelsperger, Alan Johnstone, and George S. Mower as wardens.[22]

It was apparent to all that the Republican strategy for 1878 would be not to nominate candidates for statewide offices because of the tremendous popularity of Governor Hampton. Instead, the Republicans planned to concentrate on several congressional seats and the state legislature. In Newberry, the Republicans hoped to get at least one seat in the House of Representatives and several county commissioners.

In April, a County Convention of Colored People was held at the Hoge School on Caldwell Street. The fifty-three delegates present resolved not to renew the antagonism between the white and colored people, but expressed their determination to withhold support from any Democratic candidate who would not promise formally to give the freedmen proper representation.[23]

In April the *Newberry Herald* endorsed Hampton's re-election but wanted the other state officers rotated. The State Democratic Executive Committee suggested primary elections; the county convention adopted a primary plan, but then rescinded its action and decided to use the convention system again. Because of the strong feelings engendered by this debate, the *Newberry Herald* warned that the Democrats were not as united or as strong as in 1876 and that the Republicans, while quiet, intended to make a fight for the legislature. The Democrats were a minority and had to attain unity, it said. This could not be done if Independent candidates were encouraged.[24]

When the State Democratic Convention renominated the entire Hampton slate, the governor warned that Republicans would attempt to win the Legislature. At the first campaign meeting in Greenville, he delivered his famous dictum that an Independent was worse that a Radical:[25] "The greatest of these (dangers), in my apprehension, is that of the Independent movement. He who sets up his own individual judgment as a rule of action, and refuses to act in full and perfect accord with our platform, in spirit as well as in letter, is an Independent, and an Independent at this crisis in our affairs is worse than a Radical."

The county Republican Party met first on August 1, with all delegates being black except Dr. Constantia, of whom the *Newberry Herald* contemptuously said he was practicing on the government reservation near Maybinton, that no one knew whence he came or his race, but that he had a black wife. The apparent purpose of the Republicans was to destroy the Democratic Party by nominating a mixed ticket. The Republicans reconvened in September with D. R. Phifer being the only white delegate present. Phifer advocated another meeting and advised that if the Republicans would nominate a ticket composed of the best Democrats and Republicans he would support it.[26]

The Republicans met a third time on October 10 with only one white delegate present, James C. Leahy. Although Leahy advocated that no nominations be made, the convention selected several candidates: Z. W. McMorries and Belton B. Boozer for the House; Wesley R. Brown and Henry Kennedy for county commissioners; and J. A. Henderson for coroner. The executive committee was authorized to name others; the stage was set to try to divide the Democrats.[27]

The Democrats needed little help. Having split sharply over the question of whether to nominate by primary or convention, the party was even more fragmented when a shooting match occurred in the convention itself. Captain D. A. Dickert, member of the "Suber" faction, and Colonel T. J. Lipscomb of the "Johnstone" faction were wounded as a result of a quarrel over control of the convention. It was necessary to adjourn before settling the ticklish question of seating delegates from the town. The *Newberry Herald* deplored the division in the party and demanded that both C. H. Suber and George Johnstone be dropped as candidates for the House. County Chairman J. F. J. Caldwell, law partner of Suber, implored the Democrats not to divide while "a crafty and remorseless enemy watches these divisions with gloating eyes."[28]

Three weeks later the convention met again; obviously much work had been done behind the scenes. General Y. J. Pope, not a delegate, was accorded the privilege of the floor, and, in the interest of harmony, he withdrew the claims of the Johnstone delegates to be seated. Immediately, on motion of Captain John McCarley, Dr. W. M. Dorroh, George Johnstone, and C. H. Suber were nominated for the House of Representatives. Without further ado, the convention nominated Colonel William Lester, Andrew J. Livingston, and J. C. Swittenberg as county commissioners, Henry S. Boozer as school commissioner, Jacob B. Fellers as probate judge, and E. C. Longshore as coroner. Convention President W. D. Hardy then adjourned the convention.[29]

Immediately efforts were made to field an Independent ticket. First a ticket was proposed that retained Dorroh and Suber as candidates for the House and named John T. Peterson as the third House candidate; Samuel W. Cannon, W. W. Houseal, and Andrew J. Longshore for county commissioners; John A. Chapman for school commissioner; and Silas Johnstone for probate judge. Longshore indignantly stated in an open letter that he was for the regular ticket and would refuse to serve if elected. Dorroh and Suber, while not spurning any votes, published cards indicating they were the candidates of the Democratic Party and were pledged to the whole ticket.[30] Chapman also refused the nomination as school commissioner.

As the election drew near, the Republican executive committee named still more candidates: Peterson for the House, L. B. Maffett for county commissioner, Alfred Denson as coroner, J. B. Boyd as school commissioner, and Silas Johnstone as probate judge. Despite such efforts, the vote resulted in the election of the entire Democratic ticket by a larger margin than in the recent special elections.[31] The *Newberry Herald* of November 13, 1878, rejoiced that for the first time in ten years Newberry was free from every taint of Radicalism. Native white Newberrians felt that they had indeed been delivered from evil.

7

The Conservative Regime

The General Assembly elected Wade Hampton to the United States Senate in November 1878. Three months later, W. D. Simpson of Laurens became governor. When he became chief justice in September 1880, Simpson was succeeded by Thomas B. Jeter of Union. In the gubernatorial campaign of 1880, Hampton backed General Johnson Hagood of Barnwell as his gubernatorial candidate, in order to head off General Martin Witherspoon Gary, the only figure of statewide stature who dared to disagree with Hampton.

Gary was a fiery, brilliant, brave man who contributed largely to the redemption of the state in 1876. An ambitious man, he was not content to remain a state senator even though he was undisputed leader of Edgefield County. He felt entitled to a higher office when he saw the two other members of the triumvirate of 1876 promoted to seats in the national arena. Bitterly disappointed at being defeated by Hampton's forces for the governorship, he retired from active politics and died in April 1881. The Conservative regime would not be seriously challenged again until Ben Tillman of Edgefield captured the Democratic Party of South Carolina.

For a decade the Conservatives sought to recreate the ante-bellum past. As William Cooper remarks in his study of the era, "for them, (the Conservatives) the best of all possible worlds had existed in ante-bellum South Carolina. To build anew what they revered in that commonwealth became their cardinal purpose. While ante-bellum South Carolina was their ideal, the Confederacy was their touchstone."[1]

The result was a complete lack of any awareness of social problems, of any program for reform, of any legislation to aid in solving the state's agrarian needs. For the most part the Bourbons looked not to the future, but to the past. The nationwide murmuring for agricultural relief was not audible to their ears. It did not occur to them that anything could or should be done to alleviate the suffering caused by the national depression. However, they were eager to build cotton mills and railroads and worked closely with outside interests in a widely heralded campaign to "industrialize" the South.

Hagood's undistinguished term gave way to that of Superintendent of Education Hugh S. Thompson, who served nearly four years before accepting a federal appointment in July 1886. Thompson was succeeded briefly by John C. Sheppard of Edgefield, and he by John Peter Richardson, chief executive from 1886 to 1890.

In May 1879, the Confederate monument was unveiled on the State House grounds. Public subscriptions of $16,000 paid the cost of this memorial. William Henry Trescot wrote the memorable lines that were carved on the side of the monument:[2]

> Let the stranger,
> Who May in Future Times
> Read This Inscription
> Recognize That There Were Men
> Whom Power Could Not Corrupt,
> Whom Death Could Not Terrify,
> Whom Defeat Could Not Dishonor,
> And Let Their Virtues Plead
>   For Just Judgment
> Of the Cause in Which They Perished.
>   Let the South Carolinian
>   Of Another Generation
>   Remember
> That the State Taught Them
> How to Live and How to Die,
> And That from Her Broken Fortunes
> She Has Preserved for Her Children
> The Priceless Treasure of Their Memories,
>   Teaching All Who May Claim
>   The Same Birthright
> That Truth, Courage and Patriotism
>   Endure Forever.

The state having set the pattern, Newberry erected its shaft to the memory of her dead heroes the following year. The Survivors Association began the task of securing funds for a monument during the Reconstruction years. Finally in August 1879, the contract was let to a local firm, Leavell and Speers, and plans were made for a suitable dedication. On June 30, 1880, the monument was unveiled. General Y. J. Pope, president of the Survivors Association, presided; General John D. Kennedy of Camden delivered the oration; and J. F. J. Caldwell, author of the *History of Gregg's Brigade*, read a special ode that he composed for the occasion.[3]

Soon after the end of the Civil War, the Order of the Patrons of Husbandry, or Grange as it was commonly called, was organized to improve the social, cultural, and educational life of rural Americans. In the South, the Grange also tended to allay sectional animosities and hasten the economic rehabilitation of the farmers. The *Rural Carolinian*, edited by Dr. Daniel Harrison Jacques, began a vigorous campaign in the interests of the Grange. The Order only began to flourish locally, however, after David Wyatt Aiken of Abbeville was appointed deputy at large for the Southern states in December 1871.[4]

Under the leadership of Colonel Aiken and his successor, Dr. John A. Barksdale of Laurens, 332 local Granges were chartered in South Carolina, with a membership of more than 10,000.[5] In Newberry County the first Grange was organized at Pomaria on June 14, 1872, with Thomas W. Holloway as master.[6]

A state Grange was organized on October 9, 1872. James N. Lipscomb of Newberry served as master of the state Grange from 1874 to 1887, and Thomas W. Holloway of Pomaria served as its secretary.[7]

James Nathan Lipscomb was born at White Hall, Abbeville District, on April 11, 1827, the son of John and Sarah Marie Bonham Lipscomb. After graduation from South Carolina College in 1848, he settled at Chappell's Depot as a planter. He served as lieutenant colonel, 2nd Cavalry Regiment, during the Civil War and was active in the Hampton Campaign of 1876. He was elected to the state Senate from Newberry County in that year. He then served as county auditor, 1880–82, and as secretary of state for South Carolina, 1882–86. A trustee of South Carolina College, commissioner of agriculture, and master of the state Grange, he lived a most useful life. Married three times, he died in Bryson City, North Carolina, on June 14, 1891.[8]

Thomas W. Holloway was born in Newberry County on March 28, 1829. Orphaned at an early age, he worked for the Greenville and Columbia Railroad, as cashier of the Bank of Newberry, and as a

merchant and farmer at Pomaria. For many years he served as secretary of
the state Grange, secretary of the State Agricultural and Mechanical Society, and member of the board of trustees of Newberry College. Recognized as one of Newberry's most useful citizens, he was twice married, first
to Martha Folk, and then to Angella V. Counts. Upon his death on January 20, 1903, he was survived by his second wife and by five children.
Henry C. Holloway, Esquire, of the Newberry Bar was a child of his
second marriage, as was a daughter, Mrs. Edward Thorpe, while Professor
J. B. O'Neall Holloway, Mrs. Luther Fellers, and Mrs. E. W. Hipp were
children of his first union.[9]

First in the *Rural Carolinian* and later in the *News and Courier*,
Aiken urged farmers to cut down their cotton acreage, plant more small
grains, rotate crops, diversify, and practice farm economy. He urged an
increase in livestock, and the improvement of the strain by buying
Merino sheep, Jersey or Ayreshire cattle, and a crossbreed of Essex and
Berkshire hogs. Crying out against crop liens and purchases on credit,
he warned farmers not to buy what they could raise themselves. He also
recommended cooperative buying and selling.[10]

The Grange advocated the creation of a state department of agriculture and the raising of the federal Bureau of Agriculture to cabinet
status. Both of these aims were achieved,[11] but when the Grange ven-
tured into politics, it lost favor and degenerated into a fraternal organization. It was, however, a forerunner of the farmer's revolution in South
Carolina in 1890.

In 1878 the Newberry Agricultural and Mechanical Society was orga-
nized with John C. Wilson as president. Other officers were Thomas W.
Holloway, John McCarley, John R. Spearman, Sr., and William D.
Hardy as vice presidents and George S. Mower as secretary-treasurer. In
November of that year it held the first fair in Newberry since 1859.
There were 760 entries and the fair was termed a great success.[12]

The number of entries rose to 1,311 in 1880. Two years later the
Newberry Agricultural and Mechanical Association succeeded the society as a joint stock company with the object of buying the fairgrounds.
Unfortunately, the association was forced into liquidation in 1886,[13] and
this ended the first effort to revive the very successful agricultural society
that had flourished in Newberry before the Civil War.

The Farmers' Alliance, one of several organizations spawned in the
latter half of the nineteenth century by agricultural distress, made its
appearance in South Carolina in 1887.[14] A county Farmers' Alliance was
organized in Newberry in 1888, with W. D. Hardy of Maybinton as its

president and county organizer. By July 11, 1889, there were fifteen alliances in the county.[15]

Among the leaders of the Alliance were W. D. Hardy, Jefferson A. Sligh, Dr. W. E. Lake, John T. Duncan, and Joseph L. Keitt. William Dixon Hardy, son of W. E. and Catherine Hardy, was born near Maybinton, Newberry District, on April 20, 1841. Educated at the North Carolina Academy under General Stephen D. Lee, he lived in Spartanburg until he entered the Confederate army with the Spartan Rifles, 5th South Carolina Volunteers. He served as sergeant-major and then as adjutant of the 5th Regiment until the surrender at Appomattox.

Active in the Hampton Campaign, he was president of the Newberry County Democratic Convention in 1878 and 1880. He also was a representative from Newberry County and master in equity. Married to Frances Booker Sims of Union County, he died at the great age of ninety-one on October 16, 1932, survived by seven children.[16]

Jefferson A. Sligh, son of Jefferson and Mary Nancy Griffith Sligh, was born in Newberry District on November 26, 1835. Educated at Newberry College and at the Lutheran Seminary, he was pastor of St. Paul's Lutheran Church near Pomaria for forty years. He served in the 13th Regiment, South Carolina Volunteers, as a sergeant. After four years in the House of Representatives, Sligh defeated John C. Wilson in a close race for the state Senate in 1884. Four years later he was defeated for reelection by Y. J. Pope in an even closer race.

In 1892, he was elected to the Senate but resigned that year upon being elected to the Railroad Commission. He was president of the county Alliance, but was defeated by Keitt for the presidency of the state Alliance in 1895. He and Keitt were elected as the Reform delegates to the state Constitutional Convention in that year. Sligh was a member of the board of trustees of Newberry College for many years. He married first Alice Rebecca Kibler and second, Lydia Clemtine Setzler. Sligh moved to Columbia after his retirement from politics; he died there on August 7, 1917.[17]

Dr. William Elijah Lake was born in Newberry District on October 28, 1852, the son of Benjamin Drayton and Rebecca Conwill Lake. After graduating from Newberry College in 1878 and from the Medical College of the state of South Carolina in 1881, he settled in the St. Luke's section of the county. He was president of the county Alliance in 1893 and 1894. Although Dr. Lake took an active part in the farmers' movement, he held no political office. He later moved into town and died there at the age of seventy-seven, on January 31, 1930. He was survived by his wife, the former Julia Anne Schroeder of Walhalla, and his six children, Edwin O. Lake, W. E. Lake, Mrs. A. R. Morris, Mrs. T. F. Suber, Mrs. T. W. Morgan, and Miss Mary Ellen Lake. At the time of his death he was the oldest physician practicing in Newberry.[18]

John Thomas Duncan, son of Baruch and Sarah Duckett Duncan, was born in Newberry County on September 18, 1862. He entered the reform movement early on, being elected one of the directors of the state Alliance Bank and to the House of Representatives in 1892. Re-elected in 1894, he was expelled from the House in 1896 for holding dual office. He had accepted an appointment in the secretary of state's office while still a member of the House. He was promptly elected chairman of the County Democratic Executive Committee and later that year he was graduated in law at the University of South Carolina. During the rest of his life he made twelve races for governor and for the U.S. Senate; he was never elected but he had the satisfaction of preventing Governor John Gary Evans's elevation to the Senate on two occasions. He married Louise Tompkins. Duncan died at a Columbia hospital on June 18, 1938, survived by his son, Daniel T. Duncan, and his daughter, Sara Duncan Olsen.[19]

Joseph L. Keitt served as president of the county Alliance and then filled two terms as president of the state Alliance in 1895 and 1896.[20] Keitt was a son of Colonel Ellison S. Keitt and Caroline Wadlington Keitt. Born in Columbia on April 1, 1857, he was educated at the Virginia Military Institute, from which he graduated in 1877, and in law at Columbia University, from which he graduated in 1881. He practiced law only a short time before devoting himself exclusively to his planting interests. He married Anna Coe of Virginia and they had three children, Trent (Mrs. E. B. Purcell), Anna Coe (Mrs. Edgar Hart), and Joseph L. Keitt, Jr.[21]

Keitt served as senator from Newberry County, being the first person who was not a Confederate veteran to be elected to office in Newberry after Reconstruction. He was one of the Tillmanites elected to the Constitutional Convention of 1895. He embraced the alliance program with vigor and supported it both in the press and on the stump.

The Alliance program, much more politically oriented than the Grange, included the abolition of national banks, free and unlimited coinage of silver, prohibition of alien ownership of land, limitation of national revenues to necessary expenditures of government, the printing of fractional paper currency, nationalization of communication and transportation systems, and the sub-treasury plan. The latter was simply a forerunner of the commodity credit plan enacted by the New Deal; it involved the deposit of staple commodities in federal warehouses and loans equal to eighty percent of the value of such commodities.[22]

Because of the problems that farmers encountered in the 1880s and the resulting hard times, many of them embraced the various features of the Alliance agenda. That the railroads and telegraph companies remained privately owned monopolies was a real accomplishment for the spokesmen for private enterprise. Most farmers would have nationalized them.

Before the end of the Conservative regime the farmers of South Carolina ceased to regard the Grange as the panacea for their economic problems and turned to the Alliance. They yearned for a more dynamic organization that would improve the lot of agriculture. Cotton brought less than ten cents a pound for twenty years, commencing in 1881. Credit, the lien system, and high interest rates were the bane of farmers everywhere.

Benjamin Ryan Tillman, brilliant pamphleteer, dynamic stump speaker, and ruthless politician, appeared on the state scene when he addressed a joint meeting of the Grange and the state Agricultural Association at Bennettsville in 1885. He electrified his audience and began his systematic attack upon the existing order.

Pretending to eschew political preferment, Tillman wrote a series of letters to the Charleston *News and Courier*. He aroused the farmers of South Carolina, stimulating them to demand an agricultural experiment station, an agricultural college, and freedom from so-called Bourbon rule.

Fortunately for Tillman, the will of Thomas G. Clemson provided the opportunity of establishing an agricultural college. Clemson, the son-in-law of John C. Calhoun, devised Fort Hill plantation, consisting of 814 acres, and the sum of $80,000 for the establishment of a separate state agricultural college. Tillman and six others were named life trustees, with power to name their successors, and the legislature was to elect six other trustees. The devise was accepted by the General Assembly in 1889.[23]

One of the six original trustees elected by the legislature was Alan Johnstone, a Newberry farmer.[24] Son of Chancellor Job Johnstone and his second wife, Almira Amelia Dewalt, he was born in Newberry on August 12, 1849. Educated at the University of Virginia, he was active in the business and civic affairs of Newberry throughout his long and useful life.

In 1892, he was elected a life trustee of Clemson and for many years was chairman of the board of that institution. He also was an alderman of the town of Newberry, representative from the county, chairman of the city school board, president of Farmers Oil Mill, and elder of Aveleigh Presbyterian Church.

For twenty years he was senator from Newberry County. He served as president pro tempore of the Senate for eight years and was chairman of the Senate Finance Committee for twelve years. Senator Johnstone married Lilla Rall Kennerly of Newberry; they had ten children of whom seven survived: Thomas K. Johnstone, Alan Johnstone, Jr., J. Malcolm Johnstone, Mrs. George McCutcheon, Mrs. T. L. Mills, Mrs. W. W. Coleman and Mrs. J. W. Roundtree.[25]

While the Conservative era in South Carolina is generally regarded as one where time stood still and faces were turned to the past, this was not true in Newberry. Here the business leaders determined that the county would have more than a pure agricultural economy. The first steps were taken during Reconstruction when the National Bank of Newberry was organized on June 3, 1871, with a capital of $100,000. Robert L. McCaughrin was elected president, John B. Carwile, cashier, T. S. Duncan, assistant cashier, and Fair, Pope and Pope, solicitors.

The board consisted of McCaughrin, Carwile, J. B. Palmer, G. T. Scott, W. H. Webb, Y. J. Pope, J. N. Martin, Robert Moorman, and John T. Peterson.[26] The bank opened in the old banking house of the defunct Bank of Newberry on the Public Square; the building is now, a century later, occupied by First Federal Savings and Loan Association.

The *Laurensville Advertiser* commented that Newberry was a wide-awake place and that "it does more business and better business than any place in the upcountry, never failing to satisfy the demands of the public in every particular."[27]

As though living up to this judgment, the Newberry Cotton Exchange was organized in October 1875, with twelve directors. W. G. Mayes was elected president, A. J. McCaughrin, superintendent, and J. M. Johnstone, assistant superintendent.[28] Although the exchange soon foundered, the fact that it was established indicates the strength of the Newberry cotton market and the progressive outlook of Newberry's citizens.

The business leaders had to cope with a series of disastrous fires that threatened the existence of the town. After the fire of 1866 destroyed much of the business section, the stores had barely been rebuilt when an even worse fire of March 8, 1877, destroyed some twenty stores. The total loss was estimated at $150,000, while the insurance coverage was only about $60,000.[29]

Two years later the town suffered once more when a blaze started at Keene's tin shop on Main Street and burned ten stores south of Caldwell Street. The Courthouse was scorched and required extensive repairs by Osborne Wells. It was then that he designed the bas relief on the facade of the Old Courthouse.[30]

In 1883 a fire destroyed Mollohon Row, which faced the square between Main and Boyce streets.[31] This row of old buildings had miraculously escaped the fires of 1866 and 1877 when all the other buildings in that block had been destroyed.

The spirit of the town showed in the construction of even better buildings to replace those burned. Two hotels were completed in 1879. J. P. Pool and his son-in-law, O. L. Schumpert, erected the Newberry Hotel on Caldwell Street, while J. A. Crotwell built the three-story Crotwell Hotel on College Street at the head of Boyce Street.[32]

G. L. Norman was architect for the Newberry Hotel. He was also architect for the Opera House, construction of which was commenced the following year. Upon completion of the new hotels, the Crotwell Hotel was leased to J. Hart Blease while the Newberry Hotel was leased to A. W. T. Simmons. Dr. S. F. Fant moved his drug store into the corner store under the Newberry Hotel, and Harvey Reese established his barber shop under it on Caldwell Street.[33]

On November 3, 1880, the council awarded a contract for building the new Opera House. Local granite was quarried at Rikard's, two miles from town, while bricks were furnished from the brickyards of Pool, Fellers, Crotwell, and Wells. Wells was hired to superintend the brickwork in the new building, W. A. Cline to supervise woodwork, and George Gilliland to cover the roof. Eugene Cramer of Columbia was given the contract to paint and furnish the scenery.[34]

Although George Hacker of Charleston furnished the doors and sashes, no blinds were included. E. C. Plumer of Columbia agreed to light the Opera House for $469. He installed a thirty-light, patented "Columbia Portable Gas Machine." Atop the tower was placed a weather vane in the shape of a gar fish four feet long; why this primordial and repulsive fish was chosen is not known. A Seth Thomas clock was installed in the tower,[35] and finally a fire bell was placed there. Since the bell was installed during the term of Mayor George Benedict Cromer, it was called "Big Ben."[36] The Opera House cost $30,000.00.[37]

The new Opera House was dedicated in February 1882 during the administration of J. P. Pool. Young John Pope spoke for the citizens of the town, while President George Holland spoke for the college, and O.

L. Schumpert for the Thespian Club. C. G. Jaeger read an Ode written by him especially for the occasion. Music was rendered by a Mrs. Bailey of Newberry and Mrs. Warren R. Davis of Columbia.[38]

The Opera House served as the real social center of the community in the late nineteenth century. Not only did touring players perform on its stage, but also meetings, dances, college commencement exercises, and musicals were held in the spacious auditorium. A false floor was laid across the tops of the seats in the orchestra section for dancing, and the chaperones were seated in the boxes.

One memorable Commencement Ball began at nine in the morning because torrential rains the night before prevented the ball's being held at the usual time. There were a great many out of town guests, the orchestra was engaged, and the Lotus Club determined not to be outdone. The local newspaper reported that the ball lasted from nine until three in the afternoon and was a great success. That night a ball for the older set was also highly successful.[39]

In 1879, Newberry's population was about 2,500; the town had fifty-three stores, including six barrooms.[40] Two years later, G. M. Girardeau made a map of the town that consisted of four wards, divided generally by Pratt (now Main) Street and Caldwell Street. By 1889, the population had increased to almost 4,000 and the number of stores to seventy-five.[41]

Commencing in 1878, a determined group of local businessmen began agitating for the establishment of a cotton factory.[42] At a public meeting held in May of that year a committee of five under the chairmanship of Robert Lusk McCaughrin was elected to assess the situation and promote a local mill.[43]

The selection of McCaughrin was a wise one. He was the leading business figure in the county from the end of the war until his death in 1896. Son of Thomas and Letitia Lusk McCaughrin, he was born in Chester on September 1, 1834. He came to Newberry in 1854 to serve as bookkeeper of the old Bank of Newberry. After seeing service in McGowan's Brigade, CSA, as a captain, he returned to Newberry and in 1871 established the National Bank of Newberry. He was elected president of Piedmont Mills in Greenville but declined this honor because he was unwilling to leave Newberry. He also served as president of the Columbia and Greenville Railroad and of the Laurens Railroad.

McCaughrin married first Anna P. Kirkpatrick, whose father was president of Washington and Lee University, and, secondly, Laura E. Nance of Newberry. An elder in the Presbyterian Church, he took an active part in redeeming the state during Reconstruction, serving as a member of the Taxpayers' Convention.[44]

McCaughrin pushed the new enterprise with vigor and by May 1883 more than $157,000 had been subscribed. In that month a board of eleven directors was chosen, and he was elected president of Newberry Cotton Mills, with George S. Mower as secretary.[45]

The new company bought the five acres on which John B. Carwile's residence was located for $4,500 and the adjoining twenty-five acres from William Langford for $2,000. Lockwood and Green, the architects for Piedmont Mills, were retained to design the new plant. W. T. Davis of Greenville, builder of Piedmont Mills, was awarded the contract to build the Newberry factory. Pool and Banks contracted to furnish 1,250,000 local bricks for the building.[46]

The Newberry Cotton Mills erected the first plant in America entirely dependent upon steam.[47] All of the mills built before it were built on rivers or streams and operated primarily by water power. Within a few years the plant was operating at full capacity of 320 looms and 10,000 spindles. The mill employed 250 people and used fifteen bales of cotton a day.[48] The only sour note sounded about this new industry was the protest of the *Newberry Herald* about the unfairness of the law exempting new factories from taxation for ten years.[49]

The Newberry Cotton Seed Oil Mill and Fertilizer Company was organized in 1890. L. W. Floyd was general manager, T. M. Neel was vice president, and George S. Mower was attorney. The mill was equipped with electric lights and it was announced that it would operate twenty-four hours a day.[50]

It was during this period that Newberry College was returned from Walhalla by the Lutheran Synod of South Carolina. Various communities vied in offering land, money, and other inducements for the relocation of the college. Columbia, Anderson, Lexington, Walhalla, Prosperity, and Newberry made offers. On the second ballot the Synod decided to accept Newberry's offer of $15,870, plus ten acres of land or the privilege of buying the old site for $2,500.[51] Newberry College reopened in Newberry on September 19, 1877. Tuition was $25 in the Junior Preparatory Department, $35 in the Middle Department, and $40 in the Senior Preparatory Department. College tuition was $50, while incidental expenses were set at $5, and board, including room, fuel, and lights, was $13 per month.[52]

The town continued to grow during this period. The *Newberry Herald* proudly reported in 1877 that Newberry was the fourth largest post office in South Carolina in point of business; only Charleston, Columbia, and Greenville transacted more business.[53] Newberry also had the distinction of being one of the first large post offices to have a postmistress. Mrs. Elizabeth Goggans Herbert, widow of Captain Chesley W. Herbert, was appointed and served from April 1885 to March 1890.[54]

From 1876 to 1890 the county's officeholders, however, were, with two exceptions, veterans of the Confederate service. The two exceptions, Joseph L. Keitt and John Martin Kinard, were sons of veterans. Most of the officeholders during the Bourbon era had been maimed in the war. Probate Judge Fellers lost an arm at Second Manassas; Treasurer Martin H. Gary an arm at Knoxville; Coroner E. C. Longshore a leg at Knoxville; Commissioner A. J. Livingston a leg at the Wilderness; and Commissioner J. Drayton Smith an arm at Knoxville.[55] All of them served in county offices at the same time.

Newberry County held its first Democratic primary election in 1880.[56] By that time the last "carpetbag" officeholder, ex-judge of probate J. C. Leahy, had departed from the county.[57] The Democrats felt strong enough to permit a primary, and their confidence was justified in the easy victory their nominees won in the general election. It was the last effort to defeat the local Democratic ticket in the general election for many years.

In 1882 the county was shocked to learn that Captain U. B. Whites, Hampton's appointee as county treasurer, had absconded with county funds. He was charged with embezzling $8,000. After a mistrial, he pleaded guilty to failing to turn over money to his successor and was sentenced to serve twelve months or pay a fine of $2,000. He paid the fine.[58]

The county was also shocked in March of 1887 when George Johnstone killed John B. Jones in Trial Justice H. H. Blease's courtroom.[59] Both men were attorneys and both were from leading Newberry families. Johnstone was the son of Chancellor Job Johnstone and Jones the son of Major Lambert Jefferson Jones, then the Nestor of the Newberry Bar. The newspapers of South Carolina were merciless in their attacks upon such conduct by lawyers. Newberry was sharply divided in its opinion as to whether Johnstone should be convicted.

Johnstone was bound over by the coroner's jury and tried for murder at the November term of General Sessions Court. Represented by Y. J. Pope, O. L. Schumpert, and J. Y. Culbreath, he was acquitted promptly.[60] Many Newberrians never forgave him for having goaded Jones into losing his head and firing first.

The shooting incident followed Johnstone's race for Congress by only a year. Newberry, unfortunately, had two candidates in the same race and Judge James S. Cothran of Abbeville defeated Johnstone and James N. Lipscomb in the congressional caucus.[61] Despite criticism for his lack of delicacy, Cothran remained on the circuit bench during the campaign.

8

The Tillman Era

The last decade of the nineteenth century was a period of great political and economic activity—a time of ferment that had lasting effects on Newberry County. Politically, it was the era of Tillman.

Benjamin R. Tillman waged a shrewd campaign for the office of governor. Pretending to have no personal ambition, he succeeded, through his brilliant pamphleteering and harsh oratory, in becoming the best known spokesman for the farmer's movement by 1890. In January of that year the so-called Shell Manifesto called for a convention to be held in March to suggest candidates for state offices. Although the manifesto was issued over the name of Dr. George Washington Shell, president of the State Farmers Association and clerk of court of Laurens County, Tillman later admitted that he had written it.

W. H. Wallace, the editor of the *Newberry Observer*, printed the manifesto on the front page of the January 30, 1890, issue of his paper, but he wrote a strong editorial opposing its object and calling on Democrats to nominate openly and not by factional caucus. The County Farmers Convention met on March 15 and by a two-vote margin endorsed the nomination of candidates at a state convention.[1]

Although the Newberry delegates disregarded this advice the state convention determined to do so by a vote of 121 to 114.[2] This result was finally announced after sufficient votes were changed after the motion apparently lost by a single vote. Thereafter the Farmers Association became known as the "Reform Movement."

The Reform ticket for the 1890 election consisted of these candidates: Tillman for governor; Eugene B. Gary of Abbeville, lieutenant governor; James E. Tindal of Clarendon, secretary of state; Young John Pope of Newberry, attorney general; W. D. Mayfield of Barnwell, superintendent of education; Dr. W. T. C. Bates of Orangeburg, state treasurer; William H. Ellerbe of Marion, comptroller general; and Hugh Farley of Spartanburg, adjutant and inspector general. In experience, background, and education these candidates compared favorably with their predecessors.

Tillman and the Reformers waged a vigorous campaign throughout the state; it was the first county-to-county campaign at which all candidates for state office appeared, and the practice continued until the middle of the twentieth century when television caused its demise. The tour reached Newberry in June and the Reformers received an enthusiastic reception.[3] Several of the later meetings were riotous but Newberry's was well behaved.

The incumbent county delegation consisted of Senator Y. J. Pope and Representatives R. T. C. Hunter, J. Malcolm Johnstone, and George S. Mower. Pope was a candidate for attorney general, while Hunter did not seek re-election. Johnstone and Mower did.

The Tillman forces held a well-publicized caucus in August 1890 and passed judgment upon all the candidates for the House of Representatives. Thomas W. Keitt, John W. Scott, C. L. Blease, W. D. Hardy, and John T. Duncan were determined to be acceptable to the Tillmanites. These gentlemen, together with Johnstone and Mower, were candidates in the primary which was won by Scott. In the second primary, Hardy and Blease, Tillmanites, defeated Johnstone and Mower, anti-Tillmanites.[4]

This was the first victory of the colorful and magnetic "Colie" Blease. He had been defeated for the House in 1888, had graduated from Georgetown University law school, and had returned home to practice law. It was the beginning of a long political career which would carry him to the offices of governor and United States senator and which would see him converted from a strong Tillman follower to a determined Tillman adversary.

In the same primary George Johnstone, brother of Malcolm, defeated D. K. Norris, the Tillman candidate for Congress from the Third District. His margin of victory was only twenty-two votes in the district but 377 votes in Newberry County.[5]

When the State Democratic Convention met after the primary it nominated as its candidates for state office those who had won in the primary. Because of being nominated for attorney general, Y. J. Pope immediately resigned as state senator from Newberry County; in the ensuing special primary Joseph L. Keitt, Tillmanite candidate, defeated J. F. J. Caldwell, the anti-Tillmanite, by a vote of 682 to 535 votes, thereby succeeding Senator Pope.[6]

In the general election in November, Tillman defeated A. C. Haskell by a vote of 1,694 to 344 in the county and by a vote of 59,150 to 14,828 in the state.[7] He then became the undisputed political leader of South Carolina, and he remained a devisive but dominant political force until his death in 1918.

Tillman's greatest services to the state were his support for Clemson in its infancy and his founding of Winthrop. Both institutions have made significant contributions to the welfare of South Carolina, and Tillman's recognition of the need for them and his vision in planning for the education of South Carolina's youth were important.

On the other hand, he infuriated the Conservatives by unseating Senator Wade Hampton and by replacing many of the state's officeholders with Tillmanites. The fact that J. L. M. Irby was selected to succeed Hampton added insult to injury. Irby was a politician of great ability but tremendous vices. But he was responsible for the success of the March convention, had served as state chairman of the Democratic Party in the Tillman campaign, and had to be rewarded. The vacancy on the Supreme Court caused by Chief Justice Simpson's death in 1891 and Justice McIver's elevation to the chief justiceship was filled by the election of Attorney General Y. J. Pope over Circuit Judge William Wallace, speaker of the Wallace House during Reconstruction.

Tillman's acceptance of a free railroad pass, after having attacked the practice, caused much resentment among both friends and foes. The Bourbons boiled at his arrogance and greed for power; they determined to block his re-election.

In March 1892 the anti-Tillmanites met in Columbia to select a ticket. Former Governor John C. Sheppard, lawyer and banker of Edgefield, and James L. Orr, Jr., lawyer and textile executive from Greenville, were chosen as candidates for governor and lieutenant governor. Newberry's delegates to this meeting were J. F. J. Caldwell, A. J. Livingston, P. C. Smith, A. J. Gibson, L. P. Miller, W. H. Hunt, Jr., John M. Suber, and Thomas W. Holloway.[8]

The ensuing campaign was bitter. Tillman demanded that the "driftwood" legislature be replaced with true Tillmanites. In 1888 Tillman had demanded a statewide primary; in 1890 and 1892 he refused such a vehicle, insisting on the convention system of nominations. Accordingly, the county-to-county tour was made by all the candidates, but electors were chosen to attend the state convention.

Newberry's campaign meeting was held at Helena, and bloodshed was barely averted. Leroy F. Youmans of Barnwell, the anti-Tillmanite candidate for secretary of state, clashed with Tillman. The speaker's stand collapsed and the meeting was called off to prevent violence.[9]

In Newberry the Tillmanites were victorious, but by a small margin. Tillman electors won by a vote of 1,170 to 832. The Tillmanite candidates for the House of Representatives, "Colie" Blease, John T. Duncan, and W. D. Hardy, were elected over J. M. Johnstone, L. P. Miller, John C. Wilson, and John W. Scott.[10] Congressman George Johnstone outpolled the Tillman candidate, A. C. Latimer of Belton, in Newberry County 1,206 to 781 but lost the congressional district.[11]

"Colie" Blease was made floor leader of the Tillman forces in the House of Representatives in 1892. A former Newberrian, Ira B. Jones, who was destined to oppose Blease when he sought re-election as governor twenty years later, was chosen speaker of the House. Dr. Sampson Pope was re-elected clerk of the Senate.

Tillman's second administration was known chiefly for the unique Dispensary Law that was enacted only three months after the voters had expressed themselves in favor of prohibition in a statewide referendum. Convinced of the impracticability of prohibition, Tillman decided to enact a law that would create a public monopoly and at the same time close barrooms and saloons. He did not foresee the graft and corruption that would later surface in the administration of the law.

The Newberry County Board of Liquor Control, named under the Dispensary Law, consisted of Jacob Senn, W. C. Sligh, and J. A. C. Kibler. R. C. Maybin was appointed dispenser.[12]

Governor Tillman appointed many constables to enforce the Dispensary Law, the chief constable for Newberry County being D. A. Dickert. It was a most unpopular system of liquor distribution and critics of Tillman inflamed public opinion. Finally the so-called Dispensary War erupted in Darlington in April 1894. When Governor Tillman called out the state militia to restore order in Darlington, a number of militia units refused to go. Among them were the Newberry Rifles, commanded by Captain Silas J. McCaughrin, who resigned and turned their arms over to the governor.[13]

Sixty new military companies were promptly organized. Five of them were from Newberry—the Newberry Reform Rifles, commanded by Captain F. C. Graddick; the Enoree Rifles, Captain John T. Duncan; the

Prosperity Rifles, Captain I. H. Witherspoon; the Hopewell Rifles, Captain W. P. Davis; and the Pomaria Rifles, Captain W. T. Hatton.[14]

During the Dispensary War, in order to increase support for the governor, some of the leading Tillmanites in Newberry secured a charter for the Reform Publishing Company. This company published the *Voice of the People*; Frank V. Capers and A. P. Bedenbaugh were the original editors.[15]

Tillman's liquor law was finally declared constitutional and was operated without scandal during the remainder of his term. He eagerly shifted his base to Washington, however, after being elected to the U.S. Senate over Senator M. C. Butler in December 1894. Tillman was determined to have a new constitution adopted before leaving for Washington, to ensure that the blacks would have no voice in government. By the remarkably close margin of 27,497 to 25,680 votes the electorate called a constitutional convention into session in 1895.[16]

Dr. Sampson Pope, an early Reformer and clerk of the state Senate from 1890 to 1893, was one of four or five candidates seeking to succeed Tillman as governor. He and James E. Tindall, the secretary of state, proposed a general primary in 1894, but Tillman and the other candidates, John Gary Evans and William Ellerbe, refused, and the state Executive Committee called a convention to nominate state officers.

Refusing to go before the convention or to bow to Tillman, Pope ran as an Independent against Evans, the nominee of the convention and hence of the Democratic Party, which, in effect, had been taken over by Tillman's reform movement. Pope was endorsed by a number of newspapers, including the *Newberry Observer*. Although defeated by a vote of 34,781 to 16,824, Pope was said by the late W. W. Ball to have "probed Tillmanism to its shallow bottom." Writing of *Bleaseism* in a series of articles appearing in the *Greenville News* in 1930, George R. Koester had the following to say about Pope:[17]

> Pope had been one of the wheelhorses of the Reform movement in its early days. He was a man of the most intense convictions and believed most firmly that South Carolina Democracy had been controlled by a ring, dominated by the old aristocracy. You remember I said in a preceding chapter that the Reform movement was originally a movement for the correction of party abuses. He went into the Reform movement to break up a ring and he was not content with substitution of one ring for another. He did not think that anything had really been gained by such an exchange. I fought Pope as I always fight any independent, because the

most important thing in South Carolina politics is to keep the white men solidly together.

No misuse of party power can justify a movement outside the party, for once the white men are divided both sides will attempt to win by use of the Negro vote, which then will become the political arbiter. While I condemned Pope's independent movement and fought for Evans, solely as the party nominee, I felt that Pope was a sincerer man and a truer Reformer than the man who had secured the party nomination by methods that smack too strongly of the very ring rule the Reform movement started out to destroy.

Pope's mistake was in not staying inside the Democratic party and submitting for the time being to what he considered wrong while keeping up his fight within the party. Had he done so, it is entirely probable that he, and not Ellerbe, would have succeeded Evans in 1896.

Pope, of course, continued to press the attack. He contested the election on the ground of fraud, presenting 200 affidavits of electors who had voted for him at the Aiken box where he had received only seventy-six votes. His petition, signed by a number of Newberrians, was presented to the U.S. Senate by Senator Butler.

He inserted this card in the local newspaper that shows his determination and his courage:[18] "Having received some threatening and some letters of advice from unknown parties, I desire to say to them that a visit in person would come better from brave men, and in addition would save them the expense and trouble of writing. I live at Newberry and can be seen almost any week day."

Newberry determined to divide its four delegates to the Constitutional Convention equally between the Reformers and the Conservatives. A mass meeting nominated George Johnstone, George S. Mower, J. A. Sligh, and W. C. Sligh, but in the balloting Johnstone and Mower were elected as Conservatives, J. A. Sligh and J. L. Keitt as Reformers.[19]

Determined to oppose Tillman in every way possible, J. F. J. Caldwell and Dr. Sampson Pope brought two suits in the Federal Court. One was on behalf of James Dunbar of Newberry and sought to have the Dispensary Law declared invalid. The other suit was to prevent the election of delegates to the Constitutional Convention.

Before the election was held, Major Caldwell and Dr. Pope went to Clarksburg, West Virginia, where they secured from Circuit Judge Nathan Goff an injunction restraining the election of delegates to the Constitutional Convention. They also secured a temporary restraining order and Rule to Show Cause directed to the State Board of Control as to the validity of the Dispensary Law.[20]

The next month Judge Goff heard arguments in Columbia; he sustained Caldwell and Pope on every issue in both cases. In June the Circuit Court of Appeals reversed Goff, and the Constitutional Convention was held without further delay.[21]

Tillman's bitter attacks on the existing order resulted in dividing families and alienating friends. Although his faction was a majority in Newberry County, the Tillmanites were not able to take control of all the county offices. Among those who defeated the Reformers were Senator Mower, who served in the state Senate for eleven years commencing in 1893, and A. J. Gibson, who was elected clerk of court over W. D. Hardy in 1896.

Meanwhile, the Conservatives were effecting many business changes in the county. A Board of Trade was first organized in Newberry in 1888. In 1890 its officers were W. T. Tarrant, president; G. W. Summer, vice president; E. H. Aull, secretary-treasurer; and an executive committee consisting of W. E. Pelham, James A. Burton, Dr. O. B. Mayer, Jr., W. H. Hunt, Jr., and John C. Goggans.[22]

In that same year the Prosperity Board of Trade was organized with Dr. R. L. Luther, president, and E. O. Counts, secretary-treasurer. The building of the Columbia, Newberry, and Laurens Railroad through Little Mountain caused that village to be incorporated in 1890,[23] and it activated the economic development of Prosperity and Newberry.

Whitmire, on the Georgia, Carolina and Northern Railroad, was incorporated in December 1891. It had five stores at that time; the first town officials were John P. Fant, intendant, and Dr. R. R. Jeter, H. E. Todd, Charles Tidmarsh, and B. F. Morrow, wardens.[24]

Helena, on the Greenville and Columbia Railroad, was incorporated in 1897. Coleman L. Blease was elected intendant, while the wardens were B. E. Julien, James F. Glenn, Welch Wilbur, and I. D. Schockley.[25]

In 1891 the Newberry Savings Bank was chartered with an authorized capital of $15,000, the incorporators being the directors of the National Bank of Newberry.[26]

With the objective of providing fire protection at low cost to the farmers of the county, the Farmers Mutual Insurance Association was organized in 1894. The original officers included Captain H. H. Folk as president, John W. Scott, James F. Todd, and J. Epps Brown.[27] As of June 30, 1990, it had $113 million insurance in force. Its present officers are George B. Wedaman, president, and Allen C. Jenkins, secretary-treasurer. The association now serves Newberry and all contiguous counties.

A third bank was founded in 1896 by local businessmen led by John M. Kinard.[28] The Commercial Bank became Newberry's strongest financial institution, being the first local bank to have resources of $1 million and the only one to weather the Great Depression.

John M. Kinard was the only president of the Commercial Bank; he served until the bank merged with South Carolina National Bank in 1931. He was born at Kinards, in Newberry County on May 17, 1862, the son of Captain John Martin and Elizabeth Lavinia Rook Kinard. His father was killed at the Battle of Strasburg in 1864. He was educated at Newberry College and at the University of South Carolina.

Upon the sudden death in 1887 of his stepfather, Captain J. Y. McFall, he was appointed to serve the remainder of McFall's term as clerk of court; he continued in this office until 1896 when he declined to offer for another term. Instead, he organized The Commercial Bank.

Kinard also served as director of Newberry Cotton Mills, Oakland Mills, Mollohon Manufacturing Company, the National Loan and Exchange Bank of Columbia, the South Carolina National Bank, Newberry Knitting Mill, and many local businesses. He was president of the South Carolina Bankers Association and active in the American Bankers Association.

He married Margaret Lee Land of Augusta. They had five children, John Martin Kinard, Jr.; Robert Land Kinard, who died in infancy; Elizabeth, who married John T. Norris; Margaret, who married Joseph L. Keitt, Jr.; and Rook, who married Arthur H. McCarrell. He died on June 28, 1933.[29]

Upon R. L. McCaughrin's death, J. N. Martin succeeded him as president of the National Bank of Newberry and as president of the Newberry Mill. Martin only lived for three years after succeeding McCaughrin. James Newton Martin, son of William and Jane Wilson Martin, was born in the county on February 14, 1832. He served as lieutenant in Company E, Third South Carolina Regiment and at the end of the war returned to Newberry to engage in business. He married first Sarah Blair and then Bernice Russell. He died on May 31, 1899, survived by his second wife and eight children, Foster N. Martin, Jane M. Sloan, Sarah Moriat Martin, Lalla Leona Martin, Bernice Tekoa Martin, Daisy Douschka Martin, Jamco Eleanor Martin, and James Newton Martin.[30]

The Western Union Telegraph Company opened an office in Newberry in 1891; this gave Newberry two telegraph lines to Columbia. The digging of an artesian well and the installation of electric lights took place in the last decade of the century.[31]

A coffin manufacturing company was organized in 1898. The Carolina Manufacturing Company was located between Main and Harrington streets west of McKibben (now Nance) Street. It not only made caskets but it also dealt as a wholesaler in undertaker's supplies. M. A. Carlisle was president, James J. Lane, secretary, and John W. Taylor, superintendent.[32]

This same decade saw the last hangings at the Newberry County Jail. Anna Tribble, convicted of murdering her bastard child, was the first person hanged in Newberry since Reconstruction. She was the second woman ever hanged in Newberry; the first was the slave Fanny, who poisoned the Robert Stewart family before the war.[33]

Two others died on the gallows during this decade. Aaron Duffie was hanged in 1896 for the murder of James Hargrove, and the following year Tourney Lyles was hanged for assaulting Miss Jane Willard at Whitmire. Lyles admitted his guilt to a black preacher before the trap was sprung.[34]

A much-needed postal service commenced in the county as the nineteenth century came to an end. Rural free delivery routes from Prosperity, with Frank V. Capers serving on alternate days, were the first started in Newberry County in 1899. Two years later, similar routes were established from the town of Newberry to Townships 5 and 6 with W. G. Peterson as carrier at a salary of $500 per year.[35]

In 1893 the Confederate veterans of the county organized the James D. Nance Camp with Captain Jesse Wistar Gary as commander; Dr. R. C. Carlisle as lieutenant commander; J. F. J. Caldwell as 2nd lieutenant commander; Thompson Connor as 3rd lieutenant commander; C. F. Boyd as adjutant; Dr. Sampson Pope as surgeon; Reverend E. P. McClintock as chaplain; G. F. Long as treasurer; and N. H. Young as color sergeant.[36]

Four years later Captain William Smith Langford, graduate of The Citadel in the class of 1894, organized the Newberry Guards. The members of the unit volunteered for service in the Spanish-American War, leaving Newberry by train for Columbia in May 1898. The officers and non-commissioned officers were First Lieutenant R. H. Wearn, Second Lieutenant B. M. Aull, First Sergeant T. H. Pope, Second Sergeant J. Guy Daniels, Third Sergeant T. O. Stewart, Jr., Fourth Sergeant F. D.

Mower, Corporal James Renwick, Drummer W. H. Hunter, and Quartermaster George C. Jones.[37]

When the Newberry County Memorial Hospital was built, Captain Langford, who was very popular with his men, made a generous contribution in their honor. The plaque, which is in the foyer of the current Newberry County Memorial Hospital, lists the volunteers of Company B, 1st South Carolina Volunteers.

On July 23, 1898, Captain Silas J. McCaughrin organized Company G of Colonel Wilie Jones's Second Regiment. This company included many Newberrians as well as men from adjoining counties. The roster of the unit hangs in the Newberry National Guard Armory. The officers were First Lieutenant Edward C. Horton and Second Lieutenant Robert F. Dukes. Caldwell E. Fant was first sergeant, George S. Noland, quartermaster sergeant and John L. Finley, Morgan T. Mooney, Owens P. Saxon, and Andrew B. Stoudemire, sergeants.[38]

One of the volunteers from Captain Langford's Company, Levi E. "Chink" Folk, remained in the regular army for twenty-five years. He was one of only five intrepid men who volunteered to nurse yellow fever victims and to be human guinea pigs for Colonel Walter Reed in his efforts to learn the cause of that disease in 1901.

Folk retired from the service in 1923 as a technical sergeant; in 1931 he was awarded a gold medal for "Conquest of Yellow Fever" and a monthly pension of $125 by Congress. On February 8, 1936, Folk died at the age of sixty-six.[39] Son of County Auditor Levi E. Folk, he was a genuine hero.

Another Newberrian who was honored for his services before the beginning of the new century was Brigadier General Ernest Garlington. Son of General A. C. Garlington, he was born in Newberry on February 25, 1853. He attended first the University of Georgia where his father was educated; after two years at that institution he received an appointment to West Point from which he was graduated in 1876. He won the Congressional Medal of Honor at Wounded Knee, South Dakota, on December 29, 1890. Garlington served as inspector general of the U.S. Army from 1906 until his retirement in 1917. He died in October, 1934, survived by his widow, Anna B. Garlington.[40]

9

Blease

Coleman Livingston Blease, at the age of twenty, made his first political race in 1888. Although the Constitution of 1868 provided that a member of the House of Representatives should be twenty-one years of age, the House was the judge of the qualifications of its members, and the young candidate must have thought that he would be seated if he won. Since he lost, the House did not have to resolve the question. The boldness he displayed in making that race, however, portended things to come.

In the 1888 race, John Malcolm Johnstone, George S. Mower, and Robert T. C. Hunter were nominated and later elected.[1] This was the first of many contests between the Johnstones and the Bleases for political control of the county and for leadership of the local Bar. The struggle continued for more than half a century.

Two years later Blease defeated Johnstone when the latter ran for re-election.[2] Blease was reelected in 1892 but was defeated in 1894 and 1896[3] despite having served as Tillman's floor leader in the House of Representatives during his second term as governor. Twenty years later he and Tillman became bitter enemies.

Blease, son of Henry Horatio and Mary Ann Livingston Blease, was born in Newberry on October 8, 1868.[4] Several Blease brothers moved to Newberry from Edgefield before the Civil War and established themselves in this county. David Duncan Wallace, never friendly to the Bleases, characterized them as being of "good middle-class English descent." Basil Blease was Newberry's first volunteer for service in the Civil War. Thomas Wainwright Blease built the jail in 1854. Henry Horatio Blease was a respected magistrate and livery stable keeper. It was in his courtroom on the public square that George Johnstone killed John Jones in 1887.

Married twice, Henry Horatio had eight children by Mary Ann Livingston, including Cole and Henry Horatio Blease, Jr., known as Harry. By his second wife, Elizabeth Satterwhite, he had five children, including Eugene S. and Cannon G. Blease. All made the most of their opportunities and all took active parts in the political affairs of South Carolina and of Newberry County.

The Johnstones were among the county's ruling ante-bellum families. Chancellor Job Johnstone was the owner of some 5,000 acres and the master of 147 slaves at the time of his death in 1862.[5] He ruled his agricultural empire from Coateswood, located at the edge of the courthouse village. He too was twice married, first to his cousin, Eliza Meek Johnston of Fairfield, by whom he had three children, including Silas Johnstone, long a leader at the local Bar; and then to Almira Amelia DeWalt of Newberry, by whom he had six children, including George, John Malcolm, and Alan. The two broods were not friendly; indeed Silas, leader of the first set of siblings, and George, acknowledged leader of the second, opposed each other in several political contests.

By the time Cole Blease emerged as a political factor, George Johnstone was an established leader. He actively participated in the Hampton campaign of 1876, served as a legislator from 1878 until 1884, and was chairman of the Ways and Means Committee of the House of Representatives. At the Bar he was recognized as an extremely able advocate.

John Malcolm Johnstone, who crossed swords with Cole Blease in 1888 and 1890, was a Confederate veteran who had attended the University of Virginia after the war. He was appointed consul at Paramaribo, Brazil, in 1894 and ceased to be a local political factor after that foreign service. He died unmarried in February 1904.[6] The third Johnstone, Alan, entered the political arena a little later but became and remained one of the strongest figures in state government as chairman of the Senate Finance Committee, president *pro tempore* of the Senate, and chairman of the board of trustees of Clemson College. These were the men young Cole Blease challenged before he was admitted to the Bar.

Cole attended Newberry College and the University of South Carolina; he left both institutions under a cloud, having been accused of plagiarism in his speeches.[7] In fairness to him, it should be pointed out that it depended upon the accuser's politics as to whether Blease was guilty of schoolboy indiscretions or more serious offenses. He left the University of South Carolina just before his first and unsuccessful campaign. After his defeat he entered Georgetown University and graduated in law in 1889.[8]

Returning to Newberry he was admitted to practice and entered into a partnership with his older brother Harry. Harry, born on February 4, 1865, was educated at The Citadel and at Newberry College. Following his admission to the Bar in 1886, he graduated in law from Georgetown University in 1887. The brothers practiced together until 1893 when Harry moved to Anderson.[9]

After being defeated for the House in 1896, Blease was elected intendent of Helena in the off year of 1897; he was the first to head the government of that village after its incorporation. In 1898 Cole Blease was elected once again to the House of Representatives.[10]

Two years later he ran for the office of lieutenant governor, finishing fifth in a field of five; James H. Tillman, nephew of B. R. and son of George D. Tillman, was elected in the second primary over John T. Sloan, senator from Richland County. In 1902 Sloan, Blease, and Frank B. Gary, former Speaker of the House of Representatives, were candidates for the same office. Blease was eliminated in the first primary.[11]

After being defeated by Jim Tillman in 1900, Blease remained friendly with him. Following the fatal shooting of N. G. Gonzales, editor of the *State*, by Tillman on January 15, 1903, Blease and George Johnstone were retained to defend him, along with George W. Croft, Patrick H. Nelson, O. W. Buchanan, W. T. Sharpe, G. T. Graham, George R. Rembert, and Efird & Dreher. Solicitor J. William Thurmond, G. Duncan Bellinger, Andrew Crawford, William Elliott, Jr., I. L. Asbill, and L. T. Sturkie prosecuted the defendant. James F. Byrnes was hired as a special stenographer by the *State*.[12] The trial was held in Lexington and resulted in Tillman's acquittal. One of the unverified stories about this case is that Blease had a photographer circulate through the county with pictures of the principals. He supposedly reported to counsel the reaction of members of the jury panel to pictures of Senator Tillman and Gonzales thereby giving counsel information as to their leanings and possible bias. The trial was unusual in that George Johnstone and Cole Blease were associates and not adversaries.

Undaunted by his two defeats for lieutenant governor, Blease offered for the state Senate from Newberry in 1904. He defeated Arthur Kibler for that office. He was joined in the senate by his younger half-brother, Eugene S. Blease, as Senator from Saluda County, but the latter resigned in 1906 following a personal tragedy in which Senator Eugene

Blease killed his brother-in-law. Cole Blease was elected president *pro tempore* and served in this capacity during the terms of 1907 and 1908.[13]

He ran for governor in 1906, running third behind Martin F. Ansel of Greenville and Richard I. Manning of Sumter. A fourth candidate was A. C. Jones of Newberry, who received only 898 votes.[14]

At the end of Governor Ansel's first term Blease tried to unseat him. As Frank Jordan observed, "Blease served notice of the events to come in 1910," although he was handily defeated in 1908.[15]

Blease had to wait two years before he could try a third time for the office of governor. During the interim he was elected mayor of Newberry in the off year of 1909.[16]

The election of 1910 was marked by close races and charges of fraud. At the age of forty-two Blease was elected governor over Claudius C. Featherstone of Laurens, the candidate of the prohibitionists, by the narrow margin of 5,000 votes. James F. Byrnes of Aiken defeated J. O. Patterson of Barnwell for Congress from the Second District by the even closer margin of forty-four votes amid charges of ballot stuffing and other irregularities.[17] These two winners would oppose each other fourteen years later.

Blease was probably elected because of an eleventh hour attack on him by the *State* newspaper, featuring a cartoon representing Blease as a buzzard with outstretched wings whose pinions were marked "dispensary grafters, ignorance, race prejudice, lawlessness, blind tigers, injustice, class prejudice and demogogy." The carrion's head was that of Blease; it circled a woman's figure representing South Carolina and was armed with a sword labeled "the ballot."[18]

A third candidate for governor in 1910 was John T. Duncan of Newberry. This was the first of his eight campaigns for the office of governor. Duncan, son of Baruch Duncan and his second wife, Sarah Duckett Duncan, was born on September 18, 1862. He became active in the Farmers Movement and in the politics of Newberry County. Defeated for the House of Representatives in 1890, he was elected to that body in 1892 and 1894. Because he accepted employment in the Secretary of State's office he was expelled from the House for dual office-holding in February 1896. Elected chairman of the Newberry County Democratic Party, he ran for the U.S. Senate that year in order to defeat Governor John Gary Evans, whom he despised.[19]

Blease's first term as governor was tempestuous. His bombastic messages to the General Assembly, domineering attitude toward state officials, disregard of the responsibility of senators to advise and consent to his appointments, running battle with the Supreme Court in the matter of appointing special judges, lavish use of the veto power, freely used pardon power, and vituperative attacks on the press created determined enemies. His support of the old dispensary system and removal of the commission appointed by Governor Ansel to liquidate the dispensary added fuel to the flames.

In short, he offended nearly everyone but his supporters; they followed him fanatically and blindly. The race issue served as a very effective political weapon for him. His frequent tirades in defense of lynching found favor with many in the state; they agreed that it was the only honorable means of dealing with the black rapist. When a mob in Anderson County lynched Willie Jackson, accused of raping a white woman, the governor congratulated the leader of the mob. In a speech a few weeks later he stated his disbelief that a jury would convict any member of the mob but if that happened he promised that he "would wire pardons to those convicted."[20]

When Blease ran for re-election he was opposed by two other Newberry natives; this is the only campaign of modern times in which all the candidates for a statewide office were born in the same county. Chief Justice Ira B. Jones resigned from his high judicial position to make the race. The third candidate, John T. Duncan, made the second of eight campaigns for governor.[21]

Ira Boyd Jones, son of Charles Milton and Mary Jane Neel Jones, was born on December 29, 1851. He attended Newberry College and then was graduated from Erskine College in 1870; he taught school and read law. Admitted to the Bar in 1873, he practiced first at Newberry and then at Prosperity. Moving to Lancaster in 1875, he became active in the affairs of that county.

Jones was speaker of the House of Representatives from 1890 to 1894; vice president of the Constitutional Convention of 1895; justice of the Supreme Court from 1896 to 1910; and chief justice from 1910 until 1912.[22]

In the bitter campaign of 1912, Blease carried Newberry County with 1,623 votes to 1,447 for Jones and 46 for Duncan. In the state Blease received 71,552 votes or 50.9 percent of the votes cast. Jones received 66,478 votes, and Duncan 2,385 votes. Blease carried twenty-six counties, Jones carried seventeen, and Chester County ended in a tie.[23]

Early in his second term, Blease won a major victory by forcing a hostile General Assembly to close the hosiery mill at the state penitentiary. He also succeeded in returning most convicts to the control of the various counties to work on the public roads. During his four years in office, he extended clemency to 1,743 convicts; in the closing days of his second term he issued a pardon to 1,000 persons whom he had earlier released from prison.[24]

In order not to be succeeded by Richard I. Manning, Blease resigned five days before the end of his second term. Lieutenant Governor Charles A. Smith succeeded him instead of Manning.

While generally hostile to the state colleges, except for Winthrop and The Citadel, Blease articulated the desire to prevent duplication and proliferation of courses, thereby creating a more efficient system of higher education. His leadership in acquiring the Medical College of Charleston as a state institution saved the school and was a genuine service to the people of South Carolina.

On balance, Blease's administrations produced little constructive legislation but instead fanned the fires of factionalism within the state. The constant carping criticism kept him off balance and undoubtedly caused him to do things and to make statements impulsively that he simply could not later admit were wrong; once having taken a position his pride would not permit him to change it.

It was inevitable that sooner or later Tillman and Blease would part political company. They did in the campaign of 1912 when Tillman turned against Blease just three days before the primary election. From then until Tillman's death in 1918 they were at war; Blease rejected Tillman's efforts to persuade Blease to bridle his tongue. Tillman supported Ellison D. Smith in his race for reelection to the U.S. Senate against Blease in 1914. Smith carried Newberry County by a vote of 1,611 to 1,476. And in 1916 Tillman supported Governor Richard I. Manning's campaign for reelection as governor. Blease carried Newberry County by a vote of 1,642 to 1,559.[25]

Having convincingly demonstrated his political strength in the extremely close race against Governor Manning in 1916, Blease prepared to tackle Senator Tillman when he came up for reelection in 1918. His ally, John P. Grace of Charleston, established a daily newspaper, the American, which would support Blease.[26] His friends began early to organize in their communities. Blease himself made a series of speeches against world War I. However, Blease misjudged the temper of the people as well as their support of President Woodrow Wilson.

In an extremely bitter speech delivered at Pomaria on July 27, 1917, Blease denounced America's entry into the war. He spoke in a section of the county that had been settled by immigrants from Germany and only a few miles from Jolly Street where Blease was the unquestioned political leader, but he made a serious error. He was pilloried over South Carolina as "the traitorous pro-German Cole L. Blease."[27]

The long-awaited head-to-head contest between Tillman and Blease never developed. Tillman died on July 3, 1918, and the vacancy for the full term attracted Blease, Nathaniel B. Dial of Laurens, and James F. Rice of Anderson. The election for the short term was contested by Christie Benet, Thomas H. Peoples, and W. P. Pollock. Pollock and Dial won. It was Blease's most humiliating defeat; Dial carried Newberry County over Blease by a vote of 1,387 to 1,346.[28]

During Blease's long political life, from his first defeat for the House of Representatives in 1888 until his final defeat for governor in 1938, Newberry County voters were fairly evenly divided between Bleasites and anti-Bleasites. Even when he could poll a majority for himself, he was unable to prevent his opponents from being elected in his native county. Alan Johnstone, for example, served as senator from 1908 to 1928, repulsing the bids of staunch Bleasites to defeat him in 1908, 1912, 1916, and 1920. There were others.

South Carolina's leading historian of an earlier generation, David Duncan Wallace, a native of Newberry where his father was editor of the *Newberry Observer*, wrote that "the strength of Blease's appeal was not any platform of measures, but his personality and viewpoint."[29] Blease was a conservative in legislative policy despite his violence of speech and his tolerance of lawlessness.

During the decade between leaving the governor's office and entering the U.S. Senate, Blease and Bleasism continued to be the dominant issue in South Carolina politics. Another able historian has recently written an account of these years.[30] It (the account) includes his denunciation of President Wilson, opposition to prohibition, open and public endorsement of lynching, and opposition to entering World War I. Despite his unpopular positions, he still retained the support of more than a third of the state's electorate.

When Blease left the governor's office, he moved from Newberry to Columbia. There he enjoyed a statewide criminal law practice. Bold, articulate, and possessed of a deep understanding of human nature, he was a formidable advocate. The late Clinton T. Graydon, himself one of the state's great trial lawyers, often said that Cole Blease was not at his best unless his cause was desperate, but, when it was, he had no superior.

In July 1919, Congressman Asbury F. Lever of the Seventh Congressional District resigned to accept a position with the U.S. Department of

Agriculture. A special election was ordered to fill the vacancy and Blease promptly announced his candidacy in the general election. He stated that he had been robbed in the Democratic primaries in 1914 and 1916 and that he could not receive fair treatment at the hands of the state's Democratic officials.[31]

When he asked his supporters to abstain from participating in the primary so as to be eligible to vote for him in the general election many of his staunch supporters refused to follow him. The *Newberry Observer* stated editorially that "independentism means an appeal to the Negro vote" and that Blease was among the first to maintain that bolting the party was an unpardonable sin in South Carolina.

Race relations that summer were worse in South Carolina and in America than at any time since the 1890s. A race riot resulted in three deaths in Charleston, and a lynching was narrowly averted in Newberry. Speaking before the South Carolina Historical Association in 1978, Dr. Daniel W. Hollis stated:[32] "Late in August Representative James F. Byrnes, alarmed by the demands of the National Association for the Advancement of Colored People in behalf of Negro veterans, made a speech in Congress in which he bluntly informed the blacks that the war had in no way changed the racial attitudes of whites. Byrnes advised Negro veterans who could not live in the United States without political and social equality to depart for Africa or any other country they wished."

Blease abruptly withdrew from the campaign in mid-August. He never gave any satisfactory explanation for his withdrawal. Senator Dial, who expected Blease's opposition in 1924, said that "I am not surprised that a man who was disloyal in 1918 would bolt the party and encourage Negroes to vote."[33] It was ironic that the man who had been regarded as a Negro hater because of his statements in favor of lynching where white womanhood was violated should be publicly attacked for advising the blacks to "stand by their leaders" and for daring to repudiate the Democratic primary.

In 1920 Blease did not seek office. This was the only time between his first race for the House of Representatives in 1888 and his election to the U.S. Senate in 1924 that he was not a candidate for county or state office. Instead, Blease endorsed his old adversary Ellison D. Smith, for reelection to the U.S. Senate "because he thought he was the best candidate."[34]

The anti-Bleasites who thought that Blease's political career was over were wrong; shortly after the 1920 general election in which Harding was elected President, Blease commenced making a series of political speeches preparatory to running for governor in 1922. He led in the first primary with 44.8 percent of the vote; taking Newberry County from Blease, Thomas G. McLeod defeated him in the second primary by a vote of 100,114 to 85,834.[35] The vote showed that Blease was far from finished as a political leader.

The 1924 race for the U.S. Senate attracted the incumbent Senator Nathaniel B. Dial, Congressman James F. Byrnes, former Superintendent of Education John J. McMahan, and former Governor Blease. The 1922 race showed his rivals that their problem was surviving the first primary. They attacked each other, and Blease conducted a dignified campaign, even acting as peacemaker when Dial and McMahan had a fight at Gaffney.

Blease led in the first primary, followed by Byrnes. In the second primary no holds were barred. When Byrnes advertised that the Aiken Ministerial Association and the officers of St. Thaddeus Episcopal Church endorsed his active role in the affairs of that church, twenty men from Charleston inserted an advertisement in the *Charleston Evening Post* three days before the second primary election that probably changed the course of the election. These men described themselves as schoolmates of Congressman Byrnes at St. Patrick's Roman Catholic School who had served with him as altar boys at St. Patrick's Church. They said they were supporting him because of his faith in Christian ideals and because his life demonstrated that "a man can rise from the lowest to the loftiest state in spite of race, class or creed prejudice."[36]

John P. Grace, Irish Catholic leader of Charleston and ally of Blease, was responsible for this endorsement of the former altar boy who had left the Roman Catholic Church. Broadsides of the endorsement were circulated in the upcountry where they would hurt Byrnes. Blease stated that he had not injected the religious issue into the campaign; since Byrnes had done so, he reaped his reward.[37]

Senator Dial refused to endorse Byrnes. Hollis says that he "was so angered by what he regarded as the devious tactics of Byrnes and McMahan, that he preferred the election of a man that he had once denounced as a traitor."[38]

Blease defeated Byrnes by a vote of 100,738 to 98,467. Each carried twenty-three counties. The vote in Newberry County was 3,311 to 2,552 in favor of Blease.[39]

Six years later Blease was opposed for reelection by Byrnes, who had moved to Spartanburg, and Solicitor Leon W. Harris of Anderson. After leading in the first primary by what appeared to be a safe margin, Blease was defeated in the second primary by Byrnes; the vote was 120,755 to 116,264.[40]

As a senator, Blease's courage in supporting the nomination of Judge John J. Parker of North Carolina to the Supreme Court was praiseworthy in a time when many other Southern congressmen ran for cover. He was instrumental in creating a third federal judgeship for South Carolina, but was unable to have his former law partner, Congressman Frederick H. Dominick, appointed to the post.

Blease was always a controversial figure. He made no lasting contributions to the government of the state or nation but he excelled in a period when personal politics prevailed. No one who knew him was neutral in his feelings about Blease. He still is either despised or loved a third of a century after his death.

"Where Tillman was harsh, Blease was affable; where the old farmer was abstemious, the new leader was intemperate; where the former was careless in dress, the latter was meticulous; and where the self-educated agrarian leader was at ease among the English classics from which he quoted liberally, the champion of the mill workers, though having a formal education that extended through law school, was virtually unread." Thus did Tillman's biographer compare the two men.[41]

Perhaps it would be more accurate to say that whereas few loved Tillman, Blease's followers adored him. He repaid their devotion with absolute loyalty. Tillman alienated all of his principal supporters; only John Gary Evans attended his chief's funeral as a pallbearer—and perhaps as a mourner. When Blease was an old man, Colonel Wyndham Manning, son of his greatest adversary, asked members of the General Assembly to elect the former governor to the Unemployment Security Commission; his reason was that no former governor should be impoverished. It is doubtful that this ever would have been done for Tillman. Blease's conduct was exemplary as a member of the commission.

Both men capitalized on the "strain of violence" that runs through South Carolina.[42] Both openly justified violence when necessary to enforce the majority view of South Carolina whites. Both were dictatorial. Blease was an impulsive, warm-hearted man, while Tillman was cold, ascetic, and selfish. Cole Blease was not the only member of his family to be prominent in state affairs and influential in Newberry County. His half-brother, Eugene S. Blease, served as mayor of Newberry, member of the House of Representatives, associate justice of the state Supreme Court, and chief justice of South Carolina until his voluntary retirement in 1934. In 1942, Judge Blease ran for the U.S. Senate against Senator Burnet R. Maybank; he was defeated by the narrow margin of 6,000 votes in his first and only statewide race.[43]

Another half-brother, Cannon G. Blease, was the most popular member of the family in Newberry County. Son of Henry Horatio and Elizabeth Satterwhite Blease, he was born in the town in 1884. His father having died when he was eight years old, he was able to attend Newberry College for only a short time before going to work, first as a magistrate's constable, then as a rural mail carrier, and at the age of twenty-one as magistrate.

In 1912 he was elected sheriff of Newberry County and continued in that office until ill health forced him not to offer for reelection in 1936. Active in fraternal and civic affairs, he was a consistent member of the Methodist Church. He married Minnie Lee Adams in 1902; they had one child, Colie, who married Richard L. Baker. Sheriff Blease died at the age of fifty-four on August 20, 1938.[44]

Of fifteen statewide campaigns, Cole Blease was elected in three, twice as governor and once to the U.S. Senate. Three times he led in the first primary only to lose in the second primary. He generally polled his maximum strength in the first primary. As long as he lived, Blease had a core of Bleasites who would vote for Cole regardless of the opponent.

Blease was active in various fraternal orders and served as Grand Master of the Independent Order of Odd Fellows of South Carolina, Grand Sachem of the Improved Order of Red Men, Dictator of the Loyal Order of Moose, and Chancellor Commander of the Knights of Pythias.

He married Lillie B. Summers of Anderson. They had no children. After her death he married Caroline Floyd Knotts; they soon separated. Governor Blease died on January 19, 1942, and is buried in Rosemont Cemetery in Newberry.

10

The New Century

At the beginning of the twentieth century Newberry appeared to have a bright future. The population of the courthouse town was 4,607, or double what it had been at the end of the Civil War. Newberry College had been returned to the town and was recognized for its cultural and educational leadership in the community. The daily schedules for trains on Newberry's two railroads made it easy not only to ship cotton and other products but also to commute to Columbia.

In the previous quarter-century Newberry had established a cotton mill, a steam roller mill, a bonded cotton warehouse, a cotton seed oil mill, three banks, and two newspapers. Its wide-awake business leaders were planning further economic development and soon proceeded to implement their plans. A knitting mill, a shuttle factory, a steam laundry, two bottling plants, a daily newspaper, a fourth bank, two more cotton mills, and an oil mill were established before World War I.

Unfortunately, not all of them succeeded. The Newberry Knitting Mill, chartered in 1900, built its plant on Caldwell Street south of Scott's Creek and at the site of Bandusian Spring.[1] It failed and was liquidated in 1905.[2] The Newberry Shuttle and Handle Company, also incorporated in 1900, met the same fate. The daily newspaper, the *Evening Telegram*, lasted only a few months.[3]

The National Bank of Newberry also met with difficulty. When James N. Martin died in 1899, control of the National Bank and of the Newberry Cotton Mills passed to other hands. The Carlisle group took over the bank and maintained control for almost ten years. Milton A. Carlisle succeeded Martin as president of the bank but resigned in 1908, was indicted in 1909, and was convicted of malfeasance in office by the United States Court in Greenville in 1910. Sentenced to serve five years in prison, he served a portion of his sentence in the Newberry County Jail before being pardoned by President Woodrow Wilson. He was succeeded as president of the bank by Budd Cade Matthews who continued in that office until the bank failed on July 1, 1929.[4]

Thomas J. McCrary replaced Martin as president of the Newberry Cotton Mills. A native of Clinton who married Clara Johnstone he lived in the Johnstone family home, "Coateswood." While attempting to cross a fence there in 1905, he was killed by a gun he was carrying.[5] He was succeeded by Zacheus F. Wright, who continued in that position until the plant was sold to M. M. Claremont in 1946.

Wright, son of Robert H. and Mary F. Bowers Wright, was born in Newberry on March 21, 1869, and lived his entire life in the town. After graduating from Newberry College in 1888, he first operated a bookstore and then was cashier of the Commercial Bank. He served as director of all three local cotton mills and of the Commercial Bank. He was mayor of Newberry for nine years, a member of the South Carolina Highway Commission at the time when Governor Olin D. Johnston attempted to seize the Highway Department, a trustee of Newberry College, and president of the Chamber of Commerce. Never married, he died in October, 1949.[6]

Of great importance to Newberry's economic welfare was the Mollohon Manufacturing Company. Incorporated in 1901 with an authorized capital of $300,000, its capital was increased to $500,000 in 1903.[7] The original officers were George W. Summer, president; Z. F. Wright, vice-president; and E. B. Wilbur, superintendent and general manager. They served as directors along with Dr. James McIntosh, D. H. Wheeler, J. N. McCaughrin, and C. E. Summer.

The contract for constructing the mill was awarded to John F. Grandy, and work was commenced in Andrew McCaughrin's pasture on the south side of the railroad tracks in September 1901. The mill was completed in July 1902, with 300 looms and 1,100 spindles.[8]

George Walter Summer was the youngest, and Charles Edward Summer the oldest, of three sons of George W. and Martha Epting Summer, the middle son being John Harrison Summer. All three were born in the Dutch Fork and moved to Newberry in the 1880s where they became leaders in agriculture and business. They organized Summer Brothers, and that firm operated a large general mercantile store, conducted a lien business, ran a cotton gin at Jalapa, and farmed over 2,500 acres with seventy plows.

About 1905 John Harrison Summer withdrew from the family business and operated a haberdashery until shortly before his death at the great age of ninety in 1951. During part of this time his son, Thomas Roy Summer, was in business with him. J. H. Summer, married first to Huldah Cromer, had by her eight children—George Leland, Elbert Hugh, John Ernest, Thomas Roy, Verna Kohn, Mary Delila, Annie Julia Wise, and James Harrison. After his first wife's death, he married Mary Alice Swittenberg, by whom he had one child, Jane Ragland.[9]

The other two brothers continued to operate Summer Brothers until the firm failed in the Great Depression. George W. Summer served as president of Mollohon Manufacturing Company until it was sold to the Kendall Company in 1926. He was also president of the Newberry Bonded Warehouse, founder of Newberry Lumber Company, an original director of the Commercial Bank, an original director of Security Loan and Investment Company, and owner of the Newberry Hotel. Active in the civic and religious life of Newberry, he served as trustee of Newberry College and as president of the Chamber of Commerce. He married Polly Levinia Long; they had seven children, Eugenia S. Wise, George W., Jr., Oscar, Gilbert, William Carroll, M. D., Grace, and Robert Earl. George W. Summer died on May 24, 1944, aged eighty-two.

Charles E. Summer was president of Summer Brothers and director of Oakland Mill and Newberry Savings Bank. He served as an alderman and then for twenty-five years as commissioner of public works. He married first Leonora Sease, by whom he had three children, Clarence T., Agnes S. Mayes, and Susie S. Haltiwanger. His second wife was Mary Jane Sease, his first wife's sister; by her he had five children who lived to maturity— Elmer, Charles Forrest, Ruby S. Hanna, Kate S. Caldwell, and Rosa Lee S. Moore. He died on February 20, 1948, aged eighty-nine.[11]

Another local business tied closely to agriculture was the Farmers Oil Mill. Organized in May, 1904, with W. K. Sligh as president and John H. Wicker as manager, its plant was constructed on Drayton Street just south of Halcyon Grove.[12] For the next forty years it would grind the county's wheat flour and corn meal. It would process cotton seed and sell ice and coal. The firm was liquidated during World War II.

While George Summer and his associates were erecting the Mollohon Mill in Newberry, William Coleman of Union County and his associates and kinsmen were converting the little village of Whitmire on the Seaboard Railroad near the Enoree River into the county's second-largest town. They completed the Glenn-Lowery Mill in 1902 and established a bank, the First National Bank of Whitmire, in that same year.[13]

Coleman was a dynamic businessman with political ambitions. He was an unsuccessful candidate for governor in 1922, his bank failed, and he lost his cotton mill to the J. P. Stevens Company after a bitter court battle in the 1920s.[14]

Two new financial institutions, the Security Loan and Investment Company and the Mercantile Exchange Bank, were established in 1905. In March the Commercial Bank group, with some outside capital, organized a finance and insurance company with quarters on the corner of College and Boyce streets. The officers were W. H. Hunt, president; John M. Kinard, vice-president; and J. N. McCaughrin, secretary-treasurer.[15]

The Security Loan and Investment Company was organized by virtually the same local businessmen who, through the Newberry Real Estate Company organized in 1903, developed the eastern section of the present town of Newberry. That company acquired 200 acres, including the old Chancellor Caldwell-Major L. J. Jones home on Main Street.[16] New streets were cut—McCaughrin Avenue, Mayer Avenue, Hunt Street, Kinard Street, and others—and lots were sold. Many of these purchases were financed by this new company.

W. H. Hunt was succeeded by William Adney McSwain, native of Cross Hill and graduate of the University of Kentucky, and active in civic affairs. When McSwain was elected state insurance commissioner in 1918,[17] he was succeeded by James Henry West, native of Graniteville and furniture dealer in Newberry. West was chairman of the board of Kentucky Central Life and Accident Insurance Company of Louisville. When he died in 1941 he was succeeded by Thomas L. Hicks, native of North Carolina. Hicks sold the company shortly before his death in 1973 to Kenneth Brown. The company failed due to embezzlement by the new owner, who pleaded guilty to that crime. Thus ended the life of a strong company which served Newberry for almost three-quarters of a century.

The Mercantile Exchange Bank, founded in June, 1905, did not last that long. It failed on April 11, 1931. The first officers were J. D. Davenport, president; R. C. Carlisle, vice-president; and M. L. Spearman, cashier. Other directors were George B. Cromer, J. A. Senn, George C. Glasgow, Charles J. Purcell, Edward R. Hipp, and A. F. Brown. The bank's quarters were located on Main Street next to Gilder and Weeks Drug Store.[18]

Davenport moved to New York soon after the bank was founded, and Edward R. Hipp served as president until his death in 1910.[19] Hipp was born in Pomaria and operated a large wholesale grocery. He married Mary Elvira Holloway; their children were Rear Admiral Thomas E. Hipp, Dr. Edward R. Hipp, Jr., Mrs. A. J. Bowers, Jr., Mrs. Homer Schumpert, and Mrs. Jesse O. Willson.

Upon Hipp's death, Henry Lakin Parr, native of Fairfield County, became head of the Exchange Bank. Parr, along with Frank R. Hunter and their associates, secured the franchise to construct an electric railway in and adjacent to the town of Newberry and to furnish heat, light, and power generated by electricity or gas.[20] Nothing came of this effort.

Parr was successful, however, in constructing the five-story office building on the corner of Main and College streets in 1918.[21] First known as the Exchange Bank Building, it has been known as the Parr Building since its purchase by James N. and Henry L. Parr, grandsons of the builder. A branch of North Carolina National Bank occupied the banking quarters on the first floor until the summer of 1987.

Henry L. Parr died on October 7, 1931, at the age of sixty. He married Mary J. Boyd, who survived him with their three children, Callie Boyd Parr, Eddie Mae Parr Baker, and Azilee Parr Patrick.[22]

One of the original directors of the Exchange Bank, Charles Joseph Purcell, native of Augusta, Georgia, was postmaster of Newberry from 1902 until 1913. During his tenure, two events of importance occurred in the town—the initiation of residential mail delivery and the construction of a handsome new post office.

In 1908 J. Claude Dominick, A. J. Bowers, Jr., and B. H. McGraw were appointed as the first city carriers of the Postal Service; they made two or three deliveries a day to houses and stores. And in 1909 the site of the new post office at the corner of Friend and College streets was selected, and the building was completed and opened in May 1913.[23] It is now the Newberry-Saluda Regional Library.

Purcell married Lavinia Rook McFall; they had eight children, Edward B., Mildred Davis, Helen Cooley, Elizabeth West, James McFall, Rook Brown, Charles Joseph, Jr., and Louise Wright. Purcell was a prominent merchant in the town until his death on September 23, 1928, at the age of sixty-seven.[24]

Another development occurred in the communications system of the town when Southern Bell Telephone and Telegraph Company acquired for the second time the local telephone franchise in 1903.[25] It had secured the franchise in 1882 but then surrendered it in 1896.[26] L. W. Floyd acquired the Newberry franchise and then the Clinton, Spartanburg, Greenville, Greenwood, Union, and Prosperity franchises. In

1903 he sold his entire system to Southern Bell.[27] By 1909 there were 819 telephones in the county and 382 in the town of Newberry. The first local telephone directory was published in 1915; there were then 513 telephones in the town.[28] In 1906 a native Newberrian, James Epps Brown (1867–1925), son of Dr. Thomas C. and Martha Epps Brown, was made general manager of Southern Bell. He became president in 1919 and chairman of the board in 1924.[29]

In 1910 Newberry's third cotton mill was built. Oakland Mill was constructed on the Fair place north of Newberry College. The original officers were W. H. Hunt, president; John M. Kinard, vice-president; and F. N. Martin, secretary. Other directors were Z. F. Wright, George S. Mower, Charles E. Summer, Dr. George Y. Hunter, James A. Burton, and I. H. Hunt.[30]

Walter Herbert Hunt (1861–1927) was born in Newberry, the son of Walter Herbert and Susan McCaughrin Hunt. He attended Newberry College, was admitted to the Bar in 1883, and thereafter practiced at Newberry and Spartanburg. He was president of the State Baptist Convention, Security Loan and Investment Company, and Oakland Mill, and a director of Newberry Cotton Mill, Mollohon Manufacturing Company, and the Commercial Bank. He was a trustee of both Newberry College and Greenville Woman's College. Married to Lucy Baxter, he was survived by her.[31] There were no children.

George Sewall Mower (1853–1921), another of the mill's organizers, was also one of Newberry's most useful citizens. The son of Duane and Cynthia Mower, he was born in Greene, Maine. His parents moved to Prosperity before the Civil War, and they sent him back to Maine to attend college; he graduated from Bowdoin, read law, and practiced in Newberry for the rest of his life.

His was a varied and successful career. Representative and senator from Newberry County; anti-Tillman member of the Constitutional Convention of 1895; Grand Master of Masons in South Carolina; trustee of the Newberry graded schools, Erskine College, and Newberry College; director of Newberry Cotton Mill, the National Bank of Newberry, the Commercial Bank, the Newberry Savings Bank, Oakland Cotton Mill, and of many other firms, he was one of Newberry's most influential leaders. He married Fannie D. Jones; they had four children, Frank D., M.D., McHardy, Myra Cannon, and Helen Martin.[32]

Foster N. Martin (1870–1936), son of James N. and Sarah Blair Martin, and son-in-law of Mower, was born and reared in Newberry. He was trustee of the Newberry schools from 1893 to 1910, serving as chairman for the last nine of those years. He was director of both the Newberry Cotton Mill and Oakland Cotton Mill and a partner in the firm of West-Martin Furniture Company.

In his latter years he taught his own children and their friends about the flora and fauna of this area. He used Lynch's Woods as his classroom and the tours he conducted are still remembered by those who had the opportunity of accompanying this accomplished botanist. He was survived by his wife, the former Helen Mower, and their seven children, George, Foster, M.D., Frances Goette, Sarah Nichols, Mary Caroline McAlister, James Blair, M.D., and Cynthia.[33]

James A. Burton (1862–1925), son of Henry and Betty Maylie Burton, was another native-born businessman. Educated at Newberry College, Captain Patrick's Academy, and South Carolina College, he became depot agent at Newberry and then president of Carolina Manufacturing Company before establishing a very successful real estate and insurance business. He was one of the large landowners of the county and was held in high regard as a public-spirited civic and church leader. He married Edna Goode Griffin, by whom he had six children, Mary Caroline Renneker, Elizabeth Bryson, Richard Lee Burton, James A. Burton, Jr., Margaret Thomson, and Goode Waters.[34]

By 1913 the county had eleven banks—the National Bank, the Commercial Bank, the Exchange Bank, and the Savings Bank in Newberry; the Bank of Prosperity and the People's National Bank in Prosperity; the First National Bank of Whitmire; the Farmers and Merchants Bank of Little Mountain; the Bank of Pomaria; the Farmers Bank of Chappells; and the Farmers Bank of Silverstreet. Obviously a county with a population of 30,000 could not support that many banks. The Farmers Bank of Silverstreet was closed by the state bank examiner in 1915.[35] The others survived until after World War I.

During these early years of the new century three remarkable young women of Newberry distinguished themselves as educators. Euphemia and Mary Law McClintock were daughters of Dr. Ebenezer Pressley McClintock and Elizabeth Young McClintock. He was an Erskine graduate, Confederate veteran, and pastor of the Thompson Street Associate Reformed Presbyterian Church from 1871 to 1906.

Born in this county on February 18, 1866, Euphemia was educated at Newberry Female Academy and at Woman's College in Baltimore (later known as Goucher), from which she was graduated in 1893. A member of Phi Beta Kappa and for some years a trustee of Goucher, she was president of the College for Women in Columbia, South Carolina, from

1902 until that institution merged with Chicora College in 1915. After World War I she founded the Erskine School in Boston. She died on February 27, 1953, and is buried in Rosemont Cemetery in Newberry.[36]

Her sister, Mary Law, was also born in Newberry. She was also educated at Newberry Female Academy and at Goucher College from which she was graduated in 1895. She then obtained a Master of Philosophy degree from the University of Chicago in 1902. She was head of the Department of English of the University of Florida from 1896 to 1901. She later became principal of Miss McClintock's School in Boston in 1908. She died unmarried in January 1925 and is buried in Rosemont Cemetery, Newberry.[37]

The third female educator from Newberry during this period was Lucy Williams McCaughrin, daughter of Robert Lusk and Laura Nance McCaughrin; she was born in Newberry on February 15, 1877. Her maternal ancestors included Major Frederick Nance and Colonel Robert Rutherford, both of whom were prominent figures in early Newberry.

Educated at Newberry Female Academy, the College for Women in Columbia, and Converse College, she began to lose her hearing while still a young lady. To help pass the time, she purchased a kiln in 1897 and for about twenty years painted quality china.

By 1915 she realized that even a hearing aid would not keep her from becoming a social outcast. She once wrote that "there were ever before my mind pictures of the deafened of old, those who had stirred our hearts to pity but whom we did not know how to help and so had left to shrivel and die in their chimney corners."

With characteristic determination she resolved to learn lip reading; she went by herself first to Providence, Rhode Island, to Miss Pattie Thomason; then to Boston to the Bruhn School of Lip Reading; and then to the Kinzie School of Speech Reading in Philadelphia.

She became a teacher of lip reading and taught in a number of cities before going to Columbia in 1933, where she taught both children and adults in her own private school and as executive director of the Columbia Hearing Society. She was instrumental in persuading the General Assembly of South Carolina to make, in 1940, its first appropriation for teaching the deaf except for Cedar Springs School for the Deaf and Blind.

She joined forces with the Junior League of Columbia which also pioneered work in the early detection of deafness. Finally at the age of seventy she returned to Newberry where she lived until her death on May 6, 1962. She too is buried in Rosemont.[38]

This charming gentlewoman of compassion and determination served as southeastern vice president of the American Society for the Hard of Hearing. She was truly a Southern pioneer and her good works still live. In October 1979, the Newberry branch of the Hearing and Speech Center of Columbia dedicated its headquarters to her memory.

While the business leaders of the community were trying to diversify the county's economy, the women of the town were attempting to improve Newberry culturally and aesthetically. In 1904 a group headed by Mrs. Joseph E. Norwood organized the Newberry Library Association. The library was established on the second floor above C. and G. S. Mower's store on College and Main streets. Membership dues were fixed at one dollar per year. Besides Mrs. Norwood as president, the other original officers were Mrs. W. H. Hunt, vice president; Mrs. R. D. Wright, secretary; and Miss Helen Mower, treasurer.[39]

After World War I, the library was moved to the first floor of the Community Hall. It became a part of the state library system and today, as the Newberry-Saluda Regional Library, occupies handsome quarters in the old post office building on Friend Street.

In February 1907 Mrs. L. W. Floyd, as president of the Women's Club, called a meeting at which Mrs. Rufus Fant of Anderson organized a Civic League. Mrs. R. D. Wright was elected president; Mrs. L. W. Floyd, first vice president; Mrs. Owen McR. Holmes, second vice president; Mrs. J. E. Norwood, secretary; and Miss Fannie McCaughrin, treasurer.[40] The objectives of the league were to beautify the town and to keep it clean. The league meant much to the town and it is regrettable that it ceased to exist in 1982, ending three-quarters of a century of service to Newberry.

Soon after the Civic League was founded, Newberry had its most destructive fire. On March 29, 1907, fire started about 11:45 a.m. at the store of R. C. Williams on Friend and College streets. Spreading rapidly to the east, it burned five square blocks, destroying ten stores, twenty-two residences, two churches, several livery stables, and between fifteen and twenty outbuildings and servant's houses. It burned up Main Street from College Street to a point east of Calhoun Street. On the north side of Main Street the F. N. Martin house, Dr. James M. Kibler's home, and St. Luke's Episcopal Church were spared. On the south side of Main, Mrs. Humbert's home was not burned. A quarter of a mile away from the nearest burned building, the McCaughrin house, the Blackwelder house, the Parr house, and the F. Z. Wilson house caught fire but were saved. Owen McRee Holmes's house on Walnut Street caught fire five times but survived.[41]

Although the fire was costly, Newberry turned at once to its rebuilding, and C. C. Davis constructed a number of well-built residences. The Associate Reformed Presbyterian Church was moved from the corner of Main and Thompson streets to the corner of Main and Calhoun streets. There a new church was built at a cost of $13,000; it was designed by Frank Milburn, the architect for the new courthouse, and it was constructed by C. C. Davis.[42]

Henry L. Parr and M. L. Spearman bought the Crotwell Hotel in 1918, and announced plans to make it an up-to-date hotel with all modern conveniences. A few months later, George W. Summer bought the Newberry Hotel for $100,000.[43] But thoughts of economic growth had to take a back seat when America entered World War I in April 1917. Although Newberry had no National Guard unit to send to the war, many young men volunteered and many others were drafted.

Among the World War I soldiers to be decorated was Lieutenant William Osce Coleman of Chappells, who received the Distinguished Service Cross, the Silver Star, the Croix de Guerre, the Italian Cross, and the Victory Medal with five citations.[44] He was the son of A. P. and Katherine Holloway Coleman; he lost an arm in the war. After the war, he served as a representative from Greenwood County before moving to Oklahoma City where he managed the municipal airport.

Another was Captain James A. Burton, Jr., Signal Corps, 4th Division. He received the Distinguished Service Cross and was cited three times in General John J. Pershing's Orders for conspicuous bravery in battle.[45]

Lieutenant Eugene E. Stuck, who served in the infantry and in the aviation corps, was awarded the Silver Star, and he, too, was cited for distinguished service by General Pershing. Captain William E. Bickley, Jr., of the Medical Corps, United States Army, was also awarded the Silver Star. There were others whose service was worthy of note.

Those from Newberry County who died in the war were:[46]

Arthur Baker	Henry Coleman
Francis Earle Boazman	Ben Collins
Walter Calvin Brooks	James Collins
Clyde Brown	Bennie Cook
Carl Chester Bundrick	Haskell Briggs Cromer
Porter Byrd	Otis Lawton Crooks
Roy Caughman	Edmund Deketlaer
George Coleman	Victor Ernest Digby

Ben Duckett
George Lawson Duncan
Thomas Owens Duncan
Bennie James Folk
George W. Hairston
Nathaniel Harp
Charley Harris
Charles S. Haynes
Marion Haynes
John W. Hill
Lonnie Holly
Grady Howard
Brady Johnson
James Keitt
Jehu R. Livingston
Ernest McHardy Longshore
Lonnie Marvin Mills
Clyde Mize
William M. Mobley
Tarrance Moon

Brox Nelson
John Nesby
Horace Ruff, Jr.
William Leslie Sample
Willie Sator
George Adam Shealy
Rudolphus Shettleworth
Milton Shirey
Joshua Ward Motte Simmons
Jacob O'Merle Singley
John Sligh
Henry Smith
John Bluford Smith, Jr.
Colie L. Stevens
Vandora Edwin Stuck
Curtis D. Trammell
Isaac Williams
Nathaniel Williams
Willie Wise

11

The Depression Years

Newberry's depression came in 1921, a decade before the Great Depression. The boll weevil appeared in South Carolina during World War I, causing havoc in every county in the state. Cotton, which was the economic mainstay of Newberry County, plunged in price from thirty-three cents a pound in 1920 to thirteen cents a pound in 1921. Although the price rose to about twenty-seven cents a pound in 1923 and 1924 these years were the exceptions; the price of cotton remained depressed until World War II. Newberry's economy suffered for twenty years.

During this period there were numerous foreclosures of farm mortgages. Black labor moved off the farms to the towns and then to the North and West. The county's black population fell from 20,641 in 1920 to 14,242 in 1940. Farms were abandoned and lien merchants went out of business.

The county's banks could not survive; they commenced failing even before the Great Depression hit America. First to fail was the People's National Bank of Prosperity. When it closed on March 14, 1925,[1] it was reorganized and reopened as The Citizens National Bank. The latter survived for only six years.

Meanwhile, the Farmers and Merchants Bank of Little Mountain failed in 1927, the National Bank of Newberry on July 1, 1929, and the Bank of Pomaria in March 1930.[2] Rather than risk failure, the management of the Farmers Bank of Chappells voluntarily liquidated that institution; the cash reserve was more than adequate to pay all depositors and creditors.[3] The Exchange Bank of Newberry, however, failed on April

11, 1931. The Bank of Prosperity and the Citizens National Bank of Prosperity failed in 1931,[4] leaving Prosperity without banking facilities.

This left the Commercial Bank as the only bank in the town of Newberry—a situation that some of the business leaders could not tolerate. In order to provide a second bank in the county seat, these businessmen persuaded the Peoples State Bank of South Carolina to open a branch facility. The local advisory board was announced in May 1931; the bank failed in January 1932.[5]

During 1931 the Commercial Bank merged with the South Carolina National Bank and occupied the handsome quarters on the corner of Boyce and Caldwell streets that it had built in 1923. Until World War II the only banks in the county were the South Carolina National in Newberry, the American Bank in Whitmire, and the Prosperity Depository. The latter was organized by John F. Clarkson and his associates in 1933.[6]

Another financial institution organized by the Clarkson group was the Newberry Building and Loan Association. This was founded in 1929 by John F. Clarkson, Dr. C. D. Weeks, M. O. Summer, A. S. Paine, I. II. Hunt, E. A. Carpenter, James W. Johnson, J. E. Stokes, and J. W. Earhardt, Jr. as incorporators. In 1935 the association was federalized, becoming the Newberry Federal Savings and Loan Association.[7] Just before World War II, it built and occupied new quarters on College Street across from the courthouse.

The first years after the armistice saw a plethora of new organizations established in Newberry. In November 1919, American Legion Post 24 was founded with sixty-six members. The original officers were Hal Kohn, commander; Dr. John B. Setzler, vice commander; J. Dave Caldwell, adjutant; McFall Wise, finance officer; and Joseph L. Keitt, Jr., historian.[8] This was the first modern veterans group to be formed, and it remains the strongest such organization in the county today since the veterans of World War II, the Korean War, and the Vietnam War decided generally to affiliate with the Legion rather than form organizations of their own.

The State Department of the Legion held its third annual convention in Newberry in 1921, at which time Mrs. L. W. Floyd was elected president of the South Carolina American Legion Auxiliary,[9] she was the first of three Newberrians to fill that position. The others served much later, Alma Cole Dufford being elected in 1947,[10] and Ruth Ethridge Anderson in 1957.[11]

Ola Clark Floyd, daughter of Dr. Richard P. and Adeline Piester Clark, was born in the county. She was an active civic worker, helping to organize the Civic League and serving as its president, and also serving on the City Board of Health, as a trustee of Rosemont Cemetery, and as a member of the committee to plan and erect a World War Memorial in Newberry.

Her husband, Lou Washington Floyd, son of John and Lou Washington Anderson Floyd, was a prominent business leader until his death on May 3, 1922. He was the founder of Newberry Cotton Seed Oil and Fertilizer Company, a director of the Commercial Bank, a trustee of the city schools, and the owner of telephone franchises in Newberry and a number of other cities until he sold his system to Southern Bell Telephone Company. He was survived by his widow and four sons, Richard Clark, John Clark, Washington Clark, and Louis Clark Floyd. His widow died on December 6, 1928.[12]

In March 1920, Newberry's first service club was organized. The original officers of the Newberry Rotary Club were Z. F. Wright, president; George B. Cromer, vice president; B. L. Dorrity, secretary; T. Roy Summer, treasurer; and J. Ernest Summer, sergeant-at-arms.[13] Ralph B. Baker was the last surviving charter member at the time of his death in 1983.

Newberry's second service club, the Kiwanis Club, was established two months later. Its original officers were William S. Matthews, president; W. W. Cromer, vice president; and Ernest A. Carpenter, secretary.[14]

The Newberry Lions Club was organized in October 1928, with twelve charter members. The first president was the Reverend M. C. Dendy. John F. Clarkson succeeded him.[15]

The Newberry Jaycee Chapter was organized in April, 1941. The original officers were Gerald C. Paysinger, president; P. Duncan Johnson, Jr., vice president; Felix B. Greene, Jr., secretary; Robert R. Bruner, Jr., treasurer; and Roy Clary, Floyd Lane, and Jacob Wheeler, directors.[16]

All of these service clubs are active and useful to the community. Other service clubs, the Civitan and the Exchange Clubs, were organized after World War II.

During the early 1920s, efforts were made to provide recreational facilities for Newberry despite the agricultural recession. The Country Club of Newberry was organized in 1921. Its original officers were Z. F. Wright, president; L. G. Eskridge, vice president; and Walter B. Wallace, secretary-treasurer. The directors were these officers and T. Roy Summer, T. K. Johnstone, White Fant, and Welch Wilbur of Newberry; Dr. George Y. Hunter of Prosperity; and W. M. Sherard of Whitmire.[17]

In 1922 the club purchased a tract of 55 acres about three miles north of town from Welch Wilbur and built a spacious clubhouse, a nine-hole golf course, and a lake for swimming. When the clubhouse was destroyed by fire in 1939, it was immediately rebuilt.[18]

During the same period Newberry organized a Class D professional baseball team and became a part of the Carolina League; other teams were Anderson, Abbeville, Greenwood, Laurens, and Union. The caliber of play was said to be better than that in other leagues with a higher classification. Perhaps the most memorable game was one between Newberry and Union that lasted for twenty-one innings. Al Shealy, a Newberry College great who later pitched for the Chicago Cubs, went the whole way for Newberry; the game ended in a two-to-two tie. The local team used the facilities of Newberry College. O. H. "Red" Johnson was president of the Newberry club;[19] he was succeeded by William G. Mayes. The league lasted only two years.

The local textile companies had teams in the Mid-State League. West End, Oakland, and Mollohon fielded good teams and used college stars to augment local talent. At that time baseball was truly the national sport, and there was much interest in these local teams.

In 1923 the Newberry County Fair Association was organized with Dr. C. D. Weeks, president; Mrs. S. W. Brown, vice president; T. M. Mills, secretary; and P. D. Johnson, treasurer.[20] The annual fair continued for many years under the auspices of the County Fair Association.

Dr. Clarence Douglas Weeks, native of Clarendon County, moved to Newberry in 1895. Son of James W. and Julia Felder Weeks, he was graduated in pharmacy from the University of South Carolina in 1891. After working for Dr. Pelham, he purchased Dr. Peter Robertson's interest in the firm of Gilder and Robertson in 1900; thereafter until his death at the age of seventy on November 6, 1943, he operated the leading drugstore of the town under the name of Gilder and Weeks.

A public spirited, useful citizen, Dr. Weeks served for many years as trustee of the city schools, member of the city bond commission, vice president of Newberry Federal Savings and Loan Association, and member of the Rotary Club and the Chamber of Commerce. He was a communicant and warden of St. Luke's Episcopal Church; for years his generous and unpublicized aid kept the church going. He was survived by his widow, Nancy Pool Weeks, and two daughters, Caroline Padgett and Julia Stokes. His widow died on October 19, 1977, at the great age of ninety-eight.[21]

Pope Duncan Johnson, son of James W. D. and Mary Wilson Johnson, was born at Jalapa. A veteran of the Spanish-American War, he served as deputy to Sheriff M. M. Buford before becoming a clerk at the wholesale store of Edward R. Hipp. Following the latter's death in 1910, Johnson and J. Thaddeus McCrackin established the Johnson-McCrackin Company. It operated a general mercantile store and engaged in farming for years.

Active in the affairs of the community, Johnson was trustee of the city schools, a Mason and Shriner, an active member of the First Baptist Church, and a member of the advisory board of Peoples State Bank. He married Eleanor Duckett of Clinton, who survived him by almost half a century. He died on October 9, 1936. They had four children, P. D. Johnson, Jr., Edna J. Kirkegard, Mary J. Smith, and Thomas D. Johnson.[22]

In 1924, Whitmire had growing pains and some of its leaders attempted to establish a new county to be named "Carlisle County."[23] The county seat would, of course, be Whitmire. The county would consist of areas of Newberry, Laurens, and Union counties. Nothing came of this effort because the proposed county was too small.

The following year the Newberry County Hospital was formally opened, capping a thirty-year effort to secure medical facilities.[24] Its history is explained in the chapter on Public Health.

Another sign of progress was the new water system, also completed in 1925. This facility, which pumped water from a point on Bush River three miles from town, had a 1,000,000 gallon reservoir and two concrete filters capable of holding 500,000 gallons each.[25] Homer W. Schumpert, the superintendent of the water and light system from 1907 until his retirement in 1953, was responsible for this and many other improvements in Newberry.

Born in Newberry, the son of J. Frederick and Alice Werts Schumpert, he was graduated from Clemson College and worked for the General Electric Company until he accepted the superintendency of public works of Newberry. His father served as sergeant-at-arms of the South Carolina Senate from 1903 to 1927. He was widely known and greatly loved as "Uncle Homer." He undoubtedly taught more youngsters to ride horses and to swim than anyone in the history of the county. A faithful member of the Lutheran Church of the Redeemer, he married Louise Hipp. They had no children. She died in 1969 and he died on April 17, 1975, at the age of ninety-one.[26]

In 1925 the Kendall Company of Boston, Massachusetts, bought the Oakland Cotton Mill. W. H. Hunt continued as president until his death in April 1927. He was succeeded as president by James Nance McCaughrin who died suddenly on December 8, 1927, at the age of forty-nine.[27] The son of Robert L. and Laura Nance McCaughrin, he was born in Newberry on January 18, 1879. A graduate of Princeton University, he entered into the business life of Newberry at an early age and in many capacities. He was vice president of Mollohon Manufacturing Company and a director of the Newberry Cotton Mills, the Commercial Bank, and the Security Loan and Investment Company at the time of his death. As an elder and deacon, he was active in Aveleigh Presbyterian Church. Married to Margaret Gibson of Newberry, he was survived by her and by four children, Albert Gibson, Laura Nance, Margaret, and Elizabeth McCaughrin.

A short time later the Kendall Company bought Mollohon Manufacturing Company. Both the Oakland and Mollohon plants were thereafter operated as parts of the Kendall organization, which also owned plants in Pelzer, Camden, and Edgefield, South Carolina, and Paw Creek, North Carolina.

Ten years after the end of World War I, a committee was appointed to secure a memorial to those who died in that war. The lower part of the Public Square, the block bounded by Main, Boyce, Nance, and McKibben streets, was selected as the site and a memorial park established with a monument on which appeared the names of most of those who died in the war. A memorial mass meeting was held at the courthouse on October 19, 1919.[28]

The census of 1930 showed that the town of Newberry had a population of 7,228, an increase of 22 percent since 1920. It also showed that Whitmire had 2,763 inhabitants and Prosperity 844. There were seven other incorporated villages in the county—Helena with 596 inhabitants, Kinards with 273, Pomaria with 263, Little Mountain with 244, Silverstreet with 221, Chappells with 174, and Peak with 154.[29]

However, the improved roads then being constructed were to sound the death knell of the little villages. Newberry's first paved road was between the county seat and Prosperity; a contract for this section was let in 1926 at a cost of $171,000.[30] Within ten years a network of paved roads extended over the county. In addition to the primary roads built by the state Highway Department there were many miles of farm-to-market roads paved by bond issues and federal funds.

One of the leaders in road improvement was J. Marion Davis, member of the State Highway Commission. Born in Newberry, he went to work in Newberry Cotton Mill in 1886 after dropping out of school. He became superintendent of the mill in 1901 and continued in that capacity until his death on April 14, 1933, at the age of sixty-one. He served as mayor of Newberry and was active in civic and church affairs. A local park is named for him. He married first Lillie McGowan by whom he had four children, Kay, Frances Clisby, Edward, and Arnold. He later married Mayme E. Jones, by whom he had one daughter, Frances Marion.[31]

Another leader in road improvement was Henry Holland Ruff, county supervisor of Newberry County. During his administration, 1930–1940, the farm to market roads of the county were paved. Son of Walter Franklin and Molly Leitzsey Ruff, he was born in Newberry County and lived there all of his life. He served as trustee of St. Phillip's School, magistrate, and commissioner as well as supervisor. Married to Talu Lominick, he died on December 12, 1972, at the age of eighty-six, survived by his two daughters, Ruby R. Barber and Naomi R. Epting.[32]

In the early '20s it was evident that motor transportation would soon challenge the primacy of railroad passenger transportation. It could not succeed until the advent of paved highways, but earlier attempts were made. In January 1923 that enterprising Newberrian, Hal Kohn, organized the Newberry County Bus Line. With Howard P. Overby as the first driver the line made two round trips between Newberry and Whitmire on Monday through Friday and three round trips on Saturday. In October James G. Brown was operating a Hudson passenger car as a bus between Newberry and Columbia twice each day.[33] When the roads were paved, commercial buses took over from these pioneer vehicles.

The first decade after World War I ended on a nostalgic note. For many years the Newberry Fire Department was recognized as one of the best, if not the best, in South Carolina. It consistently won contests with the other volunteer departments in South Carolina.

Symbol of the department was Old Joe, Newberry's famous fire horse first acquired in 1904. His faithful keeper was Malcolm Lesesne who drove Joe to countless fires and in numerous contests. Old Joe never had a whip laid on him and no one ever shouted at him. He probably won more first money than any fire horse in the South. He died on May 9, 1930, and was buried in a grave 10 feet deep by the side of the fire station. The town fire bell tolled thirty-five times, once for each year of his life.[34] His death marked the end of an era.

The Great Depression compelled all elements of Newberry County to think in terms of survival. President Franklin D. Roosevelt brought his persuasive leadership to the nation; few who heard him say in his first inaugural address that "the only thing we have to fear is fear itself" are likely to forget it. He prevented revolution, and in doing so he transformed this nation.

The Civilian Conservation Corps gave employment to young men who would otherwise have been idlers. One of fifteen camps established in South Carolina was Camp John Belton O'Neall, located just south of Newberry on Ebenezer Church Road.[35]

The Works Progress Administration (WPA) gave employment to many who could not obtain work. The Public Works Agency built projects which were needed and also primed the economic pump. Alan Johnstone of Newberry was an early associate of Harry Hopkins in this program and became general counsel of the Federal Works Agency.

In 1934 members of the Johnstone family conveyed 168 acres known as Lynch's Woods to the town and county of Newberry in return for the satisfaction of all taxes owed on approximately 600 other acres belonging to the estate of George Johnstone.[36] The land was to be used as a park. A Newberry County Park Commission was established by legislative act; two of its members were to be named by the legislative delegation of the county, two by the town council, and the fifth by the other four.[37]

T. E. Davis, Homer Schumpert, and H. B. Wells served as the Committee for Development of Lynch's Wood Park.[38] With WPA labor, they laid out the roads; built barbecue pits, picnic tables, and concession stands; and preserved the pristine beauty of a most unusual area that had long been known for its flora: dogwood, black haw, syringa, judas, yellow jessamine, bloodroot, hepatica, anemone, wild azalea, saxifrage, bluets, chrisogenum, cinquefoil, moss pink, violets, and many varieties indigenous to other parts of South Carolina. It was also the home of many kinds of birds. The beauty of the unusual area has been preserved to the present day.[39]

Henry B. Wells died soon after the park was opened on July 19, 1940. Born in Newberry on April 26, 1874, he was the son of Osborne and Cornelia Schumpert Wells. He was a member of the Newberry Fire Department for fifty years, serving as chief of the department for thirty-five years. In 1940 an appreciation dinner was tendered him at the Country Club of Newberry for this service to the community. He served in many other ways, being a trustee of the city schools, a member of the Newberry Park Commission, a member of the Rotary Club, and master of Amity Lodge No. 87, AFM. He married Mary Fulmer; they had two children, H. B. Wells, Jr. and W. Fulmer Wells.[40]

Davis and Schumpert continued to serve on the Commission for many years. They earned the gratitude of the community for their work. Thomas Edward Davis, son of C. C. and Sarah Greneker Davis, was born in Newberry on May 5, 1899. His father was a master builder and erected many of the houses still standing in Newberry. T. E. Davis attended The Citadel and then entered the automobile business in Newberry. He had the Chevrolet and Buick agency in Newberry. He married Mildred Purcell and they had three children. Their son, Lieutenant Thomas E. Davis, Jr., graduated from Clemson College and was killed in World War II. Their daughter, Mary Ann, married T. Gates Beckwith; and a third child died in infancy. He died in 1962 and his widow in 1981.[41]

The Rural Electrification Act was of inestimable value to the farmers. Because of it, living became more bearable and comfortable in the rural areas. Newberry took full advantage of this program. Of a total of 592 miles of electric lines in South Carolina in 1938, Newberry County had 101 miles. Of 302 miles under construction that year Newberry had 52.[42] The Newberry Electric Cooperative has been extremely successful in supplying power to the rural parts of Newberry County at a low cost. T. William Hunter, the attorney for the local cooperative from its organization until his death in 1979, served as president of the National Association of Rural Electrification Authorities.

The United States Forest Service commenced acquiring lands between Whitmire and Newberry during the Depression. The lands had been planted in cotton so long that they had become unproductive and were badly eroded. Farmers could not pay their taxes and were eager to sell their lands. The government acquired some 54,000 acres within a period of some five years. The county receives one-fourth of the revenue from forest products in lieu of taxes.

The Social Security Act guaranteed some compensation to elderly or disabled workers, the Federal Deposit Insurance Act guaranteed the safety of individual bank accounts, and the Federal Employment Insurance Act guaranteed partial compensation to unemployed workers. Before these could take effect, there was much unrest among the textile workers of Newberry.

In 1934 a general textile strike was called by Francis J. Gorman against all Southern textile mills in an attempt to gain recognition of the United Textile Workers Union. The cotton mills in Newberry went on strike, but there were no local issues involved, and the strike lasted only a few weeks. There was trouble in some parts of South Carolina involving the

"Flying Squadrons" of workers and Governor Blackwood called out the South Carolina National Guard, but there was no violence in Newberry.

However, in 1936 a strike was called by the union led by "Red" Smith at the Mollohon Plant. This time local issues were involved, chiefly concerning the "stretch-out," an increase of work without additional pay. "Stretch-out" passed into oblivion when the minimum wage law was enacted. The people of the community were divided in their opinions as to the merits of the struggle. Some sided with management but many more thought that insensitive mill officials sent to Newberry from the northeastern states contributed greatly to the difficulty.

The strike continued for six months and the community suffered from the long shut-down. Its scars remained visible for many years.

The strike was finally settled when "Red" Smith agreed to resign as head of the local union. The members voted to pay fifty cents per week each to support him but, of course, this did not continue for long. Shortly after Smith resigned, A. S. Paine was fired by Kendall as manager of the Mollohon Plant; whether his termination was a *quid pro quo* for Smith's resignation is disputed, but the fact remains that Mollohon reopened and there was no more trouble.

Marcus Wilton Todd, a native of North Carolina, was transferred from Paw Creek to become manager of the Mollohon Plant in early September 1936, and William H. Tedford was brought in as assistant manager. J. Ed McConnell succeeded Smith as spokesman for the union. These men worked together harmoniously, and Mollohon had no more serious labor trouble.

Todd was with the Kendall Company for twenty-eight years, being moved from Mollohon to Pelzer in 1946. Later he was manager of Newberry Cotton Mills after it was sold by local interests. A veteran of World War I, he died in Winston-Salem on May 26, 1967, survived by his widow, the former Mary Wingard, and three children, Mary Anne DuPree, M. W. Todd, Jr., and Robert E. Todd.[43]

McConnell, son of J. Frank and Katherine Yochem McConnell, was born in Spartanburg. He worked at Mollohon for fifty-one years and served as a colonel on Governor Thurmond's staff and as a member of the City Council of Newberry. A member of Epting Memorial Methodist Church, he died on May 20, 1978, survived by his widow, the former Addie Mae Maw, one son, E. F. McConnell, and four daughters, Bert McEntire, Connie Wright, Grace Harvey, and Kitty Abrams.[44]

Tedford, a native of Tennessee, was educated at the University of Tennessee and at the Georgia Institute of Technology. Tedford retired as manager of Mollohon in 1972. He married Sara Cromer of Newberry and they have two sons, William, Jr., a professor at Southern Methodist University, and Timothy, graduate of the United States Naval Academy and an officer in the United States Navy.

Two recreational facilities were made available to the people of the county in the 1930s. The municipal swimming pool was completed in May 1935.[45] Located in the Margaret Hunter Park, it gave the children of the county a place to swim for a very small fee and served the community well for many years.

Mrs. John H. Summer, known to Newberrians as "Miss Mamie," was responsible for the beautification of the park and for the construction of the pool as well as for the renovation of the old courthouse as the Community Hall and many other worthwhile improvements. During her lifetime she preserved the beautiful shade trees that bordered the city's streets; after her death successive city managers hacked some down and topped others with impunity. They did not dare during her lifetime.

"Miss Mamie" was awarded the degree of Doctor of Humane Letters by her alma mater, Newberry College. A plaque was placed in her memory in the Community Hall. These are small rewards for the contributions she made to Newberry's welfare. Since her death on January 29, 1959, aged seventy-one, she has been sorely missed.

That part of the Johnstone tract lying on the west side of Highway 76 Bypass was converted into the Newberry Fairgrounds in 1935. On it were constructed exhibit buildings for crafts, cattle, and poultry; a race track; stables; and the American Legion Building. The Newberry County Fair was conducted annually on these grounds under the auspices of the American Legion Post. For some years the fair was conducted jointly by Newberry and Saluda counties but this arrangement eventually was terminated. The tract has been used for the Shrine Club's horse show and weekly automobile races.

In 1936 Marvin E. Abrams was elected to the state Senate over J. Kess Derrick in a hotly contested election in which Governor Olin D. Johnston took part. Senator Abrams commenced twenty years of service in that position, a record equalling that of Senator Alan Johnstone. He provided sound and progressive leadership to the county in a time when the legislative delegation ran the local government, and he served the state with distinction.

The son of Thomas Worth and Josephine Scott Abrams, he was born in Whitmire on March 1, 1884. Graduating with first honors at Newberry College in 1903, he became a business and civic leader in his hometown, serving as chairman of the board of trustees of the local schools, chairman of the Board of Stewards of Whitmire Methodist Church, and worshipful master of Roseboro Lodge, AFM.

Elected to the House of Representatives in 1932, he served four years in that body before becoming a state senator. He was twice a delegate to the Democratic National Convention and a trustee of Winthrop College. Following his retirement from the Senate in 1956 he was appointed a member of the South Carolina Public Service Authority. He died on July 27, 1966.

He was married twice, first to Fannie Mae Henderson, and after her tragic death, to Dewey Malone Abrams. He and his first wife had six children—Thomas Worth, Josephine, James Henderson, Marvin Eugene Abrams, Jr., Lucy Frances A. Lorick, and Margaret A. Gibson. They and his second wife survived him when he died at the age of eighty-two.[46]

J. Kess Derrick, son of Julius P. and Missouri Caroline Derrick, was born in the county on May 1, 1880. Educated in the field schools of his community, he became the leading citizen of the lower part of the county by dint of hard work. A compassionate, generous spirit caused him to aid those less fortunate then he, and he worked untiringly to improve the lot of his neighbors and his county. He married Lavinia S. Wessinger who died on November 27, 1932. After being elected to the House of Representatives in 1934, he was unsuccessful in his quest for the Senate in 1936.

Two years later he was elected to the House once more and served until his sudden death on September 24, 1943; he was survived by his only child, Carroll Derrick. He and Senator Abrams cooperated unselfishly with each other and the other members of the county delegation, R. Aubrey Harley, Thomas H. Pope, Jr., and the latter's successor, Julian A. Price.[47] Newberry had a strong and able legislative delegation during this time.

In 1939 the county sponsored its sesquicentennial celebration with great success. All organizations and communities cooperated to conduct a week-long observance. Religious services opened the event on Sunday, April 30, at the municipal stadium with the sermon being delivered that evening by Dr. R. E. Grier, president of Erskine College.

A Youth and Pet Parade was held on Monday, followed by a band concert at the stadium by the Newberry Cotton Mill Band, and later by the "Cavalcade of Progress." The latter was a historical pageant with a cast of over 600 people directed by the John B. Rogers Company. The pageant was repeated on Wednesday and Thursday nights.

Other events included a dance, a square dance, a parade, speeches by Governor Maybank and other notables, a barbecue, and May Day at Newberry College. A special sesquicentennial edition of the *Newberry Observer* containing 104 pages of historical sketches was a valuable memento of the celebration.[48]

The Sesquicentennial Committee was composed of Z. F. Wright, honorary chairman; Thomas H. Pope, Jr., executive chairman; George K. Dominick, Mrs. Robert D. Wright, Mrs. R. Herman Wright, and Thomas E. Epting, vice chairmen; C. C. Hutto, treasurer; and John F. Clarkson, secretary.[49]

In September 1939, Newberry's first National Guard unit since Reconstruction was federally recognized as Battery I, 263rd Coast Artillery Regiment. Captain Thomas H. Pope, Jr., commanded the unit, and 1st Lieutenant John C. Billingsley was executive officer.[50]

This unit later became Battery C, 107th Separate Coast Artillery Battalion (Antiaircraft). It was inducted into federal service on February 10, 1941. On the evening of February 19, a public dinner was tendered the battery by the citizens of Newberry. Mrs. Mamie S. Summer, with the help of the community leaders, organized the affair, which was due primarily to her efforts.

The next day Battery C formed at the corner of Main and Glenn streets and marched down Main Street to the Union Station before a vast crowd of well-wishers. At the station the unit boarded the train for Camp Stewart, Georgia, where it expected to train for a year.

Meanwhile, as the storm gathered in Europe, the United States Congress enacted the Selective Service Act. In October 1940, two Selective Service Boards were established in Newberry County.[51] Board Number 58 consisted of Jake R. Wise, chairman, William Scott, and Dr. Frank R. Hunter. Its clerks were Pauline Fant Meek, Julia Dickert, and Ellouise S. Setzler. Board Number 59 consisted of John A. Mayer, chairman, Dr. George Harmon, and Virgil Shealy. Its clerks were Lucille Harmon, Constance Armfield, and Macy Davis King.

The first selectees drafted from the county were Klugh Woodrow Sanford and Jessie Floyd Hiller, who left for camp in December 1940.[52]

12

World War II and
Postwar Development

Japan's attack on Pearl Harbor unified America. Hundreds of men and women from Newberry County enlisted. The Selective Service boards drafted more men, and Newberry County's National Guard unit— Battery C of the 107th Antiaircraft Battalion, then at Camp Stewart, Georgia, for a year's service—was retained for the duration. It saw overseas service in England, North Africa, Sicily, and Italy. Altogether more than 3,775 men and women from the county served in the armed forces.

They acquitted themselves well in Europe, the Mediterranean, and the Pacific. While all of them did their duty, many rendered distinguished service. For example, Captain S. Downs Wright, U.S. Navy pilot, was awarded the Navy Cross and the Distinguished Service Cross. Lieutenant Colonel Edward D. McCrackin of the U.S. Army won the Distinguished Service Cross in the invasion of North Africa. Colonel Tom W. Suber of Whitmire received two Silver Stars and the Bronze Star for service in the Pacific, while Sergeant George R. Owens received the Silver Star for service in the invasion of Sicily.

Others were prisoners of war, including O. Doyle Long, Jack B. Workman, Lykes Henderson, Edward A. Thomasson, Hugh King Boyd, Jr., Thomas V. Cromer, James E. Harrison, Russell B. Koon, Marion E. Wicker, Homer L. Wicker, Marvin R. Graham, Larry J. Bouknight, Claude E. Dominick, and Paul A. Finney.

The war years at home involved rationing of gas, food, and tires. The civilians worked hard to produce agricultural products and manufactured products. Except for the war effort, little could be accomplished in the way of expanding the local economy until the advent of peace.

137

When peace came with the defeat of the Axis powers, local veterans returned home with broadened views and a desire to make something of themselves. Having been to places they had never heard of before the war, they lost some of their provincialism. They wasted no time in taking their places as leaders in the community.

The Great Depression ended with World War II. Of equal importance to the South was the end of freight-rate discrimination. For generations the Northeast, known as the "Official Territory," was favored by freight rates over the South and the West. For example, it cost 39 percent more to ship goods from Newberry to the same point than it did from the Northeast, although the distance was equal. If the South was ever going to be able to compete with the Northeast, this freight differential would have to be erased.

In 1939 the Interstate Commerce Commission instituted investigations into the validity of the existing freight rate standards for interstate railroad traffic in the United States. It notified Congress that the commission would carry out its mandate that unlawful rates be removed and it created a uniform classification for all the territories, meanwhile reducing the rate difference from 39 percent to 19 percent. The United States Supreme Court held that discriminatory rates were illegal.[1]

The effect of this ruling was immediate in South Carolina. From 1947, when the order went into effect, until 1950, this state registered an increase in manufacturing value of 370 percent, while the national average was 204 percent. New industrial expansion in South Carolina cost over $425 million and created 50,000 new jobs and annual payrolls of $100 million.[2]

Thus, with the advent of peace, the end of the Great Depression, and the equalizing of freight rates, the South was ready to join the industrial revolution at last. But Newberry County was not to secure any new industry until 1964, with the exception of Prosperity Manufacturing Company and Setlow's Old School Manufacturing Company.

This was due to the action of former U.S. Senator Charles E. Daniels. In the fifteen years after World War II, he was the most influential South Carolinian in attracting new industry, locating the plants, and building them with his construction company. He openly stated that he would not assist in locating any plant in Newberry County until the non-union counties were surfeited. He adhered to his policy until 1960. On October 10, 1960, he spoke at a luncheon sponsored by the Newberry Development Board and stated he had helped locate some 200 plants in South Carolina and that his ambition was to locate one industry in every county. He then announced that Newberry would get some new industry.[3]

Meanwhile, the Kendall Company had in 1950 doubled the size of its Oakland Plant at a cost of some $4,000,000.[4] This was welcome news indeed to the community and ensured the county of at least one modern textile plant. As an inducement for renovation, the city approved a resolution that the plant would not be incorporated into the city.

Newberry's oldest textile plant, the Newberry Cotton Mill, was sold in 1946 to M. M. Clairmont, the stock bringing $261 per share.[5] Local dividends ceased and a paternalistic management gave way to a new and harsher regime. Clairmont then sold the company to an Armenian, named Dabakarian, and it became obvious that the plant soon would be closed. The company filed for bankruptcy in 1982, the assets were auctioned, and the main building, not razed until 1990, became an eyesore.

Meanwhile, the three local textile plants, and the J. P. Stevens Plant at Whitmire, sold all of their mill houses to their employees.[6] Those who occupied them were given the right to purchase them. The streets and utilities were donated to the towns. This divestiture was good for many reasons. It made taxpayers out of the workers, instilled a pride of ownership, and resulted in many physical improvements to the property. It eliminated a source of friction between owners and tenants, and reduced any negative feeling between those living in the town and those living in the villages. Sociologically and politically the results have been wholesome.

Although little new industry settled in Newberry for almost twenty years after World War II, a number of local businesses were started by returning veterans. New banking institutions helped provide the financing of these ventures.

At the beginning of the war the only bank in Newberry was the South Carolina National. Prosperity had the Prosperity Depository, and Newberry had the Newberry Federal Savings and Loan Association.

During the war one new financial institution, the Commercial State Bank at Whitmire, was founded by Clarence Claud Hutto. The former manager of the South Carolina National Bank in Newberry, he was a useful citizen and influential business leader. Transferred to Anderson to manage a larger branch of the South Carolina National Bank, he decided to return to Newberry County. He then established the Commercial State Bank, which has become, after a series of mergers, the Whitmire Branch of the North Carolina National Bank.

Hutto, who married Sarah Hipp of Whitmire, also became vice-president of Meek-Hutto Lumber Company and Whitener Lumber Company. Generally recognized as a brilliant financier, he died at the early age of forty-nine on April 29, 1952, survived by his wife and two children, Mary Lee and C. C. Hutto, Jr.[7]

In September 1946 the Newberry County Bank was organized by a group of local businessmen with A. J. Bowers, Jr., president; Allen W. Murray, vice-president; and Joe M. Roberts, cashier.[8] For many years this was the only locally owned commercial bank in Newberry; later it became, after several mergers, the Newberry branch of the North Carolina National Bank of South Carolina.

Bowers (1889–1967), a native of the county, was a graduate of Newberry College, veteran of World War I, postmaster from 1920 to 1924, and owner of a general insurance agency. Although replaced by Murray as president after one year in office, he remained a director until the bank's merger with State Bank and Trust Company. He served as president of the Country Club of Newberry, Representative from Newberry County, director of Newberry Cotton Mill, and trustee of Newberry College. He married Roslyn Hipp; they had two daughters, Rosemary and Edna Louise.[9]

Murray (1894–1964) was a Georgian who graduated from Emory College and moved to Newberry in 1920. He took an active part in the social and business life of Newberry, serving as master of Amity Lodge No. 87, AFM; as president of the Kiwanis Club; and as president of the Chamber of Commerce, the Newberry Lumber Company, and Murray Lumber Company. Married to Elizabeth Woodle, at his death he was survived by her, one daughter, Helen Lafayette Gray, and a grandson, Murray Gray.[10]

The other executives of this bank before its merger were James N. Beard and Joe M. Roberts. Upon Murray's death the former became chairman of the board and the latter president of the bank. For many years Beard was one of Newberry's leading merchants, being president of the Belk-Beard Company. He served as a trustee of Erskine College and as president of the Newberry Chamber of Commerce. A leader in the Associate Reformed Presbyterian Church, he was married to the former Martha Whitesides of Gastonia, North Carolina. They had two children, J. N. Beard, Jr., and Joseph Franklin Beard.

Roberts, a native of Pensacola, Florida, graduated from Georgia Tech and was an examiner for the Federal Deposit Insurance Corporation before coming to Newberry to manage the new bank. He was chairman of the Clinton-Newberry Natural Gas Authority, president of the

Kiwanis Club and the South Carolina Amateur Golf Association, and a director of the South Carolina Chamber of Commerce. After the merger of the Newberry County Bank, he served as senior vice-president of the State Bank and Trust Company and its successor, Bankers Trust of South Carolina, until his death on July 10, 1974, at the age of sixty-five. He was survived by his wife, the former Ruth Kline, and three children, June R. Shealy, Joe N. Roberts, Jr., and Clyde B. Roberts.[11]

In 1947 a third local financial institution, the State Building and Loan Association, was organized by Ralph B. Baker, J. Dave Caldwell, Dr. Hugh B. Senn, R. Aubrey Harley, and Thomas H. Pope.[12] First housed in the offices of Caldwell, it later purchased and moved into the old banking quarters of the defunct Newberry National Bank. Louis C. Floyd later became a director, and, after Dr. Senn's death in 1952, Pinckney Newton Abrams resigned as county auditor to become managing officer and secretary-treasurer of the association. The association was successfully operated until its merger with Standard Savings and Loan Association of Columbia. In 1983 Standard sold its Newberry branch to First Federal Savings and Loan Association of Greenville, which continues to operate it under the local management of Harold Folk.

Caldwell (1893–1966) was a native of the county, graduate of Newberry College, veteran of World War I, president of the Newberry Rotary Club and the Chamber of Commerce, commander of American Legion Post No. 24, and a member of the Selective Service Board during World War II. A great lover of flowers, he was active in the Camellia Society and transformed the grounds around his country home into a beautiful garden. He sold the three mill villages in Newberry as a realtor. Married to Kate Summer, he had no children.[13]

Abrams (1912–69), also a native of the county, was one of the most popular officials ever to serve Newberry County. He went to work at an early age to help support his widowed mother, working in the Bank of Chappells, as a storekeeper, and as magistrate at Chappells. He was elected county auditor in 1936 and continued until he resigned in 1953. During this time he served as president of the South Carolina Association of Auditors and Treasurers and was for many years chairman of the county Democratic Party. Later he served as president of the South Carolina Savings and Loan League and as master of Amity Lodge No. 87, AFM. A public spirited, generous man who had countless friends, he suffered from ill health in the last years of his life and committed suicide in 1969. He was survived by his wife, the former Ruby Ruff, and a half-sister, Viola D. DeHart, and mourned by all who knew him.[14]

The Prosperity Depository, established in 1933 by the Clarkson group, was converted to the Bank of Commerce in 1963.[15] In 1974 it merged with Southern Bank and Trust and is now the Prosperity Branch of First Union National Bank. Jacob A. Bowers was vice-president and cashier of the Depository and president of the Bank of Commerce. He continued as executive officer of the bank after its merger and served until his retirement.

Newberry's first radio station, WKDK, was established in May 1946 by the Clarkson group.[16] John F. Clarkson was president; C. A. Kaufmann, executive vice-president; and George Martin, chief engineer. James F. Coggins of Anderson took over the management of the station in 1949 and now owns the company. It has been a successful venture.

Coggins has been extremely active in community affairs, serving as president of the Rotary Club, the Chamber of Commerce, and the county Development Board. He, his wife, the former Marcia Parke, and his son, James P. Coggins, all participate in the broadcasting. Ernest Ray Gilliam, Sr., has been chief engineer for many years.

In 1949, during Andrew Pickens Salley's administration as mayor, Newberry employed its first city manager.[17] Edward L. Blackwell came to Newberry from Florence. A native of Darlington County, he had served in the United States Corps of Engineers during World War II and later as city manager of Florence. He was to stay twelve years and introduce some efficient reforms in the municipal government.

Among the new businesses established by local citizens during this period (1945–1964) and still flourishing are Carter & Holmes, Senn Trucking Company, Cannon Construction Company, Fulmer Building Supplies, Dickert Lumber Company, Bergen's, West Electric Company, and Eagle Construction Company.

Of these the most unique and one of the best known is Carter & Holmes. William C. Carter and his first cousin, Owen McRee Holmes, started a small floral shop shortly after the war. They soon became the largest orchid growers in the South. The company occupies large greenhouses on Mendenhall Road, and visitors from all over the United States and, indeed, from Japan and other countries are attracted to the exotic plants and flowers now grown here and shipped all over the world.

Both Carter and Holmes are natives of the county and graduates of Newberry College. Carter married Mary Ellen McLaurin, while Holmes married Rae Hughes. The latter couple has one child, Owen McRee IV, who is an attorney in Atlanta. Both Carter and Holmes are active in community affairs. Both were founding members of the Newberry County Historical Society and Holmes has served as president of that organization. Carter, chairman of the county Park Commission, has now retired, but Holmes operates this interesting business with the help of some twenty-eight employees.

Another widely known, and the largest locally owned business, is Senn Trucking Company. Established by Angus D. Senn and his brother, Billy P. Senn, as a small trucking outfit in 1955, it has developed into a national flatbed carrier operating in all states east of the Mississippi River. It has diversified into vans and currently owns some 85 percent of its rolling stock. The remaining 15 percent of its 300 vehicles are under contract. The company employs more than 300 people.

The company utilizes the most modern computer systems and has terminals in other states. A family operation, the two original partners still manage the business with the assistance of their sons. The business was incorporated in 1960 and occupies handsome quarters on Highways 34 and 121.

In 1949 Edward O. Cannon established a construction company in Newberry. Cannon, an engineering graduate of the University of South Carolina and a Naval officer in World War II, was recalled to the service during the Korean War. However, he returned to Newberry and expanded his company. It became one of the largest commercial building firms in the Midlands and enjoys an excellent reputation. Cannon has now retired, but is president of the Newberry County Historical Society and a generous benefactor of Newberry College. His wife, the former Elizabeth Huffman, died on November 25, 1984, survived by her husband and two daughters, Linda and Ann. His son-in-law, C. Otis Taylor, Jr., a native of Columbia and graduate of the University of South Carolina, now operates the company with fifty employees. The Taylors have three children, Cannon, Otis, III, and Amelia.

During the post-war decade, Al Spotts organized Eagle Construction Company, which employs 119 people and specializes in road building, and J. W. Dickert and Earl Dickert established Dickert Lumber Company, Inc., with sixty employees. It is the largest locally owned lumber company in the county.

Billye L. West opened a small electric business that has become a multi-state operation employing fifty people. He also has other interests, including a marine center, a development company, and a dealership for Star Metal Buildings.

Another local business important to Newberry is Ira T. Cousins, Inc. The late Ira T. Cousins, after many years as a cotton buyer and ginner, built the first liquid fertilizer plant in South Carolina. In 1960 he added a seed processing plant. Today the company is recognized for certified seed sold throughout the South.

Upon Cousins' death, his sons Warren and Walter took over the operation. Both are graduates of Clemson and served in the U.S. Army. Warren has served as president of the South Carolina Seedsmen's Association and been recognized as seedsman of the year. Walter, a member of the local board of Citizens and Southern National Bank, has been named conservationist of the year for South Carolina and is a member of the South Carolina Land Resources Conservation Commission and chairman of the Newberry County Soil Conservation Committee.

Jacob S. Fulmer, native of the county and veteran of World War II, established a building supply company upon returning home from service. He has expanded it into one of the largest and best-run businesses in the county.

P. Duncan Johnson organized his company in 1955 when the old Johnson-McCrackin interests were divided. He was for years the distributor in Newberry for International Harvestor, now Case-International, and for Holland. In 1990 he took over the John Deere distributorship and reorganized the company as Johnson Equipment Co., Inc. Since his retirement, the company has been under the management of his son, Gordon B. Johnson, and continues to be successful in the farm machinery business; Gordon Johnson is president of the Farm Machinery Dealers Association of the Carolinas.

Earl H. Bergen, native of North Augusta, graduate of Newberry College and former Naval officer, opened a men's clothing store in Newberry in 1948. He expanded his business to include a separate ladies' shop, a gift shop, and a store in Chester. A former member of the House of Representatives and the Highway Commission, he has now turned over the operation of his several businesses to his children but still maintains an interest in them.

Paul Whitaker opened Whitaker Floor Coverings in 1947 and has steadily enlarged his business. Today the company is located on Winnsboro Road and employs twenty people. Whitaker's son, John Paul Whitaker, is now president of the corporation.

During the post-war period various natives brought recognition to the county. In athletics Billy O'Dell, Mike Livingston, and John

Buzhardt played major league baseball, as did Johnnie Werts before the war. After being the star pitcher in the All-Star Game of 1958 by retiring fifteen batters in succession,[18] O'Dell was honored by a well attended dinner at the Country Club of Newberry.

Miss Rankin Suber, daughter of Mr. and Mrs. Walter S. Suber of Whitmire, won third place in the Miss America Pageant at Atlantic City. Mrs. E. Gordon Able, Mrs. Ralph Parr Baker, and Mrs. Thomas Littlejohn headed the South Carolina Medical Auxiliary, and Mrs. Richard L. Baker was president of the Garden Club of South Carolina. John Wainwright Chappell served as president of the Children of the Confederacy, and Mrs. L. E. Gatlin was selected as South Carolina Mother of the Year. Most recently, Police Chief Andrew Shealy has served as president of the state Law Enforcement Association, and John Long as president of the South Carolina Soybean Association; Long is now treasurer of the American Soybean Association.[19]

The Newberry Historical Society was organized in 1964[20] and has been a force for good in the community. Through its efforts a number of historic landmarks have been designated and suitably marked.

During the post-war period the Newberry County Airport was constructed 3 miles from town. A modern water filtering plant was built in 1973 on the Saluda River, from which pure water is supplied by the city of Newberry to itself, the town of Saluda, and the Newberry Water and Sewer Authority. A new waste water treatment plant was constructed by the city on Bush River in 1984.

The city has a well-run recreation department, and it is augmented by a family YMCA opened in 1986. A good eighteen-hole golf course, the Mid-Carolina Country Club, provides a second eighteen-hole golf course for the county, the older one being the Country Club of Newberry that opened soon after World War I. Whitmire has a nine-hole course.

Very few homes were built in Newberry from World War I until World War II, but a large number of subdivisions have opened since then. All have been on the eastern side of the city which is building toward Interstate 26.

In 1968, through the efforts of Congressman William Jennings Bryan Dorn and local leaders, the old post office building on the corner of College and Friend streets was secured for the Newberry-Saluda Regional Library. It is a well-built structure and makes a splendid library. Bookmobiles travel through the two counties, a boon to rural readers.

In 1984 a savage tornado swept up Main Street, resulting in the destruction of St. Luke's Episcopal Church and a number of downtown stores. The church has been reconstructed, but the business section of the town bears the marks of the storm.

In 1945 the Newberry County Hospital became the Newberry County Memorial Hospital. Public subscriptions for new construction amounted to $51,000 and the trustees of the hospital set aside sufficient funds to provide a suitable memorial to the dead of World War II on the hospital grounds.

A memorial commission was named by the Hospital Board that included representatives of the American Legion posts in Newberry and Whitmire, the Veterans of Foreign Wars posts in Newberry and Whitmire, and of the American Legion Auxiliary and the Auxiliary of the Veterans of Foreign Wars in Newberry. Albert G. McCaughrin was named chairman, the other members being E. Maxcy Stone, Albert Farah, George Duncan, Sudie Dennis, and Eva Dorrity Welling. Jake R. Wise, as county service officer, coordinated the activities of the commission. Irvine Leslie drew the plans and Carolina Royal Blue Granite Company was awarded the contract for the memorial.

The Newberry County Memorial Hospital was dedicated on May 30, 1951, and a memorial was erected on the hospital grounds[21] where it remained until 1982 when it was removed to Memorial Square opposite the Opera House. The hospital had been moved to a new location and the memorial was not being kept in good condition.

On the memorial are two panels of bronze on which the following names of those who died in World War II are inscribed:

James C. Allen	John Coleman Carlisle
Harry N. Anderson	George C. Clamp
Robert H. Anderson, Jr.	Ira L. Clamp, Jr.
Great Brittain Arrowood	Floyd E. Cook
Henry P. Baker	Dewey O. Cromer
Carol E. Banks	William T. Crosby
Carroll Bedenbaugh	Sewell W. Crouch
Lorenzo D. Bedenbaugh, Jr.	Charles Douglas Crump
Thomas Bellue	Fred J. Cumalander
James W. Bolton	Lawrence H. Davis
Clarence O. Bouknight	Thomas E. Davis
Howard E. Boulware	Thompson Calvin Dennis
Edward E. Brock	Grady M. Derrick
Olin L. Bundrick	Dewey W. Duffie

Robert Y. Evans
Heyward H. Fellers
Richard H. Fellers
Robert C. Fellers
Paul S. Floyd
Thomas E. Folk
Floyd A. Fulmer
Vassel L. Gallman
Floyd V. Gilliam
William Glasco
Albert Glascow
William Bennet Goodman
Thomas W. Graddick
Charles H. Grant
Doyle W. Griffith
William J. Grogan
Elijah W. Harrison, Jr.
James R. Hayes
Edwin O. Hentz
James E. Hentz
Clarence D. Hunter
Johnnie T. Hutcherson
James A. Johnson
Roosevelt Johnson
William T. Jones
Rupert E. Koon
David P. Leopard
Alfred M. Little
Alvin E. Livingston
Howard L. Livingston
Ashley C. Long
Homer L. Long
Carl C. Martin
John B. Mayes

Robert P. McCall
William L. McCullough
William S. McMurray, Jr.
Jimmie G. Metchicas
Lewis Midyette
Gus T. Mills
John M. Morris, Jr.
John H. Moseley, Jr.
Carl E. Nichols
Robert P. Norris
Thomas M. Owens, Jr.
Fred L. Paysinger
Hubert Praylow
Winfield O. Price
Marion E. Reed
Bennie T. Roton
James L. Sanders
Harold A. Senn
Bernard E. Shealy
James M. Shealy
Mendel W. Shealy
Noah I. Shealy
James P. Singleton
Maxie Spearman
Ralph H. Summer
Lawrence E. Summers
Hubert L. Swygert
John Thracker
Virgil Washington
Clarence R. Wise
David H. Wise
Grady L. Wise, Jr.
Howard Yon

Before the memorial could be dedicated, the community faced the realization that the country was at war again, this time in Korea. Private First Class George Frank Morris, nineteen years old from the Prosperity section, was killed.

Although no memorial has yet been erected to the memory of those who died in service during the Korean War the following men should be honored:

Charles J. Bartley	Nathan Holman
Eddie Burton	Horace J. Longshore
Odell Caldwell	Roy E. Mayer
James Odis Clamp	George Frank Morris
Ralph D. Davis	Julian Tribble
William D. Franklin	Donald C. Vinson
William E. Garnett	Hughie A. White
George E. Gary	James Whitener
Harry H. Griffin	

The period before 1965 was one of preparation for future diversification. Electric power had been available for new industry for years. Natural gas became available with the establishment of the Clinton-Newberry Natural Gas Authority in 1953; this utility now serves Newberry County, most of Laurens County, and a part of Spartanburg County. Water became available in the rural areas with the establishment of the Newberry Water & Sewer Authority in 1963. These utilities are crucial, of course, to industrial development.

Newberry County continues to be primarily an agricultural county although great efforts have been made to diversify the economy. The late John F. Clarkson contributed more to this effort than any other individual. Since his death the search for new industry has been led by James F. Coggins and J. Thomas Johnson, who is currently a member of the State Development Board.

Johnson, a native of Columbia, came to Newberry in 1977 as an employee of Newberry Federal Savings and Loan Association. A graduate of the University of South Carolina, he has been extremely active in community affairs, having served as president of the Newberry County Historical Society, president of the county Development Board, and chairman of the Bicentennial Committee. Newberry College gave him the Algernon Sidney Sullivan Award in 1987. He is president of Newberry Federal Savings Bank. Married to the former Sarah Elizabeth Biggs, he has a son, J. Thomas Johnson, Jr., a midshipman at the United States Naval Academy, and a daughter, Sarah Ashford Johnson. They are active members of Central United Methodist Church.

At this time a number of industrial plants give much-needed employment. Some are intimately connected with agriculture, and others are not. Of the former group, ISE America, Inc. processes eggs; Newberry Feed and Seed Center handles animal feed; Bedenbaugh Seed Co., Inc. of Prosperity deals in seed and feed; Counts Sausage Co. of Prosperity processes pork and beef products; and Ira T. Cousins, Inc., sells fertilizer and certified seed.

Louis Rich, which is the county's largest employer, employs 1,200 people. It processes turkeys that are delivered daily from several states. Other agri-businesses include Champion International, Georgia-Pacific, Westvaco, Federal Paper Board, Dickert Lumber Co., Inc., Haltiwanger Lumber Co., Inc., John R. Frazier, Inc., H. M. Hentz & Son, and Derrick Lumber Co. of Little Mountain, all of which deal with the timber industry.

Textile plants include American Fiber and Finishing, which employs 675; J. P. Stevens, Inc. of Whitmire, which employs 330; Kayser-Roth Hosiery, Inc., which employs 800; Setlowear, Inc. of Prosperity, which employs 290; Glenn Manufacturing of Whitmire, which employs 60; and Damon International, Ltd., which employs 85.

Of these textile plants, American Fiber and J. P. Stevens, Inc. are pre-World War II installations, while the others are new. Oakland Cotton Mill was organized by local interests in 1912 and acquired by the Kendall Company in 1925.

Renovated in 1950, the mill was successfully operated under the leadership of Southern managers. These were D. O. Carpenter, L. Hart Jordan, and G. Robert Hawkins. Hawkins, graduate of Clemson University and a member of the U.S. Marine Corps in World War II, was the first native Newberrian to manage the mill after World War II. He did an excellent job until his retirement. He is married to the former Caroline Huffman and they have three sons, Robert, Jr., Bruce, and William.

In 1985 the mill was sold to J. J. Kizer and E. C. Shotwell. It is now American Fiber and Finishing Company, Inc., and its manager is Gilbert Webber. J. P. Stevens, Inc. was constructed as Glenn-Lowry Manufacturing Company in 1902 and became the wholly owned subsidiary of West Point-Pepperell, Inc. in 1988.

Other non-textile plants established since 1965 include Shakespeare, which produces communications antennas and employs 157 people; Nekoosa Packaging Plant, which makes corrugated containers and employs 108 people; Norris Industries, which produces automobile wheel covers and employs 310 people; Pleasurecraft Marine Engine Co., which manufactures Sunliner pleasure boats and has fifty employees; Glassmaster Co., maker of fiberglass products and employer of forty-seven people; Precision Fiberglass Industries, which employs twenty-four people; Metal Masters, which employs twenty-six people; and Hobby Construction Company and Hobby Timber Resources, employing seventy-five people.

Announcement was made in January 1990 that Federal Paper Board would construct a plant below Prosperity for the manufacture of extrusion coating. The plant will cost between $15 million and $20 million and it will initially employ fifty persons.

In recent years the county acquired two additional banks. The Citizens and Southern National Bank was opened in Newberry in 1978, with a local board consisting of Dr. James E. Wiseman, Jr., Dr. Robert E. Livingston, III, Craig W. Morehead, Walter B. Cousins, and John Hammond. Later additions include Don Dowling, Dr. Hubert H. Setzler, Jr., and Gary T. Pope. Michael G. Davenport was the original manager and was succeeded in 1987 by John W. Britton, Jr.

In 1987 local interests organized Midlands National Bank with banking offices in Prosperity and Chapin. The original directors were Jacob A. Bowers, Jr., Monte Bowers, David Bowers, J. Walter Hamm, C. Gurnie Stuck, Earl H. Bergen, J. Dan Hamm, Jr., Rodney Griffin, C. W. Ellett, Terry Koon, and Heyward Shealy. David Bowers is the managing officer.

These two new banks brought the number of financial institutions in the county to seven: South Carolina National Bank, North Carolina National Bank, the Citizens & Southern National Bank, First Union National Bank, Newberry Federal Savings Bank, Midlands National Bank, and First Federal of South Carolina. Of these, Newberry Federal Savings Bank is the largest locally owned financial institution.

Chartered by the state of South Carolina in 1930, it became Newberry Federal Savings and Loan Association in 1935 and Newberry Federal Savings Bank in 1988. The original board of directors in 1935 consisted of John F. Clarkson, president; M. O. Summer, vice-president; E. B. Purcell, secretary-treasurer; J. K. Willingham, Dr. C. D. Weeks, and Clarence C. Hutto. Clarkson was succeeded by Willingham as president, and he by J. Thomas Johnson in 1984.

John Keister Willingham, son of James H. and Maggie McCullough Willingham, was born in Newberry on September 12, 1908, and died on October 12, 1987. He married Aurelia Watkins; they had two children, Joan and John Keister. Willingham was associated with Newberry Federal Savings and Loan Association for more than fifty years. He was president of the South Carolina Savings and Loan League and of the

Southeastern Group of the U.S. Savings and Loan League and a member of the local advisory board of the South Carolina National Bank. He was a member of the Newberry Rotary Club and of Cannon Creek ARP Church.

The current directors are Johnson, Paul M. DeLoache, Arthur E. Morehead, Robert W. Owen, Keitt Purcell, and Thomas H. Pope; Waldo C. Huffman is director emeritus.

Newberry Federal has branches in Saluda, Batesburg, Chapin, Prosperity, and on Wilson Road. Its assets are currently some $165 million, and it is a full-service banking institution.

In addition to Station WKDK, Newberry now has two other locally owned radio stations. WKMG, an AM station, was established by Connie Gowen and Roscoe Bedenbaugh. Station WNMX, an FM station, was opened in 1988 by Mr. and Mrs. Hayne Davis.

In the 1960s America was embroiled in the war in Vietnam. Although a division of public support resulted in demonstrations against war, none occurred in Newberry. Men and women from this county entered service and did their full share in supporting the general government. Not accorded the attention they deserved, it was not until 1986 that the Vietnam Memorial was established in Memorial Square by American Legion Post 24. Rodney Griffin, operator of a local construction company, led the effort to pay tribute to those from this area who died in the war. Alvin Jackson, as commander of American Legion Post 24, was instrumental in the erection of the marker.

The memorial in Newberry honors the following who died in their country's service during the Vietnam War:

Jerry M. Achey	Albert D. Owens
Michael R. Agnew	Leonard C. Pitts
Clifton Edward Arnold	Melvin Reeder
Jesse R. Baker	Leonda Sartor
William G. Coates	Bruce E. Saxon
James W. Crenshaw	Bobby Lewis Singley
Dennis G. Farmer	Robert A. Street
David Gibson	Bobby Ray Trapp
Allen S. Kohn	Curtiss Eugene Walker
Thomas I. Long	Carol E. Williams
Wilbur E. Magbee	

Part II

13

Agriculture

At the outbreak of the Civil War, Newberry's economy was based solidly on cotton. Negro slaves outnumbered whites by almost two to one; eleven planters in the district each owned more than 100 slaves.[1] There were 841 farms. The district was producing 17,476 bales of cotton and 452,191 bushels of corn. Livestock was valued at almost a million dollars.[2]

Five years of war played havoc with the economy. The farms suffered from neglect, the land eroded, and the livestock was seriously depleted. Buildings and fences fell into disrepair, and farm tools became scarce.[3]

To compound their problems, farmers had difficulty in inducing the freedmen to work their lands. A labor force was essential to survival, and various methods were tried. Some landowners hired hands for wages, some rented their lands to the freedmen, and others entered into sharecropping arrangements.

Most farmers in Newberry County preferred to pay wages to their workers. The prevailing wages after Reconstruction were eight dollars a month or fifty cents a day. Landowners furnished wagehands with shelter, rations, and firewood, and gave each family a garden patch and the privilege of raising poultry and keeping a pig and cow.[4]

During the first years of peace, sharecropping agreements required the approval of the military.[5] Much dissatisfaction resulted from the division of the harvest between landowner and tenant. Until it was disbanded, the Freedmen's Bureau approved contracts and tried to arbitrate disputes. A sample contract is shown in Appendix I. Bureau officials also encouraged the freedmen to work.[6]

When the Bureau passed into oblivion, no further effort was made to provide governmental supervision for the making of labor contracts. By that time sharecropping had come to mean a system in which the land-owner furnished land, fertilizer, seed, mules, shelter, rations, and garden patches for the use of the tenant, while the tenant furnished the labor. At the end of the crop year the cost of fertilizer, seed, ginning, and rations was paid first, and then the balance of the proceeds of sale was divided. The tenant generally received from a third to a half of the net proceeds.[7]

The least popular system was that of renting land either for a fixed number of bales of cotton or for a percentage of the cotton crop. In the nineteenth century the rental in Newberry County was usually from 100 to 300 pounds of cotton per acre. Some owners rented a one-horse farm of 30 acres for two bales of cotton while others required a fourth of the crop as rent. Not many landowners liked to rent their lands because renters were prone to exhaust the soil and fail to keep up the fences and other improvements.[8]

An agricultural inventory made in 1868 showed that in Newberry County only half as many acres were cultivated as on the eve of the Civil War, only half as much cotton and grain was produced, and the live-stock was seriously depleted. Only a third as much honey, wine, and butter was produced as in 1860; only two-thirds as much wool and a tenth as much beeswax was produced. No silk cocoons were grown.[9]

The depression of 1873 added to the plight of the farmers. Many were forced into bankruptcy. Dispossessed farmers were forced into tenancy. Since few blacks owned land, most of them became tenants.[10] With cotton bringing less than ten cents a pound during most of the last quarter of the nineteenth century, tenants simply could not pull themselves out of economic bondage. This was the era of the lien merchant, high inter-est rates, no conveniences, and hard work to survive. By 1900, sixty-one of every hundred South Carolina farmers were tenants.[11]

The leading Negro in the county was Lewis Duckett of Cromer Township. His story as told to a reporter of the *Greenville News* was reprinted in the *Newberry Herald* of February 23, 1881:

> I was freed in 1865 but continued working with my former master for one year, making that year nothing beyond my living. From that time until April 1867 I rented land from Mr. Duncan, taking one-third of the crop. I sold my share in April 1867 and realized enough from it to put me through the following year and had over $400, which I lent out at 15 per cent interest. While renting land at a cash rent of $1200 a year, I was

burned out, losing 60 bales of cotton and 1400 bushels of cotton seed. 1 commenced buying land in 1869 and have continued adding to my original purchase of 130 acres and now own 796 acres. I own besides 8 head of stock, 10 milk cows, 4 yearlings and 25 hogs. My crop this year made on the part of the farm I manage myself is 61 bales of cotton, averaging 600 lbs. to the bale, 1000 bushels of corn, and 80 bushels of red rust proof oats. My renters made 57 bales of cotton, 700 bu. of oats and 150 bu. of wheat.

Duckett was an unusual man who proved that industry and economy could produce results. He was respected by both whites and blacks and, when the Newberry Agricultural Society was organized in 1878, Duckett and J. P. Sims, another black leader, were admitted to membership.[12] In that same year Duckett was elected president of the Christian Association organized at Flint Hill Church.[13] In 1880, he became chairman of the Executive Committee of the Future Progress Society[14] and in that year he was a Republican candidate for county commissioner.[15]

During the latter part of the century some effort was made to get away from total dependence on cotton. John R. Spearman, a planter of the Silverstreet community, brought the first Guernseys to South Carolina in 1880. He was one of the initial members of the American Guernsey Cattle Club, and he registered "Bemba 500" as the first purebred Guernsey bull bred in South Carolina.[16] However, it was to be many years before cattle would vie with cotton in Newberry County.

In 1883, Colonel A. P. Butler, state commissioner of agriculture, made the first serious effort by any government official to analyze the resources, people, and institutions of South Carolina. He employed Harry Hammond, who concluded that farm conditions had improved in Newberry County and attributed this in part to The National Bank of Newberry, saying that "under the excellent and judicious management of its president, Robert L. McCaughrin, the operations of this bank have added largely to the prosperity and independence of the county, which, besides leading in cotton production in proportion to its area, is, in many regards, the most thriving in the region."[17]

Newberry County farmers, however, were attracted to Populism because of the economic squeeze in which they found themselves. The lien system, the low price of cotton, and the uncertainty of labor made their livelihood a precarious one.

As the nineteenth century drew to an end, Newberry farmers still clung to the one-crop economy that had long existed. In 1899, the county produced more than 24,000 bales of cotton; it brought only seven cents a pound and amounted to much less than a million dollars. Livestock was worth just half its value of 1860. Poultry was beginning to be a significant economic factor,[18] but milk and beef cattle were still relatively unimportant.

One new crop was produced in Newberry County at the end of the century. A Tobacco Growers Association was formed in 1899,and it brought W. F. Harrell of Florence to Newberry to help the group.[19] The next year 3,540 pounds of tobacco were grown on lands of Osborne Wells, C. J. Purcell, C. W. Bishop, S. P. Crotwell, and E. P. Pawley.[20]

The twentieth century has seen an agricultural revolution in New-berry County. Cotton is no longer grown commercially. Poultry, beef cattle, dairying, and forest products are the chief money makers for Newberry farmers. Soybeans are a secondary crop. The story of these changes and the men who made them possible is the story of agriculture in this century.

Cotton continued to be Newberry's only money crop until World War II. The boll weevil, the depression of 1921, the Great Depression of 1930, low prices, the exhaustion of the soil, competition from irrigated farms in the West, and the rising costs of labor and production resulted in the elimination of cotton as a cash crop.

In 1909, nine Newberry County farmers raised cotton as demonstra-tors, and they produced more than 1,400 pounds per acre.[21] The follow-ing year 75,662 acres were planted in cotton,[22] the largest in the county's history. When America entered World War I, the price of cotton soared and local farmers were more affluent than at any time since 1860. Pros-perity lasted only a short time before the boll weevil and the depression of 1921 took their toll. Although 35,000 bales of cotton were produced in Newberry County in 1920,[23] by 1944 only 12,000 bales were har-vested.[24] Cotton lost its importance to the county's economy by the end of World War II.

By 1966 cash receipts from cotton only amounted to $179,000; in that year receipts from soybeans were $293,000.[25] By 1975 there was only one cotton farmer left in the county; Harrison Reeder planted 4 acres of cotton in that year. Thus ended King Cotton's reign in Newberry County.

Meanwhile, despite efforts to improve the production of corn, the county total decreased. In 1917, Ernest Brooks of the O'Neall section won first place in a statewide corn-growing contest. He produced 89 bushels of corn an acre at a cost of seventeen cents a bushel.[26] Eight years later Willie Pat Boland of Pomaria won a silver cup presented by the Southern Railway Company for the ten best ears of corn grown in the Southeast. He was given a trip to Washington where he was honored guest at a luncheon given by the Chamber of Commerce on one day and was presented to President Coolidge at the White House the next day.[27]

However, despite these good showings in contests, corn production continued to decline. In 1900, the county produced one-third of a million bushels but after 1955 the annual yield took a sharp drop and by 1973 only 197,000 bushels were being produced. In 1979, 202,500 bushels were produced but in 1987, the number was 125,500 bushels.[28] Most of the corn produced was used for silage and is not included in these figures.

Soybeans were not introduced until the 1960s. In 1960 only 26,400 bushels were grown in the county;[29] by 1971 the yield had risen dramatically to 211,000 bushels. In 1979 the yield was 398,000 bushels, but in 1987 it dwindled to only 137,400 bushels.[30]

In 1900 poultry was valued at $20,241. The number of eggs produced was 222,140 dozen.[31] By 1920 the county was producing 290,097 dozen eggs[32] but by 1940 this number had nearly doubled to 566,122 dozen.[33] Two decades later the number had risen to 2,492,637 dozen.[34] By 1970 Newberry County was the number one county in South Carolina in production of chickens and eggs. The value of its eggs rose to $8,777,000 by 1974,[35] to $9,732,000 by 1977, to $16,670,000 by 1980, and to $17,056,000 by 1987.[36]

Much of the advance in chicken and egg production is due to the efforts of three families in Newberry—the Waldrops, the Senns, and the Cooks. David C. Waldrop and his brothers, Ralph and Jefferson, established a local egg plant in Trinity community in 1952. It prospered and so did a feed mill that the Waldrops developed.

Merging with the Senn brothers, Frank and George Foster, the Waldrops moved their operations to Newberry where they established a modern feed mill and egg plant. Central Soya, one of the giants of the feed industry, subsequently merged with this local company and operated a large, fully integrated facility in Newberry until 1982 when the facility was acquired by a Japanese-backed company, ISE-America. ISE has its own hatchery, breeder farms, feed mill, egg processing plant, and sales force. David C. Waldrop organized the local plant and served as its first manager until his retirement in 1976. John R. Hammond succeeded him as manager, but Waldrop remained a vice president of the company until 1978.

The Waldrop brothers are sons of the late Jefferson C. and Vesta Pitts Waldrop. Born in the county, they have worked hard and done well.

David C. Waldrop, the oldest brother, operates Trinity Farms with his son, David, Jr., and son-in-law, James W. Kesler. He has a large Jersey herd. Possessing vision and daring, he has become one of the most influential farmers in South Carolina and at the same time has helped to establish Newberry as the leading laying chicken and egg producing county in South Carolina. The Saluda River Farm owned by Waldrop, his son, and his son-in-law has the largest egg producing unit in the county; it has 300,000 layers.

Appointed by President Ford in 1975 as a member of the Farm Credit Commission, Waldrop represented the southeastern states on this important agency. He has served on the Palmetto Production Credit Association Board, the South Carolina Dairy Commission, the Newberry Electric Cooperative Board, the Central Electric Cooperative Board, the Advisory Board of Bankers Trust of South Carolina, and the Newberry County Water and Sewer Authority. Married to Jewel Ellenberg of Greenwood, they had two children, David C. Waldrop, Jr., former chairman of the Newberry County Council and current legislator, and Lynda Kesler, who died in 1986. In 1982 more than 400 friends attended a testimonial dinner at the Newberry Armory tendered Waldrop and Clifford T. Smith for their contributions to the county's agricultural progress.

Frank Senn, son of J. Foster and Elizabeth McMillan Senn, was born in Newberry County and educated in local schools. He was one of the pioneers in hatching eggs and selling them to Southeastern Poultry Company in Batesburg. Later, he joined with the Waldrop brothers to build the local feed mill and egg plant that have meant much to Newberry County.

After the merger with Central Soya, Senn withdrew to continue in the dairying and egg producing business with his two sons, Charles and Frank M., Jr. They have an egg producing unit operated in conjunction with ISE America, having 70,000 laying hens. Frank Senn was for some years president of the Farmers Mutual Fire Insurance Association and is a former chairman of the board of the Newberry County Memorial Hospital and a former member of the County Soil Conservation Committee. He married Audrey Senn.

The Cook brothers, Max and Harold, are sons of Sam and Eunice Halfacre Cook. Harold married Ola Burton of Newberry, while Max married Dorothy DuBose of Wilmington, North Carolina. They established an independent business in 1969 and are among the largest independent egg producers in Newberry County, keeping a flock of 100,000 laying hens. The Cook brothers process and package their eggs, which they sell to a number of chain stores and numerous retail stores.

Others who maintain large laying flocks are James Quattlebaum, Ralph Cromer, James Long, Haskell Long, Joe Kesler, Dave Greenslade, Travis Moore, Gerald Dukes, Mrs. Eugenia Johnson and her son John Mitchell Johnson, the Neel brothers, and Trinity Farms.

Another phase of ISE's business involves the raising of pullets from day-old chicks. Growers of pullets include Johnnie Pitts, Jimmy Haltiwanger, Irons brothers and the Greenfield Farms of Joseph Watters. Frank Senn is the largest producer of pullets, having 200,000 of them.

Turkeys became an important part of Newberry's economy during World War II and continued to be for twenty years. The industry was established by Waldo C. Huffman, who returned to his native county in 1939 after managing Thornwell Orphanage's turkey operations for five years.

Son of the late John A. and Floyd Aull Huffman, he was born in the Little Mountain section. He graduated from Clemson College in 1925. Married to Sara Setzler of Pomaria, he has two daughters, Caroline H. Hawkins and Evelyn H. Pridgen.

Huffman set up a sharecropping system by which he helped many farmers raise a profitable crop. From an annual production of 3,553 turkeys in 1939,[37] the number rose to 30,130 by 1949,[38] to 107,527 by 1959,[39] and to 141,087 in 1964.[40] Income from turkeys exceeded a million dollars a year, and Newberry County was at that time one of the largest producers of turkeys in South Carolina.

Huffman organized and was first president of the South Carolina Turkey Federation. He also served for ten years as a member of the South Carolina Marketing Commission, helped build the new Farmers Market in Columbia, and for many years was a director of the Newberry County Bank and its successor, Bankers Trust, and of Newberry Federal Savings and Loan Association. At the time of his retirement, he was first vice president of the National Turkey Federation.

After Huffman retired in the early 1960s, the turkey crop dropped dramatically. Today this important agricultural activity is being revived. In 1989 four producers turned out 290,000 turkeys. They were Carl B. Setzler and his sons, Carl, Jr., and Charles; Earl Bozard and his son, Bryan; Tom Riser; and Dr. J. J. Malnati and his grandson, Ricky Doran. Newberry Feed and Farm Center, Inc. produced 16,000 tons of feed valued at $3,200,000 in 1989. Before the county temporarily abandoned turkey raising, Ocoma Foods erected a huge turkey-processing plant in Newberry. It is now owned by Louis Rich Company and is supplied with turkeys from South Carolina and other states, processing 5 million turkeys a year.

At the beginning of the century Newberry County had only 2,691 milk cows and 3,943 beef cattle. Out of 1,000,000 gallons of milk produced, less than 10,000 gallons were sold, the rest being consumed at home. All dairy products were valued at $80,864.[41]

Among the early dairies was Innisfallen Dairy owned by Andrew J. McCaughrin[42] and later by his nephew, Silas J. McCaughrin. Its herd consisted of purebred Jerseys and was managed by G. M. Berry. When the Mollohon Manufacturing Company was organized in 1909, the dairy was sold and the mill built on the property. This dairy was perhaps the first to deliver milk to the people of the town; old-timers remember that Silas McCaughrin did so with large containers from which the various customers dipped pitchers of milk.

Other early dairymen were Joe Williams, the black undertaker; Thomas Meek Neel at Springfield; Robert G. Smith, who established his Dry Creek Dairy Farm in 1915 at Kinards; Welch Wilbur, near the current site of the Country Club of Newberry; Ed Senn, on the Belfast Road; and Wright Dennis in the Hartford section. And as has been mentioned, John R. Spearman pioneered with purebred Guernseys in 1880.

After World War I, the dairies supplying the town were those of Neel, Williams, and Dennis, and Sanitary Dairy owned by George W. Summer and operated by Jesse Frank Hawkins. After his father's death, Neel's dairy was operated successfully for many years by his son, T. Collier Neel. Meanwhile, Clifford T. Smith established his model Valley Farm Dairy and C. B. Parr established Head Spring Dairy, which was later taken over by his son, Henry L. Parr. William E. Senn succeeded his father in the Senn Dairy and Leon Dennis succeeded his father in the Dennis Dairy.

The Smith-Lever Act, named for Senator Hoke Smith of Georgia and Congressman Asbury Frank Lever, Newberry College graduate from the Dutch Fork, made possible the teaching of agriculture by demonstration. County agents and home demonstration agents taught farmers how and what to produce and farmers' wives how to make comfortable homes for their families. The Extension Service was the result of the Smith-Lever Act.

Thomas Marion Mills, appointed on March 1, 1914, served as

Newberry County's first county agent. A native of the county, graduate of Lenoir College, and school teacher in Newberry schools for twenty-three years, he served as county agent for fifteen years. During World War II he returned to help his successor. Mills also was secretary-treasurer of the Newberry County Terracing Association, trustee of O'Neall School, and superintendent of the Sunday School of Zion Methodist Church. He died at the age of eighty-three on February 15, 1953. He first married Sallie Long and then Ruth Lindler Meetz. He was survived by his second wife and his only child, Carroll S. Mills, son of his first wife.[43]

Mills's successor as county agent was Paul Bryson Ezell. A native of Blythewood, Richland County, he was a graduate of Clemson, veteran of the 30th Infantry Division during World War I, and teacher of vocational agriculture in Spartanburg County before assuming the duties of county agent on March 1, 1929. He served as Newberry County agent for twenty-eight years and was active as deacon of the First Baptist Church of Newberry and in the affairs of American Legion Post 24 until his death on January 2, 1972. He married Helen Johnson; they had two children, Ernest J. Ezell and Louise E. Dawkins.[44]

Newberry's third county agent was Albert F. Busby. Native of Anderson County and graduate of Clemson College in dairying, he served as assistant county agent in Lancaster County for three years and in Chester County for four years. He was transferred to Newberry County in the same capacity in 1957; the following year he succeeded Ezell. In January 1971 he resigned and purchased the Senn Dairy on the Belfast Road. Busby, with his sons and nephew, operated this fine Jersey dairying operation until the cattle were sold under the government program looking toward a reduction in dairy cattle. He became area extension agent-dairy for Newberry and several adjoining counties and continued in this position until he retired in 1985. He married Clarice Hobson, who died in 1978; they had three children, A. Foster Busby, Jr., Hobson Busby, and Amy Busby. He married Melvina Hobson Sprunt in 1982.

Busby was succeeded as county agent by Henry L. Eason. A native of Sumter County, graduate of Clemson College in animal husbandry in 1951, assistant county agent of Laurens County for eleven years, and area specialist in livestock for Lancaster, York, Chester, and Fairfield counties for five years, he came to Newberry as county agent in 1972. His title was Newberry County extension leader; he retired in 1985. Eason married Frances Rickmond of Asheville and they have three children, Linda, Bob, and Joe.

Philip O. Epps succeeded Eason as county extension leader. Born in

Charleston, he graduated from Clemson University in 1968 with a B.S. in Forestry; in 1972 he received a B.S. in Wood Science from North Carolina State University and in 1983 a master's degree in Agricultural Education from Clemson University. He served in Germany with the U.S. Army Corps of Engineers from 1968 to 1971, worked in private industry from 1971 to 1974, and joined the Extension Service in 1975. Active in Central United Methodist Church affairs and in the U.S. Army Reserve, he married Judith Halfacre, a native of Newberry.

Newberry's white home demonstration agents from 1914 to the present were Fannie Holloway (1914), Willie Mae Wise (1915–1920), Bessie Campbell (1921), Marian Farish (1921), Daisy Berrie Denning (1921–1924), Ethel Counts (1925–1951), Margie Davis Freeman (1951–1959), Mildred Koger Holliday (1959–1980), and Ruby Carolyn Johnson (1980–1983).[45]

Black home demonstration agents were Laura Whitney Jeter (1938–1943), Naomi Shuler (1944–1946), and Lillian Saunders (1946–1972).[46]

Assistant and associate county agents who have served Newberry are T. F. Cooley (1930–1935), J. L. King (1935–1942), G. J. Mobley (1937–1939), S. A. Williams (1942–1943 and June 1944), J. E. Fagan (1943–1983), W. A. Ridgeway (1944–1957), H. L. Bailey (1947–1948), B. J. Gill (1949–1971), J. O. Donkle (1955–1983), Robert C. McDaniel (1958), Walter Walker (1958–1963), T. J. Bryson (1963–1966), Steve A. Quinn (1968–1969), Jack R. Queener (1970–1975), J. Ray Holliday (1985–1988), Howard Dillon, Jr. (1972–present), Philip O. Epps (1975), and Larry Elmore (1989–).[47]

The present area dairy agent is Michael J. Lovelace (1985–); the area livestock agent is John Irwin (1988–); and Paul Howe (1982–85), Dayne Barron (1985–88), and Brad Sanders (1988–89) have served as forestry agents.

Newberry was the first county in South Carolina to hire a dairy specialist. R. D. Steer came to Newberry in 1920 and his activity was of great benefit to the dairy interests. In May 1922, the Newberry Creamery was chartered. C. T. Summer was the first president; Dr. W. D. Senn, vice president; and T. M. Neel, secretary-treasurer.[48]

The company was reorganized a few years later, and James W. Johnson took over the active operation. He persuaded Jack Hove of Wisconsin to help him and the creamery became highly successful. For many years "Newberry Maid" butter was a popular item throughout the state. After the deaths of Johnson and Hove, Maurice Moseley, son-in-law of Jack Hove, managed the enterprise until it was closed in 1978.

At the outbreak of World War II a group of leading dairymen of the county organized the Newberry Grade A Milk Cooperative, Inc.[49] The founders were C. B. Parr, T. Collier Neel, J. F. Hawkins, W. E. Senn, and Neal W. Workman. Its purpose was to enable the local dairies to handle their output in a more economical manner than individual processing and selling entailed. Unfortunately, the venture failed.

In the same year that the cooperative was established (1942), the Borden Company erected a processing plant for grade "C" milk in Newberry. This plant was next door to the cooperative and prospered for a while but then closed. While neither the Borden plant nor the cooperative lasted more than a few years, they helped the farmers of the county since they offered outlets for dairy products. After these plants closed, local dairymen commenced selling to Pet, Coble, Sealtest, and other chain processors.

By 1960, the county produced 14,000,000 pounds of milk, valued at $2,000,000;[50] by 1980, 77,024,000 pounds, valued at $11,380,000; and by 1987, its dairy products were valued at $11,804,000.[51] Newberry has become the second-highest South Carolina county in milk production, next only to Orangeburg.

Three of Newberry's farmers have been placed in Clemson's Agricultural Hall of Fame—Jesse Frank Hawkins, Callie Boyd Parr, and Clifford T. Smith. Jesse Frank Hawkins was born in Newberry County on November 21, 1887. He was the son of Pierce M. and Mary Jane Swindler Hawkins. He attended the country schools of the county and took a one-year course at Clemson College. Returning to the county, he first operated the Sanitary Dairy for George W. Summer, and then his own dairy; he kept a herd of purebred Guernseys. He was one of the first to sell milk to the residents of the town, delivering to the homes every morning.

He married Anna Dickert of Newberry, and they worked together devotedly for half a century. Industrious, high-principled, and unselfish, he contributed a great deal to the community and to his county. He served four years in the House of Representatives and eight years in the Senate of South Carolina.

Senator Hawkins was active in Ebenezer Methodist Church, serving as chairman of the board, and in farm affairs, he was designated a master farmer and was master of Hartford Grange, director of Clinton Production Credit Association, and president of the Newberry County Cooperative Breeding Association. He was director of the Newberry County Bank and of the Newberry Boys' Farm. More importantly, he helped foster everything of benefit to the farmers of Newberry.

It is fitting that the modern, well-equipped nursing home in Newberry is named the J. F. Hawkins Nursing Home in his honor. He was a
self-made man in the best sense of the word; by dint of honesty and
industry he acquired a competence; he died October 30, 1971, at the age
of eighty-five; after making ample allowance for his wife, he bequeathed
the remainder of his estate to charitable organizations. His farm was
taken over by Marvin H. Hamm whose son, Perry, operates it very successfully today as Myrtledale Farm.

Callie Boyd Parr, son of Henry Lakin and Mary Boyd Parr, was born
in Newberry County on October 18, 1902. He was graduated from Newberry College in 1920 and for a short time was receiver of The Farmers
and Merchants Bank of Little Mountain. Later he returned to his birth-
place near Head Spring and established his dairy. He also managed Standard Warehouse in Newberry. Using purebred Jerseys, he became a
leader in dairying in South Carolina, and was president of the South
Carolina Jersey Club.

In 1958, his health failed and he turned over the farm to his son,
Henry L. Parr. After his retirement, he was active in the South Carolina
Rose Society, which he served as president. Married to Mary Nance of
Newberry, he was the father of five sons, James Nance, C. B., Jr., Henry
L., W. W., and David. He died in 1981, and his wife in 1980.

Clifford T. Smith, son of I. M. and Florence Cromer Smith, was born
at Valley Farm on May 14, 1906. His father died in 1919. He graduated
from Clemson College in 1927 and came back to Valley Farm. By dint of
hard work and intelligent management he made it pay. Acquiring the
interests of his mother, brothers, and sisters, he kept expanding his operations. Paying off the mortgage on the farm, he added other acreage
and bought the most modern dairy equipment. He served as president of
the South Carolina Jersey Cattle Club, director of the Newberry Electric Cooperative, director of Newberry County Memorial Hospital, trustee of the local schools, member of the Advisory Board of the South
Carolina National Bank, and deacon of the Bush River Baptist Church.

He has been a leader in the agricultural affairs of South Carolina.
Active in the affairs of Clemson University and a Master Farm Family
winner, he received the Distinguished Service Award from his alma
mater in 1979, and the Rural Rehabilitation Commission established a
scholarship in his name at Clemson. Married to Helen O'Dell of Pickens, he is father of three daughters, Sylvia (Mrs. Charles Lee Crook),
Linda (Mrs. Edgar Eugene Jones, Jr.), and Mary Helen (Mrs. Harry
Ragland). In 1970, he sold Valley Farm Dairy to W. C. McGinnis.

William E. Senn, son of Edward and Carrie Smith Senn, was another leader in the dairy movement. Born in Newberry County, he was educated at Newberry College, from which he graduated in 1929. His father having died, he succeeded to the operation of the family dairy on Belfast Road. By his industry and attention to duty he succeeded in buying out the interests of his mother, brother, and sisters and in establishing one of the finest dairies in the county.

He has served as president of the South Carolina Jersey Cattle Club, chairman of the Board of Deacons of old Bush River Baptist Church, director of Newberry Electric Cooperative, and in other community enterprises. He married Ruth Bedenbaugh, and they have one daughter, Patsy Ruth (Mrs. Engrum Lee Johnson, Jr.). He retired in 1971 after selling his farm to A. F. Busby, former county agent.

Henry L. Parr has operated Head Spring Dairy with great success, winning many awards for producing milk. A graduate of Clemson College, he has been named a Master Farm Family winner. He married Mittie Bryan of Aiken, and they have four children. Henry, Jr., finished Furman University and graduated with honors in law from the University of Virginia. Mary Boyd graduated from Erskine and is married to Dr. Daniel Whitesides. Boyd Hobson graduated from Clemson University and then studied veterinary medicine at the University of Georgia. Calhoun B. also graduated from Clemson University.

It is not only the men of Newberry County who have been recognized for their leadership roles in agriculture. Mary Ellen Kempson Griffith Blackwell served as president of the South Carolina Farm Women in 1950. Born on a farm in Saluda County, she was first married to Senator Joe Griffith of that county; they had one daughter, Mary Jo, who married Roger Gibson and now lives in Washington, where she is an attorney. Following Senator Griffith's death, Mrs. Griffith married the late Gordon D. Blackwell, for many years the manager of the Newberry branch of Thomas and Howard Company. Widowed twice, she lives in Newberry.

Newberry County farmers have favored Jerseys until the last few years. Newberrians who have served as president of the South Carolina Jersey Cattle Club are C. B. Parr, C. T. Smith, W. E. Senn, W. C. McGinnis, and A. F. Busby. McGinnis, a native of Mecklenburg County, North Carolina, is a graduate of North Carolina State University and managed a large farm in Cherryville, North Carolina, before coming to Newberry. He increased Valley Dale herd to about 323 cows and then bought a large farm known as White Plains in Laurens County. McGinnis was president and a member of the board of directors of the American Jersey Cattle Club, member of the National Dairy Board, president of the National Dairy Herd Improvement Association, and has been active in promoting the dairy industry in South Carolina. He is married to the former Frances O. Smith of Raleigh.

Other major Jersey cattlemen include Stanley Baker, owner of Sand Hill Farm; Henry L. Parr of Head Spring Farm; David C. Waldrop of Trinity Farms; Henry Anderson of Sweet Springs Farm; and Dr. Julio John Malnati of Bush River Jerseys Farm. Baker bought Sand Hill Farm from James M. Clary, a former Newberrian who was an extremely successful food broker in Greenville, and who died in 1981. Dr. Malnati, a licensed veterinarian in Massachusetts, moved to Newberry in 1972. Since that time, he has devoted full time to developing his modern dairy known as Bush River Jersey Farm.

Perry Hamm of Myrtledale Farm is perhaps the largest Guernsey dairyman in the county. His father, Marvin Hamm, purchased the herd from Senator J. F. Hawkins, who, in turn, had succeeded to the ownership of the Sanitary Dairy of the late George W. Summer. Perry Hamm now operates the dairy.

Holsteins have become popular within the last decade. They are larger and heavier than Jerseys and Guernseys and give more milk. William D. Cromer, who owned a dairy with his son, Charles, on Whitmire Highway near Long Lane, was first to acquire a registered Holstein-Fresian herd in the county. Cromer, who married Novice Rikard of Newberry, was a director of Palmetto Production Credit Association and a leader in agricultural affairs until his death in 1981. His son, Charles, took over the dairy after his death. His neighbor, the late Mike Jenkins, was an early Guernsey dairyman.

At the time of his death in 1988, Claude M. Satterwhite of Bush River was one of the largest milk producers in the county. He changed to Holstein cows soon after William Cromer. Establishing a farm partnership with his sons, William and Wayne, he acquired a large acreage by dint of hard work and careful planning. Quiet, unassuming, and industrious, he was a fine citizen. A descendant of John Satterwhite, who in 1775 was a member of the First Provincial Congress, he married the former Mary Bonds; they had three children, their daughter, Linda, being married to James R. Sexton.

In July 1977, C. M. Satterwhite and Sons Dairy received the coveted Master Farm Family Award presented by *The Progressive Farmer* and the Clemson Extension Service.

Because of the efforts of these dairymen, Newberry County has become a major center of dairying in South Carolina. All of the farmers operate Grade A dairies. Although the number of dairies decreased after 1960, the quality and quantity of the milk produced have increased greatly.

In 1989, the following Grade A dairies were producing milk in Newberry County: Sweet Spring Farm (Henry Anderson & Son), C. J. Bishop, Sam Boozer, Leslea Farm (James Braswell & Sons), WillChar Farm (Charles Cromer), Marion Felker & Son, Green Acres Farm (Virgil and Kenneth Graham), Myrtledale Farm (Perry Hamm), Ray and Danny Graham, Rodmarlane Farm (William B. and Heyward L. Long), Beaverdam Farm (Mrs. Frances Long and Eddie Long), Bush River Jerseys (Dr. J. J. Malnati), Elliott and Lee Mayer, Bel Ivy Farm (Harold Pitts), G. I. Riddle & Sons, M. A. and J. A. Riddle, Sandhill Farm (Dr. Stanley Baker, Stanley Baker, III), C. M. Satterwhite & Sons, Allen Senn, Senn-Sational Jerseys (Frank M. Senn & Sons), Palmer Shealy, Trinity Farms (David C. Waldrop, David C. Waldrop, Jr. and Jimmy Kesler), Ralph Waldrop & Sons, Lyon Odyssey (Mark Lyon), Cackle Valley Farm (William Buford), and Headspring Farms (H. L. Parr & Sons).[52]

In 1900, forest products in the county were valued at $42,620[53] and thirty years later were worth only $120,000,[54] but the picture soon changed with the establishment of the Enoree Division of Sumter National Forest. Approximately 54,000 acres, or almost one-seventh of the county's area, the pie-shaped portion lying east of U.S. Highway 76 and north of the Whitmire-Newberry Highway, were purchased by the United States government in a period of some five years at what now appears to have been rock-bottom prices.

Many farmers were glad to sell their lands for Great Depression prices of five to fifteen dollars an acre. At least they would no longer have to pay property taxes. The federal government agreed to pay Newberry County one-fourth of its revenue from forest products in lieu of taxes. In 1989, Newberry County received $256,126.74, with one-half of this amount allocated to schools and the other half going to general county purposes.

In order to operate the Enoree Division of the Sumter National Forest, the U.S. Forest Service established a ranger office in Newberry. There has been a succession of rangers located here, the present one being Larry Cope. The first and best known was John C. Billingsley, a native of Arkansas and graduate of the University of Michigan School of Forestry, who came to Newberry in the 1930s.

Billingsley was an officer of Battery C, 107th AAA Battalion, which entered service on February 10, 1941. He saw service in the European and Mediterranean theaters, being promoted to the command of the battalion. Returning to Newberry after his release from active duty, he established a forestry consulting business and maintained his interest in the National Guard, retiring as a brigadier general. General Billingsley was killed in an airplane accident on February 3, 1971; he was survived by his widow, the former Wava Shanks, and one son, John C. Billingsley, Jr.

The South Carolina Commission of Forestry has located a district forester's office as well as a county forest ranger's office in Newberry. The present district forester is Tom Forte, while the county ranger is Watkins Martin. A network of fire towers provides a surveillance system for fires and the service has been very effective in keeping forest fires to a minimum.

Guy V. Whitener of Newberry was a member of the South Carolina Commission of Forestry, and served as chairman from 1949 to 1951.

Through the cooperative efforts of the Forest Service, the State Forestry Commission, and some large private landowners, the forests have become recreation areas. Once more the wild turkey and the deer are as plentiful as they were two centuries ago.

In the years between World Wars I and II only a few lumbermen operated sawmills and planer mills in the county. W. Sloan Chapman had a planer mill at the old Connor Place above Jalapa, Hunter H. Brown had one at Strothers on the Fairfield side of Broad River, Guy V. Whitener had a plant on College Street Extension, Newberry Lumber Company maintained a plant on Cline Street, J. Kess Derrick had a plant at Little Mountain, and Prosperity Lumber Company operated another just south of Prosperity.

During World War II, Fairfield Forest Products Company, a wholly owned subsidiary of what has become Champion International, opened an office in Newberry. Herschel Keener was its local manager; he and the old Fairfield Forest employees, E. A. Allanach, Wallace Wheeler, Andy Anderson, Eddie Duckworth, and Boose Hargrove have now moved away. William W. Walker, another employee and highly respected and beloved resident, died in 1987. Only Robert D. Coleman, Jr., H. Lee Smallwood, and Martyn Cavanaugh remain—all highly valued citizens of the county.

By 1949, the value of forest products had grown to $198,951.[55] The paper companies—Champion International, Canal Wood, Continental,

West Virginia, and International—had begun buying both pulpwood and land. Some local pulpwood dealers began acquiring tremendous acreages, generally by buying the land and then selling the timber for more than enough to pay for the land they kept.

By 1960, Newberry was third among the counties of the state in production of pulpwood; the volume that year was 85,172 cords.[56] Six years later farmers sold $514,000 worth of forest products from their lands.[57] In 1980, the delivered value of forest products in Newberry County was $17,454,000 while in 1987 the value was $26,548,000.[58]

Because of the great quantity of pine produced and the favorable rate of replacement growth in this part of the state, several new mills appeared. At a cost of some $15 million, Champion International constructed a large plywood factory near Silverstreet on the Saluda River in 1974. The plant was unionized, a long strike ensued, and the plant was closed in 1989.

While that division of Champion was having its troubles, the Timberlands Division continued as a good corporate citizen. Its relations with the local people have been excellent. The Timberlands Division maintains an office in Newberry, a modern chipping mill near Silverstreet, and a shop at Belfast. Currently its local manager is Eric Watson, its forester is Adlai Platt, the manager of the shop is Lee Walsh, and the manager of the chipping plant is Harmon Brehmer.

Other companies that have established plants in the county are Georgia-Pacific Corporation, Westvaco, and Federal Paper Board. Georgia-Pacific built a chip and saw plant near Prosperity in 1973 and two years later erected a plywood plant adjacent to it. Don Brown is the present manager of Georgia-Pacific's timber operations, Paul Fowler is manager of the plywood plant, and Michael Green is in charge of the chip and saw plant.

Southwest Forest Industries, which had merged with the Whitener Lumber Company, built a modern kiln and mill on College Street Extension in 1975. Federal Paper Board acquired this facility in 1980. Its manager is Robert O. Barrett.

Westvaco built a large chipping mill on the Columbia, Newberry, and Laurens Railroad near Kinards. Its manager is Bill Clamp, while Mahlon Moore is manager of wood procurement, and Bob Miller is manager of timberlands.

Catawba Timber Company operates a woodyard on the Columbia, Newberry, and Laurens Railroad a few miles out of Newberry. Next door is the Dickert Lumber Company which built a new mill at the old site of Vance & Dwiggins' plant in 1980. Locally owned planer mills are those of Dickert Lumber Company, Derrick Brothers at Little Mountain, and Haltiwanger Lumber Company between Newberry and Prosperity.

Following World War II, John C. Billingsley and his associates established Carolina Tree Farms which became a good-sized land holding company. It was liquidated in 1976 when it sold its lands to Catawba Newsprint Company. Among those who helped create the forest products industry in Newberry County were Billingsley, Allen W. Murray, Guy V. Whitener, J. Kess Derrick, Carroll Derrick, Alvin and Ernest Kinard, Henry M. Hentz, John R. Frazier, H. H. Brown, and W. Sloan Chapman. All are now dead except Whitener and Frazier. Others who pioneered in the pulpwood business were Earl and J. W. Dickert, Jr.; Harold and Guy Bowers; David, Jefferson, and Ralph Waldrop; William S. Hentz; and Gurnie Stuck. Others active in the lumbering industry were Seth A. Meek, J. Ralph Williams, Frank Graham, Horace and Ernest Oxner, J. W. Henderson, J. L. Koon, Clarence Robert Koon, and Charles H. Gray.

At the turn of the century beef cattle were relatively unimportant to the county's economy. It was not until the Great Depression was ending that raising cattle for sale became profitable. By 1950, there were 6,700 head of beef cattle in the county and they were worth about $1 million.[59]

In 1975 the number had risen to 25,200 and the value of the cattle to about $4 million. Newberry had become fourth among the counties of South Carolina in raising cattle.[60] In 1980 the number of beef cattle had risen to 26,400 with a value of $4,918,000. In 1987 the number had decreased to 22,250 valued at $4,851,000.[61]

Those who pioneered in raising beef cattle included T. B. Amis, A. W. Murray, Strother C. Paysinger, J. Thad McCrackin, P. Duncan Johnson, Jr., I. M. Smith, George Young, John Robert Suber, and Hamp Sease and his sons. Of these only Johnson and Tom Sease are still alive.

T. B. Amis, a former football star at Georgia Tech and a former football coach at Furman, moved to Newberry County about 1930. Settling on Indian Creek, he established a model Hereford ranch and his efforts encouraged others. T. B. Amis died in 1964.

J. T. McCrackin, son of S. P. and Ida Bonds McCrackin, was born in the county and lived there all of his life. The Johnson-McCrackin Company, which succeeded the Ed Hipp firm, dealt in livestock, farm machinery, and supplies, and operated a cotton warehouse and large farms for many years. McCrackin was one of Newberry's leading agribusiness men until his death at the age of seventy-four on May 24, 1959. Member of the Lutheran Church, a Mason and Shriner, he was one of the organizers of the Newberry County Bank. He married Margaret Matthews and they had six children, Edward D., J. T., Jr., Thomas B., Evelyn Brooks, Eliza Parr, and Caroline Workman Henderson.

Sometime before McCrackin's death, the Johnson-McCrackin Company was liquidated. The farm machinery business was assigned to P. D. Johnson, Jr., who, operated, under the name of P. D. Johnson and Company, the International Harvester franchise in Newberry from 1956 to 1990. A graduate of Clemson College in 1936, he married Elizabeth Blackwell; they have three children, Elizabeth Kohn, an attorney practicing in Dallas; Pope Duncan, III, an attorney practicing in Columbia; and Gordon B. Johnson.

Gordon B. Johnson, who was born on June 17, 1951, graduated from Clemson University in 1973. Entering the business with his father, he became manager of the company in 1980. He also was an officer in Builder's Headquarters of Newberry, Inc. until he sold his interest in that company. In 1989 he served as president of the Carolinas Farm and Power Equipment Dealers Association. He married Anne Laboone Griffith of Barnwell, and they have two children, Laurie Elizabeth and Gordon Blackwell Johnson, Jr. They attend Aveleigh Presbyterian Church.

McCrackin's close friend was Strother C. Paysinger, another native Newberrian. The son of Benjamin T. and Julia Strother Paysinger, he graduated from Newberry College, served in World War I, was active in the American Legion, and was a member of the First Baptist Church. Founder of the Newberry Oil Company, he operated the City Filling Station and had large farming interests; he was another organizer of the Newberry County Bank. He married Marion Daniel, and they had three children, Margery Williamson, Dr. B. Daniel Paysinger, and S. D. Paysinger. He died in Newberry on April 4, 1976, at the age of seventy-six.

His son, S. D. Paysinger, was born on November 11, 1924. He attended The Citadel but left to serve in World War II as an officer in the Army Air Force. He married Martha Johnstone; they had twin sons, Alan and Strother. After he was divorced, S. D. Paysinger married Eleanor Weir Clarkson. He is a collector of coins and gems; he sold his oil dealership in 1989 but continues to be active in raising beef cattle.

Other Hereford cattlemen include Carl B. Setzler and Sons, Harold Pitts, Robert C. Lake, Vernon F. Epting, J. W. Henderson, Burton Sease, Boyd Smith, and J. C. Lester.

Black Angus herds are maintained by Horace L. Boozer, Jr., Willie B. Piester, Milton F. Boland, and Richard Crump. Walter and Warren Cousins have Charolais. Others, of course, raise cattle but these are the principal cattlemen in the county.

In the closing years of the twentieth century, Newberry is still an agricultural community. The county's income from agriculture forms its economic backbone. Instead of cotton, the crops are now chickens and eggs, milk products, beef cattle, soybeans, and forest products. Its lands are still green and rolling, dotted with farm ponds and pastures.

The number of farm units had dropped to 836 by 1969,[62] while the average size per farm had risen to about 180 acres.[63] By 1980 the number of farms had declined to 820, with an average acreage of 157,[64] and by 1987 to 660 with an average acreage of 165.[65]

Two services provide professional help to the farmers of the county. The Agricultural Stabilization and Conservation Committee (known as ASCS) administers subsidy programs for various crops, maintains aerial photographs of the county, and encourages the farmers to practice better methods.

For many years Thomas M. Abrams served as county executive director; upon his retirement Keith Ritter succeeded him. James Richard Young is minority advisor. For many years J. C. Lester, A. F. Busby, and Harold Pitts served as members of the Committee. All have retired, and the present members are Heber Long, chairman, Howard Earl Meetze, and Frank M. Senn, Jr.

A second federal body, the Soil Conservation Service, is responsible for providing technical assistance in constructing ponds and lagoons and in terracing Newberry's rolling, sloping land. The service shares the costs of making these improvements with the farmer and also shares the cost of applying fertilizer and lime for cover crops to prevent erosion. The county soil conservationist is Craig O'Dell. The county committee in charge of this work consists of Walter B. Cousins, chairman, Henry Eason, S. D. Paysinger, and Ed Chandler. J. Thad McCrackin, Jr., served for many years until his death in 1988.

At the same time, the Federal Land Bank of Columbia, Palmetto Farm

Credit Association (successor to the Palmetto and Clinton Production Credit Associations), and the Farmers Home Administration have made needed capital available to the farmers, both for long-term loans on homes and land and for short-term crops. The Newberry Electric Cooperative has furnished cheap electricity to the farms, and the Newberry County Water and Sewer Authority has begun covering the county with water lines to bring water to the farmers.

14

Education

In 1860 the private academies and a number of one-teacher schools supported by private subscriptions constituted the school system in the district.[1] Poor children were enrolled in all of them by the commissioners of the Free Schools, who paid their tuition from the small annual appropriation as far as the money would go. In 1860 forty-two teachers were paid four and a half cents a day per student by the commissioners. That year 547 students were educated at public expense.[2]

During the war years the number of teachers receiving state aid for needy pupils declined to fifteen in 1864–1865. Daily tuition rose from four and a half cents to eleven cents per pupil in the last year of the war. The number receiving benefits under the Free School Act declined to 185, and the number of schools in the district shrank from thirty-three to fourteen.[3]

In the uncertain days that followed the cessation of hostilities education was, with a few exceptions, largely neglected. In February 1866, the Reverend John J. Brantley, the generally beloved pastor of the First Baptist Church, opened the Newberry Female Collegiate School.[4] It continued until Mr. Brantley left Newberry in 1867 to become Professor of Belle Lettres and Modern Languages at Mercer University.[5]

In April 1867, the Reverend J. Taylor Zealy, who succeeded Brantley as pastor of the First Baptist Church, opened the Newberry Female College in the house built by W. F. Nance and known later as Gildercrest.[6] The college operated for two years with the commencement exercises being held in the courthouse in June 1867 and 1868. Four young ladies were graduated in the former year and five in 1868.[7]

Also in 1867 the Freedmen's School was established on Caldwell Street in the town of Newberry.[8] This school was named the Hoge School in honor of "carpetbagger" Solomon L. Hoge.[9]

In 1866 Thomas Duckett established the Liberty Hall Academy near the Laurens County line. He operated this school successfully for some years, advertising in 1872 that students would be prepared for any college. The school term was 200 days, tuition for primary studies was $30, for English grammar it was $40, while for Latin and Greek it was $50 a term. Board could be procured at $12 per month.[10]

In addition to these academies, Newberry had other institutions for young people. Although the Female Academy was operating under the guidance of the Reverend J. B. Hillhouse in March 1869, Captain A. P. Pifer, former captain of General R. E. Lee's bodyguard, became principal later that year.[11] He continued his association with the Female Academy for many years; it was located on College Street. In 1869 tuition for the primary class was $10; for the junior class, $15; and for the senior class, $20. French, German, Spanish and music were taught in addition to the regular subjects.

Hillhouse became principal of the Male Academy when Captain Pifer succeeded him at the Female Academy; the male academy was located on Harrington Street. He was succeeded by James C. Hardin as principal of the Male Academy in 1871; W. C. Brooks became principal in 1872.[12]

Another exception to the general neglect of education was the establishment of the Crosson Field School by John Thomas Pressley Crosson on his farm near Prosperity. According to the account published in the SesquiCentennial edition of the Newberry Observer, on April 28, 1939, Crosson, a graduate of Erskine College in 1855 and a veteran who served in Company G, 13th S.C.V., organized this school for the benefit of his entire community. The first teacher was Miss Jane Martin, a graduate of Due West Woman's College, and the student body soon grew from 15 to 115 pupils. Crosson and those patrons who could afford to do so supported the school and paid all of its expenses. Poor children were welcomed and educated.

In 1868 a constitutional convention met in Charleston to draft a new constitution for South Carolina. It was generally recognized that one of the most important problems confronting the delegates was that of public education. Governor Orr urged the convention to provide for the general education of the blacks as well as for that of the whites.[13]

Compulsory attendance, integration, the establishment of school districts, state support, local support, uniform textbooks, and the certification of teachers were considered. B. Odell Duncan of Newberry argued strongly against compulsory attendance and integration.[14] He lost both battles.

Compulsory attendance was required "after the system of public schools had been thoroughly and completely organized and facilities afforded the inhabitants of the State for the free education of their children." In retrospect it is difficult to understand how the convention could have acted more wisely in attacking illiteracy than by postponing the assault until facilities were available.

Although the Constitution as adopted provided that publicly supported schools and colleges should be open and free to all children without regard to race, the blacks did not force the issue after the Constitution was adopted.[15] They served notice, however, that they would try to integrate the schools when the opportunity came. Meantime, they were satisfied with the establishment of a system of free public schools. The new laws had much to commend them to the citizenry.

A state superintendent of education was to be elected for a four-year term and school commissioner elected for each county. The superintendent and the county school commissioners comprised a state board of education. Counties were to be divided into school districts, and the public schools were to be supported by a state appropriation and by a poll tax levied upon every male adult.[16] Local school districts were to be encouraged to supplement these state taxes with local levies.

Each county commissioner was to appoint two persons to assist him in examining and certifying teachers. The county board of examiners was to name three trustees for each school district. Hopefully, the schools would be operated for a term of nine months when funds would permit. Uniform textbooks were to be furnished students at 10 percent above cost; trustees were authorized to furnish books free of charge to those unable to pay.[17] South Carolina was the first state to adopt uniform textbooks on a state-wide basis.[18]

Justus K. Jillson, a native of Massachusetts and a member of the Convention of 1868, served as state superintendent of education from 1868 to 1877. He was honest, sincere, and anxious to establish a workable system of public education.[19] When he took office he declared that "the education of *all* the children of *all* classes and castes is indispensable to the highest and best welfare of the community."

Despite the rascality rampant in state government during this period, the incompetence of many teachers, and the cupidity of some county commissioners of education, Jillson improved the educational opportunities of South Carolinians. He recommended repeatedly that the school year be fixed and defined by state law, the state superintendent be authorized to appoint school examiners, school trustees be elected, and county treasurers be required to set aside and retain sufficient funds to cover the estimated cost of operating local schools.[20]

He forthrightly listed the four main causes for the lack of success of the common schools as being the lack of qualified and efficient teachers, the inefficiency and unfitness of school officials, the apathy and lack of interest of the general public, and the inadequacy of school funds. In elaborating on these causes, he advocated the election of local trustees, the appointment of school commissioners, appointment of a state super-intendent, and the reduction of the number of schools.[21] In prophetic terms he deplored the proliferation of one-teacher schools and the certi-fying (because of expediency) of unqualified persons to teach. His recom-mendations were ignored. His annual reports read like those of some of his successors more than a half-century later.

During the first year the public schools were in operation the school age population of Newberry County was in excess of 5,000. However, the forty-six schools in the county reported an average attendance of only 1,000 white children and 240 black children. Only four schools for black children were in operation, the principal one being the Freed-men's School taught by the Reverend Simon Miller on Caldwell Street in the town of Newberry. The others were at Joe Bedenbaugh's near Frog Level, Mary Jane Waldrup's in Moon Township, and at Jalapa.[22]

The only brick building used for a school at that time was the Female Academy in Newberry. The other schools were either of log or frame construction. Of the forty-two teachers, thirty-eight were Southern whites and four were Southern blacks.[23] Average salaries paid are not available for 1869 but two years later they were $35.61 per month for male teachers and $24.13 per month for female teachers. The total spent for forty-four teachers was $6,760 in 1871. The schools in Newberry County operated for five months that year. One frame school building was erected that year at a cost of $30.[24]

Jillson pointed out that the state of New Jersey, with a school popula-tion of 265,000, appropriated $2,227,000 for its schools while South Carolina, with a school population of 206,000, only raised $250,000! The next year he called the system "a reproach to those who claim to be its friends and advocates."[25]

During Jillson's administration as state superintendent, four men served as school commissioners for Newberry County—two whites,

William Summer and Jesse C. Smith, and two blacks, Munson S. Long and Harry B. Scott. The ablest of the four was William Summer, the Pomaria horticulturist; but he was thrown from his buggy and seriously injured and was thereby prevented from performing his duties during most of his term.[26] No mention of the other three appears in the reports of the state superintendent of education, and the local newspapers said little regarding their activities. The two examiners who served on the county board during this period were J. C. Leahy and A. P. Pifer.

By the end of Jillson's term, the average attendance had increased from 1,240 to 1,939; of these 1,296 were blacks. The number of county schools had increased from forty-three to fifty-four, the number of black teachers from four to twenty-three, and the budget for the schools had been raised to about $10,000 per year.[27]

Hugh S. Thompson, elected superintendent of education on the Hampton ticket, postponed the opening of the schools until January 1878. He recommended establishing high schools by local tax levies, establishing a state board of examiners composed of the superintendent and four persons appointed by the governor, empowering the state board to review decisions of county commissioners, eliminating the burden of furnishing textbooks to those unable to pay, and requiring county auditors to make an annual census of school age children in each school district except during years when federal and state censuses were taken.[28]

Thompson subsequently reported that the schools made progress in the first year. Attendance increased 10 percent during 1878.[29] The county Boards of Examiners were working well. In Newberry J. C. Boyd was the new county commissioner, and the two members appointed by the State Board of Examiners were Frederick Werber, Jr., alumnus of Washington and Lee, and George S. Mower, alumnus of Bowdoin College. They continued to serve as examiners for some years and rendered fine service.

Textbooks adopted for use in the state included John Woods Davidson's *History of South Carolina*.[30] Davidson was a native of Newberry, a graduate of the South Carolina College, and a writer and critic who enjoyed a regional reputation.

For a number of years the black teachers of the county tried sporadically to organize a teacher's association. In 1881 a group was formed under the leadership of D. H. Maffett, president; B. W. Nance, secretary; and Munson S. Long as the third member of the committee to draft rules and regulations. Two years later the black teachers were reported to have organized the Teachers Association of Newberry County with P. W. Dawkins, president; J. S. Stewart, vice president; A. E. Hampton, secretary; G. W. Guignard, assistant secretary; T. W. Stewart, treasurer; and J. B. Arnold, chaplain. However, it was not until his annual report for 1885 that County School Commissioner Sale stated that a group had been organized during the year and was meeting once a month.[31] By 1900 this body apparently had disbanded.

Meanwhile the white teachers were reported to be organizing a county teachers' association in 1885, but no further mention is made of such a group until 1899. In that year sixty-three members held seven meetings with an average attendance of thirty-five. S. J. Derrick, later to become president of Newberry College, was president of the county association, with Miss Lilla Johnstone as secretary.[32]

From the election of Hampton to the adoption of the Constitution of 1895 the common schools had a difficult time. The public was generally apathetic, funds were inadequate, teachers were poorly trained, and the educational opportunities were severely limited. Illiteracy continued to plague South Carolina. Against a national average of 17 percent illiterates in 1880, the average among South Carolina whites was 21.9 percent, the average among South Carolina blacks was 78.5 percent, and the average for South Carolina was 55.4 percent.[33]

During these years Thompson was followed as state superintendent in succession by Colonel Asbury Coward, James H. Rice, and W. D. Mayfield. The school commissioners for Newberry County were J. C. Boyd, Henry S. Boozer, G. G. Sale, Arthur Kibler, Thomas W. Keitt, and F. W. Higgins. Those who served as examiners were George S. Mower, Frederick Werber, Jr., George B. Cromer, T. S. Moorman, G. G. Sale, and W. K. Sligh.

Two steps were taken during the 1880s that had far-reaching influence on public education. To improve the quality of teaching, summer institutes were conducted in different parts of the state and skilled professionals taught the public school teachers; the response was good.[34]

The other development was the supplementing of school funds by local tax levy. As a one-crop agricultural economic unit Newberry County could only raise taxes by ad valorem property assessments. Property valued at one million dollars will return $1,000 in taxes for each mill of tax. Newberry's tax levy for schools in 1883, for example, was two mills; the assessed value of taxable property was $4,395,001. Consequently, the amount raised for schools that year was $8,790. The poll tax produced $4,684, thus making about $13,000 available to the schools.[35]

As the number of schools and teachers increased, however, the funds from property taxes had to be spread thinner and thinner. Thus, by 1893, the $15,200 expended for teachers' pay only permitted an average monthly salary of $27.60 for male teachers and $26 for female teachers. In that year, Newberry County had seventy-two white and fifty-eight black teachers. Of 102 school houses, only four were brick, nineteen were log, and seventy-nine were of frame construction.[36]

In a special election held in 1890 the citizens of the town of Newberry voted to establish a graded school system to be supported by a special tax. In the same election a trustee was elected from each of the four wards to serve with the seven trustees of the Male and Female Academies. These eleven constituted the first Board of Trustees of the Graded Schools. J. F. J. Caldwell was elected chairman, and W. H. Wallace, secretary.[37]

The new board immediately elected J. F. Brown, graduate of Wofford, as superintendent, the Misses Octavia Garlington and Fannie Leavell as teachers, and the Misses Allic Cozby, Mallie Wheeler, and Fannie N. Baxter as assistant teachers in the white school. Andrew P. Butler was elected principal of the Hoge School for blacks, with the Misses Mary Tillman and Josephine Kennedy as assistants.[38]

The graded schools took over the Male and Female Academies and the Hoge Institute. In the 1870s white boys and girls attending private primary classes went to Miss Fannie Elmore's school or that of Mrs. J. H. Gaillard, while in the 1880s they went to Miss Mattie McIntosh's school or Joseph S. Reid's school.[39] When they got a little older the boys attended either the Male Academy[40] or the preparatory department of Newberry College,[41] while the girls went to the Female Academy.[42]

The Hoge Institute thrived during the entire post-war period, the student body numbering about 300. Principals of the school included H. R. Morrill, W. H. Thomas, E. E. Green, B. W. Nance, D. H. Maffett, T. R. Holmes, W. B. West, and W. S. Johnston.

In 1891 the *Newberry Observer* reported that the graded schools were exceeding expectations and that a new building was needed. The Atlanta architectural firm of Bruce and Morgan drew the plans for the new Boundary Street School. It was completed and occupied in January 1892.[43]

Frank Evans became superintendent in September 1891 and remained in that position until he was elected superintendent of the Spartanburg graded schools in 1895. He was succeeded by W. H. Wallace of the Columbia College faculty. In 1899 Wallace was elected president of the Association of State Graded Schools Superintendents, but in June 1900 he resigned to become editor of the *Greenville News*. Burr H. Johnstone was elected superintendent to succeed Wallace.[44]

Prosperity, the second-largest town in Newberry County, established the Prosperity Academy in 1873 with S. E. Caughman as principal. Six years later the Prosperity High School evolved out of the academy. C. W. Welch, who later became one of the first professors at Clemson College, was the principal.[45] By 1889 the school was housed in a handsome and commodious building. The Reverend Andrew J. Bowers was principal and John E. Edwards and Miss Lillian Luther were the teachers of a student body of 100.[46]

In 1893 John A. Chapman's *School History of South Carolina* was issued from the presses of Aull and Houseal in Newberry. It was promptly adopted by the State Board of Examiners for exclusive use in the public schools of South Carolina.[47] Thus the approved state history, written by a Newberrian, succeeded the approved state history written by James Woods Davidson, another Newberrian.

A new constitution for the state was adopted in 1895. Article XI, dealing with education, provided for a state superintendent of education to be elected every two years, the establishment of a state board of education to be appointed by the governor for a four-year term, the General Assembly to provide by law for the appointment or election of all other school officers and for the salaries of school officers, the establishment by the General Assembly of a liberal system of free public schools and the suitable division of the counties into school districts, the assessment of a poll tax to be used for school purposes, and separate schools for children of the white and black races and a positive prohibition against integration. It also provided that all the net income derived by the state from the sale or license for the sale of liquors, except so much as was allowed to the counties and municipalities by the General Assembly, should be used for education.

At the end of the century Newberry County had fifty-seven school districts. Each district operated a white school and a black school except Mt. Zion, which had only a white school. There were only two white schools with more than one teacher—Newberry, which had eleven teachers and 527 pupils, and Prosperity, which had three teachers and 136 pupils. There were two black schools with more than one teacher—Newberry, with three teachers and 334 pupils, and Garmany, with two teachers and 206 pupils.[48]

The white schools in the county averaged sessions of six and a half months. The white teachers received an average of only $208.63 per session. As poor as was their pay, however, it far exceeded the average of $90.63 paid the black teachers. The black schools averaged sessions of five months.[49]

The enrollment in the country's public schools in 1899 was 3,240 white and 4,220 black pupils.[50] There were another 100 blacks enrolled in the St. Luke's Episcopal Mission School on Lindsay Street in Newberry[51] and forty white males in the preparatory department of Newberry College. The average attendance at the public schools was 2,257 white and 3,419 black students.[52]

As Harry Ashmore so well said:

If the South did little to provide an education for Negroes in those post-war years, it did little more for the whites. There were, of course, compelling practical reasons for its failure. The stricken region was entirely by-passed by the industrial revolution which was transforming the face of America and creating great concentrations of wealth in the North and the newly-opened West. The South remained an agricultural province, and a conquered one, and poverty was almost universal. There simply was no economic base upon which to build an adequate system of public schools where none had existed before.[53]

This was true of the whole South but especially true of Newberry County with its one-crop agricultural economy. Property taxes could not sufficiently finance local government, state government, and public education.

Some improvement in the public school system was made in the pre-World War I years but much more needed to be done to provide adequate educational opportunity to the children of the county. The enrollment of 2,666 whites and 4,408 blacks in 1901 grew to 3,600 whites and 6,510 blacks in 1917. The average salaries paid white teachers rose from $222.12 to $391.91 per session, and those paid black teachers from $86.35 to $119.57.[54]

In 1907 an act of the General Assembly provided for the establishment of high schools. If voters approved, a local board of trustees was authorized to levy two mills in taxes to support these schools. State aid of up to $1,200 per school was provided and an appropriation of $50,000 was made for this purpose.[55]

Little Mountain organized its high school in 1907 and in 1917 was supporting it with a levy of ten and one-half mills. The district was absurdly small, measuring only 2 square miles; it was too small to support a good school without enrolling pupils from the outlying districts.[56]

Prosperity organized its high school in 1908 and supported it with a levy of six mills by 1917. It had only sixty-seven pupils in that year.[57]

Whitmire High School was organized in 1912, supported by a local tax levy of twelve mills. That district contained less than eight square miles.[58]

Newberry bought Judge Y. J. Pope's residence for a high school in 1909 but instead erected a new high school building on Martin Street in 1910.[59] The Pope home then became Speers Street Elementary School.

State High School Inspector W. H. Hand, reporting on the high schools of the state, said that "any town the size of Newberry with a three-year high school is in danger of losing its standing among high schools."[60] A four-year high school was not established in Newberry until 1919, the first class of seven being graduated in 1920.[61] By 1924, there were four four-year high schools in the county: Newberry, Prosperity, Little Mountain, and Whitmire.[62] Silverstreet and Pomaria became four-year high schools by 1928.[63] None of these schools could award state high school diplomas until they had been established as four-year schools for four years and required so many units of study, sixteen after June 1925.[64]

In 1913 County Superintendent of Education E. H. Aull strongly recommended that the number of school districts in the county be reduced from fifty-nine to thirty, one-teacher schools be consolidated, trustees be appointed, and teaching methods be improved.[65] He was defeated for reelection.

In 1915, County Superintendent George D. Brown, Jr., stated that a one-teacher school could not provide adequate education and that the efficiency of teachers could only be improved by requiring a central board of examiners to issue teachers' certificates.[66] At that time there were six schools in the county with fewer than twelve students each.

During Brown's tenure, Newberry County employed a supervising teacher for the rural schools. Miss Sadie Goggans did excellent work in this capacity until she became supervising teacher for Richland County in 1916. She reported that Newberry County had a number of incompetent teachers and that better school facilities were needed, but that she thought real improvement had been made.[67] Unfortunately, the county did not replace her when she went to Richland.

The passage of the 6-0-1 Law in 1924 was of vital importance. It required each county to use the three-mill constitutional ad valorem property tax and to levy at least a four-mill school tax to qualify for state aid. This aid paid the salaries of all teachers for six months provided the county ran its schools for an additional month.[68] In his 1927 report, State Superintendent James H. Hope stated that all high schools operated for nine months in South Carolina, and it was one of the few southeastern states in which this was true.[69]

Illiteracy and poor school attendance were still major problems. Dr. Wil Lou Gray, state supervisor of adult education, reported that 38,000 adult whites and 181,000 blacks were illiterate in 1926. She recommended a compulsory attendance law and the education of the illiterate.[70]

In his 1928 report, Superintendent Hope decried the lack of a compulsory attendance law. He said that 27 percent of all enrolled pupils were absent every day. A compulsory attendance law was finally enacted in 1937.[71]

School busing was instituted in the county in the late 1920s. By 1929, Newberry County was transporting 1,108 pupils in thirty-one buses. The average cost per pupil was $20.13. In this year there were 4,899 white and 4,890 black pupils enrolled, this being the first time that the whites were more numerous.[72]

Although some consolidation was effected in 1930, Newberry County still had only eighteen white and three black schools with more than three teachers. Two white and twenty-three black schools had only one teacher, ten white and nineteen black schools had two teachers, and six white and six black schools had three teachers. The average salaries were $1,066.52 for white and $345.93 for black teachers.[73]

In the city of Newberry, Burr H. Johnstone, W. A. Stuckey, H. L. Dean, Ernest Anderson, and Dr. James P. Kinard were superintendents during the period of 1900 to 1917. When Dr. Kinard went to Winthrop in 1917, Olin B. Cannon became superintendent of the city schools. He should be credited with the improvement made between World War I and World War II.

It was he who assembled a group of fine teachers in the Newberry city schools.[74] It was he who secured accreditation of Newberry High School by the Southern Association of Colleges and Secondary Schools, and it was he who could, and did, take pride in the fact that during his tenure, no graduate of the high school ever failed in college. He was a talented teacher of mathematics and a stern but fair disciplinarian. During the period between world wars his schools were recognized as among the best in South Carolina.

The son of Benjamin F. and Henrietta Buzhardt Cannon, Olin B. Cannon was born in Newberry, graduated from Newberry College in 1898, taught mathematics at the college for fourteen years, and became superintendent of the city schools in 1917. He served with distinction in this capacity until his death at the age of sixty-six on October 14, 1946. For many years he was a member of the County Board of Education and served as president of both the South Carolina Education Association and the South Carolina State Teachers Association. He was also lieutenant governor of the 9th Carolina Kiwanis District. Married to Mary Gibson, he had one son, Olin Benjamin Cannon, Jr.

It was Cannon who brought Harry H. Hedgepath to Newberry High School to coach. A native of Columbia who graduated from Newberry College in 1926, Hedgepath came to the high school that fall and coached three sports there until 1967, with the exception of four years in the U.S. Navy in which he became a lieutenant commander. He won five state championships.

He served as first secretary-treasurer of the South Carolina Coaches Association and continued in this office for twenty years. For seventeen years he coached the American Legion Juniors in Newberry. Following his retirement in 1967, he was executive secretary of the Newberry College Indian Club. Active in his church, he was a member of the council and superintendent of the Sunday School of the Lutheran Church of the Redeemer.

Coach Hedgepath was honored by having the stadium of the high school named for him in 1947 and by being tendered a dinner in August 1978 by his former students and players. Married to Mary Alice Hipp, he had one child, Harriett. He died on June 27, 1989.

Professor Cannon was succeeded as superintendent of the Newberry city schools by Price Kenneth Harmon, longtime principal of the local high school. Son of William Bennett and Nancy Caroline Boozer Harmon, he was born in the O'Neall community on August 16, 1895, and was educated at Newberry College (from which he graduated in 1921), Peabody College, and the University of South Carolina, from which he received his master's degree in education. He came to Newberry High School after serving as superintendent first of the Little Mountain schools and then of the Prosperity schools.

Professor Harmon served as superintendent of the Newberry schools until 1951 when he became director of the county schools. He retired in 1961 and began a second successful career as agent for a large school book company. A veteran of World War I, he served as commander of American Legion Post 24 and as president of the Lions Club. He married Bertie Fulmer in 1923; they had two children, B. Meredith Harmon, court reporter for the Eighth Judicial Circuit, and Muriel, wife of Kemper D. Lake, M.D., of Whitmire. He was the last superintendent of the city schools, that post being abolished with the reorganization of the schools of Newberry County. He died on November 15, 1987.

In 1927 a new high school building was erected on Nance Street; it is now used as the junior high school. The old high school building became the junior high school but was closed many years ago. Although condemned as unsafe, it stood as an empty and unsightly edifice for years before it was finally razed.

On the eve of World War II there were eleven accredited high schools in the county but by 1951 there were only seven. These were Newberry, Whitmire, Prosperity, Pomaria, Bush River, Little Mountain, and Drayton Street.[75] High schools at Silverstreet, Chappells, Stoney Hill, and O'Neall had been closed as the public concluded that high schools had to have larger enrollments to give a good education.

After World War II the state assumed primary responsibility for public education. The General Assembly provided for teacher certification, a statewide transportation system, larger school districts, participation in the National School Lunch Program, a $75 million bond issue for school buildings, a sales tax to support education, and a speech and hearing loss program.

When money became available from the state sales tax and the entire cost of education ceased to be borne by ad valorem property taxes, the county took steps to improve the schools. A committee of nine members was appointed to study the reorganization of the schools; the committee, consisting of R. D. Coleman, the Reverend E. B. Heidt, C. E. Hendrix, J. Alvin Kinard, P. K. Harmon, Mrs. B. O. Long, the Reverend LeGrand Moody, Clifford T. Smith, and Mrs. E. H. Spearman, was named on January 27, 1950.

In June 1951, the county was divided into seven school districts, and trustees were named for each district. Price K. Harmon was selected to head the county system. In early 1952 the County Board of Education, consisting of J. S. Ritchie, J. L. Keitt, Hugh M. Epting, R. C. Neel, Jr., L. M. Shealy, Jacob S. Wheeler, and Dr. C. A. Pinner[76] assumed the duties of the several boards of trustees of the fifty-odd school districts. The local boards were asked to act in an advisory capacity; consolidation took effect on February 9, 1952.

Initially, the County Board of Education was appointed by the governor upon the recommendation of the Newberry County legislative delegation. In 1969 the County Board of Education was made an elected body, and the office of county superintendent of education was abolished. The board was authorized to appoint a district superintendent of schools and a business manager.[77]

Meanwhile, a single, county-wide district was established and the number of schools reduced so that by 1960 only twelve elementary schools remained in the county. New school buildings were financed by bond issues, and abandoned schools buildings became community centers, thereby retaining some cohesiveness in those areas where schools no longer existed.

After World War I the office of county superintendent of education was filled successively by Clemson Wilson, Elbert H. Aull, D. L. Wedaman, George K. Dominick, Mrs. Mae Aull, C. E. Hendrix, and James D. Brown.

Clemson Wilson, son of Drayton Q. and Ella Mayer Wilson, was born in the county, graduated from Newberry College in 1913, took postgraduate courses at Peabody and the University of South Carolina, and was elected superintendent of education in 1916; he served four years.

Elbert H. Aull, who held that position from 1912–13, was elected to succeed Wilson. Colonel Aull's sketch is included in the chapter on Editors and Authors. His widow, the former Mae Amick, served as county superintendent by appointment in 1936. This is the only instance in which husband and wife have served Newberry County in the office.

David Leroy Wedaman, Sr., another native and the son of John David and Eustatia Folk Wedaman, was elected to succeed Aull. He served one term, 1924–1928. Wedaman taught school in the county and served as treasurer of the Newberry Electric Cooperative. A member of Bethlehem Lutheran Church, he married Mamie Epting and then Agnes Shealy. He died on October 27, 1961, survived by an only child, David Leroy Wedaman, Jr., who is now a member of County Council.

George K. Dominick succeeded Wedaman and served from 1928 to 1936 when he resigned to become postmaster of Newberry. He, too, was born in the county, the son of Elzie and Mary Kinard Dominick. A 1925 graduate of Newberry College, he taught school before his election. Dominick served as postmaster for eighteen years; after his retirement he was a director and officer of Newberry Federal Savings and Loan until 1966 when he moved to Aiken. He married Mary Ellen Bowers; they had two daughters, Cynthia D. Cox and Kay D. West. He died in 1981.

Mrs. Aull offered for reelection in 1936 but was defeated by Clinton E. Hendrix. Born in Lexington and a 1925 graduate of Newberry College, "Scrap" Hendrix received his master's degree from the University of South Carolina. He was principal of the Prosperity schools from 1925 to 1930 and superintendent of those schools from 1930 to 1936. After eleven years of service as county superintendent, he resigned to become state attendance teacher for two years, returning to Prosperity as superintendent from 1949 to 1958. He then served as superintendent of the Estill school system until his retirement in 1967. From 1970 to 1974 he was a member of the first Newberry County Council to operate under the Home Rule Act. Hendrix married Mary Sanders of Newberry County and had one son, Eugene Hendrix, Ph.D. After his first wife's death he married Helen Woodle Newton. He died on May 9, 1990.

Hendrix was succeeded by James D. Brown, who was appointed by Governor J. Strom Thurmond to fill the unexpired term of Hendrix. Born in the county, the son of Horace and Lily May Caldwell Brown, he graduated from Newberry College in 1926 and took postgraduate training at the University of South Carolina.

Brown interrupted his career as a school teacher to serve in the U. S. Army in World War II. He was a member of American Legion Post 24 and of a number of professional organizations. After the General Assembly abolished the office of county superintendent, he resigned in June 1969. Married to Leila Taylor Dickinson, he was survived by her when he died on August 18, 1980. She died in 1989.

Ralph E. Watkins, Jr., native of Greenville County and graduate of Clemson, succeeded P. K. Harmon as director of public schools in 1961. He holds a master's degree in education from the University of Georgia and was an officer in the U.S. Army in World War II. He served the Newberry County schools for nineteen years, retiring as district superintendent on June 30, 1980. At the time of his retirement he was president of the South Carolina Association of School Superintendents and a colonel in the U.S. Army, retired. He married Clara Stone of Seneca; they have two children, Martha W. Winchester and Beverly W. Mahon.

The next superintendent of the county schools was Hubert M. Bedenbaugh. A native of the county and a graduate of Clemson University, he holds a master's degree from the University of South Carolina and has done graduate work at the University of Chicago. For thirty-two years he was active in the South Carolina National Guard, retiring in 1980 as a brigadier general.

Bedenbaugh's life has been spent in the schools of Newberry County as teacher and administrator. Married to Gerry Riley of Saluda, he has three children, Hugh, Yvonne, and Gerald.

Bedenbaugh was succeeded by Dr. Vance O. Johnson, a native of Charlotte, North Carolina. The son of Oscar O'Neal and Ellen Armstrong Johnson, he was born on July 20, 1946, and educated at Western Carolina from which he received his B.A. in 1968 and his M.A.Ed. in 1970. He received his doctoral degree in education in 1983 from the University of North Carolina at Chapel Hill. He resigned as superintendent in 1989.

Following World War II, efforts were made to make black schools truly equal to the white schools as then required by Plessy v. Ferguson, which stood for the proposition that the Constitution was complied with if equal opportunities were provided for white and black students. The first monies available were expended in erecting new schools for blacks. These additional funds had to come from the state. A high school for blacks was erected in the city of Newberry and named for Ulysses S. Gallman, the veteran Jeanes teacher for Newberry County.

Ralph T. Williams, a local undertaker, became the first black to serve in a county office since Reconstruction when he was appointed to the County Board of Education in 1965. He served until his death in 1968. His grandfather's brother, R. E. ("Bob Dick") Williams, served as county auditor, 1874–1877.

Another black to serve on the County Board of Education was the Reverend E. E. Gaulden who was appointed in 1969 and served until 1973. Since 1974 all members of the board have been elected. Daisy Gibbs, a retired black teacher, was elected to the board in 1986.

In 1962 both Boundary Street and Speers Street elementary schools were razed to make way for new structures. In a nostalgic ceremony the old bell that had summoned pupils for so many years was installed in the yard of Boundary Street School and dedicated to Miss Gertrude Reeder, longtime principal of the old school.

Although efforts were being made to equalize the educational facilities of whites and blacks, there was no desegregation until 1970. In 1969 suit was brought in the United States District Court by the Reverend David Carter and others; Judge Charles E. Simons, Jr., issued an order approving a plan for complete integration submitted by the school board and approved by the Department of Health, Education and Welfare. All students, white and black, were assigned to the schools in their attendance areas. Teachers and administrators were employed based upon percentages, and semi-annual reports of employment and attendance were required.[78]

The school system, commencing with the 1970 term, has included three high schools—Newberry, Whitmire, and Mid-Carolina—to which all pupils go. Gallman High School became Gallman Junior High and later Gallman Middle School. A new high school for Newberry has been built on Highway 219, and the former high school is now Newberry Junior High. There are seventeen schools, all fully integrated, in the county. In 1969 there were 3,705 white and 2,933 black students. In 1981 there were 3,388 white and 2,983 black students; in 1989 the numbers were 3,384 white, 2,994 black, and 18 asian.

Both whites and blacks generally accepted the court order in good faith. The only incident to occur came in 1969 when the Reverend Carter and some of his followers tried to demonstrate on the school grounds. This demonstration quickly ended with issuance of a Rule to Show Cause why the demonstrators should not be held in contempt.

However, many citizens of the county are dissatisfied with the quality of education and feel that the level of instruction is not as good as it used to be. Others deplore the lack of discipline but realize that a permissive society and drug problems are responsible. Too little provision is made for gifted children, and some believe that not enough time is spent on fundamentals. However, Newberry County is not different from most other South Carolina counties; all are below the national averages in standardized test results.

One of the by-products of this dissatisfaction with school standards and integration is the Newberry Academy. It is the only private school in the county and has a kindergarten, an elementary department, and high school. The enrollment in 1981 was 204 students with thirteen teachers. The tuition is $1,100 per year. In 1989 it had 260 students and 24 teachers.

The academy was chartered on May 24, 1966, on application of Eugene C. Griffith, E. Maxcy Stone, and W. W. King, M.D. Commencing operations in the former West End Elementary School that year, it moved into a new building on Smith Road in 1971. Its first headmaster was Dr. James C. Kinard, former president of Newberry College; other headmasters have been Miss Sallie Lee Cromer, Herb Balcom, Briggs Cunningham, J. H. Glasgow, Mrs. Hiram Merserau, Steve McCutcheon, and Robert E. Dawkins.

Although there have been numerous dedicated educators who served in the county schools, there are several retired or deceased administrators who deserve special recognition. Robert C. Lake, Sr., J. V. Kneece, John Grady Long, R. E. Beck, Ralph H. Setzler, W. R. Lominick, and Hubert Long are among these. All are natives of the county except Kneece and Beck; all attended Newberry College except Lake.

Robert Campbell Lake, Sr., son of Kemper David and Mary Elizabeth Campbell Lake, graduated from Lenoir College in 1913, served two years in World War I, and was superintendent of the Kershaw schools until he accepted a similar position with the Whitmire schools in 1924. There he remained until he retired in 1955. He received his M.A. degree from the University of South Carolina in 1935.

Chiefly through his efforts, a new consolidated high school was built in 1929 and a number of small schools in the northern part of the county joined Whitmire's school system. The gymnasium erected at Whitmire in 1957 is named for him.

Professor Lake served as a member of the State Board of Education for eight years, as a member of the County Board of Education for twenty years, and as chairman of the South Carolina High School Athletic Association for four years. He married Susan Gaston Howze; he died on May 15, 1983, survived by three sons, Dr. Kemper D. Lake and Senator Robert C. Lake, Jr., of Whitmire, and Dr. John H. Lake of Ware Shoals.

Jules Verne Kneece, native of Lexington, graduated from Newberry College in 1924. He received his master's degree from the University of South Carolina in 1945 and did other postgraduate work at Clemson University. He came to Newberry High in 1941 after teaching in Greenville, Edgemoor, and Fort Lawn.

He became principal of Newberry High in 1946 and district superintendent in 1952, retiring from that post in 1966. For seven years he served on the county education staff. In 1974 he was named "Man of the Year" and was awarded the "Book of Golden Deeds" by the Newberry Exchange Club. He married Mildred Jones of Newberry; they had one daughter, Claudette Boland.

John Grady Long was born and spent most of his life in the Silverstreet community. Son of H. O. and Daisy Dominick Long, he graduated from Newberry College in 1925. Except for a few years when he taught at Mountville and St. Charles, he was connected with the Silverstreet schools as teacher, superintendent, and principal until he retired in 1970. He married Bessie Sanders and they have three daughters, Dorothy Stewart, Katherine Wiles, and Frances Blake.

R. E. Beck served the schools of the county for many years in a supervisory capacity. A native of Youngstown, Ohio, and a superb athlete, he was graduated from Newberry College in 1936 and received the M.Ed. degree from the University of South Carolina in 1954. After serving as an officer in the U.S. Navy, he was principal of Newberry Junior High, supervisory principal of the seven elementary schools in the city, and principal of Speers Street School before his retirement in 1975. He married Mary Frances Jones, and they had one daughter, Anne Kizer.

Ralph Setzler, son of George and Maude Halfacre Setzler, graduated from Newberry College in 1930. He taught in the county schools and served as superintendent and as principal of the Pomaria schools before his retirement in 1969. He married Sadie Sease; they had one daughter, Betty Maude Monroe. He died on September 28, 1988.

Another native of the Pomaria section who served as teacher and principal of the Pomaria school is W. R. Lominick, son of Horace and Willeze Boinest Lominick. He graduated from Newberry College in 1939 and married Katherine Coleman of Saluda. They have three children, Lorraine Deloney, Andrew, and William.

Hubert Long, son of Luther Edgar and Fannie Harmon Long, graduated from Newberry College in 1935. He was the highly respected principal of Newberry High School for some years before his retirement in 1982. He married Juanita Hunter; they have six children, Luther, Derrill, Gerald, Joseph Heber, James Edgar, and Jennie Ann Runyan.

15

Newberry College

The greatest cultural asset of the county is Newberry College. At a meeting of the South Carolina Synod of the Lutheran Church in 1828 Dr. John Bachman recommended the founding of a theological seminary and classical academy. In 1831 the synod established the seminary at the home of Colonel John Eichelberger near Pomaria. In 1834 the seminary was moved to Lexington. Newberry College was granted a charter in 1856 and the seminary became part of the new institution at Newberry.

The college opened on the first Monday in October, 1859. Dr. Bachman, South Carolina's greatest Lutheran leader, pastor of St. John's Church in Charleston for fifty-five years and a nationally recognized naturalist and ornithologist, was elected the first chairman of the board of trustees. Henry Summer of Newberry was elected secretary of the board, and the Reverend Theophilus Stork, D.D., of Philadelphia, was elected president of the college.

The college opened with 150 students and two professors in addition to Dr. Stork. Illness prevented Dr. Stork from carrying out his duties, and he resigned at the end of the first session.[1] He was succeeded by the Reverend James Allen Brown, D.D., also of Pennsylvania. He resigned early in 1861 to return to the North because of his strong Union views.

The third president, Dr. J. P. Smeltzer, D.D., of Maryland, was elected to succeed Brown. He came to Newberry on April 6, 1861, assuming the duties of president of the college and professor of theology in the seminary. He continued to operate the institution despite the problems of decreasing enrollment and financial support until 1865 when he was forced to suspend operations temporarily.[2]

During the Civil War part of the college's first building, completed in 1858, was used as a Confederate hospital. On July 9, 1865, Brigadier General Charles H. Van Wyck, his staff, and 150 men of the 56th New York Volunteer Regiment occupied the town and used the college building as headquarters. The occupation lasted until late September, 1865, when the regiment was transferred.[3] The federal troops virtually destroyed the handsome building, and in 1898 the United States paid the college $15,000 for the damages.[4]

In 1866 the synod authorized the repair of the building and appropriated $5,000 for that purpose. President Smeltzer, one other professor, and twenty-three students were present for the 1866–1867 session. Efforts to raise money were unsuccessful, and creditors of the college refused to reduce their claims.

The seminary moved to Columbia, and the college moved to Walhalla in November 1868.[5] "Only the college bell, the remnant of a library, and a few blackboards and benches" were moved to Walhalla. The synod voted to sell the campus property.

At Walhalla the enrollment remained small and the college continued to suffer financially. John Emlon Houseal of Newberry received the first baccalaureate degree in 1869[6] and twenty-one others were graduated from the college during its nine-year stay at Walhalla.

In 1877 the synod voted to move the college again and sealed bids were received from Anderson, Columbia, Lexington, Newberry, Prosperity, and Walhalla. It was decided to return the college to Newberry after the creditors cancelled their claims and the town pledged $15,870 and the gift of 10 acres of land or the privilege of purchasing the old campus for $2,500.[7]

The college was relocated on the old site and a new building, later named Smeltzer Hall, was constructed. Since it was not completed in time for the opening of the 1877–1878 session, classes were held for four months in a store building on Pratt, now Main, Street. The students boarded in houses near the campus.[8]

Dr. Smeltzer, who had headed the institution during the war and the trying Reconstruction period, resigned in 1877, choosing to remain in Walhalla. He was succeeded by the Reverend Dr. George William Holland, professor of Latin and Greek since 1874.

During Dr. Holland's presidency, Keller Hall, a boarding hall, and faculty houses were built. The administration building, which was erected in 1904, was named Holland Hall in his memory. Dr. Holland was a one-armed Confederate veteran. He served as fourth president from 1877 until his death in 1895[9] and is buried in Rosemont Cemetery. The first funeral conducted in the chapel was that of Dr. Holland, whose last words were "God bless Newberry College."[10] On the day of his funeral the ninth president of Newberry College, James Campsen Kinard, was born; he was destined to carry on in later years the great work of Dr. Holland.

Dr. Holland was succeeded by George Benedict Cromer, LL.D.,[11] who was the first Newberrian, the first layman, and the first alumnus to head the institution. The son of Thomas H. and Polly M. Cromer, he was born on October 3, 1857, and graduated in 1877. He read law with George Johnstone of Newberry and practiced with him from 1881 to 1895 and again after resigning the presidency of the college in 1904 because of poor health. One of Newberry's most distinguished sons, he was president of the South Carolina Bar Association in 1924 and mayor of Newberry from 1886 to 1890 and from 1906 to 1908. Wittenberg and Muhlenberg colleges awarded him LL.D. degrees.

During Dr. Cromer's presidency the college became co-educational in 1897; the first alumna, Margaret Johnstone (later Mrs. L. T. Mills), graduated in 1900. Dr. Cromer was instrumental in securing payment from the United States for damages wrought by the federal troops, building Holland Hall, and naming the original building Smeltzer Hall.[12]

In 1904 the Reverend James A. B. Scherer, Ph.D., LL.D., was elected to succeed Dr. Cromer.[13] A graduate of Roanoke College, he had served as a missionary in Japan. A scholar, he was author of several books, including Four Princes, Japan Today, The Holy Grail, and What is Japanese Morality?

During Dr. Scherer's presidency the college celebrated its semicentennial, enrollment in all departments reached 211 students, the first gymnasium was erected, and Carnegie Hall was built.[14] During his tenure of only four years, Dr. Scherer launched a successful endowment drive that raised $110,000.[15] He also established a technological department which was discontinued in 1915.

Upon Dr. Scherer's resignation in 1908 to become president of Throop Polytechnic Institute in California, the second alumnus of Newberry College succeeded him as the eighth president.[16] The Reverend John Henry Harms, D.D., served from 1908 to 1918. During these years, 18 acres were added to the campus between the college property and Rosemont Cemetery, the preparatory department was discontinued in 1914, a Student Army Training Corps unit was established, three intercollegiate sports were instituted, and the Newberry athletic teams acquired the name of "Indians."[17]

Two of Newberry's greatest athletes played during these early years, Fred D. MacLean and Ralph B. Baker. MacLean, a native of Youngstown, Ohio, was quarterback of the football team. Diminutive in stature, he had a fighting heart and was an inspirational leader. When World War I broke out he joined the Canadian "Princess Pat" Regiment and saw duty overseas. He returned to Newberry College in 1921 as coach and continued in that capacity for many years. MacLean Gymnasium is named for him, and he was inducted into the South Carolina Athletic Hall of Fame.

After leaving the college he was superintendent of the Episcopal Church Home for Children in York, where he rendered valuable service until his retirement. Returning to Newberry to live, he devoted his services to his alma mater and his church, St. Luke's Episcopal, until his death on November 5, 1964. Married to Woodie Bowman, he was survived by her and one son, Lieutenant Colonel Fred D. MacLean, Jr., U.S. Marine Corps.[18]

Ralph Barre Baker, son of Kenneth and Beulah Barre Baker, was born in Prosperity on October 2, 1895. He graduated from Newberry College in 1916 after starring in three sports. He was All-State in football for two years, in basketball for three years, and in baseball for four years. He was considered the greatest athlete in South Carolina while in college. In 1961 he was inducted into the South Carolina Athletic Hall of Fame, and fifteen years later was the first inductee into Newberry College's Athletic Hall of Fame.

For many years he operated a wholesale grocery firm in Newberry and then entered the insurance field. One of the founders of the State Building and Loan Asssociation of Newberry in 1947, he served as president until the association merged with Standard Savings and Loan Association in 1966. Thereafter he served as chairman of the local board until his death on January 23, 1983.

A charter member of the Newberry Rotary Club, he preserved a perfect record of attendance for sixty-two years. He was a past president of that club and of the Rosemont Cemetery Board, as well as past chairman of the Newberry Planning Board and the Newberry County Bond Commission. Married to Eddie Mae Parr, who died on January 27, 1981, they had three children, Ralph Parr Baker, M.D., Mary Baker Summer, and Henry Parr Baker, who was killed in World War 11.[19]

MacLean's successor as football and baseball coach and athletic director at the college was William D. Laval, who after a brilliant coaching career at Furman, the University of South Carolina, Emory and Henry, and Newberry, was also inducted into the South Carolina Athletic Hall of Fame.

"Tuck" McConnell coached football for four years after Laval retired. He was succeeded by Harvey B. Kirkland of the Class of 1937, a star back at Newberry. The son of Benjamin F. and Gelina F. Kirkland, he was born in Batesburg on December 2, 1913. Starting as a football coach at Bamberg High School, he coached at Carlisle Military Academy until he entered the U.S. Navy where he reached the grade of lieutenant commander. After the war he coached at Summerville from 1946 to 1951. Appointed head coach at the college, he served in that capacity from 1952 to 1967 with great success. From 1967 to 1979 he was in the Physical Education Department.

Active in Central United Methodist Church, he is a Sunday School teacher and former chairman of the administrative board. He and his wife, Elizabeth Louise, are the parents of four children, Marcia, Benji, Genevieve, and Rebecca.

The college was mobilized for war on October 1, 1918, and demobilized on December 15, 1918. This effort cost $4,000, only part of which was borne by the United States.

Dr. Harms resigned in May, 1918, to resume pastoral work, and the third alumnus of the college succeeded to the presidency. Sidney J. Derrick, LL.D., became president and served for twelve years. He previously was principal of the preparatory department and professor of history.[20]

During Dr. Derrick's presidency a new athletic field was constructed and named for Dr. Edwin Boinest Setzler. He and his son Hubert Holland Setzler, Sc.D., taught at Newberry College over a period of seventy-five years. MacLean Gymnasium was built in 1924, and Derrick Hall dormitory for men was completed in 1924.[21] In 1930 Summerland College near Leesville, which had been founded in 1912, was merged with Newberry.[22] The sub-freshman class was abolished in 1926 and the Master of Arts degree was discontinued the year before.[23] Smeltzer Hall became the dormitory for women and Derrick Hall the dormitory for men.

Dr. Derrick resigned because of poor health in 1930 but continued to teach history until his retirement. Dr. James C. Kinard, LL.D., Litt.D., and L.H.D., of the Class of 1916, became the fourth alumnus to become president. He served with conspicuous ability and dedicated loyalty for twenty-four years.

James Campsen Kinard, the son of George M. and Rena Campsen Kinard, was born in Newberry on October 1, 1895. Educated in the local schools and at Newberry College, he became a member of the college faculty upon his graduation in 1916. He was head of the Department of Natural Sciences from 1918 to 1930, dean from 1924 to 1930, and president of the college from 1930 until 1954.

Dr. Derrick stated often that the two brightest students he taught in his long career were Dr. Kinard and John K. Aull, the newspaperman and court reporter. Kinard was regarded as an exceptional teacher. The University of South Carolina awarded him the LL.D. degree, Erskine College gave him the Litt.D. degree, and Newberry College presented the L.H.D. degree to him.

Active in civic and church affairs, he served as chairman of the South Carolina Board of Public Welfare, president of the Newberry Chamber of Commerce, district governor of Rotary International, and member of the County Board of Education. He read law and was admitted to the Bar but never practiced. He married Katherine E. Efird. When he died on September 9, 1970, he was survived by his widow and two sons, James E. who was at the University of Virginia for many years, and Frank E., who is with the Commission on Higher Education of South Carolina.

During his presidency, Newberry College was admitted to the Association of American Colleges, instituted a Department of Business Administration, organized the Newberry College Singers, became fully accredited by the Southern Association of Colleges and Secondary Schools, increased its endowment and faculty, and developed a departmentalized curriculum. Also, the college debt was liquidated and the Wessels Library was dedicated. The college came under the ownership and joint control of the Synods of South Carolina, Florida, Georgia and Adjacent States in 1931.

Newberry College was one of two institutions in South Carolina to have the Naval V-12 Program during World War II. More than 1,000 young men were trained for service on the campus.

Upon Dr. Kinard's resignation in 1954, Christopher A. Kaufmann, LL.D., fifth alumnus to become president, succeeded him. He served for six years, resigning because of poor health in 1960. During his presidency a half-million dollar endowment drive was successfully completed and Cromer Hall, Kinard Hall, and Kaufmann Hall were built.

Dr. A. G. D. Wiles, chairman of the English Department at The Citadel, graduate of Gettysburg College, member of Phi Beta Kappa and holder of the Ph.D. degree from Princeton and the Litt.D. and LL.D. degrees, commenced his eleven-year term in 1960. Under his leadership the college tripled the value of its physical plant with five buildings being constructed—the Classroom Building, Brokaw Hall, the Science and Mathematics Building, the Alumni Music Center, and the A. G. D. Wiles Chapel. The number of students increased to more than 800 and the full-time faculty to fifty. He emphasized scholarship and left an enduring mark on the college.

The next president was Frederic B. Irvin, Ph.D., LL.D., and L.H.D., a veteran college administrator and former member of the diplomatic corps. He served from 1971 until he retired in 1975, a period when all independent colleges were facing serious problems. Enrollment reached a high of 865, annual giving met the projected goals, and plant improvements included the completion of the Alumni Music Center.

The thirteenth president, elected in 1975, was Glenn E. Whitesides, Ph.D., vice president for academic affairs since 1972 and graduate of Erskine College. He was successful in building a new athletic center but could not sustain enrollment in a time when an independent college operated at a distinct disadvantage in relation to public supported institutions. The Tuition Grant Program of South Carolina has enabled the private colleges to survive, but tuition costs in the independent institutions are onerous. Enrollment reached its highest point in 1979 when 883 students registered. It declined to 586 in 1985, but reached 701 in 1989.

Dr. Whitesides resigned at the board meeting held in February, 1984, and John S. Ammerell, a trustee since 1970, was appointed to serve as interim president. He served in that capacity from May 15, 1984, through January 7, 1985. On January 8, 1985, Dr. Paul F. Tillquist of St. Peter, Minnesota, took office as the fourteenth president. On January 30 he submitted his resignation, his tenure of twenty-two days being the shortest on record. The board then elected John S. Ammerell as the fifteenth president of the college. He took office on February 1, 1985, and served until June 30, 1986. He then retired and returned to his home in Miami.

Dr. Hubert Holland Setzler, Jr., was elected the sixteenth president and began his term on July 1, 1986. A native of Newberry and the son and grandson of former Newberry professors, he came to office with the greatest goodwill of both the faculty and the community. He is a graduate of Newberry College in the Class of 1962, holds an M.A. in Russian linguistics, an M.S. in education, and a Ph.D. in educational technology from Syracuse University. He also received a certificate in Russian studies from Indiana University and a certificate in instructor training and educational television.

Dr. Setzler has had vast experience as a consultant, course developer, and lecturer in several fields, working not only in the United States, but also in Saudi Arabia, Japan, and Korea. He has published many developmental testing plans, manuals, and books relating to English, Russian, science and foreign languages, and has received plaques for distinguished work from the Defense Language Institute and for contributions to KEIO University, Japan. For a period of fifteen years before becoming president of the college, he demonstrated his competence in the fields of education, instructional technology, research, and foreign languages.

During his presidency the college has been the recipient of many worthwhile gifts, enabling it to build the John F. Clarkson Swimming Pool, the O. L. Casey Student Center, and the Langford Communications Center. Newberry Federal Savings Bank presented a check for $25,000 as seed money for the pool; Dr. Clarkson, the founder and leader of the bank, was one of Newberry's most active and loyal alumni and trustees, and it was most fitting that the pool be named for him.

Mrs. Virginia W. Casey, trustee from Spring Hill, Florida, and representing the Florida Synod, made a generous contribution of $225,000 for the Student Center in honor of her husband. Herman S. Langford, a 1917 graduate and longtime Newberry businessman and former mayor, left the college more than $2 million upon his death in September 1987. This is the largest gift the college has ever received and enabled it to add a communications major in 1990 upon completion of the center. Dr. Gordon Able, a local surgeon, left the college a substantial gift upon his death in 1987. And in 1989 I. Y. Caughman, a 1928 graduate, gave the College $450,000 to endow a chair in honor of his late wife. It is apparent that the college has taken on a new spirit during Dr. Setzler's tenure. These gifts will undoubtedly stimulate others to give.

Dr. Setzler's involvement in community affairs augurs well. He is an active Rotarian and a former council member of the Lutheran Church of the Redeemer, as well as chairman of the advisory board of the Citizens and Southern Bank's Newberry branch. He is married to the former Cherie Annette Hale; they have three children, Rachel Lake Setzler, Hubert H. Setzler, III, and Heather-Lenore McCreary Setzler.

Newberry College has contributed greatly to the cultural life of the county. Its Music Department, amateur theatricals, and attraction of competent professional artists to the campus have enriched the community. Its training of teachers and professional people has had a profound influence on public education.

The relations between "Town" and "Gown" have been harmonious largely because of the active participation by faculty members in civic affairs. Many of the educators have made valuable contributions to the community but a few deserve special mention. Of the deceased academicians, E. B. Setzler, Gilbert Voight, A. J. Bowers, Sr., R. A. Goodman, Wilmer Gaver, Charles Trabert, James G. Park, F. D. MacLean, Hubert H. Setzler, Thomas E. Epting, and N. Kibler Williamson are remembered with affection. Dr. Grady Cooper, Harvey Kirkland, Red Burnette, Hattie Belle Lester, Sadie Crooks, Conrad Park, Philip Kelly, James C. Abrams, Fred Lester, Margaret Paysinger, and Milton Moore have retired but still maintain their interest both in the college and the community.

Another factor that has cemented relations between the college and the town has been the policy of having at least one non-Lutheran from Newberry on the Board of Trustees. Over the years these members have regarded their membership as an opportunity for service to both the institution and the community. They have included Y. J. Pope, George S. Mower, W. H. Hunt, E. S. Blease, Z. F. Wright, Allen W. Murray, John F. Clarkson, T. H. Pope, Carobel West Youmans, James E. Wiseman, Jr., and William C. Carter. In addition, several local Lutherans have served as trustees, including Vernon F. Epting, Dr. Robert E. Livingston, III, Dr. C. A. Dufford, Jr., and Margaret Christian Pope.

16

The Courts

The Courts of Common Pleas and General Sessions conducted practically no business during the war years. The General Assembly in early 1861 resolved that the courts should defer to the war effort. Chief Justice O'Neall cited this resolution at Spring Term 1861 and adjourned the court after passing an order providing for the drawing of jurors for the succeeding term of court. This procedure continued to be followed, with each court opening and closing on the same day. Finally the judges stopped coming, and the clerk of court would simply open and close the session.[1]

The only business conducted by the court during this period was the naturalization of Nicholas Schmitt and Samuel Cohen as citizens of the Confederate States of America in October 1861, and the recommendation of the grand jury in spring term 1862 that planters reduce their cotton acreage to one-fifth of that ordinarily planted as proclaimed by the governor.[2]

Only a handful of lawyers remained at home during these years—and they were too old to go to battle. Newberry's judges, O'Neall and Johnstone, died during the war. First to go was Associate Justice Job Johnstone, who died on April 8, 1862, after thirty-two years of outstanding service, first in the Equity Courts and then on the Court of Appeals.

Leroy F. Youmans, in his biographical sketch of Chancellor Johnstone appearing in U. R. Brooks's *South Carolina Bench and Bar*, says "that every circuit opinion in which he [Johnstone] was overruled by the Appellate Court, and every appeal opinion in which he dissented from the majority of the chancellors, have subsequently been confirmed and made established law in South Carolina." This is a remarkable record.

Youmans referred to Johnstone and O'Neall as "the great twin lights of Newberry." The other Newberry luminary, Chief Justice John Belton O'Neall, died on December 27, 1863. He was a veritable giant of both the Bench and the Bar and served with signal distinction for thirty-five years, but such was the concern of the public for the soldiers in the field that his death was almost unnoticed.

Governor Benjamin F. Perry wrote of O'Neall twenty years after his death: "No public man in South Carolina has left behind him a purer or more unsullied character than Chief Justice O'Neall. He had none of the faults or foibles which are sometimes found in the character of our greatest men. He was, in the language of General Harry Lee, describing General Marion, 'pure all over.' "[3]

Writing in the *Observer* of April 1, 1913, in a column entitled "Seventy Years Ago," Dr. Spencer G. Welch said of O'Neall, "He was a brilliant, learned lawyer and a great orator. He spoke with astonishing fluency, with a loud, clear, thrilling voice, and with perfect articulation. The writer has heard many eloquent speakers, but none who thrilled him as O'Neall did. We have been told by old men that as soon as his voice was heard in the courtroom a rush would be made to the building by people on the street. I heard a sixteen year old boy say the first time he heard him: 'That old man makes the cold shivers run over me.' "

In 1922, when the *Observer* conducted a poll to determine Newberry's greatest sons, O'Neall was selected as the greatest. Of the twelve men chosen, seven were members of the Newberry Bar—O'Neall, Job Johnstone, Young John Pope, George S. Mower, C. H. Suber, O. L. Schumpert, and George Johnstone.[4]

While Newberry's judges were dying at home, her lawyers were being killed or maimed in Virginia. James D. Nance, J. Elvin Knotts, and William D. Rutherford were killed in battle. Other members of the Bar who served the Confederacy included James H. Williams, James M. Baxter, Christian H. Suber, Samuel R. Chapman, John A. Chapman, A. C. Garlington and J. F. J. Caldwell.[5]

It was hoped that the end of hostilities would bring about resumption of the regular terms of the court and permit the lawyers who returned home from the service to take up once more their professional duties. This could not be done, however, until a new constitution repealing all statutes recognizing or regulating slavery was written and South Carolina was restored to the Union. The new constitution was adopted on September 27, 1865, without being submitted to the people for ratification.

The Constitution of 1865 provided for district courts with jurisdiction over infractions of the Black Code and over cases in which blacks were parties. The judges of these courts were to be elected by the General Assembly for four-year terms.[6] Young John Pope was elected district judge for Newberry District in 1865 although he was not admitted to the Bar until May 1866.[7] His record in this first of his judicial tasks was recognized as good. The Black Code was abolished by General Sickles in January 1866,[8] and the General Assembly later that year made the district court a court of record as well as one of limited jurisdiction.[9]

The Courts of Common Pleas and General Sessions continued to be the trial courts of general jurisdiction. While no civil cases were tried either during the Civil War or in the three years before congressional Reconstruction, criminal causes were prosecuted commencing in October Term, 1866.[10]

On July 27, 1866, the community was shocked at the brutal axe murder of Lemuel Lane. A gang of freedmen led by a white desperado named William Morris killed Lane in his bed and plundered his home. Gold valued at about $9,000 was stolen. Lane's children and a guest, J. B. Heller, escaped by fleeing into the night.

Twelve or thirteen freedmen were arrested. One, John Counts, alias Dawkins, was killed in a Columbia suburb; he had about $1,800 on his person and that money was recovered. In October several freedmen were convicted of the murder and hanged. Several months later London Jones, former slave of Major Jones, confessed to his part in three murders, including that of Lane; he was executed after implicating Belton Cline.[11]

Another group of these men was convicted of robbery and sentenced to be hanged by Judge A. P. Aldrich. Governor Orr commuted their sentences on February 27, 1867; unfortunately they escaped before they could be transferred from the county jail to the new state penitentiary.[12]

Morris, the white leader of the gang was never arrested. He went to Arkansas. Governor Orr offered a reward for his capture and issued a description of him, but all to no avail. Sixteen years later Lane's son, John, was still trying to run down his father's murderer and even had his attorney, C. H. Suber, write to Governor Hagood for a copy of the description issued by Governor Orr in 1866.[13]

In January 1868, a convention met in Charleston pursuant to an order of the military commander of South Carolina, General Canby. This convention adopted a moderate constitution that was to remain the supreme law of South Carolina for almost thirty years; it was modeled after the constitutions then in effect in the northern states.

The Constitution of 1868 re-established the Supreme Court in place of the Court of Appeals. It abolished the separate Law and Equity Courts, established a system of circuit courts having criminal jurisdiction and jurisdiction of all civil actions both at law and in equity, and provided that the circuit judges should rotate in accordance with the law enacted regarding that subject.[14]

Unfortunately, the General Assembly simply provided that a judge of another circuit could sit when requested by the resident circuit judge.[15] Thus was the spirit of the constitution thwarted during Reconstruction; in Newberry, Judge Montgomery Moses held every term during his tenure. In 1877 the legislature enacted a comprehensive act carrying out the constitutional mandate; it provided that the chief justice would annually provide for the rotation of the circuit judges,[16] and this system still is in effect. It is wholesome for suitors and advocates to have the opportunity of not having to appear before the same *nisi prius* judge all the time.

Under the Constitution of 1868 the Code of Civil Procedure was adopted in 1870.[17] It was patterned after the Field Code of New York and greatly simplified common law pleading. This code is still in effect.

Newberry was placed in the Fifth Circuit with Richland, Lexington, and first Fairfield and then Kershaw counties. In 1870, however, Newberry was shifted to the Seventh Circuit with Laurens and Spartanburg counties.[18]

The method of admitting persons to the practice of law was changed materially by the Radicals. The new act permitted any twenty-one-year-old male citizen who had either read law for two years in the office of any South Carolina lawyer in good standing, or who had graduated from any recognized law school in the United States, to be admitted to practice in the circuit or probate courts after examination. The circuit judge appointed the examiners and passed the order of admission. The examiners had to certify to the character and learning of the candidates. In addition, any person admitted in any court of record in the United States could be admitted on motion. Any attorney admitted to practice in the circuit court could be admitted to practice in the Supreme Court after two years.[19]

In 1872 the General Assembly provided for divorce on the grounds of either adultery or desertion for two years.[20] The courts did not become

Figure 1. Holland Hall, Newberry College, 1904.

Figure 2. A. G. D. Wiles Chapel, Newberry College, 1969.

Figure 3. Old Newberry Hotel, 1879.

Figure 4. Opera House, 1882.

Figure 5. Newberry-Saluda Regional Library, 1913.

Figure 6. Newberry County Courthouse, 1907.

Figure 7. Newberry County Memorial Hospital, 1975.

Figure 8. Country Club of Newberry, organized 1921.

Figure 9. Newberry Federal Savings Bank, 1969.

Figure 10. South Carolina National Bank, 1923,
and First Federal Savings Bank, circa 1853.

Figure 11. Church of Jesus Christ of Latter Day Saints, 1982.

Figure 12. First Baptist Church, 1907.

Figure 13. Central Methodist Church, 1901.

Figure 14. Lutheran Church of the Redeemer. 1965.

Figure 15. Aveleigh Presbyterian Church, 1908.

Figure 16. St. Mark's Catholic Church, 1961.

Figure 17. Associate Reformed Presbyterian Church, 1908.

divorce mills in any sense of the word; while the divorce law was in effect only a few divorce actions were brought in Newberry County.

Catherine Divver was granted a divorce from James E. Divver, and Dennis Moates, freedman, obtained one from Elizabeth Moates in 1874. In the same year Wade Hampton Coleman divorced Laura Coleman, and James W. Stockman was awarded a divorce from Josephine E. Stockman. Four years later, Virginia Livingston Carrington was unable to obtain a divorce from Sheriff John Carrington, because the divorce law had been repealed; she finally obtained it in Henderson County, North Carolina, in 1881.[21] Apparently no other divorces were granted in Newberry County until the constitutional amendment authorizing divorce became effective in 1949.

In 1869 the General Assembly provided for the codification of the statute law of the state by three commissioners elected by the legislature. The commissioners were Senator Daniel T. Corbin, Representative W. J. Whipper, and Senator Charles W. Montgomery.[22] The work was generally recognized as having been done by Corbin, but the others drew equal pay.

Corbin was an able lawyer. When elected a circuit judge, he declined because of the salary. Instead he served as U. S. district attorney. Elected to the U. S. Senate, he was not seated. When he was appointed by President Hayes to be chief justice of the Utah Territory, the Senate refused to confirm him.[23]

The *Newberry Herald* complained in 1879 of the congested calendars and advocated the establishment of a county court as the panacea. At that time there were 365 cases on the docket with 116 of them on the trial roster known as Calendar I.[24] More than a century later some Newberrians are advocating a county court; they do not have as crowded a trial calendar now to lend support to their contention.

As soon as the state could return to normalcy from radical Reconstruction, the administration of justice improved. Better judges were elected to the Bench by the General Assembly; better trained prosecutors and clerks improved the efficiency of the courts. The admission procedure was changed so that once more the Supreme Court had charge of admitting lawyers to the Bar.

It must be realized that in the last third of the nineteenth century the civil practice of law was extremely limited in the small towns of South Carolina. Tort practice did not, of course, include actions arising out of automobile or airplane accidents. There was little industry, so industrial accidents were practically non-existent, and corporate practice as known today had not then evolved. Since divorce was prohibited, there were few domestic relations cases; these involved legal separations, support, or child custody. The federal government had not then become so pervasive in business life; there were no federal income taxes, no fair labor standards act, no employment security laws, no antitrust laws. There were no loans for home building by a farmers home administration, a federal land bank, or a production credit association.

In truth, civil practice then included the drafting of wills, contracts, deeds, and mortgages; the administration of estates; suits against the railroads; actions to quiet title and to settle boundary disputes; suits to determine the validity of wills; and the giving of advice and counseling. But there simply was not enough legal work to keep all the lawyers in Newberry busy. Most of them engaged in criminal practice, which was much more lucrative then than in this day of the public defender and the probation system. Small wonder that the Newberry lawyers were complaining of dull times in 1883—there were too many to share the practice.[25]

One of the interesting men who read law in Newberry and then moved on to wider fields was John Fletcher Hobbs, "King of the Cannibals in the South Pacific." Born at Hope's Station in what is now Newberry County, he graduated from Newberry College and read law in the office of Pope and Fair. He was appointed a colonel on Governor Simpson's staff in 1879, began practice in Lexington in 1880, became a Radical in 1881, and went to Australia in 1882 to enter business.[26]

In 1884, Hobbs was a presidential elector on the Prohibition ticket in Georgia. In 1893 he was made king of two tribes of cannibals in the back country of Australia and of other cannibal tribes in the New Hebrides. Four years later he was married in New York City. He was known as the "Big Rice Bird" and was a frequent visitor to Newberry. Newberry College conferred the LL.D. degree upon him in 1908.[27]

Hobbs was reported in 1914 to have declined knighthood twice from Queen Victoria. He died in 1928[28]—the only Newberrian to have been a monarch, the only one to have declined a knighthood, and the only one to have been a cannibal chief.

On November 27, 1884, forty-seven leading South Carolina lawyers, including Christian H. Suber and Y. J. Pope of Newberry, issued a call for a convention to be held in Columbia on December 11, 1884, to organize a state Bar association. The local Bar met in Pope's office to elect delegates.[29]

The South Carolina Bar Association was organized at this convention and, of the 238 founders, twenty-one were from Newberry. This county had more charter members of the association than any other county except Charleston. George Johnstone was elected a delegate to the American Bar Association, Suber was elected vice-president for the Seventh Judicial Circuit, and Pope, Johnstone, and George S. Mower were named to standing committees.[30]

Three Newberry lawyers have served as president of the South Carolina Bar Association—George Johnstone in 1909, George B. Cromer in 1924, and Thomas H. Pope in 1964. The first two were delegates to the organizational meeting of 1884.

In 1891 a Newberrian was elected to the state's highest court when Attorney General Y. J. Pope became associate justice. A former Newberrian, Ira B. Jones of Lancaster, was elected to the Supreme Court in 1896. Thus Newberry had two members of the four on the court of last resort; before the Civil War it had two of three members, O'Neall and Johnstone. In 1898 George S. Mower was nominated chief justice, but was defeated by the incumbent, Henry McIver, by a vote of ninety-eight to fifty-one.[31]

During the period from the Civil War to the end of the century, three Newberry lawyers served as solicitor or state prosecuting attorney. Simeon Fair completed twenty-two years in that office in 1868. Osborne Lamar Schumpert, Confederate veteran and graduate of the University of Copenhagen, served as solicitor of the Seventh Circuit from 1888 to 1896. His successor was Thomas S. Sease, who served until his election as circuit judge of the Seventh Circuit in 1909.

One Newberrian was dean of a law school before the turn of the century. Burr James Ramage, son of the old clerk of court, was educated at Newberry College, Johns Hopkins, Heidelberg, and Columbia University. He was an author and writer and served as dean of the Law School at the University of the South in Sewanee, Tennessee, and as associate editor of the *Sewanee Review*. Dr. Ramage died childless in 1914 and is buried at Sewanee.

During the last third of the nineteenth century the Newberry Bar was known for its advocates and for its great property lawyers. The leading jury lawyers were the incomparable George Johnstone, the diplomatic and courtly Young John Pope, the "master of the twelve" Christian H. Suber, and the gifted Osborne L. Schumpert. Other well regarded advocates were George S. Mower and James Y. Culbreath.

The scholars included Silas Johnstone, Thomas S. Moorman, and J. F. J. Caldwell. Johnstone published an Equity Digest in 1877, while Moorman was author of *Limitations of Estates*. Caldwell was Newberry's best writer during this period.

Shortly after the turn of the century there was local agitation for a modern courthouse. At that time, Law Range was along Boyce Street between Caldwell and McKibben streets. The courthouse, which had been erected in the center of the Public Square in 1852, had little space for offices.

As a result of the public desire for a new temple of justice, a commission was established in 1906 and charged with the responsibility of building a new courthouse; this would be Newberry's fifth such building. The commission was composed of George S. Mower, chairman; Otto Klettner, John R. Perdue, W. D. Senn, C. H. Shannon, J. A. Sligh, and J. Monroe Wicker. A committee of the local Bar, consisting of Fred H. Dominick, George B. Cromer, and J. F. J. Caldwell, was appointed by the Democratic Executive Committee of the county to report on what disposition could legally be made of the old courthouse.[32] The report cannot be found.

The contract for the building was awarded to George W. Waring of Columbia, the architect being Frank P. Milburn.[33] It was completed in 1908 at a cost of $50,000 and still serves Newberry County.

A few years after the new courthouse was erected, Newberry determined to erect a new jail on the site of the old one on Harrington Street. A commission was named to look after the project; this commission was composed of J. Marion Davis, chairman; L. W. Floyd, secretary; Z. T. Pinner, M.D.; H. P. Wicker; John V. Clary; J. M. Kibler, M.D.; and J. C. Baker. James Hemphill and Ernest Summer were the architects, while the contractor was W. G. Sutherlin of Greenwood. The steel work was done by Pauly Jail Building Company of St. Louis and the heating by L. F. Waldrop and company of Rock Hill. The total cost of the jail was $68,313.93. It was completed and accepted by the county on April 8, 1919.[34]

This edifice was widely known throughout South Carolina as "the best jail in the state." When it was finally leveled in 1973, a victim of bureaucratic bungling, the citizens of the community were amazed at the durability and strength of the fortress. It vied in density with the skulls of some county officials.

During the first two decades of the twentieth century Newberry continued to furnish great advocates and lawyers known for their expertise in the field of property law. Coleman L. Blease and George Johnstone vied for leadership among the jury lawyers until the former was elected governor in 1910 and the latter suffered a stroke of paralysis in 1912. The fight between the Johnstones and the Bleases, however, extended into the third decade of the century; Eugene S. Blease and Alan Johnstone, Jr., continued the struggle until the latter accepted appointment as general counsel of the Federal Works Agency and moved to Washington.

Henry C. Holloway and Frank L. Bynum upheld Newberry's reputation for having great property lawyers. Neal W. Workman returned from World War I to become perhaps the local Bar's leading property lawyer during the period between the two world wars. Byron V. Chapman, he of the hearty laugh, and R. Aubrey Harley, of the convivial spirit, were two of the most popular lawyers ever to practice at the Newberry Bar. Frederick Haskell Dominick showed promise of being a great lawyer when he served as assistant attorney general of South Carolina. Elected to Congress in 1916, he served with distinction until his defeat in 1932; he was then too old to renew his early promise as a lawyer but remained a congenial companion and bon vivant.

In 1903 Young John Pope succeeded the stricken McIver as chief justice. Ill health compelled him to retire in 1909. At that time there was no pension system for South Carolina judges, and too often jurists felt that they had to remain on the bench when physically disabled because of the salary. Pope's voluntary retirement was taken as another indication of his high sense of duty. In two years he was dead.

For eighteen years Pope sat on the Supreme Court and took an active part in its labors. Regarded as a pure, just, able, and impartial judge, he merited the affection and respect of the South Carolina Bar. Open and guileless, he had no personal enemies. He was termed "Newberry's most distinguished citizen" by the local newspaper when he died.[35]

Inevitably old Law Range disappeared after the removal of the courthouse. For some time after World War I most of the offices were relocated in the Exchange Bank Building or closer to the new courthouse. Many of the old law offices were razed, but now most of them have once more been relocated, this time in first-floor offices.

In 1926 two members of the Newberry Bar, Eugene S. Blease and Isaac H. Hunt, vied for the associate justiceship that became vacant that year.

Eugene Satterwhite Blease, son of Henry Horatio and Elizabeth Satterwhite Blease, was born in Newberry on January 28, 1877. Graduated from Newberry College in 1895, he taught school for two years and read law. In 1898 he was elected superintendent of education for Saluda County; he also edited the *Saluda Sentinel*. In that year he was admitted to the Bar and managed the Saluda office of the firm of Blease and Blease. In 1900 he was elected to the House of Representatives and in 1905 to the Senate from Saluda County.

He resigned from the Senate, moved back to Newberry and entered into a partnership with H. H. Evans. Later he practiced in partnership with his half-brother, Harry H. Blease, but in 1917 moved to Houston, Texas, where he practiced for a short time. Returning to Newberry, he was elected mayor in 1919. In 1921, he defeated H. H. Evans for the House vacancy caused by the death of George S. Mower. He was re-elected in 1922 and did not run in 1924.

In 1926 he was elected associate justice of the Supreme Court over his fellow townsman, I. H. Hunt. Elected chief justice in 1931, he served with distinction until he resigned because of his health in 1934. During his eight years on the Supreme Court he demonstrated his analytical mind, his sound knowledge of the law, and his industry. He was a popular and respected judge.

Blease's partner before he went on the Supreme Court and after his retirement was Steve Campbell Griffith. Born in Saluda County and educated at the University of South Carolina and at Georgetown University, he first located at Greenwood and then moved to Newberry. He was an excellent, well-grounded lawyer, and a fine complement to Blease. As a comparatively young man, he was elected to the Circuit Court in 1945 and served with distinction until compelled to retire because of ill health in 1967. He died in 1972.

Judge Griffith was the first member of the Newberry Bar to be elevated to the circuit bench since 1860. Judge Moses was living in Sumter when elected circuit judge for the Seventh Circuit. He lived in Newberry after his election. Judge Sease had been a member of the Newberry Bar but had moved to Spartanburg while circuit solicitor; he was elected to the circuit bench while living in Spartanburg.

Judge Francis B. Nicholson of Greenwood succeeded Judge Griffith when he resigned in 1967. He served until 1985.

The Eighth Circuit, to which Newberry County had been transferred from the Seventh Circuit, was given a second judge in 1976, and Judge James E. Moore was elected and still serves. He was educated at Duke University, receiving his B.A. degree in 1958 and his J. D. degree in 1961. He represented Greenwood County in the House of Representatives from 1969 to 1976.

Judge Thomas L. Hughston, Jr., was elected to succeed Judge Nicholson in 1985 upon the latter's death. He was educated at The Citadel, receiving his B.A. degree in 1965, and at the University of South Carolina, receiving his J. D. degree in 1968. He represented Greenwood County in the House of Representatives from 1977 to 1985.

In 1977 the General Assembly created forty-four new Family Court judgeships, of which three were assigned to the Eighth Circuit composed of Newberry, Laurens, Greenwood, and Abbeville counties.

The three judges elected to the Family Court bench in this circuit were Walter T. Lake of Newberry, Curtis G. Shaw of Greenwood, and William J. Craine of Laurens. Upon Judge Shaw's election to the Court of Appeals in 1983, he was succeeded by William C. Charles, Jr., of Greenwood. Upon Judge Lake's retirement in 1988, he was succeeded by John M. Rucker of Newberry.

In 1979 the General Assembly created a Criminal Court of Appeals consisting of five judges. One of those elected was Senator Robert C. Lake, Jr. This court never functioned because the Supreme Court held that four of the five elected judges were disqualified for being in the General Assembly at the time the act was passed. In 1982 another act was passed which established a Court of Appeals consisting of six judges. They qualified on September 1, 1983, and have contributed greatly to the administration of justice in South Carolina.

Newberry did produce a law school dean in the twentieth century. William H. Wicker, son of John H. and Mary Paysinger Wicker, graduated from Newberry College. He then graduated from the law school of Yale University in 1920 and earned a master's degree in law from Harvard University in 1925. In 1946, he was made dean of the University of Tennessee Law School after teaching at the University of South Carolina for four years. Following mandatory retirement from the University of Tennessee, he continued to teach at a number of law schools as visiting professor.

Two Newberrians, Thomas S. Sease and Byron V. Chapman, served as solicitor during this century. Sease continued in that office until elected a circuit judge in 1909. Chapman served during World War II; Hugh Beasley was elected to the office in 1936, and when he entered the United States Navy in 1942, he asked that Chapman be appointed in his stead. Beasley resumed the office after returning from service.

Solicitor Beasley was defeated in 1952 by William Townes Jones, Jr. Both were from Greenwood. Solicitor Jones was graduated from the University of South Carolina, receiving his L.L.B. degree in 1949. After representing Greenwood County in the House of Representatives for two terms he was elected solicitor and served with signal success in that office until 1984. After serving for thirty-two years, he did not offer for re-election. His son, William Townes Jones, IV, was elected without opposition, re-elected without opposition, and is now the circuit solicitor.

As the Great Depression drew to an end, the Newberry Courthouse was enlarged. The commission appointed pursuant to legislative act consisted of Eugene S. Blease, chairman; Zacheus F. Wright, vice-chairman; Tabor L. Hill, secretary; C. W. Bedenbaugh, J. Kess Derrick, James C. Duncan, and J. W. Hipp.[36] This commission retained a Prosperity native, Heyward S. Singley, AIA, a Columbia architect, to draw the plans for the annex, and awarded the building contract to F. E. Moore Lumber Company. The annex enabled the county to continue using the courthouse instead of scrapping it.

At the end of World War II the county delegation refurbished the courtroom, utilizing the services of William G. Lyles, a native Newberrian and an outstanding architect, and of Leland Welling, the artisan who handcarved and built the beautiful wainscoting and judge's dais. Welling was the talented grandson of Osborne Wells, who created the bas relief on the old courthouse. During the period of renovation of the present courtroom, court was held once more in the old courthouse or Community Hall.

17

Bench and Bar

Since 1860 Newberry has had some 150 lawyers. A description of them follows in the order of their admission to the local Bar with those deceased being first mentioned and then the present members.

Simeon Fair, son of William Fair, was born in the Stoney Hill section of Newberry District on November 17, 1801. Admitted to the Bar in 1824, he first practiced in partnership with the great advocate, John Caldwell. In 1836 he served as lieutenant in the Seminole War. After serving some years in the House of Representatives, in 1846 he succeeded James J. Caldwell as solicitor of the Middle Circuit; he continued in that office until October 1868 when the Radicals replaced him. In 1860 he was one of Newberry's four delegates to the Secession Convention.

After the war, Colonel Fair was the "Nestor" of the Newberry Bar until his death on July 15, 1873. He married Mary Butler Pearson on December 23, 1840; she died on December 31, 1867. Their children included Sallie Fair, who married Colonel William Drayton Rutherford, and later Chief Justice Pope; William Young Fair; James D. Fair; and John S. Fair.[1]

Henry Summer, son of Captain John and Mary Houseal Summer, was born at Pomaria on April 11, 1809. Graduating from South Carolina College in 1832 and being admitted to the Bar in 1833, he located first at Lexington and then in Talladega, Alabama. His older brother, Nicholas, bequeathed his law library to Henry on condition that he return to South Carolina and practice at Newberry. This he did.

On December 22, 1846, Summer was married to Frances Mayer, daughter of Major Adam Mayer of Lexington District. He served two terms in the House of Representatives and was elected to represent the Third Congressional District in the Southern Congress that was called to meet in 1851, but never convened. Summer was active in the establishment of Newberry College and served as trustee and secretary of the board.

In 1865 Summer was a member of the Constitutional Convention called to amend the state constitution, but later that year was defeated for the House of Representatives.

During the war, Summer moved back to his farm near Pomaria. Unfortunately, it lay in Sherman's path and was destroyed. He moved back to Newberry where he died on January 3, 1869, survived by his widow and three children, John Adam, Mary (who later married Dr. James K. Chapman), and Catherine (who later married the Reverend Mr. Kyzer and then J. B. T. Scott).[2]

Lambert Jefferson Jones, son of Elijah Jones, was born in Newberry District on July 17, 1816. His parents having died, he was reared in the home of his guardian, John Belton O'Neall. He married Mary Eliza McHardy, another ward of Judge O'Neall.

Jones was graduated with honors from Brown University, where he was a member of Phi Beta Kappa. After reading law with O'Neall, he was admitted to the Bar in 1839. He was commissioner in equity for twelve years and a member of the House of Representatives for several terms.

Jones had three sons and a son-in-law who practiced law in Newberry —Benson M., John B., Lambert W. Jones, and George S. Mower. Jones died at the age of eighty-one on July 15, 1894. His wife died on December 15, 1894.[3]

James H. Williams, son of James and Isabella Shuttleworth Williams, was born in Newberry District on October 4, 1813. His grandfather was killed at Ninety Six during the American Revolution; his father was a captain in the War of 1812; and he served in the Seminole War of 1836. A self-educated man with a natural bent for the military, he organized and led with distinction Company L, Palmetto Regiment in the Mexican War.

Admitted to the Bar in 1843, Williams served as intendant of Newberry for four terms, commissioner in equity for four years, and member of the House of Representatives. Williams built the beautiful mansion on Main Street, which was later owned by Ralph B. Baker. He acquired large land holdings in Arkansas and was in that state when appointed colonel of the Third South Carolina Regiment. Returning home to bivouac at the Lightwood Knot Springs near Columbia, he trained his troops and led them to Virginia.

In 1862 the regiment was reorganized, and Colonel James N. Nance was elected in his stead. Colonel Williams returned to South Carolina and commanded the Fourth and Ninth regiments of state troops until the end of the war.

In 1865 Williams was defeated as delegate to the Constitutional Convention and then elected to the state Senate. Two years later he moved to Arkansas; there he was prominent in political affairs and served as a delegate to the Arkansas Constitutional Convention of 1874. He married Jane Duckett of Newberry District and died on August 21, 1892, in Rocky Comfort, Arkansas.[4] His granddaughter, Mrs. Loy D. England, was clerk of court for Little River County, Arkansas, in 1970. No descendants live in Newberry County.

Albert Creswell Garlington was born in Oglethorpe County, Georgia, on June 9, 1822. He was the son of Christopher and Eliza Aycock Garlington. First honor graduate of the University of Georgia in 1843, he was admitted to the South Carolina Bar in 1844. He read law under C. P. Sullivan, Esquire, of Laurens and practiced there until 1848. In that year he married Sally Lark, daughter of Dr. Peter Moon, and moved to Newberry. Here he enjoyed a large practice and also edited the *Sentinel* for a year. Elected to the House of Representatives and then to the Senate, upon secession he became secretary of the interior and a member of the Executive Council. He was then elected adjutant general of the state and in 1864 was a leading candidate for governor. He served in the field as major of the Holcombe Legion while adjutant general. A great orator, General Garlington was a powerful advocate in the courtroom and a stump speaker of rare ability. He divided his talents after the war between the practice of law and editing a newspaper. One of his sons, Brigadier General Ernest A. Garlington, was a graduate of West Point and inspector general of the U. S. Army. Other children were Octavia, wife of William Y. Fair, and Meredith William Garlington. General Garlington died on March 25, 1885.[5]

James M. Baxter, son of William and Nancy McGowan Baxter, was born in Laurens District on September 7, 1825. After graduation from Erskine College, he read law under General Garlington and was admitted to the Bar in 1849. On May 17, 1860, he was married to Frances, daughter of Drayton Nance, Esquire. In 1861 he entered the service as major of the Third South Carolina Volunteers and was subsequently promoted to lieutenant colonel of that unit. After the reorganization, he was transferred to the Conscript Department, in which he served until the end of the war.

Major Baxter aspired to no political office but was intendant of Newberry for two terms. General Canby, as military governor, declared his office vacant in 1868 and appointed the "scalawag" Montgomery in his place. Later that year the voters of Newberry reinstated Major Baxter.

Recognized as the leader of the Bar, both in the county and judicial circuit, Baxter was a most successful lawyer. He devoted his talent in full measure to the profession.

He was a member and ruling elder of Aveleigh Presbyterian Church for years prior to his death on February 5, 1881. He was survived by his widow and three children—William Baxter, Lucy, wife of Walter H. Hunt, Esquire, and Frances, wife of Dr. James McIntosh.[6]

Silas Johnstone, son of Chancellor Job Johnstone and his first wife, Eliza Meek Johnstone of Fairfield District, was born in Newberry on May 30, 1822. Admitted to the Bar in 1851, he practiced with Christian H. Suber until he was elected commissioner in equity in 1856. He held this office until it was abolished in 1868. In 1879 Governor Simpson appointed him master in equity and he served continuously in this position until 1895. Johnstone compiled and had published an Equity Digest in 1877.

He was intendant of Newberry in 1865 and elected Grand Master of Odd Fellows in South Carolina in 1873, becoming Grand Representative to the Sovereign Grand Lodge of that order in 1875.

Johnstone and his half-brother, George Johnstone, opposed each other in a bitter race for the House of Representatives in 1878. The feeling between the two half-brothers was unusually intense and must have made their practice at the same small Bar unpleasant. In 1895 one of George Johnstone's former law students was appointed master after only three years at the Bar.

In 1896 Silas Johnstone was appointed U. S. commissioner (a minor judicial position in which he issued arrest warrants, fixed bail, and tried minor offenders). His wife, the former Elizabeth Randell, daughter of Colonel Theodore Randell of Chester District, died in January, 1895. He died in Newberry on July 24, 1899, survived by five sons and two daughters—Randell Johnstone, Paul Johnstone, Dr. Theodore Johnstone, Dr. Albert P. Johnstone, Burr Harrison Johnstone, Mrs. John W. Coppock, and Miss Sallie Johnstone.[7]

Christian Henry Suber, son of Solomon and Elizabeth Stockman

Suber, was born near Pomaria on September 4, 1828. He graduated from South Carolina College in 1848, read law with Henry Summer, and was admitted to the Bar in 1851. He formed a partnership with Silas Johnstone that continued until the latter was elected commissioner in equity in 1856. He then practiced with General Garlington and later, for many years, with J. F. J. Caldwell.

During the war Suber was a major first in the Fourteenth South Carolina and then in the Quartermaster Service, sometimes in Virginia and sometimes in South Carolina. He served five terms in the House of Representatives and was active in the Democratic Party during the dark days of Reconstruction. A great favorite in society, Major Suber was well known throughout the Southeast. He died unmarried on March 12, 1890, after suffering a stroke of paralysis on February 23, 1890. His partner, J. F. J. Caldwell, published a memorial that shows the great esteem in which Major Suber was held and the affection which the citizens had for him.[8]

James Fitz James Caldwell, son of Chancellor James J. and Nancy Morgan McMorries Caldwell, was born in Newberry District on September 19, 1837. He graduated from South Carolina College in 1858 and read law under General James Simons in Charleston, being admitted to the Bar in 1859. He then studied law in Germany at the University of Berlin.

Entering the service as a private in Company E, Third South Carolina, he later served in Gregg's First South Carolina as a lieutenant. Severely wounded at Fussell's Mills and slightly wounded at Gettysburg, he served with distinction. In 1866 he wrote *The History of a Brigade of South Carolinians, Known First as "Gregg's", and Subsequently as "McGowan's Brigade."*

Major Caldwell wrote some fugitive verse and in 1906 published a novel entitled *The Stranger*. He was always interested in literature and sound scholarship. He was proud of his role as trustee of South Carolina College, and greatly pleased to be known as the oldest alumnus of the college in the last years of his life.

When he returned home from the war, he first tried to teach but in 1869 began the practice of law and was a partner of Major Suber until Suber's death in 1890. In 1877 Caldwell became chairman of the County Democratic Party when General Y. J. Pope resigned following his nomination to the House of Representatives. In 1890 he ran for the state Senate as an anti-Tillmanite but was defeated by Joseph L. Keitt in a close race. This was his only political campaign.

Major Caldwell was married to Rebecca Conner, daughter of Francis Conner of Cokesbury, in 1875. They had no children. A few years after Suber's death, Caldwell moved to Greenwood where he formed the partnership of Caldwell and Park. While living in Greenwood, he offered for the Supreme Court associate justiceship that became vacant in 1903, but he was defeated by Charles A. Woods.

In 1906 Major Caldwell returned to Newberry. Two years later he served on the special committee to determine what disposition could be made of the old courthouse. In 1912 Mrs. Caldwell died. The major followed her on February 3, 1925. For years he served St. Luke's Episcopal Church as warden and as vestryman, and his funeral service was held there. The *Observer* said of him, "He observed the courtesies of a day long ago and to the last bore without abuse the grand old name of gentleman."[9]

John Abney Chapman, son of John and Sophia Abney, was born on March 9, 1821, in what is now Saluda County. After teaching school, he read law and was admitted to the Bar in 1855. He located at Newberry and in 1858 became associate editor of *The Rising Sun*, continuing his practice until he entered the service. After serving six months as a private in Company G, Second Regiment of State Troops, near Pocataligo, South Carolina, Chapman joined Company G, Nineteenth South Carolina Volunteers.

After the war, Chapman hung out his shingle once more in Newberry. Newspaper work and writing appealed to him more than the law, and he sought the more congenial field. For years he ran a bookstore in Newberry. He assisted the late vice president of the Confederacy, Alexander H. Stephens, in preparing *Stephens' History of the United States*.

He wrote Part II of *The Annals of Newberry*, *The History of Edgefield*, *The Veil*, and school histories of South Carolina and of the United States.

In 1845 he married Mary A. Chapman. They had six children, of whom five survived him—John W. Chapman, Mrs. D. H. Boulware, Mrs. Walter Herbert, Miss Sophie Chapman and Miss Lily Chapman. He died in September, 1906.[10]

Young John Pope, son of Thomas H. and Harriett Neville Harrington Pope, was born in Newberry on April 10, 1841. He was graduated from Furman University in 1860 and began to read law under Chief Justice O'Neall, as had his father before him. When he heard the call to arms, he volunteered as a private in the Quitman Rifles, Company E of the Third South Carolina Volunteers. He served gallantly and was made first sergeant of the company and then adjutant of the regiment. He was wounded seven times and lost an eye at Cedar Creek, but served until the end of the war.

Returning home, he resumed the study of law. Before he was admitted to the Bar in 1866, he was elected district judge of Newberry District and served in that office until it was abolished in 1868. He then formed a partnership with Colonel Simeon Fair and his brother, Dr. Sampson Pope, under the firm name of Fair, Pope, and Pope.

In 1872 he succeeded Wade Hampton, Jr., as president of the South Carolina Club, which gave an annual ball and supper in Columbia from which "scalawags" and "carpetbaggers" were excluded. In 1874 he was married to Sallie Fair Rutherford, daughter of his partner and widow of Colonel Rutherford of the Third South Carolina.

After Colonel Fair's death, Young John Pope practiced with his brother; John S. Fair joined the firm in 1874, making it Pope, Pope, and Fair. In 1874 Pope was elected intendant of Newberry and served in this office for five terms. He also was county chairman of the Democratic Party in 1876 and rendered yeoman service in the Hampton campaign. He was one of the three nominees for the House from Newberry who withdrew their claims to office in order to secure a majority for Hampton. The next year, 1877, he was elected to the House to fill the unexpired term of W. H. Thomas, an expelled member.

In 1888 Pope was elected state senator in a very closely contested race with the Reverend J. A. Sligh. In 1890 he was elected attorney general and in 1891 became associate justice of the Supreme Court. He was elevated to chief justice in 1903 and labored on the court until compelled to retire because of his health in 1909. He served for many years as a member of the Board of Trustees of Newberry College. The University of South Carolina conferred the degree of LL.D. upon him in 1905.

Chief Justice Pope died on March 29, 1911, survived by his widow, a daughter, Neville P. Blacksbear, and a step-daughter, Kate Stewart Rutherford Johnstone. He lived a life of distinguished service and was one of Newberry's greatest sons.[11]

In a moving tribute at his memorial services in the Supreme Court, Major J. F. J. Caldwell said concerning his role during the dark and forbidding time:

> He was a conspicuous member of that band of Carolinians, who, for more than ten years, contended against the brutal tyranny and beastly corruption; who kept alive, against all odds, the fire of patriotic sentiment; and

who finally achieved deliverance from both external and internal oppression. He, with men of zeal and tenacity of purpose, fought unceasingly in his native county, at great personal risk, the forces of enemies as unsparing as they were formidable, and he contributed largely to the final triumph of right over wrong.[12]

Thomas S. Moorman, son of Robert and Mary L. Kenner Moorman, was born in Newberry on March 24, 1842. He graduated from Wofford College in 1860 and volunteered for service with the "Quitman Rifles," Company E, Third South Carolina. He served in Kershaw's Brigade until the end of the war, attaining the rank of first lieutenant. He was wounded at the Battle of the Wilderness.

Returning home, Moorman read law, was admitted to the Bar in 1866, and entered into a partnership with Colonel Simeon Fair. Later he practiced with O. L. Schumpert and then with Lewis W. Simkins. In 1889 he was appointed librarian of the Supreme Court and moved to Columbia.

He was author of Limitations of Estates and was regarded as a scholar and able property lawyer. During the Hampton campaign of 1876 he took an active part for the restoration of the Democratic regime.

Moorman was married to Marie Wardlaw and, after her death, to her sister, Janie Wardlaw. By his first wife he had six children, Mae, Robert, Joseph, Thomas S., Wardlaw, and Reuben Moorman. He died in Asheville, North Carolina, on August 6, 1902.[13]

Benson Miles Jones, son of Lambert J. and Mary Eliza McHardy Jones, was born in Newberry on April 29, 1843. After serving throughout the war as a private in Company G, Second Calvary Regiment, South Carolina Volunteers, he read law and was admitted to the Bar in 1866. He practiced with his father until his death on October 17, 1876. He was survived by his widow, the former Lillie Woodfin, and a daughter, Grace, who later married her cousin, Oscar Mauldin.[14]

Samuel R. Chapman served in Company E, Third South Carolina, as a sergeant. He was well liked and regarded as having excellent literary attainments. He was appointed magistrate upon his return from service, was elected a delegate to the State Democratic Convention of March 1868, and made a member of the Central Executive Committee of the party for Newberry County. He died of acute rheumatism at the age of thirty-one on February 21, 1869. The Prosperity Lodge, AFM, adopted and published its tribute of respect to him.[15]

William R. Spearman was admitted to the Bar in 1866 and ran his card in the Weekly Herald of June 27, 1866, as attorney and magistrate. He had attended The Citadel and served in Company A, Battalion of State Cadets during the war. In November 1866, he and Henry Summer were partners. He was still active at the Bar in January 1868, but then dropped out of sight.[16]

John F. Spearman was admitted to the Bar in 1866 and was actively practicing in January 1868; a few months later he announced that his office was at the "lower end of Law Range." He, too, attended The Citadel and served in Company A, Battalion of State Cadets during the war. After June of that year there is no further mention of him in either newspapers or court records.[17]

Charles B. Buist, who lost a leg at Secessionville in 1862, moved to Newberry soon after and remained until his death on March 24, 1892. He was unmarried. In 1867 he ran his card as attorney at law. He was elected town clerk and treasurer in January 1878, and was re-elected in 1879. He became coroner in 1888 and died during his first term in that office.[18]

James Yarborough Culbreath, son of William and Behethland Yarborough Culbreath, was born on December 26, 1843, in what is now Saluda County. He was educated at The Citadel. After serving in Company B, Battalion of State Cadets, he read law under Colonel Simeon Fair. Shortly after his admission to the Bar in 1867 his father died and he returned to the family farm where he lived until 1875. In that year he returned to Newberry where he practiced for the rest of his life.

He was married to Abbie Merchant, daughter of Sampson C. Merchant, in 1871. They had no children. In 1882 he formed a partnership with his brother-in-law, W. E. Merchant, which lasted for a few years. Later he formed a partnership with Carroll J. Ramage, who conducted the Saluda office of the firm commencing in 1898.

Mrs. Culbreath died on February 12, 1904, and her husband on December 3, 1904.[19] One of the stalwarts during the election of 1876, Culbreath never sought public office but devoted himself to his profession. He was regarded as an excellent lawyer.

Carl Gustave Jaeger, born and reared in Germany, was graduated from the University of Heidelberg. He fled from Germany in 1848 to escape persecution and settled at Cokesbury as professor of music in the female college there. He was a master of many languages, proficient in theology, law, and medicine, and an accomplished musician.

After the war he moved to Newberry, was admitted to the Bar, and was made register in bankruptcy in place of Henry Summer, deceased. He remained in Newberry until 1885 when he moved to Columbia.

When the Newberry Opera House was dedicated, Jaeger read a special ode that he wrote for the occasion. Jaeger was one of the most cultivated men who ever lived in Newberry. He died in Columbia on January 28, 1897, and subsequently was buried by Amity Lodge, A.F.M., in the Masonic Square at Rosemont Cemetery.[20]

Dr. Sampson Pope, son of Thomas H. and Harriet Neville Harrington Pope, was born in Newberry on October 15, 1836. He attended The Citadel, accompanied Colonel James Glenn on his survey of the boundaries of Kansas, survived an attack of cholera while in the West, and attended Jefferson Medical College in Philadelphia. He spent a year as an intern at Pennsylvania General Hospital and then received his M.D. degree from Jefferson.[21]

Returning to Newberry he commenced the practice of medicine but volunteered for service when the call to arms was given in 1861. Enlisting in the Rhett Guards, as Company B, First South Carolina Volunteers was called, he rose to command of that unit. In 1862 he resigned, transferred to the Medical Department, and became senior surgeon of Sorrell's Brigade with the rank of major.[22]

After the war, he returned to Newberry and commenced the practice of medicine. His inquiring mind drove him to the study of law, and he was admitted to the Bar in 1868. He became a partner of Fair, Pope, and Pope in July of that year and continued to practice until 1877 when he moved to Texas. The Newberry Bar on January 16, 1877, adopted a tribute of respect to him.[23]

During Reconstruction he was one of the leaders who worked indefatigably for the restoration of democratic government. He was especially active during the campaign of 1876. Returning to Newberry from Texas, he resumed the practice of medicine. Although active in politics until 1896, he really never practiced law again although he attacked the registration law and the dispensary law in the United States courts; he was admitted to the Bar of the Circuit Court in order to appear in that forum.[24] (For more information about Dr. Pope see Chapter 22.)

In 1869 Samuel Furman was admitted to the Bar by order of Judge James L. Orr. He practiced a few years in Newberry and served for a short time as trial justice in 1871.[25] Nothing further is known about him.

In 1871 William S. Tillinghast was admitted to the Bar by order of Judge Moses.[26] He never practiced in Newberry.

Osborne Lamar Schumpert, son of Jacob Kinard and Harriet Abney Schumpert, was born in Newberry District on January 26, 1845. He was educated at Pagesville Academy and at Newberry College and then, at the age of sixteen, entered the Confederate service. Volunteering as a private in the Quitman Rifles, Company E, Third South Carolina, he served with distinction and was severely wounded.

After the war, he attended the University of Copenhagen from which he was graduated. He returned home, was admitted to the Bar in 1871, and entered into a partnership with Thomas S. Moorman. After serving one term in the South Carolina House of Representatives in 1884–1885, he was elected solicitor of the Seventh Judicial Circuit in 1888. He served eight years in this important position but was defeated for reelection in 1896.

In 1898 he was an unsuccessful candidate for governor. The following year he entered into a partnership with Henry C. Holloway that continued until Colonel Schumpert's death.

He served for years as adjutant of the James D. Nance Camp, United Confederate Veterans, which showed the esteem in which he was held by his comrades. He was master of Amity Lodge, A.F.M.

In January 1876, Colonel Schumpert was married to Mamie E. Pool, daughter of Jordan P. Pool. Their daughter, Thyra S. McClure, predeceased him; his widow and son, Aumerle Schumpert, survived him when he died on December 10, 1910.[27] Colonel Schumpert was one of Newberry's great lawyers.

George Johnstone, Newberry's greatest trial lawyer, was born in Newberry on April 15, 1846, the son of Chancellor Job Johnstone and his second wife, Amelia DeWalt Johnstone. He attended The Citadel and was a boy soldier of the Confederacy, serving in the Battalion of State Cadets.

After the war he attended the University of Edinburgh. Returning to Newberry, he studied law under Colonel Simeon Fair, was admitted to the Bar in June 1871, and commenced his spectacular career. He first entered into a partnership with Y. J. Harrington; after the latter's early death, he practiced from time to time with Francis W. Fant, George B. Cromer, Cromer and J. Brooks Wingard, and R. H. Welch.

He was active in the campaign of 1876 and was an indefatigable worker for Hampton. Later he served as a member of the House of Representatives and then a term as the congressman from the Third District. He was unsuccessful in his race for the U.S. Senate in 1908.[28]

It was as a lawyer and not as a politician that Johnstone made his mark. One of the organizers of the South Carolina Bar Association, he served as its president in 1909. He frequently appeared in the state and federal courts of South Carolina and was recognized as one of the great trial lawyers of the state.

His greatest weakness was his arrogance. He was vitriolic and insulting and took advantage of witnesses in a fashion that would not be tolerated today. In 1886 he goaded into a duel young John B. Jones of the Newberry Bar and killed him in the Magistrate's Court of Henry Blease.[29]

In 1896 he was married to Kate Stewart Rutherford. They had no children. Stricken by apoplexy in 1912, Johnstone lived until March 8, 1921.[30] He died at his home on College Street.

The South Carolina Bar Association, in adopting a resolution regarding his death, stated:

> He disliked the routine of the law office. He chafed under the restraint of mere authority but was disposed to cut straight through the rule and its trappings and seek the reason for the rule. He believed in trial by jury, and he was at home on the hustings and in the forum. He was a great trial lawyer. He had acute powers of analysis, and great skill in the examination of witnesses. He never took notes of testimony. Bold, fearless, virile, aggressive, self-confident, it was his policy to put his adversary on the defensive and then drive him. Apt at repartee, quick in retort, a master of invective . . . he was at his best and was filled with the gaudium certamins when his case seemed desperate and others thought it lost. . . . It is very doubtful whether the South Carolina Bar of other generations ever produced his superior.[31]

Ira Boyd Jones, son of Charles Milton and Mary Jane Neel Jones, was born in Newberry on December 29, 1851. Following his graduation from Erskine College in 1870, he taught school; while teaching, he read law and was admitted to the Bar in 1873.

He first practiced law in Newberry while at the same time acting as associate editor of the *Herald*. He then moved to Prosperity where he practiced while teaching school. In 1875 he moved to Lancaster, South Carolina, where he lived until his death in December 1927.[32]

He was speaker of the House of Representatives, 1890–1894; vice president of the Constitutional Convention of 1895; justice of the Supreme Court, 1896–1910; and chief justice, 1910–1912. He retired from the court in order to make the race for governor in 1912, being defeated by another Newberrian, Coleman Livingston Blease, in one of the bitterest campaigns ever waged in South Carolina.[33]

After his defeat, Judge Jones practiced law and edited the *Lancaster News*. He was married to Rebecca Wyse of Edgefield County.

On January 31, 1873, Young John Harrington was admitted to practice by Judge Montgomery Moses. Harrington was the son of Dr. William Henry and Sarah Strother O'Neall Harrington and was born in Newberry on November 11, 1851. He entered into partnership with George Johnstone; the two partners were admitted to practice before the Supreme Court in May 1875. During the Hampton campaign, Harrington was an active Democrat. Unfortunately he died of typhoid fever in December 1876 at the early age of twenty-five.[34] He was a grandson of Chief Justice O'Neall and resembled him in many particulars.

John S. Fair, son of Simeon and Mary Butler Pearson Fair, was born in Newberry on May 10, 1852. He was admitted to the Bar in 1874 and formed a partnership with Y. J. Pope and Dr. Sampson Pope under the firm name of Pope, Pope, and Fair. He served for many years as town clerk and treasurer but retired from the firm when appointed trial justice in 1881. He moved to Cokesbury in 1894 and became postmaster there. He died on June 12, 1911, at Cokesbury and is buried at Rosemont Cemetery in Newberry. He was married to Hannie Herndon of Cokesbury; they had four children.[35]

William H. Thomas, a Pennsylvania mulatto who was principal of the Hoge Institute, was admitted to the Bar by Judge Montgomery Moses on January 30, 1874. He was the first of his race to be admitted to the Newberry Bar. In 1875 Thomas was appointed trial justice by Governor Chamberlain and the next year he was elected to the House of Representatives. He did not get to complete his legislative term because of being expelled by the House in 1877.

Thomas was arrested in May 1877 and charged with improper use of funds while a trial justice. He left Newberry and in 1878 was appointed consul at St. Paul de Loando on the west coast of Africa. He was convicted *in absentia* and never returned to Newberry.[36]

Milton Anderson Carlisle, son of Thomas A. Carlisle, was born in Union District on September 7, 1841. Educated at South Carolina College, he left before graduating with a company of college cadets; the college awarded him an A.B. degree in 1906. He later enlisted in Company E, Palmetto Battalion, Light Artillery.

Carlisle moved to Mississippi where he was admitted to the Bar and practiced until 1874 when he returned to South Carolina. Admitted to the local Bar on motion on July 8, 1874, he commenced to practice in Newberry. He was elected president of the National Bank of Newberry in June 1899, to succeed James N. Martin, deceased. He was also president of Peoples National Bank of Prosperity. He gave up the practice of law for banking but had a tragic career; he was convicted of violating banking laws. He died on March 11, 1920.

Carlisle married Rosa A. Renwick, daughter of Colonel J. S. Renwick. They had four children, Edwin A. Carlisle, Renwick Carlisle, Mrs. R. M. Kennedy, and Mrs. J. W. Kennedy.[37]

George Sewell Mower, son of Duane and Cynthia Allen Mower, was born in Maine on April 20, 1853. His parents moved to South Carolina before the war and operated a clothing store first in Prosperity and then in Newberry. Mower was educated at Bowdoin College, from which he received a B.A. degree in 1873 and an M.A. in 1876. Erskine College, which he served as trustee and treasurer for many years, conferred the LL.D. degree upon him in 1918.

He read law with Lambert J. Jones and practiced law with him for a few years. He was admitted to the Bar in 1875 by Judge Moses. For the last thirty years of his life he was in partnership with Frank L. Bynum. He maintained the most complete law library of any lawyer in Newberry and was the first to have a typewriter.[38]

Mower was elected to the House of Representatives six times and served for twelve years in the Senate. He was speaker *pro tem* of the House in 1911–1916. Senator Mower was one of four delegates from Newberry County to the Constitutional Convention of 1895. He aspired to the bench and offered for chief justice against the incumbent Henry McIver in 1898, but was defeated by a vote of ninety-eight to fifty-one.[39]

Active in many fields, Senator Mower was grand master of Masons in South Carolina, and was for many years on the Board of Trustees of Newberry College. He was a devoted churchman, being a member of the Associate Reformed Presbyterian Church.

He married Fannie D. Jones, daughter of Lambert J. and Mary Eliza McHardy Jones, on June 13, 1876. She died on March 10, 1910, and he on July 25, 1921. He was survived by four children, Mrs. Foster N. Martin, Dr. Frank D. Mower, McHardy Mower, and Mrs. Henry T. Cannon.[40]

Others admitted to practice by Judge Moses in 1875 were Augustus P. Pifer, Joseph D. Boston, James C. Leahy, and James L. Blease. Captain Pifer, born in Virginia on August 3, 1839, first honor graduate of Roanoke College, and a member of the Bar of that state, came to Newberry to teach school. When Virginia seceded, Pifer immediately returned to his home state to enter service. He was captain of Lee's bodyguard, scouts, and couriers.

Returning to Newberry after the war, he was admitted to the Bar on motion since he had been admitted in Virginia. However, he continued to teach school, serving as principal of the Newberry Academy until 1888 and then serving as a college president in Virginia. He returned to Newberry to engage in the insurance business and remained there until his death on May 18, 1907. He was survived by his widow, the former Lucy Fair, daughter of Dr. Drury Fair of Selma, Alabama, and one son, Drury Fair Pifer.[41]

James C. Leahy, originally from Ohio, settled in Newberry after the war and was elected probate judge in 1870. He continued in this office until 1879. He was admitted to the Bar in 1875 and after returning to Tiffin, Ohio, in March of 1879, he married and moved to Kansas. In 1882 he was elected county attorney of Ellis County, Kansas.[42]

Joseph D. Boston was born in slavery in the state of Virginia. Before the war he belonged to William D. Reagin of Newberry District. Boston was at various times a preacher, teacher, and politician. He was a member of the House of Representatives from 1868 to 1876. While a legislator, he was admitted to the Bar. The Journals of the Courts of General Sessions and Common Pleas show that Boston had little practice.

In the campaign of 1876 Boston voted for and worked for Hampton. From then until his death from consumption on February 2, 1880, he taught at the Hoge School. Boston was the most respected of the Radical legislators from Newberry.[43]

James Lambert Blease, son of James Hartwell and Mary Rebecca Covar Blease, was born on October 30, 1853. He was admitted to the Bar in 1875 but his health was frail, and he died at the age of thirty-five on July 29, 1889. He had been an invalid for several years. He was active for the Democrats in the Hampton campaign of 1876.[44]

Thomas P. Slider, admitted to the Bar in 1853, had not practiced law for years but was appointed trial justice for the town by Governor Chamberlain. His first wife, the former Ellen Ring, died on April 9, 1871, and he married T. W. Gilder in 1873. He advertised in 1875 that he was trial justice and attorney at law; however, two weeks later he advertised an "intelligence office" or employment bureau. He did not really practice law in Newberry after the war; he moved to Atlanta and died in that city.[45]

William Henry Wallace, son of John Wallace, was born at Belfast on November 4, 1848. He was one of the boy veterans of the Confederacy, serving in Company H, Fourth Regiment of State Troops. After the war, he entered Wofford College and received his A.B. degree in 1871 and his M.A. in 1873. He taught at Columbia College from 1873 to 1876 when he was admitted to the Bar and located at Newberry to practice law. He rendered great service during the Hampton campaign.

He soon became co-editor of the *Herald* and then in 1883 the editor of the *Newberry Observer*. He served as president of the State Press Association in 1891 and then as superintendent of the Newberry schools for five years commencing in 1896.

He then became editor of the *Greenville News* but because of ill health resigned that position and returned to Newberry to edit the *Newberry Observer* once more.

Wallace married Alice Lomax of Abbeville, who died on September 25, 1920. He died on May 16, 1924, survived by one child, the great historian, David Duncan Wallace.[46] Although he spent few years in the practice of law, Wallace contributed greatly to the desire for law and order in the county. He was a great force for good in the state.

Frederick Werber, Jr., son of Frederick and Louise Bobo Werber, was born in April 1853. Educated at Washington and Lee, he was admitted to the Bar by Judge Northrop on May 11, 1876. Earlier that year he was married to Fannie W. Roach of Atlanta, Georgia. In 1878 he was elected clerk of the new Board of County Commissioners. He later moved to Washington, D.C., and practiced law there until he accepted a civil service appointment. After retiring from the government, he resumed private practice in Washington with his son-in-law, Ralph C. Case. He died in March 1925, survived by his widow; a son, Waldemar Werber; and his daughter, Mrs. Case.[47]

Francis William Ederington Fant, son of Oliver Hazard Perry and Elizabeth Jones Fant, was born on February 24, 1853. Educated at Furman University and at the law school of the University of Virginia, he was admitted to the Bar in January 1877. Locating at Newberry, he formed a partnership with George Johnstone that was dissolved in 1879. A few years later he moved to Spartanburg to practice; in 1884 he was appointed a trial justice there.

Fant returned to Newberry in 1895 but then moved to Whitmire where he lived until his death on February 1, 1933. He saw service in Company G, Second South Carolina Infantry in the Spanish-American War. A noted sportsman, he brought the celebrated horse "Henry Clay" to Newberry in 1879.

Fant married first Elizabeth White of Richmond, Kentucky, by whom he had one son, White Fant. Later he married Lizzie Clark, by whom he had a daughter, Dorcas Fant.[48]

On September 8, 1877, five young men were admitted to practice in the circuit courts by Judge T. J. Mackey. They were C. D. Barksdale, James C. Clary, Lambert W. Jones, James C. Packer, and Lewis W. Simkins.

C. Douglas Barksdale was from Laurens. He read law with his uncle, Major Baxter, in Newberry so stood the examination for admission to the local Bar. He returned to Laurens upon his admission but came back to Newberry to practice in September 1879. Within six months, Governor Simpson appointed him to the position of master for Laurens County, and he returned to his native county.[49]

James C. Clary read law in the offices of Johnstone and Fant and then was admitted to the Bar. In February 1878 he moved to Laurens to practice. He later practiced in Greenville but died unmarried at the age of forty-two in April 1898. He died at the home of his sister, Mrs. Lowndes Ferguson at Reno, Laurens County.[50]

Lewis W. Simkins was born in Newberry District near Chappells. He first located in Newberry after being admitted to the Bar. He and Milledge L. Bonham, Jr., purchased the *News* and published it for about a year. When they dissolved their partnership in 1880, Bonham moved to Abbeville to practice law, while Simkins remained in Newberry and formed a partnership with Thomas S. Moorman. He moved to Laurens in 1884 to run the firm's office there. He died in Laurens in February 1903 at the age of forty-eight. He married Addie Moorman of Newberry, and they had three sons and a daughter.[51]

James C. Packer was an Englishman who located in Newberry and advertised in 1873 as a house, sign, and decorative painter. Governor Hampton appointed him trial justice for the town in February 1877. He resigned this office in 1883, announcing that he was in charge of the clerical work in Y. J. Pope's office. He died on May 15, 1885, survived by his widow, Mary E. Packer.[52]

Lambert Whitfield Jones, son of Lambert J. and Mary Eliza McHardy Jones, was born in Newberry on January 13, 1855. Educated at Mercer University from which he graduated in 1875, he was admitted to practice in the circuit courts by Judge Mackey in 1877 and by the Supreme Court in 1881. He practiced in partnership with his father until the latter's death in 1894 and thereafter by himself. He was awarded the degree of LL.D. by the Court of Common Pleas, Judge C. C. Featherstone presiding, in February 1941, in recognition of the fact that he and his father practiced for more than 100 years in Newberry.

Jones was married first to Jeannie Herndon of Cokesbury. She died on December 13, 1895, survived by three children, Herndon C. Jones, Benson M. Jones, and Anne Dunbar Jones. He next married Jeannette Merriman by whom he had no children. He died on August 29, 1948, at the age of ninety-three.[53]

A future chief justice, Milledge L. Bonham, Jr., moved to Newberry from Ninety Six in 1879. He and Lewis W. Simkins published the *News* for a year and also engaged in the practice of law. In 1880 he moved to Abbeville to practice law.[54]

In 1880 three Newberrians were admitted to the Bar—Stephen B. Fowles, R. C. Maybin, and James K. P. Goggans. Fowles immediately moved to Beaufort and hence never practiced at the Newberry Bar.[55]

Robert Charles Maybin read law in the office of Moorman and Schumpert. He did not practice law actively and died in October 1911. He was survived by his widow, Susan Halfacre Maybin, and three daughters, Mrs. Wilson, Miss Verna Maybin, and Miss Teresa Maybin.[56]

James K. P. Goggans, son of David and Emily Davidson Goggans, was born in Newberry District on November 3, 1850. Graduated from Furman University in 1874, he taught school and read law in the office of Suber and Caldwell. He completed the law course at the University of Virginia in 1879 and was admitted to practice the following year. He practiced first with D. O. Herbert and then with W. H. Hunt, Jr.

Goggans married Sarah L. Gary and had three children, John C., James, and Eva G. Copeland. He was mayor of Newberry and extremely active in the business affairs of the community. He died of pneumonia in St. Louis in 1896.[57]

G. W. Abney of Edgefield settled in Newberry to practice in September 1880, but there is no further reference to him in the newspapers.[58]

Jacob Brooks Wingard, son of Job Franklin and Martha Auger Wingard, was born in Lexington District on August 24, 1856. After graduating with honors from Newberry College, he read law under George Johnstone. Upon being admitted to the Bar in 1881, he entered the partnership of Johnstone, Wingard, and Cromer. Later he moved to Lexington and was active in law and politics.

He married Lula Rice Hutcheson of Charlotte Courthouse, Virginia. They had three children: Brooks Johnstone Wingard, a lawyer; J. Frank Wingard; and Daniel Wingard. He died in March 1927 at the age of seventy-one.[59]

The other member of the last mentioned firm was George Benedict Cromer, one of the most distinguished men produced in this county.

Born on October 3, 1857, he was the son of Thomas H. and Polly M. Cromer. He graduated from Newberry College in 1877, read law under George Johnstone, and practiced with him after being admitted to the Bar in 1881.

Dr. Cromer received the degree of LL.D. from Wittenberg and Muhlenberg colleges. He served as president of Newberry College from 1896 to 1904, and one of its buildings is named in his memory. He was chairman of the Board of Trustees of Newberry College, a presidential elector in 1928, president of the Newberry Rotary Club, and chairman of the Newberry Hospital Board. He also was mayor of Newberry from 1886 to 1890 and again from 1906 to 1908. Dr. Cromer was one of the founders of the South Carolina Bar Association in 1884 and served as its president in 1924. He was a great lawyer and a man of splendid character.

He married first Carolyn Julia Motte who died on April 26, 1888. They had two children, Carolyn Cromer and Marguerite C. Moise. He then married Harriet Susan Bittle who died on December 1, 1911. They had two children, Beale Holland Cromer and George Benedict Cromer. Dr. Cromer died on September 25, 1935, at the age of seventy-eight.[60]

George Gilmer Sale, son of Dr. T. A. and Lucy Montgomery Sale, was born in Abbeville on September 4, 1852. After graduating from the University of Georgia, he came to Newberry College as professor of mathematics in 1879. Admitted to the Bar in 1881, he practiced law or taught school for the remainder of his life. In 1883 he was associate editor of the *News*, and served a term as county superintendent of education. In 1905 he moved to Chesterfield to teach but returned to Newberry to practice law three years later.

He was married to Kate Huiett. They had three sons, George Gilmer Sale, Jr., Wilbur Maclin Sale, and Frederick L. Sale, and one daughter, Blanche, who died when only fourteen. He died at the age of seventy-six on June 11, 1929.[61]

Joseph Lawrence Keitt, son of Colonel Ellison S. and Caroline Wadlington Keitt, was born near Columbia on April 1, 1857. He graduated from Virginia Military Institute and the Law School of Columbia University in New York City. He was admitted to the Bar in 1881 and opened an office in Newberry, but soon forsook the practice for the life of a planter.

Appointed trial justice to fill an unexpired term in 1886, he was later that year elected to the House of Representatives. In 1890 he was elected to the Senate to fill the unexpired term of Y. J. Pope upon the latter's election as attorney general. In 1895 he was a delegate to the Constitutional Convention. For more than thirty years, Senator Keitt was president of the Farmers Mutual Insurance Company of Newberry. He was also president of the Farmers Alliance of South Carolina and active in all agricultural organizations.

He was married in 1883 to Anna Harrison Coe of Virginia. They had three children, Joseph Lawrence Keitt, Jr.; Fannie Trent, who married Edward B. Purcell; and Anna Coe, who married Edgar L. Hart. Senator Keitt died on September 6, 1927.[62]

In 1882 six Newberrians were admitted to the Bar—M. C. Galluchat, W. Ernest Merchant, D. O. Herbert, J. B. Jones. E. H. Aull, and H. H. Evans.

Minor C. Galluchat of Manning, South Carolina, was operating the Newberry Hotel just before his admission to the Bar. He gave up his lease on the hotel and moved back to Manning where he had a success-ful practice.[63]

W. Ernest Merchant, the son of Sampson C. and Rebecca Merchant, was born in Newberry District on January 17, 1861. Following admission to the Bar, he formed a partnership with his brother-in-law, James Y. Culbreath. However, he did not practice long before turning his atten-tion to agriculture. He married Alma Piester, the daughter of Dr. Rich-ard P. Clark, and lived at Jalapa until his death on October 18, 1909.[64]

D. Oscar Herbert, son of Captain Chesley W. and Elizabeth Goggans Herbert, was born in Newberry District in 1857. He was educated at Wofford College and the Law School of Vanderbilt University. He was admitted to the Georgia Bar in 1881 and to the South Carolina Bar in 1882. He commenced to practice in Newberry with his uncle, J. K. P. Goggans. In 1887 he accepted employment as a post office inspector but three years later located at Orangeburg; there he practiced in partner-ship with his brother-in-law, W. L. Glaze.[65]

He practiced in Orangeburg for forty years and was president of that Bar at the time of his death in February 1930. A veteran of the Spanish-American War, he served as a colonel in the state militia. Colonel Her-bert was married to Julia Salley. They had six children.[66]

John Belton O'Neall Jones, youngest son of Lambert J. and Mary Eliza McHardy Jones, was born in Newberry on December 18, 1859. After his graduation from Newberry College in 1880, he read law with his brother-in-law, George S. Mower. Following his admission to the Bar, he practiced in Newberry until his death in 1887.

Jones was killed by George Johnstone in a shooting which occurred during the trial of a trifling case in the court of Trial Justice Blease. Both attorneys were armed and both fired their pistols. The press of the state was very critical of the entire affair and the community was divided in its sentiments. Johnstone was tried for murder but was acquitted. Jones died on April 2, 1887, at the age of twenty-seven. He was not married.[67]

Elbert Herman Aull, son of Jacob Luther and Julia Haltiwanger Aull, was born on August 18, 1857. Following graduation from Newberry College and admission to the Bar, he decided to locate in Greenwood to practice and to edit the *Saluda Argus*, but the next year he returned to Newberry where he formed a partnership with General A. C. Garlington. He was one of the organizers of the state Bar Association but after Garlington's death turned his attention to publishing.[68]

He was elected president of the State Press Association in 1895 and served in this capacity for sixteen years. He edited the *Newberry Herald and News* for many years and served as county superintendent of education.[69]

He was first married to Alice Kinard by whom he had three sons, John Kinard Aull, James L. Aull, and Herman Aull, and a daughter, Alice Aull. Colonel Aull's second wife was Mae Amick; they had five sons, Elbert J., Luther, Francis, Julian, and Phillip. Colonel Aull died on October 27, 1929.[70]

The last of the six admitted to the Bar in 1882 was one of the most colorful characters who ever lived in Newberry. Henry Herbert Evans was born on Sullivan's Island in 1852 and was reared in Charleston. He was the son of Samuel N. and Mary Butler Evans who moved from Charleston to Newberry about the time of the war.

Evans read law in the office of Pope and Fair. After his admission to the Bar, he moved to Laurens where he was elected intendant in 1884. He became chief of police for the town of Newberry in 1891 and four years later was elected mayor. He served several terms in the House of Representatives from Newberry County and was first a member of the state Dispensary Board and then its chairman.[71]

In 1907 he formed a partnership with Eugene S. Blease when the latter moved from Saluda to Newberry.[72] Later he practiced alone until he retired and devoted himself to planting.

Evans was married to Sarah Ellen Hunter of Laurens County. She died on October 15, 1922, and he on August 18, 1925. They had ten children—Mrs. Landon Townsend, Mrs. J. N. Stone, Mrs. William Brooker, Lurline, Mildred, Rex, Frazier, Roscoe, James, and Beverly Evans.[73]

Two Newberrians were admitted to the Bar in 1883—Mordecai Foot, Jr., and Walter Herbert Hunt, Jr. Foot was the son of an old Newberry merchant. After practicing in Newberry for six years, he moved to Atlanta where he was successful.[74]

Hunt, son of Walter Herbert and Susan McCaughrin Hunt was born in Newberry on April 16, 1861. He attended Newberry College which later conferred the LL.D. degree upon him. He was active in all phases of community life, serving as president of the Baptist State Convention, trustee of both Newberry College and Greenville Women's College, and director of the three local textile plants, the Commercial Bank, and the Security Loan and Investment Company. He organized and was president of Oakland Mills from 1911 until his death on April 9, 1927.

One of the organizers of the state Bar Association, Hunt practiced first with J. K. P. Goggans; then with his brother, Isaac H. Hunt; and then for two years in Spartanburg with S. T. McCravey. He returned to Newberry in 1901 and practiced thereafter with his brother and James B. Hunter under the name of Hunt, Hunt, and Hunter. They had a tremendous practice. Colonel Hunt was married to Lucy Baxter, daughter of Major James M. Baxter of the Newberry Bar. They had no children.[75]

In 1884 T. R. Holmes was admitted to the Bar. He was principal of the Hoge Institute in Newberry and never actively practiced here.[76]

Henry Horatio Blease, Jr., son of Henry H. and Mary Ann Livingston Blease, was born in Newberry on February 4, 1865. He was the first of three brothers to be admitted to the Bar from Newberry. Educated at The Citadel, where he was a beneficiary cadet, and at Newberry College, he was admitted to the Bar in 1886. He then attended Georgetown University from which he graduated in law in 1887.

He practiced alone and then in partnership with his brother, Coleman L. Blease, until he moved to Anderson in 1894 to practice alone. The following year he moved to Staunton, Virginia, where he practiced until 1913 when he returned to Newberry to form a partnership with his half-brother, Eugene S. Blease. He continued to practice in Newberry until his death on March 18, 1921. He was survived by his widow, the former Maggie Koiner of Staunton, and one son, Marion, who died unmarried.

Harry Blease, as he was known, was active in the Methodist Church and in the Prohibition movement. He never sought public office but served as magistrate in Newberry following his father's resignation from that office.[77]

David Ramseur Phifer was born in North Carolina in April 1839. Educated at Davidson College and at the College of William and Mary, he served in the 33rd North Carolina Regiment until severely wounded at New Bern. He married Sarah Whitmire of Newberry District and moved to Newberry in 1869. A staunch advocate of Negro suffrage, he became an active member of the Radical group that controlled Newberry County.

He was defeated for the office of intendant of the town in 1870. The next year he was appointed chairman of the Board of County Commissioners; in 1872 he became county treasurer and continued in that office until 1874.

In 1882 he went to the Dakota Territory in order to obtain a divorce. While there he was admitted to the Bar and practiced a short time in Yankton. He returned to Newberry and was admitted to the Bar in 1889 on motion. In 1889 he went to Washington to try to secure the appointment as postmaster of Newberry. He died there in April 1889 at the age of fifty and is buried in Rosemont Cemetery in Newberry.[78]

Coleman Livingston Blease, son of Henry Horatio and Mary Ann Livingston Blease, was born in Newberry on October 8, 1868. Educated at Newberry College, the University of South Carolina, and Georgetown University, he graduated from the latter with a law degree in 1889. He was then admitted to the Bar and formed a partnership with his brother, Harry. In 1890 he was married to Lillie Summers of Newberry; they had no children.

Having a love for politics, he was engaged in campaigning for office virtually all of his adult life. He served as mayor of both Newberry and Helena, speaker *pro tem* of the House of Representatives, president *pro tem* of the Senate, governor of South Carolina, and U.S. senator.

Active in fraternal orders, he was head of the Odd Fellows, the Red Men, the Moose, and the Knights of Pythias in South Carolina and represented the first three of those groups in their national governing bodies.

Senator Blease located in Columbia after completion of his term as governor. He enjoyed a statewide practice, specializing in criminal law. The late Clint T. Graydon of Columbia, who was associated with Blease in his practice, stated that Senator Blease was at his best when the case seemed hopeless, and that he regarded Blease as a superb trial lawyer when confronted with a real challenge.

In 1940 he was elected to the South Carolina Unemployment Security Commission. All factions joined in giving the old warhorse a sine-cure in his declining years. He died on January 19, 1942, and was buried beside his wife in Rosemont Cemetery, Newberry.[79]

In 1889 S. B. Lathan opened an office in Prosperity where he was principal of the school.[80] There is no further mention of him as a lawyer in the county.

The following year Butler W. Nance and W. T. Williams, graduates of Allen University and native Newberrians, were admitted to the Bar. They did not practice in Newberry.[81]

Franklin Lyles Bynum, son of John Thomas and Margaret Frances Worthy Bynum, was born in the Maybinton section of Newberry County in 1868. After attending Newberry College, he read law and was admitted to the Bar in 1891. For several years he was U.S. commissioner and served as special associate justice of the Supreme Court of South Carolina. He practiced in partnership with George S. Mower until the latter's death and thereafter alone until his retirement. He died unmarried on September 23, 1950, at the age of eighty-three.[82]

Thomas Sidney Sease, son of John L. and Martha Fike Sease, was born in Newberry District on August 25, 1867. Educated at Newberry College and the University of South Carolina, he graduated from the latter with a Bachelor of Arts and a law degree. Admitted to the Bar in 1892, he was in the office of Johnstone and Cromer until he was appointed master in equity in 1895. He then practiced alone and later in partnership with Frederick H. Dominick.

He was elected solicitor of the Seventh Circuit in 1896 and continued in this office until he became judge of that circuit. He was circuit judge from 1909 until 1948. He moved to Spartanburg after being elected solicitor and remained there until his death on May 9, 1952. Judge Sease was married first to Lula Caughman of Edgefield County and then to Eunice P. Calhoun of Abbeville.[83]

Isaac Hamilton Hunt, son of Walter Herbert and Susan McCaughrin Hunt, was born in Newberry on May 3, 1868. He attended Newberry College, South Carolina college, and Eastman's Business School in Poughkeepsie, New York. After reading law in his brother's office, he was admitted to the Bar in 1894 and formed a partnership with his brother, Walter.

From 1900 to 1927 the firm was Hunt, Hunt, and Hunter. Following Walter Hunt's death, the firm was dissolved. In 1929 he formed a new partnership with John F. Clarkson that continued until I. H. Hunt's death on July 16, 1935.

Hunt was a member of the House of Representatives in 1926–1927. During his term he was defeated for the position of associate justice of the Supreme Court by another Newberrian, Eugene S. Blease.

Active in fraternal affairs, he was master of Amity Masonic Lodge in Newberry, head of Pulaski Lodge, IOOF, and a Shriner. A devoted Baptist layman, he filled many posts of responsibility in the State Baptist Convention and the Reedy River Baptist Association. He was a trustee of Furman University, the Baptist Hospital at Columbia, and the Southern Baptist Theological Seminary. I. H. Hunt was married to Unity Gibson, daughter of Major and Mrs. Albert J. Gibson of Newberry County. They had no children.[84]

John T. Duncan, son of Baruch Duncan, was born in Newberry County. He graduated from the Law School of the University of South Carolina and was admitted to the Bar in 1896. He practiced in Columbia and was editor of the *Reporter* in that city. After being away from Newberry for a great many years, he moved back to the town and lived at the Newberry Hotel during the last years of his life. He died on June 18, 1938.[85]

Eugene Satterwhite Blease, son of Henry Horatio and Elizabeth Satterwhite Blease, was born in Newberry on January 28, 1877. Graduated from Newberry College in 1895, he taught school for two years and read law.

In 1898 he was elected superintendent of education for Saluda County; he also edited the *Saluda Sentinel*. In that year he was admitted to the Bar and managed the Saluda office of the firm of Blease and Blease. In 1900 he was elected to the House of Representatives and in 1905 to the Senate from Saluda County.

Following a personal tragedy, he resigned from the Senate, moved back to Newberry, and entered into a partnership with H. H. Evans. Later he practiced in partnership with his half-brother, Harry H. Blease, but in 1917 moved to Houston, Texas, where he practiced for a short time.[86]

Returning to Newberry, he was elected mayor in 1919. In 1921, he defeated H. H. Evans for the House vacancy caused by the death of George S. Mower. He was re-elected in 1922 but did not run in 1924.[87]

In 1926 he was elected associate justice of the Supreme Court over his fellow townsman, I. H. Hunt. Elected chief justice in 1931, he served with distinction until he resigned because of ill health in 1934.[88] During his eight years on the Supreme Court, he demonstrated his analytical mind and sound knowledge of the law and industry. He was a popular and respected judge.

Resuming his practice in Newberry, he formed a partnership with

Steve C. Griffith, his partner from 1924 to 1926. They had a tremendous practice not limited to Newberry County but extending to all parts of the state. After Griffith's election to the bench, Judge Blease practiced in partnership with C. Emile Saint-Amand, and later with Steve C. Griffith, Jr., and Eugene C. Griffith.

In 1942 Judge Blease made the race for the U.S. Senate, being narrowly defeated by incumbent Senator B. R. Maybank.[89]

He never again sought public office but continued in the active practice of the law until his death. He was the recognized leader of the Newberry Bar for thirty years. A safe and wise counselor, adept at analyzing a problem and finding its solution, he was a great lawyer. If he had a weakness, it was his habit of identifying himself with his client's cause and making it his own; sometimes this led to personal encounters in the trial of causes that hampered his effectiveness as an advocate. But such incidents were few. Tenacious, industrious, and possessed of a truly phenomenal memory of names and cases, he was a foe worthy of his steel.

He first married Saluda Belle Herbert in 1896 but they were divorced. Later he married Urbana Neel of Newberry. His only daughter, Saluda, died when only twenty-seven. Her only child, Jack Blease Workman, was reared by Judge and Mrs. Blease. Judge Blease died on December 27, 1963, and Mrs. Blease on August 5, 1968.[90]

Judge Blease had five contemporaries who came to the Bar within the span of three years—Robert H. Welch, James B. Hunter, Frederick H. Dominick, Henry C. Holloway, and L. C. Speers.

Robert Holland Welch, son of James and Rebecca Suber Welch, was born near Pomaria on May 14, 1874. He was a member of the first class at Clemson College, read law with George Johnstone, took summer courses at the Law School of the University of Virginia, and was admitted to the Bar in December 1896. He practiced in Newberry with the firm of Johnstone and Welch until 1904 when he moved to Columbia.

From time to time he practiced with Abney and Thomas, G. Duncan Bellinger, Joseph Nettles, and Ashley Tobias. When the Federal Land Bank was created in 1917, he became its general counsel and remained in this capacity until his death.

He served as a legislator from Richland County. One of his specialties was that of organizing new counties. He acted as attorney in the formation of five counties in South Carolina.

Welch married first Mabel Day of Newberry in 1897. She died in 1908, and he married Nettie Heath. He died in Columbia in July 1929, survived by his second wife and by four children of his first wife—Mrs. Josiah Marde, Margaret, William, and James Welch.[91]

James Bennett Hunter, son of R. T. C. and Rebecca Boozer Hunter, was born in Newberry County on July 18, 1872. First honor graduate of Newberry College in 1896, he read law with George Johnstone and was admitted to the Bar in December 1897. He located in Saluda as manager of the firm of Johnstone, Welch, and Hunter; two years later he came to Newberry as a partner in the firm of Hunt, Hunt, and Hunter.

Hunter took no interest in politics and never ran for public office. He was active, however, in the Lutheran Church of the Redeemer, and as a trustee of Newberry College, treasurer of the Endowment Fund of the College, and president of the Newberry Chamber of Commerce. He served as city attorney for many years.

Following the death of Walter H. Hunt, the firm was dissolved, and Hunter practiced alone for the last four years of his life. James B. Hunter died on December 17, 1930, survived by his widow, the former Minnie McLarnon of Chester. They had no children.[92]

Frederick Haskell Dominick, son of Jacob Luther and Georgianna Minick Dominick, was born at Peak on February 20, 1877. He was educated at the University of South Carolina and at Newberry College. He read law with George Johnstone, was admitted to the Bar in May 1898, and settled in Newberry.

He first practiced in partnership with Thomas S. Sease and then with Coleman L. Blease. He served in the House of Representatives in 1900–1902 and was assistant attorney general from 1913–1916. In the latter year he was elected to the U.S. House of Representatives and served continuously as the congressman from the Third District until 1933.

For many years he practiced in Newberry as a partner of Neal W. Workman, under the firm name of Dominick and Workman, and for a few years in the firm of Dominick, Workman, and Clarkson.

Active in fraternal work, Congressman Dominick served as master of Amity Lodge, AFM, and was a Knight Templar, Shriner, Odd Fellow, Pythian, Elk, and Red Man. He was a member of the Lutheran Church of the Redeemer.

He married Alva Segar, daughter of Congressman George Segar of Passaic, New Jersey, in 1929. They had two daughters, Joan Dominick Bartlett and Doris Dominick Sandberg. He died on March 11, 1960, and Mrs. Dominick on November 30, 1972.[93]

Henry Counts Holloway, son of Thomas W. and Angela Counts

Holloway, was born at Pomaria on September 28, 1874. He was graduated from Newberry College in 1895 and read law in the office of Johnstone and Welch. He graduated from the Law School of the University of South Carolina in 1899 and was admitted to the Bar in that year. He formed a partnership with O. L. Schumpert that lasted until Colonel Schumpert's death in 1910. Thereafter he practiced alone for the rest of his life.

In 1931 Holloway was named receiver for the Exchange Bank of Newberry. He never sought public office but devoted his every energy to the practice of law and to planting. One of the largest land owners in Newberry County, he mistakenly considered himself responsible for payment of every mortgage placed by him as an attorney; during the Great Depression he took in hundreds of acres of land and paid his clients the amounts due on their mortgages. The result was that he went from affluence to poverty in a short length of time.

A prodigious worker, he rose well before daylight and studied his cases. A well-read lawyer, he was always prepared when he went into court. He deserved better than he got.

He married Mrs. Furman Dominick when he was an elderly man. They had no children. He was killed in a tragic automobile accident as he walked along a dark street on October 21, 1957.[94]

Another Newberrian admitted to the Bar near the end of the century was Leland Coppock Speers. Educated at The Citadel and Davidson, he graduated from the latter and received a law degree from Washington and Lee. He served in the Spanish-American War. After being admitted in May 1898, he located at Greenwood. Later he became a famous correspondent for the *New York Times*. He practiced only a short time and never at the Newberry Bar. Speers died on June 23, 1946.[95]

In 1900 Thomas J. Harmon was practicing in Spartanburg. He was a native of Newberry County, the son of Godfrey and Harriett Dominick Harmon. He died at the age of seventy-two in June 1942, survived by his widow, Mildred Shortt Harmon, and two daughters, Nell and Harriett.[96]

In 1902 C. E. Saint-Amand, son of Julius Eugene and Cornelia Blease Saint-Amand of Charleston, moved to Prosperity to manage the office of his uncles, Coleman L. and Eugene S. Blease. He had been living at Kingstree for two years, having studied law there under John A. Kelley. Two weeks after coming to Prosperity, he was married to May Flagler of Kingstree, and two months later he returned to Kingstree to practice with Kelley. He died on August 22, 1951, at the age of seventy-three.[97] His son later practiced in Newberry.

McHardy Mower, son of George S. and Fannie Jones Mower, was born in the town on November 2, 1882. Educated at Johns Hopkins and the University of South Carolina, he graduated in law from the latter in 1904 and was admitted to the Bar. He practiced for only a short time and then operated the Studebaker agency for thirty-one years. He married Kate Adams and they had two daughters, Elizabeth, who married Powell E. Way, Jr., and Grace, who married Robert Duncan. McHardy Mower died on July 25, 1943, at the age of sixty.[98]

In 1909 two Newberrians were admitted to the Bar—Williams Welch and J. Oliver Havird.

Williams Welch, son of Dr. Spencer G. and Cordelia Strother Welch, was born in Newberry County on June 29, 1866. He was an artist of great natural ability and had the advantage of going to Europe in 1891 to visit the great art galleries. He received an appointment as instructor of art at the South Carolina University. Later he attended Georgetown University from which he graduated in law in 1909. His health was bad and he was an invalid for some years before his death on January 20, 1933, in Newberry. He never actively practiced at the Newberry Bar.[99]

John Oliver Havird, son of Campbell L. and Ella Blease Havird, was born on November 15, 1887. He graduated from Newberry College and from the Law School of the University of South Carolina. He located at Anderson where he practiced until he moved to Newberry in 1940. He was city attorney of Anderson and a member of the House of Representatives from Anderson County in 1928. He served as city recorder of Newberry for many years. He died on June 19, 1958, survived by a daughter, Mrs. Herman G. Carter.[100]

Byron Vivian Chapman, son of Jacob Lemuel and Elmina Dreher Chapman, was born near Little Mountain on August 18, 1877. He graduated from Newberry College and from the Law School of the University of South Carolina. At the latter, he played tackle on the 1909 football team. He commenced to practtice at Newberry in 1911. He was a state representative in 1916–17, senator in 1932–36, judge of the City Court from 1919–1932 and from 1937–1942, and solicitor of the Eighth Judicial Circuit during World War II.

Chapman also was Newberry County attorney for many years, chairman of the county Democratic Party, superintendent of the Sunday School of the Lutheran Church of the Redeemer, and a member of the

Church Council. He was married to Esther Cozene and had three children, William Jacob, Laurence D., and Mrs. C. Ray Jackson. Killed in an accident on March 7, 1960,[101] Judge Chapman was greatly loved and one of the most popular members of the local Bar in this century.

Alan Johnstone, Jr., son of Senator Alan and Lilla Kennerley Johnstone, was born in Newberry on July 11, 1890. He graduated from Newberry College in 1910 and from the Unversity of South Carolina Law School in 1912. Johnstone also studied at Harvard University, where he pursued a post-graduate course in law. Settling in Columbia, he practiced there until he left to engage in war work. He was elected to the House of Representatives from Richland County in 1914 and served in the Seventy-first General Assembly; his father was at that time the senator from Newberry County.

After World War I, Johnstone settled at Baltimore where he engaged in social work until he returned to Newberry in 1928. While in Maryland, he became a close friend of Harry Hopkins, a leading figure in Roosevelt's administration.

He was appointed general counsel of the Federal Works Agency and served in this important position until he resigned in 1948 to campaign for the U.S. Senate. After his defeat by Burnet Maybank, he returned to Washington and engaged in the private practice of law until his death on January 6, 1966.[102]

A felicitous writer and an excellent orator, Johnstone could have been a leader of the Bar if he had devoted himself to the law. In many respects he was like his uncle, George Johnstone.

He married Lalla Rook Simmons of Newberry. They had two daughters, Martha and Lalla Rook. Mrs. Johnstone died in 1961. One grandson, Alan Johnstone Paysinger, lives in Newberry.

Neal Wells Workman, son of Henry and Martha Elizabeth Wells Workman, was born near Chappells on May 24, 1885. He attended Meridian College in Mississippi and graduated from Plains College in Plainview, Texas, in 1909. After studying at the University of Chicago, he obtained his Master of Arts and Bachelor of Laws degrees from the University of South Carolina in 1913. He was admitted to the Bar in that year and formed a partnership with Frederick H. Dominick.

He was elected to the House of Representatives in 1914. In 1916 he ran for the Senate against Senator Alan Johnstone and was defeated in a very close race by only sixty-seven votes. He served as first lieutenant in the American Expeditionary Forces in Europe; after the war, he attended lectures at Oxford University before returning to Newberry to his practice.

In 1920 he again ran for the Senate against Alan Johnstone, Sr., and again he was defeated. In 1924 he ran for probate judge, was elected, and served in this office for the remainder of his life. In 1928 he was elected chairman of the Democratic Party for Newberry County and held this important position until his death.

When world War II came, Judge Workman commanded Company M, Second Regiment, Home Defense Force. He died suddenly on July 6, 1945, at the age of sixty, survived by his widow, the former Geneva Thornton Dickert, and his step-son, Elbert J. Dickert.[103]

Quiet, unassuming, and scholarly, Neal Workman was recognized as an extremely able lawyer. He specialized in property law and had few equals, and no superiors, in this exacting field. Kind to young lawyers, he earned their affection as well as their respect.

In 1914 Charles Paschal Barre was admitted to the Bar. Son of Samuel Calhoun and Mary Catherine Bowers Barre, he was born at Prosperity and was graduated from Newberry College. He graduated from the University of South Carolina Law School in 1914 and immediately located at Newberry. The following year he was appointed county superintendent of education, replacing George D. Brown who resigned to accept a position with the State Department of Education. At the end of his term he retired to devote his full attention to his practice.

In 1917 he entered Officers Training School and was commissioned; he was discharged as a first lieutenant and settled in New York. Admitted to the Bar of that state in 1921, he practiced in New York City for more than forty years. He died unmarried on June 17, 1972, at the age of eighty-three. He is buried at Prosperity Cemetery.[104]

Soon after World War I two lawyers from Tennessee practiced in Newberry. Edgar James Green settled in Newberry in 1919. His kinsman, Roy Garrison, joined him here in 1922; they practiced as the firm of Green and Garrison. Garrison returned to Tennessee after a few years. Green was disbarred in December 1930, on the petition of the Newberry Bar.[105]

Steve Campbell Griffith, son of Richard C. and Mary Campbell Griffith, was born in Saluda County on October 13, 1898. He was educated at the University of South Carolina and at Georgetown University, from which he received the LL.B. degree in 1922 and the LL.M. degree in 1923. He practiced a short time in Greenwood and then moved to

Newberry where he opened an office in 1924. In 1925 he formed a partnership with Eugene S. Blease that was interrupted by Blease's election to the Supreme Court in 1926 but resumed in 1934 when Blease resigned as chief justice.

Recognized as a safe counselor well versed in the law and as an able advocate, he enjoyed a wide practice. He was elected to serve the unexpired term of J. Kess Derrick as state representative in 1943. He was reelected to the House without opposition in 1944 and served until his election as judge of the Eighth Judicial Circuit on April 11, 1945. He served with distinction until his retirement on February 28, 1967.

For the last five years of his life, he suffered with fortitude an incurable disease. He died on July 31, 1972, survived by his wife, the former Bertie Hambright of Clover, and two sons, both members of the local Bar, Steve C. Griffith, Jr. and Eugene Cannon Griffith.

John F. Clarkson, son of the Reverend G. Floyd and Nancy Ansel Clarkson, was born at Walhalla on May 25, 1903. He graduated from Newberry College in 1923 and from Furman University Law School in 1929. He was admitted to the Bar in 1928. Locating at Newberry, he entered partnership with I. H. Hunt and practiced with him until the latter's death. Thereafter, he practiced in the partnership of Dominick, Workman, and Clarkson; then with Clarkson, Hunter, and Harley; and then with Clarkson, Hunter, and Clarkson.

He was awarded the LL.D. degree by Newberry College. He founded and was chairman of the board of Newberry Federal Savings and Loan Association and established radio station WKDK in Newberry. Active in civic and church affairs, he was a member of the State Development Board and potentate of Hejaz Temple, AAONMS. He married Elizabeth Hopke and was the father of two daughters, Jacqueline Templeton and Beverly Ivester. He died August 20, 1980.

T. William Hunter, son of George F. and Veda Sheldon Hunter, was born at Prosperity on November 15, 1906. He graduated from Newberry College in 1926 and from the University of South Carolina in law in 1934. He was admitted to the Bar in 1933. He practiced first in the partnership of Hunter and Harley, then with Clarkson, Hunter, and Harley, and then with Clarkson, Hunter, and Clarkson.

He served as a member of the House of Representatives, 1955–1960; president of the National Rural Electric Cooperative Association; and county attorney. He married Leila Knotts of North, South Carolina, and they had two daughters, Margaret Ann McCarthy and Diane Clary. He died December 25, 1979.

Joseph C. Hiott, son of Judge and Mrs. James Capers Hiott of Calhoun County, was admitted to the Bar in 1931, following his graduation in law at the University of South Carolina. He located in Newberry and practiced law alone until his death. He ran for the House of Representatives in 1936 but was unsuccessful.

He was a member of the Baptist Church, the Newberry Country Club, and the Masonic Order. He married Annette Golson, who survived along with two children, Llewellyn and James Capers Hiott. He was killed in an automobile accident near Walterboro on November 1, 1939 at the age of thirty-two.

Berley Metts Havird, son of B. M. Havird, of Silverstreet, graduated from the University of South Carolina with the B.A. and LL.B. degrees. Admitted to the Bar in 1934, he came to Newberry to practice in February 1935. He then taught school at Spring Hill for the 1935-1936 session. He was defeated that year when he ran for the office of magistrate. Shortly afterward he accepted a civil service appointment and moved to Columbia where he still lives.

Russell Aubrey Harley was born on December 2, 1908, in Barnwell, the son of John and Bessie Morris Harley. Educated at Furman University and the University of South Carolina, he located at Newberry upon graduation and admission to the Bar in 1934.

Here he practiced first in partnership with T. William Hunter; later the firm became Clarkson, Hunter, and Harley. After some years of individual practice, he formed a partnership with James N. Parr, and still later with his son-in-law, James Verner. At the time of his death on March 22, 1974, he was senior member of Harley and Verner. At various times others were associated with him—John S. Huggins, Wilson Yates, and Senator Robert C. Lake, Jr.

Entering fully into the life of his adopted community, he was elected to the House of Representatives only four years after arriving in Newberry. He served as state representative from 1938 to 1948, being elected without opposition three times. In 1956 he was elected state senator, after having served this judicial circuit as highway commissioner.

For the last twenty years of his life, Aubrey Harley served as attorney for the city of Newberry. He also was president of the Newberry Bar Association for several terms.

Active in business as well as in government, he was one of the organizers of the State Building and Loan Association. He served that institution as attorney and director until its merger with Standard Savings and Loan Association—and thereafter he was attorney and advisory director of Standard until his death. He also helped organize Carolina Tree Farms and served as president of that company for years.

In December 1934, he married Helen Esdorne of Walterboro. She survived along with three children, Martha Dahl Verner, Dr. Russell Aubrey Harley, Jr., and Charles Harley. The Harleys liked to entertain their friends, and Aubrey Harley had a rare ability to make them feel at home.

A leading member of this Bar for four decades, he was well liked and popular both with his colleagues and his clients. He made friends easily —more importantly, he retained them. Considerate of others, he did not resort to trickery but was open, guileless, and honorable. Able to see both sides of a question, he would determine what was fair and reasonable—and offer to settle on that basis. He realized that a trial is not always the best solution to a problem.

Felix Bailey Greene, Jr., was born in Columbia in 1917. Educated at the University of South Carolina, from which he received a law degree in 1940, he was admitted to the Bar and located in Newberry. He practiced as an associate of Thomas H. Pope until the beginning of World War II. He served with the Eighty-second Airborne Division in the European and Mediterranean Theatres.

When the war ended, Greene returned to Newberry and practiced in partnership with Thomas H. Pope under the firm name of Pope and Greene until 1956. In that year he moved to Beaufort where he was judge of the Family Court and the Civil and Criminal Court of Beaufort County.

Judge Greene married Jean Dobson of Greer; they had two children, George and Mary Martha. He died in 1980.

C. Emile Saint-Amand, son of C. E. and May Flagler Saint-Amand, was born in Wilmington, North Carolina, in 1907. Educated at Duke University, from which he received both his academic and law degrees, he was admitted to the Bar in South Carolina in 1931.

He located at Gaffney and represented Cherokee County in the House of Representatives in 1933–1934. In 1945, he moved to Newberry to form a partnership with his great uncle, Eugene S. Blease. This firm continued until 1952 when Saint-Amand returned to Gaffney.

He married Alice Littlejohn of Gaffney; they have two children, Nathan Saint-Amand, M.D., and Amelia, both of New York City.

Frank E. Jordan, Jr., a native of Columbia, was educated at the University of South Carolina. Upon his graduation from its Law School in 1940, he was admitted to the Bar. He practiced a short time before entering the U.S. Marine Corps, in which he distinguished himself in the Pacific area.

Following the war he settled at Rock Hill but soon moved to Newberry to practice with the firm of Clarkson and Hunter. He was elected to the House of Representatives from Newberry County in 1950 but resigned to accept appointment as assistant U.S. district attorney in Greenville. Later he served as clerk of the Court for the Western District of South Carolina before moving to Columbia to enter private practice.

Jordan was author of *The Primary State*. He married Margaret Davies of Columbia; they had four children, Frank E. Jordan, III, Caroline, Margaret, and Sarah. He died in Columbia in 1976.

Charles Rook Counts, son of Charles Herbert and Alice Kinard Counts, was born in the St. Phillips section on October 27, 1920. He graduated from Newberry College in 1940, taught school, and entered military service in July 1942 as a private. He was successively promoted to captain and upon his release entered law school. He graduated in law from the University of South Carolina in 1948 and the following year located at Newberry as the associate of Frederick H. Dominick.

He re-entered the U.S. Army in 1949, receiving a commission in the Judge Advocate's Department. He was a colonel, stationed at Fort Jackson. Colonel Counts married Mary Penick of Wichita Falls, Texas. They were the parents of three children, Charles Edward, Kenneth Clifford, and Sally Lynn. He died in 1980.

Eugene Wilson Yates, Jr., son of Eugene Wilson and Alice Wet Yates, was born in Winnsboro in July 1923. After three years at The Citadel, he volunteered for service during World War II and became an officer in the U.S. Army Air Corps.

Upon release from active duty, he entered the Law School of the University of Virginia and was graduated in 1948. He located at Newberry and was associated with R. Aubrey Harley. He remained in Newberry for several years and then moved to Rock Hill to practice. He is now an insurance executive in Lexington, Kentucky. He married Isabel McCants of Winnsboro, and they have four children.

James Nance Parr, son of Calhoun Boyd and Mary Nance Parr, was born in Newberry on July 1, 1926. He was educated at the University of South Carolina academically and in law; he received the LL.B. degree in 1950. Returning to Newberry he practiced alone for some years, then in partnership with R. Aubrey Harley, and then alone again. He served for years as public defender of Newberry County. A member of Wig and

Robe, president of the Country Club of Newberry, and a member of the Rotary Club, he died on February 21, 1983. Married to Betty Jo Poston, of Johnsonville, he was survived by her and their children, Lee Poston Parr Deas and James N. Parr, Jr.

Rembert Dantzler Parler was born at Bamberg on December 8, 1930. He was admitted to the Bar in 1954 and located at Newberry where he practiced with the firm of Pope and Schumpert. He was educated at the University of South Carolina both academically and in law. He practiced in Newberry until 1965 when he moved to Spartanburg to engage in practice with the firm of Butler, Chapman, and Parler. He married Shirley Hardeman; they have three children, English, Rembert, and Catherine Parler.

E. Maxcy Stone, son of Harry and Clara Wicker Stone, was born on November 17, 1918. He graduated from Newberry College in 1940 and served in the U.S. Army during World War II. Following his discharge, he attended for a short time the University of Virginia and the University of South Carolina law schools. He was elected probate judge of Newberry County in 1948 and served for sixteen years. After reading law, Stone was admitted to the Bar in 1958; he practiced first alone and then entered the partnership of Blease, Griffith, and Stone.

He married Theresa Robins and they were the parents of four children, Karen Theresa Robertson, Mary Robins Stone, Nazanovitch Stone, and David Maxcy Stone. He died April 27, 1978.

Steve Campbell Griffith, Jr., son of Judge Steve C. and Bertie Hambright Griffith, was born in Newberry on June 14, 1933. He graduated from Clemson College in 1954 and, after service as an officer in the U.S. Army, from the Law School of the University of South Carolina in January 1959. Admitted to the Bar in 1959, he entered practice in partnership with Eugene S. Blease, his father's former partner.

He was elected to the House of Representatives in 1960 and served one term. In 1965 he accepted the appointment as assistant general counsel for Duke Power Company and moved to Charlotte, North Carolina. He is now vice president and general counsel of the company. He married Mary Stanley Salley of Newberry; they have two daughters, Jane and Salley Griffith. Later he married Elizabeth Earhardt Sokovitz.

His brother, Eugene C. Griffith, was born in Newberry, on February 1, 1936. Educated at the University of South Carolina, from which he graduated in 1957, he served as an officer of the U.S. Navy. Upon being released from active duty, he entered the Law School of the University of Tennessee and then transferred to the University of South Carolina, from which he received the LL.B. degree in 1962.

Returning to Newberry, he consecutively entered the partnership of Blease and Griffith; Blease, Griffith, and Stone; Griffith, Mays, Foster, and Kittrell, with offices in Newberry and Columbia; and finally, at the time of his death, Griffith and Kittrell. He was elected to the state Senate in 1966 and served one term. He served as a director of the Newberry Academy, the United Fund, and the Newberry branch of the South Carolina National Bank, as a member of the Board of Trustees of Epworth Children's Home, and as president of the Newberry County Bar Association and the South Carolina Young Republicans. He was an active member of the Central United Methodist Church and was Newberry city attorney from 1980 until his death on April 20, 1990. Griffith was a talented trial lawyer and had a large practice. He married Anne Bruner and was the father of two children, Eugene Cannon Griffith, Jr., a 1990 graduate of the Law School of the University of South Carolina, and Leeann Griffith, who teaches school.

Elliott Duborg Thompson was born in Alexandria, Virginia, on February 17, 1936. He was educated at the University of Maryland with a B.S. in 1960, and at the University of South Carolina with a J. D. in 1967. He was admitted to the Bar in 1967 and located at Newberry. There he practiced with Pope and Schumpert until 1973 when he moved to Columbia. He married Eleanor Page; they have three children, Elliott, Page, and Robert.

Ronnie A. Hightower was born in Saluda in 1943. Educated at Furman University and the University of South Carolina, he was admitted to the Bar in 1968. He located at Newberry and practiced with the firm of Blease, Griffith, Stone, and Hightower. He accepted appointment as an assistant U.S. attorney in Charleston and moved to that city in 1973. He married Jane Wells, of Greenwood; they have two children, Lindsey and Wells. He now practices in Lexington.

Thomas C. Dillard, son of James Ray and Ruth C. Dillard, was born in Whitmire in 1942. He graduated from Newberry College in 1970 and from the University of South Carolina Law School in 1973. He was admitted to the Bar in November 1973 and located at Whitmire where he practiced as an associate of Robert C. Lake, Jr. He has now moved to Union where he practices alone. He married Bertha Yarbrough, and they have one daughter, Anna Ruth.

William Levern Pyatt, son of Charlie and Sarah Gilliard Pyatt, maintained an office in Newberry for several years. He was born in Conway on August 30, 1950. He received his B.A. from Morehouse College in 1972 and his J.D. from the University of South Carolina in 1975. Since his admission to the Bar in 1975, he has been engaged in private practice in Columbia and Newberry.

He married Lou Ann Rush Pyatt and they have two children, Sarah Ann-Marie Pyatt and Caroline Denise Pyatt.

Cheryl H. Bullard, daughter of Monroe Jackson Harris, Sr., and Vera Helen Sanford Harris, was born in Newberry County on December 19, 1952. She graduated from the School of Nursing of the University of South Carolina in May 1975. After her marriage to Dr. P. D. Bullard, she entered the Law School of the university and received her J.D. degree in May 1982. After graduation, she was an attorney for the South Carolina Department of Mental Health. In March 1986, she became an associate of Pope and Hudgens, P.A., and continued the practice in Newberry with that firm until she and her husband moved to Columbia in 1988.

The lawyers living in Newberry County in 1990 with their dates of admission are: Thomas H. Pope, 1938; Walter T. Lake, 1949; Robert C. Lake, Jr., 1949; John S. Huggins, 1950; Robert D. Schumpert, 1951; Gordon N. Clarkson, 1953; Joseph W. Hudgens, 1956; Raymond K. Wicker, 1959; James S. Verner, 1962; Walton J. McLeod, III, 1964; Rudolph C. Barnes, Jr., 1967; Richard M. Kenan, 1969; John M. Rucker, 1969; William F. Partridge, Jr., 1970; Marvin F. Kittrell, 1971; Samuel M. Price, Jr., 1974; Thomas H. Pope, III, 1974; Adele J. Pope, 1974; Margaret Christian Pope, 1975; Henry P. Bufkin, 1975; Gary Tusten Pope, 1976; Henry Summer, 1976; Walter B. Summer, 1976; William J. Smith, 1976; Joy R. Mann, 1978; Robert C. Lake, III, 1983; and James N. Parr, Jr., 1984.

Thomas H. Pope was born at Kinards on July 28, 1913. He is the son of Dr. Thomas H. and Marie Gary Pope and graduated from The Citadel in 1935. He studied law at the University of South Carolina and received the LL.B. degree in 1938.

Elected to the House of Representatives after his freshman year in law school, he was reelected in 1938. Serving overseas with the 107th Anti-aircraft Battalion, he received a battlefield promotion to lieutenant colonel from General George S. Patton. Elected to the House while still in service, he served the unexpired term of Judge S. C. Griffith and then two more terms. He was speaker of the House, 1949–1950. He ran unsuccessfully for governor in 1950 and has not offered for public office since.

He has served as president of the South Carolina Bar Association, president of the South Carolina National Guard Association, chairman of the Foundation of Independent Colleges, vice chairman of the Board of Trustees of Newberry College, president of the Association of Citadel Men, and Grand Master of Masons in South Carolina. A special circuit judge in both 1955 and 1956, he was chairman of the South Carolina Judicial Council. A retired brigadier general of the South Carolina National Guard, he is a graduate of the Command and General Staff College. In 1969, he received the LL.D. degree from Newberry College and in 1977, the LL.D. degree from The Citadel.

He is a director emeritus of the Citizens and Southern National Bank of South Carolina, a former director of the State-Record Company, and a director of Newberry Federal Savings Bank (formerly Newberry Federal Savings and Loan Association) and the Carolina Motor Club. He served on the State Ports Authority from 1958 to 1965 and on the South Carolina Commission of Archives and History from 1965 to 1975. He received the Algernon Sydney Sullivan Award from Newberry College in 1976 and the Durant Distinguished Public Service Award from the South Carolina Bar Foundation in 1983.

In 1983 the Newberry National Guard Armory was dedicated to him and the men he led to World War II, the structure being named the Thomas H. Pope, Jr. Armory.

For the first volume of *The History of Newberry County* he was awarded the certificate of Commendation of the American Association for State and Local History in 1974. He married Mary Waties Lumpkin of Columbia, and they have three children, Mary Waties (Mrs. Robert H. Kennedy, Jr.), Thomas Harrington Pope, III, and Gary Tusten Pope.

Walter T. Lake, son of Edwin O. and Bessie Nichols Lake, was born at Newberry on July 6, 1923. He graduated from Newberry College in 1945 and in law from the University of South Carolina in 1949. He located at Newberry and practiced alone here except for four years when he served as a member of the South Carolina Industrial Commission. In 1977 he was elected family court judge of the Eighth Judicial Circuit and served in that capacity until his retirement in 1988.

He represented Newberry County in the House of Representatives, 1949–1952 and 1969–1974. He married Annelle Ruff of Newberry, and they have two children, Susan Annelle, a member of the South Carolina Bar, and Walter Thomas, Jr.

Robert Campbell Lake, Jr., son of Robert C. and Susan Gaston Howze Lake, was born at Whitmire on December 27, 1925. He received the LL.B. degree from the University of South Carolina in 1949 and since his admission to the Bar has practiced in Newberry County. He was an associate of the late R. Aubrey Harley in Newberry, and then established his own office in Whitmire. He is senior partner in the firm of Lake and Lake, with offices in Newberry and Whitmire.

He served in the U.S. Army in 1944-1945, was elected senator in 1969, and served in that body until 1985. Active in civic affairs, he was potentate of Hejaz Temple and is an elder in the Presbyterian Church. He married Carolyn Young Gray of Whitmire, who died January 21, 1989. They had three children, Robert C., III, Samuel Young, and Linda (who died at the age of twenty-three on April 9, 1973).

John Summer Huggins, son of Dr. H. H. and Marie Summer Huggins, was born at Pomaria on May 1, 1926. He graduated from Newberry College in 1946 and in law from the University of South Carolina in 1950.

He located at Newberry and practiced in the office of R. Aubrey Harley and then alone. Elected to the House of Representatives in 1952, he served one term. Later he entered the U.S. Rehabilitation Service and gave up active practice. He is married to the former Doris Lynn Gunter of Estill, and they have two children, John Summer Huggins, Jr., and Nancy Lynne H. Wessinger. He has an office at Irmo and since his retirement from government work practices there.

Robert D. Schumpert, son of Claude and Myrtle Dennis Schumpert, was born in Newberry on October 28, 1927. Educated at Newberry College and the University of South Carolina, he received the LL.B. degree from the latter in 1951. After a year in Atlanta with the Office of Price Administration, he returned to Newberry in 1952 to practice with the firm of Pope and Greene. The firm later became Pope and Schumpert, and he continued in active practice until May 1973 when he suffered a severe stroke. He served as president of the Newberry Bar Association; member of the Board of Bar Examiners, 1969-1973; member of the Supreme Court Commission on Grievances and Discipline, 1964-1967; and member of the Law School Committee of the South Carolina Bar Association for many years.

He retired from active practice in 1975 but is of counsel to the firm of Pope and Hudgens. Married to Probate Judge Margaret Hutchinson Schumpert, he is the father of five children, Susan, Young, Dennis S. Byrd, Lucia S. Renwick, and Claude.

Gordon N. Clarkson, son of the Reverend G. Floyd and Nancy Ansel

Clarkson, was born at Cokesbury on August 1, 1914. He graduated from Newberry College in 1935, read law under T. William Hunter, and was admitted to the Bar in 1953. He served two years in the U.S. Air Force during World War II.

He was a member of the firm of Clarkson, Hunter, and Clarkson until the death of his partners. Since then, he has practiced by himself. Married to Innis Mims of Newberry, he has one daughter, Nancy Elizabeth Ragsdale.

Joseph W. Hudgens, son of Joseph W. and Fannie Gilreath Hudgens, was born at Taylors, South Carolina, on May 21, 1932. He graduated from Furman University in 1954, received his LL.B. from the University of South Carolina in 1956, and was awarded the B.D. degree from Southeastern Baptist Theological Seminary in 1963.

He served as clerk to the late Chief Justice C. A. Taylor and to his successor, Chief Justice Joseph R. Moss. After supervising the Legal Aid Office in Greenville, he moved to Newberry in 1973 where he practices in the firm of Pope and Hudgens. He was chairman of the Committee on Character and Fitness, South Carolina Supreme Court for many years and chairman of the State Board of Youth Services, of which he is still a member. He married Judy Sweetland of Spartanburg. They have two children, Toni and Celena.

Raymond K. Wicker, son of L. D. and Ruth Dominick Wicker, was born in Newberry on June 27, 1930. He graduated from Newberry College in 1951 and from the Law School of the University of South Carolina in 1959. He also studied at the University of Maryland and the University of Oklahoma. Commissioned a captain, he entered the Judge Advocate's Department of the U.S. Army in 1964, retiring as a colonel in 1985. Following the death of Eugene C. Griffith, he became a member of the firm of Griffith and Wicker, with offices in Newberry. He was formerly county attorney for Edgefield County, maintaining his office in Johnston.

James S. Verner, Jr., son of the late Assistant Attorney General James S. and Ann Marshall Verner, was born in Columbia on July 17, 1937. Educated at the University of South Carolina, he received the B.A. degree in 1960 and the LL.B. degree in 1962. He practiced in Spartanburg, Columbia, and Hartsville before coming to Newberry in 1970 to form the partnership of Harley and Verner. He served as city attorney of Newberry for some years. He now practices alone and is public defender for Newberry County.

Married to the former Martha Dahl Harley, he is the father of three boys, Charles Vermuele, James Spencer, and Russell Aubrey Harley Verner.

Walton J. McLeod, III, son of Walton J. and Rhoda Lane McLeod, was born at Walterboro on June 30, 1937. He was educated at Yale University, B.A. 1959, and at the University of South Carolina, LL.B. 1964. After serving as clerk to Judge Clement F. Haynsworth, Jr., of the Fourth Circuit Court of Appeals, he practiced with the firm of Pope and Schumpert in Newberry.

He then became assistant district attorney for South Carolina and is now general counsel for the South Carolina Department of Health and Environmental Control. McLeod was also magistrate of Little Mountain District until he resigned in 1981. He was then mayor of Little Mountain for several terms. Married to the former Julie Hamiter of the music faculty of Newberry College, he lives at Little Mountain; they have one child, Walton James McLeod, IV.

Rudolph Counts Barnes, Jr., son of Rudolph C. and Ella Carson Barnes, was born in Columbia on September 16, 1942. He received his B.A. degree from The Citadel in 1964, his J.D. degree from the University of South Carolina, and the M.P.A. from the latter in 1979. After serving two years on active duty in the U.S. Army, he became a partner in the firm of Barnes, Alford, Stork and Johnson in Columbia where he practiced from 1971 to 1986. He was a member of the Columbia City Council and Central Midlands Regional Planning Council.

In 1986 he moved to Prosperity and established the firm of Barnes and Bufkin, but he now practices alone. He is a member of the Newberry County Water and Sewer Authority Board, vice-president of the Mid-Carolina Chamber of Commerce, and an active member of Zion United Methodist Church.

He married Jeanette Wall. They have three children, Rudolph C. Barnes, III, Tracie, and Ashley.

Richard Maxwell Kenan, son of Judson Glenn and Archel C. Glenn Kenan, was born in Greensboro, North Carolina, on March 10, 1940. He graduated from the University of North Carolina, B.S. 1962, and from the University of South Carolina, J.D. 1969. He served in the U.S. Navy as an officer, 1962-1965.

He located at Newberry, practicing first with the firm of Pope and Schumpert and then by himself. He was a member of the South Carolina House of Representatives, 1974-1976. He first married Lillian Sinclair Kemper of Newberry, and they have two children, Clifton MacLaine and Richard Kemper. He is now married to June B. Brooks.

John M. Rucker, son of Marvin J. and Sarah Bouknight Rucker, was born in Newberry on October 22, 1944. He was educated at the University of South Carolina, receiving the B.S. degree in 1966 and the J.D. degree in 1969. He first settled in Clinton, where he practiced for a short time, and then moved to Newberry where he was engaged in general practice until his election as family court judge in 1988. He served as a member of the House of Representatives, 1976–1980. He married Harriett Lee, and they have two sons, John Brandt Rucker and Wylie Marvin Rucker.

William F. Partridge, Jr., son of William F. and Clara Eskridge Partridge, was born in Newberry on July 16, 1945. Educated at The Citadel, from which he graduated in 1967, and at the University of South Carolina, from which he received the J.D. degree in 1970, he served four years as an officer in the U.S. Air Force.

He returned to Newberry in 1974 and practiced with the firm of Pope and Hudgens until 1984 when he established his own office. He married Ilene Stewart of Lillington, North Carolina, and has one daughter, Allison, and a son, William Franklin, III.

Marvin F. Kittrell was born in Daytona Beach, Florida, on October 3, 1941. Educated at Furman University, B.A. 1963, and at the University of South Carolina, J.D. 1971, he received his LL.M. degree from the University of Florida in 1976. He served in the U.S. Navy from 1965 to 1968. A former member of the firm of Griffith and Kittrell, he is a member of Central United Methodist Church. He is now a member of the South Carolina Workers Compensation Commission, having been appointed by Governor Campbell in 1990. He married Julia Wagner and has one daughter, Erika, and a son, Benjamin.

Samuel M. Price, Jr., son of Samuel M. and Selma Brown Price, was born in Newberry on November 6, 1949. He graduated from Wofford College in 1971 and received the degree of J.D. from the University of South Carolina in 1974. Following admission to the Bar in November 1974, he located at Newberry and practices by himself. He married Ann Renwick, and they have three children, Jonathan McGill Price, Samuel McGowan Price, III, and Meagan Renwick Price.

Thomas Harrington Pope, III, son of Thomas H. and Mary Waties Lumpkin Pope, was born in Columbia on March 30, 1946. He graduated from Episcopal High School in 1964, the University of the South in

1968, and the Officer Candidate School of the U.S. Navy in 1969. He served in Vietnam as commanding officer of a swift boat and received a unit citation and the Bronze Star.

Upon his release from active duty, he graduated from the University of South Carolina in 1974, receiving the J.D. degree. He practiced in Columbia with the firm of Glenn, Porter, and Sullivan until he returned to Newberry in 1977. He is in the firm of Pope and Hudgens, has served as president of the Newberry Historical Society and as senior warden of St. Luke's Episcopal Church, and is a member of the Kiwanis Club. He was elected to the state Senate in 1984 and re-elected without opposition in 1988.

His wife, Adele Jeffords Pope, daughter of John Cotesworth and Laura Hammond Jeffords of Columbia, graduated from Mary Baldwin, received her master's degree at the University of Virginia, and graduated in law from the University of South Carolina, receiving her J.D. degree in 1974. She was a partner in the firm of Haynsworth, Marion, McKay, and Guerard in Columbia, specializing in estate planning. She now practices alone. They have one son, William Harrington, and one daughter, Jane Marshall Pope.

Gary Tusten Pope, younger son of Thomas H. and Mary Waties Lumpkin Pope, was born in Columbia on August 15, 1949. He graduated from Episcopal High School in 1967 and the University of the South with a B.A. in English in 1971. He graduated from Washington and Lee University in law, receiving his J.D. degree in 1976. Admitted to practice in Virginia and South Carolina, he practices with the firm of Pope and Hudgens and is Newberry County attorney.

He married first Leslie Lander; they have one daughter, Helen Harrington. He then married Margaret Ann Christian, daughter of Dr. Richard and Martha Stelling Christian of Greenwood. She graduated from Emory University and the Law School of the University of South Carolina. She serves as trustee of Newberry College and is a partner in the firm of Sinkler and Boyd in Columbia, specializing in bond practice. They have three children, Gary Tusten Pope, Jr., Elizabeth Christian Pope, and Ann Stelling Pope, and are active members of the Lutheran Church of the Redeemer. He has served on the Church Council.

Henry P. Bufkin, son of Benjamin I. and Frances Doris Bufkin, was born in New York City on May 31, 1943. After graduation from the University of Bridgeport (Connecticut) in 1965, he entered the U.S. Army. After twenty years of service, he retired as lieutenant colonel in the Judge Advocate General's Department. He received the M.B.A. degree from Alabama A. and M. in 1972 and the J.D. degree from the University of Tulsa (Oklahoma) in 1975.

In 1986 he formed the partnership of Barnes and Bufkin in Prosperity and in 1990 established his own office. A member of Our Lady of the Lake Catholic Church, he is active in the Boy Scouts, Little Mountain Ruritan Club and Little Mountain Elementary School Parent Teachers Organization. Married to Jane Susan McArthur Bufkin, he has three children, Daniel P., Michael F., and Jeanne S. Bufkin.

Two brothers, Henry Baker Summer and Walter Baker Summer, were admitted to the Bar in 1976. They are the sons of C. Walter and Mary Baker Summer; Henry was born in Columbia on February 7, 1947, and Walter in Newberry on July 3, 1948.

Henry Summer graduated from Newberry College, B.S. in 1969, and from the University of South Carolina, J.D. in 1976. He became a CPA in 1973, and after practicing accounting with J. W. Hunt & Co. of Columbia for two years, opened his own accounting office in Newberry. He has been treasurer of both the Newberry Historical Society and the Newberry Easter Seal Society and was a founding member of the Board of the Newberry YMCA.

He married Sue Davis of Newberry, and they have three children, Walter Munson, Janie Marie, and Buford McCary Summer. They are members of the Associate Reformed Presbyterian Church, of which he is a former treasurer and deacon.

Walter Summer graduated from Newberry College, B.S. in 1969, after which he worked in the General Accounting Office in Washington for four years. He graduated from the University of South Carolina, J.D. in 1976, after which he practiced law with John Bolt Culbertson in Greenville until 1981 when he opened his office in Newberry. He retired because of ill health in 1987. Walter formerly was married to Rose McDaniel Heatley. They have one child, Kate Summer.

William J. Smith, son of George Thomas and Corinne Martin Smith, was born in Newark, New Jersey, in 1947. He graduated from Clemson University with a degree in electrical engineering in 1969 and from Georgetown University, J.D. in 1973. He was a patent examiner in the U.S. Patent Office from 1969 to 1975. He is a member of the Board of Directors of the Newberry Council on Child Abuse and Neglect. A member of the South Carolina Bar and a patent attorney, he operates a TV shop in Newberry.

He married Rande Yates, who is secretary to Circuit Judge Carol Connor in Columbia. They have one child, Benjamin.

Joy R. Mann, daughter of Jesse George and Marian Williams Rushe, was born in Graniteville on May 24, 1936. She received her B.S. degree from Newberry College in 1956, her master's degree in education from the University of South Carolina in 1973, and her J.D. degree from the same institution in 1978.

She married Richard A. Mann, from whom she is divorced. They have three children, Richard Anthony Mann, Jr., Anna Joy M. Fletcher, and Marian Elizabeth Mann.

Mann practices law from her office in Prosperity with Herbert E. Buhl, III, of the Columbia Bar, under the firm name of Buhl and Mann.

Robert Campbell Lake, III, son of Robert C. Lake, Jr., and Carolyn Othella Young Lake, was born in Union, South Carolina, on February 13, 1958. He graduated from the University of South Carolina, B.S. in 1980 and J.D. in 1983.

He was clerk to Judge James M. Morris for a year and an associate of his father until January 1989, when he became a partner in the firm of Lake and Lake. He maintains membership in the Whitmire Presbyterian Church. He married the former Gerda Hallman; they have two children, Gerda Hallman Lake and Robert Campbell Lake, IV.

James Nance Parr, Jr., son of James Nance and Betty Jo Poston Parr, was born on July 7, 1959. He was educated at the University of South Carolina, receiving both the B.S. and J.D. degrees in 1984. After practicing several years with Lester L. Bates, Jr., in Columbia and as legal counsel for Wells American Corporation in West Columbia, he returned to Newberry in 1988 and now practices here.

18

Editors, Authors and Artists

Before the Civil War, Newberry had five newspapers, the *Sentinel*, the *Newberrian*, the *Mirror*, the *Conservatist*, and the *Rising Sun*, but never more than two of these were published at the same time. During the war years only the *Rising Sun*, published by Thomas F. Greneker and Thomas P. Slider, served the local community. When Greneker entered the Confederate service, he sold his interest to his brother, Richard H. Greneker.[1] The *Rising Sun* was discontinued in early 1865, being succeeded by the *Tri-Weekly Herald*.[2]

The Greneker brothers published this newspaper until it became the *Weekly Herald* in June 1865, and then the *Newberry Herald* in 1866.[3] The great fire of that year, which destroyed more than half of the business section of the county seat,[4] consumed both the newspaper office and the home of Richard H. Greneker located on the southwest corner of Main and College streets.[5]

The brothers dissolved their partnership and went their separate ways for some time. Thomas F. Greneker continued to publish the *Newberry Herald*, while Richard H. Greneker and Thomas P. Slider established the *Progressive Age* in 1873.[6] The latter failed in 1876[7] and was succeeded by the *Newberry News*, founded by R. H. Greneker, Jr. and W. P. Houseal in 1878.[8]

In May 1875 the State Press Association was organized at a meeting held in the Hibernian Hall in Charleston.[9] Thomas F. Greneker was the first treasurer of this group and held that office for several years. Later Colonel Elbert H. Aull served as president of the association for sixteen years, from 1894 to 1909.[10]

In 1879 Milledge L. Bonham, Jr., future chief justice of South Carolina, moved to Newberry to form a partnership with Lewis W. Simkins, also a lawyer, to publish the *Newberry News*.[11] After a year they sold the paper to R. H. Greneker and his son.[12] In 1884 the *Newberry Herald and News* appeared after the two Greneker-owned papers merged.[13]

In 1883 W. H. Wallace, W. P. Houseal, and J. H. M. Kinard founded the *Observer*.[14] A third weekly, the *Voice of the People*, established as a partisan Tillman organ, was published by the Reform Publishing Company with Frank V. Capers and Arthur E. P. Bedenbaugh as editors.[15] The *Newberry Herald and News* was acquired by Elbert H. Aull and W. P. Houseal in 1887.[16] This press also commenced publishing the *Lutheran Visitor* in that year.[17]

T. F. Greneker, pioneer Newberry newspaperman, died on December 3, 1889, at the age of sixty-three. He was a member of the Methodist Church and was ill for some years before his death.[18]

In the first year of the new century another early Newberry newspaperman died at his home in Helena.[19] Richard H. Greneker, son of Captain Thomas Greneker, was born in Charleston in 1832. He came to Newberry in 1859 to work for his brother, T. F. Greneker, and as noted, was associated with various local newspapers. He was an active communicant of St. Luke's Episcopal Church.

William H. Wallace, who had left the editor's chair of the *Newberry Observer* in 1893, returned to that post in 1901. He resigned as editor of the *Greenville News* because of ill health. A few months after his return, the local newspaper became a semi-weekly rather than a weekly.[20]

The first of three daily newspapers in Newberry was established in May 1904 with John K. Aull as editor. Wallace, in announcing its advent, commented that "it is a five column four-page paper, very neatly printed and presenting altogether quite a creditable appearance." Aull's partner in this venture was William B. Seabrook,[21] later to become famous as the author of *Asylum*.

The *Evening Telegram* was discontinued in December 1904, and it was almost twenty years before a second attempt was made at publishing a local daily. This was the *Evening Midget* that lasted only a few months during 1923. The last attempt at publishing a daily occurred in 1937; in that year S. L. Goodman and A. L. Thompson published the *Daily Herald* for five months.[22]

E. H. Aull continued in the newspaper field as editor and publisher of the *Herald and News* until he sold the paper to the Armfield brothers, Otto F. and Ira B., in 1928. Ira Armfield withdrew from the paper in

1936, and the next year Otto sold the paper to Goodman and Thompson of Virginia. In turn they sold the paper to John W. Earhardt, Sr., who combined it with the *Newberry Observer*.[23]

After disposing of the *Herald and News*, O. F. Armfield established the *Sun* in October 1937. His son Frank succeeded him as publisher but in 1972 the *Sun* was discontinued.[24] Since that time Newberry has had only the *Newberry Observer*, now a tri-weekly, and a throw-away one known as the *Diversified Printer*.

As the second town in the county, Prosperity had an active press after the *Reporter* was established in 1885 by E. H. Aull and Milledge S. Hallman.[25] That paper became the *Press and Reporter* when Frank V. Capers acquired it.[26] Later E. O. Counts became editor and L. S. Bowers business manager. Two other papers in that town before 1900 were the *Prosperity Adviser* edited by I. D. Witherspoon and the *Prosperity News*. The latter's demise was announced in May 1899.[27]

Prosperity, however, has had a number of short-lived papers during the twentieth century. These include the *Voice of the People*, which was moved from Newberry in 1900; the *Prosperity Eagle Eye*, established in 1901;[28] and the *Prosperity Citizen*, organized in 1961.[29] Prosperity has had no newspaper in recent years.

In 1911 Whitmire had the *Whitmire News*, with Albert Young as editor, but the paper failed in March 1912. It was re-established in February 1934 and was edited by Mrs. W. W. Lewis until May 30, 1935. Later that year Ann Duckett attempted to revive the paper but was unable to publish more than a few issues.[30]

In the 1960s William C. Armfield published several papers including the *Whitmire News* and the *Prosperity Citizen*. He then retained his job printing shop and sold his papers to the *Clinton Chronicle*. The *Whitmire News* was discontinued in 1989. The *Whitmire Courier* is now being published by the owner of the the *Diversified Printer*.

In 1922 the *Observer* became the joint property of W. H. Wallace, J. W. Earhardt, Sr., and Arthur H. Counts.[31] In that year, the paper conducted a contest to name Newberry's greatest citizen. John Belton O'Neall won, the other five of the six greatest being O. B. Mayer, Sr., George W. Holland, Robert L. McCaughrin, Young John Pope, and George S. Mower.[32]

Two years later William Henry Wallace died. Son of John and Martha Wallace, he was born at Belfast on November 4, 1848. He graduated from Wofford in 1871, after having served the Confederacy as a boy soldier. He taught at Columbia College, was superintendent of the Newberry city schools for five years, and practiced law in Newberry. Founder of the *Newberry Observer*, he served for some time as editor of the *Greenville News*. He married Alice Lomax of Abbeville. After she died on September 25, 1920, he lived with his brother, Robert G. Wallace, in Newberry. He had one son, David Duncan Wallace, Wofford teacher and South Carolina historian.[33]

Another founder of the *Newberry Observer*, James H. M. Kinard, died in November 1910, at the home of his daughter in Augusta. Born in Newberry on November 3, 1847, he was the son of Solomon P. Kinard, antebellum postmaster of the village. He spent his life as a printer and continued with the paper he had helped found until 1909 when his health compelled him to retire. He was survived by two sons, George M. Kinard and Julian H. Kinard, and two daughters, Mrs. Elmo S. McNeill and Ethel Kinard.[34]

The third founder of the *Newberry Observer* was William Preston Houseal, the well-known "Dutch Weather-Prophet." Born in Newberry on July 30, 1856, he was the son of William Walter and Eliza Caroline Barre Houseal. Educated at Newberry College, he was awarded the degree of Litt. D. by that institution in 1934.

He became a printer's apprentice in 1873, then founded the *Newberry News* in 1878 and the *Newberry Observer* in 1883. He published the *Lutheran Visitor*, first in Newberry and later in Columbia. As a partner in the firm of Aull and Houseal, he printed *The Annals of Newberry*, second edition, and a number of other works.

Possessed of a remarkable memory and a facile pen, he contributed a number of articles to the local newspapers. In 1881 he married Catherine Anna Rives, and they had four children, Vera, Edward Bennett, William Walter, and Ainsley Rives (Mrs. Lane Bonner). He lived to the ripe age of ninety and died in September, 1946.[35]

Another longtime worker on the *Newberry Observer* was John Wolfe Earhardt, Sr. Born in Lexington on January 8, 1867, he was the son of John Wolfe and Joanna Mariah Eloise Harman Earhardt. He came to Newberry to work as a compositor.

Alderman and mayor of Newberry, representative from Newberry County, commissioner of public works, secretary of Amity Lodge, AFM, for twenty-six consecutive years, he was a leading and useful citizen of this community.

He married Jessie Copeland, who died on December 6, 1937. Mayor Earhardt died on July 9, 1949, at the venerable age of eighty-two. He was survived by two sons, J. W. Earhardt, Jr. and George B. Earhardt, and by four daughters, Mrs. H. L. Huffman, Miss Eloise Earhardt, Mrs. I. M. Satterwhite, and Mrs. G. R. Kluttz. At the time of his death, and for many years before, he was the publisher of the *Newberry Observer*.[36]

John Wolfe Earhardt, Jr., succeeded his father as editor and publisher of the *Newberry Observer*. Born in Newberry on August 25, 1906, he was educated in the local schools and graduated from Newberry College with a Bachelor of Arts degree in 1926. After serving as head of the English Department in the Allentown Preparatory School, Allentown, Pennsylvania, for 1926–1927, he returned to Newberry as a reporter for the *Newberry Observer* in 1928. He remained with the paper in various capacities until the newspaper was sold to the State-Record Company of Columbia on July 1, 1979, which in turn sold the paper to Knight-Ridder in 1986.

Married to the former Frances Elizabeth Bedenbaugh of Prosperity, he had one daughter, Elizabeth Griffith. A member of the Lutheran Church of the Redeemer and active in the fraternal and business affairs of the community, he died on February 15, 1989.

The present editor of the *Newberry Observer* is Ollie Thomas Moye. A native of Anderson County, he worked first for the *Anderson Daily Mail*. In 1956 he joined the news staff of the *Newberry Observer* and became editor in 1979. He is married to the former Alicia Bonds; they have two sons, Michael Thomas and Timothy Bonds Moye. The family attends Macedonia Lutheran Church.

The longtime editor of the rival newspaper, the *Herald and News*, was Elbert Herman Aull. The son of Jacob Luther and Julia Haltiwanger Aull, he was born on August 18, 1857. After graduating from Newberry College and being admitted to the Bar, he settled in Greenwood to practice law and edit the *Saluda Argus*; the next year he returned to Newberry to form a partnership with General A. C. Garlington. Although one of the organizers of the South Carolina Bar Association, he devoted himself to publishing a newspaper after Garlington's death.

Elected president of the State Press Association in 1895, he served in this capacity for sixteen years. He edited and published the *Newberry Herald and News* for many years and also served as county superintendent of education.

He was first married to Alice Kinard by whom he had three sons, John Kinard, James L., and Herman, and a daughter, Alice Aull. Colonel Aull's second wife was Mae Amick. They had five sons, Elbert J., Luther,

Francis, Julian, and Phillip. Colonel Aull died on October 27, 1929. Just a year before his death he sold his newspaper to the Armfield brothers as has been recounted.

His son, John Kinard Aull, was even better known than his father. Born in Newberry on February 17, 1884, he was a brilliant, though dissipated, genius. First honor graduate of Newberry College in 1902, he became secretary to Governor McSweeny in 1903. The next year he edited Newberry's first daily, the *Evening Telegram*. He wrote well and often charmingly. After serving as secretary to Governor Blease and to Congressman Dominick, and after several stints as court reporter, he was correspondent for the *Newberry Observer* and other newspapers.

He married Kate Tompkins of Edgefield and upon his death on February 3, 1940, he was survived by her and one daughter, Julia Kate (Mrs. Jackson Nims). He was buried in Rosemont Cemetery in his family's square.[37]

Another notable figure in the local newspaper group was the late Otto F. Armfield. He was born at Tradesville, Lancaster County, on April 11, 1895, the son of William Joseph and Mollie Snipes Armfield. He learned the printing trade as a youth and followed it for many years. He and his brother, Ira Burton Armfield, bought and operated first the *Saluda Standard* and then the *Newberry Herald and News*, which was purchased from E. H. Aull in 1928.

In 1936 Armfield sold this paper to Goodman and Thompson. He continued in the job printing business for a short time but found the urge too strong to resist so he established the *Sun*. He wrote a column that appeared on the front page of the weekly and was eagerly awaited each week. It was the most candid and courageous journalism ever to appear in a Newberry paper.

He finally tired of crusading and turned the *Sun* over to his son, Franklin. Thereafter he dealt in real estate and spent much time fishing, but he made his mark in local journalism. Armfield died on August 15, 1970, survived by his widow, the former Ruth Carrie Thrower, and four children, Allie Constance, Otto Franklin, Jr., Doris Ruth Sanders, and William Clay.[38]

A good many books have been written by Newberrians since 1860. While most of them have been histories, the number includes a few novels, some poetry, and one biography.

One of Newberry's most gifted writers was Dr. Orlando Benedict Mayer, Sr. Son of Adam and Mary Counts Mayer, he was born near Pomaria on February 24, 1818. He graduated from the South Carolina

College in 1837 and from the Medical College of Charleston. He then located in the Dutch Fork but later went to Europe where he studied at the universities of Edinburgh, Paris, and Heidelberg. He settled in the town of Newberry in 1846 and lived there for the rest of his life.

He was married three times—first to Mary David of Fairfield, then to Carrie DeWalt, and finally to Mrs. Louise Kinard. By his second wife he had five children, one of whom was Dr. O. B. Mayer, Jr. Besides teaching physiology and hygiene at Newberry College for many years, he was a musician and patron of the arts.[39]

Before the Civil War he contributed many stories to literary magazines, including *Russell's Magazine*. Among his contributions were "The Voice, the Hand and the Silhouette," "The Music Girl of the Rue de la Harpe," "Aberhot Koselhantz, the Wizard Gunsmith," and "The Cob-Pipe: A Tale of the Comet of '43."[40]

Leland Cox, in his critique of antebellum Charleston magazines at the Reynolds Conference in 1974, said of Mayer: "The best of Russell's contributions is also perhaps the least well-known. Nevertheless it is with the stories of O. B. Mayer that the final refinements are added to the realistic and humorous materials that were printed in Charleston's magazines . . ."[41]

Mayer wrote the "Dutch Fork Sketch" for the *Herald and News*, which was edited by James E. Kibler and published in 1982 as *The Dutch Fork*, and a book he was working on at the time of his death which appeared posthumously. It bore the rather formidable title *Malladoce, the Briton; His Wanderings from Druidism to Christianity*.[42] He also wrote *John Punterick* (a novel of Life in the Old Dutch Fork) that was edited by James E. Kibler and published in 1981 as Volume 7 of the South Caroliniana Series.

Dr. Mayer was named as one of the six greatest Newberrians in the poll conducted by the *Newberry Observer* in 1922. He died in Newberry on July 16, 1891.[43]

Two brigade histories were written by local residents, one in 1866 and the other in 1899. *The History of a Brigade of South Carolinians, known first as Gregg's and subsequently as McGowan's Brigade* was written by J. F. J. Caldwell. Despite a long and forbidding title, it is interestingly presented and was characterized by the late Dr. Douglas Southall Freeman, author of *R. E. Lee* and *Lee's Lieutenants*, as "altogether the best history of a brigade in Lee's Army. A wise, well-written book, which should be republished."[44] The latest edition of this volume was published by the Morningside Press in 1985.

Caldwell also wrote a novel, *The Stranger*. It was not a best-seller when it was published in 1906 and today is unknown. His education made him a master of language, and he wrote charmingly in his fugitive pieces to newspapers and in his eulogies. He simply was not a novelist but a historian. For additional information about Caldwell's career, see the biographical data in Chapter 17.[45]

The History of Kershaw's Brigade was written by D. Augustus Dickert. Published by the E. H. Aull Company of Newberry in 1899, it was termed by Freeman as "the account of a famous Brigade of McLaws Division, First Corps."[46] Dickert also wrote interesting newspaper accounts from time to time of local events. One of these was the story of Marie Boozer, Countess de Pourtales, whom he termed "The Sorceress of the Congaree."

Dickert was a boy captain in the Third South Carolina. He combined his writing with a legendary daring; the story of his riding his horse up the steep steps of the old courthouse during Reconstruction is still told locally. The shooting scrape he had with T. J. Lipscomb broke up a county convention and threatened to divide the Democratic Party in Newberry.[47] He ran for public office several times but was not successful. This fiery, interesting figure died at the age of seventy-four in October 1917. Three children survived—J. Roland Dickert, Mrs. Amos Wells, and Lucile Dickert.[48]

John A. Chapman, a part-time lawyer, wrote *Part Second: The Annals of Newberry, History of Edgefield County, History of South Carolina*, and a book in blank verse, *Within the Veil*. All except the last were published in Newberry, being printed either by Aull and Houseal or by the E. H. Aull Company. His *History of South Carolina* was adopted for use by the schools of South Carolina in 1893.[49] It succeeded the official history written by another Newberrian, James Wood Davidson. For more details about him see Chapter 17.

Davidson, son of Alexander and Sarah Davidson, was born on March 9, 1829, in the Enoree section of Newberry District. He graduated from the South Carolina College, B.A., in 1852; he received an M.A. in 1855. Before the Civil War he taught school in several different villages and in Columbia.

He served as adjutant, 13th South Carolina Regiment, seeing service in Virginia. After the war he wrote *A School History of South Carolina* that was adopted for use in the schools of the state in 1878.[50] He also wrote *Living Writers of the South* that has been characterized justly as "incondite and curious, but interesting"; it is certainly highly informative about important matters not to be learned of elsewhere.

After living and working as a journalist for ten years in New York, he married Josephine Allen, a widow, and moved to Lake Worth, Florida. There he served in the state Constitutional Convention of 1886, and in the state legislature in 1887. He published *The Correspondent*, a handbook for writing letters; *Florida of Today*; and *The Poetry of the Future*. The latter was undoubtedly his best work; as a literary critic he excelled, and it is an urbane volume. At the time of his death on June 23, 1905, he was compiling a dictionary of Southern authors.[51]

John Brown Carwile wrote *Reminiscences of Newberry*, which was published in 1890 and republished by the Newberry County Historical Society in 1970. Born in Newberry District on November 24, 1825, he was the son of John Schuyler and Elizabeth Williams Carwile. He read law in the office of Thomas H. Pope, Esquire, but when the tutor died suddenly, the young clerk abandoned law to enter business as a merchant and then as a banker.

Carwile's book is not a history but a collection of charming vignettes of personal recollections. His contribution to the preservation of Newberry's history is an extremely valuable one. He married first Mary Calmes; after her death, he married Kate Birdsall. Carwile died in 1897, survived by two children, Will and Daisy. None of his descendants is now living, and the name is extinct in Newberry.[52]

James Pinckney Kinard, son of John Martin and Lavinia Rook Kinard, was born at Kinards, Newberry District, on July 17, 1864. He attended Newberry College and The Citadel, being graduated from the latter in 1886. He was headmaster of the Newberry Male Academy before returning to The Citadel as assistant professor of English. After receiving his Ph.D. at Johns Hopkins, he taught at Winthrop and The Citadel, was president of Anderson College, superintendent of the Newberry city schools, and dean and president of Winthrop. Dr. Kinard wrote *English Language and Literature*, *Our Language*, a play entitled *Mortmain*, and edited *Old English Ballads*. The first two were textbooks and were used in the public schools of the state.

He married Lee Wicker of Farmville, Virginia, and they had six children, Lavinia (Mrs. O. P. Smith), James P. Kinard, Jr., Oscar Wicker Kinard, Katharine Kinard, Nellie Kinard, and Henry Harrison Kinard. He died in June 1951, and is buried in Rosemont Cemetery. He was the oldest living graduate of The Citadel at the time of his death.[53]

Edwin Boinest Setzler, son of Dr. George A. and Elizabeth Cromer Setzler, was born on June 28, 1871. He graduated from Newberry College in 1892 and received his Ph.D. degree from the University of Virginia in 1902. Awarded the Litt.D. by Presbyterian College in 1924, he was recognized as a leading authority on Old English. He was author of numerous publications, including *Notes on English Grammar, Notes on Anglo-Saxon Versification, An Introduction to Advanced English Syntax, High School and College English Grammar Manual,* and *The Jefferson Anglo-Saxon Grammar and Reader.* He married Una Lake, longtime teacher of English in the Newberry city schools. They were parents of Dr. Edwin L. Setzler, dean of Lenior Rhyne College, and of Hubert Holland Setzler, Sc.D., for many years a member of the Newberry College faculty. Dr. Setzler died on December 10, 1939; Mrs. Setzler, on August 3, 1966.[54]

Howell Meadors Henry, son of Hugh P. and Martha H. Boozer Henry, was born in Newberry on August 18, 1879. He received a Bachelor of Arts degree from Newberry College in 1898, and from Vanderbilt University a Master of Arts degree in 1908 and a Ph.D. degree in 1913. He spent his life teaching at Emory and Henry College where he served as professor of history and political science and as dean. He wrote *Police Control of the Slave in South Carolina* as his dissertation; it was published in 1914. An active Methodist, he married Addie Folk of South Carolina. They had two children, Howell Kirkland and Hugh Fort Henry.

George Leland Summer, son of John Harrison and Huldah Cromer Summer, was born at Pomaria on November 16, 1881. He received both the Bachelor of Arts and Master of Arts degrees from Newberry College and was active in many fraternal and patriotic societies. At one time he was cashier of the Newberry Savings Bank and then was secretary of Mollohon Manufacturing Company. Later he was agent for several life insurance companies.[55]

Summer's avocation was genealogical research. He wrote *Newberry County South Carolina Historical and Genealogical* in 1950. Unfortunately he did not authenticate his historical facts: and, because of this his statements must be checked. Nevertheless, his work is valuable despite this defect.

He married Caroline Nancy Mayes; they had four children, George Leland, Jr., Harry Thomas, William Mayes, and James Elbert Summer. He died on April 27, 1956.[56]

Eloise Welch Wright edited *A Confederate Surgeon's Letters to his Wife,* first published in 1911. Her father, Dr. Spencer Glasgow Welch, was surgeon of the Thirteenth South Carolina Volunteers. Mrs. Wright was born in Newberry on October 4, 1874, the daughter of Dr. Spencer G. and Cordelia Strother Welch. She was active in civic affairs and in the Methodist Church. She served as president general of the United Daughters of the Confederacy. The wife of Robert Downs Wright, she had two children, Troxelle (Mrs. Hunter H. Brown) and Captain Spencer Downs Wright (U.S. Navy). She died on December 23, 1973, at the age of ninety-nine.[57]

Carl Julien, son of B. E. Julien, merchant and postmaster of Helena, moved from the county following service in World War I. Born in 1897, he began working for the Southern Power Company (now Duke Power) while still in high school, joined a Greenwood National Guard unit, and soon found himself in uniform. Upon returning to civilian life, Julien and his bride, the former Jessie Annie Fouche of Greenwood, settled briefly in Newberry where he helped organize a Boy Scout troop. In the early 1920s, aided by veterans' benefits because of an eye injury while in the armed forces, Julien enrolled at Clemson and—even though he lacked a high school diploma—completed the requirements for a civil engineering degree in only three years.

Much of his adult life was spent working with the state highway department, although in the 1930s his photographic skill, especially pictures of wild flowers and historic sites, began to attract widespread attention. A series of photos that appeared in the State led to illustrations in several books, among them ex-Governor Duncan Clinch Heyward's Seed from Madagascar (1937) and Beatrice St. Julien Ravenel's Architects of Charleston (1944).

A wizard with his camera, he worked professionally from 1943 to 1956, during which time he published a number of books. Each volume had a co-author who wrote the narrative, while Julien provided the photographs. His best-known works include Ninety Six with the late Harry L. Watson, Beneath So Kind a Sky with Chapman L. Milling, and Look to the Rock with Daniel W. Hollis.

He returned to highway work in 1956, retiring in 1962. Julien died fifteen years later in Greenwood, survived by his widow and two adopted sons. Few of those who marveled at his photographic skill realized that, after World War I, Julien had vision in only one eye.

Lillian Adele Kibler, daughter of the late Dr. James Mathias and Emma Elizabeth Wertz Kibler, was born in Newberry on August 16, 1894. She was educated at Winthrop College, B.A. 1913; Randolph-Macon Woman's College, B.A. 1915; and Columbia University, where she received both a master's in history in 1937 and a doctorate in 1943. At Columbia she was a student of Allen Nevins, the great historian. She was elected to Phi Beta Kappa at Randolph-Macon in 1947.

She taught history at Newberry High School before securing her master's degree at Columbia. Later she was chairman of the Department of History at Converse College from 1942 to 1962, when she retired as professor emeritus.

In 1946 her definitive biography, *Benjamin F. Perry: South Carolina Unionist*, was published. It received many favorable reviews and is a scholarly appraisal of a great Carolinian and his times. She wrote the official story of Converse, entitled *The History of Converse College*, which was published in 1973.

Dr. Kibler was a gifted teacher and a distinguished historian. From her retirement until her death in May 1978, she made her home in Newberry with her sister, Miss Julia Kibler, also a great teacher.

Robert Gordon Halfacre, son of Edwin Harvey and Lela Mae Ruff Halfacre, was born in Newberry on June 22, 1941. After attending Lexington High School, he graduated from Clemson University with a B.S. in landscape horticulture in 1963. After receiving his master's from Clemson, he earned his doctorate in horticulture from Virginia Polytechnic Institute and State University in 1968. In 1974 he received the degree of M.L.A. from North Carolina State University.

Dr. Halfacre and his wife, Carolyn, have two children, Angela Carolyn and Gordon Robert Halfacre. He has taught at North Carolina State and since 1974 at Clemson University where he is associate professor of horticulture.

Dr. Halfacre is the author of three books—*Carolina Landscape Plants* (1971), *Keep 'Em Growing* (1972), and *Fundamentals of Horticulture* (1975)—and a recognized authority in his field. A gifted writer, he is also a fine teacher; he received the Outstanding Teacher Award from North Carolina State in 1970.

James Everett Kibler, Jr., was born in Prosperity on June 24, 1944, the son of James E. and Juanita Connelly Kibler. He was educated at the University of South Carolina, receiving his B.A. degree in 1966 and his Ph.D. in 1970. He joined the English Department of the University of Georgia in 1970 and has remained there, becoming a full professor in 1982.

Kibler is a prolific writer specializing in Southern literature. He is particularly interested in the Dutch Fork section of South Carolina and is president of the Dutch Fork Press. He has edited two of Dr. O. B.

Mayer's books, *John Punterick: A Novel of the Old Dutch Fork* (1981) and *The Dutch Fork* (1982). He also edited *Fireside Tales: Stories of the Old Dutch Fork* (1984), *A Carolina Dutch Fork Calendar: Life and Manners in the Olden Times* (1988); *The Selected Poetry of William Gilmore Simms* (1990); and *Dictionary of Literary Biography,* volume 6, *American Novelists Since World War II, Second Series* (1980).

He is the author of *Pseudonymous Publications* of William Gilmore Simms (1976); *The Poetry of William Gilmore Simms: An Introduction and Bibliography* (1979); and, with Keen Butterworth, *William Gilmore Simms: A Reference Guide* (1980). In addition, he has written numerous articles and contributions to published books. Altogether, he is Newberry's leading author in this century.

Juanita Hitt, daughter of Jesse J. and Willametta Hogg Hitt, was born and reared in Newberry. Following her graduation from Newberry College in 1926, she took special courses in music at the University of South Carolina and at Cape Cod, Massachusetts. For many years she was instructor of music in the schools of Newberry and achieved statewide recognition for her work.

A member of many patriotic organizations, she has won several national awards for her historical papers. During the state's tricentennial celebration, she published her first book, a biography of her grandfather, Newton Thomas Hogg; later she published three others—*Colonial Churches in the Thirteen Original Colonies, Southern Miscellany,* and *Mama's Cook Book.*

J. Irby Koon, son of John Henry and Martha Wilson Koon, was born in the O'Neall section of the county. Educated at Lenoir College and at Newberry College, from which he was graduated in 1908, he taught school and then became a newspaperman. He was city editor of the *State* and the author of a book entitled *They Stoned Ma Hayden.* He was never married and died on May 4, 1947, being interred in the cemetery of Mt. Olive Lutheran Church in this county.

Thomas H. Pope's first volume of this history was published in 1973. He and General John C. Henagan were co-authors of *The History of the 107th Separate Coast Artillery Battalion (AA),* which was published in 1982.

George Carter Abrams, son of Clark Ivy and Sallie Eliza Reagin Abrams, was born in the county on January 3, 1913. He graduated from Newberry College in 1935 and was a veteran of World War II. After the war he served in the South Carolina National Guard and was employed by P. D. Johnson and Company until his retirement. He compiled and published an interesting and exhaustive genealogy entitled *The Abrams Family, 1945–1979.* In 1982 he compiled and edited volume one of *Newberry County South Carolina Cemeteries.* It is an extremely valuable source of information to genealogists.

He married first Julia Alethia Halfacre, who died on April 21, 1954, and then, Tommie McCain Johnson. He and his second wife had two children, Clark Ivy Abrams II and Mary Tommie Abrams Morrison. He died on October 2, 1986.

Clarence McKittrick Smith, Jr., wrote *Waymarks: A History of Aveleigh Presbyterian Church 1835–1985.* George Carter Abrams prepared the appendices and index. Smith was born at Kinards on December 13, 1913, the son of Clarence McKittrick and Agatha Caroline Smith. Educated at Newberry College, B.A. *magna cum laude* 1934, Harvard University, M.A. in history 1937, and Duke University where he pursued his doctoral training, he was author of the volume on hospitalization in the official history of World War II. He taught at Newberry College and served in the U.S. Army. At the request of his uncle, J. W. Smith, he gave up his academic career to return to Newberry to manage the Smith Motor Company in 1954.

Successful in business, he retired in 1979. He has been president of the Rotary Club, the Newberry County Historical Society, and the Indian Club. He married Helen Parker, and they have two children, James William McKittrick Smith and Caroline Bridgers Smith. They are active members of Aveleigh Presbyterian Church of which he is an elder.

Cynthia Martin, daughter of Foster N. and Helen Mower Martin, was born in Newberry on August 6, 1918, and educated at Newberry College from which she graduated *cum laude* in 1939. She served as a WAC sergeant in World War II. She is a photographer and worked with her brother-in-law, Leon Nichols, until she retired. In 1980 and 1983 she published *Newberry As It Was,* Volumes 1 and 2, charming and nostalgic collections of photographs made before World War I.

Other native authors are James Alvan Brown and his daughter, Jane Brown Bunn. He is the son of John Alvan and Edith Rose McGill Brown and was born in Newberry County on April 17, 1924. He graduated from Newberry High School and received a certificate in business from Newberry College in 1941. After serving as a staff sergeant in the U.S. Army during World War II, he farmed and operated a dairy until his retirement. He is an elder of Newberry ARP Church.

Brown married Carolyn Hentz, daughter of William S. and Lillie Helena Cromer Hentz. Their daughter Jane was born on August 1, 1959, and graduated from Newberry College in 1980. She is active in patriotic organizations and is a facilities engineer with Southern Bell in Charleston. She married Norman Wayne Bunn. In 1981 James Brown and Jane Bunn published a very readable and interesting genealogy entitled *The Sims Brown Family of Newberry County 1750–1981*.

In 1985 Charlie M. Senn published *A History of Trinity United Methodist Church 1835–1985*. It is well done and interesting. He was born in the county on June 12, 1913, the son of Jesse Foster and Elizabeth McMillan Senn. A graduate of Newberry College and a veteran of World War II, he devotes most of his time to genealogical research and history.

Histories of other churches in Newberry County have been written by Newberrians. They include *The History of Central Methodist Church* by L. Clifton Graham, *The History of the First Baptist Church* by James Aull, and *The History of The Lutheran Church of the Redeemer* by Julia Kibler.

Other writers who lived in Newberry County at some time but who were not natives were Erskine Caldwell, author of *Tobacco Road*; William B. Seabrook, author of *Asylum*; Mary Fowles, author of *The Golden Fleece, A Sequence of Songs*, and *A Hero's Last Days*; James A. B. Scherer, president of Newberry College and author of *Four Princes, Japan Today, Young Japan, The Holy Grail*, and *What is Japanese Morality?*; Mrs. L. M. Sale, author of *The Saddest of All is Loving*; and Frank E. Jordan, Jr., author of *The Primary State*.

In 1987 Glenda Bundrick and Andy Suber published the very valuable reference book, *Newberry County South Carolina Probate Estate Abstracts, Volume 1*. Mrs. Bundrick is the wife of Donald Bundrick and is active in genealogical research. Dr. Suber practices veterinary medicine in Columbia; his family came from Newberry County.

The most recent work by a Newberrian is the *Bicentennial History of Newberry*, which was published by the Newberry County Historical Society in 1989. Its editor was JoAnn Cousins, daughter of the late Ira T. Cousins and Bernice McMichael Cousins. She was born in Newberry on March 19, 1928, graduated from the University of South Carolina and Emory School of Medical Technology, and returned to Newberry after early retirement. She has restored a late nineteenth century farm house and is active in community activities.

Newberry has had few artists of note. Dr. Charles H. Kingsmore, born in Savannah in 1823 and reared at Abbeville Courthouse, was graduated as a physician at Castleton, Vermont, in 1844. After practicing a short time at Due West, he abandoned medicine for the more congenial profession of painting. After studying art in Italy, he settled in Newberry before the Civil War, combining photography with portrait painting. Possessed of a rare genius, he painted portraits of many Newberrians, including Chief Justice O'Neall, John S. Carwile, and Dr. James Kinard. He remained in Newberry until after the war, when he moved to Augusta, Georgia, where he died on May 14, 1873.[58] Dr. Kingsmore married Harriet Schumpert, daughter of Jacob and Harriett Abney Schumpert.[59]

Albert Capers Guerry opened a studio in Newberry in 1883 and received so many commissions that he moved his family here in September of that year. The local newspaper reported that he had seventeen commissions for portraits during the first few months. Many of his portraits, including that of General Martin Gary, hang in the State House in Columbia. Among his local portraits were those of George S. Mower, Colonel W. D. Rutherford, Mr. and Mrs. R. L. McCaughrin, Colonel Renwick, Mrs. J. N. Martin, Dr. George Keitt, and Joseph L. Keitt. Ten portraits were commissioned by Colonel E. S. Keitt. Guerry was one of the most prominent portraitists in the South. Sadly, the local newspaper reported him destitute and in need of work ten years later.[60]

The third portraitist was Williams E. Welch, whose sketch is included among those of members of the Bar. He taught art at Columbia College and at the University of South Carolina. Among his works was a full-length portrait of Thomas G. Clemson commissioned by the General Assembly of South Carolina. Welch studied art in New York and in Europe.[61] His health failed and he made his home with his sister, Mrs. Robert Downs Wright, for some years before his death on January 20, 1933.

Newberry had no more artists of note until after World War II when local artists organized the Power House Alley Art Club. Two merit mention.

William Frank Lominack, Jr., son of W. Frank and Bessie Kinard Lominack, was born on December 23, 1918. Educated at Newberry College, he entered service with Battery C of the 107th Separate Coast Artillery Battalion (AA) on February 10, 1941. At Camp Stewart he won the marksmanship contest in the battalion. He was given a medical discharge and returned home to enter the hardware business with his father. He retired in 1985.

He took art lessons from Robert Mills at the Dutch Door in Columbia and was a member of the Power House Alley Art Club in Newberry. His watercolors and pen and ink drawings have attracted much attention and have been very favorably received. His painting of the Newberry County courthouse hung in the governor's mansion during Governor Riley's tenure. His rendering of the Opera House is the frontispiece and is on the dust jacket of this volume.

A gun collector, expert marksman, and artist, he has been active in the Lions Club, the Newberry Pistol Club, Amity Lodge No. 87, A.F.M., and Hejaz Temple of the Shrine. Married to the former Margaret Kern, he has three children, William F. Lominack, III, Peggy Epps, and Lynn Parnell. The Lominacks are members of Central United Methodist Church.

Genell Murphy Boozer was born at Adel, Georgia, on February 24, 1923. The only child of Eldridge Gresham and Nellie Floy O'Keefe Murphy, she was educated at Wesleyan Conservatory in Macon, the University of Florida, and the University of South Carolina. She is a talented artist in both oil and charcoal and specializes in flowers. Her paintings have been widely exhibited and hang in the houses of prominent citizens as well as in institutions.

She married Thomas Blair Boozer, Jr. They have four children, Barbara Ann Shipman, who is also an artist; Carole Sydney Miller; Thomas Blair Boozer, III, a jewelry designer; and Melissa Genell Boozer Lane, a periodontist's assistant.

19

Newberry's
Business Community

In 1860 Newberry District had a population of 20,879, of whom one-third were white. Its economy was based upon cotton, and most of the inhabitants lived on farms. There were only two incorporated towns, Newberry Courthouse and Frog Level. Railroad stations existed at Pomaria, Silverstreet, Saluda Old Town, Chappells, Helena, Jalapa, and Kinards. A store or two had been established at each of these stations, and there were small stores scattered through the countryside.

In 1860 Newberry Courthouse had 1,637 residents, of whom half were white, thirty-five were free Negroes, and the rest were slaves. The village had grown greatly since the Greenville and Columbia Railroad reached it in 1852. Newberry College had been established in 1859; the Laurens Railroad had been built with its terminus at Helena; two newspapers were being published, the *Conservatist* and the *Rising Sun*, and a third, the *Weekly Herald*, would soon be established. The Bank of Newberry was thriving, five local churches had been built, and the town had a variety of stores.[1] The Bank of Newberry closed during the war and left the town without banking facilities. And, of course, other businesses also closed.

Dry goods and clothing stores that advertised in the local newspapers included S. J. Sloman, G. D. Smith, E. S. Coppock, A. M. Riser, J. J. Amick, S. T. Agnew & Co., H. H. Marshall, M. Foot, W. & J. Sultzbacker, G. M. Thomson & Co., Houseal and Amick, W. D. Goggans, and W. M. Hatton. Drug stores were operated by Dr. W. K. Griffin, W. F. Pratt and Nance, Land and Bruce, and Williams and Ferguson.

Boozer, Peoples & Co. had a hardware store, while Stiles Hurd operated a furniture and carriage business. Patrick Scott and A. M. Riser advertised as merchant tailors. H. H. Blease sold harness, stoves, and tinware. E. S. Bailey & Co. and Summerfield Montgomery had jewelry stores, and grocers included Hunt and Brother, S. L. Smith, J. N. Martin, and W. G. and J. B. Mayes. W. J. Duffie had a good book store, and Dr. C. H. Kingsmore had a photography studio and also painted portraits. Land and Werts had a shoe store, while Mrs. J. P. Morgan and Mrs. E. C. Christian were milliners. George Larsen operated a restaurant and fish market, and R. M. Dean ran a livery stable.[2]

In June 1866 one-half of Newberry's business section was destroyed by fire. Although the local newspaper opined that times were dull, that there was no business, and that the streets were deserted, the burned business section was rebuilt within a year. The same newspaper proudly reported in 1869 that there were eighty places of business, large and small, in the little town.[3]

Robert Stewart was the leading merchant of the town until his death in 1869. His brick store on the corner of Pratt (now Main) and Caldwell streets faced the Public Square and had a long wooden annex behind it running along Caldwell Street. Here he conducted a successful business for nearly half a century. Carwile says that he studied the wants and needs of his customers more closely than any other merchant of his day and that he sold the best quality of goods.[4]

Upon Stewart's death, his place of business became that of Pettus W. and Reuben S. Chick. The street now known as Cheek Street was named Chick for Pettus Chick, who built the house on College Street now occupied by Dr. C. A. Dufford.

The National Bank of Newberry was organized in 1871, giving the town banking services that had ceased to exist when the old Bank of Newberry closed its doors. The streets were marked by street signs and kerosene jets lighted the business section.[5]

In 1871 the *Newberry Herald* reported that the *Laurens Advertiser* stated that "Newberry is a wide awake place. It does more business and better business than any place in the upcountry, never failing to satisfy the demands of the public in every particular." From September 1870 to September 1871, 24,406 bales of cotton were shipped from Newberry depot. It was reported in 1873 that "Newberry next to Charleston is the largest cotton market in the State, and not only is more cotton bought and shipped from here, but the production of the staple is greater."[6]

A business directory published in the *Newberry Herald* in 1873 listed the following businesses:[7]

R. C. Shiver and Co., McFall and Pool, P. W. and R. S. Chick had dry goods stores; Lovelace and Wheeler, M. Foot, J. D. Cash, Thomas Cook, J. M. Wilson & Co., T. F. Harmon, and A. A. Nathan operated dry goods and grocery stores; John A. Chapman had a book and stationery store; and W. T. Wright sold stoves and tinware. R. Y. Leavell and W. H. Harris were furniture dealers, L. R. Marshall had a restaurant, and W. H. Wiseman a photography studio. J. R. Leavell and L. M. Speers sold monuments; Webb, Jones and Parker, buggies and wagons. John A. Chapman was listed also as the seller of cotton gins, while William C. Chase & Co. and A. J. McCaughrin & Co. were commission merchants. G. T. Scott, F. E. Salinas, Mayes & Martin, Leavell & Spearman, and William C. Chase & Co. were cotton buyers and grocers.

A. M. Wicker, A. D. Lovelace, A. M. Bowers & Co., J. C. Wilson, and J. E. Webb & Co. sold groceries and canned goods, while John F. Speck was a jeweler and Wright and Coppock sold men's clothing. Mrs. D. Mower and Mrs. M. Hunter had millinery shops, Dr. S. F. Fant operated a drug store, Z. L. White was a gunsmith, and J. B. Leonard & Co. sold wines and whiskey.

Newberry was not alone in being hurt by fire. In July 1873, fire destroyed the business section of Prosperity, until shortly before then known as Frog Level. The dry goods merchants in that town were H. S. Boozer; Wise, Whites and Co.; Heller & Shealy; Luther & Dominick; Bowers, Wheeler and Co.; and L. C. Kibler. The grocers were F. Bobb, Wheeler and Mosely, J. M. Kibler, and P. P. Beacham. J. C. Counts operated a furniture store, while J. L. Counts was the undertaker. Simpson, Maffett and Co. operated the drug store; Miss Mattie Stone was the milliner.[8]

These merchants conducted their businesses in barns and other temporary quarters while rebuilding. The *Newberry Herald* reported that Prosperity was being rapidly rebuilt, and by 1877 it was said to have twelve business houses. New ones mentioned included those of A. L. Wyse, S. L. Fellers, J. B. Fellers, W. S. Birge, Kibler and McFall, and W. Green.[9]

The greatest danger to the business section of the towns was fire. To meet this threat, the Hook and Ladder Company was organized in Newberry in 1875. The town council appropriated $200, the Greenville & Columbia Railroad gave $100, and the insurance companies doing business in the town donated $100 for equipment.[10]

A year later this firefighting company prevented a disastrous blaze. But it was unable to cope with a terrible fire in March 1877, when many residences and stores were destroyed.[11] Among the twenty stores that burned were those of M. Foot, W. E. Pelham, B. H. Cline & Co., Henry Burns, McFall & Pool, O. A. Havird, L. R. Marshall, and Chapman & Crawford.

Despite the fires, Newberry continued to prosper.[12] In February 1879 another fire consumed ten stores and caused two others to be razed. Newberry, however, showed its determination to overcome such obstacles by erecting the Newberry Hotel and the Crotwell Hotel in 1879, the Opera House in 1882, and the Newberry Cotton Mill in 1883.[13]

This building program created a local brick making business, with J. P. Pool, J. A. Crotwell, B. H. Cline, and Osborne Wells being the leaders. It also resulted in the stores being built of brick instead of wood. At that time, Newberry, with a population of 2,342, was the seventh largest town in South Carolina. The local telephone system was put in operation on June 26, 1882.[14]

In June 1883 a new fire company, the "Excelsior," was organized and its new engine was named "Young John" for Mayor Y. J. Pope. The company was unable to save Mollohon Row in July but did render good service, saving the Newberry and Crotwell hotels.[15] This fire company was the beginning of the Newberry Fire Department.

A Board of Trade was organized in July 1888;[16] it was the forerunner of the local Chamber of Commerce. Prosperity followed suit by organizing a Board of Trade in 1890.[17]

By 1889 the merchants of Newberry included the following:[18]

W. H. Harris, B. H. Cline, B. H. Lovelace, J. Mittel, A. L. Knighton, H. C. Summers, A. M. Bowers, J. W. Kibler & Co., Proctor Todd, C. and G. S. Mower, Paul Johnstone, L. P. W. Riser, Otto Klettner, John Donahue, F. R. Wallace & Co., Summer Brothers, T. Q. Boozer, Caldwell Brothers, and W. A. Kinard were grocers.

O. H. P. Fant, George McWhirter and J. N. Martin were wholesale grocers, while J. S. Russell, M. Foot, Jr., D. M. Ward, J. Mann, Thomas F. Harmon, Joseph Brown, Floyd & Purcell, and W. T. Tarrant had general merchandise stores.

Dry goods stores were run by Gary, Cook and Carwile, Wooten and McWhirter, Minter & Jamieson, Joseph Brown, M. S. Epstein, Davis & Goggans, Summer Brothers, C. L. Havird, Thomas T. Tarrant, C. and G. S. Mower, and L. P. W. Riser.

There were three book stores—those of J. W. Chapman, W. H. Hunt, Jr., and T. F. Greneker, and the art store of R. C. Williams. S. P. Boozer & Co. and Peoples and Johnson had hardware stores.

Louis Crede operated a bakery, and S. B. Jones a restaurant. There were four drug stores—those of W. E. Pelham, Robertson and Gilder, Cofield and Lyons, and Belcher, Houseal and Kibler—and two men's clothing stores, those of Wright and J. W. Coppock.

L. M. Speers and R. C. Chapman were undertakers, and Fant and Buford, J. B. Martin, and F. A. Schumpert sold carriages and buggies.

Edward Scholtz and J. W. Montgomery had jewelry stores, while J. D. Smith, D. R. Phifer, and H. H. Blease ran livery stables. J. W. Smith was a gunsmith and J. Taylor had a wagon and carriage factory.

W. T. Davis ran a sash, door and blind factory, and D. B. Wheeler sold sewing machines. A. J. Sproles dealt in tinware, Dominick & Lovelace ran a grist mill, and W. H. Blats had a shoe shop.

Blacksmiths included Tom Williams, Elijah Phillips, Charles Cannon, and Joe Hines. Saloonkeepers were D. M. Ward, D. W. Fant, E. C. Summers, A. M. Bowers, Otto Klettner, Jordan Green, and T. Q. Boozer.

O. McR. Holmes and A. J. McCaughrin sold fertilizer, and cotton buyers were W. H. Stapleton, O. McR. Holmes, J. N. Martin, and W. J. Lake.

S. P. Boozer & Son, E. A. Scott, James F. Glenn, W. T. Tarrant, James F. Todd, and James A. Burton were insurance agents, and Carlisle and Lane were realtors. W. M. Lane and S. B. Aull were cotton weighers, and Harvey Reese was the town barber.

Newberry's prosperity attracted merchants from elsewhere. Louis Crede from Prussia owned a bakery and confectionery. Otto Klettner from Germany had a saloon and grocery and served as Newberry's mayor. James A. Mimnaugh from Ireland was a successful dry goods merchant. Dennis and Chris Athanos, John Pappas, Gus Metchicos, and S. P. Trakas from Greece had restaurants and confectioneries. The Busy Bee Cafe, operated by the Athanoses, was open twenty-four hours a day and became Newberry's most popular eating place in the twentieth century.

A number of progressive Jewish merchants operated dry goods stores. Nineteenth century merchants included Mordecai Foot, Joseph Mann, Joseph Brown, Louis Morris, M. Foot, Jr., and M. S. Epstein, while twentieth century Jewish merchants included Taylor Vigodsky and his sons, Harry and Joe, Philip Daitch, J. Levy, B. P. and I. C. Kurtz, Alex Golinsky, Isidor Kaplan, and Al Rabin. All are now dead except Joe Vigodsky and Al Rabin, both of whom moved away from Newberry.

The leading merchants around the turn of the century were the Summer brothers. They operated stores and warehouses, including a retail grocery, a dry goods and clothing store, a hardware store, a grain warehouse, a cotton warehouse, a fertilizer warehouse and a buggy and wagon warehouse. In addition they farmed several thousand acres and helped establish the Mollohon and Oakland Mills.[19]

Newberry merchants enjoyed their greatest prosperity from 1890 to 1930. During this period the population grew from 3,000 to 7,278. The number of merchants rose correspondingly, and the establishment of Mollohon and Oakland Mills provided many jobs.

This was the era of the lien merchants. The cotton farmer arranged with a merchant to furnish him with seed, fertilizer, food, farm supplies, and clothing for himself and his "hands" on credit. The farmer would give the merchant a lien on his cotton crop, and a settlement would be made when the cotton was ginned and sold. Many lien merchants made big profits, but the system depended on reasonable prices for cotton as well as good crops.

Summer Brothers, Purcell & Scott, Edward R. Hipp, Johnson-McCrackin Company, H. M. Bryson, R. D. Smith & Co., and George C. Hipp were among the lien merchants in the town. In the outlying villages the general stores also engaged in the lien business.

In 1920 Newberry County produced 35,000 bales of cotton. The price that year was 32.7 cents a pound, and local agricultural leaders openly advocated holding the crop until the price rose to 50 cents a pound. Instead of rising, the price plummeted to 13.1 cents a pound in 1921. And the dreaded boll weevil infested the county with the result that production costs rose and the yield declined. Many farmers were ruined and some lien merchants, including Summer Brothers, failed. The Great Depression finished the lien business.

Around the turn of the century the merchants who advertised most frequently in the *Observer* were C. and G. S. Mower, M. A. Renwick, O. M. Jamieson, Copeland Brothers, A. C. Jones, Flynn's Cash Store, and George I. C. McWhirter, all of whom sold dry goods; Scott and Carlson, merchant tailors; Eduard Scholtz, jeweler; W. A. Young, who had perfumes; W. G. Mayes, who ran a book store; J. H. West, R. Y. Leavell, and the Kibler, Dennis and Company, furniture; William Johnson, hardware; Miss Bessie Riser, millinery; J. Z. Salter, photography studio; M. A. Spehl, bakery; L. M. Speers, monuments; Otto Klettner, general merchandise; E. Cabiness, meat market; J. A. Russell, R. B. McCarty, S. B. Jones, Counts and Dennis, B. W. West, The Smith Company, E. L. Polgren, C. J. McWhirter, and Todd and Cozby, grocers; and J. D. Davenport, fertilizer.

A more complete list of Newberry's merchants appears in the January 8, 1904, issue of the *Observer*, which reported a large mass meeting called to discuss the town's new business license ordinance. All businesses in town were said to be represented, and most were opposed to the law.[20] The minutes of the town council for February 1, 1904, show that the protest was received as information and the mayor was instructed to reply to it. The business license ordinance was not repealed.

Newberry again suffered from a disastrous fire in March 1907. Five square blocks were destroyed with the loss of ten stores, two churches, and twenty-two residences.[21] The local fire department was credited with saving the rest of the town.

This fire, however, did not impede progress for long. The burned sections were quickly replaced, and the town's business continued to prosper. Local merchants organized the Chamber of Commerce in 1906, and in 1908 the sidewalks were paved and city mail delivery was instituted with two deliveries a day.[22]

The roads of the county were paved in the 1930s, and the displacement of the horse and buggy by the automobile was a severe blow to the villages of Pomaria, Little Mountain, Silverstreet, Chappells, and Kinards, but these changes stimulated the growth of Newberry, Whitmire, and Prosperity as trading areas. The population of Newberry grew from 7,278 in 1930 to 9,216 in 1970.

The leading merchants of Pomaria in the early decades of this century were M. E. K. Glymph, Alvin and Ernest Kinard, Hub Lominack, and Dick Hipp. Of Little Mountain, they were the Derrick Brothers, J. B. and J. Kess, the Wise Brothers, and the Bolands. Silverstreet's merchants were Mayer Havird, Otto Nichols, and O. W. Long. At Chappells, John B. Scurry and A. P. Coleman were leading cotton buyers; LeRoy Holloway, H. W. Dipner, and A. P. Werts ran general stores; and John Wilson had a barber shop. Kinards had three stores—Smith Brothers, Oxner's and Dominick's—in addition to a barber shop and two cotton gins. All of them are now gone.

The leading ladies' dry goods merchants of Newberry during this period included Carpenter's, successor to C. and G. S. Mower; Harry Vigodsky's The Fashion; Efird's Department Store; Belk-Beard Company; and B. C. Moore & Sons Department Store. P. E. Anderson and B. T. Anderson had dry goods stores. Men's clothiers included J. H. Summer, R. C. Perry, T. Roy Summer, J. H. Clary, Johnson Hagood Clary, G. C. Clamp, and Earl H. Bergen. R. H. Anderson, Leroy Anderson, and A. D. Garner had shoe stores; Hal Kohn and Fred Thomas, book stores. Thomas P. Johnson, Frank Lominack, R. M. Lominack, L. G. Eskridge, Haskell Wright, and Ben Chapman and Chester Hawkins had hardware stores. J. J. Langford, Herman S. Langford, Ben T. Buzhardt, G. B. Summer, Marvin O. Summer, Adrian Summer, Gurnie Summer, Richard L. Baker, G. Leland Summer, Jr., and first Maxwell Brothers & Quinn and later Maxwell Brothers and Lindsay, and John Lindsay had furniture stores. Some forty-odd grocery stores were operated by local businessmen, the leading stores being those of R. G. Wallace, W. O. Wilson, Boozer Brothers, and Paysinger Brothers.

Local automobile dealerships included those of J. W. Smith, C. T. Summer, T. E. Davis, A. J. Patrick, Shealy Motor Co., D. L. Hayes, H. A. Kemper, R. B. Baker, Clarence McK. Smith, H. B. Kirkegard, and J. H. Davis. Oil distributorships included those of Durrett Lipscomb, Buddy Lipscomb and later Arthur E. Morehead, who handled Gulf products; C. D. Coleman, and his son C. D. Coleman, Jr., who sold first Pure Oil and then Phillips 76; Strother C. Paysinger and his son, Strother D. Paysinger, who marketed first Sinclair and then Union 66; C. T. Summer, who distributed Shell; Harry Dominick and later T. W. Hunter, who handled Texaco; George Martin, who handled Sinclair; S. W. Brown, Jr. and then Burnest Neel, who distributed Amoco; and Aubrey Davis and later Preston Kunkle, who handled Standard Oil.

Insurance agencies included Purcell's, R. E. Summer & Company, Bowers and Floyd, L. D. Gardner, Robert Lister, and Durrett Lipscomb.

The Johnson-McCrackin Company conducted a farm implement and general merchandise business until it was dissolved in 1950. P. D. Johnson & Co. became a farm implement and machinery business at that time. Other such businesses were conducted by J. Ellerbe Sease, Ralph Shealy, Burnest Neel, and Wilson Road Tractor & Equipment, Inc.

Palmetto Cotton Company was established when the Kendall Company purchased Oakland and Mollohon Mills. J. D. French of Massachusetts was its first manager; upon his retirement he was succeeded by Hugh E. Wessinger, a native of Newberry, son of J. Olin and Jessie Hill Wessinger and graduate of Newberry College. He married Elizabeth Townsend, and they have three sons, Hugh, Jr., Townsend, and Lee Wessinger. Hugh Wessinger retired in 1989, being succeeded by Jimmy Ray Pruitt. The company's name was changed to Kendall Cotton Company in 1972, and the office was moved to Wilson Road after the Oakland Mill was sold to American Fiber and Finishing Company.

The face of downtown Newberry began to be changed with the opening of the Newberry Shopping Center in 1970. This started the flight of business from downtown. Other shopping centers have since been developed on Wilson Road, anchored by the chain groceries and chain department stores, and some local businesses have also located on the bypasses. Because of the shopping centers, Newberry is still a large trading center.

The tornado that struck the business section of the town in March 1984 hastened the decline of downtown Newberry. The stores destroyed and those that had to be razed have not been replaced because the center of business has moved to Wilson Road and it was therefore not economically feasible to do so.

Now the Market Basket is the only grocery supermarket remaining downtown; the small groceries that were operated on Main Street and in the Mollohon, West End, and Oakland sections have closed. The chain groceries, Winn-Dixie, A & P, Food Lion, and Bi-Lo, are on Wilson Road.

The only large clothing stores remaining downtown are Belk's, B. C. Moore & Sons, and Bergen's. Lominack's Drug Store and Newberry Drug Store are still on Main Street.

Harold Edgar Anderson, son of LeRoy and Kitty Edgar Anderson, and a graduate of The Citadel, and his wife, the former Mary Correll, operate Anderson's Shoe Store and Anderson's Dress Shop. He is a third-generation Newberry merchant. They have two daughters, Meg and Kate, and the family attends St. Luke's Episcopal Church.

Downtown remains home for the lawyers, Purcell's, C. T. Summer, Inc., Turner's Jewelers of Newberry, Inc., Woolbright's and Emerson Jones (florists), three dry cleaning establishments, Lindsay Furniture Company, Heilig-Myers Furniture Company, Nichols Studio, the finance companies and banks, Garner's Shoe Store, and a few other small stores. Whether downtown Newberry can be revived is doubtful. This is the common problem of most cities.

One of the successful businesses to remain downtown is Purcell's, established by Edward B. Purcell in 1930 and with a history under other names going back to the turn of the century. Purcell (1899–1974), son of Charles J. and Lavinia McFall Purcell, had a long career of public service. An elder in Aveleigh Presbyterian Church, he served as mayor, councilman, and commissioner of public works. A director of Newberry Federal Savings and Loan Association and the Newberry branch of South Carolina National Bank, he married Trent Keitt; they had three children, Keitt, E. B. Purcell, Jr., and Trent P. Coleman.

Keitt Purcell succeeded his father as head of Purcell's, member of the board of the Newberry branch of South Carolina National, director of Newberry Federal Savings Bank, and elder of Aveleigh Presbyterian

Church. A graduate of The Citadel, he married Myrle Hill of Sumter; they have a son, Trent, and two daughters, Julie and Lucille P. Hursey. Trent, also a graduate of The Citadel and former regular Army officer, is in the business with his father. He married Yvonne Edwards.

Ben P. Stewart, vice-president of Purcell's, has been with the firm for more than forty years. He married Nelle Harmon; they have one son, Ben P. Stewart, Jr., and two daughters, Gay S. Durham and Joy S. Whisnut.

Of Newberry's mayors and intendants since 1860, eighteen have been merchants.[37] Of these, J. J. Langford and Herman S. Langford are the only father and son to serve. Of those serving since 1941, six of eight have been merchants; all six are now deceased. There is only one surviving former mayor. The following were mayors in this modern era: H. S. Langford, E. B. Purcell, D. L. Hayes, A. P. Salley, J. E. Wiseman, C. E. Kinard, E. H. Layton, and C. A. Shealy, Jr.

At the beginning of World War II, Herman S. Langford was mayor. He owned and operated a furniture store until he died unmarried in 1987. He left a large estate, most of which he left to Newberry College (his alma mater), the Lutheran Church of the Redeemer, the Lowman Home, and the Lutheran Orphanage in Virginia. His bequest to Newberry College is the largest ever received by that institution.

Langford was succeeded by Edward B. Purcell, and he by Dave L. Hayes. Hayes was a native Newberrian who for many years operated an automobile dealership. Son of William C. and Alma Williams Hayes, he served as chairman of the board of the John de la Howe School and was an active member of Central Methodist Church, the Newberry Lions Club, and the County Development Board. He received the Sertoma Award for Service to Mankind in 1982 and was a director of the local Advisory Board of the South Carolina National Bank. Married to the former Catherine Smith of Union, he died childless on September 18, 1985, aged eighty-three.

Andrew Pickens Salley, son of Andrew Pickens and Mary Stoney Salley of Columbia, was the next of the eight to become mayor. He was manager of the local branch of the South Carolina National Bank, and was prominent in community affairs, although he lived in Newberry for only eight years. He was senior warden of St. Luke's Episcopal Church, president of the Chamber of Commerce, and president of the Rotary Club. He died on May 9, 1950, survived by his widow, Mary Stanley Salley and two daughters, Mary Stanley and Catherine Pickens Salley.

The next to serve as mayor was James E. Wiseman, son of Dr. C. B.

and Margaret Wray Wiseman; he was born in Henrietta, North Carolina, and attended the University of North Carolina. Moving to Newberry in 1932, he was manager of the Newberry Hotel and then of the Wiseman Hotel until his retirement in 1971. He served as Newberry city recorder, president of the Country Club of Newberry, and chairman of the Community Hall Commission. He died on February 15, 1989, at the age of eighty-three, survived by his widow, Lorna Wilson Wiseman, and his son, James E. Wiseman, Jr.

Cecil E. Kinard, Ernest H. Layton and Clarence A. Shealy, Jr., were the most recent mayors. Kinard, son of George W. and Frankie Alice Rikard Kinard, operated a restaurant for many years. He died in office on September 30, 1979, after having served on the city council for thirty-five years. An active member of O'Neal Street United Methodist Church and the Newberry Volunteer Fire Department, he was a Mason and a Shriner. Kinard, seventy-nine years old, was survived by three children, C. Edward Kinard, Charles E. Kinard, and Carolyn K. Williams.

Ernest H. Layton, son of Charles F. and Nannie Hair Layton, operated a store on O'Neal Street for many years with his brother, Olin. He was an active member of O'Neal Street United Methodist Church, a Mason and Shriner, and a member of the board of Rosemont Cemetery Association. He died on October 7, 1978, aged seventy-two, survived by his widow, Dessie M. Layton, and two children, Charles Ernest Layton and Sue Layton Davenport.

Clarence A. Shealy, Jr., an insurance agent with Liberty Life Insurance Company, Newberry native and Newberry College graduate, was elected in 1968. He served, generally without opposition, longer than any of Newberry's mayors, but was defeated in 1990 by Ed Kyzer, a newcomer to politics. Shealy married Joanne Bobb; they have two children, Clarence, III, and Sue Ellen. They attend Epting Memorial United Methodist Church.

The city manager system is generally regarded as superior to the mayor-councilmen system whereby part-time officials attempt to solve problems that grow more intricate every decade and where a great deal of "log-rolling" results. Newberry's city manager system has brought more efficiency to city government. The present city manager, W. A. Harvey, a graduate of the University of South Carolina, commenced his service in Newberry in 1977.

Prosperity has continued to have a small but select number of local merchants whose stores compare favorably with those of much larger towns. Prosperity Furniture Company, organized by D. H. and Allen Hamm, continues to be one of the leading furniture stores in this part of the state. D. H. Hamm's sons, Dan and Walter, carried on the business after their father's retirement. Dan is now sole owner. J. Asbury Bedenbaugh is a longtime employee and civic leader. His father, J. Moody Bedenbaugh, was postmaster of Prosperity for many years and was an active land surveyor.

J. Walter Hamm was born on August 1, 1925. Educated at The Citadel and the University of South Carolina, he joined Prosperity Furniture Company and remained active in that business until he sold his interest after forty-four years. He married Frances Rudisell; they have three children, J. Walter Hamm, Jr., David, and Nancy. He has been active in many civic organizations and has served as mayor and councilman of Prosperity since 1959, chief of the fire department, and chairman of the Newberry County Water and Sewer Authority since 1964. He is active in Wightman United Methodist Church and a most useful citizen.

Glenn Hamm and his son, Ladison, operate a modern, well-stocked hardware store. Other local businesses include Prosperity Drug Company, owned by Arlen Stuck; Counts Sausage Company; the Back Porch, a local restaurant; Martin's Farm and Garden Center; James Mills's Piggly Wiggly; and James Dawkins's grocery.

Prosperity has always been a close-knit, self-sufficient community with good locally owned businesses. Today it continues this tradition with excellent stores, three banking institutions, a dentist, and the Lovelace Family Medical Center. It is fortunate to have local industries such as Kayser-Roth, Norris, and Georgia-Pacific near the town. The new Federal Paper Board Plant will be nearby, and the announcement that Greenwood Industries soon will establish a plant initially employing fifty people is encouraging.

After Whitmire's incorporation in 1891, the town grew rapidly. The local cotton mill provided employment and a good payroll. In the days of railroad travel, Whitmire was on the main line between Atlanta and the North. Local business served the needs of the area around the town. Indeed Whitmire developed so well that local leaders attempted to organize Carlisle County with Whitmire as the county seat in 1924; that effort failed because the proposed county was too small to meet constitutional requirements.

Whitmire's leading businessmen were Z. H. Suber, M. E. and T. J. Abrams, the Scotts, Joe Simpson, J. W. Hipp, the Millers, Drs. Duckett and Gary, Sam and George Young, and John Robert Suber. Whitmire's population rose to 3,272 in 1940, and the business section grew with the population.

For a number of reasons over which Whitmire leaders had no control the town started shrinking in size and as a trading center. By 1950 the population was 3,006; in 1960 it was 2,663, and by 1980 it had dropped to only 2,038.

The establishment of the Sumter National Forest, which took a large area in that section, reduced the rural population around Whitmire. The curtailment of the Aragon-Baldwin work force and the elimination of railroad passengers were factors. The fact that Whitmire was not on a main highway such as an interstate was another. The failure of the small industries built after the war to live up to expectations was also a contributing factor. With these adverse conditions, the local businesses could neither expand nor hold their own. Not much local business is left.

In 1939 W. E. Baker and his son Elmer R. Baker organized a construction business. It has done well and has been active within a sixty-mile radius in erecting residences and commercial buildings. The firm, which is now incorporated with Elmer as chairman and Edgar Baker as president, not only conducts a construction enterprise but also operates a builders supply company. Roche Pharmacy, Miller's Hardware, and Cody Owens's Lawn & Garden Center are locally owned stores. NCNB maintains a branch bank, Young Chevrolet operates a garage and sales department, and Whitmire Furniture & Appliance, Inc. has its store. Whitmire's future is not bright unless outside industry can be attracted to locate there.

20

The Churches

The advent of peace presented a perplexing problem to the black and white members of the existing church congregations in Newberry District and of the entire South. Local denominations represented were Lutheran, Methodist, Baptist, Presbyterian, Associate Reformed Presbyterian, and Episcopal. Before Appomattox all included members of both races, albeit the blacks had no real voice in church government.

The ultimate decision of whether the existing state should continue, or whether the blacks should withdraw and form their own separate churches, rested of necessity with the blacks. However, the leaders of the various faiths felt their responsibility keenly as evidenced by the discussions held at various church meetings.

In 1866 the Lutheran Synod was asked by its president, the Reverend Thaddeus Street Boinest of Newberry District, to lay down a general rule for the Lutheran churches, stating that "most of our sister denominations have recommended their separate and distinct organization and this is perhaps the best course that we can pursue in reference to them (the Freedmen)."[1]

Boinest's recommendation was not accepted; the Synod determined to "retain the same relation to the freedmen as we have heretofore done." Gradually the number of black communicants declined until by 1869 there were not enough to report in the parochial statistics.[2] After Reconstruction the Synod turned its attention again to the problem but it was too late. Blacks had decided to organize their own churches.

The other denominations were equally concerned. The Baptist State Convention in 1866 appointed a strong committee consisting of J. C.

Furman, P. C. Edwards, William Williams, J. A. Broadus, and Basil Manly, Jr., to study the problem. The committee recognized the obligation of Baptists "in regard to the instruction of the Colored People," and at the same time acknowledged that they would prefer, in certain localities, to be organized into separate churches. The committee recommended that the blacks be permitted to remain in their current church connection or to form their own separate congregations; in either case the white Baptists should help their black brethren in any way possible.[3]

In 1877 the representatives of the recently organized black Baptist State Convention were officially received at the white convention, which appointed two brethren to bear their fraternal greetings to the Negro State Convention.[4]

Although for three years the Methodists were able to report "the refreshing news" that many blacks were joining the mixed congregations, each year of freedom showed a steady decline in the number of blacks who belonged to the old white churches. By 1867 the 40,000 black members of the Methodist churches in South Carolina had fallen to 8,275 and by 1873 to 653. Baptist, Presbyterian, and Episcopal churches had similar losses.[5]

Meanwhile, the African Methodist Episcopal Church and the independent Negro Baptist churches grew apace. Simkins and Woody concluded that "the winning of religious independence by the Negro was perhaps the most momentous social change of Reconstruction";[6] this change became permanent. They also point out that for each white sect there is now a corresponding black sect with approximately the same proportion of the race in it. However, this is not true of Newberry County where twenty-four percent of the whites are in the Lutheran church but none, or few, blacks are in that denomination. Generally speaking, the blacks belong to the evangelical and not the liturgical churches.

Two Northern denominations, formed before the Civil War, were able to attract most of the black Methodists in Newberry County. The African Methodist Episcopal Church, organized in Philadelphia in 1816, was most successful and remains today the dominant Methodist denomination among the blacks. The other was the African Methodist Episcopal Zion Church, organized in New York City in 1796. The Southern Methodists established several churches in Newberry County under the name of the Colored Methodist Episcopal Church of America. This was authorized by the General Conference of the Methodist Episcopal Church South in 1866.

The Northern Presbyterian Church also organized several black churches in the county, including Calvary Presbyterian and Oak Grove Presbyterian near Sligh's.[7] The Baptists simply left their old churches and established separate churches unaffiliated with the Southern Baptist Church.

Only three black churches were built in the town of Newberry before G. M. Girardeau completed his map of the town in 1881: the African Methodist Episcopal Church on Caldwell Street, now known as Miller's Chapel; Bethlehem Baptist on College Street; and Calvary Presbyterian on Caldwell Street.[8] In July 1869, Edward K. Christian conveyed a small lot of one-eighth of an acre to Joseph Boston, John Jones, Joseph Jones, Edward Young, and William Robertson as trustees of the African Methodist Episcopal Church in the town of Newberry; the following February Burrell Raines gave to the same trustees the adjoining one-quarter acre.[9]

In 1872 G. T. Scott conveyed a small lot on the south side of Scott's Creek on College Street to Elder Ira Lewis, Dred Rutherford, Joe Kinard, and James Baxter as trustees of the Colored Bethlehem Baptist Church. The first church building was completed the following year on this land. In 1901 the church purchased six lots across the creek and erected the present handsome edifice. In 1919 a parsonage lot on Vincent Street was bought.[10]

Calvary Presbyterian was organized a few years later. In 1879 James Ratley, Simeon Young, and M. S. Long as trustees took title to a lot on Caldwell Street for the church. In 1903 Elijah Phillips, Jr., Charles F. Beecher, and Jason Jones, as trustees of Calvary Church (black Presbyterian) conveyed the property to the Calvary Presbyterian Church.[11] Of those three churches, Calvary has ceased to exist. The other two are among the strongest congregations in the county.

The African Methodist Episcopal churches in Newberry County form the Newberry District of the Columbia Conference. The Reverend W. B. Williams is the presiding elder of the Newberry District. Mrs. Genell Ruff of Newberry is a member of the General Board of the African Methodist Episcopal Church, which has world-wide jurisdiction over all African Methodist Episcopal churches. The present African Methodist Episcopal churches composing the Newberry District are divided into stations, circuits, and missions.

The stations, with their pastors in 1989, are Trinity, the largest, the Reverend Melvin Coleman; Miller's Chapel, the Reverend Harold E. Hunter; Shiloh, the Reverend Johnny Byrd; and Wateree, the Reverend Lemuel L. Washington.

Circuits consist of the following churches, with their present pastors also listed: St. James Circuit, St. James and St. Mark, the Reverend J. H. Bates; Providence, the Reverend H. A. Hinton; Pine Grove, the Reverend Michael Harp; Mt. Moriah Circuit, Mt. Moriah and Lower Mt. Olive, the Reverend F. M. Moses; Elisha Circuit, Elisha and Cross Road, the Reverend Jeremiah Wilson; Helena Circuit, Brown Chapel and St. Mary's, the Reverend Lonzo Stephen; Pleasant Grove, the Reverend Daniel L. Simmons; St. Matthew, the Reverend Morgan Bruce Reeves; Mt. Olive Circuit, Upper Mt. Olive and Mt. Zion, the Reverend Dallas Jones; Hannah Circuit, Hannah and Lever Chapel, the Reverend Lorenzo Dinkin; Mt. Hebron, the Reverend M. H. Jenkins; and St. Paul, the Reverend William Brunson.

Sweet Spring and Mt. Nebo are missions, their pastor being the Reverend Lonzo Stephen.[12]

The African Methodist Episcopal Zion Church in America has established its churches in Whitmire and the surrounding countryside. These include Cedar Grove near Cromer's Cross Roads; Trinity in the Maybinton section; Whitmire in the town; and Bruce Tabernacle in Whitmire.[13]

The Colored Methodist Episcopal Church in America organized Zion on the Holley's Ferry Road and congregations in Prosperity and on James Street in Newberry.[14]

In October 1876 the New Enoree Baptist Association was organized in Newberry.[15] It is the dominant organization of black Baptist churches in the county and consists of twenty-one churches in Newberry County and Tucker's Chapel in Union County. Its congregations are not large, generally averaging less than 150 members each. The Reverend Nura Ray Matthews serves as moderator of this association.

The constituent Newberry County churches of the New Enoree Baptist Association with their pastors in 1989 are: Antioch below Prosperity, no pastor at the present time; Little Beaverdam at Helena, the Reverend R. C. Crump; Bethlehem on College Street, Newberry, the Reverend James Williams; Boozer Chapel in the Hartford community, the Reverend J. B. Bouknight; Bush River in the Bush River community, the Reverend G. W. Brinkley; Calvary on the Newberry-Whitmire highway, the Reverend Sammie Robinson; New Enoree near Keitt's Crossroads, the Reverend Claude H. Tolbert; Fellowship in No. 3 Township, the Reverend Willie Starks; Flint Hill near Whitmire, no pastor at the present time; James Hopewell in the Hartford community, the Reverend Sammie R. Robinson; Little River on the Newberry-

Chappells highway, the Reverend M. C. Burrell; Metropolitan near Boyd's Crossing, the Reverend Dorothy Davenport; Mt. Zion in Helena, the Reverend W. B. Ellis; New Hope in the Long Lane community, the Reverend Dolphus Rayford; Renwick Grove in the Long Lane community, the Reverend R. C. Crump; Seekwell in the Maybinton section, the Reverend William Clark; Sims Chapel on Indian Creek, the Reverend Nura Ray Matthews; St. John on the Newberry-Pomaria road, the Reverend W. D. Samuel; St. Matthew in Sunset Park, Newberry, the Reverend George Pendergrass; and Welch Zion on the Newberry-Silverstreet highway, the Reverend William Boyles.[16]

The Vaughansville Baptist Association, of which the Reverend Richard Crump is moderator, includes these churches and pastors: Old Beaverdam near Jalapa, the Reverend Tommy Rush; Vaughansville near Chappells, the Reverend Willie Evans; Belmont in the Longshore community, vacant; Mt. Moriah just off East Main Street in Newberry, the Reverend Mrs. A. Lyles; and Scurry Spring Hill near Chappells, the Reverend Lue Wash Cannon.[17]

The Gethsemane Association includes Fairview on the Newberry-Winnsboro highway. Other Baptist churches that apparently do not belong to any of these three associations are: St. Mary's near Pomaria, Mt. Bethel on the Newberry-Winnsboro road, Suber Chapel near Whitmire, New Bethlehem in No. 7 Township, Victory on U.S. 176 near Brown's Crossroads, and St. Matthew No. 2 of Fairfield County on Benedict Street, Newberry.[18] It is possible that some of these churches are no longer in existence.

In addition to these black congregations, there have been a great many fundamentalist churches organized in the county. Some of these are Triumph The Church and Kingdom of God in Christ; Triumph Church of the New World; Mt. Olive Righteous Church of God; House of Prayer; United House of Prayer for All People Church on the Rock of the Apostolic Faith; Mt. Olive Holiness Church; Mt. Olive Righteous Church of God; and the Church of God in Helena.[19] Some no longer exist but they have left a colorful contribution to our language in their very names.

The Protestant Episcopal Church established St. Luke's the Physician in 1894 and purchased property on Lindsay Street in 1899.[20] It conducted a private school for blacks for some years. Later the name of the mission was changed to St. Monica's, and a new church was built on South Street. However, shortly after this building was constructed the church was merged with St. Luke's in the 1970s.

While black churches proliferated, the established white denominations also added new congregations. The Lutherans increased from twelve churches before the Civil War to twenty-six in the county today. One out of four residents of Newberry County is a Lutheran.

The antebellum Lutheran churches are St. John's, St. Paul's, Bethlehem, St. Matthew's, St. Luke's, Mt. Zion, St. James, Beth Eden, Colony, Macedonia, Church of the Redeemer, and Grace. The churches organized since 1865 are Mt. Tabor, St. Phillip's, Mt. Olivet, Mt. Pilgrim, Bachman Chapel, Mt. Hermon, Holy Trinity, Mayer Memorial, Silverstreet, Pomaria, Summer Memorial, Bethany, St. Timothy, and Faith.[21]

St. John's, organized in 1754 by the Reverend John Gasser as a Reformed church, is the oldest congregation in present-day Newberry County. The church became Lutheran and has served as such for more than two centuries. The first log church was replaced by another log building that in turn was replaced by the famous "White Church" in 1809. The latter still stands as the oldest frame Lutheran Church in South Carolina and was the special pride of the late W. D. Summer, Sr. He left a handsome bequest for its upkeep.

In 1950 a modern brick church was erected across the road from the historic "White Church." A new parsonage was erected in 1956 and a parish education building was constructed in 1967.

The membership consists of 198 confirmed members. This church has given one son to the ministry, the Reverend Alton C. Clark, for many years chaplain of the South Carolina House of Representatives. The present pastor is the Reverend J. Henri Bishop.

St. Paul's was organized in 1761 by the Reverend Joachim Bulow on land granted to him. Among the pastors, the Reverend Frederick Joseph Wallern was one of the founders of the "Corpus Evangelicum" of 1787. In 1824 the Reverend S. Herschner, while pastor, was secretary and first treasurer of the South Carolina Synod.

For many years St. Paul's formed a parish with St. Phillip's and Bachman Chapel but in 1962 became a self-supporting church. The present handsome stone church was dedicated in 1938, and the present parsonage constructed in 1963. The parish building was erected in 1954. St. Paul's has given the following sons to the ministry: Herman Aull, William Berley, Elijah Elmore, J. Eusebius Berley, M. J. Epting, S. J. Riser, G. A. Riser, R. E. Livingston, W. K. Sligh, H. P. Counts, T. B. Epting, E. K. Counts, Lewis Koon, and G. A. Hough.

Its membership consists of 423 confirmed members. The Reverend

R. Delano Ricard served as pastor until October 15, 1989, when he assumed the position of executive director of Lutheran Conference and Retreat Ministries of the South Carolina ELCA. His successor has not been named but the Reverend George T. Moore is interim pastor.

Bethlehem's first house of worship was erected in 1816 under the guidance of its first pastor, the Reverend Godfrey Dreher. The date its congregation was organized is unknown.

The church was the site of two meetings of Synod, in 1855 and 1863. At the first, which lasted six days, it was decided to locate the Lutheran College at Newberry.

The present church building was constructed in 1881 and remodeled in 1942. An educational building was erected in 1936, and a new parish building in 1962. The church, formerly a part of Bethlehem parish, became self-supporting in 1969. It has 168 confirmed members. The Reverend Steven D. Jackson is the present pastor.

St. Matthew's was organized as "Heller's Church" in 1827. Located on Broad River ten miles northwest of Pomaria, its founder was the Reverend J. D. Scheck. Destroyed by a cyclone in 1844, it was rebuilt two years later.

For many years this church was in Bethlehem Parish with Bethlehem and Pomaria, but it became self-supporting in 1969. It has given two sons to the ministry: Thomas F. Suber and E. A. Felker. It has 130 confirmed members. The Reverend F. Adolf Kleindt is pastor.

In 1828 St. Luke's, the largest rural Lutheran church in South Carolina, was organized by the brilliant young Lutheran divine, the Reverend J. G. Schwartz. One of the charter members, John Enlow, gave the land on which the present or fourth church stands. It was completed in 1955; the parsonage was built in 1962.

St. Luke's has given the following sons to the ministry: S. R. Shepard, Levi Bedenbaugh, Wilson Bedenbaugh, J. S. Elmore, Jacob Hawkins, I. P. Hawkins, Z. W. Bedenbaugh, C. P. Boozer, W. E. Pugh, P. E. Shealy, J. A. Shealy, Clyde Bedenbaugh, Vernon Frick, Larry W. Smith, and Gerald Whitman Smith. It has 592 confirmed members. The pastor is the Reverend Larence A. Dooley.

St. James, first known as Liberty Hill in Laurens County, was organized in 1840 by the Reverend Herman Aull. It was moved to Jalapa, Newberry County, in 1889 and dedicated as St. James. When the church building was struck by lightning and destroyed in 1941, it was rebuilt and dedicated, free of debt, the next year. In 1960 a brick-veneer educational building was constructed; it too was free of debt when dedicated. It has 182 confirmed members, and the pastor is the Reverend Herbert L. Wood, Jr.

Beth Eden was organized in 1843 by the Reverend G. H. Brown; the church building was dedicated that year. For the first century, the church flourished, but the Sumter National Forest encompassed the church and cemetery and stifled the existence of the congregation. The church is in a parish with St. James, but many of its former members have united with other congregations. Beth Eden now has forty-eight confirmed members. The Reverend Herbert L. Wood, Jr. is also pastor of this church.

Colony was organized in 1845 by the Reverend William Berley. Originally in a parish with St. Paul's and St. Luke's, in 1902 it became part of Beth Eden Parish with Mayer Memorial and Beth Eden churches. In 1910 St. James took the place of Mayer Memorial in Beth Eden Parish, which continued in this form until 1958 when Colony secured a full-time pastor of its own.

Through the generosity of Mr. and Mrs. S. V. Shevlin, both of whom were killed in a railroad crossing accident in 1951, the present, and third, church building was erected. An Allen organ and chimes were installed in 1957 and 1958.

This church has given the following sons to the ministry: H. A. McCullough, Sr.; his nephew, I. E. Long; J. B. Bedenbaugh; and Andrew David Eargle. Colony has 234 confirmed members, and the pastor is the Reverend Paul B. Williams.

Macedonia was founded in 1847 while it was located in Lexington County. The Reverend George Haltiwanger, Sr., was the first pastor. The present church building replaced the original one in 1914. It stands near the edge of Lake Murray on a beautiful site. The creation of the lake in the late 1920s caused many of the members to move to other sections, and the church lost almost two-thirds of its membership. Today the church is in Newberry County because the portion of Lexington County lying north of the lake was annexed to Newberry.

Macedonia has furnished three sons to the ministry—S. C. Ballentine, A. W. Ballentine, and George David Swygert. It has 226 confirmed members. The Reverend Randall S. Derrick is pastor.

The Church of the Redeemer was organized under the name of "Luther Chapel" on July 10, 1856, in the old courthouse in Newberry by the Reverend Thaddeus Street Boinest, later to be president of the South Carolina Synod. There were twenty-one charter members.

The first church building on Caldwell Street was struck by lightning about 1869. It was repaired and used until 1890 when the church was moved to its present location on Boundary and Wilson streets. There its name was changed in 1897.

The present beautiful church was erected in 1965 at a cost of about $455,000. A Schantz pipe organ was installed the next year at a cost of $30,000. Upon the laying of the cornerstone of the new church, January 10, 1965, Julia M. Kibler published *The History of the Lutheran Church of the Redeemer, Newberry, South Carolina, 1853–1964*.

Sons and daughters of this church who have been in full-time service include: Paul E. Scherer, W. C. Schaeffer, Jr., H. Brent Schaeffer, Mrs. Mary Lou Bowers Gray, Oscar Blackwelder, A. H. Boozer, William Peery, Gilbert Goodman, James Lee Shealy, Charles J. Shealy, Jr., A. D. Owens, H. A. Dunlap, A. J. Bowers, Sr., and John C. Peery.

Redeemer has 552 confirmed members. The Reverend Robert M. Van Horne, D.D., is the present pastor.

The twelfth and last church organized before the Civil War was "Newville, Frog Level" in 1859 by the Reverend William Berley. At the end of the war Newville, Colony, and St. Paul's formed a parish which continued until 1872, when Newville became self-sustaining.

In 1878 the church changed its name to Grace. A few years earlier Frog Level had become Prosperity. In 1892 Grace formed a parish with Mt. Tabor that continued until 1914, when Grace became a separate parish. The parish building was completed in 1951 and its church building was erected in 1974.

Grace has been host to Synod five times, to the Womens Missionary Society four times, and to the State Luther League twice. P. E. Wise was treasurer of the Synod for thirty years and his successor, A. H. Kohn, held that post for twenty-two years. Other leading layman were Rufus Counts and Kenneth Baker.

The church has given the following to full-time church service: M. M. Kinard, J. D. Kinard, A. J. Bowers, Sr., V. Y. Boozer, James L. Shealy, Al Potter, Day B. Werts, Charles B. Dawkins, E. H. Kohn; Mrs. Charles B. Dawkins, Mrs. Gertrude Simpson Leonard, C. E. Norman, Sister Lilie Leckinger, and Lottie Wyse.

It has 241 confirmed members. The Reverend Gary A. Loadholdt is pastor.

Mt. Tabor, located a mile north of Little Mountain, was organized by the Reverend J. A. Sligh in 1880. He served as pastor for the first twelve years while pastor of St. Paul's. In 1892 the church was put in a parish with Grace and remained in that status until 1914, when joined in a parish with Mt. Pilgrim and Mt. Olivet.

The church erected a brick building in 1925 and dedicated it, debt free, in 1927. A new brick parsonage was constructed in 1949 and a parish education building in 1962. The church became self-supporting in 1965.

Sons of the church given to the ministry are: L. P. Boland, Voight Cromer, and H. W. Dowd. Its membership is 296 confirmed members. The Reverend W. Osborne Herlong, Jr., is pastor.

In 1881 the Reverend H. S. Wingard organized St. Phillip's Church between Newberry and Pomaria. The church building was dedicated the following year when the church had thirty confirmed members.

The church became independent in 1948. It constructed its third church building in 1962, having built a parsonage in 1948. It has given one son, Virgil Cameron, to the ministry and has 361 confirmed members. Its present pastor is the Reverend Wilbur D. Miller.

Mt. Olivet was formed in the O'Neall section of the county in 1882 by the Reverend C. A. Marks with seventeen charter members. The present church was built in 1890 on a site given by Mrs. Anna Cason. The construction of Lake Murray in 1929 caused the dislocation of many members of the church. With ten confirmed members, it is the smallest Lutheran congregation in the county. The Reverend Stephen M. Thrash is pastor of Mt. Olivet and Mt. Hermon.

Mt. Pilgrim, with thirty-two charter members, was organized on February 22, 1880, by the Reverend J. D. Bowles. A. H. Miller donated 4 acres to the new church, which was dedicated in 1885 and used for forty years. A new building, erected in 1934, continues to be used. Mt. Pilgrim became self-supporting in 1965. It has 145 confirmed members and the Reverend Alton C. Clark is the present supply pastor.

Bachman Chapel is located about four miles north of Prosperity. It was organized in 1886 by the Reverend J. A. Sligh with forty members. It became self-sustaining in 1965 and has 255 confirmed members. The Reverend James F. Shealy is the present pastor.

Mt. Hermon at Peak was organized in 1889, with thirty-three members, by Dr. J. B. Fox of the Newberry College faculty. The first church was built in 1890, and the church was in Bethel parish until 1926.

A new church was erected in 1958 on land donated by Mrs. G. A. Swygert. Dr. C. H. Pinner, Jr., gave the architect's fee. In 1964 a parish was formed with Mt. Olivet, Chapin. It has 107 confirmed members.

Holy Trinity, Little Mountain, was organized in 1891 with thirty-four charter members as a part of the Tennessee Synod by the Reverend J. K. Efird. The second church was built of brick in 1917, and an educational building was constructed in 1962.

In 1895 the congregation was received into the South Carolina Synod and put in a parish with Macedonia. This church has given to full-time service the Reverend J. Virgil Long, L. P. Boland, J. Obert Kempson, H. D. Chapman, James Franklin Shealy, and Mrs. James B. Griffith. It has 470 confirmed members. The Reverend John E. Pless is now pastor.

Mayer Memorial, Newberry, was organized in 1899 with twenty-five charter members. The building was a gift from Dr. O. B. Mayer, Jr., in memory of his father; the land was donated by Newberry Mills. The church and all of its records were destroyed by fire in 1919. The church was rebuilt, and in 1957 the present brick structure was erected.

Initially the church was in a parish with Beth Eden and Colony; then it formed a parish with Summer Memorial. In 1929 it became self-supporting. It has given to the ministry Louis E. Bouknight, D. M. Shull, Jr., and George T. Willis. Mayer Memorial has 300 confirmed members. The Reverend Floyd E. Sides is pastor.

Silverstreet was established in the village of that name in 1908 with twenty-five charter members. A building was erected in the next year and pastors were supplied from the faculty of Newberry College. The first pastor was the Reverend S. P. Koon. The church became self-supporting during the pastorate of the Reverend Thomas F. Suber who began his labors there in 1919. A new church was built in 1951. One son of the church, the Reverend L. Boyd Hamm, was given to the ministry. It has 271 confirmed members, and the pastor is the Reverend D. Rodney Gunter.

Pomaria, located in the town of.that name, was organized by the Reverend J. J. Long in 1910, with twenty-four charter members, who came from the congregation of Bethlehem. In 1911 a modest church was built that served until 1955 when the present brick edifice was erected. In 1969 Pomaria became self-supporting; it has 148 confirmed members. The Reverend Donald L. Safrit, Jr., is pastor.

Summer Memorial was given by the Summer Brothers, C. E., J. H., and George W., as a memorial to their parents, George W. and Martha D. Summer. It was formed in the Mollohon Mill village in 1910 with twenty-six charter members. The original building was replaced in 1952. A self-supporting congregation, Summer Memorial has given two sons to the ministry—George Benet Shealy and Guerry Alvin Fulmer. Its membership is 286 confirmed members. The Reverend John F. Weaver is pastor.

Bethany, which serves the Oakland community, was organized in 1936. Gilbert Goodman, the son of Dr. R. A. Goodman, started holding services in the Oakland School House while he was a seminarian. Later, Dr. E. B. Keisler, then pastor of the Redeemer and later president of Central Theological Seminary, continued this work until the congregation was organized.

The Reverend J. B. Harman, D.D., was the first pastor. The church building was completed in 1938 and the church became self-supporting in 1954. It has 143 confirmed members and the Reverend C. William Flowers is pastor.

St. Timothy, Whitmire, was organized in 1939, with fifty charter members, as a part of the Union-Whitmire parish. The church building was completed in 1948. Its membership is fifty confirmed members. The Reverend J. Paul Rimmer is pastor.

The newest Lutheran church in the county and the fifth in the town of Newberry is Faith. Organized in 1961 by the Reverend Shelton Moose, it had seventy-four confirmed members. A church building was purchased after a non-Lutheran congregation was disbanded. A parsonage was dedicated in 1963 and an educational annex erected in 1971. It has 137 confirmed members. The Reverend J. Gordon Peery is pastor.

Newberry County's oldest Presbyterian church is Little River-Dominick, which was established as Little River in 1764 by the Hanover Presbytery meeting in Augusta County, Virginia. The Reverend James Creswell was the first minister; Colonel James Williams, Angus Campbell, and James Burnside were its first elders.[22]

Its congregation, including members of the Hunter, Griffin, Simpson, Nance, Caldwell, Luke, Crawford, Williams, Clarke, Golding, and Burnside families, furnished civil and military leaders of this section of South Carolina before the Civil War. It was one of fifty-four churches belonging to the South Carolina Presbytery during the short life of the Confederate States of America.

The original church building was located next to the old cemetery; the latter has been restored by Champion International. After the Civil War the building was moved into Laurens County near Milton, a distance of some four miles from its original site.

Meanwhile in 1913, the Dominick Presbyterian Church was established about twelve miles from Newberry and south of the Belfast Road. It remained a small church, and the congregation of Little

River dwindled. The two congregations agreed to unite and did so in 1938; the new church, known as Little River-Dominick, boasted of 101 members. A new church was erected by the congregation on land donated by Champion International; in 1947 a manse was erected on land given by Patrick Dickson. The church began to grow and has thrived ever since. Members of the Davenport, Johnson, Stewart, Boozer, Livingston, Oxner, Harmon, and Simpson families are members of this church. The Reverend Lawton Daugherty, a former pastor of this church, returned to Little River-Dominick as pastor in January 1990.

The second-oldest Presbyterian church in the county is Aveleigh.[23] Founded in 1835 and first located at Hunt's Crossroads, now the intersection of Highways 34 and 76 Bypass, the thirty-one charter members are listed in the first volume of this work. The famous Reverend Moses Waddell was the first minister. In 1852 the church was moved to the corner of Calhoun and Martin streets in Newberry.

Destroyed in the Great Fire of 1907, Aveleigh was rebuilt on the same site. A well equipped educational and recreational annex was constructed at the rear of the church in the past decade.

Aveleigh has long been a leading church in the South Carolina Presbytery. It now has a membership of 277, being the largest Presbyterian church in the county. The Reverend David F. Jones, D.D., is the present pastor.

Smyrna, located about six miles from Newberry on the Belfast Road, was organized in 1839 by the Reverend R. C. Ketchum and the Reverend M. D. Fraser.[24] The original seventeen members came from the Boozer, Senn, and Clary families.

Three sons of this church have been given to the ministry—the Reverend John I. Boozer, the Reverend Fred Boozer, and the Reverend Woodrow Hassell.[25] The present membership is 203. The Reverend Gaynor Phillips is the pastor.

Morris Chapel at Chappells was organized in 1887 with thirty-three members.[26] The first minister was the Reverend T. B. Craig; the original elders were George T. Reid and William R. Smith, and the first deacon was John R. Scurry. This church was disbanded about 1930.

Whitmire Presbyterian was organized in 1905, the first elders being James E. Yarborough, L. R. Brannon, and R. H. Burton.[27] The church was erected in 1908, a manse was later built, and a new Sunday School building added in 1925. The present membership is 136. The Reverend Steve Mayes, D.D., is pastor of Whitmire and McCullough.

McCullough Presbyterian was formed in 1948.[28] Located on the New-berry-Whitmire Highway, it has twenty-five members.

The newest Presbyterian Church in the county is Queen's. Organized in 1954 as Queen's Memorial Chapel, it is located on the Whitmire-Newberry Highway about five miles from Newberry and has fifty-six members.[29] The Reverend Charles Gahagan is pastor.

The Baptists are the third-oldest denomination in the county. The first church was Enoree in 1768, the second was Bush River, organized in 1771,[30] and the third, Lower Duncan's Creek, was established in 1786. Other antebellum Baptist churches were Cross Roads, First Baptist of Newberry, Bethel, and Fairview. Since the Civil War, seven churches have been established—West End, Chappells, Glenn Street, Hunt Memorial, Central, College Street, and The Master's.

All of these except Bethel are located north or west of a line extending from Higgins Ferry on the Saluda to Ashford Ferry on the Broad. This part of the county was settled by the English and the Scotch-Irish. The lower part of the county, where the Lutherans predominate, was settled by the Germans.

The first organization of Baptist churches was the Congaree Association, founded in 1771 and dissolved about 1778. Only Bush River was a member of this association. It was succeeded by Bethel Association (1789–1876). Bush River, Cross Roads, Enoree, and Lower Duncan's Creek were members of Bethel for a few years. Enoree then joined Salem Association (1845–1863), but transferred to Fairfield Association (1863), and then to Reedy River Association (1826 to date). All of the other Newberry County churches became early members of Reedy River Association.[31]

After the Baptist State Convention was organized in 1821, First Baptist of Newberry was the first separate church admitted to membership; it became a member in 1833. Bush River was the second, joining in 1834. Two Newberrians have served as president of the State Convention—John Belton O'Neall, from 1858 until 1863, and Walter Herbert Hunt, from 1910 to 1913. Both were members of First Baptist, Newberry.[32]

Enoree, which was originally located at Littleton's Ferry on Enoree River, was later moved to its present location near Keitt's Crossroads. The church building was an attractive frame building that has recently been brick veneered, and the membership of 148 is active and flourishing. The Reverend John Hipp, III, is pastor.

Bush River, mother church of First Baptist, Cross Roads, Fairview, and other churches continued its leadership into the twentieth century.

It occupies a handsome building complete with an educational annex and maintains a well-kept cemetery with the aid of trust funds established for this purpose. It has a present membership of 207. The Reverend John Thomas Morrow is pastor.

Lower Duncan's Creek was moved to Whitmire in 1902 and renamed First Baptist, Whitmire. It is the second-largest Baptist Church in the county with 491 members. The present supply pastor is the Reverend Louie B. Wynn of Greer.

Cross Roads, organized in 1807, is located a few miles from Chappells. The nineteen members occupy the old church building and are proud of its past. It is the smallest Baptist congregation in the county. The Reverend Thomas G. Daum is pastor.

First Baptist, Newberry, with 650 members is the largest Baptist church in the county. It has been regarded as one of the strongest churches in this part of South Carolina since its organization in 1831.[33] The Reverend Charles Nanney, pastor until he resigned because of ill health in 1981, was succeeded by the Reverend Kenneth W. Harmon.

Mt. Zion, organized in 1832, was disbanded after World War II. None of the congregation now survives.

Bethel, organized in 1840, now has 164 members. It is located on the Holley's Ferry Road about six and one-half miles south of Prosperity. The Reverend E. E. Smith is pastor.

Fairview, established in 1859, is located a mile from the Laurens County line near Indian Creek. It has a congregation of 145 members. The Reverend Frank Cooper is pastor.

These are the seven antebellum Baptist churches in the county. Seven others have been organized since the Civil War. West End, which was established in 1887, is located in the Newberry Mills section of Newberry. It has a present membership of 314. The Reverend Roy J. Flynn is pastor.

Saluda at Chappells, established in 1892, is the next-to-smallest church in the county with only sixty-nine members. The Reverend James Holston is pastor. Glenn Street, organized in 1903 in the Mollohon Mill section of Newberry, is the third-largest Baptist congregation in the county with 451 members. The Reverend John Elmer Smith is pastor.

Hunt Memorial serves the Oakland Mill community of Newberry. Established in Oakland in 1913, it was renamed in 1937 in honor of Walter H. Hunt, late president of Oakland Mill. It has 283 members, and the pastor is the Reverend Colon Wehmeyer.

Central is the second Baptist church in Whitmire. Founded in 1945, it has 119 members. Its pastor is the Reverend Boyd Duckett. College Street was established in 1954. The fifth Baptist church serving the county seat, it has 142 members. The Reverend Boyd Duckett is pastor. The newest church, and the third Baptist church in Whitmire, is The Master's. It was organized in 1967 and has 109 members. The Reverend Allen Bratcher is pastor.

The Associate Reformed Presbyterians are the fourth-oldest denomination in the county. The Reverend John Renwick from County Antrim, Ireland, was the leader of the sect that founded King's Creek and Cannon's Creek churches in the early 1770s. These were the mother churches of the Associate Reformed Synod of the South. From them sprang Mt. Bethel, Gilder's Creek, Prosperity, Head Spring, Newberry, and Unity Churches. Only Newberry and Cannon's Creek remain.

Newberry was founded in 1854 on a lot given by Dr. Thomas W. Thompson. The church was known as Thompson Street Church until destroyed in the Great Fire of 1907. The church was rebuilt at its present location at the corner of Main and Calhoun streets and renamed.[34] Its membership is 280. The Reverend Edward L. Bland is pastor.

Cannon's Creek was moved from its original location to a point on the Newberry-Prosperity Highway in 1948. The Prosperity Church was abandoned and its members united with Cannon's Creek. It has sixty-seven members. The Reverend Gary L. Pierstorff is pastor.

The United Methodists have fifteen churches in Newberry County. They are the fifth-oldest denomination, having first appeared in the late eighteenth century. They were heartened by the visits of the great Bishop Francis Asbury, who encouraged the founding of Mt. Bethel Academy as well as the early churches.

Ebenezer (Maybinton), the first Methodist church founded in the county, was organized in the 1780s. Its third meeting house was razed in the 1970s; no regular services had been held for some time. The community from which its membership was drawn has become part of the Sumter National Forest, and the old families that constituted its membership have moved. It is a pity that this ancient landmark has been destroyed. Only the old cemetery remains to mark its existence.

Most of the Methodist churches in the county are in Greenwood District; four are in Columbia District.[35] The latter includes New Hope, established about 1795 near Broad River; Mt. Pleasant, organized in 1822 near the Enoree River; Wightman, first organized in 1848 as Bethesda and later renamed and moved to Prosperity; and Zion, formed in 1813 and located on the road from Prosperity to Batesburg.

The Greenwood District includes Central, Epting Memorial, Lewis Memorial, O'Neal (sic) Street, Trinity, Sharon, and Whitmire; three churches in the Newberry Circuit (Ebenezer, Lebanon, and New Chapel); and Capers Chapel.

Central, the second church of any denomination to be founded in the village of Newberry, was established in 1833. It has the largest congregation of any church in the county with 746 members. Originally named Newberry Methodist, it became Johnstone Street Methodist in 1900 and was renamed Central when the present church building was completed in 1901. Central owns an entire city block and has a well-appointed brick church building with an educational annex.[36] The Reverend Mitchell Houston is the pastor.

Epting Memorial, named for the late James F. Epting, was organized in 1902 by the Reverend G. E. Edwards.[37] It has 332 members. Its pastor is the Reverend Barry Brown.

Lewis Memorial, organized in 1912 as Oakland, serves the Oakland section of the city. It was renamed for the Reverend W. H. Lewis who served as pastor of it and Epting Memorial.[38] It has 317 members. The Reverend Harry R. Workman is now pastor.

O'Neal Street, organized in 1891 as Second Methodist, was renamed for the street on which it is located. That street was named for John Belton O'Neall, but the city authorities insisted upon using the variant spelling. Its name was changed in 1895. The Reverend S. A. Nettles was the first pastor.[39] O'Neal Street now has 341 members, and its pastor is the Reverend Richard Rogers-Berry.

Trinity, founded in 1835 when the old churches of Shady Grove and Kadesh merged, is located in the Silverstreet section.[40] It has 287 members. It has given three sons to the ministry—Rex V. Martin, James H. Martin, and M. E. Boozer. The Reverend Carl Ritter is pastor.

South of the town is Ebenezer. First known as Watson's Camp Grounds, it was organized in 1814.[41] It gave the Reverend J. B. Kilgore to the ministry. Ebenezer has 109 members and is one of the churches in the Newberry Circuit. The Reverend Walter S. Green serves as pastor for the three churches in the circuit.

Lebanon, another church in Newberry Circuit, was established in 1875 in Caldwell Township.[42] It has seventy members but has given three sons to the ministry—G. A. McGraw, Walter H. Henry, and J. Matthew Henry.

The third church in Newberry Circuit, New Chapel, was organized in 1830 by Isaac Herbert.[43] Although it now has only thirty-three members and is the smallest Methodist church in the county, it has furnished a large number of its sons to the ministry—Thomas G. Herbert, J. Marion Boyd, George M. Boyd, David P. Boyd, Walter I. Herbert, Thomas G. Herbert, Jr., Chesley C. Herbert, George Pierce Watson, and Robert C. Boulware.

Whitmire, organized in 1892, resulted from the transfer of many members of old Mt. Tabor and Ebenezer (Maybinton); it was the first church organized in Whitmire following its incorporation in 1891. It is the second-largest Methodist church in the county with 437 members. The Reverend Harry Goewey is pastor.

Sharon, located at Kinards, was formed in 1854. It shares a pastor with Hopewell in Laurens County and has a membership of forty-five. The current pastor is the Reverend Jack Fenner.

Capers Chapel, located just inside the county below Pomaria, has fifty members. It was named for Bishop William Capers. The Reverend Jerry M. Price is pastor.

Of the four United Methodist churches in the Columbia District, New Hope is the oldest. Organized near Broad River in 1795, it has 137 members. The Reverend Jerry M. Price is pastor.

Zion, founded in 1813, was moved to its present site on the highway from Prosperity to Batesburg in 1829. It has 321 members. The Reverend Ben M. Gafford is pastor of Zion and Wightman.

Mt. Pleasant, located near Keitt's Bridge on the Enoree River, was established in 1822. Its membership numbers 201. The Reverend Kermit Shrawder is pastor.

Wightman in Prosperity emerged from Bethesda, which was located about a mile out of Frog Level. Both church and town changed names. Wightman has 200 members.

St. Luke's, the only Episcopal church in the county, was organized in 1846. Its beautiful gothic building was built in 1855 and was consecrated in August of that year by the Right Reverend Thomas F. Davis, Bishop of South Carolina.[44]

The building was vandalized during the Civil War and for many years was on the verge of being closed. Captain N. B. Mazyck, a gallant Confederate officer who was railroad station agent at Newberry, and a handful of the faithful preserved the church.

Later, Major J. F. J. Caldwell, Dr. C. D. Weeks, and Professor Wilmer

Gaver of the Newberry College faculty kept the tiny congregation together.

After World War II there was a renaissance brought about largely through the efforts of Andrew Pickens Salley and T. E. Davis. The church acquired a rectory, a parish house, and a resident vicar, the Reverend Edwin B. Clippard, who was ordained to the priesthood in the church in 1952.

The 1950s and 1960s were happy years for St. Luke's. The congregation grew steadily, worked together, and advanced the work of the Church Triumphant. One son, R. Houseal Norris, was ordained a priest. Vicar during the 1970s was the Reverend Frederick C. Byrd, now Archdeacon of the Diocese of Upper South Carolina.

The church was demolished by the tornado of 1984. Fortunately, through the generosity of other churches in Newberry, citizens of the town, and benefactors from South Carolina and elsewhere, it has been rebuilt in the gothic style of the former building.

Soon after the church was destroyed, the Reverend George Vought was sent to St. Luke's for a year. Chaplain of the Brooks School in Massachusetts, he took a sabbatical to serve the church. He did an outstanding job of reuniting the various factions in the congregation and in completing the church edifice. When he died suddenly in February 1986, the entire town mourned. His influence is still felt among Episcopalians.

After Mr. Vought's death there was no resident vicar until the Reverend John A. Brown, Jr., came in the fall of 1986. He continued the good work and it was generally regretted that he resigned in 1989 to enter the counseling field in Columbia. The Reverend Dr. Jerry Van Drew came to St. Luke's in 1990.

Clayton Memorial Universalist Church, known as the Halfacre Church, was organized in 1907. Named for the Reverend Daniel Bragg Clayton, the church was built on lands owned by the late David Halfacre. In 1881 a tract of 1 acre was set aside as a family burial ground,[45] and on this tract the heirs later established the church. It now has about forty members. The Reverend Rhett D. Baird and the Reverend David Vaughn are the present pastors.

St. Mark's Catholic Church was organized in 1956. In that year a beautiful lot on Boundary Street was purchased,[46] and the church building was completed and consecrated by J. J. Russell, Bishop of the Diocese of Charleston. Those instrumental in establishing the church included Arthur E. Morehead, the late Walter J. Regnery, and the late William Turner. At present the church is served by Father Sidney J. Gilly. The present membership of St. Mark's is about 100.

A Church of Jesus Christ of Latter Day Saints was founded in 1975. The church occupies an attractive building on Glenn Street. Its membership comes from Newberry and Saluda counties and numbers about seventy.[47]

Fundamentalist sects appeared in the county just before World War I. First to come were the Pentecostal Holiness churches which were organized in Chappells, Silverstreet, Newberry, and Whitmire.[48] The First Pentecostal Church in Newberry, located at the corner of Pope and Nance streets, has been in the same location for more than sixty years. Its pastor is the Reverend Dan Lewis, and it has fifty-five members.

The Church of God established churches in Whitmire and Newberry[49] just before World War II. The Newberry church occupies a nice brick building on College Street near Rosemont Cemetery. Its pastor is the Reverend Daniel Nash and it has eighty-four members.

The First Church of God also has formed branches in Newberry and Whitmire, while the Church of Christ has a church on U.S. 76 outside Newberry. The Reverend Louis Rushmore is its pastor; it has thirty-five members. The First Assembly of God has a church on Glenn Street, Newberry.[50]

Other sects are the Wesleyan Methodist Church, with churches in Newberry and Whitmire, the Church of the Nazarene, the Primitive Baptists, and the Free Will Baptists. In Prosperity the Independent Bible Baptist Church, with the Reverend Tom Martin as pastor, has been functioning for some years.[51]

The Southern Methodists are represented by Mt. Bethel Southern Methodist Church and Morris Chapel Southern Methodist Church. The Reverend Cecil Rourk is pastor of Mt. Bethel, which has a membership of about fifty. The Reverend Leecy Bright is pastor of Morris Chapel.

There are some 150 churches in Newberry County. This is an extremely large number to serve a population of less than 32,000 people.

21

Medicine and Public Health

Most of Newberry's physicians served in the Confederate Army either as surgeons or as line officers. Only the old and the physically unfit remained at home to care for the civilian population. Those who did had no access to hospitals and no public health department to help with preventive medicine. Medical care was primitive.

Peace brought even more problems. When freedmen moved into town, they lived in crowded houses under unsanitary conditions. By 1885 the death rate among blacks was 38.49 per 1,000, more than double that of the whites.[1] There were no agencies to improve sanitation or to teach personal hygiene. This could only be done by the physicians individually.

In December 1865 the doctors organized the District Medical Association with Dr. Pressley B. Ruff as president, Dr. James McIntosh as vice-president, and Dr. Sampson Pope as treasurer. Not surprisingly, they adopted a minimum fee schedule on December 26, 1865.[2]

Five years later, on March 21, 1870, the association was reorganized. It underwent a second reorganization in 1878, becoming the Newberry County Medical Society.[3] During this entire period there were about thirty physicians in the county.

The problems Newberry experienced with unlicensed physicians and an absence of a public health agency were general throughout the state. Finally in 1878 the State Board of Health was established, and in 1882 a law was enacted requiring physicians to register with the clerk of court. Although many Newberry County physicians have failed to register during the past century, the Register is still the best available record of local physicians, their dates of license, and, for the registrants of the early years, their medical colleges.[4]

Also in 1882 the town of Newberry established a Board of Health; it originally consisted of nine members, with two members from each ward and the ninth member from the town at large.[5] The first chairman of the Board of Health was Dr. James McIntosh, who served until 1889.

Dr. McIntosh was a native of Society Hill in Darlington County. Born on February 28, 1838, he graduated from the South Carolina College in 1857 and from the Medical College of South Carolina in 1860. After serving as a line officer with the 8th South Carolina Regiment and then in the Medical Department as a surgeon in the Civil War, he married Frances Higgins and settled in Newberry. He served as president of the South Carolina Medical Association in 1874.

Dr. O. B. Mayer, Jr., succeeded Dr. McIntosh as chairman of the Board. He, too, served as president of the state medical association, doing so in 1886. He and Dr. McIntosh are the only Newberry physicians to head the state association. Each of them had a son who also served as president of the state medical association—Dr. James Higgins McIntosh and Dr. Orlando B. Mayer; both were practicing in Columbia when elected.

Others who served as chairman of the Board of Health in its early years included Dr. J. K. Gilder, Dr. W. G. Houseal, Dr. J. M. Kibler, and Dr. P. G. Ellesor.

In 1890 a town ordinance required physicians to report deaths and births, and in 1894 a health inspector was employed to help the board enforce the health laws. Town council employed a public vaccinator when smallpox threatened in 1882 and 1897,[6] but there was no countywide machinery to improve public health until 1920.

Efforts were made to protect the public from untrained and unlicensed physicians. In 1891 Governor Tillman appointed Dr. W. D. Senn, Dr. C. T. Wyche, and Dr. R. C. Carlisle as a County Board of Medical Examiners.[7] This board could license a physician if satisfied of his competence even if he had not graduated from a recognized medical college. A decade later the State Board of Examiners took over the licensing function.[8]

There was no hospital or public clinic in the county until 1925. Early in the twentieth century efforts were made to establish a hospital. Without a hospital, the local doctors had to send patients to Charleston or Columbia for specialized treatment or surgery. There were, of course, only general practitioners in Newberry, and there was nothing to attract a surgeon or an internist. To provide proper local health care, a hospital was a necessity.

The physicians attempted to mold public support for a hospital. In 1911 a committee was appointed to investigate the cost. Two weeks later the Newberry Hospital Association was formed with Dr. W. G. Houseal as president and Dr. W. E. Pelham, Jr., as secretary,[9] but World War I stopped all work on the problem.

The cause of a local hospital was helped greatly by the establishment of the County Health Department in 1920. Dr. Roy F. Finney came to Newberry as the first health officer; Jacob R. Wise was employed as sanitarian and Miss Theresa Lightsey as county health nurse. Dr. Finney remained only a short time, being succeeded by Dr. E. P. Nnotts, who in turn was succeeded in 1924 by Dr. H. G. Callison.[10]

A mass meeting was held on December 11, 1923, over which Dr. W. G. Houseal presided. A strong board of directors was chosen for the Newberry County Hospital Association with Dr. George B. Cromer as chairman.[11] The next month the board elected a medical advisory board consisting of five local physicians, Drs. Houseal, Pope, Kibler, Mayes, and Mower. Dr. John B. Setzler was elected secretary of the board of directors.[12] Very wisely, the physicians were not made members of the board, but in their advisory capacity they greatly assisted in the planning for the new hospital.

A twenty-five bed hospital was constructed on Hunt and Kinard Streets, at a cost of $62,000. All of the costs were paid by voluntary contributions from interested citizens. Various rooms were furnished by local organizations and individuals. Among the latter, Captain W. Smith Langford gave the equipment for the operating and sterilizing rooms in memory of the men who served under his command in the Spanish-American War, and R. Herman Wright furnished a special room in memory of his mother.[13]

The hospital was formally opened on December 22, 1925.[14] By an act of the General Assembly in 1927, the Newberry County Hospital was incorporated, and the corporation took over all assets and assumed all liabilities of the hospital association.[15]

Dr. H. Grady Callison, the county health officer, was superintendent of the hospital for six years before he moved to Augusta, Georgia, in 1932. Jake R. Wise of the Health Department became secretary of the hospital board and served until his death. Much of the progress in public health is due to their efforts.

Dr. Callison, son of J. W. and Amanda Hollingsworth Callison, was born in Greenwood County on March 10, 1889. He graduated from the Medical College of South Carolina and the next year became county health officer in Newberry. In 1932 he moved to Augusta to become commissioner of health for Richmond County and the city of Augusta. He later returned to South Carolina and to the South Carolina Department of Public Health. In 1948 he became director of the Anderson County Health Department and continued in that position until his death on December 8, 1964. He married Ethel Jaeger, who survived him with three children, H. G. Callison, Jr.; Eugenia, who married the Reverend Houseal Norris of Newberry; and Carolina Callison, M.D.[16]

Jacob Ramage Wise, son of George Herman and Melverda Ramage Wise and a native of Saluda, graduated from Clemson College in 1916, served as sergeant-major in the 81st Infantry Division in World War I, and came to Newberry in 1920 to help establish the County Health Department. In addition to his duties as sanitarian and secretary of the hospital board, he was county service officer from the creation of the post until his death on October 5, 1967. Active in the American Legion and the 40 and 8, his life was one of useful service. He married Julia Summer and they had no children. The *Newberry Observer*, in an editorial following his death, stated that he was one of Newberry's best loved and most useful citizens.[17]

In 1932 Dr. Hugh B. Senn became county health officer, being succeeded in 1934 by Dr. J. Claude Sease. Dr. Sease served longer than anyone else and was greatly beloved. Upon his death in 1960, Dr. Von Long became Newberry's last resident health officer and served until he retired in 1978. Sketches of these three doctors appear in the chapter on physicians of the county.

In 1938 the Newberry County Board of Health was established under the control of the State Board of Health. It consisted of three members, one appointed by the county legislative delegation, one appointed by the city council of Newberry, and the third to be selected by the first two members. It was to elect the county health officer and to assume the duties of all municipal boards of health in the county. Its secretary was to be the secretary of the county health department.[18]

Following World War II, the hospital was enlarged to sixty beds and became the Newberry County Memorial Hospital in honor of the servicemen of World War II. Appropriate dedicatory services were held with the principal address being made by Brigadier General James C. Dozier, longtime adjutant general of South Carolina and Congressional Medal of Honor recipient.[19]

Again in 1963 the hospital was enlarged, this time to a seventy-two bed capacity.[20] Although still operated under its charter as an eleemosynary corporation, the institution was supported by a local tax levy and also received aid from the Duke Foundation. However, the hospital simply could not fill the needs of the community unless it was enlarged and better equipped.

Members of the board during the crucial years when the community was made aware of the importance of a new hospital were Thomas P. Buzhardt, Gerald C. Paysinger, Jacob A. Bowers, Margie Y. Leaman, Earl W. Dickert, John E. Caldwell, A. E. Morehead, Jr., Harrison Reeder, Edward Rollins, Robert D. Schumpert, Doris Setzler, and Dr. B. M. Montgomery, chief of staff.

Special recognition should be given Buzhardt, Paysinger, Bowers, Morehead, and Schumpert. The first four served as chairman during the critical years of 1971 to 1976 and they succeeded in securing a favorable vote in the referendum of 1972 for construction of a new hospital. Schumpert helped with the legal issues.

Buzhardt, native Newberrian and graduate of Newberry College, served in the U.S. Navy, worked for the South Carolina National Bank, was office manager at Mollohon Mill, and director of finance for the city of Newberry. A former chairman of Newberry County Council and chairman of the Hospital Board in 1971, he now farms in the Hartford section. Married to the former Eunice Frances Burgess, he has a son, Tommy, and a daughter, Jane.

Paysinger, another native son and graduate of Newberry College, served four years in the U.S. Army and was captain of Field Artillery, 78th Lightning Division, in World War II. A successful merchant, active member of the Lutheran Church of the Redeemer, and chairman of the County School Board from 1959 to 1980, he was chairman of the Hospital Board in 1972 and 1973. He and his wife, the former Virginia Alice Thompson, have established scholarships at both Newberry and Columbia colleges. They have three daughters, Nancy Virginia, Jane Thompson, and Alice Louise.

Bowers, another native of the county and graduate of Newberry College, has been a banker except when he was with the U.S. Air Force during World War II. He commenced his banking career with the South Carolina National Bank, then was executive vice-president of the Prosperity Depository, and later president of the Bank of Commerce that he successfully merged with Southern Bank and Trust. He was city executive of the latter until he retired. In 1988 he helped organize the

Midlands National Bank, which he serves as chairman of the Board of Directors. An active churchman, civic and business leader, he served for fifteen years on the hospital board. Son of J. A. and Ola Bowers, he was born on January 26, 1919, and married Margie Wilson. They have four children, Andy, David, Monte, and Betsy Ruff.

Morehead, native of Memphis, Tennessee, graduate of the University of South Carolina, captain of the latter's football team, and officer in the U.S. Navy during World War II, moved to Newberry after the war. First he operated the local Studebaker agency and then became the local Gulf Oil distributor. Active in St. Mark's Catholic Church and many civic organizations, he has served as chairman of the board of Newberry Federal Savings Bank and the hospital board. He has been president of the Newberry Chamber of Commerce, the Country Club of Newberry, and the Lions Club, as well as commander of Post 24, the American Legion. He is married to Nelle Lipscomb, and they have three children, Harriette Swearingen, Judge A. E. Morehead, III, and Craig W. Morehead.

In view of a constitutional amendment adopted in March 1973, it was necessary to carry a test case to the Supreme Court to determine the validity of the bond issue relative to the hospital. Fortunately the special bond issue was upheld.

The city of Newberry and the county allocated large portions of the money being returned to them under the revenue-sharing plan of the central government to assist in financing the construction. In June 1974 the county council agreed to underwrite any deficit and a contract was let. A new 102-bed hospital was erected at a cost of $6 million on a lot on Kinard Street.

The effect of the well-equipped institution on the medical services of the community was immediate. Newberry now has two surgeons, a pathologist, a radiologist, two specialists in internal medicine, an orthopaedic surgeon, two opthalmologists, a urologist, and two pediatricians, in addition to the physicians who have family practices. Other urologists and opthalmologists maintain offices near the hospital, which they staff on certain days.

Administrators of the hospital during these critical years were Lawrence Richardson, Clem G. Beasley, and Joe Pettus. In 1979 the hospital entered into a management contract with the Hospital Corporation of America. The first administrator after this change was Charles Morgan, who served from 1979 to 1983. Morgan was succeeded by Donnie J. Weeks, a native of Barnwell and a graduate of the University of South

Carolina. He was administrator of the Barnwell County Hospital from 1973 until he came to Newberry in 1983.

The members of the board serve without pay and deserve recognition for their efforts. Besides those mentioned, the following have served as chairman since Dr. G. B. Cromer: Z. F. Wright, G. K. Dominick, Waldo C. Huffman, H. A. Kemper, Thomas C. Dillard, Frank Senn, John Caldwell, William D. Kibler, John F. Scurry, Jr., Henry Reeder, and Clara Wertz.

In 1990 the members of the board were Sinclair Kenan, Jake Arant, Jr., Hazel Clark, Elmer R. Baker, Jerry Alewine, Louie Derrick, Ladison Hamm, John Scurry, Jr., Henry S. Reeder, V. Odell Ruff, Mark A. Davis, M.D., Ann Threatt, and Fred J. Weir.

The current chairman, Fred J. Weir, Jr., was born in Newberry on March 6, 1928. The son of Fred J. and Helen Bedenbaugh Weir, he graduated from Clemson with a B.S. in textile manufacturing in 1949. After a training program at Clinton Mills, he was an engineer with Newberry Mills, Inc., the Kendall Company, and Greenwood Mills, retiring in 1987 as vice president of Customer Service. He has served as director and president of the Newberry Lions Club and of the Newberry Jaycees, and as member of the council of the Lutheran Church of the Redeemer. He married Mary Lou Anderson, and they have three children, Fred J. Weir, III, and twins, Robert Harold Weir and Thomas Anderson Weir.

22

The Physicians of the County

On the eve of the Civil War there were eight physicians in active practice in the town of Newberry. These were Drs. William Brown, Thomas W. Thompson, P. B. Ruff, O. B. Mayer, David E. Ewart, D. C. Glenn, Sampson Pope, and E. B. Ferguson.[1] Of these, Drs. Pope, Ewart, and Glenn volunteered for and served in the Confederate forces. Drs. Brown, Ruff, Mayer, and Thompson continued in practice, and nothing further is known of Dr. Ferguson.

Dr. William Brown was born in Ireland about 1816 and his wife, Mary, was born in Baden about 1824. He bought a lot on Caldwell Street in 1853 and advertised it for sale in January 1870. According to the public records, he sold the property in 1874. He did not join the other physicians in publishing a fee scale in December 1865, nor is he included in the membership of the medical association. He is included in the census of 1870. There is nothing in the public records or the local newspapers to indicate where he went from Newberry.[2]

Dr. Thomas W. Thompson graduated from the Medical College of South Carolina in 1835. He settled in Newberry and practiced with great success until his death in January 1865, survived by his wife, Sara Ann, and two sons, Thomas A. and John M. Thompson.[3]

Dr. Pressley B. Ruff was born in the district on December 21, 1801. Graduating from the Medical College of South Carolina in 1832, according to the register, but in 1830 according to the Centennial Memorial, he settled in the town. When the district medical association was organized in December 1865, he was elected its first president. Dr. Ruff built the beautiful brick home on Boundary Street now owned by Mrs. O. M. Cobb.

Dr. Ruff married twice. By his first wife, Esther Lorick (1816–1850), he had four children: Mary Alabama, who married Captain John M. Kinard; John J., who died in Confederate service; Frances Harriet, who died unmarried; and Ann B., who died in infancy.

He married second Harriet Catherine Thompson of Fairfield (1819–1887). Dr. Ruff died on December 28, 1890, at the age of eighty-nine, at that time the oldest citizen of Newberry.[4]

Also practicing in the town was Dr. Orlando Benedict Mayer, Sr. Born near Hope's Station in what was then Lexington District on February 24, 1818, he was a graduate of South Carolina College in 1837 and the Medical College of South Carolina in 1840. After studying in Europe, he settled in Newberry in 1849. Dr. Mayer married first May Davis of Fairfield, second Caroline DeWalt, and third, Mrs. L. C. Kinard. Active in the Lutheran Church and a teacher at Newberry College, he was a leader in his profession. His son, Dr. O. B. Mayer, Jr., was his partner in medicine; his grandson, third of that name, is a prominent retired physician in Columbia now. Dr. Mayer died on July 16, 1891.[5]

Dr. David E. Ewart was born in Columbia on April 30, 1830, and graduated from the Medical College of South Carolina in 1851. After studying in Paris, he married Laura Graham of Newberry and commenced his practice there.

He volunteered for service and was commissioned surgeon of the Third South Carolina Volunteer Regiment. Later he resigned and was commissioned assistant surgeon, Confederate States Navy. He contracted yellow fever and died aboard the gunboat Chicora in Charleston harbor in September 1864.[6]

Dr. Daniel C. Glenn, son of John F. and Edna Glenn, was born in the district. He settled in the town in March 1859. He, too, volunteered for the Confederacy and saw hard service. After the war he returned to Newberry, but was unable to practice long because of his health. He died on June 28, 1873, survived by his widow and two children.[7]

Dr. Sampson Pope, son of Thomas H. and Harriet Neville Harrington Pope, was born in the town on October 15, 1836. Educated at The Citadel and Jefferson Medical College, he served an internship at Pennsylvania General Hospital before returning to Newberry to practice in 1858. He volunteered for service in Company B, First Regiment, South Carolina Volunteers, on January 6, 1861. Commissioned successively as third lieutenant, first lieutenant, and captain of that company, he saw hard service in Virginia. He later transferred to the Medical Department and was senior surgeon of Wright's Brigade.

At the end of the war he returned to his practice in Newberry. Later he read and practiced law with his brother, Y. J. Pope, and Colonel Simeon Fair from 1868 to 1877. In the latter year he moved to Texas but returned to Newberry in 1881 when he resumed the practice of medicine there. He married his first cousin, Helen Harrington. He died on April 22, 1906, while his widow died on August 12, 1906. They were survived by a son, Dr. Thomas H. Pope, and a daughter, Sarah, who married Paul E. Anderson.[8]

In 1862 Dr. Thomas L. Ogier, born in Charleston of French ancestry and a graduate of the Medical College of South Carolina in the class of 1830, purchased the W. F. Nance mansion (now known as Gildercrest). He was Confederate director of medical services for three southern states. Whether he practiced in Newberry is not known, but he was a vestryman of St. Luke's Episcopal Church. In 1868 he sold the house and returned to Charleston where he died in 1900 at the age of ninety.[9]

At the end of the war, Dr. Benjamin F. Kilgore, member of the class of 1841 at the Medical College of South Carolina and surgeon of the Thirteenth Regiment, South Carolina Volunteers, was in charge of the Confederate hospital housed in the Newberry College building.[10]

On December 4, 1865, the physicians of the district met at the courthouse to organize a district association and to agree upon a fee scale. Dr. P. B. Ruff was elected president, Dr. James McIntosh, secretary, and Dr. Sampson Pope, treasurer. It was agreed that they would charge $1 for a visit in town and mileage of 50 cents per mile during daylight and $1 at night; $1 for a prescription; $20 to $50 for obstetrics; and $20 in advance for treatment of gonorrhea or syphilis.[11]

Members of the new society were Drs. P. B. Ruff, O. B. Mayer, Sampson Pope, B. F. Watkins, W. T. McFall, G. W. Garmany, C. H. Sondley, J. A. Bond, J. W. McCants, William C. Sondley, A. B. Pitts, D. C. Glenn, J. M. H. Ruff, T. B. Kennerly, and James McIntosh.[12] Of these, P. B. Ruff, Mayer, Pope, Watkins, Garmany, Glenn, and McIntosh lived and practiced in the town.

Dr. George W. Garmany settled in Newberry in June 1865, announcing that he had an office at Mrs. Ewart's. Chapman said that he served first as a private and then as surgeon of the 62nd North Carolina Regiment. He moved to Sumter in 1882 but soon returned to Newberry where he died on December 19, 1890, at the age of fifty.[13]

Dr. McIntosh was born in Darlington District on February 28, 1838. He graduated from South Carolina College in 1857 and from the Medical College of South Carolina in 1860. He served first in the line with the 8th South Carolina Regiment and then in the Medical Department as surgeon. He married Frances Higgins and settled in Newberry after the war. Here he practiced until 1901 when he became president of the Newberry Savings Bank. He remained active in that bank until it merged with the Exchange Bank in 1919. While he was practicing medicine, he served as president of the South Carolina Medical Association in 1874.

By his first wife, Dr. McIntosh had two children, Dr. James H. McIntosh and Mrs. George Buell. His second wife was the former Sarah Burt Rook; they had two children, Margaret and Murray McIntosh. Dr. McIntosh died on February 26, 1919.[14]

Dr. B. F. Watkins first practiced in the Broad River section of the county but located in Newberry in April 1865. He joined the District Medical Association in December of that year but left Newberry in 1866.[15]

Dr. John Calhoun Caldwell, son of John and Abigail O'Neall Caldwell, was born in the town on September 19, 1817. After graduating from the Medical College of South Carolina in 1840, he located at Newberry. He then moved to Greenville County where he practiced until his mother died in February, 1866. He returned to Newberry in order to settle her estate and resumed his practice there. However, a short time later he returned to Greenville County. He married Ellen Drucilla Owen and died on March 28, 1904, being buried at Gowansville.[16]

Dr. Jerome D. Bruce was born in Moore County, North Carolina, on July 23, 1836, and graduated from Jefferson Medical College in 1856. He served as a surgeon in the Confederate Army. Coming to Newberry in November 1867, he practiced for a short time before moving to Prosperity where he opened a drugstore. He later moved to Green Cove, Florida. After the death of his first wife, he married Alma Werber of Newberry in 1892. He retired to Newberry in 1911. The date of his death is not known.[17]

Dr. Samuel Franklin Fant was a native of the county, having been born near Whitmire on August 23, 1827. He was the son of William and Mildred Edrington Fant. He located in Newberry to practice medicine but gave up the practice to operate a drugstore before 1870. In that year he was listed as a druggist in the census. He was the first to occupy the quarters on the corner of Main and Caldwell streets under the Newberry Hotel when the new building was completed in 1880. Shortly before his death, he sold his business to Drs. Cofield and Lyons. Dr. Fant married Frances Lyles; he died on October 8, 1886, survived by his widow and four children: Ione, who married Silas J. McCaughrin and was a substantial benefactor of Rosemont Cemetery; Lois; Caldwell Edrington; and Maude.[18]

Only five physicians were actively practicing medicine in the town in 1870.[19] They were Drs. William Brown, P. B. Ruff, O. B. Mayer, G. W. Garmany, and James McIntosh. Dr. Sampson Pope was then practicing law and Dr. Daniel C. Glenn was incapacitated. However when Dr. John Thompson Darby of Columbia came to Newberry in 1873 to remove a cancerous womb from a black, his successful operation was witnessed by Drs. McIntosh, Garmany, Fant, Pope, Wallace, and Abney of the town and by Drs. Carlisle and Renwick of the county.[20]

Dr. C. W. Abney settled in the town in August 1872, but did not remain long. He was not listed in the census of 1880 nor is there further newspaper reference to him.[21]

Dr. Andrew Wallace, son of Colonel William Wallace of Columbia, was born there in 1848. He practiced in Newberry from 1872 to 1878 when he moved to Greenville. He practiced there successfully and died at the age of sixty-eight in August 1916.[22]

Three physicians mentioned in the local newspapers as practicing in the county but about whom little has been learned are Dr. Charlton H. Sondley, Dr. W. C. Sondley, and Dr. John L. Speake. All graduated from the Medical College of South Carolina in the classes of 1852, 1854, and 1860, respectively. Both Dr. C. H. Sondley and Dr. W. C. Sondley attended the organizational meeting of the District Medical Association in December 1865. Dr. C. H. Sondley's body was found near the Johnstone Cemetery just outside the town in 1876 and the newspaper reported that it was not known whether he had committed suicide or had been accidentally killed while hunting.[23] No further mention is made of either Sondley.

Dr. John L. Speake, son of George and Rebecca C. Speake, was born in the district on January 16, 1836. After graduating from the Medical College of South Carolina in 1860, he volunteered as a private in Company D, 3rd South Carolina Battalion. Later he was transferred to the Medical Department and served as assistant surgeon and then surgeon of the 15th South Carolina Infantry Regiment.

In 1870 Dr. Speake was elected treasurer of the County Medical Association when it was reorganized. However, he was not listed as a physician in the county in 1870. He signed the register in 1885. He married Hattie Fellers and apparently lived in Laurens County and practiced in both counties.[24]

Dr. John M. Thompson, son of Dr. Thomas Thompson of Newberry, was born in the village. He graduated from Jefferson Medical College in 1872 and first settled in the town. Thompson then moved to Silverstreet community where he practiced until 1889 when he moved to Ocala, Florida, where he had a successful career.[25] He served as president of the Newberry County Medical Society from 1878 to 1880.

Dr. Orlando Benedict Mayer, Jr., son of Dr. O. B. and Caroline DeWalt Mayer, was born in Newberry on March 23, 1853. Graduating at the Medical College of South Carolina in 1874, he joined his father in general practice. He was president of the South Carolina Medical Association in 1886, being the second Newberrian to hold this office. From 1899 to 1907, he was a member of the State Board of Medical Examiners. He was a trustee of Newberry College and vice president of the Commercial Bank. He married Harriett Jones and was survived by her and three children, Dr. O. B., Cornelia, and Harriett (Mrs. William R. Reid).[26]

Dr. John C. Halfacre was born in the district on October 25, 1851. He graduated from the Medical College of South Carolina in 1874 and located near Pomaria. He married Lula Neel, who died in 1912. Dr. Halfacre moved to the town in 1891 and died on September 20, 1916. He was survived by seven children, Paul S., Frank H., Ruth, Mary Frances, Lula Neel, Hulda Halfacre, and Eunice H. Hipp.[27]

Dr. James A. Cofield was born in Union District on June 25, 1844. He enlisted at the age of eighteen in Company D, 7th South Carolina Infantry Regiment and served until the surrender at Appomattox. He graduated from the Medical College of South Carolina in 1874 and settled in Newberry County. After practicing in Prosperity and the Maybinton section, he moved to the town in 1886; he and Dr. Lyons purchased the drugstore of Dr. S. F. Fant in that year. Two years later Dr. Cofield died on November 3. He was survived by his widow, the former Mary Bethune, who taught history and political science at Columbia College for sixteen years. She died in May 1911.[28]

Dr. Dargan Strother Pope, son of Thomas H. and Harriet Neville Harrington Pope, was born in the village on September 24, 1850. He was educated at Furman University and Jefferson Medical College, graduating in medicine in 1875. He opened his office in Newberry in February of that year; in 1877 he and Dr. J. C. Wardlaw opened a drugstore. He was elected secretary of the medical society upon its reorganization in 1878. In 1879 he moved to Columbia to become assistant physician at the penitentiary. He married Florence Brooks Sims of Columbia on December 22, 1881. Following her death, he married Ethelind Goss of

Union. Dr. Pope became physician at the penitentiary in 1881 and continued in that office until 1889; thereafter he practiced in Columbia until his death on April 24, 1926. He was greatly beloved and mourned. He was survived by his widow and three children, Ethelind, Nancy Harrington, and Dr. D. Strother, Jr.[29]

In 1875 Dr. Joseph McMorries located in the town. Born in Newberry, he was taken to Mississippi when he was five years old. He was of the McMorries and Holman families. In 1877 he patented a new hypodermic syringe but apparently moved from the county before 1880.[30]

Dr. James K. Gilder, son of Dr. James K. and Louisa Neel Gilder, was born in the district on February 28, 1856. He was graduated from the College of the City of New York in 1878 and settled in Newberry. Dr. Gilder married Jessie Fant. He was an extremely popular and highly regarded physician; he was also in the drug business, first with Dr. Peter Robertson and later with Dr. C. D. Weeks. He died on April 6, 1920, survived by his widow and four children, Dr. J. K. Gilder, Jr., Mrs. O. H. Johnson, Pauline Gilder, and Fant Gilder. Dr. Gilder first lived on the northwest corner of Boundary and Drayton streets and then at Gildercrest.[31]

Dr. William Elijah Lake was born in the district on October 18, 1852. He graduated from Newberry College in 1878 and the Medical College of South Carolina in 1881. He settled in the St. Luke's section but later moved to the town. He married Julia Anne Schroeder of Walhalla. He died at the age of seventy-seven on January 31, 1930, being the oldest physician in Newberry. Dr. Lake was survived by his widow and six children, Edwin O., W. E., Mary Ellen Lake, Mrs. A. R. Morris, Mrs. T. F. Suber, and Mrs. T. W. Morgan.[32]

In 1886 two relatives graduated in medicine from the University of Maryland and settled in the town. Dr. James Mathias Kibler, son of Drayton Washington Tucker and Julia Ann Barre Kibler, was born in the district on April 10, 1860. Educated at Newberry College, from which he received the B.A. and M.A. degrees, he married Emma Elizabeth Werts. He served as trustee of Newberry College and was a member of the American, state, and county medical organizations, the Sons of the American Revolution, and the Country Club of Newberry. He died at the age of seventy-six on April 19, 1936, survived by his widow and five daughters, Mrs. F. W. Chapman, Mrs. Vernon H. Wheeler, Mrs. H. E. Holley, Miss Julia, and Miss Lillian Kibler.[33]

The other graduate of 1886 was Dr. Walter Gustave Houseal. The son of William Walter and Eliza Caroline Barre Houseal, he was born in the town on May 14, 1861. He graduated from Newberry College in 1881, received his M.A. degree from that institution in 1884, and married Sarah Wright. He served as a trustee both of Newberry College and the Medical College of South Carolina; he was also vice president of the Exchange Bank. Upon his death on September 15, 1929, he was survived by his widow and four children, Walter Gustave Houseal, Jr., Dr. Robert W. Houseal, Mrs. John C. Goggans, and Mrs. W. Fitzgerald Rutherford.[34]

Dr. Daniel W. Reid was born in Newberry District on October 10, 1826. He graduated from Erskine in 1847 and from the Ecletic Medical College of Massachusetts in 1849. Dr. Reid married Elizabeth Amanda Bradley of Abbeville District, practiced in the town until 1857, and then moved to Georgia. After the war he studied theology at Due West and lived in Shelby County, Tennessee, returning to Newberry in 1888. He died in Newberry in February 1910.[35]

Dr. Edwin Olin Hentz was born on June 12, 1864, in the New Hope section. He graduated from Newberry College and in 1889 from the Medical College of South Carolina. He married Fannie Caldwell and practiced at Walton until he moved to the town in 1921. He practiced in Newberry until his death in November 1937. Dr. Hentz, a gentle, beloved physician, was survived by two sons, Dr. E. O. Hentz, Jr., and William E. Hentz, and two daughters, Mrs. Homer Daniel and Mrs. Georgia Welborn.[36]

Dr. Zebulon W. McMorries was born in Greenville, Alabama, and graduated in medicine from Meharry Medical College in 1883. He settled in Helena and was Newberry's first black physician. In August 1889 he was appointed mail clerk and forsook the practice of medicine. He died in Charleston on December 4, 1905.[37]

Dr. Arthur Teague, a native of the county, graduated in medicine from New York University in June 1890. He was granted his license to practice in August.[38]

Dr. James Higgins McIntosh, son of Dr. James and Frances Higgins McIntosh, was born in Newberry on October 3, 1866. He was educated at Newberry College and Johns Hopkins and graduated from the College of Physicians and Surgeons of New York in 1888. He returned to Newberry in 1891 to practice in partnership with his father. Five years later the partnership was dissolved when the elder Dr. McIntosh retired from practice to engage in banking. Dr. James H. McIntosh married Frances Nance Baxter; they had seven children, James, Baxter, Frances, Martha, Dorothy, Walter Hunt, and Nancy. He moved to Columbia in

1900 where he enjoyed a large and successful practice until his death on September 2, 1944. This beloved physician was presented a silver pitcher and goblets by the Columbia Medical Society in 1942. In the same year his portrait was presented to the Columbia Hospital.[39]

Dr. J. H. McCullough was licensed to practice in 1891 by the Newberry County Board of Medical Examiners. He was born in the county in 1870, son of Henry and Jane Bailey McCullough; he was graduated from Southern Medical College. After practicing in the town for some years he moved away, living in Philadelphia, Newark, and Spartanburg. Dr. McCullough returned to Newberry in 1937 and practiced until his retirement. He died on June 28, 1952, at the age of eighty-two, survived by three sons, Dr. H. B. McCullough, Dr. Malloy A. McCullough, and L. G. McCullough.[40]

Dr. Thomas William Smith, son of J. Drayton Smith and Catherine Summer Smith, was born and reared in the county and was educated at Newberry College and the Louisville Medical College from which he graduated in 1891. He practiced in both Newberry and Laurens counties but principally in the town of Newberry from 1902 until his death at the age of sixty-eight in September 1937. He served as president of the county medical society and as chairman of the Newberry Board of Health. Dr. Smith was survived by his widow, the former Ermie Mahon of Union; two daughters, Mrs. F. G. Wright and Mrs. James F. Epting; and one son, Mahon Smith.[41]

A classmate of Dr. Smith at Louisville from Newberry County was Dr. Thomas J. Hunter. He settled at Trenton, Edgefield County.[42]

Dr. Andrew L. Longshore, son of Levi F. Longshore, was born and reared in the county. Following his graduation from the College of Physicians and Surgeons of Baltimore in 1893, he settled in the Trinity section to practice. In 1899 he was married to Sara Emma Riser, daughter of Sheriff W. W. Riser. He moved to Newberry to practice in January 1902, and died at the age of thirty-three of typhoid fever on May 28, 1902. Dr. Longshore was survived by his widow and one daughter, Hulda, who later married Drayton Nance.[43]

Dr. Pettus Gray Ellesor, son of Thomas and Elizabeth DeWalt Ellesor, was born in the county on January 2, 1869. His mother died when he was an infant, and he was reared by relatives, the Johnstones, at Coateswood. He graduated from the Medical College of South Carolina in 1894 and settled at Newberry. He was appointed a member of the State Board of Medical Examiners in 1909 and served as president of the county medical society in 1912. Dr. Ellesor married Jane Vance of Clinton; he died in August 1922, survived by his widow and one daughter, Martha Vance Ellesor.[44]

Dr. Ellesor's classmate in medicine from Newberry was Dr. Israel Brown, who in 1895 settled in Norfolk, Virginia, to practice.[45] Dr. Gustavus Werber, another native of Newberry, graduated in medicine at Columbia University, Washington, D.C., in 1894. He moved to Washington where he practiced medicine and served in the government pension office as a special examiner. Dr. Werber married Catherine Moses of Sumter. He was a scientific farmer and owned much land in this county. He died on June 12, 1929, and was buried at Sumter.[46]

Dr. Van Smith, native of Anderson County, was born on September 8, 1859, and graduated from Atlanta Medical College in 1885. He settled in the Trinity section of Newberry County in 1888. Ten years later he moved into Newberry and established a drugstore on the corner of Main and McKibben streets. He acted as mayor when John W. Earhardt, Sr., resigned in 1904 to take his seat in the House of Representatives. In 1913 Dr. Smith moved to Whitmire to practice medicine and run a drugstore. The following year he was elected mayor of Whitmire. In 1920 he moved to Beaufort to operate a truck farm. Dr. Smith married Lilla Bee, who died on April 6, 1922; he died on April 17, 1950, survived by an only child, Colonel Claud Cleveland Smith.[47]

Dr. W. A. Dunn was born in Sumter County on September 2, 1864. He graduated from Louisville Medical College in 1892 and settled at Pomaria to practice. He was elected intendant of Pomaria in 1903. That year he swore out a warrant for Dr. W. T. Dickert for practicing at Sligh's without a license; Dr. Dickert then went off to medical school and obtained his diploma from the Medical College at Chattanooga, Tennessee. Dr. Dunn subsequently moved to Newberry and was killed in a train accident in Newberry in March 1928. Dr. Dunn was twice married, first to Lucy Whaley, who bore him two daughters, Mary and Lucy; and secondly, to Elliott Duncan, who survived him along with two daughters, Ella and Alliene, and one son, William E. Dunn.[48]

Dr. J. W. Nance, son of Major J. K. G. Nance, was born in the county. He graduated from the Medical College of South Carolina in 1900 and settled in Newberry. Six months later he moved to Lake City, Florida, where he formed a partnership with his brother-in-law, Dr. D. R. Julian. He married a daughter of Luke Sease of Newberry who survived him, with three children, upon his death in September 1912.[49]

Three physicians lived in Newberry only for a short time around the turn of the century. Dr. S. L. Cash was practicing in town in 1897, for in

August of that year he was one of three physicians to pronounce a felon dead after being hanged at the county jail.[50] The next month Dr. B. A. Daniels announced that he was opening an office next door to the Crotwell Hotel and would treat eyes, ears, throat, and nose.[51] Dr. John Gregg McMaster, son of George H. McMaster of Winnsboro, graduate of the Medical College of South Carolina in 1903, settled in Caldwell section to practice in January 1904. The following year he moved to the town; in March he was elected secretary and treasurer of the county medical society. He moved to Florence in October 1905.[52]

Dr. C. Eugene Stephenson, a black physician who graduated from Meharry Medical College in Tennessee in 1903, was a native of Dorchester County. He settled in Newberry and was reported to have had a fine practice. Dr. Stephenson married a daughter of the Reverend Joshua Wilson, postmaster of Florence, South Carolina.[53]

Another black physician of this period was Dr. W. T. Smith, graduate of Howard University in 1887 and native of Columbia. He was living in Newberry in November 1899.[54]

Dr. William Ellerbe Pelham, Jr., son of Dr. W. E. and Brantley Leavell Pelham, was born in the town on January 25, 1879. He graduated from the Maryland School of Pharmacy in 1900 and from Tulane University in medicine in 1905. He and Dr. Frank D. Mower formed a partnership in 1911. He was elected secretary of the Newberry Hospital Association in that same year. Dr. Pelham married Azile Pool and was survived by her and three children, Ellerbe, Brantley, and Heyward. Dr. Pelham died during the influenza epidemic in October 1918.[55]

Dr. Frank Duane Mower, son of George S. and Fannie Dunbar Jones Mower, was born in the town in 1879. He was educated at Newberry College, Johns Hopkins, and Tulane Medical College. He graduated from the latter in 1907 and located in the town where he practiced for thirty years. He entered the U.S. Army on August 10, 1917, and was discharged as a major on July 15, 1919. He was a surgeon in the 306th Field Signal Battalion, 81st Division. He served as president of the county medical society and as surgeon for the Southern Railway Company. Dr. Mower married Nina Seay who survived him with three children, George, Rachel, and Helen. Another son, Frank D. Mower, Jr., was killed in a tragic vehicle accident in 1927 at the age of eight. Dr. Mower died on March 20, 1937.[56]

Dr. J. Alex Meldau, native of Sumter, was licensed to practice in 1900. He settled at Newberry in 1907 and remained until 1917. In August of that year he moved to McClellanville; his wife died there in 1929.[57]

Dr. Ernest Harrison Moore practiced in the county from 1907 until his death in 1962 and enjoyed a large practice. Since he lived in the Mt. Bethel community, his biography is given in the section devoted to the physicians of Caldwell Township.

Dr. Thomas H. Pope, son of Dr. Sampson and Helen Harrington Pope, was born in the town on July 7, 1876. Educated at Newberry College and the Medical College of South Carolina, he graduated from the latter in 1908. He settled at Kinards where he practiced until 1920 when he moved to Newberry. He served as trustee of the Medical College, president of the county medical society for a number of years, and president of the district medical association. His compassion and rectitude caused him to be highly respected in his community and greatly beloved by his patients. He married Marie Gary of Abbeville and, upon his death on August 6, 1943, he was survived by her and an only child, Thomas H. Pope, Jr. Mrs. Pope died on July 22, 1964.[58]

Dr. John Bachman Setzler, son of Dr. George A. and Elizabeth Cromer Setzler, was born near Pomaria on November 30, 1879. He was educated at Newberry College and the University of Virginia, graduating from the latter in 1910. He settled in Newberry and became secretary of the county medical society. He served as an officer in the Medical Corps of the U.S. Army during World War I and later became a lieutenant colonel in the Officers Reserve Corps. He returned to Newberry where he practiced until 1927; he then entered the public health service and was health officer first of Dillon County and then of Richland County. In 1933 he resigned to become medical director of Carolina Life Insurance Company. Dr. Setzler was a member of Phi Beta Kappa and the Raven Society at the University of Virginia. He died unmarried on November 9, 1949.[59]

Dr. Everard S. Blackshear, a native of Georgia who married Neville Pope, daughter of Chief Justice Y. J. and Sallie Fair Pope, opened an office in Newberry in September 1911. He did not remain long, however, moving to Florida and then entering the Medical Corps of the U.S. Army. On July 21, 1946, he died in Charleston, survived by a second wife and a son, Colonel John Pope Blackshear, a graduate of the U.S. Military Academy.[60]

Dr. Hugh B. Senn, son of Dr. W. D. and Hennie Boozer Senn, was born in the county on August 17, 1888. Educated at Newberry College and at the Medical College of South Carolina, he graduated from the latter in 1913. He settled at Silverstreet. Dr. Senn served as health officer for Beaufort and Newberry counties and returned to Newberry to practice in 1937. He married Mecie Timmerman and was survived upon his death on October 6, 1952, by her and two daughters, Mrs. Dorothy S. Corbett and Mrs. Virginia S. Hassell.[61]

In the same year Dr. Senn graduated, Dr. John Kieffer Wicker, son of John H. and Mary Paysinger Wicker, graduated from Tulane University in medicine. He, too, received his academic education at Newberry College. He opened an office in the town but left to serve in the Medical Corps, U.S. Army, during World War I. He returned to Newberry to practice and served as president of the county medical society. He lost his health and died on July 10, 1972, after being hospitalized for many years. He married Ola Tolbert; they were divorced.[62]

Dr. Robert Lusk Mayes, son of William Glenn and Nancy Jones Mayes, was born in Newberry. Educated at The Citadel and the University of Maryland in pharmacy, he was employed by his brother as druggist until he entered medical school in 1910. He graduated from Jefferson Medical College in 1914. He returned to Newberry and practiced medicine until his death, unmarried, on February 23, 1930.[63]

Dr. William Edward Crooks, native of the county and son of Joseph Lawton and Ida Elizabeth Crooks, graduated from the Medical College of South Carolina in 1916. He settled in the county but soon entered the Medical Corps of the U.S. Navy. He served for eighteen years and then opened an office in Newberry. He later returned to the Navy and, following his retirement, lived in Newberry until his death on September 27, 1967, at the age of seventy-eight. He married Jessie Rutherford; they had two daughters, Mrs. E. Paul Smith and Mrs. Sloan Rankin.[64]

Dr. John Lewis Duckett, a native of the county, was licensed in 1914 and opened his office in Newberry. He continued a successful practice in the town until he moved to Greenwood in August 1923. He was the fourth black doctor to practice in Newberry.[65]

Dr. William Calvin Brice, son of T. W. Brice of Edgefield County, saw service in World War I. He was educated at Presbyterian College and the Medical College of South Carolina. He settled in Newberry but remained only a short time before moving to York. Dr. Brice married Vera Gooding of Ware Shoals. He died in York at the age of thirty-five in 1935.[66]

Dr. Robert Wright Houseal, son of Dr. W. G. and Sarah Wright Houseal, was born in Newberry on November 13, 1892. Educated at Newberry College, B.A. 1910, University of Virginia, M.A. 1911, and Johns Hopkins University, he received his degree in medicine from the latter in 1918. In 1924 he came to Newberry to practice in partnership with his father. He was most successful and enjoyed a very fine practice until he accepted a commission as captain in the Medical Corps in June 1942. After the war he was chief of medicine at the Veterans Administration Hospital in Columbia until his retirement. Newberry College awarded him the honorary Sc.D. degree in 1957. He married Esther Wilcox, who died on October 6, 1969; they had one child, Robert W. Houseal, Jr. Dr. Houseal died on June 11, 1975.[67]

Dr. Chauncey M. Rakestraw of Chester moved to Newberry in 1925 to practice surgery. He did not remain long; he died in Red Springs, North Carolina, on January 10, 1931.[68]

Dr. Augustus Theodore Neely, native of York County and son of Adolphus T. and Nonie Coulter Neely, was graduated from the Medical College of South Carolina in 1913. He specialized in diseases of the eyes, ears, nose, and throat and settled in Newberry in 1921. He was elected president of the county medical society in 1933. Dr. Neely married Margaret Ogilvie; and, upon his death at the age of sixty-four on February 1, 1952, was survived by her, by a son, A. T. Neely, Jr., and a daughter, Mrs. Clarence W. Senn. He was a deacon in Aveleigh Presbyterian Church.[69]

Dr. E. Gordon Able, native of Norway and graduate of the Medical College of South Carolina in 1924, settled in Whitmire. After a successful general practice there, he took postgraduate training in general surgery at the Louisiana State University School of Medicine in New Orleans and located in the town of Newberry in 1932. He married first Alice Brennecke by whom he had one son, E. Gordon Able, Jr.; following the death of his first wife, he married Elizabeth Dowling. After enjoying a large practice, Dr. Able retired from his active practice as a surgeon in 1970. He died on September 13, 1987, leaving a large estate, most of which was bequeathed to Newberry College, the Newberry County Memorial Hospital, several churches, and to other charitable organizations.

Dr. Von Anderson Long, son of Lawton S. and Lilla Werts Long and native of the county, graduated from Clemson in 1932 and in medicine from the Medical College of South Carolina in 1937. He married Elizabeth Ruff and moved to the town of Newberry from Prosperity to practice in 1952. Dr. Long accepted the position of county health officer in 1960; he held this position until his retirement in 1978. They had three sons, Von, Jr., David Lawton, and Dr. Elmer Gordon Long. Dr. Long died on November 17, 1985.

Dr. Madison Edward Parrish was graduated from Furman University in 1926 and from the Medical College of South Carolina in 1932. He returned to Newberry, where he signed the Register on December 20, 1932; he then took special training in radiology and became chief of radiology at Tuomey General Hospital in Sumter. He died on December 17, 1961, and was buried in Johnston.[70]

Dr. Julian Edward Grant was born at Bennettsville, South Carolina, on April 11, 1900, son of Jacob and Josie McCullough Grant. Educated at Claflin College, he received a B.A. degree from that institution in 1925. He then entered Meharry Medical School, Nashville, Tennessee, from which he received his M.D. degree in 1929. Dr. Grant interned at General Hospital Number 2, Kansas City, Missouri, in 1929–1930. Licensed to practice in Tennessee and in South Carolina, he has practiced medicine successfully in Newberry for more than forty years.

A trustee of the Newberry Housing Authority, he is a member of the Palmetto State Medical Association and the National Medical Association. Dr. Grant married Grace Clementine Funchess. They had four children. He was honored at a testimonial dinner by Newberry citizens on July 8, 1977.

Dr. Foster Newton Martin, Jr., son of Foster Newton and Helen Mower Martin, was born in Newberry on September 1, 1907. He graduated from Newberry College and received his M.D. degree from the Medical College of South Carolina in 1932. He settled in Newberry for general practice in 1933 but left in 1938. After practicing in Charleston and New Orleans, he returned to Newberry in 1954. He later went back to New Orleans where he died on January 31, 1983.

Dr. Martin's brother, Dr. James Blair Martin, also graduated at the Medical College of South Carolina and is now a surgeon in Charleston. His son, Dr. Frank Foster Martin, graduated from the Medical College of South Carolina in 1963 and practices internal medicine, with a subspecialty of gastroenterology, in Charleston.

Dr. Foster Martin married Abbey LaRoche and they had three children, Dr. Frank Foster Martin, Emily Allen Brown, and Kenneth Douglas Martin. His second wife was Delma Kennerly; they had one daughter, Cynthia Theresa.[71]

Dr. Arthur W. Welling, son of J. L. and Ruth Wells Welling of Newberry, was born on June 10, 1911, and opened an office in the town in 1938. He was educated at Newberry College and the Medical College of South Carolina in the class of 1936. He served a two-year internship at the Youngstown (Ohio) General Hospital before coming to Newberry. Dr. Welling married Eva Dorrity of Newberry, served in the U.S. Army

overseas, and returned to Newberry to practice. They had two daughters, Eve and Patricia. After his divorce, he married Mary Willis. He died
in Knoxville, Tennessee, on November 28, 1987, and was buried in
Memorial Gardens in Newberry.

Dr. Robert E. Livingston, Jr., son of Robert E. and Sunie Johnson
Livingston, was born in the Bush River section of the county on
November 12, 1913. Educated at the University of South Carolina and
the Medical College of South Carolina, graduating from the latter in
1939, he interned and was a resident at Greenville General Hospital,
after which he settled at Fountain Inn. In 1943 he moved to Newberry
and engaged in a large general practice. He took special training in diseases of the eyes, ears, and throat at Polyclinic Hospital in New York and
specialized in this field in partnership with his son, Dr. Robert E. Livingston, III, until his retirement in 1988. He married Pauline Wise and they
have one son and two daughters, Christie (Mrs. Harvey Wilkinson) and
Polly (Mrs. Hayne Davis).

Dr. Reyburn W. Lominack opened his office in Newberry on November 1, 1944. He was born in the town on October 26, 1916, the son of
William Frank and Bessie Kinard Lominack. He was educated at Newberry College and the Medical College of South Carolina, graduating
from the latter in 1942. He served as a lieutenant in the U.S. Army
Medical Corps in World War II. Dr. Lominack married Elizabeth
Wieters of Charleston. He practiced very successfully in Newberry until
his death on November 22, 1955. Dr. Lominack was survived by his
widow and three children, Reyburn, Lisa, and Robert.

Dr. Virgil Wright Rinehart, native of Saluda, graduated from Wofford
College in 1927 and from the Medical College of South Carolina in
1931. He moved to Newberry in 1941. He served as president of the
county medical society and as chief of staff of the Newberry County
Memorial Hospital. He was married twice, first to Josephine Morris, and
then to Carrie Thompson, widow of Dr. Davis of Columbia. Dr. Rinehart had two children, Virgil, Jr., retired lieutenant commander, U.S.
Navy Air Corps, and Martha Jo. He died December 29, 1978.[72]

Dr. Arthur J. Katzberg, a native of Brooklyn, New York, settled in
Newberry in 1946 after serving in the U.S. Army. He enjoyed a large
practice but moved to Clinton in 1955. He is married to the former Mae
Weir and practiced at Whitten Center in Clinton until his retirement.

Dr. Ralph Parr Baker, son of Ralph Barre and Eddie Mae Parr Baker,
was born in Newberry on July 31, 1918. He was graduated from Washington and Lee University in 1940 and from Duke University in medi-

cine in 1943. Dr. Baker served as captain, U.S. Army Medical Corps in World War II. He then took extensive training in pathology and surgery at George Washington University School of Medicine and at various hospitals in the Washington area. He returned to Newberry in 1950 and engaged in the practice of general surgery until forced to retire because of ill health.

Dr. Baker was a Fellow, American College of Surgeons, past president of the Newberry County Medical Society and of the Third District Medical Society, and a member of various national and state medical associations.

Dr. Baker married Elizabeth Renwick. They had five children, Elizabeth, Mary, Ralph, Erwin, and Catherine. Elizabeth, Mary, and Ralph graduated in medicine, while Erwin graduated in dentistry, and Catherine attended law school. He died on August 29, 1988.

Dr. Elbert J. Dickert, another native Newberrian and the son of Elbert J. and Geneva Thornton Dickert, was born on October 1, 1921. He graduated from Newberry College in 1942 and from Tulane University in medicine in 1945. He interned at Columbia Hospital and served as a medical officer in the U.S. Army before locating in Newberry in October 1948. He is a member of the American and South Carolina medical associations, the Newberry County Medical Society, and the American Academy of Family Physicians. Dr. Dickert practices family medicine in partnership with Dr. Long. He married Mary Layton and they have two sons, Neal Workman, an attorney in Augusta, and David, an accountant in Jacksonville, Florida.

Dr. Cornelius A. Dufford, Jr., was born in Newberry on July 10, 1921, the son of C. A. and Alma Cole Dufford. Educated in the local schools and at Newberry College, he received his B.A. degree at the latter institution. He then graduated from the Medical College of South Carolina and interned at Newark City Hospital. He later served a residency in pediatrics at the Richland County Memorial Hospital before settling in Newberry in 1950. Here he specializes in pediatrics. Dr. Dufford has served as a Newberry College trustee and president of the Country Club of Newberry.

Dr. Benton McQueen Montgomery, Jr., son of Dr. Benton McQueen and Mana Claffy Montgomery, was born in Kingstree on February 17, 1920. He graduated from The Citadel in 1941 and from the Medical College of South Carolina in 1944. He served as captain, U.S. Army Medical Corps, in World War II. After the war, he took postgraduate training in internal medicine at the Medical College of South Carolina

Figure 18. Bethlehem Baptist Church, 1901.

Figure 19. St. Luke's Episcopal Church, 1986.

Figure 20. Miller Chapel AME Church, circa 1891.

Figure 21. Valley Farm, circa 1880, home of Mr. and Mrs. C. T. Smith.

Figure 22. Home of the late Fay Murray Gray, 1966.

Figure 23. Mower-Keitt House, circa 1890,
home of Mr. and Mrs. Robert Barber.

Figure 24. Maybin-Pool House, circa 1871, home of Mrs. Price J. Padgett.

Figure 25. Mendenhall, 1960, home of Mr. and Mrs. W. C. Carter.

Figure 26. Holmes-Baker House, circa 1883, home of
Mr. and Mrs. Thomas H. Pope, III.

Figure 27. Home of Mr. and Mrs. Keitt Purcell, 1965.

Figure 28. Edward R. Hipp House, circa 1900,
home of Mr. and Mrs. Harry Cromer.

Figure 29. Houseal-Harrington-Burton House, circa 1850, home of Mrs. Marion Spigener.

Figure 30. J. H. Summer House, circa 1910, home of Mr. and Mrs. Alexander C. Cuthbertson.

Figure 31. Luther House, Prosperity, circa 1880, home of Mrs. J. D. Luther.

Figure 32. Glasgow-McCrackin House, circa 1910,
home of Mr. and Mrs. William Leland.

Figure 33. Regnery House, circa 1950, home of Mr. and Mrs. Allen Murphy.

Figure 34. Oakhurst, circa 1890, home of Mrs. W. E. Matthews.

and at James Walker Memorial Hospital. He located in Newberry in 1951 and engaged in the practice of internal medicine until 1977. In that year he accepted an appointment as director of the Family Practice Clinic in Greenwood. Dr. Montgomery taught at the Medical College of Georgia and was a trustee of the Medical University of South Carolina. He was a Fellow of the American College of Physicians, and a Diplomate of the American Board of Internal Medicine. Lander College conferred an honorary doctorate upon him. He married Ingeborg Ferus Schulla; they had two children, Benton McQueen, III, and Erika M. Mays. He died a much beloved and respected physician on March 18, 1989.

Dr. James A. Underwood, Jr., son of James A. and Annie Mae Brown Underwood, was born on October 23, 1920. He was graduated from the U.S. Naval Academy in 1942 and served as a line officer in the U.S. Navy. He graduated from the Medical College of South Carolina in 1954. Dr. Underwood served his internship and residency at Greenville General Hospital and, after practicing for two years in Greenwood, located in Newberry in 1957. He was engaged in general practice with Dr. Elmer E. Epting, Jr., and Dr. John W. Green until his retirement in 1986. Dr. Underwood married Rosalyn Sanders of Newberry; they have six children, Patricia, Nancy, Elizabeth, Jeanne, James A., III, and Julie.

Dr. William Wyman King, Jr., son of Dr. W. W. and Gertrude Matthews King, was born on December 28, 1929, at Elizabethton, Tennessee. He graduated from the University of South Carolina in 1952 and from the Medical College of South Carolina in 1956. He interned at Richland Memorial Hospital and settled in Newberry in 1957. Dr. King married first Adele Allston; they have three children, William W., III, Janice, and Luke. He later married Brenda Gatling and moved to Walterboro where he is director of Emergency Service at the local hospital.

Dr. Sydney E. Carter, son of James H. and Addie Cribb Carter, was born in Georgetown on December 9, 1928. He graduated from The Citadel in 1950 and served as 1st lieutenant, 3rd Infantry Division, in Korea. He graduated from the Medical College of South Carolina in 1961. Following internship and residency at the Medical College Hospital, he located in Newberry and engaged in general practice until 1970. He then took postgraduate training at the Medical University Hospital in cardiology and internal medicine. He returned to Newberry in April 1972, and engaged in the practice of internal medicine and cardiology until his death on January 7, 1975. Dr. Carter married Elizabeth Baker; they had two sons, Sydney, Jr., who died tragically in an automobile accident in 1974, and Richard Baker Carter.[73]

Dr. E. Eugene Epting, Jr., son of Elmer E. and Naomi Ruff Epting, was born in Newberry on October 9, 1939. He graduated from Newberry College in 1961 and from the Medical College of South Carolina in 1967. He served as lieutenant commander, U.S. Navy, 1968–1970, following his residency at Greenville General Hospital. He returned to Newberry in 1970 and is engaged in general partnership with Dr. Green. Dr. Epting married Donna Thackeray; they have three children, Holland, Page, and Kimberly.

Dr. Robert E. Livingston, III, son of R. E. and Pauline Wise Livingston, was born on July 3, 1941. He was educated at the University of South Carolina and at the Medical College of South Carolina, graduating from the latter in 1965. He was a lieutenant in the U.S. Navy. After extensive postgraduate training in ophthalmology at Grady Hospital in Atlanta, he returned to Newberry to engage in his specialty in partnership with his father. Active in community affairs, he was an at-large trustee of Newberry College. He married Georgette DuTart; they have two children, Robert E., IV, and Sunie Elizabeth.

Dr. Everett M. Hughes, son of E. H. and Jean Sanders Hughes, was born at Union on January 31, 1935. He graduated from the Georgia Institute of Technology in 1957 and from the Medical College of South Carolina in 1962. He then took special training in radiology and located in Newberry on July 1, 1972, as chief of radiology at the Newberry County Memorial Hospital; he is a Diplomate of the American College of Radiology. He married Marjean Davis; they have three children, Margaret Jean, Mary Legare, and Michael Sanders.

Dr. Richard Anthony Mann was born in Washington, D.C., on September 26, 1932. Educated at Newberry College, from which he received the B.S. degree in 1959, and at the Medical University of South Carolina from which he received the M.D. degree in 1964, he interned at Columbia Hospital. He served residencies in general surgery at the University of Louisville Hospital, the Medical University of South Carolina, and Spartanburg General Hospital. Certified by the American Board of Surgery in 1970, he settled in Newberry and is on the staffs of Newberry County Memorial Hospital and of the Lexington County Hospital. He married Joy R. Rushe; they are divorced.

Dr. Thomas Chlingman Littlejohn, Jr., was born in Cowpens, South Carolina, on September 22, 1926. He received his B.S. degree in Business Administration in 1947 and his J.D. degree in law in 1949 from the University of South Carolina. Locating at Gaffney, he engaged in the practice of law there for five years. He represented Cherokee County in the House of Representatives in 1950–1952, and in the latter year was president of the Cherokee County Bar Association.

Dr. Littlejohn graduated from the Vanderbilt University School of Medicine in 1959 and specialized in pathology after completing his post-graduate training. He was pathologist for Newberry County Memorial Hospital. A member of numerous medical societies and associations, he was licensed to practice law in South Carolina and to practice medicine in Georgia, North Carolina, South Carolina, Maryland, Tennessee, and Kentucky. He served in the U.S. Army Air Corps and as a major in the Tennessee National Guard. He married Madge Floyd and they had two daughters, Debbie and Christie. Dr. Littlejohn died on July 23, 1982.[74]

Dr. David Andrew Marsh was born in Worthing, Sussex, England, on November 9, 1929. He received his B.A. degree in 1960 from Columbia Bible College and his M.D. degree in 1968 at the University of London's Royal Free Hospital School of Medicine. After interning at Southlands Hospital in Sussex, England, he served residencies in general surgery at Watts Hospital, Durham, North Carolina, the North Carolina Baptist Hospital in Winston-Salem, and Greenville General Hospital in Greenville, South Carolina.

Dr. Marsh is a member of the British Medical Association. He moved from Newberry in 1979, having practiced here for only a short time.

Dr. Elmer Gordon Long, son of Dr. Von A. and Elizabeth Ruff Long, was born in Newberry on July 18, 1943. He received a B.S. degree from Clemson University in 1965, and an M.D. degree from the Medical University of South Carolina in 1970. He interned at Roanoke (Virginia) Memorial Hospital and held a residency in family medicine at the Medical University of South Carolina.

Locating in Newberry in 1973, Dr. Long is engaged in family practice in partnership with Dr. Dickert. He is married to Elizabeth Norris, and they have two children, John Norris and Elizabeth Kinard.

Dr. Thomas W. Behrmann, son of Fremont W. and Jeannette M. Behrmann, was born in Bay City, Michigan, on October 17, 1947. He was graduated from the University of Michigan with a B.S. degree and from the University of Michigan Medical Center with the M.D. degree. After serving an internship and a residency in general surgery at St. Joseph Mercy Hospital in Ann Arbor, Michigan, he settled in Newberry in 1977 where he had a general surgical practice until 1988. He now practices in Columbia but lives in Newberry. Dr. Behrmann married Sandra Sue Gibson; they have one child, Chris.

Dr. P. D. Bullard, Jr., son of P. D. and Helen Parrish Bullard, was born in Bainbridge, Georgia, on July 17, 1942. He graduated from Presbyterian College with a B.S. degree and from Vanderbilt University School of Medicine with the M.D. degree. He interned and served residencies in both surgery and obstetrics-gynecology at Tripler Medical Center in Hawaii. He located in Newberry in 1978 but moved to West Columbia in 1988 where he specializes in obstetrics and gynecology. Dr. Bullard has two children, Richard and Jennifer, by a previous marriage. His wife is the former Cheryl Harris, a native of Newberry County and member of the South Carolina Bar.

Dr. John W. Green, son of the Reverend Walter S. and Marjorie Strickland Green, was born in Danville, Virginia, on December 7, 1950. He was graduated from Wake Forest University with a B.A. degree and from the University of Virginia School of Medicine with the M.D. degree. After serving an internship and residency in the Greenville Hospital System, he joined the partnership of Underwood and Epting and now practices family medicine with Dr. Epting. He married Diane Martin, and they have three children, Katherine Elizabeth, Scott Christian, and John, Jr.

Dr. C. M. Jones, Jr., son of C. M. and Alma Brooks Young Jones, was born in Seneca, South Carolina, on January 1, 1948. He was graduated from Clemson University with a B.S. degree and from the Medical University of South Carolina with the M.D. degree. After serving a residency at the U.S. Air Force Medical Center at Wright-Patterson Air Force Base, Dr. Jones came to Newberry in 1979 and formed a partnership with Dr. Dickert and Dr. Long for family practice. He married Grace Ruth Chaplin, and they have two children, Meredith and C. M. Jones, III. He left Newberry in 1986.

Dr. Lawrence F. McManus, son of Michael Joseph and Mary Ann Early McManus, was born in New York City on January 4, 1940. He graduated from Manhattan College with a B.S. degree and from the New York Medical College with the M.D. degree. After an internship at Walter Reed General Hospital, a general surgery preceptorship at Tripler General Hospital, and a three-year orthopaedic residency, he commenced the practice of orthopaedic surgery in Columbia. He came to Newberry in 1979 to practice orthopaedic surgery, but had to retire because of his health. He is married to Kathleen O'Conner, and they have four children, Larry, Chris, Kathy, and Debbie.

Dr. John M. Thompson, son of Robert C. and Katharine Riddle Thompson, was born in Charlottesville, Virginia, on April 9, 1948. He graduated from Florida Southern College with a B.S. degree and from

George Washington University with the M.D. degree. After serving an internship and residencies at the Medical University of South Carolina, he came to Newberry in 1978 where he practices internal medicine. He married Carol Lady; they have two sons, Brian and Alan.

Dr. Mark A. Davis, son of W. M. and Ruth Boggs Davis, was born in Durham, North Carolina, on December 25, 1951. He received his B.A. degree from Newberry College and the M.D. degree from the University of Miami School of Medicine. He served his internship and residencies in internal medicine at the University of Alabama Hospital and Clinic; he then had a Fellowship in Primary Care Internal Medicine at the same institution. In 1981 he joined Dr. Thompson in a partnership practicing internal medicine. Dr. Davis is married to the former Mary Emily Buddin; they have four children, Terry, Amy, Leslie and Patrick.

Joel Steven Sexton, M.D., was born on May 1, 1936, the son of Charles Frank and Nuel McAmis Sexton of Spartanburg. He was graduated from the University of Virginia, served three years in the U.S. Navy, and received M. S. and M.D. degrees from the Medical College of South Carolina. He taught and practiced forensic pathology in Charleston until 1983 when he moved to Newberry. He enjoys a large statewide practice as a forensic pathologist and serves as pathologist for the Newberry County Memorial Hospital. Since 1972, he also has been coach of the pistol team at The Citadel. He is a member of Central United Methodist Church.

Married to the former Lu Lynn Galt, he has four children, Sibyl Lynn Wessler, Steven Lawrence Sexton, Susan Lucinda Sexton, and Sheila Louise Sexton.

Dr. John Spearman Floyd, III, son of John S. and Lucy Elizabeth Derrick Floyd, was born in Fairfield County on November 11, 1933. He graduated from Newberry College with a B.S. in 1954, and from the Medical College of South Carolina with an M.D. in 1958. He interned at Spartanburg County Hospital, 1958-1959, served a residency at the U.S. Naval Hospital in Great Lakes, Illinois, 1962-1965, and served in the U.S. Navy until 1968.

Dr. Floyd was in private practice in Charleston until 1984 when he moved to Newberry. He specialized in obstetrics and gynecology and was a Fellow of the American College of Obstetrics and Gynecology and a Diplomate of the American Board of Obstetrics and Gynecology.

Married to the former Julia Myers, they had four children, Charlotte Elizabeth, John S., III, Frank Myers, and Julia Ann Floyd. Dr. Floyd died on November 14, 1989.

Dr. Arthur R. Collins, son of Arthur R. and Mabel Alverson Collins, was born in Union on November 26, 1933. He graduated from The Citadel, B.S. in 1955, and from the Medical University of South Carolina in 1959. He specializes in pediatrics.

Dr. Collins is a member of the First Baptist Church, the Civitan Club, the Association of Citadel Men, and the DSS Treatment Team. He is the father of two sons by his first marriage, Gary Russell Collins and David Patrick Collins. His second wife is Joyce Evelyn Petts.

A recent addition to the physicians of the county is Dr. Earl Alford. He was born in Spartanburg, on January 7, 1935. After graduating from Presbyterian College in 1955 and from the Medical University of South Carolina in 1959, he was a surgical resident at Spartanburg General Hospital in 1963, at Grady Memorial Hospital in Atlanta in 1964, and at Oteen Veterans Administration Hospital near Asheville, North Carolina, in 1966.

He moved to Newberry in April 1989. He married Markay VaNess, and they have four children, Celia, Duncan, Tochie, and Earl Alford.

The newest physician to locate in Newberry is Dr. Jan Keith Hull, a urologist, who came in 1989. A native of Bowling Green, Ohio, where he was born on May 26, 1936, he was educated at Bowling Green State University, B.A. 1958, and at the University of Cincinnati College of Medicine, M.D. 1962. He interned and was a resident in General Surgery at St. Vincent Medical Center in Toledo, Ohio. Later he was in the U.S. Army Medical Corps as a general surgeon, specializing in urology.

Dr. Hull is certified by the American Board of Urology and is a member of the American Urological Association, the American College of Surgeons, and the Association of Military Surgeons. He has published a number of articles in his field. He has two children, Elise and Erica.

The Physicians of Caldwell and Maybinton Townships

At the end of the war, Drs. D. William Hatton, J. W. McCants, and Thompson Wilson were practicing in Caldwell Township. When the census of 1870 was taken, they were the only physicians listed in that township and Dr. J. M. H. Ruff the only one practicing in Maybinton. Within the next decade, Drs. James A. Cofield, L. B. Bates, and George Douglass settled in the area; Bates located in Caldwell Township and the other two in Maybinton. By 1880 only Dr. Hatton, Dr. Douglass, and Dr. Ruff were still active in the area.

Dr. James W. McCants died on August 10, 1871, at the age of fifty-two. Born in Fairfield District, he was graduated from the Medical College of South Carolina in 1844 and settled in the Caldwell section. He was one of the founders of the State Medical Association in 1848 and of the Newberry District Medical Association in 1865. He practiced in the county until his death.[75]

Dr. D. William Hatton, a native of Newberry District and graduate of the Medical College of South Carolina in 1840, practiced all of his life in this section of the county. Chapman in *The Annals of Newberry*, says that he was wealthy until ruined by the war and that he died in poverty.[76]

Dr. Thompson Wilson was born in the district on April 26, 1823. He first married Sarah Clark, born on July 3, 1823, who died on December 7, 1857. They had two children, Margaret and Mary. He later married Lydia P. _____, who survived him. Dr. Wilson died on May 17, 1871. Both he and his first wife are buried in Head Springs Cemetery.[77]

Dr. J. M. H. Ruff was born in the district on May 23, 1836. He graduated from the Medical College of South Carolina in 1857, married Elvie C. Suber, and served in the Confederate Army, first as a lieutenant in Company E, Third Regiment and then as a surgeon. He died at his home in the Mt. Pleasant community on December 17, 1907, survived by two daughters, Mrs. G. B. Caldwell and Miss Lizzie Ruff.[78]

Dr. James A. Cofield, a native of Union County, settled first in the Maybinton section, but soon moved to Prosperity and then to Newberry where he died in 1888.

Dr. Lucius B. Bates located in the Caldwell section in January 1872. After serving as president of the county medical association in 1875, he became dissatisfied and moved to Orangeburg in 1882. He sold a large farm at Brown's Cross Roads before moving.[79]

Dr. George Douglass was born in Goshen Hill, Union District, on November 1, 1850. He graduated from the Medical College of South Carolina in 1877 and settled in the Maybinton area. He developed a large practice but, when Whitmire was incorporated, he moved there. He died in 1907, survived by his widow, Leonora E. Stuck Douglass, and three children, George A., Francis K., and Mary Lou Douglass.[80]

Dr. Thomas C. Brown was a resident of Caldwell Township but did not actively practice medicine. Born in Newberry District on May 29, 1836, he was the son of Thomas Jefferson and Anna Chapman Brown. He graduated from Erskine College in 1859 and then in 1861 from the Medical College of South Carolina. After serving as surgeon, Third South Carolina Regiment during the Civil War, Dr. Brown returned home to give his attention to farming. Elected state senator in 1880, he suffered a paralytic stroke in 1884. He died unmarried on June 26, 1891.[81]

During Reconstruction, Dr. F. L. Von Constantia lived and practiced in Maybinton. He was reported as having a black wife and as living on the government reservation (lands of the South Carolina Land Commission) in 1878. Nothing more is known of him.[82]

Another bright young physician who was cut off at an early age was the very promising Dr. Edward George Keitt. Born on February 22, 1855, the son of Ellison S. and Caroline Wadlington Keitt, he graduated from Wofford College in 1873 and from the College of Physicians and Surgeons in Baltimore in 1881. He served an internship in Baltimore and then returned to Newberry County. He practiced for only seven months before he died of intermittent fever on September 2, 1882.[83]

Dr. J. F. Lyles, who lived near Maybinton, died on September 8, 1879.[84] It is not known whether he lived in Union or Newberry County. Certainly he practiced in both.

In 1886 Dr. G. Bartow Caldwell graduated from the College of Physicians and Surgeons in Baltimore.[85] He married Minnie, daughter of J. M. H. Ruff. Dr. Caldwell died intestate on July 3, 1901, survived by his widow and three children, James Wilson Caldwell, Joseph Elvira Caldwell, and George Bartow Caldwell.

Dr. Wilson Caldwell Brown, son of Colonel J. C. S. and Lavinia Cannon Brown, was born in Newberry District on February 3, 1861. He graduated from Erskine College in 1882 and from the Medical College of South Carolina in 1888. He married Elizabeth Chalmers and settled in the Mt. Bethel community to practice. However, in 1896 he turned his attention to farming. In 1910 he served for a few months as president of the Farmers Bank of Prosperity. For many years he was chairman of the County Board of Equalization and active in the rural electrification movement. Mrs. Brown died on April 24, 1936. Dr. Brown died at the age of ninety on July 1, 1951, survived by his daughter, Mrs. E. H. Moore, and his son, Chalmers Brown.[86]

Dr. J. F. Coleman settled in Maybinton in 1902, boarding with Berry Richards. He was licensed to practice in June of that year.[87] No medical school was listed.

Dr. John Gregg McMaster, son of George H. McMaster of Winnsboro, was graduated from the Medical College of South Carolina in 1903 and settled in the Caldwell section that year. He practiced there for two years before moving into the town of Newberry.

Dr. Ernest Harrison Moore, son of L. G. and Mary Ellen Harrison Moore, of Spartanburg County, was born on October 18, 1880. He graduated from Wofford and then from the Medical College of South Carolina in 1907. Settling first at Dead Fall in Newberry County, he practiced there until he married Novice Brown, daughter of Dr. W. C. Brown, in 1912. He then moved to the Mt. Bethel community where he lived until his death at the age of eighty-one on February 9, 1962. Mrs. Moore died on July 9, 1953. He was survived by his son, Wilson Moore, and his daughter, Mary Elizabeth Watters. Dr. Moore was one of the last of the old-time country doctors and was greatly beloved. He served as president of the county medical society, as president of the Kiwanis Club, and as chief of staff of the Newberry Memorial Hospital.[88]

The Physicians of Cromer Township

According to the 1870 census four physicians were then practicing in Cromer Township. They were Drs. R. C. Carlisle, E. A. Blackburn, W. F. Robertson, and Marcellus A. Renwick.[89] Although not listed because they had retired, Dr. Thomas B. Kennerly and Dr. James A. Bond were active in that area shortly after the war.

Dr. Thomas Barclay Kennerly, son of Samuel and Elizabeth Hall Kennerly, was born in Lexington District on March 7, 1831. He was educated at Cokesbury Institute in Abbeville District, read medicine in Columbia under Drs. Wells and Fair, and graduated from the Medical University of the City of New York in 1845.

He married Martha, daughter of Richard Samuel and Margaret Turner Law Brown, and settled near Baker's Crossroads. He practiced medicine and farmed until his death on October 31, 1884. His wife died on December 4, 1881. They had six children, Sims Edward Kennerly, Lilla Rall Kennerly Johnstone, Margaret Law Kennerly Todd, Samuel Brown Kennerly, James Law Kennerly, and Amelia Katherine Kennerly Hardy.[90]

Dr. Ephraim Allen Blackburn graduated from the Medical College of South Carolina in 1847 and lived near Liberty Hall until his death in May 1881.[91]

Dr. Warren F. Robertson, graduate of the same institution in 1859, practiced in the Mollohon section until his death at the age of seventy-six in January 1896. He was survived by his widow, the former Carrie Ruff, and one son, John Robertson. Mrs. Robertson, a sister of Dr. J. M. H. Ruff and Moorman Ruff, died in February, 1917.[92]

Dr. Marcellus Adolphus Renwick, son of Colonel John S. and Mary Toland Renwick, was born in Newberry District on April 30, 1846. He left Erskine College to enlist in Company M, Twentieth South Carolina Volunteer Regiment. He graduated from the Medical College of South Carolina in 1868 and studied in Europe before returning to the Long Lane section to practice. He was married first to Mary Irvin of Hendersonville, North Carolina, and later to Kitty Jones. He abandoned his practice in 1893 and entered the mercantile business with J. D. Davenport. Later he became a farmer. When he died on July 6, 1918, at the age of seventy-three, he was survived by his second wife; by four children of his first marriage, Irvin, Hugh, James, and Mrs. Wyckliffe Austin; and by five children of his second marriage, Margaret, Elizabeth, Marcellus, George, and Mildred Renwick.[93]

Dr. Richard Coleman Carlisle was born in Union District on December 5, 1835, the son of Thomas A. and Kittie P. Teagle Carlisle. He was educated at The Citadel, graduating in 1855, and at the University of the City of New York, graduating there in 1861. He served in the Seventh South Carolina Regiment, CSA, until the surrender at Greensboro. After the war, he lived in Newberry County until his death on August 21, 1906. He married Emma E. Renwick, daughter of Colonel J. S. Renwick, on September 16, 1869. He was active in his profession and was elected president of the Newberry County Medical Society in 1881. He was a member of Amity Lodge, AFM, and King's Creek Church. He was survived by his widow and five children.[94]

Dr. William M. McCarley graduated from the Medical College of South Carolina in 1880. He returned to his native county to practice and was admitted to membership in the Newberry County Medical Society on November 1 of that year. He was elected a delegate to the South Carolina Medical Association in 1881 and 1882. Dr. McCarley married Ida V. Calmes of Greenville on April 17, 1881. Dr. McCarley died on July 9, 1884, at the age of twenty-eight.[95]

The Physicians of Reeder Township

At the end of the war, Reeder Township had four physicians, J. H. Williams,[96] R. P. Clark, John K. Gary, and William M. Dorroh. Of these, Williams and Dorroh were not listed as practicing in the census of 1870. The other two were, along with J. Pinckney Johnson.

The senior of this group was Dr. John King Gary. Born on March 8, 1808, in Newberry District, he was the son of Captain West and Frances

Griffin Gary. After graduating from the Medical College of South Carolina in 1830, he settled at Gary's Lane. He married his cousin, Rebecca, the daughter of Captain Jesse and Mary Reeder Gary. Their five sons served in the Confederate Army, one being killed and another losing an arm. One son, Captain Jesse Wistar Gary, was graduated from the Medical College of South Carolina in 1860 but never practiced his profession. During the desperate days of Reconstruction, Dr. John K. Gary was nominated for the House by the Democrats in 1868; he was not a politician but he recognized his duty to his community and consented to run. Dr. Gary died on March 30, 1880; Mrs. Gary died on April 23, 1887, aged seventy-seven.[97]

Their children were Dorsey Leonidas, Thomas West, Martin Hillary, Jesse Wistar, John C., Elizabeth Louisa, and Josephine, who married John A. Watts of Laurens.

Dr. Richard Pinckney Clark was born in Newberry District on December 30, 1814, the son of George and Katherine Leavell Clark. He graduated from the Medical College of South Carolina in 1839, married Sarah Adeline Piester, and by the outbreak of the war was devoting himself to planting. He resumed his practice after losing a fortune in the war and continued it until his death at the age of eighty on December 8, 1894. He had four daughters, Margaret Catherine Swittenberg, Alma Piester Merchant, Talulah Adeline Aull, and Ola Floyd.[98]

Dr. James Pinckney Johnson was born in the district on May 7, 1840. He graduated from the Medical College of South Carolina in 1861. Shortly thereafter he enlisted in Battery D, James's Third Battalion. Later he transferred to the medical department where he served as surgeon until the end of the war.

Married three times, he died at his home near Fairview Church on September 16, 1912. He was survived by his third wife, Rachel, and two sons, Nathan Y. and Malcolm P. Johnson.[99]

Dr. William McDavid Dorroh was born on October 25, 1818. He married Lucretia Williams, the widow of G. W. Gary, and practiced in the vicinity of Bush River Baptist Church. He devoted himself to farming and forsook medicine after the war. He served as delegate to the Taxpayers Convention in 1874; in 1876 he was nominated for the House by the Democrats and was a member of the Wallace House. However, the Newberry democratic nominees were not seated for reasons already recounted. Dr. Dorroh was elected to the House in 1878. He died December 10, 1897, aged eighty-one. His wife, Lucretia, died in 1888.[100]

Dr. John William Folk, son of Levi E. and Elizabeth Counts Folk, was born at Pomaria on January 1, 1852. Educated at Newberry College and the Medical College of South Carolina, he graduated from the latter in 1874. He settled at Jalapa but for about twenty-five years served as quarantine officer at Georgetown, living on South Island and enjoying the hunting and fishing. Upon his retirement from the post, he returned in 1909 to Newberry County, locating at Jalapa. There he practiced and farmed as long as he was able. He married Hariett Adelle Fogle of Barnwell; after her death in 1881, he married Beulah Smith. Dr. Folk was the father of fourteen children. He died on February 1, 1938, at the age of eighty-six.[101]

Dr. W. A. Williams was reported as being in practice at Jalapa in 1870.[102] He was not listed in the census of that year.

Dr. William M. Kinard was practicing at Jalapa in 1873. He contracted cancer of the throat and died on April 3, 1877, survived by his widow and one son, William Mayes Kinard.[103]

Another physician reported to be practicing in Jalapa in 1876 was Dr. Thomas Weir.[104] He is buried in the cemetery of Duncan's Creek Presbyterian Church near Clinton.

Dr. Oliver B. Evans, son of Samuel and Mary A. Evans, was born in Charleston on August 11, 1853. His parents moved to Newberry and he graduated in medicine from the University of Georgia in 1880. He married Mrs. George T. Speake, née Mary Emma Boyd, and by her had one son, Samuel B. Evans. He lived at Kinards where he practiced until about 1909 when he moved to Maybinton. He returned to Kinards and died at his home there on August 22, 1918. Dr. Evans was a brother of H. H. Evans and E. M. Evans of Newberry.[105]

Dr. Thomas W. Smith practiced briefly in Reeder Township before he settled in Newberry. Dr. Thomas H. Pope practiced at Kinards for twelve years before moving to Newberry in 1920.

Dr. William Earnest Bickley, son of Simeon and Susan Nichols Bickley, was born on July 25, 1892, in the Utopia section. He was graduated from Newberry College and from Johns Hopkins University. Licensed to practice in 1916, he settled near Jalapa[106] but soon moved to Goldville in Laurens County and from there to Pendleton. He served in both World War I and World War II and died on August 5, 1960.

The Physicians of Floyd Township

Dr. Thomas W. Boozer, native of the district, settled at Kadesh near Smyrna Church when he was graduated from the Medical College of the State of South Carolina in 1843. He was born on November 2, 1820, the son of George and Sarah Wilson Boozer. He married first Charlotte Wilson and, after her death, her sister, Sarah. They were daughters of Thomas P. Wilson. Dr. Boozer had a large number of children; those who reached maturity were Henry Wilson, Sarah, Thomas, Job, George Burder, and Lavinia Boozer Hayes. He died on August 19, 1893.[107]

His brother, Job Johnstone Boozer, was born in 1832 and graduated from the Medical College of South Carolina in 1854. He married Georgia Anne Griffin of Pendleton. After the war, he practiced for a short time in the Smyrna section but then moved to Laurens County where he was a successful doctor until his death in 1906.[108]

Dr. James W. Potter was listed among the physicians in this township in 1870.[109] He does not appear in any other records relating to Floyd Township.

Dr. John M. Thompson, son of Dr. Thomas W. Thompson, was born in the village of Newberry. He graduated from Jefferson Medical College in 1872 and returned to his native district to practice. Locating near Silverstreet in July 1873, he practiced there until he moved to Florida in 1890. He was president of the Newberry County Medical Society in 1880.[110]

Dr. Daniel Wallace Patton was born in Laurens District on October 2, 1832, and graduated from the Georgia Medical College in 1859. After the war, he located in Newberry County and practiced there until his death. He married Martha Pressley who died on February 25, 1890. Dr. Patton died on January 23, 1885, survived by his widow and seven children, Luva E. Miller, Lula J. Patton Crawford, William, John, Ebenezer, Dora, and Ava P. Patton.[111]

Many years after Dr. Patton's death, an editorial on country doctors concluded:[112] "A good physician of heroic mould and skillful training, and a lover of mankind—such a man as Ian Maclaren pictures in Dr. McClure, or such as were Dr. John K. Gary and Dr. Daniel Wallace Patton, who lived such noble lives in this county a generation ago. . . . "

Dr. J. R. Spearman was a member of the county medical association in May 1870; he was also listed in the census that year as practicing in Floyd Township.[113]

Dr. Van Smith of Anderson County settled in Floyd Township after graduating from Atlanta Medical College in 1886. However, he moved to Newberry after a few years and his sketch is included in those of the doctors there. Dr. William E. Lake, who graduated from the Medical College of South Carolina in 1881 and settled in the township, also moved to town and is identified with the physicians there.

Dr. William David Senn, a native of the county, was born in 1859 and died at the age of seventy-four on November 23, 1933. He graduated from Newberry College and the Medical College of South Carolina in 1881. He settled in the Smyrna section, married Hennie Boozer, and practiced for a half-century in the county. He later moved to the town and was living there when he died, survived by his sons, William E. Senn of Seneca and Dr. Hugh B. Senn, and by a daughter, Lucy Senn. His wife predeceased him.[114]

Dr. Andrew L. Longshore settled in the Trinity section in 1893, following his graduation from the College of Physicians and Surgeons in Baltimore. He moved to Newberry in 1902 and died there in that year. His sketch appears among those of the physicians of the town.

Dr. Hugh Boozer Senn, son of Dr. W. D. Senn, first settled near Silverstreet following his licensing in 1911. However, he spent most of his professional life in the town and is included among its doctors.

The Physicians of Moon Township

The doctors who practiced in the Chappells area in the decade following the war were J. N. Lindsey, J. W. Tribble, C. C. Higgins, T. G. White, and James Hill, Sr. Dr. Lindsey practiced at Saluda Old Town; he was living on Floyd's Plantation there in 1873 and was listed in the census of 1880 as practicing in the township.[115]

Dr. James W. Tribble, born in Laurens District, graduated from the Medical College of South Carolina in 1860 and served in the Seventh South Carolina Cavalry Regiment during the war. He then located at Chappells where he practiced for several years. He moved west but returned to Chappells. He then forsook medicine, ran a livery stable in Newberry, and became a traveling salesman for a drug concern. He married Mittie Chappell. Dying in Raleigh in September 1905, he was survived by two daughters, Mrs. Robert L. Goff and Maude Tribble.[116]

Dr. C. C. Higgins, son of Francis B. Higgins, was born in the district circa 1823. He graduated from the Medical College of South Carolina in 1846 and married Martha S. Griffin. Dr. Higgins died at his home in Vaughansville on January 18, 1876, at the age of fifty-three.[117]

In 1871 Dr. Thomas Grimke White, native of Beaufort, was practicing at Chappells Station. He had served as a lieutenant of Company F, Palmetto Battalion in the Civil War. In November 1874 he moved to Beaufort.[118]

Dr. James Hill, Sr., was born on January 23, 1783, and died on February 27, 1869. He was married twice, being survived by his second wife, Nancy, three children by this second wife—Rebecca, William A., and Susannah—and by unnamed children of his first wife. He is buried in the Hill-Proctor Cemetery near Chappells.[119]

Dr. Alexander N. Talley, a native of Columbia, moved to Vaughansville following his graduation from the Medical College of the University of Georgia in 1885.[120] Apparently, he soon moved to Columbia.

Dr. James Oliver Dickert, son of Andrew and Margaret Dickert, was born on June 8, 1833. He practiced at Chappells where he died on October 24, 1884. He married Fannie Hill, the widow of Captain W. S. Eichelberger. Dr. Dickert was survived by his wife, a daughter, Gussie, and two step-daughters.[121]

Dr. William Jordan Holloway was born in 1845 in Edgefield District. He served as a boy soldier of the Confederacy. After his graduation from the Medical College of Georgia in 1868, he settled at Chappells. There he enjoyed a large practice until he retired some years before his death. Dr. Holloway married Vicie Jennings, daughter of Dr. Joe Jennings of Edgefield County. He died on December 28, 1922, survived by two sons, Dr. William O. Holloway and Julian Leroy Holloway.[122]

Dr. Arthur Allen Madden, born in Laurens County on February 7, 1870, and educated at Georgia Medical College, settled at Vaughansville in 1891. In 1894 he moved to Columbia where he enjoyed a large practice. He was married to Nellie Watson. They had five children, including Dr. L. Emmett Madden of Columbia.[123]

Dr. W. J. Holloway was the first of four generations of physicians. His son, Dr. William Osce Holloway, was born at Chappells on August 4, 1874, and was a graduate of the University of Maryland in medicine. He located at Chappells and had a large and extremely successful practice there until his death at the age of sixty-nine on December 28, 1943. He was married to Sallie Smith, who survived him along with two daughters, Mamie H. Scurry and Sara H. Cox, and a son, Dr. William Jordan Holloway.[124]

Dr. William Jordan Holloway, son of Dr. William Osce and Sallie Smith Holloway, was born at Chappells. Educated at the Webb School in Bell Buckle, Tennessee, the University of South Carolina, and the Medical College of South Carolina, he was graduated in medicine from the latter in 1935. He interned at Orange County Hospital in Orange, New Jersey. After one year in Greenwood, he settled in Ware Shoals in

1937 and engaged in medicine and general surgery there until his retirement to his home at Chappells. He served in the U.S. Navy for four and one-half years during World War II.

Following his release from active duty, Dr. Holloway studied for eighteen months at the Medical College of South Carolina before returning to his practice at Ware Shoals. He married Caroline Peterson and they have four children, three of whom are physicians. Dr. William Osce Holloway, their eldest son, was graduated from Clemson University and then from the Medical University of South Carolina in 1963. After a surgical residency of five years at Emory University Hospital in Atlanta, he served for two years in the U.S. Air Force as a general surgeon. After a year's fellowship in vascular surgery, he settled at Greenwood. He is married to Suzy Bruner, and they have three children, William Jordan, Lindy, and Jonathan Osce.

The second son, Dr. Jordan Michael Holloway, is an orthopedist. He attended The Citadel and graduated in medicine from the Medical University of South Carolina in 1964. After serving in the Peace Corps, he spent three years as resident in orthopedics in Greenville General Hospital. After specialized training in surgery of the hand in South America and at Denver, Colorado, he is now orthopedic surgeon for the Public Health Alaska Native Hospital. He is married to Elizabeth Neil, and they have one son, David Michael.

The third son, Dr. John Teddy Holloway, graduated from Wofford College in 1966 and from the Medical University of South Carolina in 1970. After interning at Maricopa County Hospital in Phoenix, Arizona, he took submarine training and served as diving medical officer on a submarine tender in the Mediterranean. He is married to Linda Hale.

Their daughter, Barbara Caroline, is married to Franklin Lewis Smith. She is a graduate of Erskine and holds a master's degree in horticulture from Clemson University.

This is truly a remarkable family of physicians.

The Physicians of Mendenhall Township

In the first few years after the end of the Civil War, four physicians practiced in Mendenhall Township. They were Drs. S. G. Welch, A. B. Pitts, James W. Spearman, and D. A. Cannon.

Dr. Spencer Glasgow Welch, son of William and Mary Glasgow Welch, was born in Newberry District on March 12, 1834. After attend-

ing Furman University and Jefferson Medical College, he graduated in
medicine from Castleton Medical College in Vermont in 1856. During
the war he served as surgeon, 13th South Carolina Regiment in the Army
of Northern Virginia. He married Cordelia Strother, daughter of George
and Eloise Bates Strother of Edgefield District. They celebrated their
golden wedding anniversary in 1911; she died in 1915 and he in January
1916, survived by one son, Williams Welch, and one daughter, Eloise,
who married Robert Downs Wright. Dr. Welch moved from Deadfall to
Newberry in 1875. For many years he lived at Helena; after retiring from
active medical practice, he devoted his attention to farming.[125]

Little is known of Dr. Aaron B. Pitts. He was one of the organizers of
the Newberry Medical Association in 1865, and in 1867, he and Dr. J.
W. Spearman announced that in the future they would require cash
payment for their services unless their bills were paid up by Christmas.
He was listed in the census of 1870 as practicing in the township but was
not listed ten years later.[126]

Dr. James W. Spearman, born in the district about 1834, graduated
from the Medical College of South Carolina in 1858. He moved to Seneca where he died of consumption on July 28, 1882.[127]

Dr. David Albert Cannon was born in the district in 1831. He was a
graduate of the Cincinnati Medical College and practiced nearly his entire life in the New Chapel section. He was married first to Mary C.
Herbert. After her death, he married Ella Steele of Columbia on February 20, 1889. He died on April 17, 1890. One of his sons was Chesley
Herbert Cannon, treasurer of Newberry County for eight years from
1929 to 1937.[128]

Dr. William E. Lake practiced in the Utopia section for some years
after his graduation from the state medical college in 1881. However, he
moved to the town of Newberry and his biographical sketch is included
with those physicians who practiced there.

After Dr. Cannon's death, several physicians settled in the township but none remained there long. Dr. Ernest Harrison Moore located at Deadfall in 1907 but moved to the Mt. Bethel community
following his marriage in 1912. When Dr. Moore moved, Dr. W. C.
Stone, formerly of Batesburg, settled at Deadfall.[129] He boarded with
Mrs. D. G. Livingston.

The following year Dr. J. H. Henry was at Silverstreet.[130] He then
moved to Newberry and then to Whitmire. He is included among the
physicians of that town.

The Physicians of Stoney Battery Township

In the first decade after the Civil War, Drs. Kibler, McFall, Cofield, Grimball, Simpson, and Cureton practiced medicine in the Frog Level section.

Dr. Amos A. Kibler was born on June 7, 1834, and died on June 12, 1894. He married Elvira P. Moore (1838–1925).[131]

Dr. William Todd McFall, a native of Georgia, participated in the formation of the Newberry Medical Association in December 1865, was active in town politics in Prosperity, and practiced medicine there until his death at the age of seventy-one on February 4, 1898. His daughter, Ella, married Dr. E. C. Ridgell.[132]

Dr. Cofield advertised as a practicing physician at Prosperity in 1875 but later moved to Newberry and opened a drugstore there. He is included among that town's physicians.

Dr. Lewis M. Grimball, graduate of the Medical College of South Carolina in 1857 and surgeon of the 6th South Carolina Infantry Regiment, opened an office in Frog Level in January 1866, but did not remain long.[133]

Dr. John B. Simpson was born in Laurens District on December 9, 1835, and graduated from Georgia Medical College in 1861. Settling in Prosperity, he lived there until his death in September 1906 at the age of seventy-one. He practiced medicine successfully in that community for many years; after his retirement he farmed. He married Elizabeth Cook and was survived by two children, Mrs. S. D. Duncan and Miss Nannie Simpson.[135]

Dr. Cureton was attacked by a Negro named Pink Phillips in January 1876, but nothing further is known of him.[135]

The census of 1880 listed four active practitioners in the village of Prosperity—Drs. William T. McFall, Jerome D. Bruce, Asa F. Langford, and John B. Simpson. Although not listed in the census of 1880 as active practitioners, the mortality section of that census lists Dr. A. L. Oxner and Dr. Thompson Young as physicians who signed death certificates in Stoney Battery Township.[136]

Dr. Asa F. Langford was born in Lexington District on December 9, 1828. He graduated from Philadelphia Medical College in 1855 and moved to Prosperity before 1880. He had a fine practice and died at Prosperity at the age of seventy-six on December 20, 1904. In 1911, Dr. D. M. Crosson credited Dr. Langford with switching Sampson Bridges from the Mackey or Republican House to the Wallace or Democratic

House in 1876. Dr. Langford's wife, the former Susannah Rhinehart, died at the age of sixty-five on September 4, 1899.[137]

Dr. Thompson Young was born in Newberry District on February 16, 1810. He married Mary Hunter (1816–1849) and practiced for many years. While not listed as a physician in either the Census of 1870 or that of 1880, he is shown as having signed death certificates in 1880. He did not actively practice for many years prior to his death on May 8, 1894.[138]

In the 1880s Dr. John R. Langford, Dr. Jacob L. Bowers, and Dr. C. T. Wyche commenced practice in this section. Dr. Langford, the son of Dr. Asa L. and Susannah Rhinehart Langford, was born in Edgefield District on April 19, 1856, and graduated from the College of Physicians and Surgeons in Baltimore in 1885. He returned to Prosperity where he practiced with his father for some years; later he moved to Swansea where he practiced until his death on August 21, 1938. He married Jennie Johnson.[139]

Dr. Jacob L. Bowers was born in Newberry County on April 5, 1861 and graduated from the Medical College of the University of Maryland in 1888. Upon graduation he settled at Slighs near Prosperity. He married Lora Shealy in 1901 and continued to practice medicine until his death on August 28, 1933. She died on February 18, 1952.[140]

Dr. Cyril Thomas Wyche was born in Greenville County, North Carolina, on May 26, 1857. He attended the University of North Carolina and graduated in medicine at the College of Physicians and Surgeons in Baltimore. He came to Prosperity in 1882 and practiced medicine and ran a drugstore there for many years. Active in fraternal and governmental affairs, he served as vice president of the South Carolina Medical Association, chairman of the Prosperity Board of Trustees, a member of the South Carolina House of Representatives for fourteen years, speaker pro tem, mayor of Prosperity for several terms, and master of Prosperity Lodge No. 115, AFM. He was married to Carrie Sease; and, when he died on May 4, 1930, he was survived by his widow, four children, and two brothers. His sons were U.S. District Judge Charles Cecil Wyche and C. Granville Wyche, Esquire, and his daughters were Mrs. James Goggans and Mrs. Henry Forbes.[141]

Dr. Wyche's pharmacist for many years was Dr. J. A. Simpson. Dr. Simpson married Frances Kibler. Their children were Dr. O. B. Simpson, a physician; Dr. Perry D. Simpson, a druggist; C. M. Simpson; Dr. L. D. Simpson, another druggist; and Mrs. C. C. Leonard.

In 1891, Dr. Abner J. P. Julian, brother-in-law of Dr. Wyche, commenced practice in Prosperity but shortly thereafter removed to Florida. He died in Lake City, Florida, in August 1917.[142]

In 1891, Dr. George Young Hunter settled at Prosperity. He was a native of the section, was educated at the University of South Carolina and graduated from the Medical College of Tulane University in 1891. He practiced at Prosperity for more than forty years and until his death on April 30, 1936. Dr. Hunter was president of the Bank of Prosperity for twenty years and vice president of Mollohon Manufacturing Company in Newberry for the same period. He served as intendant of Prosperity and as president of the South Carolina Livestock Association. He was active in civic and fraternal affairs. He was survived by his widow, Carrie DeWalt Hunter, and three daughters, Mrs. F. Dawson Beattie, Mrs. R. K. Wise, and Mrs. John T. Walker.[143]

A physician who did not continue to practice was Dr. Robert L. Luther. Born in Buncombe County, North Carolina, on November 13, 1834, he attended the Medical College in Cincinnati and served in the Civil War in the Seventy-ninth North Carolina Regiment. He married Elizabeth Catherine Stone of Newberry County and settled in Prosperity. There he engaged in the mercantile business for many years. He died at the age of ninety on November 13, 1924, survived by his wife of sixty-three years and five children, Lillian, Mrs. George S. Bearden, E. W., R. P., and J. D. Luther.[144]

In 1898, Dr. Jacob Simeon Wheeler commenced practice in Prosperity. A native of the county, he was born on October 6, 1872, and graduated from Newberry College in 1892 and received his medical degree from Tulane University. For many years he was president of the Prosperity Cotton Oil Mill, vice president of the Bank of Prosperity, a trustee of Newberry College, chairman of the Board of the Prosperity Schools, master of Prosperity Lodge No. 115, AFM, director of the Newberry Cotton Mills, and vice president of Hunter-Wheeler Lumber Company. He also served as intendant of Prosperity for several years. He was married first to Margaret Russell and second to Lenora Corlee. He died on July 8, 1927, survived by his second wife; by two daughters of his first marriage, Ellen and Florence Wheeler; and by two sons and a daughter of his second marriage, Henry Lee Wheeler, Jacob S. Wheeler, Jr., and Kate Jennings Wheeler.[145]

At the turn of the century, two other physicians settled in Prosperity. Dr. L. George Corbett, graduate of the Medical College of South Carolina in 1883, commenced practice there in 1899,[146] while Dr. John Jacob

Dominick graduated from the Medical College of South Carolina in 1900 and returned to Prosperity to practice.

Dr. Dominick, son of John Wesley and Nancy Stilwell Dominick, was born on October 17, 1877, in the St. Luke's section. Educated at Newberry College and the Medical College of South Carolina, he became prominent in the affairs of his town and county. At various times he served as mayor of Prosperity, member of the House of Representatives, and member of the County Democratic Executive Committee. He was never married and died on April 19, 1949. He, too, operated a drugstore in Prosperity.[147]

The third drugstore in Prosperity was owned first by Dr. George Y. Hunter, Dr. Jacob S. Wheeler, and Dr. James Ira Bedenbaugh. The pharmacist was the beloved Dr. Cyril Keister Wheeler who was born in Prosperity, the son of Thompson L. and Ida Rikard Wheeler. He graduated from the Pharmaceutical College of Atlanta and was quite active in Prosperity life until he died at the age of seventy-seven on August 16, 1968. Dr. Wheeler was survived by his widow, the former Annie Day; a son, Dr. C. K. Wheeler, Jr.; and by a daughter, Mrs. Dorothy W. Stone. An active member of Grace Lutheran Church, he was a Mason, a Shriner, and a member of the South Carolina Pharmaceutical Association. He also served as mayor of Prosperity.[148]

In 1903 Dr. James Ira Bedenbaugh returned to Prosperity to practice. A native of the town and son of Warren P. and Jane Rikard Bedenbaugh, he was born on May 20, 1874, and graduated from Newberry College in 1895 and the Medical College of the University of Georgia in 1903. He practiced in Prosperity for more than a half century and was truly the beloved physician of that community. Dr. Bedenbaugh married Frances Elizabeth Wheeler, who died on February 26, 1960, after almost fifty-seven years of married life. Dr. Bedenbaugh died at the age of eighty-six on June 8, 1960. He was survived by a son, James Arthur Bedenbaugh, and by two daughters, Mrs. Fred J. Weir, Sr., and Mrs. J. W. Earhardt, Jr. He served as president of the Newberry County Medical Society, chairman of the Commission of Public Works, and a member of the town council, the local school board, and the Council of Grace Church. He was a Mason and a Shriner.[149]

Dr. Oscar Barre Simpson, son of Dr. J. A. and Frances Kibler Simpson, was a native of Prosperity. Graduating from Newberry College in 1905, he taught school for two years and then completed his studies at the Medical College of South Carolina in 1910. He located in Prosperity, married Mary Warren of Salisbury, North Carolina, and had two sons, Oscar B., Jr., and Hebart. Dr. Simpson was extremely popular, serving as mayor for several terms. He died at the age of forty-two in May 1924.[150]

Several years elapsed before another physician located in Prosperity. In 1930 Dr. Von A. Long graduated from the Medical College of South Carolina and commenced practice in Prosperity.[151] Following World War II, he moved to Newberry and then in 1960 accepted the appointment as county health officer.

Dr. William Leslie Mills, son of William Lee and Nettie Barnes Mills, was born in Prosperity on February 20, 1921. Educated at Wofford College, where he was a member of Phi Beta Kappa, and the Medical College of South Carolina, he received the M.D. degree in 1945.[152] After interning at Columbia Hospital, he served two years in the U.S. Army Medical Corps. Then, after three years of surgical residency at Bruce Hospital in Florence, he returned to Prosperity.

Dr. Mills operated the Mills Clinic and had a tremendous practice in the lower part of Newberry County until his retirement in 1988. An appreciation dinner was tendered him on July 12, 1989, attended by 200 people. Active in fraternal and civic affairs, he is married to the former Virginia Bouknight. They have two daughters, Virginia M. Boland and Leslie M. Stuck, and two sons, Michael and Dean Mills.

In 1952 Dr. Frank Wright Shealy graduated from the Medical College of South Carolina. He practiced a short while with Dr. Mills but then moved to Greenwood where he now specializes in anesthesiology.[153] Dr. Gurdon W. Counts graduated from the same institution in 1961, practiced a short while in Prosperity, but then moved to Batesburg.

In 1988 Dr. Oscar F. Lovelace, Jr., opened the Lovelace Family Medical Center at Prosperity. The son of Oscar F. and Virginia D. Lovelace, he graduated from Clemson University with a B.S. in Zoology and from the Medical University of South Carolina with an M.D. He spent three years as a resident in family medicine at the University of Virginia Hospital in Charlottesville and is a member of the American Medical Association, the South Carolina Medical Association, the American Academy of Family Physicians, and Aveleigh Presbyterian Church.

Married to the former Mary Atkinson, they have four children, Benjamin O., Spencer C., Erin V., and Luke Dantzler Lovelace.

In July, 1990, Dr. Lovelace was joined in his practice by Dr. Michael R. Emlet, a native of Pennsylvania, and a graduate of the University of Pennsylvania School of Medicine in 1987. He completed his third year of residency in family practice at the University of Virginia. He is unmarried and attends Aveleigh Presbyterian Church.

Dr. Bonnie Bass is a pharmacist at the Lovelace Medicine Center Pharmacy. She is the former Bonnie Trull, is married to David Bass, has one daughter, Rachel, and lives in Irmo. She is a 1984 Phi Beta Kappa graduate in pharmacy from the University of South Carolina.

The Physicians of Cannon Township

According to the census of 1870, there were three practicing physicians residing in Cannon Township—Dr. Levi L. Kibler, Dr. William A. Fair, and Dr. D. Hilliard Werts. A fourth physician, Dr. R. Calvin Kibler, was not listed but is referred to in the newspapers of the period.

Dr. Levi L. Kibler was born in Newberry District on January 15, 1811, and was licensed to practice medicine by the Medical Society of South Carolina in 1835. He died on August 14, 1895.[154]

Dr. William A. Fair, son of James Fair, was born in Newberry District on May 31, 1827. He graduated from the Medical College of South Carolina in 1850 and died in Newberry County on March 5, 1873.[155]

Dr. Daniel Hilliard Werts was born in the district on August 14, 1830. He graduated from the Ecletic Medical College of Cincinnati in 1858. He volunteered for Confederate service in Company H of the Holcombe Legion. After the war he settled in the Jolly Street section and practiced medicine there until his death on September 10, 1900. He married Irene Mahala Kibler (1842–1920), who survived him. A daughter, Alice, wife of Jacob Ruff, died in 1892.[156]

In the June 28, 1865, issue of the *Weekly Herald*, Julia Aull wrote a blistering letter about a band of rogues who were terrorizing the community; among them, she said, was Dr. R. Calvin Kibler. In 1882 Dr. R. Calvin Kibler was reported to have been seriously injured at Dr. J. B. Simpson's steam mill at Prosperity. No further mention of him has been found.[157]

Medicine in the village of Little Mountain meant for a half century the Seases, father and sons. Dr. John Marion Sease was born in Lexington District on December 7, 1861. He was the son of Daniel and Mary Jane Rawl Sease; his father was a Confederate soldier who died in a federal prison. Dr. Sease was educated at Newberry College, B.A. 1882 and M.A. 1886, and at the University of Maryland, M.D. 1886. He married Margaret Monts of Little Mountain and commenced his practice at Ethridge. He relocated in Little Mountain in 1891 and from that time until his death was active in the practice over a wide area. He served as president of the Farmers and Merchants Bank at Little Mountain and as master of the Masonic Lodge there. He died on November 21, 1923, survived by his widow and four children, Virgil B. Sease, Dr. John Claude Sease, Dr. Ralph W. Sease, and Elberta Sease.[158]

Dr. Ralph Willard Sease was born on March 8, 1896, and graduated from Newberry College in 1917 and from the Medical College of South Carolina in 1921. He practiced at Kingstree where he died on December 2, 1929, survived by his widow, the former Beatrice Belvin, and two daughters, Margaret and Belvin.[159]

Dr. John Claude Sease was born in Little Mountain in 1892. He was graduated from Newberry College in 1913 and from the Medical College of South Carolina in 1917. He served in the Medical Corps of the U.S. Army during World War I, returning to Little Mountain to practice with his father. In 1934 he accepted the position of health officer for Newberry County and served with great distinction in the field of public health until his death on January 31, 1960. He was never married. Dr. Sease was treasurer of Holy Trinity Church for twenty years, president and later secretary of the Newberry County Medical Society, active in Newberry Kiwanis Club, and for years on the board of the Lowman Home. He was a greatly beloved citizen of the county.[160]

The Physicians of Heller Township

Dr. Joel A. Berley was born in the Pomaria community on April 5, 1824. He graduated from the Medical College of South Carolina in 1845, and practiced in his native section until his death on December 16, 1888. He and his wife, Laura Berley, are buried in the Berley family graveyard.[161]

His son, Dr. John Eusebius Berley, born near Pomaria on January 28, 1860, graduated from the Medical College of South Carolina in 1882. He never married and ceased to practice in order to enter the ministry. Dr. Berley died on July 19, 1890.[162]

Dr. George A. Setzler, born in Newberry District on December 31, 1835, graduated in medicine from the Medical College of South Carolina in 1856. He was a surgeon in the Confederate Army and returned home where he practiced until his death at seventy-seven on March 4, 1913. He married Elizabeth Cromer (1840–1897). They had nine children: Frances Elizabeth Young; Carrie M. Folk; Thomas A.; Ida; Dr. Edwin H.; James P.; Benedict M.; Dr. John Bachman; and George W. Setzler. After his wife's death, he married Susannah Frances Setzler (1843–1906).[163]

Dr. James K. Chapman, born in Lexington District on June 8, 1845, graduated in medicine from the University of Maryland in 1869. He married Mary Summer, daughter of Henry Summer, Esquire. Dr. Chapman died on October 11, 1894, survived by three children, Louise Frances Chapman, Henry Summer Chapman, and Bennie Mayer Chapman.[164]

Dr. James D. Cannon was born on November 12, 1833. Graduated from the Medical College of South Carolina in 1856, he practiced for many years in the Pomaria section until ill health forced his retirement. He married Harriett Caroline Oxner (1842–1926) and died at the age of seventy-six in August 1910.[165]

Dr. John C. Halfacre was born in the lower part of Newberry District on October 22, 1851. He received his degree in 1874 from the Medical College of South Carolina and first settled at Pomaria. He moved to Newberry in 1891 and his sketch is included among those of the doctors in Newberry.

Dr. Edwin Olin Hentz, born in the New Hope section of the district on June 12, 1864, graduated at Newberry College and then from the Medical College of South Carolina in 1889. He practiced in Heller Township at Walton and at New Hope until 1921 when he moved to Newberry. His sketch is included among those physicians of the town.

Dr. R. Berley Epting was born at Pomaria on August 14, 1855. He graduated in medicine from the University of Maryland in 1885 and returned to Pomaria to practice.[166]

Dr. Allen Kinard was born in Edgefield County and received his medical degree from Tulane University in 1890. He located in Newberry County, married Ida Bowles, and practiced in the Pomaria section. She died on September 28, 1895, and was buried at St. Phillips.[167]

Dr. William A. Dunn was born in Sumter District on September 2, 1864. He graduated from Louisville Medical College in 1892 and settled at Pomaria. There he established a fine practice and was elected intendant. However, he moved to Newberry and practiced there until his death in March 1928.

Dr. Thomas W. Koon, a native of the county, graduated from the College of Physicians and Surgeons, Baltimore in 1893, and commenced his practice at Pomaria. He married Clemmie Toombs in 1893.[167]

Dr. Zachary Taylor Pinner was born in Arden, North Carolina, on June 2, 1878. He graduated in medicine at the College of Tennessee in 1905. Settling at Pomaria, Dr. Pinner established a very large practice, operated a drugstore, and was active in banking. He was president of the Newberry County Medical Society in 1914. He married Maude Josephine Johnson (1886–1959) of Horse Shoe, North Carolina. Dr. Pinner died on October 18, 1940, at the age of sixty-one. He was survived by his widow and his son, Beaman L. Pinner, a druggist of Asheville, North Carolina.[169]

Dr. Robert Hamilton Folk, son of William H. and Lula M. Cromer Folk, was born in the county on December 11, 1888. He was graduated from Newberry College and obtained his medical degree from the University of Maryland in 1916.[170] After practicing for a short time in Pomaria, he entered the Public Health Service. He worked in Leesville, at the State Hospital, and then practiced in Belton until his death in 1938. He married Selma Hunter of Belton, who survived him, along with a son.

Dr. William Thaddeus Dickert was born in the county on April 18, 1869, the son of Jesse and Nancy Dickert. He commenced to practice medicine before being licensed by the State Board of Examiners; indeed he was elected county physician in 1900. He settled at Sligh's where he was practicing when Dr. Dunn swore out a warrant against him for practicing without a license in 1903. With commendable determination, Dr. Dickert attended the Medical College at Chattanooga, Tennessee, and received his diploma in 1905. He was immediately licensed by the State Board but, unfortunately, died at the early age of forty-two on May 2, 1912. He married Ida, daughter of Melvin Wicker, and was survived by her, two sons, and a daughter—J. W. Dickert, Floyd Dickert, and Louise D. Hunter.[171]

Dr. Thomas Hayne Wedaman, born in the county on September 15, 1882, graduated from Newberry College in 1901 and in medicine from the University of Maryland in 1909. He married Earle Epting (1884–1938) of Pomaria and practiced there for some years before moving to Johnston. He died at the age of sixty-two on January 9, 1935, survived by his widow and one son, Thomas H. Wedaman, Jr.[172]

The Physicians of Broad River Township

For more than a half century the name of Pinner has been synonymous with medicine in Broad River Township. Dr. Carroll A. Pinner settled at Peak upon his graduation from the Medical College of South Carolina in 1917. He conducted a large practice extending over parts of four counties. There being no bridge across Broad River between Columbia and Ashford Ferry, he maintained a car on either side of the stream and walked the trestle of the Southern Railroad between Peak and Alston to make his calls. Today the Carroll A. Pinner Bridge is a memorial to this country doctor.

Dr. Pinner, son of Benjamin and Mary Johnston Pinner, was born on June 21, 1892, in Arden, North Carolina. He graduated from Christ School and attended the University of Chattanooga and the University of North Carolina. He graduated from the Medical College of South Carolina in 1917. He married Rosalie Suber. Upon his death on January 25, 1962, she survived him along with a son, Dr. C. A. Pinner, Jr., and two daughters, Llewellyn Pinner and Mrs. Don McIntosh.[173]

Dr. Carroll A. Pinner, Jr., son of Dr. Carroll A. and Rosalie Suber Pinner, was born at Peak on October 10, 1923. He was graduated from The Citadel in 1943 with a B.S. degree and from the Medical College of South Carolina with an M.D. degree in 1946. He interned at Roper Hospital and returned to Peak to engage in general practice. He served two years in the U.S. Army Medical Corps.

He was a member of the Newberry County Medical Society, the South Carolina Medical Association, the Academy of General Practice, and the American Medical Association. He was married to Harriett Eidson, also a physician, and they were the parents of five children, Carroll A., III, Mary Ellen, Judith, Laura, and George Michael. Dr. Pinner died on March 5, 1983.[174]

Dr. Harriett E. Pinner was born on October 16, 1921. She graduated from Winthrop College with a B.S. degree in 1942 and from the Medical College of South Carolina with an M.D. degree in 1947.[175] She has engaged in general practice at Peak since 1950, except for two years spent in the Public Health Service. She is a member of the Newberry County Medical Society, the South Carolina Medical Association, the American Medical Association, and the American Public Health Association. She retired in January 1990.

Dr. Carroll A. Pinner, III, son of Dr. C. A. Pinner, Jr., and Dr. Harriett E. Pinner, was born on August 8, 1945, at Charleston. He graduated from The Citadel in 1967, and from Bowman Gray School of Medicine in 1971. He interned at Greenville General Hospital and practices at Peak. He is married to Margaret Dianne Keesee. They have three children, Jenifer Withers, Benjamin Carroll, and Davis Christopher.

Dr. John Herbert Ferguson, son of Herbert Harris and June Price Ferguson, was born in Abbeville on December 3, 1954. Educated at Wofford College, B.S. in 1977, and at the Medical University of South Carolina, M.D. 1981, he had a family practice residency at the Greenville Hospital System from 1981 to 1984, being the chief family practice resident in 1984. He joined Carroll A. Pinner, III, and Harriet E. Pinner in Peak in July 1984.

A member of the South Carolina Medical Association, the Newberry County Medical Society, and the American Academy of Family Physicians, he served as president of the county society in 1988.

He is married to the former Debra Ann Clement and is the father of two children, John Matthew and Kiri Nichole Ferguson. The family are members of Lake Murray Presbyterian Church.

The Physicians of Whitmire

Dr. Francis Marion Setzler was practicing in the Whitmire area before the textile mill was built and before the town was incorporated. He was born in Pomaria on August 22, 1845, and died near Whitmire on July 29, 1905. He served in the Thirteenth South Carolina Regiment as a private. After the war, he studied medicine and graduated from the Medical College of South Carolina in 1868. He married Mary Young on July 29, 1869. He was survived by six children: James, Gist, Annie, Ella, M. H., and Mary Young.[176]

Also practicing in the area before the mill was erected was Dr. Joseph H. Hamilton. Dr. Hamilton, born at Santuc on February 24, 1853, graduated from the Medical College of South Carolina in 1875. He located first at Goshen Hill, Union County, and, after some years in Whitmire, in 1890 moved to Union where he died. He established the first drugstore in Whitmire, which was operated by his nephew, Dr. R. R. Jeter. Dr. Hamilton married Josie Hill of Spartanburg.[177]

Other early Whitmire physicians were Dr. R. R. Jeter, Dr. George Douglass, Dr. John Stokes, Dr. D. C. Turnipseed, Dr. Hugh K. Boyd, and Dr. W. L. Sims. All of them were practicing there before 1910. During the next decade others came to Whitmire, including Dr. R. G. Blackburn; his wife, Dr. Mary R. Baker; Dr. Henderson Henry; Dr. Van Smith; Dr. J. H. Moore; Dr. T. B. Wood; and Dr. W. E. Bracket. In the 1920s Dr. E. Gordon Able and Dr. H. B. Thomas located there, and in the 1930s Dr. F. L. Webb and Dr. W. L. Norville. Dr. Kemper D. Lake returned home to practice in 1946, and Dr. Roy Suber in 1952. Dr. Lawrence Hampton Craig located there in 1963. Dr. J. L. Bozard also practiced in Whitmire for about a year during that decade.[178]

Dr. Robert Russell Jeter, son of John Randolph and Ophelia Hamilton Jeter, was born in Santuc, South Carolina, on December 13, 1865. He was graduated from The Citadel in 1887 and from the Medical College of South Carolina in 1890. He practiced medicine and opened a drugstore in Whitmire.

Dr. Jeter married Agnes Morgan Coleman. They had six children: Robert Coleman, Victoria Rice, John Randolph, Agnes Morgan, Ethel Antoinette, and Russell Jeter. Mrs. Jeter died on July 28, 1936, while Dr. Jeter died on May 7, 1921. At the time of his death and for many years before, he was a prominent physician of Union.[179]

Dr. George Douglass moved to Whitmire from Union to practice; his sketch is included among the physicians who lived in Maybinton.

Dr. John Stokes of Santuc settled in Whitmire after his graduation from the University of Maryland in 1903. He later moved to Montana.[180]

Dr. D. C. Turnipseed was reported to be practicing in Whitmire in 1904.[181]

Dr. Hugh King Boyd, son of Calhoun F. and Eliza Wilson Boyd, born in the county in 1878, graduated in medicine from Tulane University in 1906. He settled at Whitmire and practiced his profession there for some years. He married Elizabeth Child; they had one child, Colonel Hugh King Boyd, U.S. Army. Dr. Boyd gave up the practice of medicine, was elected clerk of court in 1924, and served in that capacity until his death on April 18, 1954. Mrs. Boyd served as his deputy in the clerk's office; she died on April 6, 1964.[182]

Dr. William L. Sims graduated from the Medical College of South Carolina in 1886. He married Mattie Henderson and was practicing in Whitmire at the time of his death at the age of sixty-four on December 6, 1916. He was survived by a son, Caldwell Sims.[183]

Dr. R. Golden Blackburn, a native of Germantown, North Carolina, settled in Whitmire in 1910 after his graduation from the Medical College of South Carolina in that year. He married Dr. Mary Baker of Columbia at Trinity Church, Columbia, on September 13, 1911. She was a native of Marion, South Carolina. They returned to Whitmire to practice but after a few years moved to Marion.[184]

Dr. Van Smith, whose sketch is included among those physicians of the town of Newberry, moved from Newberry to Whitmire in February 1913. There he conducted an active practice, operated a drugstore, and served as mayor. In 1920 he moved to Beaufort in order to engage in truck farming.

Dr. B. Henderson Henry, son of W. J. Henry, was a native of Laurens County. He graduated from the Atlanta Medical College in 1913 and located in Whitmire.[185] He soon moved to Clinton.

In 1914 Dr. James H. Moore and Dr. T. B. Wood settled at Whitmire.

Dr. Moore was a native of Oconee County. He died in the hospital at Millegeville, Georgia, in 1954, and is buried in the Prosperity Cemetery. He was eighty-seven.[186]

Dr. Wood was born in Chester County. He went into the Army at the beginning of World War I and never returned to Whitmire.[187]

Dr. William E. Brackett commenced his practice in Whitmire in July 1919. He remained there for a number of years but then moved to Hendersonville, North Carolina.[188] In that city he specialized in the diseases of the eye, ear, nose, and throat.

Dr. E. Gordon Able settled in Whitmire in 1924 following his graduation in medicine.[189] Since the greater part of his career was spent in the town of Newberry, his sketch is included among the physicians of that town.

Dr. F. L. Webb practiced for a short time in Whitmire. He then moved to Clinton where he practiced at Whitten Village.[190]

Dr. Hilland Bernard Thomas was born in Atlanta, Georgia, on November 21, 1891. He attended Wofford College and graduated from the Medical School of the University of Virginia in 1917. He interned at the Retreat for the Sick in Richmond and at Pryor Hospital in Chester, South Carolina. After two years in the U.S. Army, he took postgraduate work in New York and settled at Whitmire. There he practiced with great success until his retirement. He was married to Kathleen Cummings of Belton; they moved there to live upon his retirement. Dr. and Mrs. Thomas had one daughter, Enola Thomas. He died on October 13, 1964.[191]

Dr. W. L. Norville, a native of Rutherfordton, North Carolina, and a graduate of the University of Tennessee Medical College, settled in Whitmire in the 1930s and developed a fine practice. He left Whitmire in the 1950s to enter the North Carolina Public Health Service. He was married to Lillie Mae Freeman; they have three daughters, Phoebe, Barbara, and Laura.[192]

Dr. Kemper David Lake, son of Robert C. and Susan Gaston Howze Lake, was born at Kershaw on February 15, 1923. He graduated with a B.S. degree from Presbyterian College in 1943 and from the Medical College of South Carolina in 1946. He interned at the Medical College Hospital at Richmond, Virginia.

Dr. Lake is a member of the Newberry County Medical Society, the South Carolina Medical Association, the American Medical Association, and the American Academy of Family Practice. He retired due to ill health in 1984. He is married to the former Muriel Harmon, and they have three children, Susan, Patricia, and David.

Dr. James Claffy Montgomery, son of Dr. Benton McQueen and Mana Elizabeth Montgomery, was born in Kingstree on June 7, 1922. After graduating from The Citadel in 1943 and from the Medical College of South Carolina, he settled at Whitmire. He remained there for several years but then returned to Kingstree. He is a brother of Dr. Benton McQueen Montgomery and married Maude E. Brounou. They have five children: James Claffy, Jr., Nancy Elliott, Elizabeth Ruth, George Rickenbaker, and David Benton Montgomery. Dr. Montgomery is a member of the Williamsburg County Medical Society, the South Carolina Medical Association, the American Medical Association, and the Southern Medical Association.[193]

Dr. Roy Bonds Suber, son of Otis B. and Elizabeth McCrackin Suber, was born in Whitmire on October 20, 1921. He was graduated from Davidson College in 1942 and from the Vanderbilt University School of Medicine in 1951. He interned at Presbyterian Hospital of Chicago and located in Whitmire. There he engaged in general practice until 1963 when he accepted appointment as director of the Whitten Village. He now practices in Clinton. He married Eleanor Rae of Chicago. They have one daughter, Lea.[194]

Dr. Lawrence Hampton Craig practiced for about a year in Whitmire after settling there in 1963. He was a graduate of the Medical College of South Carolina and subsequently moved to Saluda. He died a few years later in New York.[195]

Dr. J. L. Bozard, native of Orangeburg, was graduated from Clemson College and from the Medical College of South Carolina. He remained in Whitmire only a few years before he moved to Greenville.[196]

Following Dr. Lake's retirement, there was for a short time no resident physician in Whitmire. In 1985 Drs. Yanetti and Price opened their office there.

Robert A. Yanetti, M.D., was born in Camden, New Jersey, on October 9, 1952, the son of Robert Anthony and Gertrude Yanetti. He graduated from Clemson in 1974 with a B.S. in Zoology, received a master's degree in Zoology from Clemson in 1976, and received his M.D. from the Medical University of South Carolina in 1982. He completed a residency in internal medicine at St. Luke's Hospital in Bethlehem, Pennsylvania, in 1985 and located at Whitmire. He has offices in Whitmire and Union. He and his wife, Karen, have two children, Diana and Julia.

Dr. Robert Price was born on January 30, 1953, in Guilford County, North Carolina. He was educated at the University of North Carolina at Greensboro and at the Medical University of South Carolina, from which he received a B.S. in Pharmacy in 1976 and an M.D. in 1982. After completing a residency in internal medicine at New Hanover Memorial Hospital at Wilmington, North Carolina, in 1985, he settled in Whitmire. He moved from Whitmire in 1987.

23

The Dentists of the County

At the outbreak of the Civil War, there were two dentists in the village of Newberry. Dr. Washington B. McKellar settled there before 1850, while Dr. Richard S. Whaley arrived in 1857.[1] McKellar was named senior warden of Amity Lodge No. 87, Ancient Free Masons, when that lodge was chartered in 1853, and he was intendant of Newberry in 1856.[2] Both McKellar and Whaley served in the Confederate Army[3] and both returned to Newberry after Appomattox.

In April 1865 Dr. J. E. Dapray opened an office, announcing himself a surgeon dentist. However, he returned to Charleston in September 1866 after suffering a loss in the fire of June 1866. While Dapray's property was damaged in the estimated amount of $300, Dr. McKellar was damaged $1,000, and Dr. Whaley's dwelling, office, and his wife's millinery shop were damaged $4,000.[4]

Dr. Whaley issued a public call in July 1867 to the dentists of South Carolina to meet to organize a state dental association[5] but it was two years later before such a meeting materialized. It was held in the Columbia office of Dr. Thomas T. Moore, a native of Newberry District, who had practiced dentistry for a short time in Dr. McKellar's office in 1866. He had then gone to the Pennsylvania College of Dental Surgery, graduating in 1869 and locating in Columbia.[6]

At the temporary organizational meeting of the South Carolina Dental Association held on November 10, 1869, Dr. McKellar was elected 1st vice president and Dr. Gurdon S. F. Wright of Pomaria was named secretary and treasurer. The other officers were Dr. W. C. Wardlaw of

Abbeville, president; Dr. D. L. Boozer of Columbia, 2nd vice president; and Dr. T. T. Moore, corresponding secretary.[7]

In September 1869, Dr. John R. Thompson, graduate of the Philadelphia Dental College and native of Newberry, became associated in the practice with his step-father, Dr. McKellar.[8] When the latter died on November 26, 1869, Dr. Thompson continued to practice in Newberry for the rest of his life. The dentists of Newberry, Dr. R. S. Whaley, Dr. E. C. Jones, Dr. J. R. Thompson, and Dr. W. A. Fallaw, met to memorialize their stricken colleague.[9]

Dr. McKellar died at the comparatively early age of fifty-one, having been born on July 28, 1818. As intendant of his adopted town, an active Mason, a Confederate veteran, and a leader in his profession, he was highly regarded. He was survived by his wife, Eliza K., the widow of Robert Thompson, and two step-children, Dr. John R. Thompson and Mary B. Thompson. He is buried in Rosemont Cemetery.[10]

In April 1870, the state dental association became a permanent organization. Dr. Jones and Dr. Thompson served on the Committee on Membership, while Dr. Whaley and Dr. Fallaw were named to the Committee on Operative Dentistry.[11]

Dr. Fallaw, who practiced for only a few years, later became a traveling salesman and then entered the hotel business. He was a Confederate veteran and died at the Old Soldiers Home in Columbia in September 1918, survived by one son, Clint Fallaw. He is buried in Rosemont Cemetery.[12]

Dr. Whaley was elected 1st vice president of the South Carolina Dental Association in 1872. He died on April 17, 1874, survived by his widow, Ann, and five children. He is buried in Rosemont Cemetery.[13]

Dr. Edwin C. Jones, son of Charles M. and Mary Neal Jones, was a native of Newberry. He was born on June 7, 1848, and served as sergeant, Company H, Fourth Regiment of State Troops as a boy soldier. In 1872 he graduated from the dental school of the University of Pennsylvania and returned to Newberry to practice. He was mayor of Newberry, an active member of the A.R.P. Church, and for five years a member of the State Board of Dental Examiners. He married first Sue Harrington, by whom he had one son, George Garmany Jones. After her death, he married Julia Connor, by whom he had three daughters, Ethel, Louise Brogdon, and Helen Scarborough. Dr. Jones died on February 3, 1929, and is buried in Rosemont Cemetery.[14]

Dr. J. R. Thompson, son of Robert and Eliza K. Thompson, was born in Newberry on December 19, 1849. A Confederate veteran, he graduated from Philadelphia Dental College in 1869. He served as president of the South Carolina Dental Association in 1877. For many years he was a member of the State Board of Dental Examiners. Dr. Thompson married Adelaide Frances Scott who died in 1891. He died on his fifty-second birthday, December 19, 1901, survived by an only daughter, Mary, who married P. E. Scott.[15]

The next dentists to practice in Newberry were the two sons of Silas and Elizabeth Randell Johnstone. The elder, Dr. Albert Pope Johnstone, was born in Chester on September 15, 1847, reared in Newberry, and graduated from Philadelphia Dental College in 1872. He first located at Newberry but moved to Anderson in 1877. He was president of the South Carolina Dental Association in 1885, taught at Vanderbilt Dental College in 1888, and served as a member of the State Board of Dental Examiners from 1909 to 1914. He died on August 13, 1932.[16]

His brother, Dr. Theodore Johnstone, was born on November 29, 1855. He became a licensed pharmacist in 1878 but then studied dentistry, graduating from Baltimore Dental College in 1883. He practiced in Newberry until ill health forced him to retire a few years before his death in February 1927. His wife, the former Leila Rives, died in 1919. He was survived by an only daughter, Julia Johnstone.[17]

In 1879 Dr. T. A. Sale moved to Newberry from Athens, Georgia. He practiced in Newberry for a few years after opening his office in his residence opposite Dr. P. B. Ruff's home on Boundary Street. Later he maintained his office in the Mower Block. His wife died on March 14, 1891, and he died in Columbia in December 1893, at the age of eighty-three. He, too, is buried in Rosemont Cemetery.[18]

Two other dentists practiced in Newberry before 1900. They were Dr. J. W. Boozer and Dr. David Luther Boozer, Jr., sons of Dr. David L. Boozer of Columbia. The father, a Confederate veteran, served as president of the State Dental Association in 1884 and had three sons who were dentists; when he retired in 1900, he moved to Newberry where, with two other sons, he operated the Newberry Roller Mill. Because of ill health he moved back to Columbia where he died on June 26, 1902, at the age of sixty-five.[19]

Dr. David Luther Boozer, Jr., graduated from the University of South Carolina and from the Dental School of the University of Maryland in 1896. He practiced in Newberry for seven years but was forced to retire because of ill health. He then moved to Columbia to live with his mother until his death in May 1908. He is buried in Elmwood Cemetery, Columbia, alongside his parents and brothers.[20]

Dr. J. W. Boozer was reported to be practicing in Newberry in 1895 when he attended the annual meeting of the South Carolina Dental Association. He soon moved to Columbia where he practiced with another brother, Dr. J. Edward Boozer.[21]

In 1904 Dr. Robert Moffett Kennedy located in Newberry. The son of William M. and Rachel M. Kennedy, he was born in York on June 24, 1880. He was educated at Erskine and at Emory University Dental School. He married Bessie Renwick Carlisle of Newberry, who died on April 26, 1953. They had five children, Edwin, Robert, James, John, and Rachel. Dr. Kennedy moved to Rock Hill in 1910 but returned to Newberry in 1915. He then lived in Due West for a short time, returning to Newberry in 1917 where he practiced until his death on November 17, 1960. He was a member of the Associate Reformed Church and is buried in Rosemont Cemetery.[22]

Dr. James Ambrose Fulmer, a native of Lexington County and graduate of Baltimore Dental College, settled in Newberry in 1905. The next year he moved to Fountain Inn where he practiced until his death in April 1945.[23]

Dr. G. R. Harding, who advertised as "The Painless Dentist," had an office on Vincent Street at the "Sign of the Big Tooth" in 1905. He was not a member of the South Carolina Dental Association.[24]

Dr. James K. Gilder, son of Dr. James K. and Jessie Fant Gilder, opened an office in Newberry in 1906. Two years later he moved to Buenos Aires, Argentina, to practice but returned to Newberry in 1912. A few years later he moved to New York City.[25]

Dr. Edgar Haskell Kibler, son of Captain J. D. A. and Elizabeth Drafts Kibler, was born at Kibler's Bridge in Newberry County. He was educated at Newberry College and Southern Dental College in Atlanta. He opened his office in Newberry in 1906 and was active in community affairs until his death on February 14, 1946. Dr. Kibler was president of the local Rotary Club, an active member of the Country Club of Newberry, and a member of the Lutheran Church of the Redeemer. He was an avid golfer and hunter. He married Abbie Smith of Canada and was survived by an only child, Colonel E. H. Kibler, Jr., a graduate of West Point.[26]

Dr. Young Mosley Brown, son of George D. and Nancy Mosley Brown of Prosperity, was born on November 21, 1889. He received his B. A. degree from Erskine in 1909 and his D.D.S. from Vanderbilt University in 1913. After practicing a short time in Lake City, he settled in Newberry where he practiced until his death on January 7, 1954. He was a member of Prosperity A.R.P. Church, Prosperity Lodge Number 115, AFM, and Newberry American Legion Post 24. He served as first lieutenant, Dental Corps, U.S. Army in World War I and rose to the rank of lieutenant colonel, Officers Reserve Corps. When the South Carolina Probation and Parole Board was established in 1941, he became its chairman and served in that capacity for the rest of his life. He was president of the Southern States Parole Association and a member of the state Democratic Executive Committee from Newberry County. He was never married.[27]

Dr. Eugene E. Stuck, son of George M. and Elizabeth Wessinger Stuck, was born in Newberry County on July 26, 1890. He became a telegrapher and then entered Atlanta Dental College from which he graduated in 1910. Settling in Newberry he practiced here until ill health forced his retirement about 1940. During World War I he served in the infantry and then in the aviation corps as an officer. On July 19, 1918, he was cited for distinguished service by General Pershing. Following his discharge as first lieutenant in 1919, he returned to Newberry. On June 13, 1923, he married May Tarrant, daughter of Robert L. and Rosa Kilgore Tarrant; they were divorced. He was a member of the Lutheran Church, Amity Lodge No. 87, A.F.M., the Kiwanis Club, the Country Club of Newberry, and American Legion Post 24. He died in Greenville on March 20, 1943, and was buried in the family cemetery at Peak.[28]

Dr. John Reuben Boozer was born in Newberry in 1905 and died in his native town on June 13, 1945. He graduated from Newberry College in 1927 and from Southern Dental College in 1934. He practiced for ten years in Newberry. He served as president of the Central District Dental Society. Dr. Boozer was a Mason, a steward in Central Methodist Church, and a member of the Country Club of Newberry. He was survived by his widow, the former Elizabeth Corley, and his infant son, John R. Boozer, Jr.[29]

Dr. B. G. Qualls settled in Newberry in 1923 and practiced until his death on October 5, 1955. He was a native of Kershaw County. Dr. Qualls was survived by his widow, Ruby Scott Qualls, and two children by his first wife. He was the only black dentist ever to practice in Newberry.[30]

Dr. Fuller Alexander Truett was born in Brookneal, Virginia. Educated at Wake Forest and Emory Medical College, he served in the U.S. Army in World War II. Following his release from service in 1946, he settled in Newberry where he lived until his death on December 7, 1972.

He took a leading part in community and professional affairs, serving as president of the Southern Academy of Oral Surgery, president of the Newberry Cotillion Club, and president of the Lions Club. He was a Mason, Shriner, and Methodist. Dr. Truett married Lucy Salley Corbitt, who survived him with one daughter, Brenda T. Derrick, and one granddaughter, Kathryn. He was a prominent and beloved dentist of Newberry County.[31]

Dr. Evander M. Anderson, son of E. M. and Katie Weatherford Anderson, was born in Dillon County on December 10, 1918. He graduated from Wake Forest University with a B.S. in 1939 and from Emory University with a D.D.S. in 1947. He located in Newberry in 1947. A life member of both the American and South Carolina dental associations, past president of the Central District Dental Association, member of the American Academy of General Dentistry, and the American Academy of Dentistry International, he is a Rotarian, Mason, and Shriner. He attends Aveleigh Presbyterian Church. Dr. Anderson married Viola Wade, and they have four children, Dr. E. M., Jr., Gretchen, Robert, and Beth.

Dr. Evander M. Anderson, Jr., was born in Hartsville on July 1, 1941. He, too, graduated from Wake Forest (1963) and Emory University (1967). He married Lynda Klebold; they have three children, Andrew Wade, Nathaniel Clay, and E. M., III. He was associated for a time with his father but now practices at Chapin.

Dr. James E. Wiseman, Jr., son of James E. and Lorna Wilson Wiseman, was born in Newberry on December 13, 1933. He was educated at Wofford and the University of South Carolina; he graduated from the University of Louisville in dentistry in 1959. Dr. Wiseman located in Newberry in 1959 and now practices with Dr. William Edwards. A member of the American and South Carolina dental associations, president of the Central District Dental Association, president of the South Carolina Academy of Practice Administration, he is a former senior warden of St. Luke's Episcopal Church, a former trustee of Newberry College, and a member of the Newberry Advisory Board for the Citizens and Southern National Bank. He married Sallie John Ruff; they have four sons, James E., III, William D., David W., and John D.

Dr. E. Benton DuBose, Jr., son of Carl B. and Minnie Reynolds DuBose, was born in Columbia on May 28, 1940. He graduated from the University of South Carolina, B. S. in Business Administration and the University of Louisville in dentistry in 1970. Upon graduation he located in Newberry. He is a member of the American and South Carolina dental associations, the Academy of General Dentistry, St. Luke's Episcopal Church, and the Board of Directors of the Newberry County Council on Aging. Dr. DuBose married Lynn Fishburne; they have two sons, Steven M. and Brett B.

Dr. Charles Rogers Hook, son of Fred W. and Jacqueline Hook, was born at Sumter on September 6, 1946. He graduated from Clemson University in 1968 and the Medical University of South Carolina in dentistry in 1973. Locating in Newberry, he practiced here until he entered the missionary field. He is married to the former Ann Rush of Manning. They have three children, Martie, Lyn, and Charles Rogers, Jr.

Dr. Robert L. Brown, son of William L. and Virginia Hill Brown, was born in San Diego, California, on August 10, 1945. He was educated at Vanderbilt University and The Citadel, receiving a B. E. degree from the latter. After graduating from the Medical University of South Carolina with the D.M.D. degree, he practiced in association with Dr. Anderson but now practices family dentistry alone. He is married to Lucy Mahon.

Dr. Oliver Frank Hart, son of Dr. George and Georgia Herbert Hart, was born in Columbia on April 13, 1950. He graduated from the University of South Carolina with a B. S. degree and from the Medical University of South Carolina with the degree of D.M.D. He succeeded Dr. Hook in his practice here. He is married to Lucy Jordan; they have twin daughters, Jordan and Rebecca, and another daughter, Treva. He moved to Columbia in 1983.

Dr. James R. Williams, Jr., son of J. Ralph and Mary Lane Whittaker Williams, was born in Newberry on March 3, 1949. After receiving his B.S. degree from Clemson University, he graduated from the Medical University of South Carolina with a D.M.D. degree in 1974. He settled in Chapin upon graduation but moved to Newberry in 1977 and has since practiced here. He is a member of the Academy of General Practice, the American Dental Association, and Central United Methodist Church, and is a past president of the Newberry Rotary Club. He married Margery Lynn Hook who died in 1989. They had one daughter, Rebecca, and one son, John Ralph Williams. He later married Sally Nicholson.

Dr. Erwin R. Baker, son of the late Ralph Parr Baker, M.D., and Elizabeth Renwick Baker, was born in Newberry on February 12, 1956. He was graduated from Duke University with a B.A. in Botany in 1978 and from the Medical University of South Carolina Dental School in 1984. He located at Newberry and, after practicing for some time with Dr. Brown, opened his own office on Hunt Street.

He is a member of the American Dental Association, the South Carolina Dental Association, the Central District Dental Society, the Aveleigh Presbyterian Church, and the Rosemont Cemetery Board. President of the Newberry Historical Society in 1988 and 1989, he is a Mason and a Shriner.

Dr. Baker married Sally Davis of Rutherfordton, North Carolina, a talented musician. They have one child, William Erwin Baker.

Dr. William B. Rush, Jr., son of William B. and Sadie Smith Rush, was born in Sumter in 1953. After graduating from Clemson University and the Medical University of South Carolina in 1979, he practiced for several years in Barnwell but moved to Newberry to take over the practice of Dr. Hart upon the latter's removal to Columbia in 1983.

He is a member of the American Dental Association, the Southern Academy of Oral Surgery, the Newberry Pilots Association, and the First Baptist Church. He married Roberta Campbell, and they have three children, Rebecca, Sarah, and Will.

Dr. William B. Edwards, son of John S. and Vivian Edwards of Johnston, was born on May 30, 1950. He graduated from Clemson University, B.A. degree in psychology, obtained a master's degree in counseling from the University of South Carolina, and received the D.M.D. degree from the Medical University of South Carolina. Dr. Edwards is a member of the American Dental Association, the Central District Association, the Greater Columbia Dental Association, the courtesy staff of Lexington Medical Center, and on the staff of Newberry County Hospital. He is a member of the First Baptist Church of Johnston. He practices with Dr. James E. Wiseman, Jr.

The Dentists of Prosperity

Dentists in Prosperity before 1900 included Dr. John A. Harmon, Dr. E. C. Ridgell, and Dr. Euston N. Kibler. The latter two served as presidents of the South Carolina Dental Association. Dr. Harmon committed suicide on January 30, 1891, survived by his widow and one child.[32]

Dr. Edgar Clifton Ridgell was born in Batesburg on November 6, 1859. He studied medicine in Wisconsin for a year and then transferred to Baltimore College of Dental Surgery from which he graduated with the D.D.S. degree in 1881. He located at Prosperity but soon moved to Batesburg, where he practiced until his death on August 23, 1935. He was president of the South Carolina Dental Association in 1890, senator from Lexington County, and an extensive peach grower.[33]

Dr. Ridgell's nephew, Euston Nathalie Kibler, son of J. Middleton and Rosa Ridgell Kibler, was born in Prosperity on March 16, 1871. After studying under Dr. Ridgell in Batesburg, he entered Emory University, graduating in dentistry in 1892. He practiced in Prosperity for more than a half-century, served for sixteen years in the House of Representatives, and for eight terms was mayor of Prosperity. He was president of the South Carolina Dental Association in 1909. Unmarried, he died on December 7, 1961, and is buried in Prosperity.[34]

Since 1900, six other dentists have practiced in Prosperity—Drs. J. F. Littlejohn, George W. Harmon, Godfrey D. Harmon, John E. Wessinger, Carolyn Deanne Mainous, and Anthony Frank Chibbaro. Dr. Littlejohn located there in 1904 but remained only a short time. He was a native of Spartanburg.[35]

Dr. George Waddell Harmon, the son of W. P. B. and Martha McNary Harmon, was born in Newberry County. He graduated from Newberry College in 1906 and from Emory University in 1911. He immediately settled in Prosperity and practiced dentistry successfully until his death on March 15, 1966, at the age of eighty-one. Dr. Harmon was president of the Central District of South Carolina Dental Association, a member of Psi Omega Fraternity and Prosperity Lodge No. 115, A.F.M. He served as chairman of the Board of Trustees of the Prosperity schools, as a member of the Prosperity Town Council, and on the County Selective Service Board during World War II. He married Ruby Wallace of Atlanta, who survived him with a son, George Wallace Harmon, and a daughter, Martha Harmon Bradley.[36]

Dr. Godfrey Dominick Harmon died on February 23, 1954, at the age of seventy. He was the son of Godfrey and Harriett Dominick Harmon of Newberry County. Following his graduation at Emory University in 1916, he practiced dentistry in Prosperity until he retired because of ill health in 1939.[37]

Dr. John Earl Wessinger, son of Voight E. and Emily Cooley Wessinger, was born in Leesville on September 28, 1927. He graduated from Clemson College with a B.S. degree in 1950 and from the School of Dentistry of the Medical College of Virginia with the degree of D.D.S. in 1957. He served three years on active duty in the U.S. Naval Air Corps at the close of World War II. Locating at Prosperity, he was the town's only dentist.

Dr. Wessinger was married to Doris Lavada Koon. They were the parents of four children, Tamie Jo, Tina Leigh, John Earl, Jr., and Voight Earl. He died on April 8, 1981.[38]

Dr. Mainous, a native of Greenville, was licensed on June 15, 1981. She practiced for a short time in Dr. Wessinger's former offices.[39]

Dr. Anthony Frank Chibbaro was born in Charleston on September 23, 1956. After graduating from Newberry College in 1978 and the Dental School of the Medical University of South Carolina in 1981, he located at Prosperity in 1982. He married Julia Anne Segars.[40]

The Dentists of Whitmire

Whitmire's first dentist was Dr. R. H. Truesdale who settled there in 1904.[41] He remained only a short time, before a Dr. Hawkins came to Whitmire. In 1909 Dr. Hawkins moved to Charleston, and Whitmire was left without a dentist.[42] Later that year Dr. P. B. Hilton opened an office in Whitmire,[43] followed in 1914 by Dr. N. B. Thornton.[44]

Dr. Carl B. Busbee, native of Springfield, practiced for a short time before moving to Conway, as did a Dr. Spain.[45]

Dr. Samuel Hanna Trotti, a native of Chesterfield, was graduated from Emory University Dental College in 1933. He settled in Whitmire and continued to practice there until he entered active duty with the 107th AAA Separate Battalion (AW) on February 10, 1941. Captain Trotti served with the battalion overseas and after the war opened his office in Saluda. He was greatly beloved by the citizens of Whitmire and by the men of the 107th AAA Separate Battalion. He died in 1970, survived by his wife, the former Bertha Marsh, and two daughters, Marsha and Hannah.[46]

Dr. Alfred Bradbury Schriver, son of Dr. Alfred H. and Maude Bradbury Schriver, was born in Brewer, Maine, on November 11, 1914. He was educated at the University of Maine and at the Dental School of the University of Maryland. After interning at the Baltimore City Hospital for a year, he settled first at Hickory, North Carolina, and then moved to Whitmire in 1949. He served as a trustee of the Whitmire schools 1951–1961 and is a deacon of the Presbyterian Church. He is a member of the Southern Academy of Oral Surgery, the South Carolina Dental Association, and American Dental Association, and is active in Masonry. He married Elizabeth Byron Kincheloe of Upperville, Virginia. They have two daughters, Mrs. David Griffin and Mrs. Robert Kelly, Jr.

Dr. Rickey Lee Bledsoe, born in Augusta, Georgia, on October 20, 1952, was educated at Augusta College, the University of South Carolina, and the Medical University of South Carolina. After graduating from the latter in 1978, he practiced in Edgefield for a year. He then moved to Whitmire in 1979 and has since practiced there. He married Rosemary Perry; they have two sons, Garrick L. and William K. Bledsoe.

The Dentists of Pomaria

Pomaria has had two dentists since the Civil War. One stayed a few years, and the other for a week. Both moved to Columbia and both became president of the South Carolina Dental Association.

Dr. Gurdon F. S. Wright was born in Marion, South Carolina, on April 17, 1832. After serving in the Confederate Army, he settled at Pomaria. He was elected secretary and treasurer of the South Carolina Dental Association at the organizational meeting on November 10, 1869. He moved to Columbia in 1875 and became president of the association that year. He then practiced in Georgetown until his death on January 18, 1909.[47]

Andrew Jackson Bedenbaugh, son of Andrew Jackson and Rebecca Folk Bedenbaugh, was born in Prosperity on January 1, 1888. After graduating from Newberry College in 1910 and from the Dental School of the University of Maryland in 1913, he settled at Pomaria to practice dentistry; the local newspaper reported the opening of his office. The next week the newspaper advised that he had moved to Columbia to practice with Drs. Boozer and Boozer. He served as a first lieutenant, Dental Corps, in World War I; he practiced in Columbia after returning from service until his death on March 7, 1955. He was president of the South Carolina Dental Association in 1948.[48]

Other Dentists Who Signed The Register

Dentists who signed the Register kept by the clerk of court for Newberry County but who apparently did not practice in the county include:

Dr. James E. Britt, Jr., born in Tarboro, North Carolina, and licensed on July 12, 1960; Dr. David Wayne Bishop, born in Augusta, Georgia, and licensed on July 15, 1963; Dr. Henry James Hare, born in Newberry and licensed on July 7, 1951; Dr. James Warren Henderson, Jr., born in Newberry and licensed in August 1969, being a very successful dentist in Lancaster; Dr. R. N. Kennedy, born in Mooresville, North Carolina, and licensed on August 26, 1930; Dr. John Hayne Lake, born in Whitmire and licensed on July 31, 1951, being a leading dentist in Ware Shoals; Dr. Dennis Woodrow Newton, Jr., born in LaJunta California, and licensed on June 24, 1972, practicing orthodontry in Columbia; and Dr. Julian Wade Nichols, born in Newberry and licensed on June 28, 1975.

24

The Druggists of Newberry

Until almost the end of the nineteenth century the county's only drugstores were located in the county seat. The fire of June 18, 1866, destroyed most of the business section of the town of Newberry. The three drugstores then in operation were destroyed. While Dr. Capers lost his stock of goods, Dr. Theodore Gouin lost not only his stock but his building, and Dr. W. F. Pratt lost his stock of goods, his store building, and his dwelling.[1]

The next year Dr. Gouin and Dr. James McIntosh formed a partnership to conduct a drugstore under the name of Dr. T. Gouin. His wife having died a few months before, Dr. Gouin became homesick. In 1871 he gave up and returned to his native France.[2] Dr. McIntosh then devoted his attention to the practice of medicine and forsook the drug business.

In October 1871 two new drugstores were opened. Dr. Homer P. Tarrant and J. Ward Motte opened one of these. Motte died in 1876 and Tarrant, after an unsuccessful try at suicide, moved to Mobile, Alabama, in 1882.[3]

The other store was owned by a physician, Dr. Samuel Franklin Fant. A year after he opened the drugstore, Dr. Fant was awarded a degree in pharmacy by the University of South Carolina on June 19, 1872. A progressive merchant, he installed a new soda fountain in 1873; employed Dr. R. K. King, an accomplished Englishman, as pharmacist in 1874; and in 1880 moved his store to the corner of Main and Caldwell streets, under the Newberry Hotel.[4]

Dr. Fant continued in this location until 1886 when he sold his business to Cofield and Lyons. A short time later, on October 8, 1886, he died at the age of fifty-nine. His sketch appears in Chapter 22.

In 1875 Dr. William Ellerbe Pelham of Columbia moved to Newberry to enter the drug business. Born in Columbia on June 19, 1854, he was the son of Charles P. and Jeanne Dunlap Pelham. After graduating from the South Carolina College in 1871 and getting a degree in pharmacy from that institution in 1872, he settled in Newberry. He was married to Brantley Caroline Leavell, daughter of Colonel John R. Leavell. He remained in the drugstore until 1914 when he became an insurance agent. Dr. Pelham died on December 14, 1922. He was the father of Mrs. T. K. Johnstone, Charles P. Pelham, and Dr. William E. Pelham, Jr.[6]

Four other drugstores appeared in the town during the 1870s and 1880s. In 1873 Dr. Oliver J. Harris and Dr. Frank Green opened a store. A short time later they sold their business to Dr. Fant.[7]

In 1877 Dr. D. Strother Pope and Captain J. C. Wardlaw opened a new store. The business did not succeed, and in 1879 Dr. Pope moved to Columbia where he practiced for a half-century. In 1879 Dr. Theodore Johnstone, later a successful dentist but then a pharmacist, and R. C. Maybin formed a partnership. This business was sold to Dr. L. A. East in 1882. In 1889 the drugstore of Belcher, Houseal, and Kibler was opened. It too lasted only a short time.[8]

In February 1889, Cofield and Lyons, who had bought out Dr. Fant a few years before, sold their stock to Dr. Peter Robertson and Dr. J. K. Gilder. The firm of Robertson and Gilder moved into the corner quarters under the Newberry Hotel and conducted a successful business until Robertson's death in 1900. Dr. C. D. Weeks, who had come to Newberry to work for Dr. Pelham, joined Dr. Gilder, who was thus enabled to give his full attention to his medical practice. In 1901 the firm became Gilder and Weeks. Three years later Dr. Frank R. Hunter joined the enterprise, which became known as Gilder, Weeks, and Hunter. In 1906, however, Hunter entered the real estate business,[9] and the firm of Gilder and Weeks continued as the leading drug firm in the town until the death of Dr. Weeks in 1943. Dr. James N. Burgess purchased the store and operated it at the same location until his death in 1958.

Dr. Peter Robertson was a native of Charleston, having been born there in July 1846. He served in Hart's Battery, Hampton's Legion, during the war. He came to Newberry about 1875 and married Alice L. Hunter of Newberry in 1877. At the time of his death on January 25, 1900, he was a member of the State Board of Pharmaceutical Examiners.

Dr. Clarence Douglas Weeks died on November 6, 1943; his sketch appears in Chapter 11. One of the pharmacists who worked for Dr. Weeks for many years was Dr. Virgil M. Kizer.

Another drugstore that operated about 1900 was Reeder's Pharmacy. Dr. E. E. Platt was pharmacist there before William G. Mayes purchased the store in 1901. Mayes' Drugstore continued on the corner of Main and Nance streets. Dr. Robert L. Mayes, brother of W. G. Mayes and a licensed pharmacist, was in charge of the prescription department until he entered Jefferson Medical College in 1910. Dr. Powell E. Way of St. George, South Carolina, succeeded him as pharmacist. Mayes continued to operate the drugstore until January 1926, when he sold it to Dr. Thomas E. Rivers.[10]

W. G. Mayes, son of William G. and Nancy Jones Mayes, was born in Newberry. He was a member of the Newberry School Board for twenty years and a steward of Central Methodist Church. He married Mary Wright; they had no children and she died many years before Dr. Mayes died on March 22, 1937. At his death he was living in Statesboro, Georgia.[11]

Another druggist in Newberry just after 1900 was Dr. Van Smith. His sketch appears in Chapter 22.

When Dr. Pelham left the drugstore in 1914, he sold his stock to Dr. W. O. Miller. Miller was born near Peak on May 22, 1884, the son of William O. and Nora Miller. He began clerking for Dr. Pelham when still a boy. He attended Newberry College. His drugstore, the Newberry Drugstore, was located in the middle of the Main Street block between College and Caldwell streets. Dr. Miller married Sallie Bell Buford, daughter of Captain Munson M. Buford. The couple had no children, and she survived him when he died at the age of fifty in May 1934.[12]

Meanwhile, Dr. Powell E. Way had left his employment with Dr. Mayes and had opened his own store on the corner of Main and McKibben streets. He was very successful and in 1928 moved to Spartanburg to operate several drugstores. Later he returned to Newberry to live.

Dr. Way, son of George E. and Amanda Wannamaker Way, was born in St. George on June 3, 1884. He graduated in pharmacy from the Medical College of South Carolina in 1904. He came to Newberry in 1910. Dr. Way married Brooksie Dennis and upon his death on March 21, 1958, was survived by her and three children, George D. Way, Powell E. Way, Jr., and Sophie Way Long.[13]

In 1931 Dr. Irwin M. Satterwhite, who had been a pharmacist for ten years at Dr. Way's drugstore, purchased the Central Drugstore from

Dr. Maffett Haynie. Dr. Haynie, who had opened the store three years before, returned to Belton.

Dr. Satterwhite, son of Michael M. and Lila Matthews Satterwhite, was born in Newberry on June 4, 1896. He graduated from Newberry College in 1916 and from the Medical College of South Carolina in pharmacy in 1920. He served in the U.S. Navy in World War I. In 1952 Dr. Satterwhite was elected president of the South Carolina Pharmaceutical Association. He was a Mason, a Shriner, and a Lutheran. He married Marion Earhardt; they had one child, Irwin M. Satterwhite, Jr., who was in partnership with his father. He died on July 19, 1976.

Dr. John Erwin Renwick was born October 30, 1876, in Newberry County, the son of Marcellus Adolphus Renwick, M.D., and Mary Eliza Erwin of Hendersonville, North Carolina. For the last fourteen years of his life he was a pharmacist with the Central Drug Store in Newberry.

He received his early education in a private school, attended Erskine College, and completed pharmacy training in Atlanta. For a number of years he was secretary, treasurer, and pharmacist of the Palmetto Drug Company in Union. When his father's health failed, he sold his business and returned to Newberry County to help with his father's farm.

He was married on September 29, 1920, to Frances Mills Caldwell of Winnsboro, who died on February 16, 1930. They were the parents of three children: Frances Elizabeth, who married Ralph Parr Baker, M.D. of Newberry; Mary Catherine, who is now Mrs. Dayton Everett Hardwick, Jr., of Manlius, New York; and a son who died in infancy. Dr. Renwick was a lifelong member of the Kings Creek Associate Reformed Presbyterian Church and served as a Deacon. He was a Mason and a Shriner, belonging to the Oasis Temple, Charlotte, North Carolina. He died March 18, 1944, and is buried in the Kings Creek Cemetery in Newberry County.[14]

Dr. I. M. Satterwhite, Jr., was born in Newberry on March 1, 1922. He was graduated from Newberry College in 1943 and served in World War II. After the war, he studied at the University of South Carolina, receiving his degree of B.S. in Pharmacy in 1951. He married Ida Huiett of Columbia; they have two children, Derryll and Suzanne Satterwhite. He closed the drugstore a short time after his father's death in 1976.

Dr. J. E. Stokes purchased Way's Drugstore in 1933. Dr. Stokes had been a pharmacist for some years at the Newberry Drugstore. Dr. Stokes continued in business at the corner of Main and McKibben streets until he sold his store to Dr. Jesse Dickert. Dr. Stokes married Nellie Waites; they moved to Atlanta.

In 1939 Callie Boyd Parr sold Dr. Jesse Dickert and Dick Mims his interest in the Newberry Drug Company which the three partners had purchased from the estate of Dr. W. O. Miller. In the same year the new Cut-rate Drugstore was opened by Dr. Z. R. Knotts, Jr., and Dr. J. W. Hogue.[15]

Dr. James N. Burgess was born in Williamsburg County, the son of George H. and Ada Epps Burgess. He attended The Citadel but volunteered for the Army in World War I and left college to serve. After the war, he became a registered pharmacist and, following the death of Dr. Weeks in 1944, he moved to Newberry where he operated Gilder and Weeks Drugstore. He died at the age of sixty on September 23, 1958, survived by his widow, the former Albatiene Stalvey. Dr. Burgess was a member of the Lions Club, the American Legion, the South Carolina Pharmaceutical Association, and Aveleigh Presbyterian Church.[16] One of his pharmacists was Dr. Fred Kempson, native of Newberry County.

After the death of Dr. Burgess, Gilder & Weeks Drug Store was purchased by Dr. Joseph E. Hunter, Jr., and Dr. John G. Jackson of Columbia. Dr. P. A. Fulmer of Greer was employed as pharmacist. Later Dr. Hunter closed the Gilder and Weeks store, which had been on the corner of Main and Caldwell streets for almost a century. He then purchased the Smith's Cut-rate store and operated it until he sold that store to Drs. Ringer and Bussey and returned to the University of South Carolina where he was professor of pharmacology.

In 1933 J. Richard Lominick opened a new store under the name of Lominick's Drugstore. Born in Newberry County on July 23, 1906, he was the son of W. Pettus and Vinnie Ruff Lominick. He graduated from Newberry College in 1928, and from the University of South Carolina in pharmacy in 1931. He married Mary Martha Hickson, and they have four children, Dr. James Richard Lominick, Jr., Martha L. Rucker, Sara Bee Looney, and Cindy L. Snell.

Dr. Lominick's brother-in-law, James P. Hickson, was his partner until he died on August 1, 1965. Hickson was a native of Lynchburg, and the son of Henry Alexander and Annie Powers Hickson. He married Florence McGill Crump and was survived by her, his step-daughter, Priscilla Crump, and two sons, James P. Hickson, Jr., and Clifford Alexander Hickson.

Dr. J. Richard Lominick, Jr., was born in Newberry on August 24, 1939. He attended Newberry College for one year and then transferred to the University of South Carolina. He graduated from the latter in

1961 with a degree in pharmacy. Dr. Lominick is married to Glenda Wise, and they are the parents of two children, Lynn and J. Richard Lominick, III.

Dr. Jesse L. Dickert, son of Jacob L. and Effie Counts Dickert, was born in Newberry on July 19, 1909. He attended Newberry College. Licensed as a pharmacist in 1930, he and Dick Mims operated the Newberry Drug Company for several years. Later Dr. Dickert purchased the Stokes Drug Company on the corner of Main and McKibben streets and operated the Newberry Drug Company there for a number of years. He then practiced pharmacy in Whitmire until his retirement in 1973.

Dr. Thomas Blair Boozer, Jr., returned to Newberry and was in charge of Revco Drug Store until his retirement.

Dr. Malcolm L. Ringer, son of the late John W. Ringer, Sr., and Ada D. Ringer, was born in Newberry on July 3, 1930. After attending Newberry College for a year, he transferred to the University of South Carolina from which he graduated in 1952. He was one of the owners of the Main Street Pharmacy until the business was closed. Married to Joyce Mays, he is the father of two children, Kevin Lee Ringer and Robin Ringer Wicker.

Dr. Tony Calvin Chapman, son of the late Ben C. Chapman and Mable Hawkins Chapman, was born in Newberry on July 14, 1935. He graduated in pharmacy from the University of South Carolina in 1963. Locating in Newberry, he now owns Newberry Drug Company, Inc. Married to Margaret Wallace, he is the father of two children, Rebecca Jill and Tony Calvin Chapman II.

Dr. D. Charles Bussey, son of Leo R. Bussey, Sr., and Iris J. Bussey, was born in Edgefield County on March 21, 1939. He attended Clemson University and graduated from the University of South Carolina in 1961. He was one of the owners of the Main Street Pharmacy until he became pharmacist at the Newberry County Memorial Hospital. He married Marie Martin, and they have two children, Carol Renee and Keith Martin Bussey.

At the present time the only locally owned drugstores are Lominick's, Newberry Drug, and Lo-Rex. The chain drugstores are Eckerd's, Revco, and The Medicine Shoppe.

Dr. Ronnie Cromer owns and operates Lo-Rex. A native of the county, he was born on December 1, 1947, the son of William R. and Mabel Shealy Cromer. Educated at the University of South Carolina, he received his degree in pharmacy in 1973. He is married to the former

Linda Epting and is the father of two children, Candace and Heather. For six years after his graduation he was pharmacist at Prosperity Drug Company and then established his own store in Newberry.

Another native Newberrian, Robert Burnett Lominack, formerly was pharmacist at Eckerd's and consulting pharmacist for the J. F. Hawkins Nursing Home. Son of Dr. Reyburn W. and Irma Elizabeth Weiters Lominack, he was born on September 6, 1949, and educated at Riverside Military Academy, Newberry College, and the University of South Carolina, where he received his B.S. in pharmacy in 1979. After serving in Vietnam with the U.S. Navy, he maintains his service in the Naval Reserve. Married to the former Cynthia Diane Sease, he is the father of William Burnett and Jeannie Anne Lominack. They are members of the Lutheran Church of the Redeemer, where he is a member of the Church Council.

William Luther Brice, son of Luther Leonard and Vernara Gossett Brice, was born in Newberry on March 4, 1945. He received his B.S. in pharmacy from the University of South Carolina in 1968. He was pharmacist for Scottie's Drug Store in Newberry until the local prescription department was discontinued. After being transferred to Walterboro in 1973, he accepted employment with the state of South Carolina. He married Mary Kay Shannon, and they have two children, William Luther Brice, Jr., and Scott Workman Brice.

Many other pharmacists have worked in Newberry but have not owned their own stores, including Dr. James M. Hodgson, Dr. Joseph S. Murray, Dr. Ann Merchant Vassey, and Dr. James A. Ward, Jr.

The Druggists of Prosperity

Dr. Cyril Keister Wheeler, Jr., was born in Prosperity on October 21, 1916. After graduating from Newberry College, B.A. 1937, he entered the University of South Carolina and graduated in 1940 with a B.S. in pharmacy. Later he obtained his M.S. in pharmaceutical chemistry from the University of North Carolina in 1942. He served as a lieutenant in the U.S. Navy, 1942–1946, and returned to Prosperity where he was first his father's partner in operating the Prosperity Drug Company and then, upon his father's retirement, sole proprietor of the store until his own retirement in 1978.

Member of Phi Beta Kappa and Rho Chi fraternities, the LeConte Scientific Society, and president of the Carolina Pharmaceutical Society, he is active in Grace Lutheran Church, having served as chairman of the Church Council and of the congregation. Since his retirement, he has served as president of the Prosperity Cemetery Association. He sold the store in 1978 to Arlen W. Stuck.

Dr. Stuck, son of Christopher Ansel and Reba Wessinger Stuck, was born in the county on April 8, 1941. He graduated in pharmacy from the University of South Carolina in 1963. A Mason and Shriner, Dr. Stuck is a charter member and past president of the Mid-Carolina Country Club, a member of the state and 5th District pharmaceutical associations, and a member of St. John's Evangelical Lutheran Church. Married to the former Cynthia Lindler, he has two children, Melissa Faye and Kelly Lynn.

The Druggists of Peak

The Peak Pharmacy is owned and operated by Dr. Hammie Joe Smith. Born in Jasper County on January 29, 1928, he graduated from the University of South Carolina in 1949 with the degree of B.S. in pharmacy. He has been active in the civic and business life of Newberry County, serving as magistrate at Peak since 1967, president of the Newberry County Development Board, president of the Mid-Carolina Country Club, a member of the advisory board of Southern Bank and Trust Company, and a member of the Regional Advisory Board of First Federal of South Carolina. He is married to Imogene Counts. They have two daughters, Donna Jean S. Fulmer and Mary Jo Smith, who has graduated in pharmacy from the University of South Carolina and has joined her father as a pharmacist.

The Druggists of Whitmire[17]

The first drugstore established in Whitmire was owned by Dr. Joseph H. Hamilton and operated by Dr. Robert R. Jeter in the 1890s. In 1913 Dr. Van Smith moved to Whitmire from Newberry to practice medicine; he also opened a drugstore and operated it until he moved to Beaufort in 1920.

Another early drugstore was owned by Dr. P. B. Hilton, a dentist. Dr. Hilton moved to Rock Hill before World War I and sold his business to Dr. R. M. Duckett, Dr. J. W. Gary, J. D. Tidmarsh, and E. E. Child. The two latter purchasers soon sold their interests to Duckett and Gary.

Dr. Robert Maxwell Duckett, son of William L. and Ann Ray Duckett, was born in Newberry County in 1882. He was a pharmacist for more than half a century and, at the time of his death, was operating the Whitmire Drug Store. He served as president of the South Carolina Pharmaceutical Association, an elder in the Whitmire Presbyterian Church, and mayor *pro tem* of Whitmire for several terms. He died at the age of seventy-nine on January 23, 1961. He was survived by his widow, the former Mary Wright, by one son, R. M. Duckett, Jr., and by three daughters, Ann Duckett, Mrs. Al McCourry, and Mrs. Mary Duckett Hunter.

His partner, Dr. J. W. Gary, preceded him to the grave by only a month. Son of Samuel L. and Pelleree Mason Gary, he was born in Laurens County. A veteran of World War I, an elder in Whitmire Presbyterian Church, and a former mayor of Whitmire, he married Drucie Smith of Kinards. She died in 1958, and Dr. Gary died, aged sixty-nine, on December 22, 1960. He was survived by an only child, Mrs. Byrd Martin.

After the partners died, Thomas Malone bought the Whitmire Drug Company. Dr. Jesse Dickert of Newberry was the pharmacist for some years before his retirement. He was followed by Dr. Stephen P. Lovelace, a native of Spartanburg, who was born on November 27, 1940, and was educated at Spartanburg Junior College and the University of South Carolina. After receiving his degree in pharmacy, Dr. Lovelace moved to Whitmire in 1971 but, within a few years, the Whitmire Drug Company was closed, and he left the county.

In the 1920s Dr. Olin Busbee, a native of Springfield, operated a drugstore in Whitmire. In the 1930s a Dr. McDonald had the Economy Drug Store. For a time in the 1950s Dr. James N. Burgess had a branch of Gilder and Weeks Drug Company of Newberry in Whitmire. The venture was short lived.

The only drugstore now in Whitmire is Roche's Pharmacy. Owned by Dr. John F. Roche, a native of Abbeville and a graduate of the University of South Carolina in pharmacy in 1949, the store was established in 1949. Dr. Roche has been active in the affairs of Newberry County and currently serves as a member of the Newberry County Board of Education, of which he was chairman for many years. He is married to the former Louise Day. They have six children, Angela, Jennie, Judy, John F., Jr., Beth, and Susan.

Appendix A

Officeholders of Newberry District, 1861–1868

Senators

1860–1864	A. C. Garlington
1864–65	Robert Moorman
1865–67	James H. Williams

Members, House of Representatives

1860–62	James Nathan Lipscomb
	Christian Henry Suber
	James H. Williams
1862–64	Robert Stewart
	Christian Henry Suber
	James H. Williams
1865–66	Albert Creswell Garlington
	Ellison Summerfield Keitt
	Christian Henry Suber

Clerks of Court

| 1851–66 | Burr J. Ramage |
| 1866–68 | Elijah P. Lake |

Commissioners of Free Schools

1861   E. P. Lake, Jackson Teague, John M. Calmes, John Hair,

Sheriffs

1859–63	Nathan F. Johnston
1863–	James M. Maffett
	(died before qualifying)
1863–67	William W. Houseal
1867–72	Thomas M. Paysinger

Ordinary

| 1851–63 | E. P. Lake |
| 1863–68 | John T. Peterson |

Commissioners in Equity

| 1856–68 | Silas Johnstone |

Tax Collector

| 1860–64 | John R. Leavell |
| 1864–68 | J. B. Fellers |

Coroner

| 1861–64 | John Coate |
| 1865–68 | H. H. Kinard |

Colonel G. S. Cannon, Jacob H. Suber, Benson Counts, Jacob Singley, and William E. Hardy.

1865   E. P. Lake, Thomas Lipscomb, George S. Cannon, John M. Calmes, Reuben Lyles, Thomas Y. Wicker, Allen Hawkins, F. H. Dominick, and John Crooks.

1867   E. P. Lake, Thomas Lipscomb, George S. Cannon, John M. Calmes, Reuben Lyles, Thomas Y. Wicker, Allen Hawkins, F. H. Dominick, and John Crooks.

Commissioners of Public Buildings

1861   Silas Johnstone, James Maffett, L. J. Jones, H. H. Kinard, Dr. William H. Harrington, Wallace A. Cline, and John R. Leavell.

1863   Silas Johnstone, James Maffett, L. J. Jones, Nathan A. Hunter, Dr. William H. Harrington, Wallace A. Cline, and John R. Leavell.

1865   L. J. Jones, Nathan A. Hunter, Wallace A. Cline, John R. Leavell, Mathias Barre, James Gauntt, and James M. Baxter.

1866   Captain R. H. Wright, *vice* L. J. Jones, resigned.

1867   R. H. Wright, N. A. Hunter, W. A. Cline, John R. Leavell, Mathias Barre, James Gauntt, and James M. Baxter.

Soldier's Board of Relief

1861   Dr. Peter Moon, Robert Stewart, B. J. Ramage, Robert Moorman, George Gallman, George Wise, Daniel Goggans, Andrew J. Longshore, George S. Cannon, and Joseph Caldwell.

1862   Dr. Peter Moon, Robert Stewart, B. J. Ramage, Robert Moorman, George Wise, Daniel Goggans, Andrew J. Longshore, George S. Cannon, Joseph Caldwell, Matthew Hall, and James Maffett.

1863   Dr. Peter Moon, George S. Cannon, Joseph Caldwell, Robert Moorman, John F. Glymph, James Maffett, Matthew Hall, George Wise, Daniel Goggans, and Henry Burton.

1864   Robert Moorman, John F. Glymph, Thomas B. Rutherford, Thomas Ellisor, P. W. Counts, George Brown, Daniel Goggans, Henry Burton, George S. Cannon, Henry Whitmire, E. P. Lake, Dr. W. H. Harrington, and David C. Boazman.

Commissioners of Roads

1861   Jackson Teague, Pierce W. Harmon, Henry Whitmire, Michael Buzzard, John T. Peterson, George S. Cannon, Dr. T. B. Kennerly, O. W. Folk, and Thomas H. Crooks.

1863   Robert Moorman, William Satterwhite, Matthew Hall, Jacob

H. Hunt, Henry Burton, T. W. Caldwell, T. Henry Chappell, John L. Glasgow, and John A. Cannon.

1865   Matthew Hall, J. H. Suber, James Caldwell, John K. G. Nance, Jackson Teague, Thomas W. Holloway, A. J. Longshore, M. F. Workman, and J. F. Sims.

1866   Matthew Hall, J. Hardy Suber, James Caldwell, John K. G. Nance, Jackson Teague, Thomas W. Holloway, A. J. Longshore, M. F. Workman, and J. F. Sims.

1867   Matthew Hall, J. H. Suber, James Caldwell, John K. G. Nance, Jackson Teague, Thomas W. Holloway, A. J. Longshore, M. F. Workman, and J. F. Sims.

Commissioners to Approve Public Securities

1861   Dr. George W. Glenn, Robert Stewart, H. H. Kinard, John R. Leavell, and John B. Carwile.

1865   G. T. Scott, Peter Hair, John B. Carwile, Dr. George W. Glenn, and R. L. McCaughrin.

1866   E. S. Coppock, *vice* Dr. George W. Glenn, deceased.

1867   G. T. Scott, Peter Hair, John B. Carwile, E. S. Coppock, and R. L. McCaughrin.

Commissioners of the Poor

1867   W. W. Boozer, Thomas H. Cromer, Dr. J. W. McCants, J. B. Floyd, and John Coate.

Magistrates

Samuel Bowers	Isaac Herbert
George B. Cannon	John G. Houseal
John A. Cannon	H. H. Kinard
E. P. Chalmers	E. P. Lake
John A. Chapman	James N. Lipscomb
Samuel R. Chapman	L. B. Maffett
John Coate	P. R. Mangum
P. W. Counts	Charles W. Montgomery
James N. Crosson	Thomas S. Moorman
F. H. Dominick	John K. G. Nance
William M. Dorroh, M.D.	James E. Peterson
Eben Douglas	Y. J. Pope
Henry Halfacre	Luther Riser
William E. Hardy	John F. Spearman
Thomas F. Harmon	Josiah Stewart
J. B. Heller	Wiliam Summer
Chesley W. Herbert	Joseph M. Ward

Appendix B

Officeholders of Newberry County, 1868–1990

Senators

1868–72	Charles W. Montgomery (president pro tempore)
1872–77	Henry C. Corwin (resigned prior to 1877 session)
1877–80	James N. Lipscomb
1880–84	Thomas C. Brown
1884–88	Jefferson A. Sligh
1888–90	Young John Pope (resigned to become candidate for attorney general)
1890–92	Joseph L. Keitt
1892	Jefferson A. Sligh (resigned to become railroad commissioner)
1893–1904	George S. Mower
1904–08	Cole L. Blease (president pro tempore, 1907–08)
1908–28	Alan Johnstone (president pro tempore, 1920–28)
1928–32	Tabor Hill
1932–36	Byron V. Chapman
1936–56	Marvin E. Abrams
1956–60	Russell Aubrey Harley
1960–66	Jesse Frank Hawkins
1967–68	Eugene C. Griffith
1969–84	Robert C. Lake, Jr.
1984–	Thomas H. Pope, III

Members, House of Representatives

1868–70	Joseph D. Boston, James A. Henderson, James Hutson
1870–72	Joseph D. Boston, Henry C. Corwin, John T. Henderson

388

1872-74	Joseph D. Boston, Sampson S. Bridges, Isom Greenwood
1874-76	Joseph D. Boston, Sampson S. Bridges, James A. Henderson
1876-78	Sampson S. Bridges, Thomas Keitt (December 1, 1877—expelled for bigamy), William H. Thomas (May 1, 1877–denied seat in House), Young John Pope, *vice* Keitt, George Johnstone, *vice* Thomas.
1878-80	William M. Dorroh, M.D., George Johnstone, Christian Henry Suber.
1880-82	George Johnstone, Jefferson A. Sligh, John C. Wilson.
1882-84	William D. Hardy, George Johnstone, Jefferson Allen Sligh.
1884-86	William D. Hardy, Sampson Pope, M.D., Osborne Lamar Schumpert.
1886-88	E. P. Chalmers, Joseph Lawrence Keitt, Sampson Pope, M.D.
1888-90	Robert Thompson Carmichael Hunter, John Malcolm Johnstone, George Sewell Mower.
1890-92	Coleman Livingston Blease, William D. Hardy, John W. Scott.
1892-94	Coleman Livingston Blease, John Thomas Duncan, William D. Hardy.
1894-96	John Thomas Duncan, William D. Hardy, Cyril Thomas Wyche, M.D.
1896-98	John Felder Banks, Arthur Kibler, Cyril Thomas Wyche, M.D.
1898-1900	Coleman Livingston Blease, Herbert Henry Evans, Cyril Thomas Wyche, M.D.
1900-02	John Felder Banks, Frederick Haskell Dominick, Arthur Kibler.
1902-04	Elbert Herman Aull, John Felder Banks, Arthur Kibler.
1904-06	John Wolfe Earhardt, Francis W. Higgins, John M. Taylor.
1906-08	Elbert Herman Aull, Alan Johnstone, Arthur Kibler.
1908-10	Godfrey Harmon, Arthur Kibler, Cyril Thomas Wyche, M.D.
1910-12	Arthur Kibler, George Sewell Mower, Cyril Thomas Wyche, M.D.
1912-14	Arthur Kibler, George Sewell Mower, Cyril Thomas Wyche, M.D.
1914-16	Byron Vivian Chapman, George Sewell Mower, Neal Wells Workman.
1916-18	William Bowman Boinest, Thomas Andrew Dominick, Herbert Henry Evans.
1918-20	Herbert Henry Evans, John William Folk, M.D., George Sewell Mower.
1920-22	William Arthur Counts, Euston Nathalie Kibler, George Sewell Mower (died July 25, 1921), Eugene Satterwhite Blease, *vice* Mower.
1922-24	Eugene Satterwhite Blease, Euston Nathalie Kibler, William Rogers Watson.

1924-26	Alexander Pope Coleman, John Jacob Dominick, M.D., Isaac Hamilton Hunt.
1926-28	David Luther Boozer, Andrew Jackson Bowers, Jr., Euston Nathalie Kibler.
1928-30	William Bowman Boinest, Arthur Kibler, Zacheous Hatton Suber.
1930-32	Arthur Kibler (died February 3, 1931), Euston Nathalie Kibler, Zacheous Hatton Suber, Andrew Jackson Bowers, Jr., vice Kibler.
1932-34	Marvin Eugene Abrams, John Jacob Dominick, M.D., James Philander Setzler.
1934-36	Marvin Eugene Abrams, John Kess Derrick, Zacheous Hatton Suber.
1936-38	John Jacob Dominick, M.D., Thomas Harrington Pope, Jr., J. Claud Senn.
1938-40	John Kess Derrick, Russell Aubrey Harley, Thomas Harrington Pope, Jr.
1940-42	John Kess Derrick, Russell Aubrey Harley, Julian Arthur Price.
1942-44	John Kess Derrick (died September 24, 1943), Russell Aubrey Harley, Steve Campbell Griffith, vice Derrick.
1944-46	Steve Campbell Griffith (elected judge on April 11, 1945), Russell Aubrey Harley, Thomas Harrington Pope, Jr., vice Griffith.
1946-48	Russell Aubrey Harley, Thomas Harrington Pope
1948-50	Walter Thomas Lake, Thomas Harrington Pope (elected speaker on February 15, 1949).
1950-52	Frank Elliott Jordan, Jr. (resigned on June 4, 1951), Walter Thomas Lake, Robert Daniel Coleman, vice Jordan.
1952-54	Earl Howell Bergen, John Summer Huggins.
1954-56	Earl Howell Bergen, T. William Hunter.
1956-58	Jesse Frank Hawkins, T. William Hunter.
1958-60	Jesse Frank Hawkins, T. William Hunter.
1960-62	Daniel Paul Folk, II, Steve Campbell Griffith, Jr.
1962-64	Daniel Paul Folk, II
1964-66	Daniel Paul Folk, II
1966-68	Daniel Paul Folk, II
1968-70	Walter Thomas Lake
1970-72	Walter Thomas Lake
1972-74	Walter Thomas Lake
1974-76	Richard Maxwell Kenan
1976-80	John M. Rucker
1980-	David C. Waldrop, Jr.

Sheriffs

1867–72	Thomas M. Paysinger (removed from office)
1872	William Summer (coroner, acting sheriff)
1872–77	John J. Carrington (ousted by court order)
1877–85	D. B. Wheeler
1885–97	W. W. Riser
1897–1913	Munson M. Buford
1913–37	Cannon G. Blease
1937–45	Tom M. Fellers
1945–49	Ben F. Dawkins
1949–68	Tom M. Fellers
1968–73	B. Eugene Shealy (died in office)
1973–76	L. L. Henderson
1976–80	Raymond H. Roton
1980–88	L. L. Henderson
1988–	James Lee Foster

Clerks of Court

1868–72	Thomas M. Lake
1872–75	Jesse C. Smith
1875–77	H. Claremont Moses (appointed *vice* Smith, named county treasurer)
1876	T. J. Clayton (failed to qualify)
1877–84	E. P. Chalmers
1884–87	J. Y. McFall (died in office)
1887–96	John M. Kinard
1896–1900	Albert J. Gibson
1900–20	John C. Goggans
1920–24	James D. Wheeler
1924–52	Hugh King Boyd
1952	Gurdon Wright Counts (nominated but died before general election)
1952–57	Charles Bowers (resigned)
1957–66	Burke M. Wise (died in office)
1966–83	Mildred R. Harmon
1983–88	Ellouise S. Setzler
1989–	Jackie S. Bowers

Auditors

1868–72	Summerfield Montgomery (died in office)
1872	H. C. Corwin (resigned upon election to Senate)

1872–74	James W. Hayward (resigned)
1874–77	R. E. Williams (removed by Governor Hampton)
1877–80	Levi E. Folk (died in office)
1880	J. N. Lipscomb
1880–84	J. K. G. Nance
1884–89	W. W. Houseal (died in office)
1890–1902	Wallace C. Cromer (died in office)
1902–09	William W. Cromer
1909–15	Eugene S. Werts
1915–31	J. B. Halfacre
1931–33	Helen Halfacre (appointed to serve unexpired term)
1933–37	Herman M. Halfacre
1937–53	Pinckney N. Abrams (resigned)
1953–67	Ralph B. Black (died in office)
1967–84	Jeannette Koon Hamm
1984–	Nancy P. Owen

Treasurers

1869–72	Thomas P. Slider
1872–74	D. R. Phifer
1874	Edwin Blodgett (appointed by Governor Moses)
1874	D. R. Phifer (appointed by Governor Chamberlain, but not confirmed)
1874–77	Jesse C. Smith
1877–82	U. B. Whites (removed fron office)
1882	A. H. Wheeler (appointed for unexpired term of Whites)
1883–85	Martin H. Gary
1885–91	A. H. Wheeler
1891–1901	C. F. Boyd
1901–16	John L. Epps (died in office)
1916–28	C. C. Schumpert
1929–37	C. H. Cannon
1937–39	J. C. Brooks (died in office)
1939–41	Ralph B. Black (resigned to enter U.S. Army)
1941	Cornell Bedenbaugh (appointed to serve unexpired term; resigned to accept civil service appointment)
1941–72	J. Ray Dawkins (appointed to serve Black's unexpired term)
1973–	George W. Summer

Probate Judges

1868–70	John T. Peterson
1870–78	J. C. Leahy

1878–95	Jacob B. Fellers
1895–1903	W. W. Hodges
1903–07	John C. Wilson (died in office)
1907–12	F. M. Schumpert (resigned)
1912–16	C. C. Schumpert (resigned to offer for county treasurer)
1916–24	W. F. Ewart
1924–45	Neal W. Workman (died in office)
1945–47	Geneva T. D. Workman (appointed to serve husband's unexpired term)
1947–66	E. Maxcy Stone
1966–87	Frank H. Ward (died in office)
1987–	Margaret H. Schumpert

Masters

1878–95	Silas Johnstone
1895–1900	Thomas S. Sease
1900–20	H. H. Rikard
1920–23	J. D. Quattlebaun (office abolished)

Tax Assessors

1965–69	Walton B. Halfacre
1969–73	B. Monroe Harmon
1973–	Jimmie B. Davenport

Veterans Service Officers

1927–67	Jake R. Wise
1967–77	Gerald C. O'Quinn
1977–	Allen W. Morrison

Coroners

1868–69	H. H. Kinard (died in office on June 17, 1869)
1869–70	William Summer
1870–71	Munson S. Long (removed from office)
1871–72	William Summer (appointed to fill vacancy)
1872–74	James A. Henderson (resigned)
1874–78	James W. Eichelberger
1878–84	Euclydus C. Longshore
1884–88	John N. Bass
1888–92	Charles B. Buist (died in office)
1892	John W. Reagin, vice Buist
1892–08	Francis Marion Lindsay

1908–12	W. E. Felker
1912–24	Francis M. Lindsay (died in office)
1924	E. M. Evans, *vice* Lindsay
1924–43	Ira H. Wilson (died in office)
1943	Leroy Wilson, *vice* Wilson
1944–48	Leroy Wilson
1948–76	George R. Summer
1976–81	Leroy Wilson
1981–88	R. Coleman Bishop (died in office)
1988–	James O. Smith

School Commissioners
(later county superintendents of education)

1868–70	William Summer
1870–72	Jesse C. Smith
1872–74	Munson S. Long
1874–76	H. B. Scott
1876–78	Munson S. Long (removed from office)
1878	J. C. Boyd (appointed to serve unexpired term)
1878–82	Henry S. Boozer
1882–84	J. C. Boyd
1884–88	G. G. Sale
1888–92	Arthur Kibler
1892–94	Thomas W. Keitt
1894–1900	F. W. Higgins
1900–04	Eugene S. Werts
1904–12	J. S. Wheeler (resigned)
1912–13	Elbert H. Aull
1913–15	George D. Barre (appointed to serve unexpired term)
1916–20	Clemson Wilson
1920–24	Elbert H. Aull
1924–28	D. L. Wedaman
1928–36	George K. Dominick
1936	Mrs. Mae Aull
1936–47	C. E. Hendrix
1947–69	James D. Brown (resigned June 1969)

Supervisors

1894–96	W. A. Hill
1896–98	John M. Schumpert
1898–1900	W. A. Hill
1900–02	John M. Schumpert

1902–04	John M. Schumpert
1904–06	J. Monroe Wicker
1906–08	J. Monroe Wicker
1908–10	L. D. Feagle
1910–12	L. D. Feagle
1912–14	W. A. Hill
1914–16	James C. Sample
1916–18	James C. Sample
1918–20	James C. Sample
	(office abolished in 1920; reinstituted in 1930)
1930–32	Holland H. Ruff
1932–36	Holland H. Ruff
1936–40	Holland H. Ruff
1940–44	Eugene H. Spearman
1944–48	Eugene H. Spearman
1948–52	S. W. Shealy
1952–56	S. W. Shealy
1956–60	S. W. Shealy
1960–64	Harold B. Hendrix
1964–68	Harold B. Hendrix
1968–71	Harold B. Hendrix

Commissioners

1868–70	George Brown (resigned December 1869), T. M. Jenkins, Samuel Dogan, Matthew Gray (appointed to serve Brown's unexpired term).
1870	Simeon Young, David Hailstook, Andrew Gregory (all were convicted of misconduct in office).
1871	D. R. Phifer (resigned in April 1872 to become county treasurer), Dennis Moates, W. P. Harris, Simeon Young, (appointed to serve Phifer's unexpired term).
1872–74	Dennis Moates, Allen Rice, Thomas Keitt.
1874–76	Henry Kennedy, Wesley R. Brown, Simeon Young.
1876–78	Henry Kennedy, Wesley R. Brown, Simeon Young.
1877	L. Bates Maffett (appointed by Governor Hampton, *vice* Brown, removed).
1878–80	William Lester, Andrew J. Livingston, J. C. Swittenberg.
1880–82	J. C. S. Brown, A. J. Kilgore, William Lester.
1882–84	A. J. Livingston, J. Drayton Smith, Jacob Epting.
1884–86	Euclydus C. Longshore, A. J. Livingston, J. A. Cromer.
1886–88	P. B. Workman, J. J. Kinard, S. B. Aull.
1888–90	J. C. Perry, Jenkins H. Smith, Silas Walker.

1890–92   Jenkins H. Smith, J. J. Kinard, J. W. Smith.
1892–94   George B. Aull, J. C. Dominick, Irby D. Schockley.

The office of supervisor was created by Act 320, *Statutes at Large*, XXI, 481. The Board of Commissioners was abolished, and the Chairmen of Township Boards of Commission served with the supervisor as a newly created board. The old Board of Commissioners was recreated in 1899.

1900–02   J. Y. Floyd, Benjamin Halfacre
1902–04   Benjamin Halfacre, G. Sam Moore
1904–06   J. P. Cannon, Osborne Wells
1906–08   W. H. Wendt, Thomas J. Wilson
1908–10   Custis L. Leitzsey, L. C. Livingstone
1910–12   Custis L. Leitzsey, L. C. Livingstone
1912–14   J. W. Epting, L. C. Livingstone
1914–16   J. W. Epting, L. C. Livingstone
1916–18   S. J. Cromer, L. C. Livingstone
1918–20   S. J. Cromer, L. C. Livingstone
               (office abolished in 1920; reinstituted in 1930)
1930–32   Thomas P. Adams, C. B. Schumpert
1932–34   John R. Spearman, C. B. Schumpert
1934–36   John R. Spearman, C. B. Schumpert
1936–38   Paul H. Haile, C. B. Schumpert
1938–40   Paul H. Haile, S. W. Shealy
1940–42   Wilbur E. Epps, C. C. Lominick
1942–44   Wilbur E. Epps, C. B. Schumpert
1944–46   Wilbur E. Epps, C. B. Schumpert
1946–48   Wilbur E. Epps, C. B. Schumpert.
1948–50   J. Frank Lominack (Mrs. Irene R. Lominack, *vice* husband), C.
               B. Schumpert (Mrs. C. B. Schumpert, *vice* husband).
1950–52   J. Frank Lominack, Jr., G. T. Werts.
1952–54   T. C. McDowell, G. T. Werts.
1954–56   T. C. McDowell, G. T. Werts.
1956–58   Carman Bouknight, G. T. Werts.
1958–60   Carman Bouknight, Ross George.
1960–62   Carman Bouknight, Ross George.
1962–64   Carman Bouknight, S. Virgil Williamson.
1964–66   Ben F. Dawkins, Ross George.
1966–68   Ben F. Dawkins, Ross George.
1968–70   Ben F. Dawkins, Curtis E. Shealy

County Council

1971–72	Ben F. Dawkins, Curtis E. Shealy, C. E. Hendrix, chairman, Carman Bouknight, John Schumpert (died in office, April 5, 1972).
1973–74	Curtis E. Shealy, C. E. Hendrix, vice chairman, Carman Bouknight, chairman, David C. Waldrop, Jr., L. Bruce Wessinger.
1975–76	Charles L. Lake, Curtis E. Shealy, vice chairman, David C. Waldrop, Jr., chairman, L. Bruce Wessinger, James L. Braswell.
1977–78	David L. Wedaman, George R. Summer, Charles L. Lake, James L. Braswell, John E. Seibert, Arthur C. Sparks, chairman, Cecil E. Kinard, vice chairman, L. Bruce Wessinger (died March 22, 1978).
1979–80	Charles L. Lake, George R. Summer, Thomas P. Buzhardt, J. Milton Pitts, John E. Seibert, Arthur C. Sparks, chairman, D. L. Wedaman, vice chairman.
1981–83	Arthur C. Sparks, W. Durrett Lipscomb, J. Milton Pitts, D. L. Wedaman, J. E. Seibert, Thomas P. Buzhardt, chairman, D. Wyman Cook, vice chairman.
1983–85	D. Wyman Cook, J. Milton Pitts, Arthur C. Sparks, chairman, David L. Wedaman, John E. Seibert, W. Durrett Lipscomb, John E. Caldwell.
1985–87	D. Wyman Cook, chairman, J. Milton Pitts, David L. Wedaman, John E. Seibert, John E. Caldwell, Henry B. Summer, Robert Duckett, III.
1987–89	D. Wyman Cook, chairman, David L. Wedaman, vice chairman, John E. Caldwell, Robert M. Duckett, III, John E. Seibert, Henry B. Summer, William D. (Bill) Waldrop.
1989–	D. Wyman Cook, chairman, David L. Wedaman, vice chairmen, John E. Caldwell, Claude L. Dominick, Darrell W. Gilliam, Sr., Henry B. Summer, William D. Waldrop.

County Managers

1971– Nov. 1973	W. W. Hursey
1974–1975	James C. Cleckler
1976–1978	James D. Burwell
1979–	Edward F. Lominack, Jr.

Game Wardens

1930–32	John P. Livingston

1932–34   Frazier Evans
1934–68   G. Herman Wise (Game wardens were nominated in the Primary by Act No. 81 of the Acts of 1929 until 1952; thereafter, the County game wardens were appointed. Mr. Wise was South Carolina Game Warden of the Year in 1966.)

Magistrates, 1869–1870

J. McM. Calmes
Charles C. Chase
Samuel Dogan
G. M. Girardeau
J. B. Heller
John T. Henderson
H. H. Kinard

J. P. Kinard
M. S. Long
L. B. Maffett
James E. Peterson
A. M. Riser
Jesse C. Smith
William Summer

Trial Justices, 1870–1877

Frank C. Aldridge
R. W. Boone
C. C. Chase
Samuel Dogan
Samuel Furman
A. R. Gantt
Matthew Gray
J. B. Heller
John T. Henderson
G. P. Jacoby
James F. Kilgore
Munson S. Long
Jones Lowman
L. B. Maffett

Dennis Moates
John T. Peterson
D. R. Phifer
John D. Pitts
Adam W. Riser
J. F. Sims
T. P. Slider
Jesse C. Smith
William Summer
William H. Thomas
D. M. Ward
Frank H. Whitney
Simeon Young

Trial Justices, 1877–1895

Harry H. Blease
Henry H. Blease
H. S. Boozer
J. H. Boulware
Mordecai J. Boyd
M. M. Buford
John T. Bynun
J. B. Campbell
M. A. Carlisle
J. H. Crisp

S. S. Cunningham
Reuben S. Davidson
B. F. Day
Charles P. Dickert
John L. Epps
Levi W. Etheridge
H. H. Evans
John S. Fair
J. B. Fellers
S. L. Fellers

G. M. Girardeau
B. S. Golding
Nathan Gregory
B. B. Hair
J. B. Heller
George R. Hill
J. B. O'N. Holloway
Thomas W. Holloway
James H. Irby
James R. Irvin
J. W. D. Johnson
Joseph L. Keitt
James N. Lipscomb
Madison J. Longshore
B. H. Maybin
R. C. Maybin

James S. McCarley
A. H. Miller
James Packer
Warren G. Peterson
J. W. Reagin
Joseph S. Reid
John W. Riser
T. Levi Schumpert
G. Melvin Singley
William C. Sligh
W. F. Suber
W. W. Wallace
A. H. Wheeler
J. H. Williams
Patrick E. Wise

Magistrates, 1895–1989

P. N. Abrams
Joseph H. Adams
C. Hampton Alewine
W. P. Allen
R. M. Aughtrey
C. H. Aull
John B. Bedenbaugh
Cannon G. Blease
B. E. Bowers
J. L. Bowers, Jr.
M. R. Brooks
J. C. S. Brown
James Chesley Butler
Wilton O. Chastain
John H. Chappell
Emily Clements
Hix Connor
J. O. Counts
W. A. Counts
G. H. Cromer
W. M. Cromley
S. S. Cunningham
Braxton Bragg Davis
Ben F. Dawkins
J. Charles DeHihns

J. B. Derrick
Jodie K. Derrick
D. A. Dickert
A. Lamar Dominick
E. Haskell Dominick
H. L. Dominick
J. H. Dorroh
William M. Dorroh
Charles W. Douglas
Robert Duckett
P. B. Ellesor
J. W. Epting
Francis W. Fant
O. A. Felker
J. L. Fellers
John P. Foster
Darrell Gilliam
R. W. Glymph
W. R. Glymph
L. M. Graham
B. B. Hair
M. P. Harrington
W. D. Hatton
John Henderson
J. W. Hendrix

John J. Hentz
Ralph G. Higgins
A. J. Holt
J. R. Irwin
Arthur L. Jayroe, Sr.
J. W. D. Johnson
W. R. Keith
E. B. Kibler
J. J. Kibler
W. L. Kibler
J. A. Kinard
J. Alvin Kinard
J. T. Kinard
Barry Simpson Koon
Clarence Robert Koon
George O. Koon
John B. Lathan
A. G. Leitzsey
B. B. Leightzsey
Ronald Leonhardt
W. D. Lindler
Frank E. Maybin
Walton J. McLeod, III
S. A. Merchant
John F. Miller
A. C. Miller
A. C. Mills
R. A. Nelson
W. B. Oxner
C. B. Pitts
J. Milton Pitts
Madison Pitts
L. M. Player
W. G. Puckett
Leroy C. Pugh
William R. Reid
T. B. Richardson
J. F. Riser

J. R. Riser
W. W. Riser
James G. Roof
John W. Ropp
H. H. Ruff
W. D. Rutherford
J. C. Sample
Richard S. Sanders
William A. Schuler, Jr.
J. Henry Senn
Andrew Shealy
Eugene Shealy
Tallye Hugh Shealy
A. L. Shull
William C. Sligh
G. Fred Smith
Hammie Joe Smith
J. B. Smith
W. E. Spearman
B. P. Stewart
Roy D. Stutts
W. F. Suber
John G. Watts
E. H. Wertz
J. W. Wertz
J. E. Wessinger
Ernest A. Wheeler
J. M. Wheeler
W. B. Wicker
J. H. Williams
Claude Wilson
John C. Wilson
J. H. Wilson
J. W. Wilson
Burke M. Wise
J. Harold Wise
Z. B. Wright
J. Oscar Zobel

Appendix C

Newberry's Units in the Civil War

The Rhett Guards, Company B, First South Carolina Volunteers (Gregg's)
Field and Staff, Third South Carolina Volunteers
The Williams Guards, Company B, Third South Carolina Volunteers
The Pickens Guards, Company C, Third South Carolina Volunteers
The Quitman Rifles, Company E, Third South Carolina Volunteers
The Dutch Company, Company H, Third South Carolina Volunteers
The Newberry Rifles, Company D, Thirteenth South Carolina Volunteers
The DeKalb Guards, Company G, Thirteenth South Carolina Volunteers
Company H, Thirteenth South Carolina Volunteers
Company F, Twentieth South Carolina Volunteers
The Newberry Rangers, Company C, The Holcombe Legion (Redesignated
Company E, Seventh South Carolina Cavalry)
Company G, The Holcombe Legion
Company H, The Holcombe Legion
Company G, Second South Carolina Cavalry
Company M, Mounted Rifles, Twentieth South Carolina Volunteers
Company G, Second Regiment, South Carolina State Troops

Individual service records and Muster Rolls are in the State Archives, Columbia. Rolls are given also in John A. Chapman, *The Annals of Newberry*, Part II (Newberry, SC, 1892), and in D. A. Dickert, *History of Kershaw's Brigade* (Newberry, SC, 1899). See also A. S. Salley, Jr., *South Carolina Troops in Confederate Service*, Volume 1 (Columbia, SC, 1913).

Appendix D

Newberry's Units in the Spanish-American War

Company B, First South Carolina Volunteers (Copied from the plaque in the Newberry County Memorial Hospital)

Abrams, J. W.	Caldwell, E. R.
Allen, Walter	Cannon, C. O.
Adams, Walter	Cannon, J. P.
Aull, Herman	Cooley, J B.
Blats, Jno. W.	Copeland, W. O.
Blats, W. E.	Cromer, C. T.
Bradburn, P. M.	Denson, J. L.
Blakely, Ab	Daniels, J. W.
Brown, J. L.	Daniels, J. G.
Best, W. M.	Dreher, John E.
Bodie, M. S.	Duncan, James C.
Boyd, J. E.	Davis, J. H.
Brown, A. D.	Edwards, J. L.
Broce, Jno. H.	Eison, Julius
Boulware, Geo. P.	Farrow, W. W.
Coleman, J. T.	Fuller, R. J.
Cassidy, J. O.	Finger, Robert
Cockrell, Robert	Folk, T. N.
Cook, G. B.	Folk, L. E.
Corley, Edward	Glenn, W. P.
Cockrell, Joe	Glenn, J. O.
Cook, A. J.	Griffith, Jno. E.
Coleman, A. T.	Garrison, H. H.
Chapman, J. D.	Gray, S. P.

Grice, E. S.
Hughey, Herbert
Hooper, J. E.
Holmes, C. E.
Hipp, M. D.
Hinson, H. H.
Holt, W. W.
Hutchinson, E. C.
Hipp, W. C.
Huiett, W. F.
Johnson, P. D.
Jones, G. G.
Kilgore, J. J.
Kinard, Jno. M.
Keith, J. H.
Kirkpatrick, D. V.
Langford, W. S.
Livingston, W. T.
Livingston, J. A.
Lorrick, T. W.
Lovelace, L. L.
Langston, Jno. F.
Longshore, J. J.
Lancaster, M. C.
Mower, F. D.
Matthews, W. S.
Moore, Geo.
Martin, Charley
Mittle, David
Madden, J.
Mitchell, T. S.
Martin, Perry N.
Matthis, C. E.
Mayer, Jno.
Medlock, S. L.
McCarley, S. P.
McCafferty, J. W.
McGee, C. W.
Norris, Robert
Nelson, J. W.
Nicholson, J. C.
Ouzts, J. E.
Pope, T. H.

Price, F. L.
Paysinger, S. H.
Prather, W. W.
Pearsall, V. V.
Reeder, W. C.
Renwick, J. E.
Renwick, J. S.
Roberts, R. L.
Reeder, J. C.
Reeder, E. M.
Reddish, E. P.
Roebuck, J. M.
Stewart, T. O.
Smith, G. F.
Schumpert, A.
Spearman, R. S.
Swindler, T. W.
Strickland, Luther
Shackelford, R.
Smith, S.
Spehl, T. H.
Sloop, F. K.
Stewart, C. C.
Sheppard, D. E.
Simmons, H. L.
Sligh, Edwin
Stevenson, Miles
Swindler, W. O.
Suber, G. B.
Tiller, J. J.
Tribble, C. J.
Thompson, W.
Wise, W. B.
Ward, S. M.
Wallace, W. E.
Wallace, H. A.
Wearn, R. H.
Wearn, G. F.
Werts, W. B.
White, H. T.
Wallace, Miles A.
Weeks, J. K.
Wood, Landy

Williams, Carleton   Yarborough, W. P.
Williams, Thos. G.   Yeargin, Marion
Wix, W. A.

Company G, Second South Carolina Volunteers (copied from the list in the National Guard Armory)

Captain: Silas J. McCaughrin
Lieutenants: 1st—Edward C. Horton
                2nd—Robert F. Dukes
Sergeants: 1st—Caldwell E. Fant
                QM—George S. Noland
                John L. Finley
                Morgan T. Mooney
                Owens P. Saxon
                Andrew B. Stoudemire
Corporals: George H. Ballentine
                Herman P. Aull
                William J. Miller
                Edward A. Groves
                Leonard B. Cummings
                George F. Turner
Musicians: Snyder J. Parrott
                Watson M. Connor
Artificer: James N. Sligh
Wagoner: James S. Chalmers
Privates: Jackson J. Abrams   James F. Hinton
                Kimble P. Bailey   Wilbur C. Hipp
                Arthur Bair   William O. Huiett
                John J. Barrs   William O. Jordan
                Willie W. Barrs   David M. Malone
                Wilson A. Boyd   William D. Maybin
                Elmo G. Bramlett   James G. Miller
                Charlie Broughton   Madison D. Milam
                Frank J. Byrd   William H. McGarvey
                Samuel B. Cauble   George A. McKinney
                Kisler Collins   Leon M. Myers
                Julius J. Conally   Henry Pitts
                John Connor   Ford Roper
                George B. Cook   William J. Sloan
                John Davis   William J. Smith

Will Divver
Ransom Dewitt
William J. Deuitt
Ollie O. Eargle
Frank W. Fant
Claude P. Finley
Giff H. Finley
James Flake
Charlie E. Glenn
John D. Glynn
William M. Glynn
John L. Goers
Arthur Haney
Patrick H. Hargrove
James W. Hawkins
Armand P. Hinson

Hugo G. Spell
George Spotts
Walter A. Syfrett
Edgar W. Teague
John H. Todd
James R. Tucker
Thomas F. Turner
Jasper Ulmer
Joseph A. Watson
Thomas H. Watson
George G. Wilson
James M. Wilson
Hugo Weathers
John H. Whetsell
Thomas Woodall
Joseph Wood

Appendix E

Newberry's World War II Unit

BATTERY C, 107th SEPARATE COAST ARTILLERY BATTALION
(Antiaircraft)

Captain Thomas H. Pope, Jr.
First Lieutenant John C. Billingsley
First Lieutenant Earl Clayton Hipp
First Lieutenant Purvis W. Bane
First Lieutenant Robert L. McCrady
First Sergeant Amon J. Beckham

Staff Sergeant Julian L. Welling, Jr.
Sergeant William R. Anderson, Jr.
Sergeant Robert D. Hudson
Sergeant William F. Lominack, Jr.
Sergeant Gerald C. O'Quinn
Sergeant Albert P. Parrott, Jr.
Sergeant Powell E. Way, Jr.

Corporals

James K. Eargle
Manning E. Hutchinson
Charles H. Leaman
Alec McCarley
George A. Miller

William K. Smith
Evans F. Son
Charles F. Summer
George S. Wise

Privates First Class

Harry E. Bedenbaugh
Floyd G. Beheler
Willie D. Berley
Madison C. Bouknight
William D. Cheatham
Ira Lee Clamp
James W. Counts

James L. DeHart
Derril C. Driggers
Lonnie L. Franklin, Jr.
Earl H. Gilliam
Arthur L. Logins
G. W. Magbee
John E. Mayer

James A. McCarty
George R. Owens
Eugene J. Parker

John McC. Slice
Hubert D. Smith, Jr.

Privates

James H. Abrams
Alonzo B. Albritton
Harold Berry
Hugh G. Bouknight
J. C. Brooks
Willis P. Berry
James V. Clamp
Earl B. Davis
James W. Darby
Robert J. Brank
John L. Campbell
Walker C. Clamp
Curtis O. Chapman
John C. Eargle
Clarence M. Frier
Jacob S. Fulmer
Charles M. Hardin
Herman E. Hawkins
James W. Henderson
Thomas L. Hicks, Jr.
Robert F. Inman
Guy L. Kohn

George Koon
Isaac Y. Koon
James C. Lester
Allen W. Livingston
David L. McCullough
James E. O'Shields
Calvin F. Padgett
Eugene E. Perkins
John R. Renwick
William C. Ruff
Stancil K. Sessoms
Hugh King Shannon
James N. Shannon
Andrew D. Smith
Woodrow D. Smith
Thomas Y. Summer
Joe W. Swindler
Carl O. Taylor
Braxton W. Watkins
George W. Wicker
Charles E. Wise
Daniel C. Wright

Losses

The following men were discharged on February 10, 1941, by direction of the President by reason of physical disability as determined by the physical examination board at Newberry, South Carolina:

Private First Class William Davis Cheatham
Private First Class Earl Howell Gilliam
Private Clarence Merle Frier
Corporal Evans Ferrell Son

Appendix F

Intendants, Mayors and City Managers of Newberry

Intendants		
1860	E. P. Lake	
1861	John R. Leavell	
1862	W. G. Mayes	
1863	Thomas W. Blease	
1864	Robert Stewart	
1864	E. P. Lake	
1865	Silas Johnstone	
1866	W. G. Mayes	
1867	James M. Baxter	
1868	Charles W. Montgomery	
1869	James M. Baxter	
1870–71	T. M. Paysinger	
1872–73	J. P. Pool	
1874–76	Y. J. Pope	
1877	W. T. Tarrant	
1878–81	J. P. Pool	

Mayors		
1882–83	Y. J. Pope	
1884–85	J. M. Johnstone	
1886–89	George B. Cromer	
1890–91	J. K. P. Goggans	
1892	L. W. C. Blalock	
1893–95	Dr. E. E. Jones	

1896–98	H. H. Evans
1899–1900	O. B. Mayer
1901–02	Otto Klettner
1903–04	John W. Earhardt
1905	Dr. George B. Cromer
1906–07	A. T. Brown
1908–09	J. J. Langford
1910	C. L. Blease
1911–12	J. J. Langford
1913–19	Z. F. Wright
1920–21	Eugene A. Blease
1922–23	W. W. Cromer
1924–25	W. B. Wallace
1926–27	Z. F. Wright
1928–31	J. M. Davis
1932–41	J. W. Earhardt
1942–43	Herman S. Langford
1944–45	Edward B. Purcell
1946–47	Dave L. Hayes
1948–49	A. P. Salley
1950–55	J. E. Wiseman
1956–57	Cecil E. Kinard
1958–67	Ernest H. Layton
1968–90	Clarence A. Shealy, Jr.
1990–	Ed Kyzer

City Managers

1949–61	E. L. Blackwell
1961–62	W. C. Wallace (interim)
1962–76	Ken W. Riebe
1976	Thomas P. Buzhardt (interim)
1976–77	Thomas W. Edwards, Jr.
1977	Emily H. Mitchel (interim)
1977	W. A. Harvey

Appendix G

Intendants and Mayors of Prosperity

Intendants

1871	David Kibler (of Frog Level)
1873	U. B. Whites
1874	A. H. Wheeler
1875	Dr. R. L. Luther
1878	A. H. Wheeler
1879	Paddie Wheeler
1881	S. L. Fellers
1882	George G. DeWalt
1883	A. H. Wheeler
1884	D. H. Wheeler
1886–87	H. C. Mosley
1888	George G. De Walt
1889	A. H. Kohn
1890	H. C. Mosley
1891	Dr. C. T. Wyche
1892	H. S. Boozer
1893	J. M. Wheeler
1903	Dr. George Y. Hunter
1904–05	Dr. J. S. Wheeler
1906–07	Dr. E. N. Kibler
1908–11	Dr. J. S. Wheeler
1912–13	W. T. Gibson
1914–	Dr. J. S. Wheeler

Mayors

1915	Dr. E. N. Kibler
1916	M. C. Morris
1917	Dr. E. N. Kibler
1918	S. L. Fellers
1919	Dr. C. T. Wyche
1920–21	Dr. O. B. Simpson
1922	Dr. C. T. Wyche
1923–25	J. A. Dominick
1926	W. T. Gibson
1927	Dr. E. N. Kibler
1928	A. N. Crosson
1929–30	Dr. E. N. Kibler
1931–32	J. Sidney Wheeler
1933	Dr. C. K. Wheeler
1934	A. N. Crosson
1935	Edward O. Counts
1936	H. P. Wicker
1937–38	Dr. E. N. Kibler
1939–40	Dr. C. K. Wheeler
1941–47	R. P. Luther
1948	Dr. John J. Dominick
1949–52	Dr. C. K. Wheeler
1953–57	D. H. Hamm, Sr.
1958–65	J. A. Williams
1966–present	J. Walter Hamm

Appendix H

Intendants and Mayors of Whitmire

Intendants

1892–1902	John P. Fant
1902–05	S. A. Merchant

Mayors

1906	John P. Fant
1907	A. J. Holt
1909	S. H. Bascomb
1910	A. J. Holt
1911–12	Spencer B. Sims
	vice Holt, resigned
1913	John C. Duckett
1914	Dr. Van Smith
1915	W. F. Howard
1917	William J. Atchison
1922	W. G. Puckett
1924–30	C. G. Gilliam
1931	J. T. Gregory
1932–40	C. G. Gilliam
1940–43	Francis Douglass
1944	Dr. R. M. Duckett
1945	P. B. Dean
1946	Frank A. Senn
1948	William L. Norville
1948	Frank A. Senn
1950	J. A. Crosby
1956	Tom W. Suber
1962	Arthur Sparks
1964	Robert Baker
1972	William C. Owens
1986	J. Phillip Barrington
1988	William C. Owens
1990	John F. McCarley, resigned

Appendix I

Labor Contract, 1866–

South Carolina) Contract of Service for the year 1866
Newberry Dist) between Simeon Fair of the one part and Aaren, a person of color of the other part, for himself & his family consisting of himself, wife & children & Molly & his son Bob

The said Simeon Fair agrees to employ the entire service of the said Aaren & family during the present year as servants in husbandry on the following terms & conditions

The said Simeon Fair agrees to furnish a piece of ground containing about fifty acres known as the Pond field & part on which there is to be a house for the said Aaren & his family to live in during the time he remains in the employ of the said Simeon Fair & no longer, a horse or a mule, plough & gearing, such as are now in use on the plantation-privilege of the gin & screw & blacksmith shop— and cotton seed to plant the land (but the seed to be returned out of the said Aaren's share raised on the place in the fall to the whole amount planted) & allow said Aaren one-half of the entire crop raised on said land on the conditions hereinafter stated.

The said Aaren agrees to give the entire labor of himself & family in preparing, cultivating & gathering the crop to be planted on said land, & preparing it for division or sale—the whole of the land to be planted in cotton except the bottom land in corn, a small patch in sorghum, not more than one or two acres, & about the same quanity (sic) in potatoes if the said Aaren desires to do so. That all the crop except the cotton is to be divided when gathered—the cotton is to be ginned & packed & then sold by the said Simeon Fair & the proceeds equally divided after paying for bagging, roping, blacksmith bills, & if any guano is used on the place, or other bought manures, to be first paid; but the said Aaren shall before being paid over is to refund & pay the said Simeon Fair for any

advances made or liabilities incurred by him for the said Aaren in the way of money or provisions or otherwise. And the said Aaren further agrees that he will use skill & industry in the management of the farm, use good governnent in his family & preserve good order both in his family & on the farm, to allow no drinking, frolicking, or gambling or other disorderly assembly, or any improper conduct—to allow no deadly weapons to be concealed about the persons of himself or any of his family, and generally to conduct himself and family as good servants should do. He is to take good care of the mule or horse put in his charge to cultivate the land with-not to allow it to be ridden or used for any other purpose than that of the farm, without the consent of the said Simeon Fair. He is find (sic) his own provisions, and feed the horse or mule and to furnish his own firewood (except the privilege of getting old dead wood limbs that have fallen down), or in no instance to take or cut any live wood, and in no case to allow any rails or plank to be burned. He is also to keep the fences in good order around the land he cultivates. He is to assist the said Simeon Fair to thresh & cut his wheat crop and to assist in moving the houses to suit the division of the plantation into small farms as may directed by said Simeon Fair—and it is further covenanted & agreed that in case the said Aaren should prove unfaithful in the performance of any of the duties herein specified & required of him under this contract—that then and in that event the said Simeon Fair shall have the right to turn him off, & himself & family out of the house, & to take charge of the house and farm, and have the farm carried on for the benefit of him the said Simeon Fair—without allowing the said Aaren anything whatever or if the failure in performing his duty should only consist in not keeping the crop or horse in good condition, the said Simeon Fair may require the crop or horse to be put in good condition—& if the said requisition be not immediately complied with then he may take the horse away & employ additional labor at the expense of the said Aaren to put the crop in condition & shall continue the said Aaren or not at the pleasure of the said Simeon Fair. That the said Aaren is to take care that the crop be not lost or stolen after being gathered & whilst preparing it for sale or division. That the said Aaren is to assist in keeping the ginhouse, gearing & screw in order. The said Aaren is to have the privilege of a truck patch not exceeding one acre, for the use of himself & family without charge. This contract is to refer back to the first of January & continue to the end of the year. Signed, sealed and delivered this 2nd day of March 1866.
in presence of
W. R. Spearman   )   Aaren his mark   X   (LS)
)
J. T. Culbreath   )   Simeon Fair   (LS)
    The foregoing labor contract was approved by G. H. Zeigler, Lt., Act. Sub. Asst. Com.

Notes

Chapter 1

1. *Rising Sun*, November 21, 1860.

2. *Journal of the Convention of the People of South Carolina, Held in 1860, 1861, and 1862, Together with the Ordinances, Reports, Resolutions, Etc.*, R. W. Gibbes, printer to the Convention (Columbia, SC, 1862), 11–14. The members appointed were John A. Inglis, R. B. Rhett, James Chesnut, Jr., James L. Orr, Maxcy Gregg, B. F. Dunklin, and W. F. Hutson.

3. Ibid., 42–45.

4. Charles Edward Cauthen, *South Carolina Goes to War 1860–1865*, (Chapel Hill, NC, 1950), 70.

5. Ibid., 71.

6. To meet these responsibilities, the convention, on December 19, provided for the creation of four standing committees of thirteen members each. Simeon Fair was named to the Committee on Relations with the Slaveholding States of North America. Robert Moorman was named to the special committee to inquire how much the legislation of Congress would be abrogated by the secession of the state from the Federal Union. See John Amasa May and Joan Reynolds Faunt, *South Carolina Secedes*, (Columbia, SC, 1960), 10, 12, 14, and 18.

7. Cauthen, 80.

8. Ibid., 81.

9. May and Faunt, 26.

10. *Journals of the South Carolina Executive Councils of 1861 and 1862*, Charles E. Cauthen, editor (Columbia, SC, 1956), x.

11. Cauthen, 83; *Convention Journal*, 150, 158.

12. May and Faunt, 29–30.

13. Cauthen, 115.

14. Ibid., 115n.

15. Ibid., 115.

16. John A. Chapman, *The Annals of Newberry*, Part II (Newberry, SC, 1892), 412.

17. D. Augustus Dickert, *History of Kershaw's Brigade* (Newberry, SC, 1899), 33.

18. *Rising Sun*, January 9, 16, and February 13, 1861.

19. David Duncan Wallace, *South Carolina: A Short History 1520–1948* (Chapel Hill, NC, 1951), 529.

20. Wallace, 529; *Addresses of J. H. Carlisle, 1825–1909*. J. H. Carlisle, Jr., editor (Columbia, SC, 1910), 205.

21. *Rising Sun*, January 16, 1861. A letter from Camp Gregg, Sullivan's Island, dated January 25, 1861, and printed in the *Rising Sun* of January 30, 1861, gives the following roster of Company B, 1st SCV, the Rhett Guards, Captain Whitfield Walker, 1st Lt. J. Elvin Knotts, 2nd Lt. R. B. Ligon, 3rd Lt. Sampson Pope, Orderly Sergeant E. Douglass, 2nd Sgt. A. M. Bowers, 3rd Sgt. B. M. Blease, 4th Sgt. and Color Bearer W. P. Cromer, 5th Sgt. P. A. Aldrich; 1st Cpl. Pickens B. Watts, 2nd Cpl. William W. Boazman, 3rd Cpl. D. P. Goggans, 4th Cpl. S. B. Higgins, 5th Cpl. Hayne Williams, 6th Cpl. Thomas H. Syles; Privates: Joseph F. Abrams, Thomas A. Abrams, G. W. Beam, James W. Beard, John Blats, E. P. Boazman, D. S. Boozer, Henry Boulger, T. Pinckney Boyd, John Carr, William Henry Carter, M. Aleck Chambers, William H. Clamp, W. C. Counts, James L. Cromer, Daniel Dendy, George Denson, James Denson, H. Frank Enlow, J. C. Evans, George W. Fairbairn, Edwin Ford, Eli Franklin, George W. Franklin, W. R. Franklin, B. W. Goodman, John R. Harris, Dr. John W. Hill, R. Watts Hill, John M. Hood, P. S. Hunter, George A. Hutchinson, James A. Lathrop, Albert Erskine Lyles, William McDavid, J. C. McLemore, J. McAntee, D. H. Merchant, W. B. Pulley, Hayne D. Reid, William A. Rice, John W. Riser, W. W. Riser, William F. Ridlehuber, H. W. Ridlehuber, R. L. Ruff, A. T. Sanders, Edward T. Stephens, B. E. Strickland, Henry Summer, William Vance, Drury A. Wright.

22. Dickert, 23.

23. Cauthen, 131.

24. *Convention Journal*, 236–238. Joseph Caldwell voted against ratification; Fair, Kinard, and Moorman voted for it.

25. Cauthen, 135.

26. A. S. Salley, Jr., *South Carolina Troops in Confederate Service* (Columbia, SC, 1913), Volume 1, 235.

27. Cauthen, 136.

28. *Convention Journal*, 299, 367–369, 376, 378, 379, 793–796. Fair voted against the establishment of the Executive Council; Caldwell and Moorman voted for it; and Kinard did not vote. This was the second Executive Council and completely different from the first.

29. Cauthen, 143–144.

30. *Journals of the Executive Councils*, 107, 110, 111.

31. Cauthen, 145, 147.

32. Ibid., 165, 167.

33. Ibid., 167, 169.

34. *Journals of the Executive Councils*, 86 and 115.

35. Ibid., 221, 222, 233. Colonel Simeon Fair wrote the council in October 1862, bringing to its attention the complaint that certain Negroes from Newberry who had been sent to the coast had been retained beyond their term. The council took the matter under consideration. *Journals of the Executive Councils*, 278. James B. Floyd, Henry Burton, Henry Rikard, John M. Calmes, George W. Glenn, Thomas J. Price, Bluford F. Griffin, Chesley David, George M. Chaplin, Thomas Wilson Caldwell and Thomas B. Wadlington claimed reimbursement for slaves lost during their impressment. Most of the slaves died of typhoid fever. *Reports and Resolutions, 1863*, 352.

36. Cauthen, 171.

37. *Journals of the Executive Councils*, 122, 130, 137, 138, 141, 143, 147, and 149. See *Convention Journal*, 670–673, for discussion of the prohibition against exporting cotton.

38. Cauthen, 151.

39. *Statutes at Large*, XIII, 128. The convention expired under the terms of a resolution by which it would do so unless reassembled to meet an emergency before December 17, 1862. The legislature abolished the Executive Council and declared invalid all of its acts and orders except contracts.

40. Cauthen, 163.

41. Ibid., 164.

42. Ibid., 174–177.

43. *Tri-Weekly Herald*, March 28, 1865.

44. Cauthen, 211.

45. Ibid., 183.

46. *Reports and Resolutions of the General Assembly of the State of South Carolina, 1861* (Columbia, SC, 1861), 27–32 and 62–63. There were ten classes of property. In Newberry District, 2,280 acres were assessed at $3 per acre; 800 acres at $1.50; 12,850 acres at $1; 359,250 acres at forty cents; and 1450 acres at twenty cents per acre. The state tax in 1861 and 1862 was about $25,000 per year. So-called district police assessments for the relief of poor and for roads and bridges were $6,100 in 1861 and $2,560 in 1862.

47. Ibid., 42–43.

48. Cauthen, 188–192.

49. *Reports and Resolutions, 1863*, 40.

50. *Statutes at Large*, XIII, 20.

51. *Reports and Resolutions, 1862–63*, 62–66.

52. *Reports and Resolutions, 1863*, 40.

53. Cauthen, 192–193.

54. *Statutes at Large*, XIII, 100, 101, 218.

55. Including Brigadier General John E. Glenn, Colonel James M. Crosson, and Lieutenant Colonel Joseph S. Reid.

56. *Reports and Resolutions, 1861*, 336. Others who served in this important post were Matthew Hall, James Maffett, John F. Glymph, and Henry Burton. See *Reports and Resolutions* for 1862, for 1863, and for 1864–1865.

57. Report of Board of Soldier's Relief in Newberry District, South Carolina Department of Archives and History.

58. General Sessions Journal, 1858–1873, Newberry County; Common Pleas Journal, 1861–1873, Newberry County. The Courts of Freeholders did continue to function. One of these courts consisted of a magistrate and five freeholders; and slaves and free Negroes were only triable in such courts. The report of James E. Peterson, jailer, made in November 1862, is filed in the loose files, Department of Archives and History. It lists the names of Ellen Wadsworth, free Negro, convicted of stealing clothing and sentenced to serve ten days, and of fourteen slaves sentenced mostly for larceny but in two cases for assaulting a white man and in one for using indecent language.

59. Chapman, 459.

60. *Tri-Weekly Herald*, April 25, 1865.

61. *Statutes at Large*, XIII, 104–106. Deed Book KK, page 138, Clerk of Court's office, Newberry County. The new cemetery is now known as Rosemont.

62. James Fitz James Caldwell, *The History of a Brigade of South Carolinians Known First as Gregg's and Subsequently as McGowan's Brigade* (Philadelphia, PA, 1866), 6.

63. Dickert, 531–532. Another chronicle of the bravery of Newberry men is *Sergeant Beaufort Simpson Buzhardt's Diary* (n.p., n.d.). A member of the Quitman Rifles, Company E, 3rd SCV, he was killed before Richmond on June 29, 1862; his diary ended with its entry of two days before.

64. Caldwell, 9.

65. Ibid., 11–12.

66. Chapman, 412.

67. Caldwell, 99.

68. Chapman, 407 and 410.

69. Ibid., 417, 399, and 431.

70. Caldwell, 89.

71. Dickert, 36.

72. Chapman, 391, 394, 395, 422, and 426.

73. Dickert, 315.

74. Ibid., 279.

75. Ibid., 203, 227.

76. Ibid., 262–278 and 304–312.

77. Ibid., 530.

78. Cauthen, 131; Dickert, 176.
79. Dickert, 365.
80. Dickert, 366.
81. Chapman, 414.
82. Dickert, 367.
83. Data furnished the author by Charles E. Lee, Director, State Archives.
84. U. R. Brooks, *Butler and His Cavalry in the War of Secession, 1861–1865* (Columbia, SC, 1909), 163.
85. Chapman, 442–445.
86. Ibid., 420, 427–429.
87. Ibid., 426.
88. Brooks, 160–161, 545–546.
89. Chapman, 400–402, 417.

Chapter 2

1. The Bureau of Refugees, Freedmen, and Abandoned Lands was created within the War Department on March 3, 1865. It was destined to function for seven years. See Martin Abbott, *The Freedmen's Bureau in South Carolina, 1865–1872* (Chapel Hill, NC, 1967), 4 and 23–24.
2. Ibid., 16. But see the estimate of his character by Joel Williamson, *After Slavery: The Negro in South Carolina During Reconstruction, 1861–1877* (Chapel Hill, NC, 1965), 10–11, 30–31, and 364.
3. John A. Chapman, *The Annals of Newberry*, Part II, 455, quoting a letter from Captain F. N. Walker.
4. John Porter Hollis, *The Early Period of Reconstruction in South Carolina* (Baltimore, MD, 1905), 24.
5. John B. Carwile, *Reminiscences of Newberry* (Charleston, SC, 1890), 85–91, quoting a letter from Mrs. Henry Summer dated January 18, 1888.
6. John G. Barrett, *Sherman's March Through the Carolinas* (Chapel Hill, NC, 1956), 97.
7. Ibid., 128. General Judson Kilpatrick was as loose with his tongue as a politician after the war as he was with his morals during the conflict. After he made continued intemperate attacks upon General Nathan Bedford Forrest, the latter publicly branded him a liar and worse. Forrest's letter, dated October 28, 1868, appeared in the *Newberry Herald* of November 18, 1868, as well as in other newspapers throughout the country. It closed as follows: "I think the public will justify me in denouncing, as I now do, General Judson Kilpatrick as a blackguard, a liar, a scoundrel and poltroon. If he is the heroic figure he would have the Northern people believe him, my friend, General Basil W. Duke, at Louisville, Kentucky, is authorized to receive on my behalf any communication he may choose to make."

8. Hollis, 26.

9. David Duncan Wallace, *South Carolina: A Short History, 1520-1948* (Chapel Hill, NC, 1951), 557.

10. *Tri-Weekly Herald*, March 25, 1865. This newspaper was edited and published by T. F. and R. H. Greneker from March 21, 1865, until it became the *Weekly Herald* on June 28, 1865.

11. Hollis, 28-29.

12. Francis Butler Simkins and Robert Hilliard Woody, *South Carolina During Reconstruction* (Chapel Hill, NC, 1932), 16-17.

13. Hollis, 25.

14. *Eighth Census-Social Statistics-1860.*

15. *Ninth Census-Social Statistics-1870.*

16. Land values declined 60 percent between 1860 and 1867. Simkins and Woody, 10.

17. Abbott, 16-17.

18. Simkins and Woody, 8-9.

19. The Amnesty Proclamation is set forth in full in John S. Reynolds's *Reconstruction in South Carolina, 1865-1877* (Columbia, SC, 1905), 9-11. Those exempted from the general amnesty included former officers above the grade of colonel in the Confederate army; those who were civil or diplomatic officers of the Confederacy; officers in the Confederate service who were educated at West Point or Annapolis; and those worth over $20,000 in taxable property and who voluntarily participated in the rebellion. By subsequent proclamations of September 7, 1867; of July 4, 1868; and finally of December 25, 1868, the President proclaimed full pardon and amnesty to all. See Reynolds, 36-37.

20. See petitions in RG 94, National Archives, Washington, DC.

21. *Weekly Herald*, June 28, 1865.

22. *Weekly Herald*, July 5, 1865. The Committee of Fifteen included the Reverend J. J. Brantley, L. J. Jones, James M. Baxter, Isaac Hunt, John P. Kinard, C. H. Suber, Thomas Duckett, Burr J. Ramage, William Glenn, T. P. Slider, G. S. Cannon, Robinson Spearman, Isaac Herbert, James Fair, and Ellison S. Keitt. The Committee of Correspondence was composed of T. P. Slider, Simeon Fair, and George Dewalt, while the Committee to Raise Funds was composed of T. P. Slider and W. W. Houseal.

23. Wallace, 563; Lillian A. Kibler, *Benjamin F. Perry, South Carolina Unionist* (Durham, NC, 1946), 378.

24. *Weekly Herald*, July 12, 1865; August 9, 1865.

25. Ibid., September 13, 1865.

26. Idem.

27. Williamson, 17 and 19.

28. Chapman, 762-763; Reynolds, 6.

29. Chapman, 762. Trowbridge, for many years prior to his death, was custo-

dian of the Minnesota state capitol. The *Observer* of January 3, 1908, reported his death and identified him as the colonel of the regiment which murdered Calvin Crozier.

30. *Weekly Herald*, September 13, 1865.

31. *Journal of the Convention of the People of South Carolina, held in Columbia, SC, September, 1865* (Columbia, SC, 1865), 176–178. Other ordinances provided for the election of governor, lieutenant governor, members of the Senate and House of Representatives on the third Wednesday in October, 1865, Ibid., 173–175; for the defraying of the expenses of the convention by advancement of funds by the Bank of the State of South Carolina, Ibid., 179; for the repeal of the Ordinance of Secession, Ibid., 181; and for the division of the state into four congressional districts, Ibid., 182. Newberry was placed in the Third Congressional District with Orangeburg, Edgefield, Abbeville, Lexington, Richland, and Fairfield counties.

32. Ibid., 139–152.

33. Wallace, 564.

34. *Weekly Herald*, October 25, 1865. Henry Summer, J. P. Kinard, and J. M. Calmes were defeated.

35. Ibid., October 25, 1865.

36. Wallace, 564.

37. Emily Bellinger Reynolds and Joan Reynolds Faunt, *Biographical Directory of the Senate of the State of South Carolina: 1776–1964* (Columbia, SC, 1964), 11.

38. *Weekly Herald*, September 20, 1865.

39. Ibid., December 6, 1865.

40. Ibid., November 22, 1865; January 4, 1866.

41. Wallace, 566.

42. *Statutes*, XIII, 254. Young John Pope was appointed district judge for Newberry; the *Newberry Herald* of January 17, 1866, reported that the appointment gave general satisfaction.

43. Governor Orr's Correspondence, State Archives.

44. Thomas W. Holloway to Governor Orr, dated December 18, 1865, Governor Orr's Correspondence, State Archives.

45. C. P. Sullivan to Orr, January 7, 1866; State Archives.

46. Wallace, 566.

47. *Newberry Herald*, June 22, 1866. Fire destroyed Dr. Pratt's drugstore and the stores of Marshall Bros., Z. L. White, Stiles Hurd, R. B. Holman & Co., A. M. Wicker, Lovelace and Wheeler, S. Montgomery, C. Montgomery, Captain Boyce, G. D. Smith, Coppock and Wright, and S. P. Boozer, and the bakery of John Nesley.

48. Ibid., June 22, 1866.

49. *Statutes*, XIII, 366.

50. Ibid., 380, 401.

51. Wallace, 568.

52. Simkins and Woody, 64. On May 6, 1867, a military post was established at Newberry for the districts of Abbeville, Laurens, and Newberry. Company H, 6th Infantry, Captain J. M. McCleary, commanding, garrisoned the post at New- berry College, with three officers and seventy-six men. The post was closed but then reopened on October 15, 1868, with Company F, 8th U.S. Infantry, Captain James J. Van Horn, commanding, furnishing the garrison. This unit was succeeded by Company K, 18th U.S. Infantry, commanded by Captain James Stewart. Stewart remained in command until the post was finally closed permanently on July 7, 1875. "Returns from Military Posts, 1800–1916," Roll 839, Newberry, SC, May 1867–July 1875, National Archives Microfilm Publications, Microcopy No. 617, Washington, DC, 1965; South Carolina Archives.

53. Hollis, 63–64.

54. Simkins and Woody, 74, 78. Williamson, 372, states: "In 1867 and 1868, Union or Loyal Leagues were an important part of Republican activity in the state. Possibly, leagues had existed in South Carolina in 1865 and 1866, but it was only after the passage of the first Reconstruction Act that the organizational device was widely used. Leagues were used to indoctrinate Negroes with Repub- licanism, but they were also schools to instruct Negroes in their civic responsi- bilities."

55. *Newberry Herald*, March 20, 1867.

56. The account of the freedmen's picnic is found in the *Newberry Herald* of July 3, 10, 17, 31 and August 21, 1867.

57. Ibid., September 26, 1867; General Howard stated that the contractor who built the school was abused and threatened. See Oliver Otis Howard, *Auto- biography of Oliver Otis Howard*, 2 volumes. (New York, 1908), II, 383.

58. Hollis, 78.

59. Reynolds, 74. Others elected vice president were Wade Hampton, B. F. Perry, John A. Inglis, A. P. Aldrich, John D. Kennedy, John Bratton, and Joseph Daniel Pope.

60. Simkins and Woody, 87.

61. *Newberry Herald*, November 27, 1867.

62. Reynolds, 76.

Chapter 3

1. C. Irvine Walker, *The Life of Lieutenant General Richard Heron Anderson of the Confederate States Army* (Charleston, SC, 1917), 241.

2. L. J. Jones to Orr, May 18, 1866, Governor Orr's Correspondence File, State Archives.

3. A. C. Garlington wrote Governor Orr on April 16, 1867, that he had just returned to Newberry from Laurens District. He stated

"The "bread question" is really assuming a most alarming aspect. I am afraid there will be actual starvation unless timely aid is given. I hear of much want in this District, but I think that the condition of things is much worse in Laurens . . . I am aware that the civil authorities of the State are powerless to extend the relief called for, but the military may do much, and now is the time for them to put forth all the means at their command."

See also letters to Orr from J. M. Epps, dated April 3, 1867; from E. P. Lake, dated April 26, 1867; from Mrs. Eleanor S. Wilson, dated April 26, 1867; and from J. P. Kinard, dated May 11, 1867. All are in Governor Orr's Correspondence File, State Archives.

4. Martin Abbott, *The Freedmen's Bureau in South Carolina, 1865–1872* (Chapel Hill, NC, 1967), 40, 41, 50.

5. *Weekly Herald*, April 25, 1866.

6. Ibid., November 28, 1866.

7. Request dated December 13, 1866, from Ralph Ely, Tallahassee, Florida, with endorsements and lists, State Archives.

8. Letter to author from Mrs. S. J. Sweett, Volusia County Historical Commission, New Smyrna Beach, Florida, dated August 13, 1968.

9. *Newberry Herald*, July 11, 1866. On July 16, Silas Johnstone wrote Governor Orr for permission to go to Europe for four months to seek immigrants; he was going with George Larsen, a young Dane living in Newberry. On December 1, 1866, Johnstone asked for leave to go to Europe in January 1867; Governor Orr granted both requests on condition that Johnstone leave a competent deputy to handle the affairs of the office of Commissioner in Equity. On March 16, J. M. Baxter requested an extension of Johnstone's leave of absence until May 20, stating that he was at that time still in Europe. Governor Orr's Correspondence File, State Archives.

10. For details of the immigrants, see the *Newberry Herald*, June 5, December 4, 1867; May 13, 27, 1868; January 13, February 24, March 10, September 15, December 15, 1869. E. Merton Coulter, *The South During Reconstruction 1865–1877*, Volume VIII, *A History of the South* (Louisiana State Press, 1947), 103, states: "There was an immigration society in Newberry, South Carolina, which brought to that community 272 immigrants within the year ending in June, 1869. The nationalities of these immigrants were characteristic of the general desires throughout the South—German, Swedes, Danes, Dutch, and French."

11. Correspondence of Governor James L. Orr, South Carolina Archives, includes the letter from Duncan but not the enclosure. I cannot find any such letter in the *Charleston Daily News* for March 1867. However, Duncan's letter of February 27, 1867, addressed to Major L. J. Jones of Newberry was published by request in the *Newberry Herald* of March 20, 1867.

12. Governor Orr's Correspondence File, State Archives.

13. Family Bible of Baruch Duncan in possession of his family; Robert Norman Daniel, *Furman University, History* (Greenville, SC, 1951), 205; C. C. Brown, *General Catalog of Furman University* (Sumter, SC, n.d.), 30.

14. *Charleston Daily News*, March 9, 1868.

15. *Newberry Herald*, July 31, 1867.

16. Ibid., August 28, 1867.

17. Ibid., February 19, 1868.

18. John Porter Hollis, *The Early Period of Reconstruction in South Carolina* (Baltimore, MD, 1905), 83.

19. For these details of the convention, see *Proceedings of the Constitutional Convention of South Carolina, Held at Charleston, SC, Beginning January 14th and Ending March 17th, 1868* (Charleston, SC, 1868), 47, 49–52, 56, 266, 577, 655, 771, 807, 882–887, 890–892, 902. Also see Eric Foner, *Reconstruction: America's Unfinished Revolution, 1863–1877* (New York, 1988), 319.

20. *Statutes at Large*, XIV, 1–32.

21. Ibid., 33. For a comprehensive study of the Land Commission, see Carol K. Rothrock Bleser, *The Promised Land. The History of the South Carolina Land Commission 1869–1890* (Columbia, SC, 1969).

22. *Charleston Daily News*, February 17, 24, March 9, 1868.

23. *Newberry Herald*, March 18, 1868.

24. Ibid., February 12, 1868. General Canby had earlier appointed as magistrates in Newberry, J. G. Peterson (Special Order 191, October 28, 1867, Hqs. 2nd Military District); Jesse Smith (S. O. 210, November 9, 1867); and J. I. Hipp (S. O. 214, November 23, 1867).

25. Ibid., March 25, April 8, 15, 22, 29, 1868. Delegates to the state convention were E. S. Keitt, Simeon Fair, Y. J. Pope, and T. J. Lipscomb. Alternates were J. F. J. Caldwell and Samuel R. Chapman.

26. *Journal of the Senate*, Special Session of 1868, 9; *Journal of the House*, Special Session of 1868, 6.

27. Duncan to Scott, July 19, November 27, 1868; June 23, 1869, Governor Scott's Correspondence, State Archives.

28. Brown, 30; Walter Allen, *Governor Chamberlain's Administration in South Carolina; A Chapter of Reconstruction in the Southern States* (New York and London, 1888), 334.

Chapter 4

1. John A. Chapman, *The Annals of Newberry*, Part II (Newberry, SC, 1892), 751.

2. Francis Butler Simkins and Robert Hilliard Woody, *South Carolina During Reconstruction* (Chapel Hill, NC, 1932), 113.

3. *Journal of the House, Special Session of 1868*, 8.

4. Ibid., 53.

5. *Journal of the Senate, Special Session of 1868*, 12.

6. *House Journal*, 50.

7. Simkins and Woody, 109–110.

8. Ibid., 112.

9. Ibid., 113.

10. *Senate Journal*, 13, 14, 16, 17, 19, 26, and 30.

11. Emily Bellinger Reynolds and Joan Reynolds Faunt, *Biographical Directory of the Senate of South Carolina, 1776–1964* (Columbia, SC, 1964), 62.

12. *House Journal*, 542–545; *Statutes at Large*, XIV, 207.

13. *House Journal*, 79.

14. David Duncan Wallace, *South Carolina: A Short History* (Chapel Hill, NC, 1951), 579.

15. *Statutes at Large*, XIV, 128.

16. Ibid., 99, 376.

17. *Newberry Herald*, June 10, July 8, 1868. They were approved in General Order Number 122.

18. John T. Peterson's testimony before the Legislative Committee Investigating Conditions in the Third Congressional District. *Reports and Resolutions of the General Assembly of South Carolina, 1869–70*, 903.

19. Martin Abbott, "County Officers in South Carolina in 1868," *South Carolina Historical Magazine*. LX, (January 1959), 35.

20. Minutes, Board of Commissioners, Newberry County, 1868–1882, South Carolina Archives; *Newberry Herald*, December 23, 1868.

21. The townships were described as follows in the minutes:
Number 1, Newberry—commencing at Cappleman's and running to H. H. Folk's, thence to Senn's Mills on Bush River, thence to the fence on Timothy Creek on the Stoney Battery Road and thence to the beginning at Cappleman's.
Number Two, Caldwell—commencing at H. H. Folk's and running to Avery's Ford on Enoree River, thence to the Ashford Ferry Road at the 12 Mile post, thence to Cappleman's, and thence to the beginning at H. H. Folk's.
Number Three, Maybinton—commencing at Avery's Ford on Enoree River and running to the 12 Mile post on the Ashford Ferry Road, thence with said road to Ashford's Ferry on Broad River, thence up the said river to the mouth of the Tyger River, thence up the Tyger River to old Ford and thence with the county line to Avery's Ford on Enoree River.
Number Four, Cromer—commencing at Avery's Ford on Enoree River and running to H. H. Folk's, thence to the Laurens Line at William Young's, thence with the county line to Enoree River, and thence down the said river to Avery's Ford.
Number Five, Reeder—commencing at H. H. Folk's and running to the Laurens Line at William Young's, thence with the county line between Newberry and Laurens to Bush River, thence down said river to Senn's Mills and thence to the beginning at H. H. Folk's.

Number Six, Floyd—commencing at Senn's Mills and running in a straight line to the junction of Saluda and Little Rivers, thence up Little River to the Laurens Line, thence with said county line to Bush River, and thence down said river to the beginning at said Senn's Mills.

Number Seven, Moon—is bounded by Saluda and Little Rivers and the Laurens Line.

Number Eight, Mendenhall—commencing at Senn's Mills on Bush River and running by a straight line to the Ford on Timothy Creek on the Stoney Battery Road, thence by a straight line to the junction of Saluda and Bush Rivers, and thence by Saluda River to the junction of Saluda and Little Rivers, thence by a straight line to the beginning at Senn's Mills.

Number Nine, Stoney Battery—commencing at the Ford on Timothy Creek, on the Stoney Battery Road, and running up said creek to the public road, commonly known as the Silverstreet Road, thence with said road to Frog Level, thence with the public road known as the New Cut Road to the Lexington Line at Saluda River, thence up said river to the mouth of Bush River, and thence to the beginning at the Ford on Timothy Creek (the line of this Township to be varied so as to include the village of Frog Level).

Number Ten, Cannon—commencing at the Ford on Timothy Creek on the Stoney Battery Road, and running up said creek to the public road commonly known as the Silverstreet Road, thence with said road to Frog Level, thence with the public road known as the New Cut Road to the Lexington Line near Dominick's, thence with the said Lexington Line to Summer's, thence by straight line to Cappleman's, and thence to the beginning point on Timothy Creek.

Number Eleven, Heller—commencing at Cappleman's and running by straight line on Township Ten to Summer's, on the Lexington Line, thence along said Lexington Line to Broad River, thence up the said river to Ashford's Ferry, thence along the Ashford Ferry Road to the 12 mile stone, and thence by straight line to the beginning at Cappleman's.

22. *Newberry Herald*, January 6, 1869.

23. Ward C. Jensen, "Price Economics of What Farmers Sell," Bulletin 226, Clemson College, May 1926, 7.

24. Return of Crops, and Other Statistics of Newberry County, State of South Carolina, for the year 1868; manuscript in South Carolina Archives.

25. Jensen, 7.

26. *Statutes at Large*, XIV, 275-277.

27. Carol K. Rothrock Bleser, *The Promised Land, The History of the South Carolina Land Commission 1869-1890* (Columbia, SC, 1969), 30, 62.

28. Newberry County Deed Book PP, 63-64.

29. *Newberry Herald*, January 15, 1873.

30. Slider to Scott, Governor Scott's Correspondence File, State Archives. In the sessions of 1874 and 1875 Senator Corwin introduced joint resolutions to

pay Henry Ware & Son. Payment was never made and a joint resolution was finally passed in 1878 which recited the history of the transaction and exempted the owners from taxes for 1871-1877, inclusive, since they had been deprived of their property during this period. See *Statutes at Large*, XVI, 676.

31. *Newberry Herald*, May 19, 1875.

32. *Newberry Herald*, August 25, September 29, February 24, 1869.

33. General Sessions Court Journal 1858-1873, Newberry County, 285-286; now in State Archives.

34. Ibid., 289.

35. Slider to Scott, August 1, 2 and 11, 1868.

36. *Newberry Herald*, January 6, 1869.

37. Josephus Woodruff, Clerk of the Senate, to Scott, January 22, 1869, Governor Scott's Correspondence File, State Archives.

38. Woodruff to Scott, January 22, 1869.

39. *Newberry Herald*, November 11, 1868.

40. Ibid., July 8, 1868; January 6, 1869.

41. Ibid., September 9, 1868.

42. Ibid., October 21, 1868; Sheriff T. M. Paysinger to Scott, October 21, 22, 1868; Coroner H. H. Kinard to Scott, October 21, 1868; Simeon Fair to Scott, October 17, 1868, Correspondence File of Governor Scott, State Archives. Murtiashaw fled to Arkansas and settled there. Fitzgerald went to Texas and, while chief of police of a small town, was killed by a cowboy.

43. John S. Reynolds, *Reconstruction in South Carolina, 1865-1877* (Columbia, SC, 1905), 131.

44. *Reports and Resolutions, 1869-1870*, 615.

45. John A. Leland, *A Voice from South Carolina* (Charleston, SC, 1879), 52 and 134.

46. *Reports and Resolutions, 1869-1870*, 616. At page 619 the majority of the committee continued:

"there was a general system of intimidation in this county, the evidence, in the opinion of your committee, conclusively proves. That Bass Blease, Sim Boozer, Fitzgerald, Sam Murtiashaw, Dan Ward, and a host of others, were tools in hands of leading Democrats to intimidate and carry out their diabolical schemes, the evidence proves well. That the notorious Sam Dogan, would have been killed ere this, had it not been a question with those who desired to attack and destroy him, which of the parties would be the victim, your Committee is satisfied. That apparently a great change for the better has taken place in the County of Newberry; and that the signs of the times indicate peace, tranquility, and prosperity, must be apparent to our whole country."

47. *Statutes at Large*, XIV, 14.

48. *Reports and Resolutions, 1869–1870*, 326. Report of John B. Hubbard, chief constable.

49. *Statutes at Large*, XIV, 376.

50. Ibid., 215.

51. *Newberry Herald*, June 1, 1870.

52. *Reports and Resolutions, 1873–1874*, 549–550.

53. *Statutes at Large*, XIV, 285.

54. Ibid., 386.

55. *Newberry Herald*, April 28, 1869.

56. Ibid., November 24, December 1, 22, 1869. The identity of "Junius" is not known.

57. Ibid., November 17, December 15, 1869.

58. Ibid., January 26, February 16, March 9, 1870. Henderson to Scott, April 15, 1870, State Archives.

59. Kinard to Scott, April 19, 1870, State Archives.

60. Leland, 53.

61. *Newberry Herald*, June 1, October 5, 1870.

62. Claude G. Bowers, *The Tragic Era* (Cambridge, Mass., 1929), 359–360.

63. Wallace, 580.

64. *Newberry Herald*, June 1, 8, 22, 1870; Reynolds, 143.

65. Reynolds, 143.

66. *Newberry Herald*, September 28, October 5, 1870.

67. Ibid., October 19, November 2, 1870. The managers of the election were at Newberry Court House, Box 1, Z. L. White, Mathew Gray, Dennis Moates; at Box 2, S. Montgomery, J. P. Hutsin, T. A. Thompson; at Frog Level, W. W. Davis, James DeWalt, Sampson Bridges; at Maybinton, Isom Greenwood, J. M. Goudelock, Solomon Henderson; at Moon's, Nathaniel Peterson, Wesley Brown, Silas Nance; at Cromer's, D. R. Phifer, Bolen Gregory, Nathan Rice; and at Longshore's, J. J. Carrington, Richard DeWalt, Meredith Stevens.

68. Reynolds and Faunt, 63.

69. *Journal of the House, 1870–1871*, 3, 33, 38.

70. Wallace, 583.

71. Ibid., 579, 583; Henry T. Thompson, *Ousting the Carpetbagger from South Carolina* (Columbia, SC, 1926), 35; Simkins and Woody, 137.

72. *Newberry Herald*, October 28, 1868, noted with regret the removal from office of Solomon Kinard, postmaster for past fifteen or more years; on November 11, 1868, it reported appointment of Riser; on July 20, 1870, it announced Riser's confirmation as postmaster; on October 12, 1870, it reported his imprisonment for gross dereliction of duty and robbing the mail; on December 7, 1870, it reported his trial in Columbia; and on December 14, 1870, his conviction.

73. Ibid., May 3, 1871; on October 9, 1872, the newspaper reported that Riser had been pardoned by President Grant; on November 4, 1872, D. R. Phifer, J. J. Carrington, Joseph D. Boston, H. C. Corwin, M. S. Long, R. C. DeLarge, S.

Bridges, Isom Greenwood, Simeon Young, and Walter Gray petitioned Scott to reinstate Riser as trial justice, Correspondence File, State Archives.

74. Minutes of Board of Commissioners for Newberry County, State Archives, November 30, 1870, 49.

75. General Sessions Journal, 1858–1873, Newberry County, 328–335.

76. Ibid., 337–339, 345–346, 355. William Summer was appointed Coroner, *vice* Long, by Governor Scott. *Newberry Herald*, October 4, 1871.

77. General Sessions Journal, 1858–1873, Newberry County, 367–370.

78. *Reports and Resolutions, 1871–1872*, 241. Petition of John J. Carrington, Joseph D. Boston, John T. Henderson, Matthew Gray, A. R. Gantt, and others in Scott's Correspondence File, State Archives.

79. Commissioned April 5, 1872, Secretary of State's List of Officers Appointed and Elected, 1839–1898, State Archives.

80. General Sessions Journal, 1858–1873, 384.

81. *Reports and Resolutions, 1872–1873*, 682. Pending his pardon, Dogan requested the General Assembly to change his name, and on February 15, 1872, Scott approved the Joint Resolution changing the names of Samuel, Simon, and Columbus Dogan to Samuel, Simon, and Columbus Farrow. See *House Journal, 1871–1872*, 150, 163, and 424.

82. *Reports and Resolutions, 1872–1873*, 110.

83. *Newberry Herald*, May 24, 1871; October 4, 1871. William W. Houseal was Foreman, and other members included John H. Livingston, W. A. Cline, James Y. Harris, J. B. Fellers, J. F. Sims, W. D. Reeder, W. P. Harmon, Thomas S. Blair, Edwin C. Jones, Levi W. Bowers, P. E. Wise, J. P. Cameron, Thomas D. Buzzard, John Sheppard, and Jordan P. Pool. General Sessions Journal, 1858–1873.

84. Ibid., May 24, November 15, 1871; January 31, April 17, 1872. In July 1871, fifteen blacks resolved to "cut loose from carpet-baggers and thieves, and join hands with white native honest citizens." Ibid., July 12, 1871. In the issue of July 19, 1871, Sam Cooper, Nathan Rice, and Starling Young stated that they intended to vote only for good men, irrespective of party.

85. Ibid., September 13, November 15, December 16, 1871; Osborne L. Schumpert, attorney for the two Democrats elected, made a public statement about the refusal of F. J. Moses, Jr., and John L. Neagle, who were members of the Board of Canvassers and in Columbia when Schumpert demanded that they perform their duty. The three appointed to the board were D. R. Phifer, W. P. Harris, and Dennis Moates.

86. Ibid., March 22, 1871.

87. Ibid., May 17, 1871.

88. Reynolds, 196, 199.

89. Ibid., 200; *Newberry Herald*, April 3, 10, 17, 24, May 1, 8, 23, July 31, 1872. Among Newberrians arrested were John Merchant, Sim Malone, Hilliard Bishop, Adam Berley, Frank Lovelace, Cicero Lovelace, Frank Dodd, Eli Wall,

Dr. Ed C. Jones, Dr. William M. Kinard, Dr. Marion Setzler, Thomas P. Slider, John Houseal, Charles Sims, Thomas B. Wadlington, J. Y. McFall, Baxter Chapman, Charles Franklin, Malcolm Johnstone, Bennett Hancock, Dr. William Hatton, Grafton Laney (black), Isom Reynolds (black), Sam Young, Jeff Duncan (black), Lawson Green, Peter Gallman, William Wintz, Tony Croft, John Epps, Munson M. Buford, W. H. Eddy, J. McM. Calmes, William Calmes, Sullivan Herbert, Dr. Thomas Brown, Pat Hargrove, John Montgomery, James Packer, D. T. Newman, James Irby, former Sheriff T. M. Paysinger, Giles Higgins (black), John Duckett, Richard Duckett, John C. Odell, J. Newton Odell, Thomas H. Watson, Pinckney Bradford, John Watkins, John Wilson, Henry Chappell, John Payne, Dr. J. O. Dickert, William Smith, and Walter Andrews.

90. *Newberry Herald*, May 22, September 25, October 2, 9, 1872.

91. Ibid., February 7, 1872; General Sessions Journal, 1858–1873, 389, 391, 392, 404. Carrington was commissioned on April 13, and qualified on April 17, 1872.

92. *Newberry Herald*, August 28, 1872.

93. Ibid., September 4, 25, 1872.

94. Ibid., September 25, 1872; James Morris Morgan, *Recollections of a Rebel Reefer* (Boston and New York, 1917), 332–339. Morgan states that Tupper was convicted but later pardoned by Moses.

95. *Newberry Herald*, September 25, October 9, 1872. H. C. Corwin was nominated for the Senate; James C. Leahy for probate judge; James Henderson for coroner; Sampson Bridges and Isom Greenwood for the House and Dennis Moates and Allen Rice for county commissioners. The Boston faction's nominees for other offices were Jesse C. Smith for clerk of court; John J. Carrington for sheriff; M. S. Long for school commissioner; Thomas Keitt for county commissioner; and Joseph D. Boston for the House of Representatives. The Hutson nominees who lost included Thomas M. Lake for clerk; H. B. Scott for sheriff; the Reverend J. B. Hillhouse for school commissioner; Allen Abernathy for county commissioner; and Hutson for the House.

96. Ibid., October 9, 16, 23, 30, 1872.

97. Ibid., November 6, 1872.

Chapter 5

1. David Duncan Wallace, *South Carolina: A Short History 1520–1948* (Chapel Hill, NC, 1951), 590–592; Francis Butler Simkins and Robert Hilliard Woody, *South Carolina During Reconstruction* (Chapel Hill, NC, 1932), 126–127, 136n., 162, 465–474, 545; *Statutes at Large*, XV, 817.

2. I. W. Avery, *The History of the State of Georgia* (New York, 1881), gives a full account of Blodgett's career—he was appointed mayor of Augusta in 1867, elected superintendent of the State Road, and purchased his election to the U.S. Senate but failed to be seated.

3. Blodgett to Moses, March 13, 1873, Governor Moses's Correspondence File, State Archives.

4. Corwin et al. to Moses, March 1, 1873, and Boston to Moses, March 4, 1873, Governor Moses's Correspondence File, State Archives.

5. Printed release for the *Progressive Age* in Governor Moses's Correspondence File, State Archives.

6. *Newberry Herald*, March 19, 1873.

7. Hayward to Moses, January 31, 1874, Governor Moses's Correspondence File, State Archives.

8. Hayward to Moses, January 31, 1874, Governor Moses's Correspondence File, State Archives.

9. Josephus Woodruff, Clerk of Senate, to Moses, February 13, 1874, Governor Moses's Correspondence File, State Archives.

10. W. H. Thomas to Moses, August 21, 1874, with endorsement thereon, Governor Moses's Correspondence File, State Archives; *Newberry Herald*, September 9, 16, and December 2, 1874.

11. Ibid., November 18, 1874.

12. J. J. Carrington, sheriff, to Moses, December 2, 1873, acknowledging receipt of pardon; Governor Moses's Correspondence File, State Archives.

13. *Newberry Herald*, April 1, 1874.

14. Ibid., February 4, 1874.

15. Ibid., June 3, 1874.

16. Ibid., June 10, 1874.

17. *Newberry Herald*, August 12, 1874. Officers of the Newberry County Union were Y. J. Pope, president; R. C. Carlisle and R. L. McCaughrin, vice presidents; John C. Wilson, treasurer; and George Johnstone, secretary. Delegates to the State Union were E. S. Keitt, James N. Lipscomb, and William Ray.

18. Ibid., August 12, September 9, 1874.

19. Ibid., September 9, 1874.

20. Ibid., October 7, 1874.

21. Ibid., October 7, 1874.

22. *Newberry Herald*, October 21, 1874. All the nominees for county office were black except Leahy, candidate for probate judge.

23. Ibid., October 28, 1874.

24. Ibid., October 28 and November 4, 1874.

25. Ibid., November 18, 1874.

26. Ibid., November 18, 1874.

27. Ibid., November 11, 1874.

28. Walter Allen, *Governor Chamberlain's Administration in South Carolina* (New York, NY, 1888), states at p. viii: "That he brought to his task great force of character, a strong purpose, admirable courage, high culture, and a powerful eloquence, is generally conceded." Allen commenced his defense of

Chamberlain with his inauguration in 1874; he ignored his earlier career in Radical politics. Simkins and Woody disagree. See their estimate of Chamberlain, 560–561.

29. In his later years Chamberlain eagerly sought to change his image; he made speeches and wrote articles on Reconstruction, the Negro, and the conditions in the South. See Simkins and Woody, 544–545.

30. *Newberry Herald*, December 9, 1874.

31. *Journal of the Senate*, Session of 1874, 8, 11, 17, and 18.

32. *Newberry Herald*, November 25, December 9, 1874. Josephus Woodruff, clerk of Senate, to Chamberlain, December 7, 1874, Governor Chamberlain's Correspondence File, State Archives.

33. Ibid., January 20, February 3, 17, March 17, 1875.

34. Alrutheus A. Taylor, *The Negro in South Carolina During the Reconstruction* (Washington, DC, n.d.), 103; the *Newberry Herald*, March 24, 31 and July 28, 1875. Boston to Chamberlain, State Archives, and Chamberlain to Boston, Governor Chamberlain's Correspondence File, State Archives.

35. *Journal of the House*, session of 1876, 348. Couch, Meetze, P. Simkins, Copes, and Barnwell were appointed, 372.

36. Ibid., 442–446 and 485. The managers appointed to conduct the impeachment on behalf of the House were Speaker Elliott, General W. H. Wallace, H. A. Meetze, J. W. Barnwell, S. J. Couch, and S. J. Bampfield. Defense counsel were J. H. Rion, Leroy F. Youmans, Y. J. Pope, James M. Baxter, J. B. Campbell, and Silas Johnstone. See *Reports and Resolutions of the General Assembly of the State of South Carolina, 1875–1876* (Columbia, SC), 975–1124.

37. The account of the trial is taken from *Reports and Resolutions, 1875–1876*, 975–1124. The witnesses against Judge Moses included George Johnstone, J. F. J. Caldwell, Solicitor W. McGill Fleming, R. C. Watts, C. P. Sullivan, Dr. J. J. Boyd, R. W. Shand, Thomas M. Lake, Chief Justice F. J. Moses, Probate Judge J. C. Leahy, F. M. Trimmier, S. T. Poiner, Sheriff John J. Carrington, Ira W. Rice, Jesse C. Smith, and Samuel J. Patterson.

38. *Journal of the House*, session of 1876, 618.

39. *Newberry Herald*, March 29, 1876.

40. John A. Leland, *A Voice from South Carolina* (Charleston, SC, 1879), 141–142.

41. Rosser H. Taylor and Raven I. McDavid, *Memoirs of Richard Cannon Watts* (Columbia, SC, 1938), 36.

42. J. C. Leahy to Chamberlain, July 6, 1876, Governor Chamberlain's Correspondence File, State Archives.

43. James N. Lipscomb to Chamberlain, July 17, 1876, and W. R. Smith to Chamberlain, August 9, 1876, Governor Chamberlain's Correspondence File, State Archives.

44. T. P. Slider to Chamberlain, July 27, 1876; Will H. Thomas to Chamber-

lain, August 8, 1876; Slider to Chamberlain, August 15, September 10 and 19, 1876; Governor Chamberlain's Correspondence File, State Archives.

45. *Newberry Herald*, January 12 and 19, February 9, 1876.

46. Ibid., April 12, May 3, 1876. The County Republican Party met on April 8 and elected Senator Corwin, Thomas Keitt, and B. B. Boozer as delegates to the state convention. That body in turn elected Corwin one of the delegates to the National Republican Convention. A week later the County Democratic Convention met and elected Y. J. Pope as chairman of the Executive Committee and sent as delegates to the State Convention J. N. Lipscomb, E. S. Keitt, J. S. Hair, Y. J. Pope, T. W. Holloway, and Joseph Caldwell. The State Convention elected Sampson Pope as an alternate delegate to the National Democratic Convention. See the issues of April 19, 1876 and May 10, 1876.

47. Ibid., June 21, July 12, 1876.

48. Ibid., July 26, 1876.

49. Pope to Chamberlain. Governor Chamberlain's Correspondence File, State Archives; *Newberry Herald*, August 23, 1876.

50. General Wade Hampton was nominated as governor; other Democratic nominees were William D. Simpson of Laurens for lieutenant governor; R. M. Sims of York for secretary of state; James Connor of Charleston for attorney general; Hugh S. Thompson of Richland for superintendent of education; Johnson Hagood of Barnwell for comptroller general; S. L. Leaphart of Richland for treasurer; and E. W. Moise of Sumter for adjutant general.

51. *Newberry Herald*, August 23, 1876.

52. Ibid., August 30, 1876.

53. Ibid., September 13, 1876. Others nominated by the Republicans were R. H. Gleaves for lieutenant governor; H. E. Hayne for secretary of state; Robert B. Elliott for attorney general; John R. Tolbert for superintendent of education; T. C. Dunn for comptroller general; Francis L. Cardoza for treasurer; and James Kennedy for adjutant general. Chamberlain, Tolbert, and Dunn were white.

54. William Arthur Sheppard, *Red Shirts Remembered: Southern Brigadiers of the Reconstruction Period* (Atlanta, GA, 1940), 46. The original manuscript of Gary's plan is in the Gary papers, Caroliniana Library, Columbia, SC.

55. *Newberry Herald*, August 23, September 6 and 13, October 11, 25, 1876.

56. Ibid., September 20, 1876.

57. Ibid., September 27, October 4 and 11, November 1, 1876.

58. Ibid., October 11, 1876. Thomas Keitt, W. H. Thomas, and Sampson S. Bridges were nominated for the House; Carrington and Leahy were nominated for re-election as sheriff and probate judge; T. J. Clayton for clerk of court; M. S. Long for school commissioner; James Eichelberger for coroner; and Simeon Young, Henry Kennedy, and Wesley Brown for county commissioners.

59. Ibid., November 1, 8, 1876.

60. Ibid., November 8, 1876.

Chapter 6

1. In the Hamburg riot in Aiken County, McKie Meriwether was slain along with six blacks. See David Duncan Wallace, *South Carolina: A Short History 1520–1948* (Chapel Hill, NC, 1951), 598–599; Francis Butler Simkins and Robert Hilliard Woody, *South Carolina During Reconstruction* (Chapel Hill, NC, 1932), 486–488.

2. Ellison S. Keitt, MS *Memoirs*, Caroliniana Library.

3. *Newberry Herald*, December 13, 1876. Writing in the *Observer* of October 13, 1912, Dr. D. M. Crosson of Lexington County credited Dr. Asa F. Langford of Prosperity with persuading Sampson Bridges to go with the Wallace House.

4. *Newberry Herald*, May 23, June 19, October 24, December 12, 1877.

5. Ibid., January 3, 1877.

6. Ibid., January 10, 17, 31, February 14, 1877. John S. Reynolds, *Reconstruction in South Carolina, 1865–1877* (Columbia, SC, 1905), 436.

7. Ibid., February 21, 1877.

8. Pope to Hampton, Governor Hampton's Correspondence File, State Archives: Your Excellency's letter of the 18th inst. has received careful consideration. The following officials are now in commission in our County:

1.	Jesse C. Smith	County Treasurer	Supports Chamberlain
2.	Robert E. Williams	County Auditor	Supports Chamberlain
3.	Henry C. Moses	Clerk of Court	Supports Gov. Hampton
4.	John J. Carrington	Sheriff	Supports Doubtful
5.	James C. Leahy	Judge of Probate	Supports Chamberlain
6.	Harry B. Scott	School Commissioner	Supports Gov. Hampton
7.	Albert L. Snead	Jury Commissioner	Supports Chamberlain
8.	1) Silas Johnstone	Election Commissioner	Supports Gov. Hampton
	2) Baruch Boyd		Supports Chamberlain
	3) David F. Leahy		Supports Chamberlain
9.	1) Henry Kennedy		Supports Gov. Hampton
	2) Simeon Young	County Commissioner	Supports Chamberlain
	3) Wesley Brown		Supports Chamberlain
10.	1) James F. Kilgore	Trial Justice	Supports Gov. Hampton
	2) Dennis Moates	Trial Justice	Supports Chamberlain
	3) Joel B. Heller	Trial Justice	Supports Gov. Hampton
	4) Will H. Thomas	Trial Justice	Supports Chamberlain
	5) Frank C. Aldridge	Trial Justice	Supports Gov. Hampton

The County Treasurer, Jesse C. Smith, is drunken, a carpetbagger, and I would suggest as a proper appointment Mr. U. B. Whites of Prosperity in our County.

The County Auditor, Robert E. Williams is a negro, of small capacity. I would suggest as a proper appointment Mr. Levi E. Folk, of Longshore's in our County.

The Clerk of Court is efficient and one of our supporters. The Sheriff Jno. J. Carrington is capable of service in our behalf. I mean he can be controlled by our people.

The Judge of Probate, James C. Leahy, is capable, but an intense Radical carpetbagger. Sampson Pope Esq. was the Democratic nominee & is the contestant for that office.

The School Commissioner Harry B. Scott is a negro, but he is passably efficient, a representative of his race, popular with the whites, and has labored faithfully to induce all others to do as he has done vote & labor for Gov. Hampton. Under these circumstances, I am sure your Excellency will appreciate the feeling that moves me to make no recommendation for that office.

The Jury Commissioner, Albert L. Snead, a colored man of limited capacity, & quite unworthy to fill such an office. As his successor I would recommend Joseph M. Ward of Dead Fall in our County.

The Election Commissioners, Silas Johnstone, Baruch Boyd, and David F. Leahy. The first is a gentleman. The second is a negro, but not so unworthy altho' opposed to us. The third is a Radical carpetbagger. I would suggest John C. Wilson of the Town of Newberry as his successor.

The County Commissioners Henry Kennedy, Simeon Young, and Wesley Brown. The first is fair, tho a negro of limited education. The second Simeon Young is unworthy. I would respectfully suggest Col. William Lester as his successor. The third Wesley Brown, is unworthy. I would suggest Luther P. W. Riser, of Mollohon in our County, as his successor.

The Trial Justice, James F. Kilgore is capable & supports Law & order. No advice, recommendation as to him. The next Dennis Moates is ignorant & incapable. One Trial Justice James F. Kilgore is in Town already and there is no need for another. Dennis Moates removal is suggested.

The next is Joel B. Heller, on Broad River. His retention is recommended. The next Will H. Thomas is in Town & is a very dishonest man. I would suggest no delay in his decapitation. The next Frank C. Aldridge is no longer a citizen of our county. I would respectfully suggest as new appointments: At Frog Level or Prosperity, L. B. Maffett: At Maybinton, William D. Hardy; At Moons, Samuel W. Teague: At Mollohon, John G. Houseal.

I have endeavored not to be unmindful of the high incentive to a patriotic discharge of the duty your Excellency devolved upon me. I would in conclusion beg leave to reaprise you of the deep sincerity in the people of Newberry, without a division, in their assurance of unwavering support with men, money and all other means of your administration of the affairs of state in South Carolina.

9. *Newberry Herald*, February 7, 1877.

10. Pope to Hampton, Governor Hampton's Correspondence File, State Archives. "As Chairman of the Ex. Com. of the Democratic Party for Newberry County, I am directed to lay before your Excellency the preference of that party as ascertained in a County Convention called for that purpose, as to persons to fill the various County offices—to wit:

  X1. Trial Justice at Newberry Court House, James Packer and M. A. Carlisle

    2. Trial Justice at Maybinton—John T. Bynum

    3. Trial Justice at Liberty Hall—John W. Riser

    4. Trial Justice at Chappells Depot James N. Lipscomb

    5. Trial Justice at Frog Level S. C. Jacob B. Fellers

    6. Trial Justice at Pomaria S. C. Thomas W. Holloway

  X7. Jury Commissioner John S. Hair vice Joseph M. Ward

    8. Auditor Levi E. Folk Newberry, S.C.

    9. Treasurer Uriah B. Whites Frog Level, S.C.

  10. Supdt. State Penitentiary—Thomas J. Lipscomb

Your Excellency will be pleased to know that the appointment heretofore made by you of James Packer as Trial Justice, was after a full and thorough consideration by the Convention, almost unanimously sustained. The only alteration made was that of Joseph M. Ward as Jury Commissioner who really did not wish *that* office.

If your Excellency should be pleased to fill the above appointments & should send the appointments to me, I will see that the same reach the individuals at once—or if you should prefer to send them direct to the parties, the Postoffice of each one is that stated on the opposite page except as to *Maybinton*—that should be *Lyles Ford P. O.* Recognizing the new approach to an end of the difficulties with which your administration has been thus far hampered, & grateful to the Almighty God for the protection he has vouchsafed to you as our Ruler, I beg you will believe our people as devoted as ever.

  11. *Journal of the House*, Special Session, 1877, 36–41.

  12. Minutes of the Court of General Sessions, 1873–1883, Newberry County, 340.

  13. Ibid., 325.

  14. *Newberry Herald*, December 5, 1877.

  15. Ibid., December 12, 1877.

  16. *Newberry Herald*, November 28, 1877. Colonel Keitt recovered a verdict of six cents, which of course carried the rather substantial court costs with it. See Ibid., January 29, 1879. However, the *New York Times* then published a long, complimentary editorial about Colonel Keitt, saying among other things that Colonel Keitt was totally incapable of pursuing any object by mean or underhand methods. See *Newberry Herald* of February 5, 1879.

  17. Ibid., May 16, 1877.

18. Ibid., July 11, 18, February 28, 1877.
19. Ibid., July 25, August 22, 1877.
20. Ibid., September 5, 1877; November 21, 1877.
21. Ibid., January 2, 1878.
22. Ibid., January 16, 1878.
23. Ibid., April 24, 1878.
24. *Newberry Herald*, April 17, May 29, July 10, August 7, 1878.
25. Ibid., October 2, 1878.
26. Ibid., August 7, October 2, 1878.
27. Ibid., October 16, 1878.
28. Ibid., August 28, 1878.
29. Ibid., September 18, 1878.
30. Ibid., September 25, October 16, 1878.
31. Ibid., November 6, 1878.

Chapter 7

1. William J. Cooper, Jr., *The Conservative Regime: South Carolina, 1877–1890* (Baltimore, Maryland, 1968), 20.
2. *Newberry Herald*, May 21, 1879.
3. Ibid., August 20, 1879; June 16 and July 7, 1880.
4. J. H. Easterby, "The Granger Movement in South Carolina," *The Proceedings of the South Carolina Historical Association*, *1931*, 21–22.
5. Ibid., 26.
6. *Newberry Herald*, June 19, 1872. Other early Granges were those at Belmont, Levi E. Folk, master, and at Beth Eden, with J. P. Kinard as secretary.
7. Easterby, 25 and 26.
8. *Newberry Observer*, June 18, 1891.
9. *Observer*, January 23, 1903.
10. Claudius Hornby Pritchard, Jr., *Colonel D. Wyatt Aiken, 1828–1887, South Carolina's Militant Agrarian* (Hampden Sydney, VA, 1970), 52–72.
11. Easterby, 29.
12. *Newberry Herald*, August 21, November 27, 1878.
13. Ibid., October 13, 1880; October 5, 1882; January 6, 1886; *Statutes at Large*, XVIII, 406.
14. Francis Butler Simkins, *The Tillman Movement in South Carolina* (Durham, NC, 1926), 111.
15. *Newberry Observer*, February 21, July 11, 1889.
16. Ibid., October 18, 1932.
17. *Biographical Directory of the South Carolina Senate*, 3 volumes, N. Louise

Bailey, Editor (University of South Carolina Press, Columbia, SC, 1986), III, 1476–1478.

18. *Newberry Observer*, February 4, 1930.

19. Ibid., September 1, 1892; August 29, 1894; February 12, May 6, November 25, 1896; Frank E. Jordan, Jr., *The Primary State, A History of the Democratic Party in South Carolina 1876–1962* (n.p., n.d.), 27–37, 54 and 55.

20. *Newberry Observer*, June 26, 1890.

21. *Biographical Directory of the South Carolina Senate*, III, 857–858.

22. *Newberry Observer*, June 26, 1890. For the history of the Alliance, see Solon J. Buck, *The Agrarian Crusade: A Chronicle of the Farmer in Politics* (New Haven, Yale University Press, 1920), 111–124; and W. Scott Morgan, *History of the Wheel and Alliance, and The Impending Revolution* (Fort Scott, Kansas, 1889), 281–352.

23. Wright Bryan, *Clemson: An Informal History of the University*(Columbia, SC, 1979), 19–31.

24. *Newberry Observer*, December 19, 1889.

25. *Biographical Directory of the South Carolina Senate*, II, 841–843.

26. *Newberry Herald*, June 7, 1871.

27. Ibid., June 14, 1871.

28. Ibid., October 20, 1875. The directors were I. N. Gary, J. C. Wilson, J. S. Hair, Sampson Pope, M.D., W. T. Tarrant, S. K. Dick, J. N. Fowles, T. J. Lipscomb, W. H. Hunt, T. F. Harmon, W. J. Lake, and J. T. Peterson.

29. Ibid., March 14, 1877.

30. Ibid., February 19, March 12, 1879; May 26, 1880.

31. Ibid., July 26, 1883. A notice was tacked on a telephone post at the end of Mollohon Row warning that Mollohon Row should not be rebuilt; it was signed "Commune," and the headline in the *Newberry Herald* of August 2, 1883, referred to "Communism in Newberry."

32. Ibid., March 26, July 23, August 6, 13, 1879; February 25, 1880; and August 24, 1881.

33. Ibid., April 28, May 26, June 23, 1880; May 4, 1881.

34. Ibid., November 3, 1880; May 4, June 8, 1881.

35. Ibid., August 24, September 14, December 8, 1881.

36. *Newberry Observer*, March 28, April 18, 1889.

37. Ibid., February 28, 1889. However, in the *Newberry Herald*, July 20, 1882, it was stated that the cost was $22,000.

38. *Newberry Herald*, February 23, 1882.

39. Ibid., July 3, 1884.

40. Ibid., October 29, 1879. In addition to the six barrooms, there were twelve dry goods stores, eight groceries, and six dry goods and grocery stores. There were also two confectionaries, two furniture stores, two drugstores, two hardware stores, two book stores, three millinery shops, a bakery, two tinsmiths, one

shoe store, one saddlery and harness shop, two jewelers, two livery stables, two undertakers, and a marble yard. Professional men included twenty-two lawyers, six physicians, and three dentists.

41. *Newberry Observer*, February 28, 1889. A report to the *News and Courier* was printed on page one; this article was a civic advertisement and listed the town council (Mayor George B. Cromer and Aldermen E. C. Jones, Eduard Scholtz, George McWhirter, and B. H. Cline), professional men and operators of the various businesses. The number of saloons had increased to seven.

42. The General Assembly had passed Act 360 in 1873 to authorize the incorporation of Newberry Cotton Mills but nothing was done to carry out the plan. *Statutes at Large*, XV, 428. A new act incorporating Newberry Cotton Mills was enacted as Act 48 in 1882. *Statutes at Large*, XVIII, 69. It was under authority of this charter that the mill was organized.

43. *Newberry Herald*, May 29, 1878. The others on the committee were J. N. Martin, George S. Mower, J. D. Cash, and the Reverend H. W. Kuhns.

44. See the sketch of his life in D. D. Wallace, *The History of South Carolina* (New York, 1934), four volumes, IV, 628–629. John B. Carwile, *Reminiscences of Newberry* (Charleston, SC, 1890), in dedicating his work to McCaughrin said he did so to one "who stands pre-eminent among the benefactors of Newberry."

45. *Newberry Herald*, May 10, 1883. The original directors were D. H. Wheeler, W. T. Tarrant, James McIntosh, M. A. Renwick, George S. Mower, R. H. Wright, R. L. McCaughrin, William Langford, J. N. Martin, and James A. Crotwell from Newberry, and James H. McMullan of Maine.

46. Ibid., May 17, July 5, 26, 1883.

47. *Newberry Observer*, Sesquicentennial Edition, April 28, 1939.

48. *Herald and News*, March 31, 1887; *Newberry Observer*, February 28, 1889.

49. *Newberry Herald*, December 13, 1883.

50. *Newberry Observer*, August 7, 1890.

51. *Newberry Herald*, April 11, 1877.

52. Ibid., August 15, 1877.

53. Ibid., March 28, 1877.

54. *Newberry Observer*, April 10, 1890.

55. *Newberry Herald*, September 28, 1882.

56. Ibid., June 23 and September 1, 1880. In the latter are given the results of the primary. Frank E. Jordan, Jr., *The Primary State, A History of the Democratic Party in South Carolina, 1876–1962* (n.p., n.d.), gives 1882 as the first year for local primaries. He relied upon the *Charleston News and Courier* as his authority.

57. Ibid., March 19, 1879. He was termed an efficient officer. In the issue of December 7, 1882, it was reported that he had been elected county attorney of Ellis County, Kansas.

58. Ibid., April 13, 1882; February 8, November 1, 8, 1883.

59. *Herald and News*, March 31, 1887.

60. Ibid., April 7, November 17, 1887.
61. Ibid., September 29, 1886.

Chapter 8

1. *Newberry Observer*, March 20, 1890.
2. Ibid., April 3, 1890.
3. Ibid., June 19, 1890.
4. Ibid., August 14, 28, September 4, 1890.
5. Ibid., September 4, 1890; William H. Cooper, Jr., *The Conservative Regime: South Carolina, 1877–1890* (Baltimore, 1968), 210, inexplicably lists George Johnstone as a Tillman leader. Johnstone was one of the most prominent anti-Tillmanites in the Constitutional Convention of 1895 and made several races for Congress against such Tillmanites as Norris and Asbury Latimer. Even more difficult to understand is Cooper's insistence on spelling Dr. Sampson Pope's name as "Samson." See pages 109, 184, and 199. No other author has presumed to change Pope's Christian name.
6. *Newberry Observer*, October 16, 1890.
7. Ibid., November 27, 1890.
8. Ibid., March 31, 1892.
9. Ibid., August 25, 1892.
10. Ibid., September 1, 1892.
11. Ibid., September 1 and 8, 1892.
12. Ibid., June 15, 1893. John A. Mayer became head of the County Dispensary in 1901. See issue of February 14, 1901.
13. Ibid., February 14, April 4, 1894.
14. Ibid., May 9, 1894.
15. Ibid., April 4, 1894. The incorporators were J. A. Sligh, C. L. Blease, S. Pope, C. T. Wyche, F. V. Capers, J. A. Riser, and Job L. Hughey. The May 30, 1894, issue notes first appearance of the *Voice of the People*.
16. Ibid., November 14, 1895.
17. Ibid., August 1, September 12, October 10, 31, and November 14, 1894; William Watts Ball, *The State That Forgot* (Indianapolis, 1932), 223; *Newberry Observer*, June 17, 1930. Other installments of Koester's essay on Bleasism appeared in the issues of April 29, May 2, 13, 16, 30, June 3, 24, July 11 and 18, 1930.
18. *Newberry Observer*, March 13, 1895. Pope later joined the Republican Party and was its nominee for governor in 1896. Ibid., May 27, 1896, September 23, 1896; after his decisive defeat he took no further part in state politics.
19. Ibid., March 27, July 31 and August 7, 1895.
20. Ibid., April 24, 1895.

21. Ibid., May 8, June 19, 1895. The lead editorial of May 15, 1895, says that the movants were sustained on every point.

22. Ibid., July 5, 1888; October 9, 1890. John O. Peoples was president. For a list of merchants and businessmen in Newberry in 1889, see issue of February 28, 1889.

23. Ibid., February 6, December 11, 1890. For a list of businesses in Prosperity in 1889, see issue of January 3, 1889; Act Number 631 of the Acts of the General Assembly of South Carolina for 1890.

24. *Newberry Observer*, February 26, December 5, 1891; January 28, 1892; Act Number 945 of the *Acts of the General Assembly of South Carolina for 1891*.

25. *Newberry Observer*, April 28, 1897.

26. Ibid., February 26, 1891. The incorporators were R. L. McCaughrin, Dr. R. C. Carlisle, John B. Carwile, Dr. M. A. Renwick, John O. Peoples, R. H. Wright, J. N. Martin, J. F. J. Caldwell, and Dr. James McIntosh. All were elected directors except Carwile; Henry C. Robertson was elected instead of Carwile. Ibid., April 9, 1891.

27. Ibid., February 21, 1894.

28. Ibid., February 12, 1896. Other organizers were Dr. O. B. Mayer, L. W. Floyd, P. C. Smith, G. W. Summer, W. H. Hunt, and F. Z. Wilson.

29. Ibid., June 30, 1933.

30. Ibid., February 5 and March 25, 1896; June 1, 1899.

31. Ibid., January 8, 1891; February 19, 1896, and August 18, 1897.

32. Ibid., May 11, 1898.

33. Ibid., October 13, 1892.

34. Ibid., September 2, 1896; August 25, 1897.

35. Ibid., April 27, 1899; January 3, 1901.

36. Ibid., July 6 and September 7, 1893. Gary continued as Commander until his death in 1915.

37. Ibid., March 17, 1897.

38. Ibid., July 13 and August 10, 1898.

39. Ibid., March 29, 1923; October 6, 1931; February 11, 1936.

40. Ibid., October 19, 1934.

Chapter 9

1. *Newberry Herald and News*, August 30, 1888.

2. *Newberry Observer*, September 4, 1890.

3. *Newberry Observer*, September 1, 1892; August 29, 1894; August 26, 1896. In 1892, C. L. Blease, John T. Duncan, and W. D. Hardy were elected. In 1894, Duncan and Hardy were re-elected and Dr. C. T. Wyche was elected. In 1896, Wyche was re-elected and Arthur Kibler and John F. Banks were elected.

4. *Biographical Directory of the American Congress 1774–1971* (United States Government Printing Office, 1971), 603.

5. Box 157, Pkg. 433, Probate Court for Newberry County. In 1860, he owned 164 slaves according to Chalmers Gaston Davidson, *The Last Foray* (University of South Carolina Press, 1971), 215.

6. *Observer*, February 12, 1904.

7. Robert Burnside, "The Governorship of Coleman Livingston Blease of South Carolina, 1911–1915" (Dissertation, University of Michigan, 1963), 3–4.

8. Burnside, 4.

9. *Newberry Herald and News*, June 2, 1886; May 19, 1887; and *Newberry Observer*, January 12, 1893.

10. Ibid., April 28, 1897; August 31, 1898.

11. Frank E. Jordan, Jr., *The Primary State, A History of the Democratic Party in South Carolina 1876–1962* (n.p., n.d.), 88.

12. *State*, June 23, 1903.

13. *Observer*, September 2, 1904; Emily Bellinger Reynolds and Joan Reynolds Faunt, *Biographical Directory of the Senate of South Carolina 1776–1964* (Columbia, SC, 1964), 80, 162, 165, 182.

14. Jordan, 25.

15. Ibid., 26.

16. *Observer*, December 17, 1909.

17. Jordan, 27; *Observer*, September 20, 1910. Jordan, at 101, states that Byrnes was elected by a margin of fifty-eight votes.

18. *State*, September 8, 1910; Francis Butler Simkins, *Pitchfork Ben Tillman–South Carolinian* (Louisiana State University Press, Baton Rouge, LA, 1944), 491; and S. L. Latimer, Jr., *The Story of the State* (Columbia, SC, 1970), 87–88.

19. Jordan, 54; *Newberry Observer*, August 28, 1890, September 1, 1892, August 29, 1894, February 12, 1896, and May 6, 1896.

20. Burnside, 94.

21. Jordan, 29.

22. J. C. Hemphill, editor, *Men of Mark in South Carolina* (Washington, DC, 1907), 4 volumes, I, 194.

23. *Observer*, August 30, 1912; Jordan, 29.

24. Burnside, 183, 185.

25. Jordan, 29; Simkins, 498–499; *Observer*, August 28, 1914; September 15, 1916.

26. Daniel W. Hollis, "Cole Blease: The Years Between the Governorship and the Senate, 1915–1924," *South Carolina Historical Magazine*, January 1979, 14.

27. Ibid., 14–15.

28. Jordan, 64–67; *Observer*, September 6, 1918.

29. David Duncan Wallace, *South Carolina, A Short History* (Chapel Hill, NC, 1951), 655.

30. Hollis, 1–17.

31. Daniel W. Hollis, "Cole L. Blease and the Senatorial Campaign of 1924," *Proceedings of the South Carolina Historical Association 1978*, 54.

32. Ibid., 54, 55; *Newberry Herald and News*, August 1, 5, 1919.

33. Hollis, 55.

34. Ibid., 56.

35. Ibid., 58; Jordan, 35.

36. Hollis, 60, 61.

37. Ibid., 62.

38. Ibid., 62.

39. Jordan, 69; *Observer*, September 12, 1924.

40. Jordan, 71–72.

41. Burnside, 2, referring to Simkins, 489.

42. Simkins, 551. Simkins credits the phrase "strain of violence" to Ludwig Lewisohn in *Up Stream: An American Chronicle* (New York, 1922).

43. Jordan, 76–77.

44. *Newberry Observer*, August 23, 1938.

Chapter 10

1. *Newberry Observer*, September 6, 13, 1900; W. H. Day of Florence, George Johnstone, and R. H. Welch were the organizers. They served as directors along with B. C. Matthews, John M. Kinard, J. E. Norwood, Dr. W. G. Houseal, and C. H. Cannon.

2. *Observer*, January 21, 1905.

3. Ibid., May 13, 1904; *Newberry Observer*, June 9, 1939.

4. *Newberry Observer*, June 15, 1899, July 2, 1929; *Observer*, January 16, October 26, 1901, and October 21, 28, 1910; August 1, 1913; February 27, 1914.

5. *Observer*, September 1, 1905.

6. *Newberry Observer*, October 28, 1949.

7. *Newberry Observer*, July 4, 1901; *Observer*, January 16, 1902.

8. *Newberry Observer*, September 26, 1901; *Observer*, August 1, 1902.

9. *Newberry Observer*, March 13, 1951.

10. Ibid., May 26, 1944.

11. Ibid., February 24, 1948.

12. *Observer*, May 20, 1904. Directors were H. H. Folk, H. H. Evans, M. A. Coleman, J. Simpson Dominick, John M. Suber, B. F. Cannon, I. H. Boulware, G. C. Glasgow, and W. D. Senn.

13. *Newberry Observer*, April 28, 1939; *Observer*, February 14 and 18, 1902.

14. Frank E. Jordan, Jr., *The Primary State, A History of the Democratic Party in South Carolina, 1876–1962* (n.p., n.d.), 35.

15. *Observer*, March 7, 1905. Directors were G. S. Mower, D. C. Heyward,

John M. Kinard, Dr. O. B. Mayer, G. W. Summer, Thomas J. McCrary, Joseph
L. Keitt, W. H. Hunt, T. B. Stackhouse, Z. F. Wright, S. T. McCravy, and C. D.
Barksdale.

16. Deed Book 12 page 97, Newberry County; *Observer*, July 21, 1903.

17. *Observer*, January 18, 1918; November 6, 1923. He died in 1923.

18. *Observer*, June 13 and 27, 1905.

19. Ibid., June 28, 1910.

20. Ibid., July 1, February 4, 1910:

21. Ibid., November 8, 1918. The building cost $100,000; its architects were
Summer and Hemphill.

22. *Newberry Observer*, October 9, 1931.

23. *Observer*, May 26, 1908; April 30, 1909; May 6, 1913.

24. Ibid., September 25, 1928.

25. Ibid., January 30, 1903.

26. *Newberry Herald*, March 16, June 29, July 6, 1882; June 10, 1896; March
24, 1897. The cost was $40 per year and an additional $5 for each quarter-mile
beyond a half-mile from the central office. Original subscribers were the Columbia and Greenville R.R.; the National Bank; R. L. McCaughrin's residence;
George S. Mower's office and residence; C. & G. S. Mower's Store; G. H. Cline
and Co.; Dr. S. F. Fant's residence; A. J. McCaughrin's office; and William Langford's warehouse. The telephone system was put in operation on June 26 with
twenty-one telephones in Newberry.

27. *Newberry Observer*, June 21, 1900; *Observer*, June 27, 1902, and November 7, 1902.

28. *Observer*, October 8, 1909; *Newberry Observer*, April 28, 1939, Section K,
5. There were seventy telephones in Prosperity and forty in Whitmire.

29. *Observer*, August 14, 1906; March 4, 1919; March 31, 1925.

30. Ibid., September 13, 1910.

31. Ibid., April 12, 1927.

32. *Newberry Observer*, July 26, 1921.

33. Ibid., November 17, 1936.

34. *Observer*, February 17, 1925.

35. Ibid., October 10, 1913; July 27, 1915.

36. *Newberry Observer*, March 3, 1953.

37. *Observer*, January 20, 1925.

38. *Newberry Observer*, May 8, 1962.

39. *Observer*, March 11, 1904.

40. Ibid., February 12 and 27, 1907.

41. Ibid., April 2, 1907.

42. Ibid., June 12, 1908.

43. Ibid., November 15, 1918; December 2, 1919.

44. *Newberry Observer*, December 24, 1920.

45. *Observer*, May 27, 1919.

46. *Official Roster of South Carolina Soldiers, Sailors and Marines in the World War, 1917–1918* (Columbia, SC, 1929), Two Volumes, I, II.

Chapter 11

1. *Observer*, March 17, 1925.

2. Ibid., July 2, 1929; *Newberry Observer*, March 18, 1930.

3. *Newberry Observer*, January 13, 1931.

4. Ibid., April 14, 1931; October 13 and 23, 1931.

5. Ibid., May 5, 8, 15, 1931; January 5, 1932. Members of the local advisory board were Z. F. Wright, J. M. Davis, P. D. Johnson, E. B. Purcell, Harry Vigodsky, J. L. Keitt, and three others to be selected by them. W. B. Wallace was cashier and R. H. Wright, assistant cashier.

6. Ibid., October 2, 1931; December 22, 1933.

7. *Observer*, September 6, 1929; *Newberry Observer*, June 14, 1935.

8. *Observer*, November 4, 1919. Commanders of Post 24 have been Hal Kohn, John B. Setzler, J. L. Keitt, Elbert J. Dickert, Neal W. Workman, B. M. Scurry, Jake Wise, Henry F. Fellers, Price K. Harmon, John M. Kinard, Jr., Roy H. Elam, Thomas M. Fellers, Paul B. Ezell, Duane A. Livingston, Fred E. Adams, Tabor L. Hill, Strother C. Paysinger, J. Claude Sease, Chalmers Brown, William R. Reid, C. A. Dufford, S. Frank Sutton, T. Roy Summer, Guy V. Whitener, Thomas H. Pope, W. R. Wise, John B. Lindsay, A. P. Parrott, Jr., J. Dave Caldwell, George S. Dominick, James V. Clamp, Russell Addy, Louis C. Floyd, Felix B. Greene, Jr., Carroll Eargle, Fred Schumpert, Ray Schumpert, Eugene Stockman, Beaman Summer, Ed Wicker, L. D. Gardner, Jr., Ray Hunter, J. W. Fuller, Tommie E. Harmon, Carroll E. Looney, Bennie B. Sprouse, Doyle Gantt, James Dawkins, Wilmer Hite, George Caldwell, William M. Minick, John Smith, Alvin Jackson, and James A. Lander.

9. *Observer*, September 9, 1921.

10. *Newberry Observer*, July 18, 1947.

11. Information furnished by Mrs. Harry D. Epting.

12. *Observer*, May 5, 1922; December 11, 1928.

13. *Newberry Observer*, March 9, 1920.

14. *Observer*, February 8, 1927.

15. *Newberry Observer*, April 28, 1939.

16. Ibid., April 8, 1941.

17. *Observer*, August 9, 1921.

18. Ibid., September 5, 1922; March 6, 1923; *Newberry Observer*, March 31, 1939.

19. *Observer*, May 13, 16, July 11, October 10, 1924. Dr. W. L. "Buck" Pressley of Due West was president of the league.

20. Ibid., November 8, 1923.

21. *Newberry Observer*, November 9, 1943.

22. Ibid., October 13, 1936.

23. *Observer*, March 14, 1924.

24. Ibid., December 25, 1925.

25. Ibid., January 2, 1925.

26. *Newberry Observer*, April 18, 1975.

27. *Observer*, April 12, December 9, 1927.

28. Ibid., October 10, 1919; March 2, 1928. The committee consisted of Z. F. Wright, Mrs. Robert D. Wright, Dr. Z. T. Pinner, W. W. Cromer, T. Roy Summer, Dr. C. D. Weeks, Jacob R. Wise, Mrs. Frank R. Hunter, and Mrs. L. W. Floyd.

29. *Newberry Observer*, February 26, 1932.

30. *Observer*, May 25, 1926.

31. *Newberry Observer*, April 18, 1933.

32. Ibid., December 15, 1972.

33. *Observer*, January 23, October 18, 1923.

34. *Newberry Observer*, May 13, 1930.

35. Ibid., July 20, 1934.

36. Deed Book 40, page 495, Newberry County Clerk of Court's Office.

37. Act 735, *Acts of the General Assembly of South Carolina for 1936*. The present members of the Park Commission are William C. Carter, chairman, Mrs. John R. Frazier, and Gordon B. Johnson.

38. *Newberry Observer*, April 12, 1940.

39. The records show that Elizabeth Linch (sic) conveyed 194 acres to Job Johnston (sic) on January 6, 1849; see Deed Book DD, page 109, Newberry County. Three years earlier, on November 7, 1846, Giles C. Linch had conveyed 31 acres to Johnston; see Deed Book CC, page 285, Newberry County. All of the property was owned by the Reverend Elijah Linch, Sr., whose will, dated July 6, 1842, was admitted to probate on August 15, 1842; Estate File, Box 72, Package 184, Probate Court for Newberry County.

40. *Newberry Observer*, March 8, July 23, 1940.

41. Ibid., June 29, 1962.

42. Ibid., January 4, 1938.

43. Ibid., May 26, 1967.

44. Ibid., May 22, 1978.

45. Ibid., May 24, 1935.

46. *Biographical Directory of the South Carolina Senate, 1776–1984*, 3 volumes, N. Louise Bailey, editor (University of South Carolina Press, Columbia, SC, 1986), I, 36.

47. *Newberry Observer*, September 28, 1943.

48. Ibid., The Sesqui-Centennial Issue, April 28, 1939.

49. *Newberry Observer*, January 31, February 3, 1939. District chairmen were Chappells, Mrs. A. P. Coleman; Silverstreet, John Grady Long; Bush River, Mrs.

S. P. Harris; Whitmire, Mrs. J. G. Barnwell; Prosperity, Mrs. George W. Harmon; Pomaria, R. L. Riser; and Little Mountain, Miss Elberta Sease. Mrs. J. H. Summer was publicity chairman, Judge E. S. Blease was chairman of the Historical Committee; and George K. Dominick was chairman of the Trade Week Committee.

50. Ibid., September 26, 1939. Other members of the unit were Aman J. Beckham, Denniston J. Bedenbaugh, Jessie C. Bedenbaugh, Willis P. Berry, James E. Bodie, William G. Boozer, Madison C. Bouknight, James R. Clary, Jr., James C. Counts, Everett A. Darby, James L. Davis, Edward C. DeVore, Raymond E. Dominick, Derrill C. Driggers, Cornelius A. Dufford, Jr., James K. Eargle, John H. Glymph, Charles E. Golden, William B. Goodman, Roscoe Griffin, Joseph W. Hipp, Robert B. Hudson, Herman H. Huggins, Lee Hunt, Jimmy B. Jackson, Fred H. Kempson, Arthur L. Logins, William F. Lominack, Jr., James A. McCarty, Thomas B. McDowell, John C. Meeks, Gerald C. O'Quinn, Bennie Lee Ouzts, Osborn Padgett, Albert P. Parrott, Charles T. Price, John R. Rollins, William C. Ruff, John Slice, Hubert D. Smith, Paul N. Smith, Eston Smith, Everett R. Sturkie, Cecil J. Suits, Powell E. Way, Jr., Julian L. Welling, Robert D. Wesson, Arthur H. Wicker, Lawrence P. Wicker, James R. Williams, George R. Wise, and Jack B. Workman.

51. Ibid., October 18, 1940.

52. *Newberry Observer*, December 13, 1940.

Chapter 12

1. *New York vs. United States*, 67 S Ct. 1207, 331 US 284, 91 LEd 1492 (1947).

2. Governor Thurmond's remarks to the Governor's Conference, Charleston, SC, November 1950.

3. *Newberry Observer*, October 14, 1960. The author was master of ceremonies at the luncheon.

4. Ibid., March 14, 1950, and September 7, 1951.

5. Ibid., March 26, 1946.

6. They were sold in the following order: Mollohon and Oakland, 1947; Newberry Textile Mills and J. P. Stevens in 1949.

7. *Newberry Observer*, May 2, 1952.

8. Ibid., September 10, 1946.

9. *Newberry Observer*, November 21, 1967.

10. Ibid., October 13, 1964.

11. Ibid., July 12, 1974.

12. Ibid., June 17, 1947.

13. *Newberry Observer*, June 10, 1966.

14. Ibid., December 5, 1969.

15. Ibid., December 22, 1933.

16. Ibid., May 21, 1946.

17. Ibid., August 23, 1949.

18. Ibid., July 11, 1958.

19. *Newberry Observer*, April 6, September 14, 1954; June 1, 1956; April 14, 1959; October 8, 1957; and August 27, 1990.

20. Ibid., September 29, 1964; October 23, 1964.

21. Ibid., June 1, 1951, March 21, 1952.

Chapter 13

1. *Slave Schedule for 1860.*

2. *Agriculture of the United States in 1860; compiled from the official returns of the Eighth Census* (Washington, Government Printing Office, 1864), 214, 237, 128–131 (hereafter called the *Census of 1860*). In 1860 the Subers and Lemuel Glymph raised 2,280 pounds of rice in the Broad River bottoms, and in the same area one of the Subers raised ten bales of long staple cotton.

3. E. M. Lander, Jr., *A History of South Carolina, 1865–1960* (Chapel Hill, N.C., 1960), 106.

4. *South Carolina Resources and Population, Institutions and Industries* (Charleston, SC, 1883), 155–156. (Published by the State Board of Agriculture, it is known generally as *Hammond's Handbook*.)

5. Martin Abbott, *The Freedmen's Bureau in South Carolina, 1865–1872* (Chapel Hill, NC, 1967), 23. For an interesting, informative account of an officer assigned to the Freedmen's Bureau, see John William De Forest, *A Union Officer in the Reconstruction* (New Haven, CT, 1948).

6. The bureau's agent in Newberry in 1868 was James A. Greene who reported that he approved during the month of June contracts made by J. W. Watts, Mrs. J. A. Whitman, William McMorris (sic), and Henry Whitmire. Watts gave ten freed people one-third of all crops. Mrs: Whitman gave ten freedmen a third of the corn, cotton, wheat, and peas. McMorries agreed to furnish two hands and to give nine freed people one-fourth of the corn, cotton, pea, and hay crops but no wheat. Whitmire agreed to give five freed people one-third of the crops except for six acres of corn of which the freedmen would get two-thirds. See Roll 42, Target 6, Frame 580, Microfilm Records of the Bureau of Refugees, Freedmen and Abandoned Lands, 1865–1872 for South Carolina in State Archives.

Colonel Ellison S. Keitt realized the keen desire of the blacks for recognition so he put three former slaves in command of three corps of workers; each had the rank of major-general. His former bodyguard and a future legislator during Reconstruction, Tom Keitt, was made adjutant general to extend Colonel Keitt's orders. This quasi-military system worked so well that the following year Keitt created divisions within the corps and appointed six additional major-generals. For his account see Keitt's manuscript Memoirs in the Caroliniana Library, University of South Carolina.

7. *Hammond's Handbook*, 155–156.

8. Ibid., 155–156.

9. Return of Crops, and Other Statistics of Newberry County, State of South Carolina, for the Year 1868; the manuscript is in the South Carolina Archives. (Hereafter Return of Crops, 1868). See also *Census of 1860.*

The comparable figures for 1868 and 1860 are 44,243 bushels and 87,716 bushels of wheat; 25,940 bushels and 43,149 bushels of oats; 4,182 bushels and 13,216 bushels of Irish potatoes; 24,621 bushels and 83,599 bushels of sweet potatoes; 8,738 bales and 17,476 bales of cotton; 252,556 bushels and 452,191 bushels of corn.

Newberry farmers owned 1,740 horses in 1868 and 2,625 horses in 1860; 1,819 mules in 1868 and 2,753 mules in 1860; 3,145 milk cows in 1868 and 9,412 in 1860; 3,720 sheep in 1868 and 5,945 in 1860; and 12,454 swine in 1868 and 26,048 in 1860.

10. Of 1907 landowners in 1878, only 171 were Negroes.

11. Lander, 106. The *Newberry Herald* of February 16, 1881, made the charge that the labor system was no better in 1881 than it had been in 1865. There was "just as much higgling and bargaining between hirer and hired; the terms 'wage hands,' 'croppers,' and 'renters' are just as unsettled."

12. *Newberry Herald*, August 21, 1878.

13. Ibid., March 6, 1878.

14. Ibid., March 17, 1880.

15. Ibid., November 17, 1880.

16. *South Carolina: A Handbook* (Columbia, SC, 1927), 170.

17. *Hammond's Handbook*, 154.

18. *Census Reports, Twelfth Census of the United States Taken in the Year 1900, Agriculture, Part I, Farms, Live Stock, and Animal Products* (Washington, DC, 1902) (hereafter *Census of 1900*), Volume V, 120.

19. *Newberry Observer*, January 26 and February 16, 1899. The group consisted of C. J. Purcell, Edward Scholtz, J. D. Davenport, E. P. Pawley, J. W. White, and S. P. Crotwell.

20. *Census Reports, Twelfth Census of the United States, Taken in the Year 1900, Agriculture, Part II, Crops and Irrigation,* (Washington, DC, 1902) (hereafter *Census of 1900*), Volume VII, 571.

21. *Sixth Annual Report of the Commissioner of Agriculture, Commerce and Industries of the State of South Carolina* (Columbia, SC, 1910), 86. "A. D. Hudson produced 2400 pounds; John B. Scurry, 1695 pounds; W. D. Herbert, 1600 pounds; G. P. Boozer, 1507 pounds; and M. J. Longshore, Welch Wilbur, D. H. Stillwell, W. H. Long, and D. M. Morris, each produced 1400 pounds or more."

22. *Thirteenth Census of the United States Taken in the Year 1910, Agriculture* (Washington, DC, 1913) (hereafter *Census of 1910*), Volume VII, 519.

23. *Fourteenth Census of the United States Taken in the Year 1920, Agriculture,* (Washington, DC, 1922) (hereafter *Census of 1920*), Volume VI, 289.

24. *United States Census of Agriculture, 1950* (Washington, DC, 1952) (hereafter *Census of 1950*), Volume V, Part 16, 445.

25. *South Carolina–Cash Receipts from Farm Marketings, 1965 Revised and 1966 Preliminary* (South Carolina Crop Reporting Service, September 1967, AE304), 46.

26. *Newberry Observer*, February 13, 1917.

27. Ibid., December 11, 1925, and May 14, 1926.

28. *South Carolina Crop Statistics, 1973–1974* (South Carolina Crop and Livestock Reporting Service, June, 1975, AE382) (hereafter *Crop Statistics, 1973–74*), 4; *Agricultural Statistics for Newberry County 1979* (South Carolina Crop and Livestock Reporting Service).

29. *South Carolina Crop Statistics, State and County Data, 1960–1965 Revised* (South Carolina Crop and Livestock Reporting Service, June 1967, AE 300) (hereafter *Crop Statistics, 1960–1965*), 35.

30. *South Carolina Crop Statistics, 1965–1971 Revised* (South Carolina Crop and Livestock Reporting Service, June, 1973, AE363) (hereafter *Crop Statistics, 1965–1971*), 36; *Agricultural Statistics for Newberry County, 1979 and 1987*.

31. *Census of 1900*, V, 662.

32. *Census of 1920*, VI, 285.

33. *Sixteenth Census of the United States: 1940, Agriculture*, (Washington, DC, 1942) (hereafter *Census of 1940*), Volume I, 455.

34. *United States Census of Agriculture, 1964*, South Carolina, Bureau of the Census (hereafter *Census of 1964*), Volume I, Part 27, 305, 314.

35. *South Carolina Livestock and Poultry Statistics, 1973–1974*, (South Carolina Crop and Livestock Reporting Services, June 1975, AE383) (hereafter *Livestock Statistics, 1973–1974*), 15.

36. Article by Henry L. Eason, county extension leader, *Newberry Observer*, January 25, 1977; *Agricultural Statistics for Newberry County, 1980 and 1987* (South Carolina Crop and Livestock Reporting Service).

37. *Census of 1940*, I, 455.

38. *Census of 1950*, I, 431.

39. *Census of 1964*, I, 314.

40. Ibid., 314.

41. *Census of 1900*, V, 474, 618.

42. *Newberry Observer*, February 18, 1889.

43. Ibid., February 17, 1953.

44. Ibid., January 7, 1972.

45. Information furnished by Cooperative Extension Service of Clemson University, July 20, 1976.

46. Ibid.

47. Ibid.

48. Miscellaneous Book 4, 201, Newberry County Clerk of Court's Office; the charter was granted May 13, 1922.

49. Miscellaneous Book 8, 405, Newberry County Clerk of Court's Office; the charter was granted November 13, 1941.

50. *Agriculture of Newberry County, South Carolina* (South Carolina Crop Reporting Service, County Statistical Services No. 14, June 1962, AE221) (hereafter *Agriculture Newberry County*), 10.

51. *Livestock Statistics, 1973–1974*, 8; *Agricultural Statistics for Newberry County, 1980 and 1987.*

52. Philip O. Epps, county extension leader.

53. *Census of 1900*, VI, 679.

54. *Fifteenth Census of the United States: 1930, Agriculture* (Washington, DC, 1932) (hereafter *Census of 1930*), Volume III, 312.

55. *Census of 1950*, 454.

56. *Agriculture Newberry County*, 17.

57. *South Carolina Cash Receipts from Farm Marketings* (South Carolina Crop Reporting Service, September 1967, AE304), 46.

58. *Agricultural Statistics for Newberry County, 1980 and 1987.*

59. *Census of 1950*, I, 427.

60. *Livestock Statistics, 1973–1974*, 1 and 4.

61. *Agricultural Statistics for Newberry County, 1980 and 1987.*

62. *Selected Census of Agriculture Characteristics: South Carolina 1959–1969.* (Clemson University Extension Service, Miscellaneous Extension Publication 3, September 1972), 2.

63. Ibid., 5. The average value of land and buildings per farm was $39,400, 9. The average value of products sold per farm was $14,200, 14. Newberry County in 1969 had eighty-eight farms selling products valued at more than $40,000 per year, 21.

64. *Agricultural Statistics for Newberry County, 1980.*

65. Ibid., 1987.

Chapter 14

1. For an explanation of the operation of the schools under the Free School Act of 1811, see Thomas H. Pope, *The History of Newberry County, South Carolina*, 2 volumes (The University of South Carolina Press, Columbia, SC, 1973, 1992), I, 218–220.

2. *Reports and Resolutions, 1860*, 402.

3. Return of the Commissioners of Free Schools for Newberry District, 1 October 1864–1 October 1865, South Carolina Archives. Teachers listed were: Pagesville, Miss Fannie Elmore, seventeen students; Cannon's Creek, S. C. Connor, thirty-one students; Jalapa, M. H. Vernon, twenty students; Newberry Courthouse, E. B. Montgomery, six students; St. Paul's Church, M. E. Hall, three students; Helena, A. A. McGraw, nine students; Bond's Cross Roads, E. S. Cooper, one student; Mt. Bethel, Vinnie E. Thompson, five students; Beth-

sheba, R. S. Dominick, nineteen students; Whitman's, Jake O'Dell, eight students; Ebenezer, M. J. Boyd, eight students; Smyrna, W. P. Reeder, eighteen students; Jolly Street, Miss E. P. Moon, twenty-seven students; and Wise's, Miss S. E. Shealy, thirteen students.

4. *Newberry Herald*, February 21, 1866.

5. John B. Carwile, *Reminiscences of Newberry* (Charleston, SC, 1890), 156–159.

6. *Newberry Herald*, March 27, 1867. W. P. Houseal stated that the college was in the W. F. Nance House, *Newberry Observer* Sesqui-Centennial Issue, April 28, 1939, Section E, 1.

7. *Newberry Herald*, July 3, 1867, lists Miss Lily Barre of Newberry and the Misses Mary Holly, C. Beard, and Neelie Peake of Fairfield. The issue of June 17, 1868, lists the graduates as the Misses Eliza McCully, Margaret Wilson, Hannah Marshall, Ella Bowers, and Lou Edwards.

8. *Newberry Herald*, September 26, 1867, carried a notice of application to incorporate a freedman's school in town by Robert Toliver, Charley Cannon, James Longshore, Harvey Clark, and others. James W. White on October 10, 1869, conveyed three-fourths of an acre on Caldwell Street to Samuel Dogan, J. P. Hutsin, Joseph Boston, Burrell Raines, and Joseph Jones, trustees duly elected for school purposes, in "trust for the colored citizens." This deed is recorded in Deed Book NN, at pages 463–464, Newberry County.

9. Hoge was a native of Ohio; captain in the Union Army; member of South Carolina Supreme Court, 1868–1870, member of Congress; and comptroller-general of South Carolina. See *Biographical Directory of the American Congress, 1774–1971* (United States Government Printing Office, 1971).

10. *Newberry Herald*, December 18, 1872; the notice stated that the school would commence its seventh annual session on January 13.

11. Ibid., December 30, 1868, March 17, December 22, 1869.

12. Ibid., January 5, 1870; January 3, 1871; September 4, 1872.

13. *Proceedings of the Constitutional Convention of South Carolina, Held at Charleston, SC, beginning January 14 and ending March 17, 1868* (Charleston, SC, 1868), 51.

14. Ibid., 655 and 889–893.

15. Governor Scott stated in his inaugural address on July 9, 1868, "I would deem this separation of the two races in the public schools a matter of the greatest importance to all classes of our people." *Journal of the House, Special Session of 1868*, 62.

16. Article X, *Constitution of the State of South Carolina, 1868*.

17. *Statutes at Large*, XIV, 339.

18. Simkins and Woody, 436.

19. Ibid., 438.

20. Ibid., 442–443; *Reports and Resolutions, 1873–74*, 447; *Reports and Resolutions, 1874–75*, 391.

21. *Reports and Resolutions,* 1875–76, 478, 480.

22. *Reports and Resolutions,* 1869, 237, 453. The superintendent reported that four other schools for black children were to be furnished—one in Caldwell Township by Major J. P. Kinard; one near Wadlington by Colonel Ellison S. Keitt; one in Maybinton Township by Dr. John N. Herndon; and one in Heller Township by H. H. Counts.

23. Ibid., 237. Teachers who submitted claims for services rendered between November 1, 1868, and October 31, 1869, and whose claims were approved for payment were: Annie Boyd, C. V. Scott, Dorcas Williams, Frances Elmore, J. M. Schumpert, Lizzie Kelley, Miss D. J. Boozer, Miss Henrietta Langford, George T. Speake, Rebecca DeWault (sic), M. E. Hall, Miss E. C. Joy, John McKittrick, Z. W. Bedenbaugh, Mrs. E. C. Boland, M. L. Long, J. N. Bowchelle, Mrs. C. F. S. Wright, Mrs. Marietta Patton, D. J. Shely (sic), William H. Ruff, Simon Miller, Samuel Brooks, Rosanna E. Spence, Mrs. Elvira Kibler, Fannie Leavell, Julius D. Dreher, Eliza R. Montgomery, Mary Holloway, M. J. Peterson, J. B. Hillhouse, Elizabeth S. Herbert, U. B. White (sic), John F. Banks, Mrs. A. B. Derrick, John G. Morgan, John E. Graham, A. B. Cogburn, Sallie Maffet, and A. P. Phifer (sic). See *Reports and Resolutions,* 1870–71, 216, for the list with amounts due aggregating $2331.00.

24. *Reports and Resolutions,* 1871–72, 85 and 91.

25. Ibid., 93; *Reports and Resolutions,* 1872–73, 273.

26. *Reports and Resolutions,* 1870–71, 377, 891. Jillson reported that he had furnished Summer with $2,395 worth of textbooks for which he had not been paid.

27. *Reports and Resolutions,* 1875–76, 457, 461, 463.

28. *Reports and Resolutions,* 1877–78, 375–391.

29. *Reports and Resolutions,* 1878, Table 3 appended to Annual Report of Superintendent of Education.

30. Ibid., 321. The other textbooks selected were Reynold's Series of Readers; Appleton's Series of Readers' Swinton's Primary History of the United States, his Condensed History of the United States, and his Outlines of Universal History; Holmes's History of the United States; Cornell's books on Geography; Maury's Geography; Sanford's Arithmetic; Robinson's Arithmetic; Quackenbos's books in English Grammar, in Composition, and in Rhetoric; Webster's Dictionaries; Reynold's Series of Writing Books; Appleton's Series of Writing Books; and Swinton's Word Books.

31. *Newberry Herald,* September 28, 1881; May 10, 1883; *Reports and Resolutions,* 1886, Volume I, 66.

32. *Reports and Resolutions,* 1886, Volume I, 66; *Reports and Resolutions,* 1900, Volume II, 125.

33. Ernest McPherson Lander, Jr., *A History of South Carolina: 1865–1960* (Chapel Hill, NC, 1960), 123. See also Colyer Meriwether, Jr., *History of Education in South Carolina* (Washington, DC, 1889).

34. An institute for black teachers was held in the Presbyterian Church, Newberry, in September 1890 with forty-five in attendance. The session lasted six
days. See *Reports and Resolutions, 1891,* 377. In 1892 two institutes were held in
Newberry. Sixty-seven whites attended one and forty-four blacks the other. *Reports and Resolutions, 1893,* Volume II, 398.

35. *Reports and Resolutions, 1883,* 64.

36. *Reports and Resolutions, 1893,* Volume II, 393, 394.

37. *The Newberry Observer,* January 30, 1890. The vote was 113 to 26. The
Newberry School District was established by Act 385, *Statutes at Large,* XX,
557. The four trustees elected in the special election were L. M. Speers, Ward 1;
W. E. Pelham, Ward 2; Alan Johnstone, Ward 3; and Dr. J. K. Gilder, Ward 4.
They were nominated at a mass meeting. The other seven trustees were J. F. J.
Caldwell, W. H. Wallace, George B. Cromer, J. K. P. Goggans, George S.
Mower, N. B. Mazyck, and J. S. Cozby. Others who served on the City Board of
Trustees before it was abolished in 1952 included F. N. Martin, Otto Klettner,
John H. Wicker, Dr. Van Smith, W. S. Langford, Arthur Kibler, J. L. Keitt, Sr.,
T. Roy Summer, Dr. W. G. Houseal, John M. Kinard, W. T. Tarrant, G. M. B.
Epting, George W. Summer, J. Marion Davis, W. A. McSwain, L. G. Eskridge, J.
Y. Jones, W. G. Mayes, H. B. Wells, J. Y. McFall, Dr. C. D. Weeks, L. W. Floyd,
P. D. Johnson, G. K. Dominick, Wilton Todd, A. W. Murray, A. J. Bowers, Jr.,
D. O. Carpenter, R. Wright Cannon, J. L. Keitt, Jr., and Chalmers Brown. After
1920, the board was self-perpetuating; it made recommendations to the county
board which filled vacancies on the City Board.

38. *Newberry Observer,* May 22, 1890. The next year T. M. Hunter and Miss
Garlington were elected principals; the Misses Baxter and Wheeler and Mrs. M.
L. Tarrant were elected teachers; A. P. Butler continued as principal of the Hoge
School with the Misses Lilla Reese and L. K. Goodwin as teachers there. See the
Newberry Observer, June 25, 1891.

On August 8, 1891, Joseph Jones, Benjamin Pratt, James Hutsin, Dennis
Moates, DeWitt Johnson, and Luton Green as trustees of school property situ-
ated in the town of Newberry known as the Hoge School for the education of
black youth and children of both sexes, conveyed three-fourths of an acre to the
trustees of the Newberry School District. The deed contains a caveat from B. M.
Raines to the effect that he was one of the original trustees but had resigned
some years before and had no concern with the same. Deed Book 8, page 278,
Newberry County.

39. *Newberry Herald,* April 16, 1873; August 30, 1876; August 17, 1882; and
Newberry Herald and News, October 20, 1887.

40. See *Newberry Herald,* January 5, 1870; January 3, 1871; September 4,
1872; June 28, 1876; December 28, 1882; and May 29, 1884; *Newberry Herald
and News,* September 1, 1887; and *Newberry Observer,* February 28, 1889, for
names of the masters of the Male Academy. They included J. C. Hardin, the
Reverend J. B. Hillhouse, William Brooks, R. H. Clarkson, J. F. Brown, Miss L.

R. Cofield, James P. Kinard, and John P. Glasgow. It competed directly with the preparatory department of Newberry College during much of this period and, as a result of the small number of pupils available, both suffered.

41. In 1877 the college advertised for preparatory students. *Newberry Herald*, August 15, 1877. Six years later it had so few pupils the Male Academy was closed to help the college. Ibid., June 21, 1883. Tuition was $19 per term and board was $10 to $12 per month. Ibid., August 23, 1883.

42. Captain A. P. Pifer was principal for seventeen years commencing in 1871. He was succeeded by Miss Octavia Garlington. Some who taught in the Female Academy after the war were Miss Fannie Leavell, Professor Frederick Werber, Miss Annie Hillhouse, Mrs. Bailey, Mrs. Cunningham, Mrs. Fair, and the Misses Anna Young, Goode Griffin, Fannie Hodges, Allie Cozby, and Mamie Holbrook. Its curriculum in 1886 included English, Latin, Greek, French, German, mathematics, vocal and instrumental music, painting, drawing, and calisthenics. See *Newberry Herald*, December 30, 1868; March 17, 1869; January 3, 1871; July 5, 1876; August 21, 1884; *Newberry Herald and News*, September 8, 1886; July 21, 1887; July 28, 1887; and *Newberry Observer*, June 20, 1889.

43. *Newberry Observer*, January 15, March 19, 1891; January 7, 1892. The issue of October 22, 1891, reported the purchase of a 750-pound bell from McShane Foundry for $182.50. This bell is mounted on the campus of the present school.

44. Ibid., September 17, 1891; May 29, June 12, 1895; January 5, 1899; June 14, 1900.

45. *Newberry Herald*, November 26, 1873; September 24, 1879. Welch was assisted by D. Charlton Lake, graduate of Wofford; J. C. Boyd, graduate of Erskine; and Dr. J. D. Bruce, local physician.

46. *Newberry Observer*, January 3, 1889.

47. Ibid., August 10, 1893.

48. *Reports and Resolutions, 1900*, Volume II, 52–54, Table 1.

49. Ibid., 52–54, Table 1; 105–106; Tables 1 and 2.

50. Ibid., 117, Table 3.

51. *Newberry Observer*, June 8, 1899. James S. Daniel was chairman of the Board of Trustees of this school.

52. *Reports and Resolutions, 1900*, Volume II, 118, 123, Table 3.

53. Harry S. Ashmore, *The Negro and the Schools* (Chapel Hill, NC, 1954), 10.

54. *Reports and Resolutions, 1901; Reports and Resolutions, 1918*, Volume II, 168, 177.

55. *Reports and Resolutions, 1908*, Volume I, 896–898.

56. *Reports and Resolutions, 1918*, Volume II, 74.

57. Ibid., 75.

58. Ibid., 78.

59. *Observer*, June 4, 1909; January 4, 1910.

60. *Reports and Resolutions, 1918*, Volume II, 74.

61. *Reports and Resolutions, 1921*, Volume II, 116.

62. *Reports and Resolutions, 1925*, Volume II, 46–48.

63. *Reports and Resolutions, 1929*, Volume II, 14–17.

64. *Reports and Resolutions, 1930*, Volume II, 12.

65. *Reports and Resolutions, 1913*, Volume I, 310.

66. *Reports and Resolutions, 1915*, Volume II, 91–94.

67. Ibid., 131; *Reports and Resolutions, 1916*, Volume II, 138–139, 198.

68. *Reports and Resolutions, 1925*, Volume II, 17.

69. *Reports and Resolutions, 1927*, Volume II, 6.

70. Ibid., 51–52.

71. *Reports and Resolutions, 1928*, Volume II, 1; Act Number 344, *Acts of 1937*.

72. *Reports and Resolutions, 1930*, Volume II, 21, 61.

73. Ibid., 64, 65.

74. The author's teachers whom he remembers with affection were Gertrude Reeder, Frances Wheeler, Annie Bynum, Margaret Mooney, Marion Daniel, Caroline Melton, and Josie P. McAlhaney at Boundary Street and Elizabeth Bryson, Amie W. Swittenberg, Sudie Dennis, Julia Kibler, Lillian Kibler, Marion Jones, Mildred Livingston, Lillie Mae Werts, Price K. Harmon, Harry Hedgepath, John Brock, and Olin B. Cannon at Newberry High School.

75. *Reports and Resolutions, 1940*, Volume II, 127–131; *Reports and Resolutions, 1950*, Volume II, 81–85.

76. Others who have served as members of the County Board of Education since 1952 are Gerald C. Paysinger, James E. Young and Dr. John F. Roche, chairmen; and William Armfield, David C. Waldrop, Henry F. Mills, David Luther Ruff, W. H. Caldwell, Dan Hamm, Jr., Ralph T. Williams, J. Alvin Kinard, Gilder M. Neel, Billy Taylor, Scott Boozer, the Reverend E. E. Gaulder, James R. Sexton, Cheryl F. Bannister, Francis M. Setzler, Sudie Crump Wicker, Fred Herren, Heyward Riddle, Heyward Amick, Ann R. Price, E. Monte Bowers, Joane Willingham, Jim Braswell, John S. Frick, Daisy Gibbs, and Harriett Rucker.

77. For the evolution of the board from an appointed to an elected body, see Act Number 154, *Acts of 1951*; Act Number 719, *Acts of 1952*; Act Number 1013, *Acts of 1964*; Act Number 884, *Acts of 1970*; and Act Number 981, *Acts of 1974*.

78. See *The Reverend David Carter, et al vs James D. Brown, County Superintendent of Education, et al*, U.S. District Court, Greenwood Division, 69–546.

Chapter 15

1. For an account of the beginning of the college, see Thomas H. Pope, *The History of Newberry County*, 2 volumes (Columbia, SC, 1973, 1992), I, 221–225.

2. J. Holland Bedenbaugh, "A History of Newberry College," master's thesis, University of South Carolina, 1930, 22–25.

3. *Weekly Herald,* July 12, September 20, 1865.

4. Bedenbaugh, 87.

5. Ibid., 34. The money was not raised, and the college was moved to Walhalla.

6. Ibid., 34.

7. Ibid., 41–42; *Newberry Herald,* February 21, 1877.

8. *Newberry Herald,* June 27, 1877. G. T. Berg was the architect; Bedenbaugh, 44.

9. *Newberry Observer,* October 2, 1895; Bedenbaugh, 68.

10. Bedenbaugh, 68.

11. *Newberry Observer,* November 13, 1895.

12. Bedenbaugh, 87, 90.

13. Ibid., 94.

14. Ibid., 100, 102. Andrew Carnegie, for whom the building was named, gave $10,000 provided an additional $10,000 was raised. The building housed the Engineering Department. In 1962 the present classroom building was erected on the site of Carnegie Hall, which was razed.

15. Ibid., 99.

16. Bedenbaugh, 104, 105.

17. Ibid., 108, 114.

18. *Newberry Observer,* November 6, 1964.

19. Ibid., January 24, 1983.

20. Ibid., 118.

21. Bedenbaugh, 126, 127.

22. Ibid., 130.

23. Ibid., 127.

Chapter 16

1. General Sessions Journal, Newberry District, 1850–1873, 65.

2. Ibid., 73, 80–81.

3. Benjamin F. Perry, *Reminiscences of Public Men* (Philadelphia, PA, 1883), 203.

4. *Observer,* September 5, 1922; September 8, 1922.

5. Future lawyers of Newberry who saw service included Young John Pope, Dr. Sampson Pope, George Johnstone, J. Y. Culbreath, Thomas S. Moorman, Benson M. Jones, William R. Spearman, John F. Spearman, Charles B. Buist, Milton A. Carlisle, Augustus P. Pifer, William H. Wallace, and O. L. Schumpert.

6. Constitution of 1865, Article III, Section 1.

7. *Newberry Herald,* January 17, 1866.

8. Francis Butler Simkins and Robert Hilliard Woody, *South Carolina During Reconstruction* (Chapel Hill, NC, 1932), 57.

9. *Statutes at Large,* Volume XIII, 366.

10. General Sessions Journal, Newberry District, 1858–1873.

11. *Newberry Herald*, August 1, December 19, 1866; General Sessions Journal, Newberry District, 1858–1873, 120, 123, 124.

12. General Sessions Journal, Newberry District, 1858–1873, 127, 133; *Newberry Herald*, February 20, 1867.

13. C. H. Suber to Governor Johnson Hagood, Governor Hagood's Letterbook, State Archives, January 11, 1882.

14. Constitution of 1868, Article IV.

15. *Revised Statutes of South Carolina*, 1873, Col. XX, Chapter CV, Section 6, 498.

16. *Statutes at Large*, Volume XVI, 212.

17. *Statutes at Large*, Volume XIV.

18. *Statutes at Large*, Volume IV, 5, 72; Volume XV, 146.

19. *Statutes at Large*, Volume XIV, 96.

20. *Statutes at Large*, Volume XV, 30.

21. Journal of Court of Common Pleas, Newberry County, 1873–1880, 5, 19, 73, 406; *Newberry Herald*, September 21, 1881.

22. *Statutes at Large*, Volume XIV, 207; *Journal of House of Representatives. 1868–1869*, 542–545.

23. *Newberry Herald*, July 9, 1879.

24. Ibid., February 12, 1879.

25. In addition to those already listed as lawyers in Newberry, the following practiced in Newberry before 1900: Francis W. Fant, James C. Clary, R. C. Maybin, Lewis W. Simkins, C. Douglas Barksdale, Lambert W. Jones, James Packer, J. K. P. Goggans, Milledge L. Bonham, Jr., G. G. Sale, G. W. Abney, John B. Jones, Joseph L. Keitt, D. Oscar Herbert, Harry Blease, George B. Cromer, Walter H. Hunt, Herbert H. Evans, W. Ernest Merchant, M. C. Galluchat, Elbert H. Aull, Mordecai Foot, Jr., T. R. Holmes, Frank L. Bynum, Coleman L. Blease, S. B. Lathan, Isaac H. Hunt, Thomas S. Sease, Robert H. Welch, F. H. Dominick, and H. C. Holloway.

Those from Newberry who were admitted to the Bar before 1900 but who did not practice in Newberry during that period were Stephen B. Fowles, who located in Beaufort; John F. Hobbs, who settled first at Lexington; Butler W. Nance, graduate of Allen University; John T. Duncan, who settled in Columbia; Eugene S. Blease, who was admitted while a resident of Saluda County; James B. Hunter, who first settled in Saluda but returned to Newberry in 1900; L. C. Speers, who located at Greenwood but soon became a newspaperman in New York; and David R. Phifer, who was admitted in the Dakota Territory in 1882 while there to obtain a divorce, and who was afterward admitted in Newberry on motion in 1888.

26. *Newberry Herald*, August 6, December 10, 1879; May 26, 1880; January 12, 1881; January 26, 1882.

27. *Newberry Herald and News*, October 23, 1984; *Newberry Observer*, June 8, 1983; January 6, 1897; June 12, 1907.

28. *Newberry Observer*, May 29, 1914; December 11, 1928.

29. *Report of the Bar Convention Held at Columbia, 11th December, 1884, For the Purpose of Forming The South Carolina Bar Association* (Columbia, SC, 1885), 15–20.

30. Ibid., 20–24, 29–30. See also *Newberry Herald and News*, December 11 and 18, 1884. The charter members from Newberry were E. H. Aull, J. F. J. Caldwell, M. A. Carlisle, George B. Cromer, James Y. Culbreath, John S. Fair, J. K. P. Goggans, D. O. Herbert, Walter H. Hunt, Jr., George Johnstone, John B. Jones, L. J. Jones, L. W. Jones, T. S. Moorman, George S. Mower, James Packer, Y. J. Pope, G. G. Sale, O. L. Schumpert, Christian H. Suber, and F. Werber, Jr.

31. *Newberry Observer*, December 5, 1891; January 26, 1898.

32. *Observer*, February 13, April 9, 1906; June 9, 1908.

33. Ibid., February 5, 1907.

34. Minutes of the Newberry Jail Commission, South Carolina Department of Archives and History.

35. *Newberry Observer*, March 31, 1911.

36. Act No. 1225 of the Acts of the General Assembly of South Carolina for 1938. The renovation cost $39,000. *Newberry Observer*, January 23, 1940.

Chapter 17

1. John. A. Chapman, *The Annals of Newberry*, Part Second (Newberry, SC, 1892), 373–376; Thomas H. Pope, *The History of Newberry County* (University of South Carolina Press, Columbia, SC, 1973), I, 192, 209–211; John B. Carwile, *Reminiscences of Newberry* (Charleston, SC, 1890), 192–203; *Newberry Herald*, July 23, 1873.

2. Pope, 179, 193, 223, 285; *Newberry Herald*, January 6, 1869; Carwile, 82–91.

3. Pope, 102, 179, 182, 193; *Newberry Observer*, July 18 and December 19, 1894; Carwile, 76.

4. Pope, 102, 105, 109, 182, 194–195, 205, 274, 279; *Newberry Observer*, September 8, 1892.

5. Pope, 102, 109, 159, 195, 212, 278, 285; Carwile, 208–216.

6. Pope, 103, 150, 197; *Newberry Herald*, February 9, 1881; Carwile, 208–216.

7. Pope, 149, 182, 190, 197, 227, 228; *Newberry Herald*, January 17, 1877; November 6, 1878; January 11, 1883; *Newberry Observer*, August 10, 1899; *Cyclopedia of Eminent and Representative Men of the Carolinas*, 2 volumes (Brant and Fuller, Madison, WI, 1892), I, 280.

8. Pope, 197, 207, 210; *Newberry Observer*, March 13, 1890; Carwile, 65–66.

9. Pope, 217, 229; *Newberry Observer*, February 6, 1925.

10. Pope, 197–198; *Observer*, September 11, 1906; J. C. Hemphill, *Men of Mark in South Carolina*, 4 volumes, (Washington, DC, 1909), III, 71.

11. Hemphill, I, 213; *Cyclopedia*, I, 283; J. C. Garlington, *Men of the Time*

(Spartanburg, SC, 1902), 350; D. A. Dickert, *History of Kershaw's Brigade* (Dayton, OH, 1973, Morningside Edition), 456; *Observer*, March 31, April 4, 1911.

12. *Memorial Exercises*, South Carolina Supreme Court, June 5, 1911.

13. *Newberry Observer*, June 6, 1889; *Observer*, August 8, 1902.

14. *Newberry Herald*, November 1, 1876.

15. *Newberry Herald*, May 8, 1867; February 24, April 14, 1869.

16. *Newberry Herald*, May 16 and November 14, 1866; January 29, 1868.

17. *Newberry Herald*, June 19, 1867; January 29, March 25, and June 10, 1868.

18. *Newberry Herald*, July 31, 1867; January 23, 1878; February 5, 1879; *Newberry Herald and News*, August 30, 1888.

19. *Cyclopedia*, I, 282; *Observer*, February 16 and December 6, 1904.

20. *Newberry Herald*, February 3, 1869; February 23, 1882; *Newberry Herald and News*, February 3, 1897.

21. Pope, 271.

22. Ibid., 271.

23. *Tri-Weekly Herald*, June 14, December 26, 1865; *Newberry Herald*, April 2, 1867; April 29, July 15, 1868; January 24, 1877.

24. *Newberry Observer*, April 10, April 24, May 8, June 19, 1895.

25. Ibid., November 10, 17, 1869; May 31, 1871.

26. Ibid., October 11, 1871.

27. Hemphill, I, 347. *Observer*, December 13, 1910.

28. *Newberry Herald*, July 19, 1871; October 28, 1874; August 9, 1876; September 18, November 13, 1878; September 7, 1882; *Biographical Directory of the American Congress 1774–1971* (Government Printing Office, 1971), 1201; Frank E. Jordan, Jr., *The Primary State, A History of the Democratic Party in South Carolina, 1876–1862* (n.p. n.d.), 60–62.

29. *Herald and News*, March 31, November 17, 1886.

30. *Observer*, March 11, 1921.

31. *Observer*, January 31, 1922.

32. *Cyclopedia*, I, 245; Hemphill, I, 194; *Observer*, December 16, 1927.

33. Jordan, 28–30.

34. *Newberry Herald*, December 6, 1876.

35. Ibid., June 10, 24, 1874; January 5, 1881.

36. *Newberry Herald*, February 4, 1874; May 5, 1875; May 2, 16, 1877; February 23, July 3, 1878.

37. *Newberry Observer*, March 12, 1920.

38. *Cyclopedia*, I, 285; *Newberry Herald*, March 30, 1882.

39. *Newberry Observer*, July 31, 1895; January 26, 1898.

40. Ibid., July 26, 1921.

41. *Observer*, May 21, 1907.

42. *Newberry Herald*, September 28, 1870; July 28, 1875; March 19, July 16, 1879; December 7, 1882.

43. Ibid., July 3, 10, 1867; July 23, 1873; July 28, 1875; September 6, 1896; February 7, 21, August 29, November 28, 1877; February 11, 1880.

44. Ibid., July 28, 1875; *Newberry Observer*, August 1, 1889.

45. Pope, 105, 197, 228; *Tri-Weekly Herald*, June 21, July 5, 12, September 27, 1865; *Newberry Herald*, January 31, June 4, 1866; April 12, 1871; April 24, August 7, 1872; April 9, 1873; January 6, March 3, 17, 1875; *Newberry Observer*, February 27, 1895.

46. *Newberry Herald*, June 28, September 27, October 4, 25, 1876; December 26, 1877; December 28, 1882; January 18, 1883; *Newberry Observer*, May 7, 1891; January 5, 1899; June 14, 1900; February 21, March 14, October 31, 1901; September 28, 1920; *Observer*, May 20, 1924.

47. *Newberry Herald*, June 21, 1871; December 25, 1878; *Observer*, March 13, 1925.

48. *Newberry Herald*, January 17, 1877; July 3, 1878; January 8, September 3, 1879; *Newberry Herald and News*, October 2, 1884; *Newberry Observer*, September 11, 1895; February 3, 1933.

49. *Newberry Herald*, September 12, 1877; September 9, 1879; March 31, 1880.

50. Ibid., September 12, 1877; February 13, 1878; *Newberry Observer*, April 21, 1898.

51. *Newberry Herald*, September 12, 1877; July 31, 1878; February 26, 1879; January 21, 1880; March 13, 1884; *Observer*, February 13, 1903.

52. *Newberry Herald*, April 16, 1873; September 12, February 7, 1877; February 12, 1879; August 16, 1883; *Newberry County Cemeteries*, 2 volumes (Newberry, SC, 1985), II, 37.

53. *Newberry Herald*, September 12, 1877; February 2, 1881; *Newberry Observer*, February 14, 1941; August 31, 1948.

54. *Newberry Herald*, February 26, 1879; January 21, 1880.

55. *Newberry Herald*, January 21, 1880.

56. Ibid., January 21, 1880; *Observer*, October 24, 1911.

57. *Cyclopedia*, I, 281; *Newberry Observer*, April 22, 1896.

58. *Newberry Herald*, September 15, 1880.

59. *Observer*, March 29, 1927.

60. Hemphill, II, 87; *Newberry Observer*, September 27, 1935.

61. *Newberry Herald*, December 15, 1881; January 11, 1883; *Observer*, August 9, 1905; June 20, 1908; *Newberry Observer*, June 14, 1929.

62. *Newberry Herald*, June 1, 1881; January 5, 1882; *Newberry Herald and News*, February 24, September 15, 1886; *Newberry Observer*, July 11, 1889; January 30, June 26, September 25, October 16, 1890; May 5, October 27, 1892; July 31, 1895; July 29, 1896; September 9, 1927.

63. Hemphill, IV, 100; *Newberry Herald*, January 26, May 18, and June 8, 1882.

64. *Newberry Herald*, June 8, 15, 1882; *Newberry Cemeteries*, II, 45.

65. Hemphill, I, 269.

66. *Newberry Observer*, February 18, 1930.

67. *Newberry Herald*, December 21, 1882; *Newberry Herald and News*, March 31, 1887.

68. *Newberry Herald*, December 21, 1882; January 18, 1883; December 18, 1884; *Newberry Herald and News*, January 27, 1885; March 9, 1887.

69. *Newberry Observer*, May 29, 1895.

70. *Newberry Cemeteries*, II, 48.

71. *Newberry Herald*, June 8, 1882; *Newberry Herald and News*, August 28, 1884; *Newberry Observer*, April 30, 1891; December 9, 1896; *Observer*, April 4, 1905.

72. *Observer*, April 16, 1907.

73. Ibid., August 21, 1925.

74. *Newberry Herald*, April 26, 1883; *Newberry Observer*, December 13, 1888.

75. Hemphill, IV, 151; D. D. Wallace, *The History of South Carolina*, 4 volumes (New York, 1934), IV, 602–604; *Observer*, April 12, 1927.

76. *Newberry Herald and News*, November 13, 1884.

77. Ibid., June 2, September 29, 1886; *Newberry Observer*, January 10, 1896; *Observer*, July 4, 1913; March 22, 1921.

78. *Newberry Herald*, November 2, 1870; May 24, November 15, December 6, 1871; January 31, April 17, 1872; September 23, November 25, December 23, 1874; August 31, 1882; *Newberry Herald and News*, January 17, March 28, April 18, 1889.

79. Jordan, 25–32, 34–35, 40–43, 63–69, 71–72, 88; see Chapter on Blease in this volume; *Biographical Directory of the American Congress, 1774–1971* (Washington, DC, 1971), 603.

80. *Newberry Observer*, January 17, 1889.

81. Ibid., June 5, 1890.

82. *Newberry Observer*, September 26, 1950.

83. *Newberry Observer*, June 16, 1892; January 23, 1895; May 20, September 16, 1896; May 13, 1952; Wallace, IV, 104–105.

84. Ibid., July 19, 1935; Wallace, IV, 604.

85. See sketch in Chapter 6; Jordan, 27–37, 54–56; *Newberry Cemeteries*, II, 50; *Newberry Observer*, June 21, 1938.

86. *Newberry Observer*, September 21, 1898; *Observer*, September 2, 1904; September 12, 1905; April 13, 1906; April 16, 1907; July 4, 1913; May 15, November 13, 1917.

87. *Observer*, February 4, November 28, 1919; September 2, 1921; September 1, 1922.

88. Ibid., January 15, 1926; *Newberry Observer*, January 16, 1931; March 30, 1934.

89. *Newberry Observer*, November 2, 1934; Jordan, 76–77.

90. *Newberry Observer*, December 31, 1963.

91. *Observer*, July 30, 1929.

92. *Newberry Observer*, December 19, 1930.

93. Jordan, 105–106; Wallace, IV, 431; *Newberry Observer*, March 15, 1960; *Biographical Directory*, 870.

94. *Newberry Observer*, October 25, 1957.

95. Ibid., June 28, 1946.

96. Ibid., January 18, 1900; June 23, 1942.

97. Ibid., August 28, 1951.

98. Ibid., July 27, 1943.

99. Ibid., January 24, 1933.

100. Ibid., June 20, 1958.

101. Ibid., March 11, 1960.

102. Ibid., January 7, 1966; Jordan, 79.

103. Ibid., July 10, 1945.

104. Ibid., June 20, 1972.

105. *Observer*, November 21, 1919; *Newberry Observer*, December 16, 1930.

Chapter 18

1. *Newberry Observer*, June 6, 1939. Article by W. P. Houseal.

2. *Tri-Weekly Herald*, March 21, 1865.

3. *Weekly Herald*, June 28, 1865; *Newberry Herald*, January 17, 1866.

4. *Newberry Herald*, June 22, 1866. The fire was incendiary in origin and was started in the old Thespian Hall.

5. *Newberry Observer*, June 6, 1939. Houseal's article.

6. Ibid., February 19, 1873.

7. *Newberry Observer*, June 6, 1939.

8. Ibid., June 9, 1939. Houseal.

9. *Newberry Herald*, May 12, 1875; May 24, 1876; May 1, 1878.

10. *Newberry Observer*, July 13, 1909.

11. *Newberry Herald*, January 15, 1879; February 26, 1879.

12. Ibid., January 21, 1880.

13. Ibid., August 7, 1884.

14. Ibid., January 18, 1883.

15. *Newberry Observer*, April 4, 1894. The incorporators of the Reform Publishing Company were J. A. Sligh, C. L. Blease, Sampson Pope, C. T. Wyche, F. V. Capers, James A. Riser, and Job L. Hughey. See also issues of April 25 and May 30, 1894.

16. *Newberry Herald and News*, March 9, 1887.

17. Ibid., January 5, 1887.

18. *Newberry Observer*, December 5, 1889.

19. Ibid., March 22, 1900.

20. Ibid., February 21, March 14, and October 31, 1901.

21. Ibid., May 13, 1904, June 9, 1939.

22. Ibid., January 5, 1923, June 6, 1939.

23. Ibid., June 6, 1939.

24. Ibid., June 6, 1939. Frank Armfield carries on a job printing business in Newberry.

25. Ibid., June 9, 1939. Houseal.

26. Ibid., June 9, 1939. While Houseal states that this newspaper was discontinued in 1891, he must be in error. R. L. Whites was reported to have acquired control in 1894. Ibid., February 21, 1894.

27. Ibid., February 20, 1895, September 30, 1896, September 8, 1897, and May 11, 1899.

28. *Newberry Observer*, June 14, 1900, December 13, 1901.

29. The first issue appeared in May 1961. Publication was discontinued in July 1972.

30. *Newberry Observer*, December 15, 1911; March 1, 1912, June 9, 1939.

31. *Observer*, April 28, 1922.

32. Ibid., September 5, 1922. The second six were Job Johnstone, O. B. Mayer, Jr., C. H. Suber, O. L. Schumpert, J. P. Smeltzer, and George Johnstone.

33. Ibid., May 20, 1924. See the sketch included with members of the Bar.

34. Ibid., November 11, 1910.

35. *Who's Who in South Carolina, 1934–35*, Walker Scott Utsey, editor (Columbia, SC, 1935), 227–228; *Newberry Observer*, September 10, 1946.

36. *Newberry Observer*, July 12, 1949.

37. Ibid., February 6, 1940; David Duncan Wallace, *The History of South Carolina*, 4 vols. (New York, 1934), IV, 676.

38. Wallace, IV, 714; *Newberry Observer*, August 18, 1970.

39. *Cyclopedia of Eminent and Representative Men of the Carolinas of the Nineteenth Century*, 2 vols. (Madison, WI, 1892), I, 323.

40. *South Carolina Journals and Journalists*, edited by James B. Meriwether (Spartanburg, SC, 1975), 196–197.

41. Ibid., 183.

42. John A. Chapman, *The Annals of Newberry* (Aull and Houseal, Newberry, SC, 1892), Part II, 568.

43. *Newberry Observer*, July 23, 1891 and September 5, 1922.

44. Douglas Southall Freeman, *Lee's Lieutenants*, three volumes (New York, 1944). III, 821. Caldwell's history was reprinted by Continental Book Company (Marietta, Georgia, 1951) and by Morningside Press (Dayton, Ohio, 1984).

45. *Observer*, February 6, 1925.

46. Freeman, III, 821.

47. *Newberry Herald*, August 28, 1878.

48. *Observer*, October 5, 1917.

49. *Newberry Observer*, August 10, 24, 1893.

50. *Newberry Herald*, September 11, 1878.

51. *Dictionary of American Biography* (New York, 1959), III, 93; *Observer*, June 30, 1905.

52. John B. Carwile, *Reminiscences of Newberry* (Charleston, SC, 1890), Tricentennial reprint (R. L. Bryan Co., Columbia, SC, 1970).

53. *South Carolina and Her Builders*, edited by Ralph E. Grier (Columbia, SC, 1930); *Who's Who in South Carolina, 1934-35; Newberry Observer*, June 5, 1951.

54. *Newberry Observer*, December 12, 1939.

55. Wallace, IV, 536.

56. *Newberry Observer*, May 1, 1956.

57. Ibid., December 28, 1973.

58. *Newberry Herald*, May 21, 1873.

59. Information furnished by Ruth H. Westwood.

60. *Newberry Herald*, January 18, 1883; February 8, 1883; March 15, 1883; March 20, 1883; September 20, 1883; *Newberry Observer*, May 11, 1893.

61. *Newberry Herald*, September 20, 1883; *Herald and News*, May 12, 1887; *Newberry Observer*, May 9, 1889; September 26, 1889; April 23, 1891; and July 9, 1891.

Chapter 19

1. Thomas H. Pope, *The History of Newberry County South Carolina*, 2 vols. (University of South Carolina Press, Columbia, SC, 1973, 1991), I, 105.

2. Pope, 106.

3. *Newberry Herald*, June 22, 1866; June 5 and 19, 1867; February 24, 1869.

4. John B. Carwile, *Reminiscences of Newberry* (Charleston, SC, 1890), 29-30.

5. *Newberry Herald*, June 7, 1871; April 24, 1872; May 28, 1873.

6. *Newberry Herald*, June 14, September 27, 1871; June 11, 1873.

7. Ibid., October 29, 1873.

8. *Newberry Herald*, July 9, 1873.

9. Ibid., July 23, August 13, 1873; July 4, 1877.

10. Ibid., April 21, May 26, 1875. Officers were W. T. Tarrant, president; T. S. Moorman, 1st vice president; T. C. Pool, 2nd vice president; E. E. Salinas, 1st director; O. L. Schumpert, 2nd director; H. O'Neall Harrington, 3rd director; S. Fowles, 4th director; L. C. Moore, secretary-treasurer.

11. Ibid., March 1, 1876; March 14, 1877.

12. *Newberry Herald*, April 10, 1878. At this time there were thirteen grocery stores, five dry goods stores, three dry goods and grocery stores, four drugstores, three furniture stores, one confectionery, seven bar rooms, nine cheap lunch houses, one Noah's Ark, one tobacco and segar (sic) store, one shoe factory, two

cobbling shops, one tin and stove store, one picture gallery, two tailor shops, two merchant tailoring shops, two book stores, three printing offices, one harness and saddle store, one restaurant, one hash house, two hotels, two shaving saloons, one billiard saloon, one bathing room, one express office, three millinery emporiums, two jewelry stores, one fruit and confectionery, two dress making rooms, two livery stables, one bakery and confectionery, two hardware stores, two clothing stores, one gunsmithery, two fish dealers, one buggy dealer, one commission and guano merchant, three insurance offices, three blacksmiths, one buggy and wagon factory, one auction house, one marble yard, and two undertakers.

13. *Newberry Herald*, February 19, July 23, August 13, 1879; February 23, 1882; May 10, 17, July 26, 1883.

14. Ibid., March 26, May 14, 1879; September 29, 1880; March 23, 1182.

15. Ibid., June 21 and July 19 and 26, 1883; officers of the new company included George S. Mower, president; Ed Scholtz, vice president; I. W. Walter, 1st director; C. A. Bowman, 2nd director; George Gilliland, engineer; W. T. Jackson, asst. engineer; M. Foot, Jr., secretary; John W. Montgomery, chief of the fire department; and J. E. Brown, assistant chief.

16. *Newberry Herald and News*, July 5, 1888.

17. *Newberry Observer*, February 6, 1890. R. L. Luther was elected president and E. O. Counts, secretary.

18. Ibid., February 28, 1889.

19. Ibid., May 8, 1951.

20. Petitioners for the meeting included Edward R. Hipp, E. A. Griffin, Summer Brothers, E. M. Evans, William Johnson, S. P. Boozer, T. J. Hayes, O. McR. Holmes, H. H. McIlhenny, R. D. Smith, Dr. W. E. Pelham, Davenport and Cavanaugh, Copeland Brothers, S. J. Wooten, Livingston-Lominick Co., A. C. Thomasson, W. S. Melton, Sample & Lominick, M. A. Huiett, R. C. Sonnenburg, H. E. Todd, R. C. Williams, Cromer & McGraw, Paul Johnstone, James F. Todd, C. and G. S. Mower & Co., J. Guy Daniels, Ewart-Pifer Co., Holmes & McFall, E. H. Aull, Gilder & Weeks, W. A. Jamieson, D. L. Copeland, Blackwelder & Davenport, J. W. Kibler & Co., G. B. Summer, Shelly, Dean & Summer, J. M. Swindler, Purcell & Scott, J. A. Mimnaugh, W. G. Mayes, C. L. Havird, T. A. Williams, Louis Morris, George I. C. McWhirter, Joseph Mann, J. L. Bowers, T. Vigodsky, The Smith Co., Havird Brothers, Gus Dennis, Kibler Dennis & Co., Arthur Kibler, W. T. Tarrant, Joseph Lines, Otto Klettner, Casey & Lee, H. C. Soloman, Counts & Dickert, John W. Miller, Blair & Havird, C. J. McWhirter, J. H. Hair, J. H. West, L. C. Pitts, Alan Johnstone & Co., J. N. Bass, T. C. Pool, J. M. Counts, J. A. Black, Z. F. Wright, F. Z. Wilson, W. K. Sligh, J. W. White, J. A. Senn, B. B. Leitzsey, L. M. Speers, R. Y. Leavell, M. A. Carlisle, and James A. Burton.

21. *Observer*, April 2, 1907.

22. Ibid., March 20, 1906; April 17 and May 26, 1908.
23. See Appendix F.

Chapter 20

1. *The History of the Lutheran Church in South Carolina*, prepared and edited by the History of Synod Committee (Columbia, SC, 1971), 307–308.

2. Ibid., 308.

3. Joe M. King, *A History of South Carolina Baptists* (Columbia, SC, 1964), 255–258.

4. Ibid., 259.

5. Francis Butler Simkins and Robert Hilliard Woody, *South Carolina During Reconstruction* (Chapel Hill, 1932), 385.

6. Ibid., 395.

7. Newberry County Deed Book 7, page 329, Deed Book 66, page 386, and Deed Book 66, page 386 (hereafter Deed Books).

8. Map of the Town of Newberry, 1881, by G. M. Girardeau; photocopy of map in possession of the author.

9. Deed Book PP, page 282 and Deed Book PP page 281.

10. *Newberry Herald*, July 30, 1873; Deed Book SS page 270; Deed Book 11, page 328; Deed Book 24, page 418.

11. Deed Book AAA, page 357; Deed Book 13, page 47.

12. For deeds to these churches see: Trinity, Deed Book AAA, page 44, Deed Book 13, page 592, and Deed Book 15, page 266; Miller's Chapel, Deed Book PP, page 282 and Deed Book PP, page 281; Shiloh, Deed Book 7, page 311, Deed Book 30, page 113, and Deed Book 71, page 309; St. James, Deed Book SS, page 108, Deed Book 4, page 241, and Deed Book 42, page 574; St. Mark, Deed Book YY, page 1 and Deed Book 12, page 164; Piney Grove, Deed Book 11, page 477; Mt. Moriah, Deed Book 1, page 215, Deed Book 15, page 416, and Deed Book 71, page 375; Lower Mt. Olive, DeedBook 1, page 273, Deed Book 22, page 104, and Deed Book 85, page 55; Elisha, Deed Book 61, page 428; St. Mary's, Deed Book 2, page 479 and Deed Book 2, page 481; Pleasant Grove, Deed Book 9, page 279; St. Matthew, Deed Book YY, page 223, Deed Book 21, page 496, and Deed Book 28, page 533; Upper Mt. Olive, Deed Book SS, page 213, and Deed Book 12, page 555 (see also the *Newberry Herald*, June 11, 1873); Mt. Zion, Deed Book AAA, page 3; Hannah, Deed Book SS, page 145, Deed Book AAA, page 118, Deed Book 10, page 307, and Deed Book 65, page 350; Lever Chapel, Deed Book 7, page 22; Mt. Hebron, Deed Book 17, page 519; Sweet Spring, Deed Book 12, page 287 and Deed Book 13, page 520.
There are deeds to other AME churches which apparently are no longer in existence: Bird Stand, Deed Book 5, page 571; Tranquil, Deed Book 7, page 565; Wilson Chapel, Deed Book 19, page 311; St. Luke's, Deed Book 51, page 215

and Deed Book 51, page 217; and Mt. Zion at Little Mountain, Deed Book 66, page 372.

13. Deed Book SS, page 662, Deed Book 19, page 91, and Deed Book 80, page 110; Deed Book 23, page 65; Whitmire, Deed Book 23, page 406, and Deed Book 24, page 350; Bruce Tabernacle, Deed Book 53, page 188.

14. Deed Book 4, page 216; Deed Book 7, page 311; Deed Book 19, page 575.

15. See the constitution of the New Enoree Baptist Association, (printed 1973).

16. For deeds to these churches, see the following: Antioch, Deed Book 3, page 135 and Deed Book 80, page 12; Little Beaverdam, Deed Book 106, page 160 (this church was formerly located near Head Spring); Bethlehem, Deed Book SS, page 270, Deed Book 11, page 328, and Deed Book 24, page 418; Boozer Chapel, Deed Book 7, page 10 and Deed Book 28, page 549; Bush River, Deed Book 1, page 285 and Deed Book 10, page 590; Calvary, Deed Book 1, page 172 and Deed book 67, page 308; New Enoree, Deed Book 4, page 381; Flint Hill, Deed Book 1, page 478, Deed Book 16, page 12, Deed Book 21, page 434, Deed Book 61, page 382, and Deed Book 63, page 449; James Hopewell, Deed Book 11, page 278; Love, Deed Book 63, page 395; Little River, Deed Book 6, page 390, and Deed Book 75, page 106; Mt. Zion, Deed Book 9, page 440; Renwick Grove, Deed Book 9, page 390; Seekwell, Deed Book 9, page 331 (also see *Newberry Herald*, June 11, 1873); Sims Chapel, Deed Book 10, page 450; St. John, Deed Book 7, page 624, Deed Book 34, page 381, and Deed Book 52, page 85; St. Matthew, Deed Book 22, page 357; and Welch Zion, Deed Book 5, page 239 and Deed Book 9, page 79.

17. For references to deeds to these churches, see: Old Beaverdam, Deed Book 5, page 478 and Deed Book 65, page 21; Vaughansville Crossroads, Deed Book 12, page 411; Belmont, Deed Book 1, page 457; Mt. Moriah, Deed Book 13, page 587; and Scurry Spring Hill, Deed Book 28, page 543.

18. For references to deeds to these churches, see: St. Mary's, Deed Book 9, page 294; Mt. Bethel, Deed Book 12, page 40; Suber Chapel, Deed Book 12, page 259; New Bethlehem, Deed Book 16, page 532; Victory, Deed Book 65, page 157, and Deed Book 65, page 413; and St. Matthew No. 2, Deed Book 22, page 357.

19. Deed Book 53, page 213 and Deed Book 62, page 620; Deed Book 54, page 394; Deed Book 50, page 311; Deed Book 52, page 35; Deed Book 42, page 204; Deed Book 30, page 433; Deed Book 50, page 311; Deed Book 13, page 99.

20. *Newberry Observer*, December 28, 1898.

21. For membership and pastors of the churches see *Minutes of the South Carolina Synod*, 1989. For histories of the several congregations, see *A History of the Lutheran Church in South Carolina, supra.*

22. Lawton Daugherty, "Little River-Dominick Presbyterian Church, 1761–1961" (unpublished monograph, 1961), states that efforts were made in 1761 to persuade the Hanover Presbytery to furnish supplies to the Little River Settle-

ment. However, the Reverend Mr. Creswell was not ordained until 1764. Pope, *History of Newberry County*, Volume 1, 80, states that this church was organized in 1764, as do F. D. Jones and W. H. Mills, *History of the Presbyterian Church in South Carolina Since 1850*, (Columbia, SC, 1926), 1022.

23. Pope, I, 240–241; Jones and Mills, 982–984. Clarence McKittrick Smith, Jr., *Waymarks: A History of Aveleigh Presbyterian Church 1835–1985* (Newberry, SC, 1985).

24. Pope, I, 241. For a history of Smyrna, see Mildred W. Goodlett, *Our Heritage, A History of Smyrna Church and of the Boozers of Smyrna* (Greenville, SC, 1963).

25. Jones and Mills, 1057.

26. Ibid., 1031.

27. Ibid., 1065–1066.

28. Information furnished by Keitt Purcell, February 1980.

29. Ibid.

30. See Centennial Sermon of the Reverend Thomas H. Pope delivered on October 8, 1871, and Mrs. C. M. Smith, *History of the Bush River Baptist Church, 1771–1933* (monograph printed August 1934).

31. As to the various associations, see King, Congaree Association, 451; Bethel Association, 367–371; Salem Association, 421; Fairfield Association, 395; and Reedy River Association, 418–420. The present membership and names of the pastors were furnished the author by the Reverend Kenneth W. Harmon.

32. Ibid., 230.

33. See James L. Aull, *Historical Sketch of the First Baptist Church, Newberry, South Carolina, 1831–1931* (Newberry, SC, September 1931); *Newberry Observer*, September 25, 1956; and Juanita Hitt, *The First Baptist Church, Newberry, South Carolina, 1831–1981*, (monograph printed in 1981).

34. *Newberry Observer*, October 31, 1950.

35. The Reverend Eugene Norris furnished the present membership and names of the pastors of the churches in the Greenwood District. District Superintendent J. Chad Davis of the Columbia District furnished like information for the churches in the Columbia District.

36. L. Clifton Graham, compiler, *A History of Central United Methodist Church* (monograph printed, 1970). *Newberry Observer*, November 2, 1937.

37. Ibid., October 26, 1937.

38. Ibid., October 26, 1937.

39. Ibid., October 29, 1937.

40. Ibid., October 29, 1937; Charlie M. Senn, *A History of Trinity United Methodist Church 1835–1985* (Newberry, SC, 1985).

41. Ibid., October 29, 1937.

42. Ibid., January 15, 1935.

43. Ibid., October 29, 1937.

44. Albert S. Thomas, D. D., *The Episcopal Church in South Carolina* (Columbia, SC, 1957), 591–595.

45. Ebenezer P. Chalmers, as Administrator of Rebecca Suber, deceased vs. Perry Halfacre, as Administrator of David Halfacre, et al, Court of Common Pleas for Newberry County. Information about the church was furnished by Waldo M. Halfacre in May 1980.

46. Deed Book 70, page 194.

47. Deed Book 128, page 41.

48. Deed Book 20, page 114 and Deed Book 67, page 604; Deed Book 20, page 261 and Deed Book 38, page 476; Deed Book 24, page 441 and Deed Book 63, page 367; Deed Book 38, page 217, Deed Book 61, page 283, and Deed Book 70, page 132.

49. Deed Book 44, page 264, Deed Book 46, page 583, Deed Book 58, page 515, and Deed Book 60, page 380; Deed Book 46, page 440.

50. Deed Book 65, page 211, Deed Book 67, page 430, and Deed Book 70, page 230; Deed Book 46, page 509, and Deed Book 49, page 10; information furnished by the Reverend Mr. Hunter; Deed Book 69, page 197.

51. Deed Book 63, page 44; Deed Book 63, page 367, and Deed Book 66, page 355; Deed Book 64, page 478, and Deed Book 70, page 171; Deed Book 62, page 541, Deed Book 63, page 321, and and Deed Book 63, page 322; Deed Book 32, page 67 and Deed Book 74, page 400; Deed Book 126, page 58.

Chapter 21

1. Joseph Ioor Waring, M.D., *A History of Medicine in South Carolina: 1825–1900* (Columbia, SC, 1967), 164.

2. *Tri-Weekly Herald*, December 26, 1865. Twenty-one physicians agreed to the fee scale which included $1.00 for a visit in town; mileage of $.50 per mile in the day and $1.00 per mile at night; $1.00 for a prescription; obstetrics from $20.00 to $50.00; and $20.00 in advance for a venereal disease. Doctors P. B. Ruff, Mayer, Pope, Watkins, McFall, Garmany, C. H. Sondley, Bond, McCants, W. C. Sondley, Pitts, Glenn, J. M. H. Ruff, Kennerly and McIntosh signed the agreement.

3. *Newberry Herald*, March 30, 1870; October 16, 1878.

4. *Statutes at Large*, Volume XVII, 571 and 1173. Registration commenced on June 1, 1882.

5. Minutes of the Town Council of Newberry, June 8, 1882.

6. Ibid., June 5, 1890; June 11, 1894. (H. C. Hunter was appointed first inspector); February 2, 1882, and December 22, 1897.

7. *Statutes at Large*, Volume XX, 699, authorized county boards to license physicians, the effective date being December 24, 1890.

8. *Statutes at Large*, Volume XXIV, established a State Board of Examiners, the effective date being February 27, 1904.

9. *Observer*, May 16, 1911.

10. Ibid., June 8, 1920; March 28, 1924.

11. Ibid., December 13, 1923. Directors elected were G. B. Cromer, S. J. Derrick, W. H. Hunt, John M. Kinard, B. C. Matthews, George W. Summer, Z. F. Wright, Mrs. H. L. Parr, and Mrs. R. H. Wright.

12. *Newberry Observer*, Sesqui-Centennial Edition, Section F, 1.

13. Ibid., Section F, 1. J. C. Hemphill of Greenwood was the architect and W. F. Livingston of Newberry was the contractor. The committee which solicited these gifts consisted of Mrs. H. L. Parr, Mrs. R. H. Wright, Mrs. H. M. Bryson, Dr. W. G. Houseal, Dr. T. H. Pope, Dr. J. B. Setzler, Dr. F. D. Mower, and Dr. W. A. Dunn.

14. *Observer*, December 25, 1925. Dr. Robert S. Cathcart, Charleston surgeon and president of the South Carolina Medical Association, delivered the dedicatory address; he was introduced by Dr. Thomas H. Pope as president of the Newberry County Medical Society.

15. *Acts of the General Assembly of South Carolina for 1927*, 993.

16. *Anderson Independent*, December 9, 1964.

17. *Newberry Observer*, October 10, 1967.

18. Act Number 820 of the *Acts of 1938*.

19. *Newberry Observer*, June 1, 1951.

20. Ibid., March 5, 1963.

Chapter 22

1. Census of 1860.

2. Census of 1870; Deed Book AAA, 193, and Deed Book SS, 597; *Newberry Herald*, January 19, 1870.

3. *Centennial Memorial, Medical College of the State of South Carolina* (Charleston, SC, 1924) (hereafter *Centennial Memorial*); Probate Court for Newberry County, Box 122, Package 331; John A. Chapman, *Annals of Newberry*, Part II (Newberry, SC, 1892), 556.

4. *Centennial Memorial*; Chapman, 556; *Newberry Observer*, January 1, 1891; tombstones in Village Cemetery.

5. *Centennial Memorial*; Chapman, 567–69; *Newberry Observer*, July 23, 1891.

6. *Centennial Memorial*; Chapman, 571.

7. *Rising Sun*, March 29, 1859; *Newberry Observer*, July 9, 1873; Box 365, Estate No. 10, Probate Court for Newberry County.

8. Register of Physicians and Surgeons, Newberry County (hereafter Register); Family Bible in possession of author; G. Moxley Sorrell, *Recollections of a Confederate Staff Officer* (New York, 1905), 285.

9. *Tri-Weekly Herald*, April 20, 1865; *Newberry Herald*, May 16, 1866; *New-*

berry Observer, January 25, 1900; Joseph I. Waring, *A History of Medicine in South Carolina 1825-1900*, (Columbia, SC, 1967), 280.

10. *Centennial Memorial; Tri-Weekly Herald*, April 25, 1865.

11. *Weekly Herald*, December 26, 1865.

12. Ibid., December 26, 1865.

13. Ibid., June 7, 1865; *Newberry Observer*, December 25, 1890; Chapman, 572.

14. Register; *Centennial Memorial; Weekly Herald*, December 26, 1865; *Observer*, February 28, 1919.

15. *Tri-Weekly Herald*, April 22, 1865; *Weekly Herald*, December 26, 1865; Chapman, 562.

16. *Centennial Memorial; Newberry Herald*, February 11, and August 1, 1866.

17. *Newberry Herald*, November 20, 1867; April 15, 1868; April 23, 1873; January 17, 1877; August 27, 1879; November 22, 1883; and *Newberry Observer*, January 28, 1892, and *Observer*, March 14, 1911; Register.

18. *Newberry Herald*, December 10, 1873, June 23, 1880; *Newberry Herald and News*, June 20, 1886, and October 13, 1886, tombstones in Rosemont Cemetery; *Census of 1870*.

19. Census of 1870.

20. *Newberry Herald*, December 10, 1873; Waring, 216.

21. *Newberry Herald*, August 14, 1872, and December 10, 1873.

22. *Newberry Herald*, December 10, 1873, June 21 and August 30, 1876, and February 13, 1878; *Observer*, August 8, 1916.

23. *Centennial Memorial; Weekly Herald*, December 26, 1865; *Newberry Herald*, January 30, 1867, and February 9, 1876.

24. *Centennial Memorial; Newberry Herald*, December 5, 1866, March 30, 1869, and May 4, 1870; Register; Box 116, Package 313, Estate No. 21, Probate Court for Newberry County.

25. Register; Chapman, 556; *Newberry Herald*, January 8 and July 2, 1873; April 7, 1875; April 17 and October 16, 1878; *Newberry Observer*, December 12, 1889, and August 7, 1890.

26. Register; *Centennial Memorial*.

27. *Centennial Memorial*; Register; *Newberry Herald*, March 4, 1874; *Newberry Observer*, April 23, 1891; *Observer*, December 31, 1909, May 31, 1912.

28. *Centennial Memorial*; Register; *Newberry Herald*, February 24, 1875; *Newberry Herald and News*, September 8, 1886, and November 8, 1888; *Observer*, May 23, 1911.

29. *Newberry Herald*, March 24, 1875, January 31, 1877, October 16, 1878, January 29, 1879, October 29, 1879, October 13 and December 22, 1881.

30. *Newberry Herald*, May 5, 1875, and January 24, 1877.

31. Register; *Newberry Herald*, February 27, May 8 and December 25, 1878; *Newberry Observer*, February 28, 1889, March 2, 1898, June 13, 1901; *Observer*, March 14, 1905, and April 9, 1920.

32. *Centennial Memorial*; Register; *Newberry Observer*, February 4, 1930.

33. Register; *Newberry Herald*, September 25, 1884; *Newberry Herald and News*, September 8, 1886; *Newberry Observer*, March 28, 1889, May 15, 1890, April 21, 1936; *Observer*, January 18, 1916.

34. Register; *Newberry Herald*, September 25, 1884; *Newberry Herald and News*, September 8, 1886; *Observer*, June 2, 1911, November 19, 1915; *Newberry Observer*, September 17, 1929.

35. Register; *Newberry Herald and News*, May 19, 1886, August 9, 1888; *Observer*, February 22, 1910.

36. *Centennial Memorial*; Register; *Newberry Observer*, March 7, 1889, November 9, 1937; *Observer*, December 16, 1924 and December 8, 1925.

37. Register; *Newberry Observer*, August 15, 1889; *Observer*, December 8, 1905.

38. *Newberry Observer*, June 5 and August 28, 1890.

39. Register; *Newberry Observer*, December 25, 1890, April 8, 1896, and April 26, 1900.

40. Register; *Observer*, October 15, 1918; *Newberry Observer*, October 15, 1937, and July 1, 1952.

41. Register; *Newberry Observer*, March 5, March 26, April 16, and July 9, 1891, January 1 and July 7, 1892, December 6, 1900, and September 14, 1937; *Observer*, August 15, 1902, March 14, 1905, and February 16, 1906.

42. *Newberry Observer*, March 12, 1891, and January 26, 1898.

43. Register; *Newberry Observer*, April 20, 1893, November 16, 1899, and December 20, 1901; *Observer*, January 17 and May 30, 1902.

44. *Centennial Memorial*; Register; *Newberry Observer*, March 21, 1894, August 25, 1897; *Observer*, February 16, 1906, June 15, 1909, May 16, 1911, February 6, 1912, and August 15, 1922.

45. *Centennial Memorial*; *Newberry Observer*, March 21, 1894, and May 8, 1895.

46. *Newberry Observer*, May 2, 1894; *Observer*, April 30, 1918, and June 18, 1929.

47. Register; *Newberry Observer*, August 25, 1897; *Observer*, December 23, 1902, November 18, 1904, February 28, 1913, January 6, 1914, and October 1, 1920.

48. Register; *Newberry Observer*, April 3, 1895, January 19, 1898; *Observer*, September 4 and November 6, 1903, February 16, 1906, February 6, 1912, December 15, 1914, December 18, 1917, and March 2, 1928.

49. *Centennial Memorial*; *Newberry Observer*, April 5, July 5, and December 6, 1900; *Observer*, September 13, 1912.

50. *Newberry Observer*, August 25, 1897.

51. Ibid., September 8, 1897.

52. *Centennial Memorial*; Register; *Observer*, January 1, 1904, January 2, March 14, and October 6, 1905.

53. Register; *Observer*, January 17, 1905, April 17, 1906, and September 10, 1907.

54. Register.

55. Register; *Observer*, February 16, 1906, February 21, May 16 and June 2, 1911, December 15, 1914, December 18, 1917, and October 8, 1918.

56. Register; *Observer*, May 7, 1907, February 21, 1911, January 8, 1915; *Newberry Observer*, March 23, 1937.

57. Register; *Observer*, September 25, 1914, October 15 and 29, 1915, August 17, 1917, and September 17, 1929.

58. *Centennial Memorial*; Register; *Observer*, October 25, 1907, April 28 and July 7, 1908, May 16, 1911, July 13 and December 18, 1917, April 8, 1919, May 4, 1920, December 16, 1924, January 20 and December 8, 1925; *Newberry Observer*, March 12, 1937, August 10, 1943; *Who's Who in South Carolina, 1934–1935*, Walker Scott Utsey, editor (Current Historical Association, Columbia, SC, 1935), 375-376.

59. Register; *Observer*, October 7, 1910, February 6, 1912, September 30, 1919; *Newberry Observer*, February 3, 1933 and November 11, 1949.

60. *Observer*, September 8, 1911; *Newberry Observer*, July 23, 1946.

61. *Centennial Memorial*; Register; *Observer*, June 6 and September 16, 1913; *Newberry Observer*, June 7, 1932, January 1 and December 19, 1933, May 14, 1937, October 10, 1952.

62. *Observer*, June 10, 1913; *Newberry Observer*, January 3, 1933, January 10, 1936, and July 14, 1972.

63. *Observer*, June 16, 1914; *Newberry Observer*, February 2, 1930.

64. *Centennial Memorial*; *Observer*, July 14, 1916; *Newberry Observer*, November 26, 1937, and September 29, 1967.

65. Register.

66. *Newberry Observer*, June 14, 1935.

67. *Observer*, September 5, 1924; *Newberry Observer*, April 5, 1957, and June 13, 1975.

68. *Observer*, March 20, 1925; *Newberry Observer*, January 13, 1931.

69. *Centennial Memorial*; Register; *Newberry Observer*, January 3, 1933, and February 5, 1952.

70. Register; information furnished by Mrs. James R. Leavell.

71. Register; *Newberry Observer*, February 3, 1983.

72. Register; *Newberry Observer*, January 1, 1979.

73. *Newberry Observer*, January 10, 1975.

74. Ibid., July 24, 1982.

75. *Newberry Herald*, July 1, 1868, May 4, 1870, August 16, 1871; *Centennial Memorial*.

76. *Centennial Memorial*; Chapman, 563; *Newberry Herald*, July 1, 1868, April 10, 1872.

77. *Newberry County South Carolina Cemeteries*, edited by George Carter

Abrams (Newberry, SC, 1982), Volume One, 37; Probate Court, Box 158, Package 13.

78. Register; *Centennial Memorial; Newberry Herald*, December 26, 1865, April 16, 1879; *Observer*, December 20, 1907.

79. *Newberry Herald*, January 17, 1872, April 7, 1875, November 10, 1880, April 27, 1881, and January 5, 1882.

80. Register; *Centennial Memorial; Observer*, July 24, 1903, September 29, 1905.

81. *Centennial Memorial; Newberry Herald*, September 8, 1880, March 27, 1884; *Newberry Observer*, July 2, 1891.

82. *Newberry Herald*, August 7, 1878.

83. Ibid., September 7, 1882.

84. Ibid., September 10, 1879.

85. Ibid., March 24, 1886.

86. Register; *Centennial Memorial; Observer*, March 14, 1905, September 23, 1910, December 16, 1910; *Newberry Observer*, July 3, 1951.

87. *Observer*, May 13 and June 10, 1902.

88. Register; *Centennial Memorial; Observer*, May 24, 1907, December 16, 1924, December 8, 1925; *Newberry Observer*, February 13, 1962.

89. Census of 1870.

90. *Weekly Herald*, December 26, 1865; *Newberry Herald*, December 8, 1881, and November 16, 1884; James Alvin Brown and James Brown Bunn, *The Sims Brown Family of Newberry County 1750–1981* (Newberry, SC, 1981), 27.

91. *Newberry Herald*, June 1, 1881; *Centennial Memorial*.

92. *Newberry Herald*, April 23, 1873; *Newberry Observer*, January 22, 1896; *Observer*, February 23, 1917; *Centennial Memorial*.

93. *Centennial Memorial; Newberry Herald*, May 4, 1870; *Newberry Observer*, November 17, 1892, and June 8, 1893; *Observer*, July 9, 1918.

94. Register; *Newberry Herald*, March 2, March 30 and May 4, 1870, April 13, 1881, and April 13, 1882; *Newberry Observer*, March 19, 1891; *Observer*, February 16 and August 24, 1906.

95. *Centennial Memorial; Newberry Herald*, March 10 and November 10, 1880, April 13 and 27, 1881, April 13, 1882, and July 17, 1884.

96. His election as vice president of the Jalapa Democratic Club is reported in *Newberry Herald*, June 3, 1868.

97. *Centennial Memorial; Newberry Herald*, June 3, 1868, May 4, 1870, and April 7, 1880; *Newberry Herald and News*, April 28, 1887; *Observer*, February 27, 1903.

98. *Centennial Memorial; Newberry Herald*, June 3, 1868; *Newberry Observer*, December 12, 1894, and December 19, 1894.

99. *Centennial Memorial; Observer*, September 20, 1912.

100. *Newberry Herald*, June 3, 1868, July 18, 1877; *Newberry Herald and News*, February 16, 1888; *Newberry Observer*, October 16, 1890; *Cemeteries*, 67.

101. *Centennial Memorial*; Register; *Newberry Herald*, March 4, 1874, July 8,

1877, June 2 and November 10, 1880, April 13 and June 1, 1881, April 13, 1882; *Newberry Observer*, January 17, 1889, June 15, 1891, and February 8, 1938; *Observer*, September 24, 1909.

102. *Newberry Herald*, September 14, 1870.

103. *Newberry Herald*, April 3, 1872, September 3, 1873, January 12, 1876, and April 4, 1877.

104. *Centennial Memorial*.

105. Register; *Newberry Herald*, March 10, 1880; *Observer*, March 5, 1907, July 13, 1909, August 27, 1918, and January 8, 1929.

106. Register; *Observer*, July 14, 1916.

107. *Centennial Memorial*; *Newberry Observer*, August 24, 1893; *Cemeteries*, 80.

108. *Centennial Memorial*; *Newberry Herald*, May 4, 1870.

109. Census of 1870.

110. Register; *Newberry Herald*, January 8, July 2, 1873, April 7, September 1, 1875, April 17, October 16, 1878, May 14, 1879, November 10, 1880, and April 13, 1882; *Newberry Observer*, December 12, 1889, and August 7, 1890.

111. Register; *Newberry Herald*, June 29, 1882; *Newberry Observer*, February 27, 1890.

112. *Observer*, February 27, 1903.

113. *Newberry Herald*, May 4, 1870; Census of 1870.

114. *Centennial Memorial*; Register; *Newberry Observer*, March 19, 1891, January 26, 1932, and November 28, 1933; *Observer*, March 14, 1905, and February 16, 1906.

115. *Newberry Herald*, September 17, 1873; Census of 1880.

116. *Newberry Herald*, December 26, 1877; *Observer*, September 26, 1905; *Centennial Memorial*.

117. *Centennial Memorial*; *Newberry Herald*, January 19, 1876.

118. *Newberry Herald*, May 17, 1871, and November 4, 1874.

119. Probate Court, Box 125, Estate 12; *Cemeteries*, 132.

120. Register; *Newberry Herald and News*, July 21, 1886, and October 13, 1887.

121. *Newberry Herald*, March 30, 1882, and October 30, 1884.

122. Register; *Cemeteries*, 115.

123. Register; *Newberry Observer*, March 19, 1891.

124. *Observer*, February 27, 1903; *Cemeteries*, 115. Data about the Holloways was furnished by Mrs. William Jordan Holloway.

125. Register; *Newberry Herald*, January 9, 1867, July 1, 1868, July 27, 1870, August 11, 1875; *Observer*, July 13, 1915, and January 7, 1916.

126. *Weekly Herald*, December 26, 1865; *Newberry Herald*, November 13, 1867; Census of 1870.

127. *Newberry Herald*, November 13, 1867, March 2, 1869, and August 23, 1882.

128. *Newberry Herald*, June 5, 1878, March 30, 1882; *Newberry Observer*, February 21, 1889, and April 10, 1890.

129. *Observer*, July 9, 1912.

130. Ibid., June 3, 1913; Register.

131. *Newberry Observer*, June 13, 1894; *Cemeteries*, 90.

132. *Weekly Herald*, December 26, 1865; *Newberry Herald*, February 22, 1871, June 25, 1873, February 24, 1875, April 13, 1881, March 13, 1882; *Newberry Observer*, May 26, 1892, and February 9, 1898; *Cemeteries*, 93.

133. *Centennial Memorial*; *Newberry Herald*, January 17, 1866.

134. Register; *Newberry Herald*, June 25, 1873, March 23, 1882; *Newberry Herald and News*, February 23, 1887; *Observer*, September 25, 1906; *Cemeteries*, 122.

135. *Newberry Herald*, January 5, 1876.

136. Census of 1880, Mortality Statistics.

137. Census of 1880; *Newberry Observer*, April 23, 1891, February 11, 1892, September 7, 1899; *Observer*, December 23, 1904, and October 13, 1911; *Cemeteries*, 122.

138. *Newberry Observer*, May 16, 1894; *Cemeteries*, 99.

139. Register; *Newberry Herald*, September 25, 1884; *Newberry Herald and News*, February 3, 1886, January 26, 1888, February 9, 1888, and November 29, 1888; *Newberry Observer*, February 11, 1892; information furnished by Dan Hamm, Jr.

140. Register; *Newberry Observer*, February 21, 1901; *Cemeteries*, 149.

141. Register; *Newberry Herald and News*, March 10, 1886, November 29, 1888; *Newberry Observer*, March 19 and April 2, 1891, June 8, 1893, and May 6, 1930; *Observer*, March 14, 1905, January 16, 1914, and February 10, 1914; *Cemeteries*, 99.

142. *Newberry Observer*, February 28, 1889, May 7, 1891, and May 18, 1893; *Observer*, August 17, 1917.

143. Register; *Newberry Observer*, April 2, 1891, May 1, 1936; *Observer*, March 14, 1905.

144. *Newberry Herald*, April 13, 1881, and November 14, 1924; *Newberry Herald and News*, January 27, 1886; *Cemeteries*, 92.

145. Register; *Newberry Observer*, May 11 and 25, 1898; *Observer*, March 14, 1905, and July 12, 1927; *Cemeteries*, 98.

146. *Newberry Observer*, May 4, 1899; *Centennial Memorial*.

147. Register; *Centennial Memorial*; *Newberry Observer*, April 5, 1900, and April 22, 1949; *Observer*, March 14, 1905, and February 16, 1906; *Cemeteries*, 170.

148. *Newberry Observer*, August 20, 1968; *Cemeteries*, 97.

149. Register; *Observer*, April 3, 1903; *Newberry Observer*, March 1, 1960, and June 10, 1960.

150. *Centennial Memorial*; *Observer*, May 6, 1901, and May 9, 1924.

151. Register.

152. Ibid.

153. Ibid.

154. Ibid.; *Cemeteries*, 200.

155. *Centennial Memorial*; *Cemeteries*, 88.

156. Register; *Cemeteries*, 205; *Newberry Herald*, May 18, 1870; *Newberry Observer*, October 20, 1892, and September 15, 1900.

157. *Weekly Herald*, June 28, 1865; *Newberry Herald*, March 23, 1882.

158. Register; *Newberry Observer*, August 13, 1891; *Observer*, March 14, 1905, December 22, 1923; *Cemeteries*, 135.

159. *Observer*, December 6, 1929.

160. Register; *Observer*, July 17, 1917; *Newberry Observer*, July 3, 1934, February 2, 1960; *Cemeteries*, 135.

161. Register; *Centennial Memorial*; *Newberry Herald*, January 18, 1874; *Newberry Herald and News*, December 20, 1888; *Cemeteries*, 43.

162. Register; *Centennial Memorial*; *Newberry Herald*, March 9, 1882.

163. Register; *Centennial Memorial*; *Newberry Herald*, May 4, 1870; *Cemeteries*, 106.

164. Register; *Newberry Herald*, November 18, 1874; *Cemeteries*, 43.

165. *Centennial Memorial*; *Observer*, August 30, 1910; *Cemeteries*, 129.

166. Register; *Newberry Herald*, September 25, 1884.

167. Register; *Newberry Observer*, October 2, 1895; *Cemeteries*, 120.

168. Register; *Newberry Observer*, April 20 and November 1, 1893.

169. Register; *Observer*, December 15, 1914, January 18, 1916, and August 15, 1919; *Newberry Observer*, October 22, 1940; *Cemeteries*, 109.

170. Register; *Observer*, July 14, 1916.

171. Register; *Newberry Observer*, December 27, 1900; *Observer*, April 4, 1902, November 6, 1903, April 11, 1905, and May 3, 1912; *Cemeteries*, 208.

172. Register; *Observer*, June 18, 1909, August 15, 1919; *Newberry Observer*, January 11, 1935; *Cemeteries*, 110.

173. *Centennial Memorial*; *Observer*, July 17, 1917; *Newberry Observer*, January 30, 1962; *Cemeteries*, 156.

174. Register; *Newberry Observer*, March 7, 1983.

175. Register.

176. *Centennial Memorial*; *Newberry Herald*, April 3, 1872; information furnished by Thomas W. Abrams (hereafter Abrams).

177. *Centennial Memorial*; Abrams.

178. Abrams.

179. *Centennial Memorial*; Abrams.

180. Abrams.

181. *Observer*, August 26, 1904.

182. *Observer*, May 4, 1906, November 25, 1910, and July 18, 1911; *Newberry Observer*, April 20, 1954.

183. *Observer*, August 3, 1909, December 8, 1916; *Centennial Memorial*.

184. *Centennial Memorial;* Register; *Observer,* May 17, 1910, September 12, 1911.

185. Register.

186. Register; *Cemeteries,* 93.

187. Register; *Observer,* July 17, 1914.

188. Register; *Observer,* July 15, 1919, March 30, 1920.

189. Abrams.

190. *Newberry Observer,* January 3, 1933; Abrams.

191. *Newberry Observer,* May 28, 1935; Abrams.

192. Register.

193. Information furnished by Dr. B. M. Montgomery.

194. Register; Abrams.

195. Register; Abrams.

196. Abrams.

Chapter 23

1. Thomas H. Pope, *The History of Newberry County,* 2 volumes (University of South Carolina Press, Columbia, SC, 1973, 1991), I, 259.

2. Pope, 94, 105.

3. Neill W. Macaulay, *History of The South Carolina Dental Association, Centennial Edition, 1869–1969* (Columbia, SC, 1969), 353.

4. *Tri-Weekly Herald,* April 30, 1865; *Newberry Herald,* September 26, 1866, and June 22, 1866.

5. *Newberry Herald,* July 24, 1867.

6. Ibid., May 23, 1866, May 27, 1868.

7. Macaulay, 15.

8. *Newberry Herald,* September 15, 1869.

9. Ibid., December 8, 1869.

10. Ibid., December 1, 1869; Box 93, Package 242, Estate 2315, Probate Court for Newberry County, Estate of Robert Thompson.

11. *Newberry Herald,* April 13, 1870.

12. *Newberry Herald,* August 13, 1879; *Newberry Observer,* July 11 and December 12, 1894; *Observer,* August 2, 1910, and September 10, 1918.

13. *Newberry Herald,* July 31, 1872, and April 22, 1874.

14. *Newberry Herald,* May 1, 1872, March 1, 1876, and December 11, 1878; *Newberry Herald and News,* September 8, 1886; *Observer,* June 28, 1907, and February 5, 1929; Macaulay, 406.

15. *Newberry Herald,* February 10 and September 15, 1769, April 13, 1870, July 31, 1872, July 26, 1876, and June 13, 1877; *Newberry Herald and News,* September 8, 1886; *Observer,* December 20, 1901; Macaulay, 47.

16. *Newberry Herald,* March 24, 1875, June 13 and December 12, 1877, December 25, 1881; *Newberry Herald and News,* October 28, 1888; Macaulay, 88.

17. *Newberry Herald*, March 7, 1877, August 7, 1878, January 15, 1879, March 22 and August 2, 1883; *Observer*, February 7, 1919, and February 8, 1927.

18. *Newberry Herald*, September 24 and October 15, 1879, January 1 and September 8, 1886; *Observer*, December 27, 1893.

19. *Newberry Observer*, January 4, 1900; *Observer*, June 27, 1902; Macaulay, 80.

20. *Observer*, February 18, 1902, January 19, 1904, and May 8, 1908.

21. *Newberry Observer*, July 3, 1895.

22. *Observer*, July 6, 1904, June 28, 1907, August 2, 1910, January 29, 1915, and August 17, 1917; *Newberry Observer*, November 22, 1960; Macaulay, 397.

23. Macaulay, 397.

24. *Observer*, June 2, 1905.

25. *Observer*, November 9, 1906, September 15, 1908, and October 20, 1912.

26. Macaulay, 407; *Observer*, April 30, 1915; *Newberry Observer*, February 16, 1946.

27. Macaulay, 379; *Observer*, June 24, 1913, May 1, 1914, and April 30, 1915; *Newberry Observer*, January 9, 1954.

28. Macaulay, 434; *Newberry Observer*, March 23, 1943.

29. Register; Macaulay, 378; *Newberry Observer*, June 15, 1945.

30. Register; Box 312, Probate Court for Newberry County.

31. Macaulay, 497; *Newberry Observer*, December 12, 1972.

32. *Newberry Observer*, February 5, 1891.

33. Macaulay, 114; *Newberry Herald*, December 22, 1881.

34. Macaulay, 219; *Newberry Observer*, March 10, 1892, December 12, 1961.

35. *Observer*, October 14, 1904, July 21, 1905.

36. Register; *Observer*, June 23, 1911; *Newberry Observer*, March 18, 1966; Macaulay, 400.

37. Register; Macaulay, 400; *Newberry Observer*, February 26, 1954.

38. *Newberry Observer*, April 10, 1981.

39. Register.

40. Register; Newberry College Alumni Office.

41. *Observer*, June 24, 1904.

42. Ibid., April 16, 1909.

43. Ibid., August 3, 1909, May 17, 1910.

44. Ibid., November 13, 1914.

45. Information furnished by Tom W. Abrams.

46. Register.

47. Macaulay, 36; *Newberry Herald*, June 24, 1874; *Observer*, January 26, 1909.

48. Macaulay, 295; *Observer*, June 24, 1913, July 11, 1913, and July 18, 1913.

Chapter 24

1. *Newberry Herald*, June 22, 1866.

2. Ibid., March 27, 1867; January 25, 1871.

3. Ibid., October 4, 1871; July 27, 1882.

4. Ibid., October 11, 1871; April 23, 1873; February 18, 1874; June 23, 1880.

5. *Herald and News*, June 30, October 13, 1886.

6. *Newberry Herald*, September 15, 1875; *Newberry Observer*, December 19, 1922.

7. *Newberry Herald*, April 30, June 11, 1873.

8. Ibid., January 31, 1877; January 15, 19, 1879; September 28, 1882; *Newberry Observer*, March 28, 1889.

9. *Newberry Observer*, February 28, 1889; January 25, 1900; June 13, 1901; *Observer*, January 8, 1904; January 30, 1906.

10. *Newberry Observer*, April 5, 1900; June 13, 1901; *Observer*, September 23 and 27, 1910; January 12, 1926.

11. *Newberry Observer*, March 26, 1937.

12. Ibid., May 8, 1934.

13. Ibid., March 25, 1958.

14. Ibid., March 21, 1944.

15. *Newberry Observer*, January 20, March 28, 1939.

16. Ibid., September 26, 1958.

17. Information about the druggists of Whitmire was furnished by the late Thomas W. Abrams.

Bibliography

Manuscripts and Primary Sources

Acts of the General Assembly of South Carolina, 1861-1990.

Agriculture of Newberry County, South Carolina, South Carolina Crop Reporting Service, County Statistical Series, No. 14, June 1962, AE221.

Agriculture of the United States in 1860; compiled from the official returns of the Eighth Census (Government Printing Office, Washington, 1864).

Agricultural Statistics for Newberry County, 1980 and 1987, South Carolina Crop and Livestock Reporting Service.

Census Reports, Volume V, *Twelfth Census of the United States, Taken in the Year 1900, Agriculture, Part I, Farms, Livestock and Animal Products* (Washington, DC, 1902).

Census Reports, Volume VII, *Twelfth Census of the United States, Taken in the Year 1900, Agriculture, Part II, Crops and Irrigation* (Washington, DC, 1902).

Constitution of the State of South Carolina, 1861.

Constitution of the State of South Carolina, 1865.

Constitution of the State of South Carolina, 1868.

Constitution of the State of South Carolina, 1895.

Correspondence Files of the Governors of South Carolina, State Archives.

Deed Books, Newberry County Clerk of Court's Office.

Diary of Reverend Thaddeus S. Boinest, Newberry County, 1852-1870, 521 typed pages copied by Ellen L. Aull from the original manuscript owned by W. B. Boinest, Pomaria, SC (Historical Records Survey, February, 1939).

Family Bible of Baruch Duncan, was owned by Mrs. Ella Dunn Eleazer of Newberry, SC.

Eighth Census, Social Statistics—1860.

Fifteenth Census of the United States: 1930, Agriculture, Volume III (Washington, DC, 1932).

Fourteenth Census of the United States, Taken in the Year 1920, Agriculture, Volume VI (Washington, DC, 1922).

Grand Jury Presentments, Newberry County.

Journal of the Court of General Sessions, Newberry County, 1858–1873.

Journal of the Court of Common Pleas, Newberry County, 1861–1873.

Journal of the Court of Common Pleas, Newberry County, 1873–1880.

Journal of the Board of Commissioners of Public Buildings, Newberry County, 1828–1868.

Journals of the South Carolina House of Representatives.

Journals of the South Carolina Senate.

Journals of the South Carolina Executive Councils of 1861 and 1862, Charles E. Cauthen, editor (Columbia, SC, 1956).

Journal of the Convention of the People of South Carolina, Held in 1860, 1861, and 1862, Together with the Ordinances, Reports, Resolutions, etc., R.W. Gibbes printer to the Convention (Columbia, SC, 1862).

Journal of the Convention of the People of South Carolina, Held in Columbia, SC, September 1865 (Columbia, SC, 1865).

Journal of the Constitutional Convention of the State of South Carolina Begun to be Holden at Columbia, S.C. on Tuesday, the Tenth Day of September, anno Dominii Eighteen Hundred and Ninety-five, etc. (Columbia, SC, 1895).

Keitt, Ellison, Memoirs, Manuscript in South Caroliniana Library.

Minutes, Board of Commissioners, Newberry County, 1868–1882; State Archives.

Minutes of Court of General Sessions, Newberry County, 1873–1883.

Miscellaneous Records of Newberry County; before 1900 in State Archives, after 1900 in Clerk of Court's Office.

Muster Rolls, Civil War; State Archives.

Ninth Census, *Social Statistics*, 1870.

Plat Books, Newberry County; Clerk of Court's Office.

Proceedings of the Constitutional Convention of South Carolina, Held at Charleston, S.C., beginning January 14th and ending March 17, 1868 (Charleston, SC, 1868).

Register of Physicians and Surgeons, Newberry County, 1882–; Clerk of Court's Office.

Register of County Officers, 1841–1893, Newberry County; State Archives.

Reports and Resolutions of the General Assembly of the State of South Carolina.

Report of Board of Soldiers Relief in Newberry District; State Archives.

RG 94, National Archives, Washington, DC.

Return of Crops and Other Statistics of Newberry County, State of South Carolina, for the year 1868; manuscript in State Archives.

Returns from Military Posts, 1800–1916, Roll 839, Newberry, SC, May 1867–

July 1873, National Archives Publications, Microcopy No. 617 (Washington, DC, 1965).

Revised Statutes of South Carolina.

Secretary of State's List of Officers Appointed and Elected, 1839–1898; State Archives.

Secretary of State's List of Officers Appointed and Elected, 1899–1932; State Archives.

Secretary of State's List of Magistrates Appointed from January 1, 1933.

Selected Census of Agriculture Characteristics: South Carolina 1959–1969, Clemson University Extension Service, Miscellaneous Extension Publication 3, September, 1972.

Sixteenth Census of the United States: 1940, Agriculture, Volume I (Washington, DC, 1942).

Sixth Annual Report of the Commissioner of Agriculture, Commerce and Industries of the State of South Carolina, (Columbia, SC, 1910).

Slave Schedule for 1860.

South Carolina Cash Receipts from Farm Marketing, South Carolina Crop Reporting Service, September 1967, AE304.

South Carolina Cash Receipts from Farm Marketing, 1965 Revised and 1966 Preliminary, South Carolina Crop Reporting Service, September 1967, AE304.

South Carolina Crop Statistics, State and County Data, 1960–1965, Revised, South Carolina Crop and Livestock Reporting Service, June 1967, AE300.

South Carolina Crop Statistics, 1973–1974, South Carolina Crop and Livestock Reporting Service, June 1975, AE382.

South Carolina Crop Statistics, 1965–1971, Revised, South Carolina Crop and Livestock Reporting Service, June 1973, AE363.

South Carolina Livestock and Poultry Statistics, 1973–1974, South Carolina Crop and Livestock Reporting Service, June 1975, AE383.

Statutes at Large of South Carolina.

The Official Roster of South Carolina Soldiers, Sailors, and Marines in the World War, 1917–1918, Two Volumes, Printed under supervision of the Joint Committee on Printing, The General Assembly of South Carolina (n.p., n.d.).

Thirteenth Census of the United States Taken in the Year 1910, Agriculture, Volume VII (Washington, DC, 1913).

United States Census of Agriculture, 1950, Volume V, Part 16, (Washington, DC, 1952).

United States Census of Agriculture, 1964, Volume I, Part 27, South Carolina (Washington, DC, 1964).

Secondary Sources

Abbott, Martin, *The Freedman's Bureau in South Carolina, 1865–1872*, (Chapel Hill, NC, 1967).

Abrams, George Carter, *The Abrams Family Genealogy, 1745–1979,* (Newberry, SC, 1979).

Allen, Walter, *Governor Chamberlain's Administration in South Carolina: A Chapter of Reconstruction in the Southern States,* (New York and London, 1888).

Andrews, Sidney, *The South Since the War* (Boston, MA, 1971).

Ashmore, Harry S., *The Negro and the Schools* (Chapel Hill, NC, 1954).

Ashmore, Harry S., *Hearts and Minds* (Calvin John, MD, 1988).

Avery, I.W., *The History of the State of Georgia* (New York, 1881).

Ball, William Watts, *The State That Forgot* (Indianapolis, IN, 1932).

Barrett, John G., *Sherman's March Through the Carolinas* (Chapel Hill, NC, 1956).

Bedenbaugh, J. Benjamin, *A Centennial History of Newberry College, 1856–1956* (n.p., n.d.).

Biographical Directory of the American Congress 1774–1971 (United States Government Printing Office, 1971).

Biographical Directory of the South Carolina Senate, N. Louise Bailey, Editor, 3 volumes (University of South Carolina Press, Columbia, SC, 1986).

Bleser, Carol K. Rothrock, *The Promised Land, The History of the South Carolina Land Commission, 1869–1890* (Columbia, SC, 1969).

Bowers, Claude G., *The Tragic Era,* (Cambridge, MA, 1929).

Brooks, U. R., *Butler and His Cavalry in the War of Secession, 1861–1865* (Columbia, SC, 1909).

Brooks, U. R., *South Carolina Bench and Bar,* Volume 1 (Columbia, SC, n.d.).

Brown, C. C., *General Catalog of Furman University* (Sumter, SC, n.d.).

Brown, James Alvan and Bunn, Jane Brown, *The Sims Brown Family of Newberry County, 1750–1981* (Newberry, SC, 1981).

Bryan, Wright, *Clemson: An Informal History of the University* (Columbia, SC, 1979).

Buck, Solon J. *The Agrarian Crusade: A Chronicle of the Farmer in Politics* (Yale University Press, New Haven, CT, 1920).

Bundrick, Glenda and Suber, Andy, *Newberry County Probate Estate Abstracts,* Volume I (Newberry, SC, 1987).

Burnside, Robert, *The Governorship of Coleman Livingston Blease of South Carolina, 1911–1915* (University of Michigan, 1963).

Buzhardt, Beaufort Simpson, *Sergeant Beaufort Simpson Buzhardt's Diary* (n.p., n.d.).

Caldwell, J. F. J., *The History of a Brigade of South Carolinians, Known First as Gregg's and Subsequently as McGowan's Brigade,* (Philadelphia, PA, 1866).

Carlisle, James H., Jr., *Addresses of J.H. Carlisle, 1825–1909* (Columbia, SC, 1910).

Carwile, John B., *Reminiscences of Newberry* (Charleston, SC, 1890).

Cash, W. F., *The Mind of the South* (New York, 1946).

Cauthen, Charles Edward, *South Carolina Goes to War 1860–1865* (Chapel Hill, NC, 1950).

Centennial Memorial, Medical College of the State of South Carolina (Charleston, SC, 1924).

Chapman, John A., *The Annals of Newberry, Part II* (Newberry, SC, 1892).

Clark, E. Culpepper, *Francis Warrington Dawson and the Politics of Restoration, South Carolina, 1874–1889* (University of Alabama Press, 1980).

Coker, Elizabeth Boatwright, *La Belle* (New York, 1959).

Cooper, William J., Jr., *The Conservative Regime: South Carolina, 1877–1890* (Baltimore, MD, 1968).

Coulter, E. Merton, *The South During Reconstruction 1865–1877*, Volume VIII, *A History of the South* (Louisiana State Press, 1947).

Cousins, Joann, editor, *Bicentennial History of Newberry County* (Dallas, TX, 1989).

Cox, Lawanda, *Lincoln and Black Freedom: A Study in Presidential Leadership* (Columbia, SC, 1981).

Cyclopedia of Eminent and Representative Men of the Carolinas of the Nineteenth Century, two volumes (Madison, WI, 1892).

Daly, Louise Haskell, *Alexander Cheves Haskell: The Portrait of a Man* (Wilmington, NC, 1989).

Daniel, Robert Norman, *Furman University, History* (Greenville, SC, 1951).

Davidson, Chalmers Gaston, *The Last Foray* (Columbia, SC, 1971).

Davis, Burke, *Sherman's March* (New York, NY, 1980).

DeForest, John William, *A Union Officer in the Reconstruction* (New Haven, CN, 1948).

Dickert, D. Augustus, *History of Kershaw's Brigade* (Newberry, SC, 1899).

Dictionary of American Biography (New York, 1959).

Durden, Robert Franklin, *James Shepherd Pike, Republicanism and the American Negro, 1850–1882* (Durham, NC, 1957).

Edmunds, John B., Jr., *Francis W. Pickens and the Politics of Destruction* (Chapel Hill, NC, 1986).

Foner, Eric, *Reconstruction: America's Unfinished Revolution, 1863–1877* (New York, 1988).

Foote, Shelby, *The Civil War—A Narrative*, three volumes (New York, 1958, 1963, and 1974).

Freeman, Douglas Southall, *Lee's Lieutenants*, three volumes (New York, 1943, 1944).

Freeman, Douglas Southall, *The South to Posterity* (New York, 1951).

Goodlett, Mildred W. *Our Heritage, A History of Smyrna Church and the Boozers of Smyrna* (Greenville, SC, 1963).

Hanna, A. J., *Flight Into Oblivion* (Johnson Publishing Co., 1938).

Hemphill, J. C., *Men of Mark in South Carolina*, four volumes, (Washington, DC, 1907).

Henagan, John C. and Thomas H. Pope, *The History of the 107th Separate Coast Artillery Battalion (AA)* (Newberry, SC, 1982).

Henry, Gordon C., *A History of Newberry College, 1856–1976)* (Newberry, SC, n.d.).

Henry, H. M., *The Police Control of the Slave in South Carolina* (Emory, VA, 1914).

A History of the Lutheran Church in South Carolina, 1971–1989, prepared and edited by the History of Synod Commission, (Columbia, SC, 1988).

Hollis, Daniel W., *University of South Carolina*, two volumes (Columbia, SC, 1951, 1956).

Hollis, John Porter, *The Early Period of Reconstruction in South Carolina* (Baltimore, MD, 1905).

Holt, Thomas, *Black Over White: Negro Political Leadership in South Carolina During Reconstruction* (Urbana, IL, 1977).

Howard, Oliver Otis, *Autobiography of Oliver Otis Howard*, two volumes (New York, 1908).

Jones, F. D. and W. H. Mills, *History of the Presbyterian Church in South Carolina Since 1850* (Columbia, SC, 1926).

Jones, Lewis Pinckney, *Stormy Petrel N.G. Gonzalez and His State* (Columbia, SC, 1973).

Jones, Lewis P., *South Carolina A Synoptic History for Laymen* (Columbia, SC, 1971).

Jordan, Frank E., Jr., *The Primary State, A History of the Democratic Party in South Carolina, 1876–1962* (n.p., n.d.).

Kibler, Lillian A., *Benjamin F. Perry, South Carolina Unionist* (Durham, NC, 1946).

King, Joe M., *A History of South Carolina Baptists* (Columbia, SC, 1964).

Lamson, Peggy, *The Glorious Failure: Black Congressman Robert B. Elliott and the Reconstruction in South Carolina* (New York, 1973).

Lander, Ernest McPherson, Jr., *A History of South Carolina: 1865–1960* (Chapel Hill, NC, 1960).

Latimer, S. L., Jr., *The Story of the State* (Columbia, SC, 1970).

Leemhuis, Roger P., *James L. Orr and the Sectional Conflict* (University Press of America, Inc., Washington, DC, 1979).

Leland, John A., *A Voice from South Carolina* (Charleston, SC, 1879).

Lord, Walter, editor, *The Freemantle Diary* (Boston, 1954).

Lewisohn, Ludwig, *Up Stream: An American Chronicle* (New York, 1922).

Macaulay, Neill W., *History of the South Carolina Dental Association, Centennial Edition 1869–1969* (Columbia, SC, 1969).

May, John Amasa and Joan Reynolds Faunt, *South Carolina Secedes* (Columbia, SC, 1960).

McCullough, Paul, A History of the Lutheran Church in South Carolina (Columbia, SC, 1971).

Memorial Exercises, South Carolina Supreme Court, June 5, 1911.

Men of the Time, J.C. Garlington, editor (Spartanburg, SC, 1902).

Meriwether, Colyer, Jr., History of Higher Education in South Carolina (Washington, DC, 1889).

Minutes of the South Carolina [Lutheran] Synod, 1989.

Moore, John Hammond, The Juhl Letters to the Charleston Courier (Athens, GA, 1974).

Morgan, James Morris, Recollections of a Rebel Reefer (Boston and New York, 1917).

Morgan, W. Scott, History of the Wheel and Alliance, And the Impending Revolution (Fort Scott, KS, 1889).

Newberry County South Carolina Cemeteries, Volume One, edited by George Carter Abrams (Newberry, SC, 1982).

Newberry County South Carolina Cemeteries, Volume Two, edited by Helen W. Monie (Newberry, SC, 1985).

Newby, I. A., Black Carolinians (Columbia, SC, 1973).

O'Neall, John Belton, Bench and Bar of South Carolina, two volumes (Charleston, SC, 1859).

O'Neall, John Belton and John A. Chapman, The Annals of Newberry in Two Parts (Newberry, SC, 1892).

Perry, Benjamin Franklin, Reminiscences of Public Men (Philadelphia, PA, 1883).

Perry, Benjamin Franklin, Reminiscences of Public Men with Speeches and Addresses (Greenville, SC, 1899).

Petty, Julian J., The Growth and Distribution of Population in South Carolina (Columbia, SC, 1943).

Pike, James S., The Prostrate State (New York, 1874).

Pope, Thomas H., The History of Newberry County, South Carolina, Volume One: 1749–1860, (Columbia, SC, 1973).

Pritchard, Claudius Hornby, Jr., Colonel D. Wyatt Aiken, 1828–1887, South Carolina's Militant Agrarian (Hampden Sydney, VA, 1970).

Reynolds, Emily Bellinger and Joan Reynolds Faunt, Biographical Directory of the Senate of the State of South Carolina: 1776–1964) (Columbia, SC, 1964).

Reynolds, John S., Reconstruction in South Carolina, 1865–1877, (Columbia, SC, 1905).

Salley, A. S., Jr., South Carolina Troops in Confederate Service, Volume I (Columbia, SC, 1913).

Scott, Edwin, Jr., Random Recollections of a Long Life, 1806–1876 (Columbia, SC, 1884).

Senn, Charlie M., A History of Trinity United Methodist Church, 1835–1985 (Newberry, SC, 1986).

Sheppard, William Arthur, *Red Shirts Remembered: Southern Brigadiers of the Reconstruction Period* (Atlanta, GA, 1940).

Simkins, Francis Butler, *The Tillman Movement in South Carolina* (Durham, NC, 1926).

Simkins, Francis Butler, *Pitchfork Ben Tillman—South Carolinian* (Baton Rouge, LA, 1944).

Simkins, Francis Butler, and Robert Hilliard Woody, *South Carolina During Reconstruction* (Chapel Hill, NC, 1932).

Smith, Clarence McKittrick, Jr., *Waymarks: A History of Aveleigh Presbyterian Church, Newberry, South Carolina, 1835–1985* (Newberry, SC, 1985).

Sorrell, G. Moxley, *Recollections of a Confederate Staff Officer* (New York, 1905).

South Carolina: A Handbook (Columbia, SC, 1927).

South Carolina and Her Builders, Ralph E. Grier, editor (Columbia, SC, 1930).

South Carolina Journals and Journalists, James B. Meriwether, editor (Spartanburg, SC, 1975).

South Carolina Lives, Louise Jones DuBose, editor (Hopkinsville, KY, 1963).

South Carolina: Resources and Population, Institutions and Industries (Charleston, SC, 1883). [Hammond's Handbook].

Summer, G. Leland, *Newberry County South Carolina Historical and Genealogical* (n.p., 1950).

Taylor, Alrutheus A., *The Negro in South Carolina During the Reconstruction* (Washington, DC, 1924).

Taylor, Rosser H. and Raven I. McDavid, *Memoirs of Richard Cannon Watts* (Columbia, SC, 1938).

Thomas, Albert S., D. D., *The Episcopal Church in South Carolina* (Columbia, SC, 1957).

Thompson, Henry T., *Ousting the Carpetbagger from South Carolina* (Columbia, SC, 1926).

Tindall, George B., *South Carolina Negroes 1877–1900* (Columbia, SC, 1952).

Walker, C. Irvine, *The Life of Lieutenant General Richard Heron Anderson of the Confederate States Army* (Charleston, SC, 1917).

Wallace, David Duncan, *South Carolina: A Short History 1520–1948* (Chapel Hill, NC, 1951).

Wallace, David Duncan, *The History of South Carolina*, four volumes (New York, 1934).

Ward, C. Jansen, *Price Economics of What Farmers Sell* (Bulletin 226, Clemson College, May 1926).

Waring, Joseph I., M.D., *A History of Medicine in South Carolina, 1825–1900* (Columbia, SC, 1967).

Warner, Ezra J., *Generals in Gray* (Baton Rouge, LA, 1959).

Warner, Ezra J., and W. Buck Yearns, *Biographical Register of the Confederate Congress* (Baton Rouge, LA, 1975).

Watson, Margaret, *Greenwood County Sketches* (Greenwood, SC, 1970).

Welch, Spencer Glasgow, *A Confederate Surgeon's Letters to His Wife*, Eloise Welch Wright, editor (The Neale Publishing Company, New York and Washington, 1911). Reprinted by Continental Book Company, Marietta, GA, 1954.

Wellman, Manly Wade, *Giant in Gray* (New York, 1949).

Wells, Edward L., *Hampton and Reconstruction* (Columbia, SC, 1907).

Who's Who in South Carolina, Geddings H. Crawford, editor (Columbia, SC, 1921).

Who's Who in South Carolina, 1934–1935, Walker Scott Utsey, editor (Columbia, SC, 1935).

Wikramanayake, Marina, *A World in Shadow* (Columbia, SC, 1973).

Williams, Alfred B., *Hampton and His Red Shirts* (Charleston, SC, 1930).

Williamson, Joel, *After Slavery: The Negro in South Carolina During Reconstruction, 1861–1877* (Chapel Hill, NC, 1965).

Woodward, C. Vann, *Mary Chestnut's Civil War* (New Haven, CT, 1981).

Yearns, W. Buck, editor, *The Confederate Governors* (Athens, GA, 1985).

Articles, Monographs and Theses

Abbott, Martin, "County Officers in South Carolina in 1868," *South Carolina Historical Magazine*, LX, January 1959, 30–40.

Anderson, J. Perrin, "Public Education in Ante-Bellum South Carolina," *Proceedings of the South Carolina Historical Association, 1933*, 3–11.

Aull, James L., "Historical Sketch of the First Baptist Church, Newberry, South Carolina, 1831–1931," Newberry, SC, 1931.

Bedenbaugh, J. Holland, "A History of Newberry College," M.A. Thesis, University of South Carolina, July 1930.

Broaddus, Luther, "History of the Newberry Baptist Church, 1831–1881," Charleston, SC, 1882.

Daugherty, Lawton, "Little River-Dominick Prebysterian Church, 1761–1961" (n.p., 1961).

Easterby, J. H., "The Granger Movement in South Carolina," *Proceedings of the South Carolina Historical Association, 1931*, 21–32.

Fulmer, Verley L., "History of St. Peter's Lutheran Church (Piney Woods)," Newberry, SC, 1944.

Graham, L. Clifton, "History of Central United Methodist, Newberry, South Carolina," Newberry, SC, 1970.

Graves, Lawrence Benjamin, "The Beginning of the Cotton Textile Industry in Newberry County," M.A. Thesis, University of South Carolina, 1947.

Hitt, Juanita, "The First Baptist Church, Newberry, South Carolina, 1831–1981," Newberry, SC, 1981.

Hollis, Daniel W., "Cole Blease: The Years Between the Governorship and the Senate, 1915–1924," *South Carolina Historical Magazine*, January 1979, 1–17.

Hollis, Daniel W., "Cole L. Blease and the Senatorial Campaign of 1924," *Proceedings of the South Carolina Historical Association*, 1978, 53–68.

Kibler, Julia Marguerite, "The History of The Lutheran Church of the Redeemer, Newberry, South Carolina, 1853–1964," Newberry, SC, 1964.

Kirkland, Thomas J., "Tillman and I, Principle, Poverty, and Politics," *The State*, Columbia, SC, June 30, July 7, 14, 21 and 28, 1929.

Patton, James Welch, "John Belton O'Neall," *Proceedings of the South Carolina Historical Association*, 1934, 3–13.

Pope, Thomas H., "B.O. Duncan, Newberry Unionist," *Proceedings of the South Carolina Historical Association*, 1983.

Pope, Thomas H., "History of St. Luke's Episcopal Church, Newberry, South Carolina," Newberry, SC, 1955.

Sease, Rosalyn Summer, "A Brief History of St. John's Lutheran Church, Pomaria, South Carolina," n.p., 1970.

Singley, Phoebe Schumpert, "A Survey of Education in Newberry County, South Carolina, Prior to 1870," Master's Thesis, University of South Carolina, 1934.

Smith, Mrs. C. M., "History of the Bush River Baptist Church, 1771–1933," Kinards, SC, 1934.

Townsend, John Belton O'Neall, "The Political Condition of South Carolina," *Atlantic Monthly*, Volume 39, February 1877, 177–194.

——————————— , "South Carolina Morals," *Atlantic Monthly*; Volume 39, April 1877, 467–475.

——————————— "South Carolina Society," *Atlantic Monthly*; Volume 39, June 1877, 670–684.

Newspapers

The Rising Sun
The Newberry Herald
The Tri-Weekly Herald
The Weekly Herald
*The Observer**
*The Newberry Observer**
The Charleston Daily News
The Newberry Herald and News
The State
The Progressive Age
The Newberry News
The Reporter
The Press and Reporter
Voice of the People
The Evening Midget

The Sun
The Evening Telegram
*These newspapers changed names intermittently. *The Observer* was published 1883–1888; 1902–1919; and 1921–1929. *The Newberry Observer* was published 1889–1901; 1920; and 1930–.

Index

493

Townsend, Landon, Mrs., 233
Townships, 44
Trabert, Charles, 200
Trakas, S. P., 280
Trammell, Curtis D., 123
Trapp, Bobby Ray, 151
Trescot, William Henry, 32, 80
Tribble, Anna, 100
Tribble, James W., Dr., 346
Tribble, Julian, 148
Tribble, Maude, 346
Tribble, Mittie Chappell, 346
Trimmier, F. M., 431 n. 37
Trinity Church, 291
Trinity Farms, 166
Trinity Methodist Church, 305
Tri-Weekly Herald, 259
Trotti, Samuel Hanna, Dr., 374
Trowbridge, Charles, 22
Truesdale, R. H., Dr., 374
Truett, Fuller Alexander, Dr., 369–370
Truett, Lucy Salley Corbitt, 370
Tucker, George B., 20
Tupper, George, 56, 60
Turkeys, 158–159
Turner, William, 308
Turner's Jewelers of Newberry, Inc., 284
Turnipseed, D. C., Dr., 361
Tyler, Rockwell, 22

Underwood
  Annie Mae Brown, 333
  Elizabeth, 333
  James A., 333
  James A., III, 333
  James, A., Jr., Dr., 333
  Jeanne, 333
  Julie, 333
  Nancy, 333
  Patricia, 333
  Rosalyn Sanders, 333
Underwood and Epting, 336
Union League of America, 27, 51
Union Reform Party, 51
Union Republican Convention, 28
Union Republican Party, 33, 61
United Daughters of the Confederacy, 12, 14, 22
United Methodist churches, 304–306
United States Forest Service, 132
Unity Presbyterian Church, 304

Valley Farm Dairy, 159

Vance, William, 415 n. 21
Van Horn, James J., 421 n. 52
Van Horne, Robert M., Rev., 297
Van Wyck, Charles H., 22
Vassey, Ann Merchant, Dr., 382
Vaughansville Baptist Association, 293
Vaughn, David, Rev., 307
The Veil (Chapman), 218
Verner
  Ann Marshall, 253
  Charles Vermuele, 254
  James S., 253
  James S., Jr., 245, 253–254
  James Spencer, III, 254
  Martha Dahl Harley, 246, 254
  Russell Aubrey Harley, 254
Vernon, M. H., 450 n. 3
Vernon, T. O. P., 46
Vietnam memorial, 151
Vietnam War, 151
Vigodsky, Harry, 280, 282, 444 n. 5
Vigodsky, Joe, 280
Vigodsky, Taylor, 280, 465 n. 20
Vinson, Donald C., 148
Voice of the People, 96, 260, 261
Voight, Gilbert, 200
Vought, George, Rev., 307

Waddell, Moses, Rev., 301
Wadlington, Thomas B., 416 n. 35, 428 n. 89
Waldrop
  David, 169
  David C., 156, 157, 165, 455 n. 76
  David Jr., 157
  Jefferson, 156, 169
  Jefferson C., 157
  Jewel Ellenberg, 157
  Ralph, 156, 169
  Vesta Pitts, 157
Waldrop and Company, 208
Waldrop & Sons, Ralph, 166
Waldrup, Mary Jane, 176
Walker
  Curtiss Eugene, 151
  F. N., 18
  John T., Mrs., 352
  Walter, 161
  Whitfield, 4, 415 n. 21
  William W., 167
Wall, Eli, 428 n. 89
Wallace
  Alice Lomax, 228, 262

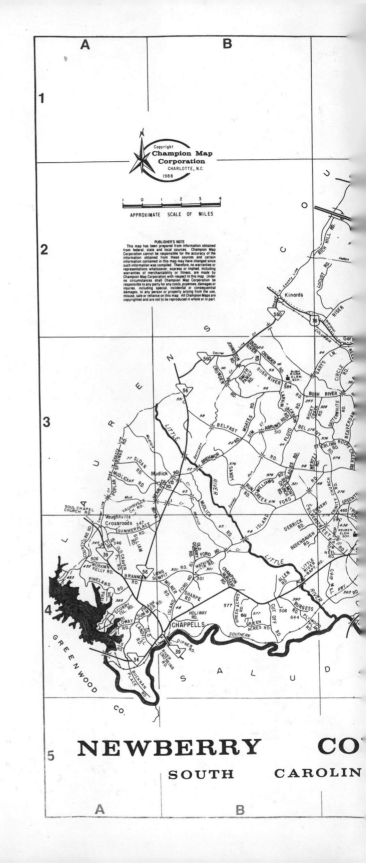

0 1 2 3 4

APPROXIMATE SCALE OF MILES

NEWBERRY CO

SOUTH CAROLIN